Rosa Luxemburg

The Complete Works of Rosa Luxemburg

VOLUME V, POLITICAL WRITINGS 3:
ON REVOLUTION—1910–1919

Edited by Helen C. Scott
and Paul Le Blanc

*Translated by Jacob Blumenfeld,
Mathias Foit, Nicholas Gray,
Henry Holland, Zachary King,
and Manuela Kölke*

VERSO
London • New York

ROSA
LUXEMBURG
STIFTUNG

Verso would like to express its gratitude to Rosa Luxemburg Stiftung for help in publishing this book

ROSA
LUXEMBURG
STIFTUNG

The publisher also gratefully acknowledges the assistance of Dietz Verlag, publisher of Rosa Luxemburg's *Gesammelte Werke*, the German source of all English translations herein

This paperback edition first published by Verso 2026
First published by Verso 2024

1 3 5 7 9 10 8 6 4 2

Verso
UK: 6 Meard Street, London W1F 0EG
US: 207 East 32nd Street, New York, NY 10016
versobooks.com

Verso is the imprint of New Left Books

ISBN-13: 978-1-78478-282-5
ISBN-13: 978-1-78478-284-9 (US EBK)
ISBN-13: 978-1-78478-283-2 (UK EBK)

British Library Cataloguing in Publication Data
A catalogue record for this book is available from the British Library

Library of Congress Cataloging-in-Publication Data
A catalog record for this book is available from the Library of Congress

Typeset in Minion Pro by MJ&N Gavan, Truro, Cornwall
Printed and bound by CPI Group (UK) Ltd, Croydon, CR0 4YY

Contents

Acknowledgments

This volume is a collective project made possible by the dedication and labor of many people and we extend our heartfelt thanks to all who have contributed. The series editor, Peter Hudis, is the capable steward of the entire Complete Works project and has provided essential resources and guidance throughout this long journey. Jacob Blumenfeld, Mathias Foit, Nicholas Gray, Henry Holland, Zachary King, and Manuela Kölke supplied the English translations of Luxemburg's German and Polish texts. Ottokar Luban generously read and provided detailed feedback on the introductory essay. Andrew Bonnell made invaluable and substantial contributions to the footnotes and translations. Lori Turner's meticulous research, editing, and language skills strengthened the glossary and entire manuscript.

Thanks also to the editorial board for their shared commitment to bringing Luxemburg's legacy to current and future generations of scholars and activists: Andrew Bonnell, Ankica Čakardić, Julia Damphouse, Jason Dawsey, Henry Holland, Peter Hudis, Manuela Kölke, Paul LeBlanc, Ben Lewis, Ewa Majewska, Dana Mills, Antonio Mota, Sandra Rein, Helen Scott, David Smith, Lori Turner, and Rida Vaquas.

We are grateful to the Rosa Luxemburg Foundation in Berlin and to the many individuals who contributed to the Toledo Fund for their support of the Complete Works project. Most of all, this volume (as well as the four volumes preceding it) would not have been possible without the direction, advice and support of Evelin Wittich and Jörn Schütrumpf of the Rosa Luxemburg Foundation, who have assisted us at each step of this project—from helping to select the materials in this volume to finding the original documents, as well as providing invaluable encouragement and assistance in all phases of our work.

Editorial Foreword

Amid a powerful upsurge in class struggle, early 1910 saw Rosa Luxemburg advocating for the use of the political mass strike in the campaign to expand suffrage, in opposition to both the right wing of the Social Democratic Party of Germany (Sozialdemokratische Partei Deutschlands—SPD) and her erstwhile comrade Karl Kautsky. In May of that year she wrote to her friends Mathilde and Robert Seidel: "During all of April, I roared through Germany with rallies and public meetings on the electoral issues. Now I am romping around in the press... And always, in between those things, there was the Russian and Polish work. So there's always enough to do. But I am personally satisfied because, after all, I enjoy life most in the midst of the storm."* Nine years later, Luxemburg was engaged in a struggle for her life against counterrevolutionary forces within the German state and the reigning SPD. On January 11, 1919, she wrote to her friend Clara Zetkin: "It is impossible to describe the way of life that I—and all of us—have been living for weeks, the tumult and turmoil, the constant changing of living quarters, the never-ending reports filled with alarm, and in between, the tense strain of work, conferences, etc., etc." Noting that these perilous conditions had interrupted many aspects of party building, she adds, "These events are a tremendous school for the masses."†

This volume frames the final decade of Luxemburg's life, tumultuous years that witnessed the collapse of the Second International, the global catastrophe of World War I, the historic early success of the Russian Revolution, the birth of the Communist International, and the outbreak of the German Revolution. During this period Luxemburg spent many years in prison, but she was also, as the writings in this volume indicate, at her place "in the midst of the storm"—writing, giving speeches, polemicizing with the party leaders, and organizing at the heart of the mass working-class socialist movement of three countries. 1910–19 is the period covered in Volume 5 of the *Complete Works*, the last of three volumes on revolution.

The *Complete Works* project organizes Luxemburg's writings into three overarching categories: Economic, Political, and Complete Correspondence. The economic writings are included in Volumes 1 and 2 (which were published in 2013 and 2015 respectively).‡ While the complete correspondence

* Georg Adler, Peter Hudis and Annelies Laschitza, eds., *The Letters of Rosa Luxemburg* (London: Verso, 2011), p. 291.

† Ibid., p. 492.

‡ Peter Hudis, ed., *Complete Works of Rosa Luxemburg: Vol. I, Economic Writings 1* (London and New York: Verso, 2013); Peter Hudis and Paul Le Blanc, eds., *Complete Works of Rosa Luxemburg Vol. 2, Economic Writings 2* (London and New York: Verso, 2015). A third supplementary volume consisting of other recently discovered manuscripts on economics is also projected.

will appear in later volumes, a companion volume was published in 2011.* The political writings are further divided into different themes: "On Revolution," "Debates on Revolutionary Strategy and Organization," "The National Question," "Colonial Policy and Imperialism," and "On Literature." Volume 3 (published 2019) contains writings on revolution to the end of 1905; Volume 4 (published 2021) covers material from 1906 to 1909. The present volume spans 1910–1919, including Luxemburg's writings on the Russian Revolution of 1917 and German Revolution of 1918–19.

By 1909, Rosa Luxemburg had already distinguished herself as a significant leader in the mass international socialist movement. The keynote of her life was revolutionary socialism. Born in 1871, the year of the Paris Commune, she grew up in Russian-occupied Poland, where she witnessed brutal conditions for the working class and experienced the national oppression of the Poles, the vicious anti-Semitism leveled against the Jewish population, and the full weight of a patriarchal society, in addition to a lifelong disability. As a teenager, she threw herself into the school opposition and the socialist movement around the illegal party Proletariat. In the context of a harsh state crackdown, she was smuggled out of Poland and went next to Zurich, where she gained both a formal university education and hands-on training in revolutionary politics, joining with many other exiled leaders of the Second International. At the age of twenty-two, she helped found what would become the SDKPiL, the Social Democracy of the Kingdom of Poland and Lithuania (SDKP), and she was still in her twenties when she moved to Berlin, where she would become one of the leading revolutionary voices in the largest party in the Second International, the SPD.

During this period tensions between the revolutionary and reformist wings of the party intensified. 1910 saw a clear rupture between Luxemburg and her ally Karl Kautsky, who increasingly wanted to restrict the work of the SPD to parliamentary activities. In a 1911 letter to Kostya Zetkin, Luxemburg refers to Kautsky's "spiritual 'bumpkinization.'"† The same year witnessed the first organized attempts to consolidate revolutionary forces within the party, with the formation of the Commission of Seven. Even while increasingly exasperated with the leadership, Luxemburg affirmed the necessity of mass organizations. In August 1911, she warned Henriette Roland Holst not to leave the Social Democratic Party in Holland: "We can't be outside the organizations of the masses, out of contact with them. The worst working-class party is better than none… Stay with the rank and file, that is our duty, we are all soldiers."‡

The turning point came in August 1914 with the outbreak of World War I, when the leaders abandoned entirely the principles of working-class

* Adler, Hudis, and Laschitza, *The Letters of Rosa Luxemburg.*

† Ibid., p. 297.

‡ Ibid., p. 311.

internationalism and anti-imperialism and instead lined up behind their government's war efforts. Luxemburg, along with other revolutionary leaders such as Karl Liebknecht and Clara Zetkin, mobilized the opposition, and in January 1916 formed the Spartacus League (*Spartakusbund*—named for a famous slave rebellion against the Roman empire). Luxemburg's antiwar activities were met with lengthy prison sentences, and she spent the best part of the war behind bars. Many of her most significant writings from this period will appear in future volumes, but this one contains her continued discussion of the mass strike, interventions in debates about Prussian suffrage, and defense of Liebknecht, who also faced persecution from the authorities without a murmur of protest from the SPD. Her words about her comrade resonate with Luxemburg's own situation: "It is clear that the government and its henchmen are planning a judicial murder of Karl Liebknecht! The hated champion of socialism, the indomitable defender of the working class, is to be assassinated by his mortal enemies; removed from the public stage, the troublemaker is to disappear into oblivion!"* The bulk of the remaining materials collected here address the Russian Revolution, which she followed avidly while incarcerated, and the German Revolution, which released her from prison and absorbed all her energies in the final months of her life. Also included here are founding statements on the German Communist Party (KPD), which Luxemburg helped launch in 1918. Much of this was written anonymously and published illegally.

When Germany was on the brink of revolution in 1918, the capitalists turned to the anti-revolutionary leadership of Social Democracy to save their system, making a deal with the now governing leaders of the SPD and the trade union bureaucrats, who joined with them against the masses struggling for social transformation. The reformists, those who claimed to shun violence in favor of a peaceful path, joined with reactionaries to send paramilitaries (precursors of the fascists) to crush worker uprisings and soldier rebellions. In January 1919, they had Luxemburg and her comrades brutally murdered; this marked a turning point for the working-class movement and the reversal of the revolutionary tide. As we argue in the introduction, this was not the inevitable outcome. There is much that can be learned from this period that came so close to world revolution, and Rosa Luxemburg's legacy continues to be a rich resource for ongoing global struggles.

* "What's with Liebknecht?"; see pp. 117, below.

Introduction: Rosa Luxemburg and the Marxist Tradition

The importance of Rosa Luxemburg to the Marxist tradition was not clear to English-speaking scholars and activists before the Second World War. With few exceptions, her writings were unavailable in translation, and secondary accounts offered, at best, only the most superficial references. In the 1960s, Anglophone readers had access to less than ten percent of her writings. Luxemburg's work has been increasingly available since then, and the ambitious *Complete Works of Rosa Luxemburg* project aims to make the entire archive available in the English language.*

Luxemburg has come to mean different things to different people, yet some of these divergent interpretations can serve to bring into focus various facets of her thought and times, with implications for our own. We must approach Luxemburg's writings with critical minds, seeking to situate texts within actual contexts while staying open to varying interpretations that might help us grasp the complexities of the realities with which she herself was wrestling. This is the approach the editors have sought to follow. A serious evaluation and utilization of Luxemburg's writings is necessarily a collective process.

I. LUXEMBURG'S REVOLUTIONARY MARXISM

To understand Luxemburg's political writings, one must grasp that *revolution* was inseparable from all that she had to say. In a sense, this conflicts with the thematic structure chosen for the *Complete Works*. Volume 5 is the final instalment of three volumes devoted to the theme of revolution, but all five volumes are of a piece with each other and the entire series. This centrality of revolution permeates the quality of Luxemburg's thought and expression, ensuring that the Marxism she personified vibrates with energy, critical-minded humor, and creativity infused with radically democratic and internationalist sensibilities.

These sensibilities animate her economic analysis, which in turn refutes the notion that capitalism can gradually be reformed into socialism. Debates over reform or revolution fermented within the SPD, which was Luxemburg's political home for most of her life. From the beginning, she fought against Eduard Bernstein's revisionist doctrine and, from 1906, the growing reformist

* Details on the slow availability and appreciation of Luxemburg's writings and ideas in English-language sources are traced in our preface to the Left Book Club edition of *Socialism or Barbarism, Selected Writings Rosa Luxemburg* (London: Pluto Press/Left Book Club, 2021), pp. ix–xiii.

and bureaucratic tendencies in the SPD. The combined economic, political, and cultural analyses one finds in Luxemburg's writings insist that such reformist moderation will prove no match for the relentless, voracious capital accumulation process, with its attendant militarism, imperialism, and—whenever necessary—authoritarian and murderous violence.

Luxemburg's understanding of revolution was forged from a lifetime of practical struggle as well as critical engagement with Marxist theory. From her youth, when she participated in the school resistance and illegal Marxist factory reading groups in Russian-occupied Poland, to the final days of her life, which were spent defending the German Revolution on the streets of Berlin, she remained committed to organizing from below. She wrote to her close friend Henriette Roland Holst, who was considering leaving the Social Democratic Party in Holland: "We can't be outside the organizations of the masses, out of contact with them ... Stay with the rank and file, that is our duty..." She was a brilliant and much sought-after speaker and journalist, but also very active in the Berlin party organization. Even when consigned to a prison cell for opposing the First World War, she continued to follow global events and intervene in current debates and actions. Not surprisingly, this commitment was repaid by tremendous respect: when released from a one-year prison sentence in 1916 she was greeted at the jail exit by women party members who later "came in massive numbers to where I live, to shake my hand. My dwelling place was and still is stuffed full with their presents."* This strong connection with the rank and file informed her political and theoretical writings, which were characterized by independence of thought and intimate knowledge of the ebbs and flows of the working-class movement.

Luxemburg's revolutionary Marxism was also shaped by her experience of oppression—as a Pole, a Jew, a person living with a disability, and a woman. Opposition to all forms of discrimination and injustice runs throughout her life and work, which roots oppression within the very foundations of capitalism as an economic system.†

---

* Adler, *The Letters of Rosa Luxemburg*, pp. 311, 355.

† In a comparative study of Rosa Luxemburg and Lorraine Hansberry, LaRose T. Parris finds that "Luxemburg's call for an anti-imperialist, socialist-feminism establishes her as a creolized theorist who was well ahead of her time." "To Be Young, Gifted and Woman: Reading Rosa Luxemburg through Lorraine Hansberry and the Black Radical Tradition," in Jane Anna Gordon and Drucilla Cornell, eds., *Creolizing Rosa Luxemburg* (Lanham, MD: Rowman and Littlefield, 2021), p. 461. Further explorations of Luxemburg's relationship to intersectional oppression can be found in Ankica Čakardić, "Social-Reproduction Theory: A Case for Luxemburgian Feminism," *Historical Materialism* 2017, Vol. 25, No. 4, pp. 37–64; Nancy Holmstrom, "Rosa Luxemburg: A Legacy for Feminists?" *Rosa Remix* (New York: Rosa Luxemburg Stiftung, 2016), pp. 32–6; and Amber A'Lee Frost, "Pick-up Artists, Ashley Madison, and Lifestyle Feminism," *Rosa Remix* pp. 37–42. Also relevant is the earlier analysis by Raya Dunayevskaya, *Rosa Luxemburg, Women's Liberation, and Marx's Philosophy of Revolution*, Second Edition (Urbana: University of Illinois Press, 1991), pp. 26–9, 89–97.

Her letters frequently reveal both independence of mind and irreverence, particularly toward routinism and orthodoxy. Writing to a close friend about the addendum to *The Accumulation of Capital*—her anti-imperialist masterpiece—her critical-minded humor turns on her beloved Marx:

> This is a work I am pretty proud of … its form is extremely simple, without any accessories, without coquetry or optical illusions, straightforward and reduced to the barest essentials, I would even say "naked" like a bloc of marble. This is, in fact, where today my taste lies. In theoretical work as in art, I value only the simple, the tranquil and the bold. That is why, for example, the famous first volume of Marx's *Kapital*, with its profuse rococo ornamentation in the Hegelian style, now seems an abomination to me (for which, from the Party standpoint, I must get five years hard labor and ten years loss of civil rights …)*

In another letter of the same period, to a dear friend who is challenging her revolutionary intransigence, she responds with wicked humor: "Your argument comes down to the following: … human beings are too cowardly and weak for such heroism, ergo one must adapt one's tactics to their weakness and to the principle 'whoever walks softly walks sensibly.' What narrowness of historical outlook, my little lamb!" She elaborates:

> There is nothing more changeable than human psychology. That's especially because the psyche of the masses, like … the eternal sea, always bears within it every latent possibility: deathly stillness and raging storm, the basest cowardice and the wildest heroism. The masses are always what they *must* be according to the circumstances of the times, and they are always on the verge of becoming something totally different from what they seem to be. It would be a fine sea captain who would steer a course based only on the momentary appearance of the ocean's surface and not understand how to draw conclusions from signs in the sky and in the ocean's depths. My dear little girl, "disappointment with the masses" is always the most reprehensible quality to be found in a political leader. A leader with the quality of greatness applies tactics, not according to the momentary mood of the masses, but according to higher laws of development …†

These "higher laws of development," which she traced in *The Accumulation of Capital*, guided her strategic and tactical orientation in relation to both the Russian and German Revolutions. As a tough-minded political analyst and a revolutionary internationalist, she perceived the two revolutions together as an interactive totality.

---

* Stephen Eric Bronner, ed., *The Letters of Rosa Luxemburg* (Atlantic Highlands, NJ: Humanities Press, 1993), p. 185.

† Adler, Hudis, and Laschitza, *The Letters of Rosa Luxemburg* p. 374.

This emphasis on the revolutionary quality of Luxemburg's Marxism may raise questions for some: although a member of the German Social Democratic Party, to what extent was she actually a Social Democrat? Was she not, instead, a revolutionary socialist? Or, as a founding member of the German Communist Party shortly before her death, wasn't she a Communist? Or did she change her mind about where she stood?

In our contemporary context "Social Democrat" often signifies "welfare state" reforms (social legislation creating a "social safety net" around such things as health care, housing, education, minimum wage, social security) within a broadly capitalist economic framework. The word "socialist" more likely implies replacing capitalism altogether with a different economic system—socialism—involving social ownership and democratic control of the economy. The word "Communist" often connotes a bureaucratic state-run economy which provides some form of "social safety net" but with neither capitalist "free market" nor democracy—though for some "communism" represents a utopia of freedom, abundance and equality.

Such distinctions are not relevant to Luxemburg's time, when Marxists saw the three terms as synonymous, with Social Democrat and socialist the more commonly used. The Socialist International, or Second International, was a world federation of socialist labor parties, often referred to as "the Social Democracy," which included a principled Marxist revolutionary wing and a more pragmatic, or opportunist, reformist wing.

Particularly given the predominance of the strong and seemingly "orthodox Marxist" German Social Democratic Party, the general view among its members was that the revolutionaries were predominant. The party had been founded, after all, on the Erfurt Program, which was committed both to the "minimum program"—immediate reforms—and the "maximum program"—overthrowing capitalism and replacing it with a socialist society. Although Luxemburg and a few others had growing misgivings from 1907 onward, "even the most consistent revolutionaries," according to Wolfgang Abendroth, "the Bolshevik faction of the RSDRP [Russian Social-Democratic Labor Party] led by Lenin, took—prior to 1914—the German Party's pseudo-revolutionary politics seriously, and Kautsky's Marxist scholasticism for real Marxism."* In contrast to their socialist and antimilitarist program and resolutions of the pre-war years, however, the majority of the German Social Democratic Party leadership, along with those of most of the Second International's affiliates, ended up supporting the war efforts of their contending governments in what they had denounced, before the fact, as a rich man's war and a poor man's fight.

* Wolfgang Abendroth, *A Short History of the European Working Class* (New York: Monthly Review Press, 1973), p. 57.

In his discussion of the resolutions of the Second International, Mike Taber observes that such revolutionaries as Lenin and Luxemburg "were not sparing in invective to label the betrayers," but also that they "never renounced the resolutions the Second International had adopted" before 1914. They were indignant over "the Second International's gap between word and deed, its hypocrisy." As more than one scholar has noted, Lenin's famous denunciation of Karl Kautsky as a *renegade* connotes the fact that the SPD's most prestigious Marxist theorist before 1914 had betrayed the principled positions that he, Kautsky, had once held in common with Lenin and Luxemburg.*

This was the beginning of a process of separation. From 1918, the word "Communist" was embraced by revolutionaries determined to draw a sharp line between themselves and such betrayers and hypocrites. From 1919, many of them joined with Lenin in founding the Communist International. In 1920, a fragmented Second International, now dominated by the reformist wing of the Social Democracy, overwhelmingly adopted a resolution dealing with "Social Democracy *versus* Communism" which sought to distinguish "between the Communist system of Moscow and the democratic system of the Second International."† In later years, as a bureaucratic Communist dictatorship crystallized around Joseph Stalin in Soviet Russia, Communism for many more people increasingly was associated with a profoundly undemocratic system. But this was not yet the case in 1918 or 1919, although we shall see that Luxemburg warned of the dangers.

The fact remained that whether she was a member of the Polish or German parties of Social Democracy or the German Communist Party, Luxemburg's revolutionary socialist orientation was consistent throughout her life. This record earned her a global reputation and continues to be a touchstone for activists up to the present. In the words of Alhelí de María Alvarado-Díaz, referencing Hannah Arendt's 1966 article "A Heroine of the Revolution": "A radical revolutionary and a fighter in the name of liberation in all its forms, Rosa Luxemburg's attitudes and intelligence can inspire a new generation of militants to rescue the ideals she herself fought for: justice, equal rights, and individual autonomy without compromise."‡

---

* Mike Taber, ed., *Under the Socialist Banner: Resolutions of the Second International, 1889–1912* (Chicago: Haymarket, 2021), p. 8. Also see Lars T. Lih, "'The New Era of War and Revolution': Lenin, Kautsky, Hegel and the Outbreak of World War I," in Alexander Anievas, ed., *Cataclysm 1914: The First World War and the Making of Modern World Politics* (Chicago: Haymarket, 2016), pp. 366–412.

† Julius Braunthal, *History of the International, Volume II: 1914–1943* (New York: Frederick A. Praeger, 1967), p. 160.

‡ Alhelí de María Alvarado-Díaz, "Heroine of the Revolution," *Rosa Remix* (New York: Rosa Luxemburg Stiftung, 2018), pp. 43–9.

II. REVOLUTIONARY EXPLOSIONS

At the start of the twentieth century, the SPD seemed to socialists around the world to be the strongest working-class party on the planet, guided by revolutionary Marxist theory and providing an inspiring model destined to lead the way to socialism, and for these reasons Luxemburg herself became a member. But Luxemburg, over time, increasingly identified problems with the model and developed an alternative. Luxemburg's biographer J. P. Nettl provides a helpful account of the genesis and significance of her growing recognition. He notes that in the decade before the eruption of the First World War, she "moved from doubts about Party policy to certainty in her formulation of alternatives." There were four successive elements in this process: "first a mass-strike doctrine, next a struggle for its application, next a dissatisfaction with Party policy against a background of personal disenchantment, and finally the development of a doctrine of imperialism."*

This final component—which incorporated acute awareness of global issues, principled opposition to colonialism, and powerful critique of imperialism and militarism—remained central to her life and work, informing her economic and political theories and organizational perspectives. The analysis of imperialism as a central component of capitalism is expressed most explicitly in her economic writings gathered in the first two volumes of the *Complete Works*, specifically the 1913 classic *The Accumulation of Capital*, which constitutes the bulk of Volume 2. Hamid Dabashi, who calls Luxemburg "the unsung hero of postcolonial theory," writes of this work: "Rosa Luxemburg demonstrated how capitalism expands the domain of its predatory operation globally to exploit resources, abuse cheap labor, expand its insatiable need for new markets, and accumulate ever-increasing surplus value. European imperialism, she suggested, was the military machinery to enable and facilitate this globalization of capital." In recent years this aspect of Luxemburg's work has received more recognition and it is our hope that the *Complete Works* will assist this development.†

---

* J. P. Nettl, *Rosa Luxemburg*, Vol. II (London and New York: Verso, 2019), pp. 493, 519–20. An overview of the German Social Democratic Party is provided by: Gary P. Steenson, *"Not One Man! Not One Penny!" German Social Democracy, 1863–1914* (Pittsburgh: University of Pittsburgh Press, 1981), Carl Schorske, *German Social Democracy, 1905–1917: The Development of the Great Schism* (Cambridge, MA: Harvard University Press, 1955), and Richard N. Hunt, *German Social Democracy 1918–1933* (Chicago: Quadrangle Press, 1970). On the social and cultural richness of this movement, see Vernon L. Lidtke, *The Alternative Culture: Socialist Labor in Imperial Germany* (Oxford, UK: Oxford University Press, 1985) and Kevin J. Callahan, *Demonstration Culture: European Socialism and the Second International, 1889–1917* (Leicester, UK: Troubador Publishing, 2010).

† Hamid Dabashi, *On Edward Said: Remembrance of Things Past* (Chicago: Haymarket, 2020), p. 197; Jane Anna Gordon and Drucilla Cornell, eds., *Creolizing Rosa Luxemburg* (Lanham, MD: Rowman and Littlefield, 2021); Filippo Menozzi and Jeremy Gilbert, eds., *Rosa Luxemburg: Capitalism, Imperialism, and the Postcolonial, New Formations* 94 (Autumn 2018). See also Alyssa

MASS STRIKE AND SOCIAL DEMOCRACY

A central component of Luxemburg's contribution to the revolutionary Marxist tradition that animates the present volume is her conceptualization of the mass strike, which came out of actual explosions throughout Eastern Europe in 1905–06, including the First Russian Revolution—working class and revolutionary upsurges Luxemburg witnessed and took part in. We see this brewing and gathering strength in her perceptive descriptions of labor ferment and class struggles (Volume 3 of the *Complete Works),* and as a theoretical orientation it explodes and finds vibrant elaboration with the 1906 classic *The Mass Strike, the Political Party, and the Trade Unions* (Volume 4). It will necessarily spill over into future volumes, for example in her important 1910 polemic with Karl Kautsky, "Theory and Practice."* In the present volume, we find not only the elaboration of the perspective but also the struggle to bring the SPD to embrace it, along with growing dissatisfaction and disenchantment over the dogged pushback and repressive reaction of the formal leadership.

Luxemburg often highlights a wild spontaneity (more accurately, semi-spontaneity), as in her 1906 pamphlet:

> The mass strike … is a phenomenon so mutable that it mirrors within itself all phases of the political and economic struggle, and all stages and moments of the revolution. Its applicability, its effectiveness and the elements of its emergence are all continually altering. It suddenly opens up new, broad perspectives for the revolution, just when the latter appeared to have gotten stuck at a choke point, and yet it fails at the very point where it is reckoned to be utterly reliable. Sometimes it flows like a broad swell, surging over the entire empire; at other times it divides into a gigantic network of narrow streams; sometimes it bubbles forth from under the ground like a fresh spring; at other times it seeps away into the ground, petering out entirely. Political and economic strikes, mass strikes and partial strikes, demonstration strikes and militant strikes, general strikes in individual branches and general strikes in individual cities, peaceful wage struggles and street battles and struggles on the barricades—all these phenomena crisscross each other, run parallel to each other, intersect with each other, flow into each other; this is a perpetually moving, fluctuating sea of manifestations. And the law of motion of these phenomena becomes evident: it lies neither in the mass strike itself, nor in the latter's technical peculiarities, but rather in the political and social relation of forces within the revolution.†

Adamson's discussion of decolonial approaches to Luxemburg's work, "Against a Single History, for a Revaluation of Power: Luxemburg, James, and a Decolonial Critique of Political Economy" in Gordon and Cornell, pp. 69–90.

* Rosa Luxemburg, "Theory and Practice: A Polemic Against Comrade Kautsky's Conception of the Mass Strike," Marxist Internet Archive, marxists.org.

† "The Mass Strike, the Political Party, and the Trade Unions" in *The Complete Works of Rosa Luxemburg*, Vol. 4, p. 303.

As Nettl explains, Luxemburg did not see the mass strike as "the final act in the overturn of society" but recognized that such upheavals had an inevitable quality. They "could not be planned" but must be factored-in as a political weapon "in the arsenal of Social Democracy." Nor was the mass strike a strike in the normal sense of the word. True, it "began as a large-scale withdrawal of labor that upset the stability of the economy and society." But it had nothing to do either with "the negotiation of better conditions" or "with conditions of work at all." In fact, people leaving work simply constituted "the pre-condition for further action," giving vent to the rage and aspirations of vast numbers of people, unleashing their energies for more revolutionary purposes. This is what Luxemburg had seen and experienced in the 1905 upheaval in Russia. Her contribution, Nettl tells us, involved "the broadness and flexibility" in how she conceptualized the mass strike. The revolutionary organization could not manufacture such actions, but it must be prepared for explosions of activity, connecting with them to advance struggles against oppression and for socialism. She saw them "not as a limited technical feat, but as a focal point of confluence for previous techniques and simultaneously as a vent for stronger action in the future."*

In the 1890s, the leadership of the SPD—headed by its "grand old man" August Bebel—had pushed back hard against militant appeals in the ranks for insurrectionary risings, including mass strikes and barricades, reminiscent of the experience of the Paris Commune of 1871. This position came out of the experience of state repression during the years 1878 to 1890, when the party had been forced underground by the Antisocialist Laws imposed by the Bismarck regime. With the end of those laws, the party adopted what came to be known as the Erfurt Program, which was shaped by Kautsky. In his discussion of the SPD before World War I, Pierre Broué explains:

> Kautsky did not renounce the maximum program, the socialist revolution, which the expansion of capitalism had made a distant prospect, but laid down that the Party could and must fight for the demands of a minimum program, partial aims, and political, economic and social reforms, and must work to consolidate the political and economic power of the workers' movement, whilst raising the consciousness of the working class.
>
> In this way, the dichotomy was created which distinguished the maximum program—revolution and socialism—from the minimum program of reforms which could be realized within the framework of the existing capitalist regimes. This separation was to dominate the theory and practice of social democracy for decades.†

* Nettl, pp. 497, 498–9, 509.

† Pierre Broué, *The German Revolution 1917–1923* (1971), trans. John Archer, ed. Ian Birchall and Brian Pearce (Chicago: Haymarket, 2006), p.17.

The party was emerging as an influential mass political force, and with rapidly growing membership, trade union strength, and remarkable electoral victories, it was determined not to be forced underground again. Over the coming decades, Broué tells us, it would become "a party so powerful that it formed a real state within the state." It "provided not just a political attitude or a way of thinking, but a framework, a way of living and of feeling."* Within this massive organization coexisted sharply different political orientations, and these differences coalesced around discussions of the mass strike.

"Mass strikes, whether general or not," notes Mike Davis, "risked becoming out-of-control conflicts that allowed the bourgeoisie to unleash their might and crush unions and roll back electoral gains." Even the aging Frederick Engels, at Bebel's behest, was persuaded to write a widely publicized introduction in 1895 to Marx's *The Class Struggles in France, 1848–1850,* in which he seemingly endorsed the SPD's pioneering development of "an entirely new method of proletarian struggle" based on trade union and electoral work.† (Such notions can, after all, be found in the *Communist Manifesto* itself). Reviewing advances in military technology that strengthened the repressive forces of the bourgeois state, Engels warned that "the powers-that-be positively want to get us to go where the guns shoot and the sabers slash." This could be taken as an endorsement of a shift away from revolutionary struggle, although this was far from Engels' intention.

The implications were the focus of Luxemburg's eloquent critique in her address to the founding convention of the German Communist Party contained in this volume.‡ Luxemburg not only explains the nonrevolutionary thrust of the reformists' current path but also traces its origins back to what she describes as the SPD's long and steady departure from its Marxist roots, even while it officially upheld its revolutionary goals:

> I am convinced—anyone who knows the works of Marx and Engels, knows the vital and revolutionary, genuine, undistorted spirit which breathes out of all their teachings and writings, must also be convinced—that Engels would have been the first to have protested against this dissipation and ruination of the workers' movement which had already taken hold in Germany decades before August 4—because August 4 did not fall on us out of the blue as an unfortunate malfunction

---

* Broué, p. 15.

† The SPD ran a doctored version of the introduction in *Vorwärts* that yoked Engels into service of their argument and removed material that affirmed the continued need for struggle in the streets. See note on p. 347 below.

‡ Mike Davis, *Old Gods, New Enigmas: Marx's Lost Theory* (London: Verso, 2018), p. 60; Luxemburg's latter-day critique of this early orientation, and of Engels's 1895 remarks, can be found on pp. 347–50, below; for background on the context out of which Bebel's orientation rose, see Vernon L. Lidtke, *The Outlawed Party: Social Democracy in Germany, 1878–1890* (Princeton, NJ: Princeton University Press, 1966).

> but was, rather, the logical consequence of that which we had experienced day by day and year by year. ("Quite right!") I am certain that Engels and Marx, if they had lived, would have been the first to protest this with all their power, and to haul the cart back with a mighty hand, so that it did not roll down into the swamp.*

Central to this address is Luxemburg's recognition of the essential role of the mass strike in the German Revolution, which speaks to extensive and ongoing debates within the party and the trade unions about its role and potential. While the SPD trade union leaders helped to popularize the notion that "the general strike is general nonsense," Davis notes that some shifts away from this outright rejection had come from pragmatists in the center and right of the Social Democratic leadership. Eduard Bernstein, for example, advanced a notion of "the defensive role of general strikes" in efforts to extend the right to vote, positing, as Davis puts it, that "union power, disciplined and well-organized, might be the best assurance that a peaceful road to socialism remained open." Among other moderate or right-wing socialist leaders, the general strike was seen "primarily as a useful safety valve for romanticized militancy. Thus the reformist Socialist leadership under [Émile] Vandervelde in Belgium twice defused pre-revolutionary crises by cleverly manipulating and prematurely ending general strikes for suffrage in 1902 and 1913."†

As can be seen from her writings in this volume (as well as in Volume 4), Luxemburg's approach was the polar opposite of this perspective. "Her crucial insights about working-class self-activity (that is to say, of unauthorized but not unled militancy)," according to Davis, "were part of a withering critique of the SPD leadership's 'parade ground' self-image as the general staff of an obedient army of trade-unionists and socialist voters." In fact, Luxemburg "was one of the first socialist intellectuals to pay careful attention to the grassroots processes of proletarian radicalization."‡

In advancing this orientation, Luxemburg confronted what Nettl describes as "the democratically masked oligarchy which existed in the SPD." Far from seriously considering the need to educate around and engage with the reality and theorizations of mass strikes, the party leadership acceded to the demands of the conservative trade union bureaucracy, and of the technocrats who ran electoral campaigns. It "strangled the discussion." Even when SPD leaders took up popular struggles to defend and expand the right to vote, they backed away from any consistent or effective militancy. Luxemburg tartly comments on this in more than one contribution in the present volume. In a 1913 speech widely reported in the mainstream German press, for example, Luxemburg works

---

* Luxemburg, "Founding Congress of the Communist Party of Germany," see p. 350, below.

† Davis, pp. 61–2.

‡ Ibid., p. 65.

through the reciprocal relationship between the party and the class. Stressing the determinant role of working-class self-activity, she calls on the party to provide crucial direction, rather than serving as an impediment, and urges preparation to lead mass action: "One cannot make a mass strike according to specific rules, one cannot regulate in advance for it, but one can foresee it and ready oneself for it, so that the situation can be exploited when it's favorable."* Sections of the elected leadership, however, continued to act as a block on mass action, as they also became steadily more conservative with regard to militarism, imperialism, and war. It soon proved impossible "to break the crust of self-absorption within which the SPD slept its leaden sleep," as Nettl puts it.†

We have noted four successive elements in Luxemburg's developing critique of the SPD: an articulation of the mass-strike doctrine, the struggle for its application, a growing disenchantment in the face of bureaucratic resistance, and, finally, the recognition of the centrality of imperialism not only in the development of global capitalism but in the fatal weakness in the very heart of the Social Democracy. "Imperialism has opened the final phase, the division of the world by the assault of capital," Luxemburg said in a May Day speech of 1913. "A chain of unending, exorbitant armaments on land and on sea in all capitalist countries because of rivalries; a chain of bloody wars which have spread from Africa to Europe and which at any moment could light the spark which would become a world fire-storm." Calling for mass strikes "as a demonstration and means of struggle for the eight-hour day, world peace, and socialism," she nonetheless seemed to predict a different outcome, but also a revolutionary hope: "Out of the world war which, sooner or later, is unavoidable, will come forth a definite and victorious struggle between the world of labor and that of capital."‡

As can be seen from items in the present volume, Luxemburg came to doubt whether the organized Social Democratic movement could be a force for working-class liberation and socialist revolution, and she was not alone in this. During the years leading up to World War I, the tensions between the reformists and the party's left sharpened, with Luxemburg and Karl Liebknecht, according to Broué, "only two of the most important figures in a current which separated itself step by step from the journalists and theoreticians who gathered around Kautsky in the course of the 'Bernstein affair' and the struggle against revisionism."§ Luxemburg broke with Kautsky in 1910, along with other key figures on the party's left. In the period leading up to 1914, Broué

* Luxemburg, "On the Political Mass Strike," pp. 79–80, below.

† Nettl, pp. 495, 516, 517, 519.

‡ Rosa Luxemburg, "The Idea of May Day on the March," in *Selected Political Writings*, ed. Dick Howard (New York: Monthly Review Press, 1971), pp. 319, 320–1; also at Marxist Internet Archive, marxists.org. (There is a minor alteration in the translation here.)

§ Broué, p. 28.

identifies the "militant workers, trade-union activists and Party members who gave the union leaders a hard time in the wildcat strikes," commenting: "These radical left-wing activists held strong positions on the eve of the War. In certain industrial centres, they enjoyed majority support among the party members and in the local Party apparatus. They also enjoyed great prestige and a wide following in the party and in the working class through their publications."* These were the militant activists who opposed imperialism and militarism and defended Luxemburg when she faced state charges for her opposition to war.

As late as June 1914, Luxemburg continued to call on the leadership of the party to become worthy of its reputation. In an appeal for more decisive action in support of the struggle for Prussian suffrage she wrote: "It is the direct duty of a fighting party like ours to trigger the masses' maximum capacity for action at every moment. And if the initiative is lacking from the center, then, in a true democratic party like ours, the initiative must come from below, from the provinces."†

The decision by SPD leaders to support the imperialist war effort was decisive in Luxemburg's break with them. "Since August 4, 1914 [the start of the First World War], German Social Democracy has been a stinking corpse." This line was attributed to Luxemburg by Lenin. While the exact words have not been found in her writings, there is more than one formulation in the present volume that expresses the same thought.‡

IMPACT OF THE MASS STRIKE CONCEPT

And yet Luxemburg could not consider the *entire* Social Democratic movement to be dead, nor was she without significant influence within it. This becomes evident when we note the views of a young working-class leader in Düsseldorf who had attended the SPD school where Luxemburg was one of the most popular teachers. Now editor of the local party paper, Peter Berten denounced those who were trying, as he put it, to turn the SPD into "a bourgeois radical reform party," insisting that "we have no cause to give up our principles and our tactics. The capitalist system with its injuries cannot be eliminated by concessions to the ruling class and its government."§

In 1913, after SPD electoral victories in Düsseldorf, he was warning that "some of our comrades seem to be of the opinion that since we won the Reichstag election everything has been achieved ... Most believe that they have fulfilled their responsibilities if they pay their dues and attend an occasional meeting." But the combination of seeking petty reforms while passively waiting

---

* Ibid., p. 38.

† Luxemburg, "Once Again the Prussian Suffrage Struggle," pp. 112, below.

‡ Taber, ed., *Under the Socialist Banner*, pp. 161–2.

§ Mary Nolan, *Social Democracy and Society: Working-Class Radicalism in Düsseldorf, 1890–1920* (London: Cambridge University Press, 1981), p. 187.

for the revolution, Berten insisted, "cannot possibly inspire and sweep along the masses. Only great goals can awaken enthusiasm and a willingness to sacrifice."*

In Berten's opinion, "only a revolutionary tactic, which always builds on the reality of class conflict and appeals to the elemental power of the masses, can waken the energy, activism, and enthusiasm of the exploited proletariat." He insisted in the *Volkszeitung* that "the mass strike is the method of struggle which is most suited to the social position of the proletariat." In his opinion, "What the proletariat possesses, in addition to its chains, is the power that does not disappear through struggle. Rather it grows until it suffices to break the chains." Mary Nolan reports that "Berten and several other functionaries were the most vociferous proponents of the mass strike, but their ideas found a sympathetic echo among comrades locally and regionally."†

Luxemburg's perspectives were shaped by such working-class activists in cities like Düsseldorf and far beyond. Luxemburg did not "invent" the mass strike and was hardly the only person either to describe its reality or to offer a Marxist theorization of it. We can find elements in the writings of others who were embedded in the working-class movement—particularly those who experienced the Russian Revolution with Luxemburg in 1905–06, including Trotsky and Lenin. What is undeniable, however, is the growing centrality of the mass strike in her political thought, and the distinctive insights she offered in her discussions of it.‡

Luxemburg's orientation had an impact elsewhere in Europe, particularly in the Netherlands among militants in the left wing of the Dutch Social Democracy, known as "the Tribunists" (after the title of their paper): Henriette Roland Holst, Anton Pannekoek, Hermann Gorter, S. J. Rutgers, and others. The reach of her influence extended well beyond Europe. Her ideas regarding mass action made their way to the United States, where Rutgers lived during the First World War. He was active in the left-wing of the Socialist Party of America and played a significant role in the beginnings of US Communism, becoming prominent for a short time in the international Communist movement.§ Some

---

* Ibid., pp. 233, 243.

† Ibid., p. 243.

‡ Nettl, p. 509. An outstanding example of other descriptions and theorizations can be found in Leon Trotsky, *1905*, second edition (Chicago: Haymarket, 2016). Aspects of Lenin's thinking (in some cases conflicting with that of some of his comrades) are laid out in Solomon Schwarz, *Russian Revolution of 1905: Worker's Movement and Formation of Bolshevism and Menshevism* (Chicago: University of Chicago Press, 1967).

§ Philippe Bourrinet traces Luxemburg's influence among Dutch Tribunists in *The Dutch and German Communist Left, 1900–1968* (Chicago: Haymarket, 2018). Her influence via Rutgers in the United States is indicated in Theodore Draper, *The Roots of American Communism* (New York: Viking Press, 1957), pp. 88–91. Also see: S. J. Rutgers, "Mass Action in Russia," *International Socialist Review*, January 1917, pp. 410–3; S. J. Rutgers, "Mass Action and Socialism," *The New International*, February 1918, p. 5; and Louis C. Fraina, *Revolutionary Socialism, A Study in Socialist Reconstruction* (The Communist Press, 1918; reprinted, New York: Cosimo, 2012), pp. 178–203.

of Luxemburg's works were published in translation in Japan in the 1920s, and, with the help of Peruvian Marxist José Carlos Mariátegui, others were translated and distributed in Spanish.* Mass strike theorizations naturally found their way into the analyses and resolutions of the early Communist International (1919–22) and of theorists and activists associated with it.†

One of the outstanding figures in this tradition, Antonio Gramsci, commented appreciatively but also critically in his *Prison Notebooks* that Luxemburg "in this little book [*The Mass Strike, the Political Party, and the Trade Unions*]—a little hastily, and rather superficially too—theorized the historical experiences of 1905 … All the same, this little book (like others of the same author's essays) is one of the most significant documents theorizing the war of maneuver in relation to political science."‡

By "war of maneuver" Gramsci means revolutionary political struggles involving direct attacks against the state, culminating in the revolutionary seizure of power and the overthrow of capitalism. Gramsci distinguishes this from what he calls "war of position," by which he means a broader, protracted conflict. In his "war of position," the working-class movement builds up its organizations and its influence (its hegemony) in social and political spheres through cultural-educational activity and winning reforms within capitalist society. While some "Gramscians" counterpose the latter concept to the former, Daniel Egan shows that Gramsci saw them in dialectical interplay—the protracted war of position ultimately culminating in a revolutionary overturn.§

Egan demonstrates that Gramsci's understanding of Luxemburg's theory is "closer to that expressed by her opponents in the SPD than her own," and that "her theory of the mass strike, far from being a model of the war of maneuver, is consistent with Gramsci's analysis of the war of position." Noting that "both Gramsci and Luxemburg understood Marxism to be a creative, living method of revolutionary analysis and practice rather than a one-dimensional dogma to be applied in a mechanical fashion," he holds that "both in turn rejected social democratic reformism" as well as what would come to be known as "Marxist-Leninist vanguardism, emphasizing instead the dialectical relationship between

---

* Hernán Ouviña, "Reading Rosa Luxemburg in Latin America," Rosa Luxemburg Stiftung, March 2020, rosalux.de.

† Luxemburg's early influence becomes obvious from combing through volumes edited by John Riddell: *Founding the Communist International Proceedings and Documents of the First Congress, March 1919* (New York: Pathfinder Press, 1987); *Workers of the World and Oppressed Peoples, Unite! Proceedings and Documents of the Second Congress, 1920* (New York: Pathfinder Press, 1991); *To the Masses: Proceedings of the Third Congress of the Communist International, 1921* (Chicago: Haymarket Books, 2016); and *Toward the United Front: Proceedings of the Fourth Congress of the Communist International, 1922* (Chicago: Haymarket, 2013).

‡ Antonio Gramsci, *Selections from the Prison Notebooks*, ed. Quintin Hoare and Geoffrey Nowell Smith (New York: International Publishers, 1971), p. 233.

§ Daniel Egan, *The Dialectic of Position and Maneuver: Understanding Gramsci's Military Metaphor* (Chicago: Haymarket, 2018), pp. 1–2, 9, 76, 113, 114.

mass action and the party." More specifically, Luxemburg's mass strike does not represent a recipe for the revolutionary seizure of power but is part of a "protracted process in which the proletariat develops a revolutionary consciousness and its capabilities to serve as the new dominant class through its own activity."*

Luxemburg articulated this with her signature figurative power in the *Mass Strike* pamphlet. Following a vivid description of the revolutionary wave spreading across Russia in 1905, she writes: "The most valuable dimension—since it is an enduring one—of this acutely revolutionary ebb and flow is its intellectual legacy: the surging intellectual and cultural growth of the proletariat, which provides an inviolable guarantee of its irresistible further progress in both the economic and the political struggle"†

CONTINUING RELEVANCE

Luxemburg's conceptualization can be applied in a variety of contexts. "Out of all her writings and speeches grew a basic democratic concept of the proletarian mass movement with an important role for spontaneity," according to Ottokar Luban, "which cannot be seen only as a purpose for itself or only as a question of the relationship between proletarian masses and their leaders—for spontaneity is only the prerequisite for creativity and the readiness for action." He adds: "Only if socialist leaders accept and encourage spontaneity in a completely democratic environment will the full creativity and strength of the proletarian masses be set free—increasing their organization, too—in the fight for political power and the subsequent building up of a socialist society."‡

Luban is here referring to "socialist leaders" and mass organizations (such as the German Social Democratic Party, with its multiple expressions and auxiliaries) corresponding to pre-1914 Germany, but Luxemburg's conceptualizations have application well beyond that specific context. Indeed, no such mass socialist organizations or movements existed in many regions swept by the mass strike phenomenon of 1905. That is also true of most of the world today.

In their introduction to the fourth volume of the *Complete Works*, the editors touch on recent developments in the United States that illustrate the relevance of Luxemburg's revolutionary conceptualizations: "the emergence of a host of new anti-racist, anti-sexist, anti-capitalist, LGBTQ and pro-environmental movements."§ We can further identify mass strike dynamics not only in such trade union struggles as the Wisconsin labor protests of 2011

* Daniel Egan, "Rosa Luxemburg and the Mass Strike: Rethinking Gramsci's Critique," *Socialism and Democracy*, 2019, Vol. 33, No. 2, pp. 46, 63, 64.

† Rosa Luxemburg, *Complete Works*, Vol. 4, p. 294.

‡ Ottokar Luban, "Rosa Luxemburg's Concept of Spontaneity and Creativity in Proletarian Movements—Theory and Practice," *International Critical Thought*, 2019, Vol. 9, No. 4, pp. 515–6.

§ *Complete Works*, Vol. 4, p. xxxii.

and the tumultuous wave of teacher strikes in 2018–19, but also in the Occupy Wall Street movement that swept through the United States in 2011–12, followed by the two powerful waves of mass Black Lives Matter mobilizations and insurgencies of 2013 and 2020.

Similar developments can be identified globally, from the "Arab Spring" to upsurges in Chile, Greece, Spain, India, Poland and elsewhere: overflowing established boundaries, breaking the rules, challenging authority, expanding the space of and support for radical-left politics, and—whether culminating in victory or defeat—often advancing a deepened radicalization and inspiring innumerable organizing efforts.*

Even within the United States, one finds a long tradition: the great labor upsurge of 1877, starting on the railroads against wage cuts and layoffs but spreading like wildfire in industrial centers through much of the country; the militant protests and battles of 1886 for the eight-hour workday that culminated in making May Day an international workers' holiday throughout the world; the 1934 insurgencies and general strikes that rocked and transformed Toledo, Minneapolis, and San Francisco, soon followed by a semi-spontaneous wave of sit-down strikes engulfing factories and workplaces, tilting the political mainstream well to the left. Despite significant social, economic, and political changes over the following three decades, there were similar insurgencies, inflected with mass strike dynamics, in the 1960s: from the early civil rights upsurge, to the campus protests and occupations, to antiwar explosions (especially in the wake of the 1970 US government escalation of the war into Cambodia), as well as—one "long hot summer" after another—the African-American rebellions in urban centers from 1963 through 1968.†

Far from becoming an obsolete relic from a bygone age, mass strikes globally have once more reached a scale only seen before at revolutionary highpoints in the last century. A major global research study of mass protests in the current period confirms this:

---

* See Sami Zemni, Brecht De Smet and Koenraad Bogaert, "Luxemburg on Tahrir Square: Reading the Arab Revolutions with Rosa Luxemburg's *The Mass Strike*," *Antipode*, 2013, Vol. 45, No. 4, pp. 888–907. The current mass actions against the military coup in Sudan are illustrative of the continuing relevance of the mass strike as theorized by Luxemburg. This is demonstrated in a November 2021 presentation by two Sudanese activists: Rabab Elnaiem, member of the Sudanese Workers Alliance for the Restoration of Trade Unions, and Muzan Alneel, cofounder of the Innovation, Science & Technology Think Tank for People-Centered Development (ISTiNAD). Their discussion illustrates many of the themes crystalized by Luxemburg: the power of mass resistance; the reciprocal push and pull between economic and political issues; the centrality of workers' democracy as a counterweight to the violence of the bourgeois state. See "Sudan Resists the Coup," *Tempest*, October 31, 2021, tempestmag.org.

† On US labor, for example, see Sidney Lens, *Labor Wars* (Chicago: Haymarket, 2009); on African-American rebellions see Manning Marable, *Race, Reform and Rebellion* (Jackson: University of Mississippi Press, 2007); on campus protests and antiwar explosions, see Van Gosse, *Rethinking the New Left* (New York: Palgrave Macmillan, 2005).

> There are times in history when large numbers of people protest about the way things are, demanding change. It happened in 1830–1848, in 1917–1924, in the 1960s, and it is happening again today … Since 2010, the world has been shaken by protests.*

One can find bitter defeats and disheartening compromises as well as remarkable victories flowing from all this. We find, however, no permanent disappearance of the mass strike phenomenon. Over time—for reasons and with dynamics identified by Rosa Luxemburg—we find that mass strike phenomena have continued to come into being in a variety of forms and around a variety of issues. Luxemburg's observations and analyses continue to have urgent relevance a century later.

III. THE REVOLUTIONARY HERITAGE

Rosa Luxemburg's political orientation was characterized by a profoundly democratic harmony of ends and means. This is telegraphed in the very opening paragraph of her classic pamphlet, *Reform or Revolution*:

> The daily struggle for reforms, for the amelioration of the condition of the workers within the framework of the existing social order, and for democratic institutions, offers to the social democracy the only means of engaging in the proletarian class war and working in the direction of the final goal—the conquest of political power and the suppression of wage labor. Between social reforms and revolution there exists for the social democracy an indissoluble tie. The struggle for reforms is its means; the social revolution, its aim.†

Genuine and radical democracy forms the vibrant link between the socialist goal and the struggle for that goal. In his classic survey *The Marxists*, sociologist C. Wright Mills notes that Luxemburg was "first of all and continuously, a revolutionary … but she was also passionately for democracy and for freedom in all the decisive meanings of those terms."‡

Democracy literally means rule by the people, a population collectively having a decisive say in the decisions affecting the lives of its members. It cannot truly exist without freedom. Freedom means control over one's life—*self-determination*: the ability to develop one's own thoughts, to express oneself

* Isabel Ortiz, Sara Burke, Mohamed Berrada, Hernán Saenz Cortés, *World Protests: A Study of Key Protest Issues in the 21st Century* (New York: Palgrave, 2022). This wide-ranging and illuminating survey of global mass protests was supported, somewhat ironically, by the Friedrich-Ebert-Stiftung New York.

† Rosa Luxemburg, *Reform or Revolution*, in *The Rosa Luxemburg Reader*, ed. Peter Hudis and Kevin B. Anderson (New York: Monthly Review Books, 2006), p. 130.

‡ C. Wright Mills, *The Marxists* (New York: Dell, 1962), p. 149.

as one wishes, to influence others and seek the influence of others, to engage in creative labor and be part of an open community "in which the free development of each is the condition for the free development of all."* For Marx, and those like Luxemburg who were inspired by him, this was central to a vision of socialism or communism, the two words initially meaning the same thing: a vision of the economy under the democratic control of the producers and consumers whose lives and labor make the economy a reality, with freedom and justice for all, a society of the free and the equal.†

During the twentieth century, a number of Communist parties took power and proclaimed the domains over which they ruled "socialism." This developed at variance with the way the word was understood by Marx and such co-thinkers as Luxemburg. "The socialism of the twentieth century, fraught as it is with backstabbing, betrayal, humiliations, subordinations, torture and murder, weighs like a nightmare on the brains of the living, but also presents opportunities that are often overlooked," according to Michael Brie and Jörn Schütrumpf, writing in 2021. "Unlike during the pre-1917 period, socialism is no longer a vague idea." The results have been grim, but also clarifying: "We now have 70 years of practice from which we can learn not only how to persistently discredit the idea of socialism, but also what socialism certainly is not."‡

Many Luxemburg scholars agree with Sobhanlal Datta Gupta that Luxemburg's thought conveys, in stark contrast to this, a "unique understanding of socialism and democracy," and many also agree with him that this is "strikingly relevant today," providing "clues to an understanding of socialism which honors the idea of democracy in a highly innovative manner." Luxemburg's notion of working-class rule, which is central to her conception of socialism, involves the existence, in an industrialized economy, of a democratic republic that is genuinely under the control of a working-class majority—buttressed by full freedom of the press, expression, and association—and supplemented by social movements (including mass action) and democratic councils in communities and workplaces.§

---

* Marx and Engels, *The Communist Manifesto*, in *Marx-Engels Collected Works*, Vol. 6 (New York: International Publishers, 1976), p. 506.

† Marx's discussion on essential aspects of humanity (species-being) relevant to his conception of socialism/communism is indicated in his *Economic and Philosophic Manuscripts of 1844*, in *Marx-Engels Collected Works*, Vol. 3 (New York: International Publishers, 1975), pp. 275–9. It is discussed in Erich Fromm, *Marx's Concept of Man* (New York: Frederick Ungar, 1961), but more recently and thoroughly in Peter Hudis, *Marx's Concept of the Alternative to Capitalism* (Chicago: Haymarket, 2013). Also relevant are Micheline A. Ishay, *The History of Human Rights, From Ancient Times to the Globalization Era* (Berkeley: University of California Press, 2008) and Brian S. Roper, *The History of Democracy, A Marxist Interpretation* (London: Pluto Press, 2013).

‡ Michael Brie and Jörn Schütrumpf, *Rosa Luxemburg: A Revolutionary Marxist at the Limits of Marxism* (New York: Palgrave Macmillan, 2021), pp. viii–ix.

§ Sobhanlal Datta Gupta, *Rosa Luxemburg* (Kolkata: Seribaan, 2015), p. 25. In addition to materials in this volume, see volume 4 of the *Complete Works*, including the introduction by

"Luxemburg's democratic insistence runs as a red thread throughout her life's work, alongside her revolutionary impetus," her biographer Dana Mills has noted. "Her legacy lived on outside of scholarly debates within the realm of German communism."*

The democracy inherent in the struggle and the goal of revolutionary socialism envisioned by many Marxists in the early twentieth century is captured in this excerpt from a 1915 polemic:

> We must combine the revolutionary struggle against capitalism with a revolutionary program and revolutionary tactics relative to all democratic demands: a republic, a militia, officials elected by the people, equal rights for women, self-determination of nations, etc. While capitalism exists, all these demands are realizable only as an exception, and in an incomplete, distorted form. Basing ourselves on democracy as it already exists, exposing its incompleteness under capitalism, we advocate the overthrow of capitalism, expropriation of the bourgeoisie as a necessary basis both for the abolition of the poverty of the masses and for a complete and manifold realization of all democratic reforms. Some of those reforms will be started prior to the overthrow of the bourgeoisie, others in the process of the overthrow, still others after it has been accomplished. The socialist revolution is by no means a single battle; on the contrary, it is an epoch of a whole series of battles around all problems of economic and democratic reforms, which can be completed only by the expropriation of the bourgeoisie. It is for the sake of this final aim that we must formulate in a consistently revolutionary manner every one of our democratic demands. It is quite conceivable that the workers of a certain country may overthrow the bourgeoisie before even one fundamental democratic reform has been realized in full. It is entirely inconceivable, however, that the proletariat as an historical class will be able to defeat the bourgeoisie if it is not prepared for this task by being educated in the spirit of the most consistent and determined revolutionary democracy.†

Sandra Rein and Peter Hudis. Also see Peter Hudis, "Rosa Luxemburg's Concept of a Post-capitalist Society," *Critique: Journal of Socialist Theory*, Vol. 40, No. 3 (2012), pp. 323–35.

* Dana Mills, *Rosa Luxemburg* (London: Reaktion, 2020), p. 163. Other relevant evaluations of Luxemburg's legacy include Evelin Wittich, "Discussions around a Monument: The Battle Around the Interpretation of History—the Example of Rosa Luxemburg," *Militarism and War* (Johannesburg: Khanya College Publishing and Rosa Luxemburg Foundation, 2004), pp. 3–11; Tanja Storløkken, "Rosa Luxemburg—Revolution and Experience," *Left Movements and Participation in Bourgeois Institutions* (Johannesburg: Khanya College Publishing and Rosa Luxemburg Foundation, 2006), pp. 3–22.

† V. I. Lenin, "The Revolutionary Proletariat and the Right of Nations to Self-Determination" (1915), excerpted in Paul Le Blanc, *From Marx to Gramsci: A Reader in Revolutionary Marxist Politics* (Chicago: Haymarket, 2016), p. 246. *From Marx to Gramsci* argues that, *despite differences*, a unified political orientation can be found in the life and works of Marx, Engels, Luxemburg, Lenin, Trotsky, Gramsci and others. Related to one of the differences between Lenin and Luxemburg (contained in this specific excerpt) is his defense of self-determination for oppressed nations—a conception that Luxemburg was inclined to challenge in the name of revolutionary internationalism.

This quotation is not from Luxemburg, but from Lenin—yet it expresses an orientation quite consistent with her own standpoint. As Peter Hudis maintains, "every serious Marxist of the First and Second International—from Marx and Engels, and from Bebel to Kautsky—fought for the creation of a democratic republic on the grounds that it is the form best suited for waging a successful class struggle against capitalism. Lenin did the same before 1914." Hudis suggests that, with the eruption of World War I, Lenin concluded this perspective "was now out of date"—but, we see from the above quotation that, in the following year, Lenin was still arguing for a radical form of democracy largely consistent with that of Luxemburg herself.*

"In 1915–1916 Lenin had thoroughly thought out the question of democracy, approaching the question from the standpoint of building socialism," reminisced his companion Nadezhda Krupskaya. "The building of socialism is not only economic building. Economics is only the base of socialist construction, its foundation, its premise; the crux of socialist construction lies in the rebuilding of the entire social fabric, a rebuilding on the basis of socialist revolutionary democracy." As Tamás Krausz has noted, democracy was "one of the cornerstones of his political concept," within which "bourgeois democracy becomes plebian democracy and then a workers' democracy (semi-state), presupposing a transformation within the power structure of the social-economic change of regimes as a whole."†

Lenin's democratic conceptualization was fundamentally compromised as the Russian Revolution of 1917 gave way to civil war, foreign invasion, counterrevolutionary terror—and the infamous Red Terror. As 1918 was about to turn to 1919, the crystallization of a one-party dictatorship was evident.‡ And in the face of this, Luxemburg forcefully advanced a critical analysis in perhaps the most essential document contained in this volume, presented here under the title "On the Russian Revolution."

THE RUSSIAN REVOLUTION

Michael Brie and Jörn Schütrumpf have aptly labeled this 1918 draft "Rosa Luxemburg's Symphony on the Russian Revolution." It is obvious, nonetheless, that it is an unfinished symphony. It is not a final draft, and one wonders how

* Peter Hudis, "Introduction: Luxemburg in Our Time," in J. P. Nettl, *Rosa Luxemburg* (London: Verso, 2019), p. xxi.

† N. K. Krupskaya, *Memories of Lenin*, Vol. II (New York: International Publishers, 1930), 189–190; Tamás Krausz, *Reconstructing Lenin, An Intellectual Biography* (New York: Monthly Review Press, 2015), p. 367.

‡ This development is highlighted in two deeply researched volumes by Alexander Rabinowitch: *The Bolsheviks Come to Power: The Revolution of 1917 in Petrograd* (Chicago: Haymarket, 2017) and *The Bolsheviks in Power: The First Year of Soviet Rule in Petrograd* (Bloomington: Indiana University Press, 2008). It is further explored in numerous works, including Paul Le Blanc, *October Song: Bolshevik Triumph, Communist Tragedy 1917–1924* (Chicago: Haymarket, 2017).

it would have ended had she been given at least an additional year of life. The Red Terror and Civil War got much worse in the months following Luxemburg's death—one imagines she would have had more to say. As Luban has confirmed, it is a myth that she was preparing to retract the profound criticisms of Lenin and the Bolsheviks contained in the pamphlet.

The source of the myth can be traced to a 1922 falling-out among some of her closest comrades. At the time, Paul Levi was breaking from the Communist movement (for reasons indicated later in this introduction), and, in the process, he published the draft of her pamphlet on the Russian Revolution, which could be seen as a justification of such a break. Clara Zetkin and Adolf Warski were maintaining their own ties with the Communist movement, and they argued that Luxemburg herself (at the time of her death a committed partisan of that movement) would have revised the pamphlet before publication.

Zetkin devoted a small book to this question, *Rosa Luxemburg's Views on the Russian Revolution*, published in German by the Communist International in 1922, and recently made available in English translation by small left-wing groups in India and the United States. An unsparing polemic with Levi, the book reproduces the main arguments in Luxemburg's critique (with generous quotes), placing these within her overall revolutionary standpoint (also presented with generous quotes). But the book also asserts that, between her writing of the unfinished draft of the critique in September 1918 and her death in January 1919, "Rosa Luxemburg had grappled her way to a changed historical evaluation." Subsequent developments in Soviet Russia, according to Zetkin, provided "a fitting reply" to Luxemburg's critique by demonstrating that "Bolshevik tactics have proved to be correct." She adds that Luxemburg's subsequent articles in *Rote Fahne*, "may indicate from her position on German affairs the close and strong inner contact she had arrived at with the Russian Revolution since September 1918." Zetkin concludes: "Rosa's entire political activity from early November 1918 until the day of her death demonstrates most effectively her later changed opinion of the controversial fundamental and tactical questions of Bolshevik politics."*

There is certainly no indication that Luxemburg intended to break with Communism, but she had, just as certainly, continued to hold the critical

---

* Clara Zetkin, *Rosa Luxemburg's Views on the Russian Revolution* (New York: Red Star Publishers, 2017), pp. 9, 35, 99, 121. According to Zetkin (pp. 10, 30, 40), Leo Jogiches had suggested the unfinished draft be burned since it no longer expressed Luxemburg's views at the time of her death—but Zetkin strongly disagreed, because "the notes could later be of interest and value," and, in fact, the critique represents "unified and coherent genuine Marxist thought, reflecting a wealth of knowledge and ideas, presenting a well-thought out and productive perspective of the historical process of development." She concludes: "Rosa Luxemburg's posthumously published observations and the questions raised by her on Bolshevist policy during the proletarian dictatorship are indeed very valuable and deserve utmost serious and thoughtful attention. This does not mean I agree with her on all counts." Indeed, much of Zetkin's book is devoted to a respectful expression and explanation of her disagreements.

opinions of the Bolsheviks and aspects of their policies of 1917–18, which are expressed in the posthumously published pamphlet. No documentation exists indicating that she was intending to significantly revise her draft. In fact, Luban is able to cite a "report by her Polish party comrade H. Walecki, a founding member of the Communist Party of Poland, who had long talks with Luxemburg at the end of November or the beginning of December 1918 in Berlin," precisely on the critical points she had drafted. The version produced in this volume appears to be what Luxemburg thought at the time of her death.*

To appreciate fully the importance of Luxemburg's critique requires a sharp focus on historical realities. We have seen that some commentators note the convergence between Luxemburg and Lenin regarding the support of democracy *before* the overturn of capitalism—but they conclude that Luxemburg differs from Lenin in her insistence on the need to *create socialism through radically democratic means*. Lenin, in contrast, is seen as representing an authoritarian, statist, top-down approach to establishing socialism in Russia's new Soviet Republic. The editors of the present volume see the matter differently.

Lenin never considered the possibility of socialism without democracy. The primary instruments of working-class democracy—which had arisen during the revolutionary workers' upsurge of 1905 (which inspired Luxemburg's mass strike orientation), and which came into being again in the early days of the February–March revolution of 1917—were radically democratic councils in the workplaces and working-class communities, designed to coordinate the revolutionary struggle and to oversee the administration of entities and areas that were under their control. While the councils aspired to include representation of Russia's vast peasantry, it was the wage-earning working class that had pride of place in the Soviet scheme. On-the-scene journalist Isaac Don Levine—at the time an admirer of the moderate Kerensky rather than of Lenin—described in June 1917 the role of what he tagged "the Council of Workmen's and Soldiers' Deputies" in the overthrow of the tsarist autocracy: "It was the workmen and soldiers that actually fought and shed their blood for the freedom of Russia." Contrasting the soviets to the far more conservative Provisional Government, he explained: "The Council of Workmen's Deputies stands for far more radical

---

* Brie and Schütrumpf, 165; Ottokar Luban, "Rosa Luxemburg's Criticism of Lenin's Ultra Centralistic Party Concept and of the Bolshevik Revolution," *WorkersControl.Net*, August 1, 2011, workerscontrol.net. In the Russian Revolution polemic, Luxemburg discusses several key questions: an understanding of and policies toward the peasantry; how to understand and deal with oppressed nationalities; and whether it was correct to dissolve the Constituent Assembly. Some of what she has to say on these matters is problematic. These sections of the polemic merit serious examination but are set aside here in order to focus on the more general nexus of democracy-socialism-revolution. For discussion of Luxemburg's support for and critique of the Bolsheviks through the lens of Walter Rodney's response, see Robin D. G. Kelley, "Walter Rodney's *Russian Revolution* and the Curious Case of Rosa Luxemburg," *Creolizing Rosa Luxemburg*, pp. 93–121.

changes in the structure of human life. It is a socialistic body. Composed of delegates of the masses and of representatives of the various revolutionary parties, the Council wants nothing less than social revolution, to be accomplished after the overthrow of autocracy in Europe… Then the capitalistic system must be attacked by the working classes of all nations as their common enemy." When he advanced the slogan "All power to the soviets!" as a prelude to the Bolshevik seizure of power, this is what Lenin was referring to.*

Hannah Arendt once wrote: "There is no doubt that Lenin suffered his greatest defeat when, with the outbreak of the civil war [in 1918], the supreme power that he planned to concentrate in the soviets passed into the hands of the party bureaucracy."† In his magisterial study *The Furies* (comparing the use of terror and violence in the French and Russian revolutions), Arno J. Mayer has expressed the tragedy of the Bolshevik Revolution more poignantly than most. He comments that of all the parties on the scene in 1917, "the Bolshevik party was by far the best organized and disciplined, as well as the most adaptable." This is balanced by his observation that "the Bolshevik project was an inconstant amalgam of ideology and circumstance, of intention and improvisation, of necessity and choice, of fate and chance." He emphasizes that "the way the Bolsheviks took power was consistent with their credo of direct and defiant action, and their authoritarian rule following Red October [1917] was bound to provoke resistances which they were, of course, determined to counter and repress." Their initial intention was to help lead the way to socialist revolution, anticipating partnership with other political forces on the working class and peasant left prepared to follow this course. More than once, Lenin stressed that the Bolsheviks were prepared to go it alone if need be. Yet even Lenin's Bolsheviks were not prepared (perhaps no party could have been prepared) for the tidal waves that would hit them. As Mayer puts it, "just as they were unprepared for the enormity of the crisis, so they were caught unawares by its Furies, which they were not alone to quicken."‡

---

* H. N. Brailsford, *How the Soviets Work* (New York: Vanguard Press, 1927), pp. 33–4; Oskar Anweiler, *The Soviets: The Russian Workers, Peasants, and Soldiers Councils 1905–1921* (New York: Pantheon, 1974), pp. 4–5; E. A. Ross, *Russia in Upheaval* (New York: The Century, 1918), p. 336; Rex A. Wade, *The Russian Revolution, 1917* (Cambridge, UK: Cambridge University Press 2000), pp. 61–66; David Mandel, *The Petrograd Workers in the Russian Revolution, February 1917–June 1918* (Chicago: Haymarket, 2018), pp. 348–51; Isaac Don Levine, *The Russian Revolution* (New York: Harper and Brothers, June 1917), pp. 227, 271, 276. It should be added that Levine was always critical of Lenin—as can be seen in his informative work *The Man Lenin* (New York: Thomas Seltzer, 1924)—and from the 1930s through the 1970s was a prominent anti-communist.

† Hannah Arendt, *Origins of Totalitarianism* (New York: Meridian, 1958), p. 319. Arendt's youth in Weimar Germany involved an immersion in an intellectual and cultural milieu permeated by socialists and dissident Communists who had been deeply influenced by Luxemburg. See Elisabeth Young-Bruehl, *Hannah Arendt: For Love of the World* (New Haven: Yale University Press, 1983).

‡ Arno J. Mayer, *The Furies: Violence and Terror on the French and Russian Revolutions* (Princeton, NJ: Princeton University Press, 2000), pp. 230–231.

The Furies to which Mayer refers are the policies and practices of terror and violence escalating during the Russian Civil War from the latter half of 1918 to 1921. As he shows, considerable violence, often involving large-scale and murderous human rights violations, was committed by enemies and also by defenders of the new Soviet regime. There was, of course, an attempt to force an authoritarian parody of "socialism" into being through a violent "revolution from above"—but this is what Stalin sought to do a dozen years later, with horrific consequences.* It is a distortion to suggest this was Lenin's orientation. Yet the "emergency measures" of Lenin and his comrades, beginning in 1918, were horrific in their own way, doing great damage—as Luxemburg warned—to the cause of socialism. And they helped create precedents and preconditions for what became known as Stalinism.

Understanding (as Luxemburg and other Marxists also understood) that backward Russia was economically too underdeveloped to create socialism, Lenin's Bolsheviks were "banking on the inevitability of the world revolution," as he explained in his August 1918 "Letter to American Workers." The spread of revolution would largely be inspired by what the Russian revolutionaries were doing, but it would also come to their rescue. Lenin and his comrades anticipated that this would sweep working-class majorities into control of industrially advanced countries, which would then join forces with the beleaguered Soviet Republic. That was also the understanding clearly expressed by Rosa Luxemburg: "The whole calculation behind the Russian fight for freedom is based on the tacit presumption that the revolution in Russia ought to become the signal for the revolutionary rising of the proletariat in the West: in France, England and Italy, but above all in Germany." Lenin emphasized: "We are now, as it were, in a besieged fortress, waiting for the other detachments of the world socialist revolution to come to our relief."†

While attempting to hold out, the Bolsheviks found that their young and fragile Soviet Republic was being invaded by foreign armies, being strangled by an economic blockade, suffering an increasingly complex and brutalizing civil war (that was financed in large measure by foreign powers), being battered by assassinations and assassination attempts, and more. In reaction to this—not

---

* C. L. R. James offered an important analysis in his landmark *World Revolution 1917–1936: The Rise and Fall of the Communist International* (New York: Pioneer Publishers, 1937). Stalin's "revolution from above" receives attention in many works, including Ronald Grigor Suny, *The Soviet Experiment: Russia, the USSR, and the Successor States* (New York: Oxford University Press, 1998), pp. 215–68; Robert C. Tucker, *Stalin in Power: The Revolution from Above, 1928–1941* (New York: W.W. Norton, 1992); Roy Medvedev, *Let History Judge: The Origins and Consequences of Stalinism* (New York: Columbia University Press, 1989), pp. 211–54; and Moshe Lewin, *Russia, USSR, Russia: The Drive and Drift of a Superstate* (New York: The New Press, 1995), pp. 82–8, 95–128.

† "Letter to American Workers," in V. I. Lenin, *Revolution, Democracy, Socialism, Selected Writings*, ed. Paul Le Blanc (London: Pluto Press, 2008), p. 300; also at Marxist Internet Archive, marxists.org; see Luxemburg, "Historical Responsibility," p. 169, below.

to "create socialism" but simply to survive—they consolidated a one-party dictatorship and established a secret police known as the Cheka, which unleashed a repressive Red Terror.*

The head of the Cheka was a recent recruit to the Bolsheviks, who under the party name "Józef" had for many years been one of Luxemburg's closest comrades in the Social-Democracy of the Kingdom of Poland and Lithuania (SDKPiL), Felix Dzerzhinsky. Writing to another Polish comrade living in Soviet Russia, she commented: "It is clear that, under such conditions, i.e., being caught in the pincers of the imperialist powers from all sides, neither socialism nor the dictatorship of the proletariat can become a reality, but at the most a caricature of both." By *dictatorship of the proletariat*, she was not referring to the Communist Party dictatorship that was being consolidated in Russia, but rather to the classical Marxist conception of political rule by the working class. "On the other hand, I'm afraid that Józef has been carried away [with the idea] that economic and political holes can be plugged up by energetically tracking down 'conspiracies' and killing 'conspirators.'" Referring to sweeping threats of "slaughtering the bourgeoisie" as "idiocy of the highest degree," she concluded that it "only discredits socialism and nothing more."†

A full understanding of Luxemburg's classic warning comes when we understand it is not simply a polemic against a "wrong" idea about socialism Lenin is purported to have, but, instead, identifies dangers that are inherent in the revolutionary struggle itself.

> That we have never been idol-worshippers of formal democracy merely means that we always distinguish the social core from the political form of *bourgeois* democracy, we have always revealed the bitter core of social inequality and lack of freedom beneath the sweet shell of formal equality and freedom—not, however, in order to discard this shell; instead we have done so in order to spur the working class not to content itself with this mere husk, but rather to conquer political power so as to fill it with a new social content. It is the historic task of the proletariat, when it comes to power, to create socialist democracy in place of bourgeois democracy—not to eliminate democracy altogether. Yet socialist democracy is not something that only begins in the Promised Land, once the substructure—the socialist economy—has been established; it does not come as a ready-made Christmas present for the obedient populace who, in the interim, have loyally supported the handful of socialist dictators. Socialist democracy commences

---

* Dynamics of what happened from 1918 onward are explored and documented in Paul Le Blanc, *October Song*, pp. 131–67.

† Luxemburg, Letter to Julian Marchlewski, September 30, 1918, in Adler, Hudis and Laschitza, *The Letters of Rosa Luxemburg*, pp. 474–5. On the life and work of Dzerzhinsky, see Robert Blobaum, *Feliks Dzierżyński and the SDKPiL: A Study of the Origins of Polish Communism* (Boulder, CO: East European Monographs,1984), and George Leggett, *The Cheka: Lenin's Political Police* (Oxford, UK: Oxford University Press, 1987).

> simultaneously with the dismantling of class domination and the construction of socialism. It begins at the very moment of the seizure of power by the socialist party.*

Democracy isn't a frosting to apply after the baking of the socialist cake. Democracy *is* the cake.

It is clear from any serious reading of her polemic that Luxemburg is neither breaking with Lenin and Trotsky and other revolutionary leaders as betrayers of the socialist ideal nor scolding them from the sidelines. *It is a critique from within.* She sees them as outstanding comrades engaged in the very same struggle to which she has committed her life, comrades who have—particularly under the pressure of events—begun to make grave mistakes which she wants to help them correct.

GERMAN REVOLUTION AND GERMAN COMMUNISM

Among those who study history, there is a notion that (as Hannah Arendt once put it) at certain moments "all roads are open."† This approach allows for speculation about what might have happened if … if … if, for example, Rosa Luxemburg had not been killed. There is a powerful tendency among some historians to resist counterfactual speculation and to see what actually happened as what was destined to happen. This naturally colors the interpretation that some have given to what Luxemburg did and failed to do. They see her "well-meaning" revolutionary efforts as inevitably doomed to defeat.

"Luxemburg got clobbered on the question of the mass strike," according to Stephen Eric Bronner (who was polemicizing with critics on his left), "and, in her stubborn insistence upon turning it into an 'offensive' weapon, she helped split the German Left, diminish her own influence within the Party, and pave the way … for the triumph of those genuinely right-wing nationalist, imperialist, careerist bureaucrats like Friedrich Ebert, who would lead the SPD into its 'great betrayal.'" This severe judgment seems to revise Bronner's discussion of the activities of her final decade in his celebratory *Rosa Luxemburg: A Revolutionary for Our Times.* Her intransigent revolutionary stance, he now seemed to be arguing, was obviously ill-considered, and by the time of her 1919 murder she was "desperate and broken." Another sympathetic biographer, Richard Abraham, has similarly reflected that "the suggestion of sectarianism, of dogmatism, even of irresponsibility is not entirely unjust" when applied to Luxemburg in her final desperate year of life.‡ Such challenges as these can have

---

* Luxemburg, p. 244, below.

† Arendt, *Origins of Totalitarianism*, p. 319.

‡ Stephen Eric Bronner, "Rosa Redux: A Reply to David Camfield and Alan Johnson," and "Moving On: New Replies to New Critics," both in *Rosa Luxemburg: Her Life and Legacy*, ed. Jason

value for scholars and activists who wish to come to grips with what actually happened in history, what was possible, and what was not. But are the critics right?

To what extent were "the roads open" to the kind of outcome for which Luxemburg and her comrades were reaching? In his earlier Luxemburg biography, Bronner rejects the notion that Luxemburg's defeat was inevitable. There actually *was* a revolutionary tide in 1918–19, he appears to be saying, and it was precisely "*to stem the revolutionary tide*" (Bronner's words) that Ebert and his right-hand man in the SPD Gustav Noske, Minister of Defense in the new government, "entered into negotiations with the military and its defeated generals, and with leading industrialists." Eric Hobsbawm explains: "The Social Democratic Party, the child of Karl Marx and Friedrich Engels themselves, had long ceased to be the dangerous revolutionary movement that its supporters and opponents had thought it to be before 1914." Under Ebert's leadership, the First World War "revealed it to be a moderate, respectable patriotic organization which loyally supported the imperial war and its aims—so loyally that its more radical elements had seceded from it." Among these more radical elements were those rallying around Luxemburg and Liebknecht in the Spartakusbund. According to historian William Pelz, "by war's end, Spartakus had grown into an organization of thousands with influence in numerous key working-class areas."*

As Evelyn Anderson has emphasized, however, "the *Spartakusbund* was weak, and … torn by internal conflicts." One central point of dispute was whether it made sense to participate in elections (which Rosa Luxemburg favored) or to boycott them (as a majority of her comrades militantly demanded). Sometimes both positions would be manifested in the same person. "I sometimes go to bed decided on boycott," confessed Karl Liebknecht, "and wake up with the conviction that we must participate in the electoral campaign." One of the more seasoned of the comrades, Eugene Leviné, was of the opinion that the Spartakusbund was too weak either to participate or to boycott, and this organizational weakness carried over into the founding of the German Communist Party (Kommunistiche Partei Deutschlands—KPD).

Schulman (New York: Macmillan Palgrave, 2013), pp. 58, 134; Richard Abraham, *Rosa Luxemburg: A Life for the International* (Oxford, UK: Berg, 1989), p. 144.

* Stephen Eric Bronner, *Rosa Luxemburg: A Revolutionary for Our Times* (University Park, PA: Penn State University Press, 1997), p. 95 (emphasis added); E. J. Hobsbawm, "Introduction" to Rosa Leviné-Meyer, *Leviné, The Life of a Revolutionary* (Farnborough, UK: Saxon House, 1974), p. vii; William A. Pelz, *The Spartakusbund and the German Working class Movement, 1914–1919* (Lewiston, NY: Edward Mellen Press, 1987), p. 286. The organization was named after the great leader of the slave revolts in the crystallizing empire of ancient Rome, Spartacus. A vibrant account of the last five years of Luxemburg's life amid the swirl of war, revolution and counterrevolution can be found in the memoir of Mathilde Jacob, *Rosa Luxemburg, An Intimate Portrait* (London: Lawrence and Wishart, 2000).

"The structure of the new party was extremely loose, indeed non-existent," comments Broué, who notes that even Karl Radek "could not help feeling that he was not dealing with a real party, [and] he was to write later 'the [founding] Congress sharply revealed the youthfulness and inexperience of the Party.'"*

Some scholars are inclined to see this as proof that Luxemburg's organization could not have added up to the revolutionary force that she envisioned. At the same time, Pelz observes that "the KPD's pro-capitalist adversaries did not share later historians' opinions that the movement was irrelevant or insignificant. Rather they sensed the potential danger a disciplined but democratic revolutionary movement represented to continued bourgeois rule." In a similar vein, Geoff Eley has argued: "The Spartacists should not be disregarded: the group's small paper membership is not the only measure of its influence, given the popular volatility and interruption of public life by the war, and in such circumstances the determined vanguardism of a few agitators could go a long way." Despite its weaknesses and repeated disruptions by the authorities, the Spartakusbund had impact. "It is primarily thanks to Rosa Luxemburg's long-time comrade Leo Jogiches" according to Luban, "that the Spartacus Group was able to effectively influence mass actions among German workers between 1916 and early 1918." This was an omen of what would unfold only a year after the deaths of Luxemburg, Liebknecht and Jogiches: the transformation of the KPD into a very substantial mass party, through merger with a majority of the left-wing breakaway from the SPD—the Independent Social Democratic Party (Unabhängige Sozialdemokratische Partei Deutschlands, USPD).†

There is no question that a majority of German workers remained loyal to their "tried and true" old bulwark, the SPD, now under the firm leadership of Ebert. The SPD continued to represent a great mass movement which, in 1919, had 1 million dues-paying members and over 11 million voters (38 percent of the electorate). Ebert and the other SPD leaders were determined to secure positive reforms for the working class, "but to do so required not only continuous pressure on the government and existing forces of order," as Geoff

---

* Evelyn Anderson, *Hammer of Anvil: The Story of the German Working class Movement* (London: Victor Gollancz, 1945), p. 40; Leviné-Meyer, p. 66; Broué, pp. 217, 222, 223.

† William Pelz, p. 289; Geoff Eley, "The SPD in War and Revolution," in *Bernstein to Brandt, A Short History of German Social Democracy,* ed. Roger Fletcher (London: Edward Arnold, 1987), p. 68; Ottokar Luban, "The Role of the Spartacist Group after 9 November 1918 and the Formation of the KPD" in *Weimar Communism as Mass Movement, 1918–1933,* ed. Ralf Hoffrogge and Norman Laporte (London: Lawrence Wishart, 2017), pp. 46, 47, 48; David W. Morgan, *The Socialist Left and the German Revolution: A History of the German Independent Social Democratic Party, 1917–1922* (Ithaca, NY: Cornell University Press, 1975), pp. 341–80. When joined by the USPD majority, the KPD "counted over 350,000 members, an array of newspapers, strong representation in the unions and parliaments, and solid bases in most of Germany's industrial areas, in Halle-Merseburg, the Ruhr, Saxony, Hamburg, and Berlin," according to Eric D. Weitz, *Creating German Communism, 1890–1990: From Popular Protests to Socialist State* (Princeton, NJ: Princeton University Press, 1997), p. 98.

Eley notes, but "also meant keeping general working-class aspirations in line. Imperceptibly, this was turning the SPD into the policeman of the working class." According to Eley, under Ebert's leadership "the bases of authoritarianism in the state and economy had been saved, indeed renewed, in their time of greatest vulnerability; and the best expressions of popular democracy had been rebuffed, even brutally repressed."*

Ebert's biographer Walter Mühlhausen notes the desperate decision by the old ruling class to replace the Kaiser with this Social Democratic "pragmatic organizer." The decision was made for the purpose of drawing the German Revolution into safe channels. Ebert was compelled to become "a revolutionary against his will"—though, in this case, a "*good* revolutionary" who would help stave off the triumph of the terrible revolutionaries, such as Luxemburg and Liebknecht. Despite his "unshakable belief in the ballot," Ebert was fully prepared to make common cause with "the military leadership [that] deployed right-wing militias (the so-called *Freikorps*) comprised mainly of demobilized soldiers who opposed democracy." Many of these would later become cadres in Adolf Hitler's Nazi movement. The quelling of the January 1919 rising "and the brutal killings of Rosa Luxemburg and Karl Liebknecht ... two days after the fighting, deepened the divide in the workers' movement," notes Mühlhausen, who adds: "Noske, supported by Ebert, proved to be a politician with an iron fist." Ebert was a Social Democratic "defender of the ballot" who remained president of the new republic until his death in 1925—yet, in fact, "was never directly elected by the people." As it turned out, "he represented an ever-increasingly bourgeois and dull republic, which was unable to reach the hearts of the people."† David Sassoon comments that "when it took charge of the government, the SPD was completely devoid of any concrete plan for a radical reform of the economy," and that it was "unable to modify the fundamental structures of power of the old regime: the army, the civil service, and the judiciary." He concludes: "The real achievement of the SPD was the creation of the Weimar Republic. Considering its tragic end, however, one should say that the SPD had handed itself a poisoned chalice."‡

Luxemburg and her comrades, then, while confronting immensely powerful forces, were hardly going up against an irresistibly popular tidal wave. Nor was their ultimate defeat preordained. More than one possibility existed—which is indicated by the rapid rise of a massive German Communist Party and movement over the next several years. Those who were closest to Luxemburg

---

* Richard N. Hunt, *German Social Democracy 1918–1933* (New Haven, CT: Yale University Press), p. 1; Geoff Eley, "The SPD in War and Revolution," p. 68; Geoff Eley, *Forging Democracy: The History of the Left in Europe, 1850–2000* (Oxford, UK: Oxford University Press, 2002), p. 169.

† Walter Mühlhausen, *Friedrich Ebert 1871–1925: A Social Democratic Statesman* (Bonn: Dietz Verlag, 2015), pp. 28, 45, 51, 54, 55, 62, 100.

‡ Donald Sassoon, *One Hundred Years of Socialism* (New York: The New Press, 1996), p. 49.

in the left-wing of the SPD joined with her to forge German Communism. Her erstwhile ally on the SPD left, Kautsky, who broke with her over the mass strike (and eventually accommodated to the Ebert leadership), acknowledged that "Rosa Luxemburg came ever closer to the Communist ideological world in the course of the [First World] War," and he expressed agreement with Radek that in 1919 "with Rosa Luxemburg, the greatest, most profound theoretical mind of Communism has died."*

The abortive 1919 upsurge, in which Luxemburg and many of her comrades perished, erupted shortly after the formation of the German Communist Party and well before it had been able to build a mass base. It was a chaotic explosion and swirl of activity lacking the organizational and political coherence necessary for a revolutionary triumph. There is no consensus regarding Luxemburg's role. According to F.L. Carsten, "not only Rosa Luxemburg, but Radek had strongly opposed the attempted seizure of power which they considered entirely premature—a hopeless undertaking that would enable the government 'to deal a blow to the Berlin movement which may weaken the whole movement for months'" (here Carsten is quoting from a report by Radek to the Central Committee of the KPD on January 9, 1919). "It is clear that the revolutionary leaders had no idea what to do next," Pelz emphasizes in his recent *People's History of the German Revolution*. "Even Rosa Luxemburg ... was initially opposed to an uprising, then unsure, decided to support a bid for power, and finally resigned in defeat." On the other hand, sifting through the evidence, Luban finds: "From Wednesday, January 8 up to and including Sunday, January 12, hence even several days after the military defeat of the rebels, she used the [KPD daily] *Rote Fahne* to promote the illusion that the Majority Social Democratic government could be overthrown.... Her fixation on long-standing arguments with the center faction of the Social Democracy ... led her to adopting a mistaken political tactic and aiming at an illusory target during these January days."†

While it is highly unlikely that a socialist revolution could have been achieved in January 1919, there is little question that revolutionary possibilities existed during the period of 1919–23. Had there been strong layers of leadership and cadres around a unified center that included Rosa Luxemburg, Karl Liebknecht, Leo Jogiches, Paul Levi, Clara Zetkin, and younger activists

---

* Karl Kautsky, "Rosa Luxemburg," in *Rosa Luxemburg, Karl Liebknecht, Leo Jogiches: Ihre Bedeutung für deutsche Sozialdemokratie* (1921), pp. 14–20; translated into English, with an introduction by Rida Vaquas, in *Prometheus* online journal, Winter 2020–2021, prometheusjournal.org.

† F. L. Carsten, *Revolution in Central Europe 1918–1919* (Berkeley: University of California Press, 1972), p. 218; William A. Pelz, *A People's History of the German Revolution* (London: Pluto Press, 2018), p. 91; Ottokar Luban, "Rosa at a Loss: The KPD Leadership and the Berlin Uprising of January 1919: Legend and Reality," *Revolutionary History*, Vol. 8, no. 4 (2004), p. 41. Luban also argues against what he considers the mistaken inclination of many to make Liebknecht the scapegoat of ultraleft errors.

associated with them (Eugene Leviné, Paul Frölich, August Thalheimer, Ernst Meyer come to mind), the years 1920, 1921 and 1923 might have culminated in far more positive outcomes. One also thinks of working-class militants such as Heinrich Brandler and especially Richard Müller, leader of the massive and militant Shop Stewards' movement. Materials in this volume show how sharply critical Luxemburg became of this movement's limitations—yet Müller's biographer notes that he soon joined the new Communist Party that she had helped form, though "he did not stay for long," expelled in a swirl of party factionalism in 1924. "The assassinations of Karl Liebknecht, Rosa Luxemburg, and, some weeks later, Leo Jogiches were a devastating blow to the young KPD," notes historian Eric Weitz. "Liebknecht and Luxemburg, for all their temperamental and political differences, were well known and effective leaders. Jogiches was a master of organizational detail. All three were solidly rooted in the traditions of the prewar labor movement."*

A slow-moving domino effect flowing from this initial loss is suggested if we examine the fate of those who were at the founding conference of the KPD. Of 127 present at this conference, 99 have been identified. Luxemburg and Liebknecht were killed two weeks later, Jogiches ten weeks after that, with three others murdered in the course of 1919. Ten seem to have dropped out of politics altogether. Of the remaining 83 people, only 29 were still active in the KPD by 1933, with 30 joining various KPD split-offs in that period.†

In 1919, Levi had come to the fore, backed by the aging Zetkin, after the deaths of Luxemburg, Liebknecht and Jogiches. Despite undeniably positive qualities and a record as one of Luxemburg's intimate confidantes and co-thinkers, Levi proved incapable of providing a leadership that the youth would follow. Active in the German Communist movement at the time, Franz Borkenau describes Levi as a brilliant lawyer with considerable political insight, "equally proficient as a speaker, a writer, and a debater." He was "very rich, widely read, and cultured," and at the same time "defiant in temperament," with an inclination to use high-handed methods to thwart or marginalize those he deemed "ultraleft." Such qualities created a gulf between him and younger leading comrades—described by another participant, Rosa Leviné-Meyer, as "a phalanx of smart, gifted youngsters, full of drive, the best intentions and

* Eric D. Weitz, *Creating German Communism, 1890–1990: From Popular Protests to Socialist State* (Princeton, NJ: Princeton University Press, 1997), p. 93; Ralf Hoffrogge, *Working-Class Politics in the German Revolution: Richard Müller, the Revolutionary Shop Stewards and the Origins of the Council Movement* (Chicago: Haymarket, 2015), p. 7. Wolfgang Abendroth once suggested that the killing of Luxemburg, Liebknecht and Jogiches "characterized the policy of systematic terror by which the German working class was consistently deprived of its best leaders." Abendroth, *A Short History of the European Working Class*, p. 73.

† Eric D. Weitz, *Creating German Communism*, pp. 93–4. Accounting for the other founding members of the KPD, between 1920 and 1933, six died and eleven faded from view for unknown reasons.

courage, but lacking political experience and links with the working class movement." They, in turn, were put off by Levi's "lordly manner, his haughty disregard for the intellectually inferior." Yet some—such as Zetkin, Luxemburg's secretary Mathilde Jacob, and working-class stalwarts (Wilhelm Pieck, Jacob Walcher, Richard Müller)—remained loyal to him in this period. While "he was never popular among the masses," according to Borkenau, "his outstanding gifts gave him pride of place" as central leader of the KPD.*

Yet he had neither sufficient political authority nor sufficient support among the majority of youthful KPD leaders to ward off the influence among them of an "authoritative" alternative, an ultraleft intriguer from Hungary representing the prestigious Communist International—Bela Kun. Levi was outvoted and marginalized. This paved the way for the disastrous "March Action" of 1921, an ultraleft fiasco animated by a "theory of the offensive" designed to force a revolution into being. This was in stark contrast to the united front orientation championed by Levi and Zetkin (advanced as well by Lenin and Trotsky in debate with other comrades in the Communist International). The March Action isolated and largely discredited the KPD within the broader working class. "In some parts of the country it even came to fights between unemployed Communists trying to enforce the general strike and employed workers who refused to down tools for a hopeless cause," according to left-wing witness Evelyn Anderson. "Hundreds of faithful Communists were killed in this abortive rebellion. Thousands were thrown into prison for their participation in the fights. And that was the end of the 'March Action.'" Before, during and after the fiasco, all this had been sharply denounced by the outvoted Levi. Its aftermath (despite Zetkin's and Lenin's vain efforts to prevent it) led to his break with the Communist movement. "Lenin's defence of Levi was bitterly resented," recalled Ruth Fischer, a central figure in "the phalanx of gifted youngsters," compelling Lenin to tread lightly regarding how hard to push against the decisions of the youthful KPD leadership that had expelled Levi.†

* Franz Borkenau, *World Communism* (Ann Arbor: University of Michigan Press, 1962), pp. 151, 155; Ralf Hoffrogge, pp. 155, 158, 160–1; Rosa Leviné-Meyer, *Inside German Communism: Memoirs of Party Life in the Weimar Republic* (London: Pluto Press, 1977), p. 15. Clara Zetkin was especially aggravated by the circle around Ruth Fischer: "The opposition does not recruit its followers from the Party's mass constituency, but rather from some circle of sophisticated functionaries possessing a mere smattering of knowledge … It is supported by broader sections of the Party only where these are clueless politically and exhibit a mere 'emotional' revolutionary sentiment." Cited in Ralf Hoffrogge, *A Jewish Communist in Weimar Germany: The Life of Werner Scholem, 1895–1940* (Chicago: Haymarket, 2018), p. 300. Also see Ralf Hoffrogge, "Class against Class: The 'Ultra-Left' Berlin Opposition, 1921–1923" and Mario Kessler, "Resisting Moscow? Ruth Fischer and the KPD, 1923–1926," both in *Weimar Communism as Mass Movement, 1918–1933*, ed. Ralf Hoffrogge and Norman Laporte (London: Lawrence Wishart, 2017), pp. 87–128.

† Evelyn Anderson, *Hammer of Anvil: The Story of the German Working-Class Movement* (London: Victor Gollancz, 1945), p. 80; Ruth Fischer, *Stalin and German Communism: A Study of the Origins of the State Party* (Cambridge, MA: Harvard University Press, 1948), p. 177. On Kun see: Borkenau, pp. 114–133, 174–175, 180, 221–223; György Borsányi, *The Life of a Communist*

Had the original collective remained intact—Luxemburg, Liebknecht, Jogiches, Zetkin, Levi—the dynamics would surely have been different, quite probably integrating rather than alienating many younger comrades and leading to a more stable early development of the KPD as it became a mass party. This could have thwarted the destructive machinations of Bela Kun, resisted the often-erratic policies promoted in the Communist International under Gregory Zinoviev, and prevented the leadership drift that ultimately paved the way for Stalinist consolidation within the KPD. The possibilities crackling through the early years of Weimar Germany might have been more effectively grasped by such a seasoned Communist leadership—with a German Revolution transforming the history of Germany, of Europe, of the working class, of Communism, and the world. "If she had not been murdered, with her concept of a humane basic democratic socialism," reflects Luban, "she surely would have influenced the political left efficiently and might have prevented or at least significantly hampered Stalinism's triumph in the Comintern."* This is not how it went. Ultimately, the void created by the death of Luxemburg and Liebknecht was filled in quite different ways by Hitler and Stalin.

TO WHOM DOES ROSA LUXEMBURG BELONG?

In the early 1920s, Luxemburg was still a central figure in the pantheon of Marxist authorities in the German Communist movement, with contending factions citing her authority to advance their counterposed positions. This had changed by the mid-1920s, however, amid a campaign under the Communist International headed by Zinoviev to "Bolshevize" German Communism. New KPD leader Ruth Fischer embraced Zinoviev's call for a monolithic "centralized organization ... carved out of stone that harmoniously and fraternally dispenses [with] the differences in their ranks. Bolshevism is Marxism in action, loyalty to the idea of the dictatorship of the proletariat, to the ideas of Leninism." She infamously compared the ideas and influence of Rosa Luxemburg to "infusions of syphilis bacilli." The mercurial and unreliable Fischer and her co-thinkers would soon be marginalized and driven out as Stalin took control of the Communist International, but Stalin also denounced Luxemburg's ideas as "a semi-Menshevik hodge-podge" leading to "a number of very serious

---

Revolutionary, Béla Kun (Boulder, Colorado: Social Science Monographs, 1993), online at archive.org. On the March Action, Levi's protests, and the consequences, see: Pierre Broué, *The German Revolution 1917–1923* (Leiden/Boston: Brill, 2005), pp. 491–552; *In the Steps of Rosa Luxemburg: Selected Writings of Paul Levi,* ed. David Fernbach (Leiden/Boston: Brill, 2011); *To the Masses: Proceedings of the Third Congress of the Communist International, 1921,* ed. John Riddell, pp. 18–23, 297–301, 422–36, 486–94, 544–6, 573–4, 1071–1101, 1104–5, 1132–52, 1174–80.

* Ottokar Luban, "The Role of the Spartacist Group after 9 November 1918 and the Formation of the KPD," in *Weimar Communism as Mass Movement,* ed. Hoffrogge and Laporte, p. 60.

political and theoretical mistakes" and requiring "the very serious criticism" of the Bolsheviks of her time and of Communists in the 1930s.*

Yet the KPD could not simply dispense with this icon of the early Communist cause. Stifling the revolutionary-democratic thrust and uncompromising critical-mindedness that were essential to who she was, they transformed Luxemburg into a safely dead martyr to be celebrated in "LLL festivals" from 1924 onward—commemorating Lenin-Liebknecht-Luxemburg—with Stalinist leader Ernest Thälmann proclaiming in 1932: "Rosa Luxemburg and the others belong to us," and Wilhelm Pieck in 1951 (now a figurehead of the East German Communist dictatorship) repeating: "Rosa Luxemburg belongs to us!"†

Among Marxist dissidents breaking away from what had become the Communist movement's Stalinist mainstream, there was a strong sense that, in fact, Rosa Luxemburg was *theirs*. In 1930, Thalheimer instructed serious-minded activists that it was a mistake to counterpose Lenin to Luxemburg. "It is not a matter of Lenin or Luxemburg, but Lenin and Luxemburg," he insisted.

> The party bureaucracy perceives Lenin and Luxemburg as opposed to each other and thereby proves that it has not understood either. We counterpose to the bureaucracy not only the formal but also the spiritual bond of these two great revolutionary champions of the working class and their closest comrades in arms, their mutual supplementary features as revolutionary leaders, as practitioners and theoreticians.

In this spirit, Paul Frölich produced one of the finest biographies of Luxemburg, in 1939. And in 1954, Isaac Deutscher, in his classic biography of Trotsky, concluded: "Of all the personalities of European socialism, nobody was in origin, temperament, and political and literary gifts more akin to Trotsky than Rosa Luxemburg."‡

---

* Mario Kessler, *A Political Biography of Arkadij Maslow, 1891–1941: Dissident Against His Will* (New York: Palgrave Macmillan, 2020), pp. 94, 98 n27; Joseph Stalin, "Some Questions Concerning the History of Bolshevism," in *Readings in Revolution and Organization: Rosa Luxemburg and Her Critics*, ed. Sobhanlal Datta Gupta (Calcutta: Pearl Publishers, 1994), p. 249.

† Eric D. Weitz, "'Rosa Luxemburg Belongs to Us!' German Communism and the Luxemburg Legacy," *Central European History*, Vol. 27, No. 1 (1994), pp. 46, 48, 56, 57.

‡ August Thalheimer, "Rosa Luxemburg or Lenin," Marxist Internet Archive, marxists.org; Paul Frölich, *Rosa Luxemburg* (Chicago: Haymarket, 2010); Isaac Deutscher, *The Prophet Armed, Trotsky: 1879–1921* (New York: Oxford University Press, 1954), p. 183. Deutscher's observation should not lead one to believe that Trotsky and Luxemburg were in any way "soulmates." While Trotsky and Luxemburg knew each other before 1917, they were not close personally—he felt a shyness in the face of her formidable brilliance and fame, while she found his arrogance and flashiness to be off-putting. However, also see Michael Löwy, "Rosa Luxemburg and Trotsky," *Against the Current*, No. 214 (September–October 2021). Luxemburg's relationship to Lenin is also captured in Elizabieta Ettinger, *Rosa Luxemburg, A Life* (Boston: Beacon Press, 1986), pp. 137–8, 165, 167–8, and more extensively in Nettl, pp. 356–57, 372, 396, 398–9, 557–60, 581, 590–1, 625–26, 782.

Among the stalwarts of the Social Democratic Party, there seem to have been very mixed feelings. To such leaders as Ebert and Noske, of course, she was "bloody Rosa," although for such former friends as Karl and Luise Kautsky she had become a well-meaning but disoriented idealist. For those on the party's left fringe, such as ex-Communist Levi, she remained a heroic, principled, insightful, martyred comrade.

By 1974, a former leftist who became Social Democratic Party leader and chancellor of West Germany, Willy Brandt, felt sufficiently bold to place her face and name on a postage stamp. Many conservative Germans were shocked, but, as one journalist observed, buying and using the stamp provided "a way for those Germans—especially younger ones—who have leftist-liberal political views to show them, without necessarily making a real political commitment." Brandt himself praised Luxemburg for her view that "human progress was possible only by democratic development, not by paternalism but by participation of the masses whose spontaneous power and creative spirit she believed in."*

Arendt once commented that the romantic-revolutionary legend of Rosa Luxemburg—"vague, confused, inaccurate in nearly all details"—would periodically "come to life whenever a 'New Left' sprang into being." She added sardonically:

> Every New Left movement, when its moment came to change into the Old Left—usually when its members reached the age of forty—promptly buried its early enthusiasm for Rosa Luxemburg together with the dreams of youth; and since they had usually not bothered to read, let alone to understand, what she had to say, found it easy to dismiss her with all the patronizing philistinism of their newly acquired status.†

At the start of the twenty-first century's second decade, however, it has become clear that increasing numbers of activists are reaching out to connect with and learn from insights, analyses, and experiences related to what Rosa Luxemburg thought and did. More than a century after her murder, the crises and catastrophes of global capitalism continue to confirm her warning that the alternative to socialist revolution is capitalist barbarism. Young workers of our era face crises that have deep roots in the history of the twentieth century and before, and that threaten the survival of the very planet itself in new and acute ways. Some

---

* Craig R. Whitney, "A Postage Stamp Raises West German Tempers," *New York Times*, March 10, 1974, p. 12, nytimes.com; Brandt quoted in Luban, "Rosa Luxemburg's Concept of Spontaneity and Creativity," p. 513. On Brandt's earlier left-wing involvement, see Willy Brandt, *In Exile: Essays, Reflections, and Letters, 1933–1947* (Philadelphia: University of Pennsylvania Press, 1971).

† Hannah Arendt, "Rosa Luxemburg: 1871–1919," *Men in Dark Times* (New York: Harcourt, Brace and World, 1968), pp. 37, 38; originally published as "A Heroine of the Revolution," *New York Review of Books*, October 6, 1966.

of the revived interest in Luxemburg's legacy has shed light on those aspects of her thought that speak to environmental concerns:

> Luxemburg could even be taken as a precocious thinker of the ecological questions that would later come to be known as eco-socialism or Marxist ecology. Her staunch defence of all living things and the land, against the violence exacted by the capitalist drive for accumulation and despoliation, seems to point in this direction.*

In one of many outbreaks of mass action for climate justice, the Glasgow COP26 gathering of the international ruling class was met by protestors from all over the world calling for "System change! Not climate change!" while trash collectors and street cleaners walked out on strike in a call for respect and decent working conditions. Most of all, Luxemburg belongs to such insurgents of today and tomorrow.

Helen C. Scott
Paul Le Blanc

---

* Hernán Ouviña, "Rosa Reloaded: Rosa Luxemburg and our Civilizational Crisis," trans. Nicolas Allen, *Historical Materialism*, January 14, 2019. historicalmaterialism.org; see also Alyssa Battistoni, "Socialism or Whole Foods: Luxemburgian Answers to Our Climate Crisis," *Rosa Remix*, pp. 70–4

Abbreviations

DDP, Deutsche Demokratische Partei—German Democratic Party
DNVP, Deutschnationale Volkspartei—German National People's Party
DVFP, Deutschvölkische Freiheitspartei—German Völkisch Freedom Party
DVP, Deutsche Volkspartei—German People's Party
FVP, Fortschrittliche Volkspartei—Progressive People's Party
ISB, International Socialist Bureau
KPD, Kommunistische Partei Deutschlands—Communist Party of Germany
KPO, *Kommunistische Partei Deutschlands (Opposition)*—Communist Party Opposition
LSDP, Lietuvos Socialdemokratų Partija—Social Democratic Party of Lithuania
NSDAP, Nationalsozialistische Deutsche Arbeiterpartei—National Socialist German Workers' Party (popularly known as the Nazis)
PPS, Polska Partia Socjalistyczna—Polish Socialist Party
PPSD, Polska Partia Socjalno-Demokratyczna Galicji i Śląska—Polish Social Democratic Party of Galicia and Silesia
PPS-FR, Polska Partia Socjalistyczna-Frakcja Rewolucyjna—Polish Socialist Party-Revolutionary Faction
PPS-L, Polska Partia Socjalistyczna-Lewica—Polish Socialist Party-Left
PPS-ZP, Polska Partia Socjalistyczna Zaboru Pruskiego—Polish Socialist Party in Prussia
RGASPI, Russkii Gosudarstvennyi Arkiv Sotsialno-Politcheskoi Istorii—Russian State Archive for Social and Political History
RSDRP, Rossiyskaya Sotsial-Demokraticheskaya Rabochaya Partiya—Russian Social Democratic Labor Party
SAP, Sozialistische Arbeiterpartei—Socialist Workers' Party
SDAP, Sozialdemokratische Arbeiterpartei—Social Democratic Workers' Party
SDKP, Socjaldemokracja Królestwa Polskiego—Social Democracy of the Kingdom of Poland
SDKPiL, Socjaldemokracja Królestwa Polskiego i Litwy—Social Democracy of the Kingdom of Poland and Lithuania
SDP, Social-Democratische Partji—Social-Democratic Party of the Netherlands
SPD, Sozialdemokratische Partei Deutschlands—Social Democratic Party of Germany
SED, Sozialistische Einheitspartei Deutschlands—Socialist Unity Party of Germany
SR, Sotsialisty Revolyutsionery—Socialist Revolutionary Party
USPD, Unabhängige Sozialdemokratische Partei Deutschlands—Independent Social Democratic Party of Germany

ZRP, Związek Robotników Polskich—Union of Polish Workers
ZZSP, Związek Zagraniczny Socjalistów Polskich—Union of Polish Socialists Abroad

1910

What Course Now?*

I.

The question of the Prussian franchise, which has been frozen and immobile for over half a century, is now a burning issue in German public life. A few weeks of energetic mass action by the proletariat have been enough to roil the old swamp of Prussian reaction, and to blow a fresh breeze through the whole of German politics.† It is impossible to solve the challenge of Prussian voting reform through parliamentary means alone, as only nationwide direct mass action is capable of creating change under current conditions. The living proof of this is clearer than ever now that we have garnered initial experiences, from the street demonstrations on the one hand, to the proceedings of the Voting Law Commission of the Prussian parliament on the other.‡

So, although the most recent majestic street demonstrations in themselves signify a welcome renewal of Social Democracy's outward forms of struggle, and have simultaneously opened up mass struggle for the right to vote in Prussia in the most vigorous manner, they also impose specific duties on the party that provides the initiative and the leadership behind them. Faced with the movement it has triggered, our party has to have a clear and specific plan for advancing the mass action that has already started. As is the case for military demonstrations, street demonstrations are usually only the preface to the proper struggle. There are cases when demonstrations achieve their goal merely through intimidating the enemy. But aside from the undeniable fact that the enemy in this case is the united Junker, *haute bourgeoisie, monarchist* reaction of Prussia-Germany, which is in no mind to capitulate to masses of people rallying in the streets, demonstrations can only apply effective pressure when backed by serious resolve, and a readiness to reach for more aggressive means of struggle if necessary. In part, this means achieving clarity regarding the course we would think of pursuing if the street demonstrations seemed not up to achieving their direct purpose.

---

* This article was first published in *Arbeiter-Zeitung* (Dortmund) I, No. 61, March 14, 1910; II, No. 62, March 15, 1910. It is translated by Henry Holland from Luxemburg's *Gesammelte Werke*, Vol. 2 (Berlin: Dietz Verlag, 2004 [Sixth Edition], pp. 289–99.

† From mid-January 1910, mass protests across Germany demanded general, equal, direct, and secret suffrage for all persons over twenty in Prussia.

‡ The commissions of the bicameral legislature—consisting of the House of Representatives [*Abgeordnetenhaus*] and of the House of Lords [*Herrenhaus*]—rejected draft changes to the Prussian franchise as submitted by the Prussian government on February 5, 1910. The government's draft was in response to pressure applied by the mass movement. It proposed only minor changes to the division of the electorate into classes and to the direct election of officeholders, while retaining a "three-class" voting law. Conflicts regarding the voting law reached their height between February and April 1910, forcing the government to withdraw its draft on May 27, 1910.

The party's experience to date has proven the necessity of complete clarity and resolve on this issue. We carried out our first experiments with street demonstrations in Prussia two years ago.* The masses showed they were equal to the challenge back then and followed Social Democracy's appeals with spirit. A breath of fresh air, a hope for a new and more effective form of struggle, a resolve not to back down, regardless of the level of sacrifice required or the intimidation brought against them—the agitated masses palpably felt all of this. And to what did this ultimately lead? The party didn't provide any more guidance, or extend or continue the action, but took quite the opposite course—again, they palmed off the masses, the general agitation tailed off, and the whole thing literally ran aground.

Read the first experiment as a finger raised in warning to our party that mass rallies have their own psychology and logic, and that politicians who want to master them are urgently advised to reckon with these factors. No force can artificially maintain expressions of the will of the masses in the political struggle at the same level long term, nor can such expressions be restrained within the same form. They have to well up, come to a head, and take on new, more effective forms. Mass action, once sparked, must move forward. And in the given moment, should the leading party fail in its resolve to supply the mass with the demands it needs, then a certain disappointment inevitably comes over that mass, its verve vanishes, and the action collapses in on itself.

We already received a small but clear warning of this kind at the start of the current campaign. When the party leadership organized those sixty-two assemblies for Berlin in January, with the intention of not combining *any* street demonstrations with these assemblies, we really were disappointed. Not nearly enough people attended, despite the agitation that had already unfolded, and it was only on February 13,† with street processions planned from the start, that the mass followed the party's appeal, in lively and immense throngs. It's obvious that the scheme of proceeding methodically each time, in a refined and detached manner, proceeding from assemblies without street demonstrations to assemblies with street demonstrations, and so on, is simply unrealistic. Social Democracy has already so shaken up the proletarian masses in Berlin and in most of Prussia's other large industrial centers that the form of mere protest assemblies for the right to vote in Prussia—with the adoption of the usual resolutions—no longer satisfies them. Today, street demonstrations are

---

* At the end of 1907 and start of 1908, the mass demonstrations for a democratic voting law in Berlin and other German cities, principally in Prussia, were at their height. Thanks to the mass agitation that preceded the election, the seven Social Democrats, including Karl Liebknecht, were elected to the Prussian House of Representatives in June 1908, despite the reactionary "three-class" voting system.

† On February 13, 1910, franchise demonstrations took place in Berlin and many other cities throughout Germany, defying a provocative proclamation by Berlin's chief of police Traugott von Jagow banning street demonstrations and threatening the use of armed force against them.

the only form of action close to being commensurate with the roaring masses' desire for deeds, and with the tense political situation.

But for how long will this be the case? One would have to have little feeling for the intellectual life of the party masses in this country, not to see clearly what is going on. Since the street demonstrations were initiated a few weeks back, they've unleashed a mood, and have concurrently and objectively created new conditions for the battlefield, that extends well beyond their present scope. This new situation demands more accentuated means, in the short and the long run.

The proceedings in the Voting Law Commission and in the plenary of the Prussian House of Representatives, and the fact that even the Center, the most demagogic of all parties, is not ashamed of destroying all hopes of serious voting law reform through their voting bloc with the Junker class—these are all responses to the superb demonstrations in the whole of Prussia.* They amount to a slap in the face for the demonstrating masses as led by Social Democracy, and one that demands a response. Once open battle has begun, each subsequent blow will have to follow from the merciless, steely logic of this same struggle. Now that the reaction, through the commission and the plenary session, has avenged itself for the mass rallies by adulterating the draft change to the voting law, the masses, under the leadership of Social Democracy, must avenge that adulteration with a new advance. In a situation like the current one, a long delay almost amounts to a battle lost, as do extended intervals between individual acts of battle and indecision in choosing the means and strategies for further struggle. It is essential to keep our enemies in suspense, and to prevent them from enjoying the illusion that we lack the courage to follow through with consequences. That said, the street demonstrations will not quickly sate the masses' psychological needs, the mood of their struggle and their animus. If Social Democracy does not resolutely take the next step, if it allows the right political moment to pass in order to avoid reaching a future solution, then it will hardly be possible for it to keep up the street demonstrations long-term: the action will ultimately falter and run aground, as it did two years ago. The examples of comparable struggles in Belgium,† in Austria-Hungary,‡ and in Russia§ confirm this analysis, showing the inevitable escalation and progress of

---

* The official platform of the Center Party included the demand for the introduction of the Reichstag voting law into Prussia. The party joined the conservatives in opposition to direct suffrage at a Voting Law Commission on February 23, 1910. See also *Gesammelte Werke*, Vol. 2, pp. 312–4.

† April 1893 in Belgium saw the first political general strike for universal suffrage in the history of the international workers' movement. Around 250,000 workers took part. The state was forced into substantially extending the right to vote in Belgium.

‡ The first political mass strike in Austria-Hungary took place in September 1905 demanding general suffrage. The ongoing protest movements forced the Austrian government to present a law to parliament in January 1907 concerning the introduction of general suffrage.

§ Under pressure from the all-Russian political general strike in October 1905 the tsar

mass action, and making explicit that it's this escalation alone that is to thank for achieving its political impact.

One further circumstance serves as an obvious reminder for Social Democracy that street demonstrations are an approach that, by themselves, will soon become superseded by the tide of events. Bourgeois democrats and left liberal elements of the bourgeoisie are already organizing street demonstrations! Naturally, everyone can see that the courage of these homeless politicians is no older than the Social Democratic initiative, and that, of course, the assemblies and street processions arranged by those pensioned officers without an army are, to a large extent, filled by none other than the Social Democratic working class. The plain fact that street demonstrations have become a necessary political means of struggle for the democratic bourgeoisie indicates that it's impossible for them to remain an adequate means of struggle for the needs of the Left Front and Social Democracy. Social Democracy can only be equal to its mission of urging all elements opposed to the property-owning classes to move forward by bringing their actions to a head, and by steadily leading the way through the decisiveness of its demands. If street demonstrations have even become a means of struggle for Breitscheid, Liszt and Co., then it's high time that Social Democracy thought about what its next means of struggle should be.*

So, all sides now pose the same question to the party: *Which course now?* And because the last Prussian Party Congress dodged this issue with a gesture that was showy rather than politically astute,† a discussion in the press and in the assemblies is now needed urgently to solve the question. The mass of party comrades in the country must weigh things up and themselves determine what should happen. Only then, only as an expression of the mass will of the party, can our battle tactics acquire the necessary weight, and the next blow acquire the necessary force.

II.

A series of resolutions and statements made by the Social Democratic working class in various centers of our movement has already provided the answer. In Halle, in Bremen, in Breslau, in the Hesse-Nassau agitational district, and in Königsberg, the comrades have loudly named the means of struggle, the

---

was forced in his manifesto of October 30, 1905, to consent to the convocation of a constituent assembly, civil liberties, and the right to vote for workers, the urban intelligentsia and some of the educated professions.

* Rudolf Breitscheid, the leader of the small bourgeois democratic party Demokratische Vereinigung, joined the Social Democratic Party in 1912 and was then active on the right wing of the party. Franz von Liszt was among the founders of the Progressive People's Party in 1910.

† At the Party Congress of Prussian Social Democracy in Berlin, January 3–5, 1910, no discussion took place about the franchise question, although delegates had submitted three motions demanding the use of the mass strike as a means of struggle.

utilization of which forces itself onto to the party in the current battle: *the mass strike.*

In principle, our party already elevated the political mass strike to a means of struggle applicable to and in Germany five years ago at the Jena Party Congress.* In passing that motion, party members were admittedly thinking about a defensive application in the first instance, about the potential necessity of protecting the existing Reichstag voting law. But we need to see this in light of the closest of connections between internal Prussian and German Reich politics, and in the light of the recent provocations and threats of a *coup d'état* by the Prussian Junkers in the Reichstag.† Indeed, considering the whole situation, it is self-evident that the current struggle is not merely about the right to vote in Prussia, but also ultimately about the right to vote in the Reichstag. If the Junkers and their minions are allowed to win against the working class this time on the question of voting rights in Prussia, their determination to put an end to the detested right to vote in the Reichstag will undoubtedly swell at an opportune moment. And vice versa: a strong and successful advance of the mass in the question of the Prussian voting law will clearly be the best and safest way for the mass to defend itself regarding the right to vote in the Reichstag.

Support for the use of the mass strike in the current campaign is, however, related to the fact that, to a certain extent, such a strike is bound to occur by itself, as a natural and inevitable escalation of mass action that has already begun and is constantly expanding. The kind of mass strike that is "produced" one fine day through a simple decree of the party, as if from a sudden shot of a pistol, is just a childish fantasy, an anarchist's delusion. But if we talk of a mass strike resulting from a month-long movement of demonstrations by huge masses of workers, a movement of growing dimensions, that places a 3-million-strong party in a dilemma: it either has to go forward at all costs, or the mass action that has begun will collapse in failure. A mass strike of this kind, born out of the inner necessity and resolve of the galvanized masses, and concurrently out of a specific political situation, carries its justification and the guarantee of its effectiveness within it.

Sure enough, the mass strike is not a magic remedy, bearing success within itself under all circumstances. We should certainly not perceive the mass strike as an artificial means of political pressure, a one-off method that the masses can apply mechanically, on command, and according to regulations. The mass

---

* The resolution passed at the Social Democratic Party Congress, September 17–23, 1905, in Jena, proposed the comprehensive application of the mass work stoppage as one of the most effective methods of struggle for the working class. However, it also restricted the application of the political mass strike essentially to the defense of the Reichstag voting law and the right to collective bargaining.

† On January 29, 1910, during the Reichstag debate on the military budget, the Conservative Elard von Oldenburg-Januschau made a direct appeal to the kaiser to breach the constitution. This prompted protest assemblies in numerous cities in Germany.

strike is merely the outer form of action that possesses its own inner development and logic, and the consequences of its further course unfolds in the closest possible relation to the political situation. The mass strike in the form of a short, one-off demonstration strike will certainly not be the final word of the political campaign that's already in motion. But just as certainly, it is *the first word* of that campaign in its current stage. Even if its further course, its length, its immediate success, and yes, even the costs and sacrifices needed for this campaign are impossible to calculate in advance with pencil and paper (as if one were reckoning costs for a stock-exchange operation), there are still situations in which it is the political duty of a party leading millions to decisively issue these demands. Without them, it's impossible to drive forward the struggle that the party commenced in the first place.

The principles of organization and of party discipline are values so elevated in a party like the German one that the extent of the initiative of the unorganized masses of the people, their spontaneous and, shall we say, improvised ability to act—which has been a significant and often pivotal factor in all previous major political struggles—are almost entirely disabled. This being the case, it behooves the party to act on the unavoidable duty to prove the value of such highly developed organization and discipline by showing, as regards large actions, that this organization and discipline can be used for forms of struggle other than parliamentary elections. It is necessary to decide whether German Social Democracy, which is built on the strongest trade union organization and the largest army of voters in the world, can bring off a mass action that has been achieved with great success at various times in little Belgium, in Italy,* in Austria-Hungary and in Sweden,† not to mention Russia. But it's also necessary to decide whether trade union organizations numbering 2 million heads in the population of Germany—together with a powerful, well-disciplined party—is just as incapable of generating a mass strike in the decisive moment as the French trade unions, hindered by anarchist confusion, and the French Party, weakened by internal conflicts.

Yet it is obvious that an action of the character and scope of the mass strike cannot be manufactured by the party alone, without the unions. It is only through a shared and unanimous effort of both branches of the organization that these can trigger a titanic action in the whole country, the only type of action worth considering in Germany. From a trade union perspective, several

---

* On September 15, 1904, a huge protest rally had taken place in Milan, which broadened into a general strike in almost all of Italy on September 17. The cause of the strike was the murder, by the police, of striking farm laborers on Sardinia and Sicily.

† From August 4 to September 6, 1909, a general stoppage was carried out in Sweden, based on a motion of the national central committee of the Swedish trade unions and carried out by all organizations affiliated to it. Seventy-five percent of workers employed in industry, skilled trades and transport took part. This strike defeated an attempt by industrialists' organizations to force unions, by means of lockouts, to agree to wage reductions during the economic crisis.

factors are now worthy of consideration. On the one hand, the western coal-mining region has been in a state of substantial ferment for some time now and is prepared for a large economic struggle. On the other hand, relations in various branches of production, including the construction industry, are so tense that the industrialists are just waiting for an appropriate excuse to enforce large-scale lockouts. At first sight, both sets of circumstances could appear to provide reasons for considering a political mass strike hardly suitable from a union standpoint. But only at first sight. Look more closely and you will see that the confluence of a comprehensive mass strike in coal mining with a political strike movement of the proletariat [in general] can only benefit both parties. In all of the proletariat's large mass movements, numerous political and economic moments interweave, and to peel them apart artificially, to try pedantically to keep them apart, would be futile and harmful. A healthy movement, capable of life, such as the current Prussian campaign, should and must avail itself of all the stockpiled social gunpowder, as all contemporary Prussian campaigns have to do. On the other hand, it could only add to the success of the miners' narrower cause if, by flowing into a wider political cause, the miners' agenda could instill yet more fear into its enemies—the coal magnates and the government. All the sooner would these actors feel forced into offering concessions in an attempt to placate the miners and to isolate them from the political tidal wave. As for the threatened lockouts, we know from countless experiences that whenever the interests of the industrialists and their ruling-class standpoint demand it, they're never short of excuses for a brutal, mass lockout, nor has a lack of half-baked excuses ever prevented them from carrying out their acts of violence. Whether or not the political mass strike takes place, lockouts are unavoidable if they continue, as they do now, to suit the industrialists down to a tee. The temporal coincidence of these lockouts with a large, political movement can only have the effect of making the workers more able to resist—despite the partial suffering caused by those lockouts—by raising up their idealism and willingness to make sacrifices.

Despite all that, the most important concern from the trade union standpoint is the following: a large mass strike action definitely faces powerful risks when it comes to the continuance of union organizations and their finances. Can and may the trade unions take on such a risk? First, the risk itself is incontestable. But which struggle, which action, which purely economic strike does not contain a risk for the workers' fighting organizations? If the numerical strength of our German unions, this most powerful construction, becomes a reason to pay greater consideration to such dangers to the struggle than do weaker unions in other countries, such as Sweden and Italy, then this would amount to a dangerous argument against the trade unions themselves. Then things would move toward the weird conclusion that the bigger and stronger our organizations become, the less we are able to act, since we become correspondingly more timid. The very purpose of the union's powerful construction would then be in question because we need these organizations as a means to an end, as arms for struggle, not as an end in themselves. Fortunately, however, this isn't a real question. In reality, the danger and risk that our union organizations are confronting are merely apparent. In reality, healthy and strong organizations can only prove their worth in a tough battle, can raise themselves out of each trial of strength with renewed strengths themselves, and thereby become larger. If a general political mass strike in the first instance results in the weakening or harming of some unions, not only will the old organizations bloom anew a short time later, but the great action will also shake up entire new layers of the proletariat. This will bring ideas about organization into new circles, which a peaceful, systematic union organization has not been able to access up to now. Or this great action will win over throngs of proletarians for our organizations, who have until now remained under bourgeois leadership in the Center Party, the Hirsch-Duncker Works' Association or the Protestant organizations.* In the case of a large, vibrant and bold mass action, the profits would weigh heavier than the losses. Right at this moment, we are witnessing an instructive example of how the most cautious union movement can, under certain circumstances, be compelled to do the right thing, throwing itself into a great fight, without fearfully weighing up the chances for profits and losses. This example is Philadelphia.† There we see stepping into battle an organization‡ that definitely counts as one of the least revolutionary, daredevil or rash in the whole International, led by a man like [Samuel] Gompers, a cool politician full of disdain for Social Democratic "eccentricities" and "revolutionary phrases." This organization will perhaps proclaim, in the very near future, a comprehensive general strike, to protect the right of 600 streetcar employees to collective bargaining. There is no doubt that the American unions are facing a large and immediate risk, in this hefty trial of strength with capital that is spreading by the hour. But who would want to condemn Gompers' steps in this case, and who will not admit that this great trial of strength can ultimately lead to the most beneficial consequences for the American workers' movement? When all

---

* The Hirsch-Duncker trade unions, founded in 1868, were liberal organizations whose leaders advocated self-help and social reform through collaboration between labor and capital. The Christian Trade Unions were founded in the late nineteenth century, initially at the local and regional levels, in response to the independent unions, which had a socialist orientation. In 1901 they joined together to form the General Association of Christian Trade Unions in Germany. Their aim was to realize trade union interests by means of social reform and while facilitating "economic peace" and "social partnership." After fierce disputes, the association's interdenominational character was established in 1912 with the papal encyclical *Singulari quadam*.

† A streetcar workers' strike had begun in Philadelphia in February 1910. See Rosa Luxemburg's speech "The Political Mass Strike and the Trade Unions), delivered October 1, 1910, in Hagen, pp. 25–42, below.

‡ The Amalgamated Association of Street and Electric Railway Employees of America, a local affiliate of the American Federation of Labor.

is accounted for, it can only benefit the German unions as a whole when those unions for once let organized capital—which has become cocky—get a clear taste of their power.

From a political standpoint, there's one more factor to consider. In 1911, we'll have the Reichstag election,* at which voters should present the general tab for the Hottentot Elections.† Our opponents have indeed worked impeccably for us to prepare the ground, with the Finance Reform.‡ For our part, however, there would be no better way of creating an illustrious starting situation [for the election] than to preface it with a large, political mass action, of a type that Germany has not yet experienced. By stirring the widest possible numbers of people, raising up idealism, and building the energy for battle to the highest extent through this action, we could achieve a level of education and of mood that would turn the coming elections into a deafening Waterloo for the ruling system.

Thus, from both the trade union and political standpoint, the same lesson applies equally: *first assess, but then dare!*

A political mass strike in Germany—obviously in this case we cannot consider Prussia in isolation, as the party masses in the rest of the Reich would surely on their own accord rush to give spirited support—a German mass strike would have the most far- and wide-reaching effect on the International; it would raise immeasurably, in all countries, courage, belief in socialism, self-trust, and willingness to sacrifice among the proletariat. Naturally, deliberations of this kind cannot be a *reason* for German Social Democracy and the German unions to resolve to apply the mass strike if it doesn't present itself from the internal situation of Germany itself. But in a profit-and-loss calculation of a potential application of the mass strike, it's permissible to allow discussion of this consideration. Until now, German Social Democracy has been the big template for the International in the fields of the parliamentary struggle, organization, and party discipline. Perhaps it can soon become a shining example of how all these virtues could combine with a resolute and stout-hearted mass action.

---

* The Reichstag election took place on January 12, 1912. Social Democracy was able to increase its number of seats to 110, compared with 43 in 1907, becoming the largest parliamentary group in the Reichstag.

† The Reichstag elections—which became known as the *Hottentottenwahl*, (Hottentot Elections, referring to the German colonial war in South-West African which was then underway)—were held on January 25 and February 5, 1907. Social Democracy increased its total number of votes from 3 million in 1903 to almost 3.3 million in 1907. Due to the superannuated division of electoral districts in combination with the bourgeois parties' voting pacts in the second ballot, Social Democracy got only 43 seats, compared with 81 in 1903. "Hottentot" was a derogatory description used by Europeans at the time to refer to the Khoekhoe people of southern Africa.

‡ On July 19, 1909, the Reichstag passed an Imperial Financial Reform, despite opposing votes from the Social Democrats, the National Liberals, and the Progressive People's Party. As four-fifths of the new taxes were indirect, the masses bore the brunt of the additional burden.

Nonetheless, there should be no expectations that a "command" to go on a mass strike will be given one fine day from the movement's high command, from the party executive and from the General Commission of the Trade Unions. Bodies that have responsibility for millions of people are—through their resolutions, which have to be carried out by *others*—tentative by their very armchair-nature. Furthermore, the decision for immediate *mass* action can only emanate from the mass itself. The emancipation of the working class can be the work only of the working class itself. This pathbreaking sentence from the *Communist Manifesto* also contains the additional significance that, even inside the proletariat's class-party, that great and decisive movement cannot stem from the initiative of a handful of leaders, but must instead stem from the commitment and resolve of the mass of party supporters.* Also, the decision to lead the current struggle for the franchise struggle in Prussia—"using all means," according to the words of the Prussian Party congress, i.e., also using the means of the mass strike—can only be taken by the widest layers possible of the party. It is the task of party and union comrades, in each town and in each electoral district, to position themselves with regard to the questions of the current situation, and to express their opinion and their will in the clearest and most open way, so that the opinion of the total organized worker mass is heard. And when that happens, our leaders are certain to be ready at their posts, as they have been constantly until now.

---

* The phrasing regarding proletarian self-emancipation is stressed in Frederick Engels's 1883, 1888, and 1890 prefaces to the *Communist Manifesto*, making use of a formulation by Marx utilized in the General Rules of the International Workingmen's Association (1864).

Party Congress of the SPD of Germany, September 18–24, 1910, in Magdeburg*

I.

Motion on the political mass strike

The Party Congress declares, in complete accord with the most recent Prussian Party Congress,† the judgment of which has been confirmed entirely by the lessons of the struggles over the franchise this past spring, that the battle over the Prussian franchise can only be led to victory by a large, decisive mass action of the working people, whereby all means, including the political mass strike, must be applied if necessary. In light of this, as regards the future renewal of the voting rights campaign, the Party Congress declares it necessary to set in motion the elucidation and propagation of the mass strike in the party press and in assemblies, and thus to accentuate the feeling of power and of political consciousness among the broadest layers of the proletariat, so that the masses are up to the great task when the situation demands it.‡

R. Luxemburg, Hänisch, Westkamp, Schöbel, Frau Lex, Grütz, Faure, Henke, Pannekoek, Wellmann, Reitze, Rauch, Elfriede Gewehr, Dröner, Schulten, Focke, Albrecht, Liebknecht, Staab, Minna Wiese, Marie Milow, Rudolph, Limbertz, Grenz, Emmel, Keil-Reichenbach, Fleissner, Graupe, Heinrich Schulz, Rohleder, Leutert, Hengsbach, Hennig, Reiwand, Örtel, Rosenfeld, Frank-Berlin VI., Fauth, Wagner, Antrick, Wassermann-Schöningen, Martin, Bromme, Neukirch, Scholich, Hoffmann, Hörsing, Dietrich, Westmeyer, Schumacher, Haug, Böhme, Castan, Ulm, Dittmann, Dißmann, Dobrohlaw, Hackelbusch, Bühler, Muth, Witzke, Arendsee

* These minutes were first published in *Protokoll über die Verhandlungen des Parteitags der Sozialdemokratischen Partei Deutschlands. Abgehalten zu Magdeburg vom 18. bis 24. Januar 1910* (Protocols of the Party Congress of the Social Democratic Party of Germany, held at Magdeburg from September 18 to 24, 1910) (Berlin: Buchhandlung Vorwärts, 1910), I, pp. 181–82, 304–07, 426–30. These minutes are translated by Henry Holland from Luxemburg's *Gesammelte Werke*, Vol. 2, pp. 451–62.

† The Party Congress of the Social Democracy of Prussia took place in Berlin, January 3–5, 1910.

‡ The Congress passed the first sentence of this motion on the franchise conflict, while the delegates involved withdrew the second sentence.

II.

Speech regarding the vote on the budget

If anything at all has proven the utter superfluity and redundancy of the motion brought by [Otto] Braun and his comrades*—and the urgent necessity of finally making a clean and clear decision here on the question of passing the budget—then it was the speeches defending the motion by [Ludwig] Frank, [Wilhelm] Kolb and other comrades. You will all admit, even when paying the greatest possible attention to these speeches, that not a single argument can be detected that attests in any convincing way to the necessity of approving the budget. (Agreement and disagreement.) Nor was a single new moment introduced into a debate on this controversial point that we've unfortunately been having in the party for the last sixteen years. What did the great speech in defense of the motion from the co-discussant Frank look like, what was it aimed at? It was a long and detailed representation of all the activities of the parliamentary group in Baden, a long enumeration of a series of proposed laws, proposed changes to laws and other similar big deeds. Frank also had to admit that our comrades in the parliament in Baden have not been able to push through adequately our principal demands in any area at all. (Agreement and disagreement.) Although, as we happily recognize, the comrades have articulated their demands in Badenese parliament, they have ultimately got back only chicken feed: they went digging for gold and were happy when they found worms instead. ("Ooh!" say the minority. Agreement from the majority.) I will respond immediately to your "ooh!" with a piece of evidence. I don't want to get drawn into a critique of all the great achievements that have been paraded for us here in all their shining glory, but you've all been able to verify that the trophy of the successful, practical politics of Badenese parliament was the famous school law.† Didn't all your hearts leap (Call: "No!"; laughter) when the speaker described how school doctors had been won? You can imagine how the abysmal health of the school-age Badenese youth has now been radically improved. (Laughter.) The other achievements in schooling were also described in detail. As a non-Badenser,‡ I don't assume the right to judge competently the new school law, passed with the support of the parliamentary group in the

* On September 16, 1910, Otto Braun proposed in *Neue Zeit* that the breach of discipline committed by the parliamentary group in Baden's regional parliament in voting for the government's budget should be dealt with by a special commission. This was brought as a motion before the Magdeburg Party Congress by several Social Democrats and was rejected by a large majority.

† On May 4, 1910, in the second chamber of Baden's regional parliament, the law on elementary school teaching was passed with all parties voting for except the Center Party. This new law placed small limitations on the influence of the clergy on schooling, it did not fulfil the demand to separate school and church, and it did not grant teachers official civil servant status (i.e., the title of *Staatsbeamte* as it was and is still known in German).

‡ "Badenser" refers to people of the region of the Grand Duchy of Baden.

Badenese parliament, but I can luckily provide you with the influential judgment of a Badenser, and even of one belonging to the group that approves this same parliament's budget. ("Hear, hear!") The same week in which I conducted my meeting in Lörrach,* the Lörrach Party paper—edited by Comrade Rösch, a friend of Kolb and Frank—published the following assessment of the Badenese school law:

> The new regulations regarding the altered law for schools have been published in the *State Bulletin* [*Staatsanzeiger*]. The law brings a series of manifold changes, but still not those changes that the complete body of Badenese teachers have long demanded, the changes needed for [the school system] to develop and thrive. Despite the law having been produced by the large voting bloc [in the Badenese parliament], the old liberal demands, including the separation of church and schools, have not been met. The new law weakens the statutory employment of school doctors: employing a school doctor is now only a requirement in schools where at least ten teaching positions cover at least three consecutive school years. The same conditions apply to the creation and filling of the post of school principal. Children who have grown up in a confessional community are obliged to attend religion lessons unless their religious education should be [formally] changed [by their parent or legal guardian]. One very important regulation for workers' families is that, dependent on parents applying, girls are allowed to finish school at Easter of the year in which they complete the fourteenth year of their lives … Moreover, the new law includes a series of important changes to the employment and payment conditions of female teachers, and also provides the essential structure of how the local municipalities and the state fund schooling. As far as can be judged to date, the population is not happy with the new school law, and above all its teachers who are dissatisfied, as it continues to deny them the rank of state civil servant. The new school law can hardly reckon on living a long life. ("Hear, hear!")

If you're dissatisfied with this assessment, please get in touch with your own colleagues from the regional parliament. This is what the most illustrious of the achievements of practical politics in the Badenese parliament looks like when a supporter of these politics shines his own light on it. The second great achievement, and the one that they mainly banged on about here, is the new municipal franchise.† Regarding this achievement, an interesting comment

* At the start of September 1910, Rosa Luxemburg had embarked on an agitation tour through Baden, and spoke in Schopfheim, Lörrach, and other localities.

† In 1910 the Social Democratic Party in the Badenese parliament not only failed to challenge a reform of the local government voting law—which included inessential changes like the lowering of the voting age from twenty-six to twenty-five, without changing the reactionary character of the voting law—but actually voted *for* the new law.

has been passed on to me, this time from a member of the regional parliament belonging to the majority grouping. In one of my public meetings in Wiesenthal,* Comrade Adolf Müller, one of the supporters of the budget, took the podium against me in a ninety-minute speech that included the following statement:

> Yes, you want to mock us for seeing it as a great achievement that we've now been granted the division of municipal voting districts into sixths instead of into twelfths. You simply don't understand our Badenese circumstances: we're already now in no position to really exploit this new suffrage law, and the reason we're not in that position is because we're not able to field enough economically independent people as candidates. ("Hear, hear!")

"Because," so said Müller, "it suffices that we field a single proletarian as a local council candidate, for him to be given the boot from his day job immediately." ("Hear, hear!"). So, these are Baden's particular political circumstances. And who allows the proletarian to be kicked out of his day job? Ask this same question in Wiesenthal to the emaciated textile workers! They'll give you the answer: "Those are our brothers in the [parliamentary] bloc: the national-liberals." (Tumultuous cries of "very good!" from the majority.) Yes, that's what these particular circumstances look like when examined more closely.

But now to the main question. Even if we were to ignore the fact that the achievements of practical politics in Baden actually boil down to a load of desperately overblown peanuts, yes, even if we were to assume that these were epoch-making measures, the question still remains: what has all this to do with approving the budget? ("Quite right!") Was the fate of any of these epoch-making laws intertwined with your final vote regarding the budget? You wouldn't dare to answer this question in the affirmative. (The minority laughs.) You also won't be able to answer affirmatively the question of whether the passing of the budget was dependent on your support. No, the support of our comrades merely contributed toward the unanimous adoption of the budget by parliament. In other words, with or without our comrades, the class state in Baden would have received these funds budgeted to it. The manner in which the budget supporters defend themselves is thus illustrative, because this is another example of how these same supporters elicited the Badenese workers' declarations of trust in the parliamentary group majority. In each location where our comrades spoke in front of workers in Baden to account

* Here, and in subsequent references to Wiesenthal's "emaciated textile workers," Luxemburg is referring to the town of Zell-im-Wiesental, in the municipality of Lörrach in Baden (today spelt without the "h" that was standard in the "thal" suffix in Luxemburg's time). It is known for its early industrial textile production and long standing radical political tradition and was one of the main stages of the 1848 revolution in Baden.

for voting for the budget, they presented a description of all their activities in the regional parliament. The question of support for the budget was not separated at any point from an assessment of all activities in the regional parliament. The Badenese workers, to whom their parliamentary representatives present the whole session of parliament as being thorough, industrious, and useful work—a fact that none of us would question—and from whom the representatives are demanding a declaration of trust, are not in a position to refuse this demand. That is because these same representatives are concurrently demanding that the workers pass judgment on the parliamentarians' overall performance. If the questions had been posed separately in meetings and assemblies in Baden, the workers would have then been in a position to judge the pure question of rejecting or approving the budget—and then, in some cases, the answer would have turned out quite differently. ("Quite right!") Yes, when one sees the Badenese proletarians, and when one appeals to them with exactly the same familiar arguments, the arguments with which we've been appealing to the proletarians' class interests for countless years in German Social Democracy, one will find just as strong an echo coming back from the workers as in other parts of Germany.

(*Chairman Dietz* draws the speaker's attention to the fact that she's already exceeded her speaking time.)

I've got twenty minutes, as I still have to justify the motion brought by my electoral district. (Calls from the audience: "No, no!") Why do you shout 'no'? Like any other independent motion, the speaker must be allocated a guaranteed twenty minutes, to justify their motion.

Chairman Dietz states, after talking with the speaker in private:

"If Comrade Luxemburg is not prepared to comply with the regulations for party business, then I must in fact appeal to the Party Congress and ask it if it is inclined to extend the speaking time. No one has submitted an independent motion. Comrade Luxemburg has, like every speaker in a discussion, ten minutes' speaking time: I permitted an extension and have already allowed her fifteen minutes."

Rosa Luxemburg, continuing:

The matter is finished; I comply. If any circumstance has proven how necessary it is to stand with utter resolve against the parliamentary group's politics in the Badenese parliament, then it's the way the Württembergian parliamentary group* has proceeded. The explanation from Kolb† and his colleagues from the regional parliament shows us just how much value the worker-masses are accorded in selecting the members of the Badenese parliament. ("Quite right!"

* The Kingdom of Württemberg, a German principality east of Baden that existed from 1805–1918, also sent representatives to the Badenese parliament.

† Wilhelm Kolb, reformist Social Democrat and chairman of the Social Democratic caucus in the Badenese state parliament.

from the audience.) This explanation shows us that our parliamentarians deal with the will of the people in exactly the way our agribusiness industrialists deal with the King, when these parliamentarians say: the people, absolutely, when they do our will. (Great outcry from the South Germans in the audience, lively applause from the majority.) It troubles you not when the workers declare that they're against your politics, and you organize a demonstration at the Party Congress in favor of the Badenese parliamentary group over the heads of the majority of the Württembergian comrades. It's evident that these parliamentarians do not in the least value demonstrations against the class state (Continuous calls to stop from the South Germans, to which the North Germans respond with calls of "quiet!") but do value demonstrations against their own workers. Frank closed his speech with an utterly correct comment…

(The calls to "finish!" are repeated so tumultuously that the speaker cannot finish the sentence that she has begun. The chairman, Dietz, requests the speaker to break off her speech; she declares that she'll comply with this request, but her words get lost completely in the din. The calls for her to stop continue to ring out among the rows of the minority. Frank calls out: "Your time is up, Comrade Luxemburg!" Laughter from the South Germans. Another group calls out, "Get off the stage!" The din swells to such an extent that the chairman threatens, if quiet does not resume, to interrupt the sitting for a short interval. Finally, Comrade Luxemburg leaves the podium to effervescent applause from the majority.)

III.

Justification for the motion on the political mass strike

A series of delegates who haven't signed our motion have declared that they completely agree in terms of the subject matter but have concerns that one word in our motion could prompt misunderstandings in certain party circles—and that's "propagation." We agree herewith that this word shall be deleted from the motion. We introduced this motion as a necessary extension to the party executive's resolution. The executive's resolution conceptualizes the question of the Prussian franchise from a general point of view. We wish to emphasize more the current point of view and the political guidelines for the struggle. Despite all the right thoughts it articulates, what's missing in the executive's resolution is sufficient recognition that we've moved a long way forward in our struggle for the right to vote in Prussia since the Prussian Party Congress. Since then, we've had the pleasure of watching the pantomime of Bethmann-Hollweg's bill, which was completely bankrupt by the end of its performance.* Alongside

---

* The commissions of the bicameral legislature—consisting of the House of Representatives (*Abgeordnetenhaus*) and the House of Lords (*Herrenhaus*)—rejected the draft changes to

that, we've experienced street demonstrations of a kind never previously seen in Germany or Prussia. The resulting situation—the parliamentary actions of the government and the bourgeois parties breaking down on the one hand, the immense upsurge in actions of the masses on the other—has not merely provided a brilliant confirmation of the basic approach of the Prussian Party Congress. It has also given the watchwords formulated at the Party Congress a much more concrete and current significance than they had at Christmas. We're talking especially about the watchword of the political mass strike. This was already adopted unanimously at the Prussian Party Congress as a recommended measure which should potentially be applied. Key lectures and speeches [at that congress] also referred to it explicitly. But events themselves have lent life to this watchword and have given it practical meaning.

Party comrades! Since the enormous spring demonstrations of the masses on the Prussian franchise question, the slogan of the mass strike has moved somewhat into the foreground of that which is of interest to our proletarian masses. Just as our Hamburg party comrades kicked things off with their successful attempt to use the mass strike as a political demonstration in January 1906,* this year the comrades in Kiel† and the comrades in Frankfurt and Hanau‡ have brilliantly executed demonstration mass strikes. And in a series of other urban centers, in Breslau, in Halle, in our Hesse-Nassau district of political agitation, in Rhineland and in Bremen, party comrades have grappled with the idea of the mass strike in the most vivacious manner, in debates which found their expression in a lively discussion of the subject in our party press this spring. To proceed in this manner is quite self-evident and could not be done differently. In the battle for the right to vote, as soon as we bring the extraordinary masses on to the stage, as soon as we organize powerful

---

Prussian voting law as submitted by the Prussian government on February 5, 1910. The government's draft bill, a response to pressure applied by the mass movement, only envisaged minor amendments to the division of the electorate into classes and the direct election of officeholders, while retaining a "three-class" voting system. This was an unequal, indirect form of suffrage, in which each eligible voter in a given voting district was categorized into three classes, according to the sum of direct taxes paid. Each class then chose, through means of a public vote, the same number of mandates for the Electoral College, which only then voted for members of parliament. This undemocratic voting system was used from 1849 to 1918 for the elections to the House of Representatives (*Abgeordnetenhaus*) of the Prussian parliament. The mass movement against this voting system reached its height between February and April 1910, forcing the government to withdraw its draft on May 27, 1910.

* On the afternoon of January 17, 1906, 80,000 Hamburg workers had downed tools to protest in assemblies and street demonstrations against limitations on the right to vote for Hamburg's parliament, the *Bürgerschaft*. This was Germany's first political mass strike.

† On March 15, 1910, around 10,000 workers from the Krupp-Howaldt-Imperial shipyard —more commonly the Friedrich Krupp Germaniawerft or simply Germaniawerft (Germania shipyard)—took part in a political half-day strike for the democratic right to vote in Prussia.

‡ A political half-day strike was called for February 23, 1910, in Frankfurt-am-Main: approximately 25,000 workers protested the denial of a democratic franchise in Prussia.

demonstrations, very soon a question arises in the masses themselves: How shall we proceed? Nobody can deny the recognition that we won't reach the goal of our struggles for the right to vote merely by way of demonstrations. It is highly unlikely that the ruling reactionaries of Prussia-Germany, responding to mere declarations of the will of the proletarian masses, will voluntarily relinquish their strongest bulwark, and, thus, a question arises naturally for the demonstrating proletarians: Do we have other, more effective weapons, if the weapon of the demonstration strike shows itself to be insufficient? ("Bravo!") Do we have other means and other roads we can go down, to apply greater and more effective pressure? Here, it is obviously our duty to give a clear answer to this question from the masses: yes indeed, you do have a more effective means, which you could propel into the situation if need be, and this is refusing to work, this is the mass strike. And something else must be added here. As soon as we organize mass demonstrations, as soon as these start to grow consistently in size and in might, we create a new playing field, on which the conclusion of the struggle over the franchise no longer depends solely on us: other factors are brought into the game instead, including our enemy's behavior. We all know how the ruling reaction met our first mass demonstrations; our memories of the saber attacks and of all the police provocations are fresh. We all know that the report published in the *Berliner Tageblatt* [Berlin Daily Paper] has not been refuted to this day. This tells how, on the day of the large demonstrations in the Tiergarten [park in central Berlin] on March 6,* the barracks of the First Field Artillery Regiment were transformed into a war camp, the troops lying in wait for an excuse to choke the peacefully and quietly demonstrating masses in their own blood. Until now, we have managed to avoid these threats being put into practice. Yes, we've managed to get the police to put their sabers back into their scabbards. But who can guarantee that we won't have to reckon with new provocations in the future, if we have to call the masses back onto the stage? On the contrary, the complete unpredictability, mindlessness and idiosyncrasy of Germany's ruling political system leaves us, as serious politicians, reckoning and being prepared for all eventualities in the struggle over the Prussian franchise. ("Quite right!") And this is where we have to give to the masses we call onto the streets to demonstrate a feeling of clear and calm security from the start: you are not delivered up defenseless to the rash provocations of the saber-waving reaction; we have a means to respond to the provocation in the most extreme case, and this means is the refusal to work, the political mass strike. Party comrades! At present we're seeing a lull in the voting law struggle, meaning the contemporary relevance of all these

* The Berlin Social Democratic Party had called for an action in Treptow Park on March 6, 1910, to demand the democratic right to vote. Because of police intervention, this was redirected into the Tiergarten. Despite the police ban on street demonstrations from February 13, 1910, the event was an impressive rally with around 150,000 demonstrators.

questions and watchwords has somewhat taken a back seat. But I hope we'll soon experience a powerful reanimation of the struggle for a new Prussian voting law. I hope and expect that our speaker, in his closing words, will allow to ring out the powerful call that I haven't heard in his speech until now:* the struggle for the right to vote in Prussia should flame up even more powerfully than it has done to date, and at the first possible opportunity. As soon as this happens, we will be confronted again with all these questions in all their vivacity, just as we were last spring. We all know that in the leading circles of our party and particularly of our unions, there's a strong disinclination against publicly discussing the mass strike question during the voting law struggle. These fears stem from an apprehension that talking about the mass strike at meetings and in the press would suffice to cause a mass strike to break out overnight, whether the moment would be opportune or not. This apprehension stretches to thinking that merely discussing the mass strike question or propaganda for a mass strike is virtually tantamount to playing with fire. Party comrades, it's high time that everyone belonging to our party realizes that this is an utterly false conception of the mass strike. And one of the aims of our motion is to create absolute clarity on this issue, to allay fears that publicly considering the mass strike question could artificially and by itself—whether opportune or not—provoke the mass strike itself. We have to overcome this false apprehension, just as the anarchistic conception of the mass strike, which fits with this false apprehension, is now long buried. A political mass strike is no phenomenon to be artificially conjured into existence by talking about it, or by propagating it as a political weapon. A political mass strike can only arise from historical conditions; a mass strike can result out of the ripeness of the political and economic situation. If there's one thing that proves that the mass strike can be discussed *ad infinitum* without that having the slightest practical success if the conditions to realize it are absent, then that's the history of the idea of the general strike itself. You know that Domela Nieuwenhuis† and other anarchists of his sort have been praising the general strike for decades as a panacea against all the ills of the current order of society, and against war. They have praised it as a means of bringing about social revolution within twenty-four hours. And whose mouths will you find "general strike" in more often today than the mouths of the French syndicalists who observe anarchistic rites? Nieuwenhuis's peddling of the general strike idea has not led to one iota of authentic success because nobody took up the cause. And the country

* Hermann Borgmann, a delegate from Berlin, gave the main speech and closing words of the voting law debate.

† Under the leadership of the Dutch Social Democrat Domela Nieuwenhuis, a left-libertarian group in the international workers' movement raised the demand that the proletariat should respond to any declaration of war with a general strike and refusal of military duty. These positions were rejected by a large majority of delegates at the International Workers' Congress in Brussels in August 1891.

today in which the general strike has moved forward least in practice is France, despite the syndicalists talking constantly about it.

Thus the history of the idea itself demonstrates that it's not the propagation, the consideration or the praising of the mass strike that can artificially call out the mass strike, but, rather, only and exclusively the ripeness of historical and economic circumstances. It's only in the last decade, in which we've seen the powerful alliance of capital into cartels, the politics of lockouts, and an incomparable escalation in class contradictions, that it's become evident that the mass strike will break out in one country after the next, not because it was once propagated by anarchists, but because historical circumstances demand it.

For us, concerning the Prussian voting law struggle, the watchword of the mass strike presents itself out of the simple fact that, in order to move this struggle toward victory, the proletariat must depend exclusively and completely on its own strength. As the most extreme form of independent proletarian political action, the mass strike is for us in Prussia-Germany concurrently the product of an exacerbation of class contradictions, of the decay of bourgeois liberalism and of bourgeois democracy, and of the alliance of all bourgeois parties against us—a product of the combined historical development of recent decades.

Conceived thus and placed upon this basis, considering the mass strike does not mean artificially conjuring up a mass strike, without a motivation and without the conditions for it to be effective, but rather means an outstanding method of enlightening the masses, an outstanding means of political education and of deepening the political approach of the proletarian masses. ("Quite right.")

So, it is not as a cure-all remedy, which only needs to be pulled out the bag in order to lead us to certain victories, that we wish to reflect on the mass strike and disseminate the idea of it. On the contrary, we have every reason to tell the masses the truth to their faces. In this point, I agree entirely with Borgmann, who thought it necessary to bring this in as an argument against our motion: that we won't be able to propel a struggle—like the one for a new Prussian voting law—to victory with a single blow. We have to prepare the masses for the fact that victory can only be achieved in a long series of heavy battles, rich in sacrifice. But precisely because we point out the full weight of the struggle before us when considering the mass strike, we cannot only fulfil the task of politically educating the working class, but also the task of education in terms of morals and mores, by appealing to the highest form of idealism, the willingness to sacrifice. When you add all that together, then you have to admit that the propagation of the mass strike, conceived in this way, also represents a good chunk of educating the masses toward socialism. ("Quite right!") Just as redundant as the fear that a mass strike could break out at an untimely moment merely because people talk about it, is the idea that its propagation already means agreeing on a binding date. Who can determine when we'll have to generate a political mass strike in Prussia-Germany? That just isn't something that is ours to determine alone. Perhaps a political mass strike can become necessary over the next one, two or even three years. But it's also possible that it becomes clear we need it after the next couple of franchise demonstrations: in addition to our own tactics, we also must consider the tactics of our opponents, the behavior of the reaction, the general atmosphere and the economic situation. Yet as this is how things stand, we cannot stipulate when and how the mass strike will be brought about. Instead, we have to admit that it could possibly become necessary within a very short period of time, from which emerges the clear duty of preparing the masses for their tasks. We also have to make certain, when the situation is ripe, that the masses do not merely reach for the weapon of the mass strike in a moving state of bitterness, but, rather, go into battle as a politically schooled and distinctly superior army of class fighters, under Social Democratic leadership. ("Bravo!") An historical manifestation like the mass strike won't allow itself to be called simply on command, but it is equally impossible to cancel it on command, when the moment's ripe for it. ("Very true!") If we neglect to prepare the masses through a thorough elucidation of the political mass strike in the context of its historical and political development, then we will only reach a situation in which the masses might plunge themselves into the mass strike in chaotic confusion, and not under our leadership. It is not us but the masses that are called upon to decide when the moment is ripe, and it is our duty to give them the intellectual weapons and clear insights into the magnitude of the struggle, into the size of the tasks, and into the casualties that are connected to that. Because in this, as in all other political struggles, we say: to be prepared is everything. (Lively applause.)

The Political Mass Strike and the Trade Unions*

Speech held on October 1, 1910, in Hagen [in Westphalia], at the Extraordinary General Meeting of the German Metal Workers' Union

Party comrades! Honorable public!

I must admit to being no less surprised than you are to have caught sight here at the extraordinary general meeting of the Metal Workers' Union of a good number of uniformed representatives of our Rulers† here on earth. I've discovered that, apart from the handful of highly placed gentlemen sojourning in this room, there's also an impressive number of police commissioners‡ and *Schutzleute*§ stockpiled in the nearest police station. (Movement in the audience.) Party comrades and honorable guests! I must admit that this surprise has affected me differently from you. It doesn't make me feel outraged—a wonderful feeling of security has come over me instead. (Ironic: "Bravo!")

Party comrades! You here in Hagen have definitely not come as far in Prussian culture as we have in Berlin; I come from the capital, Berlin, and there's a district of Berlin called Moabit.¶ That's where we learned, party comrades, that the Prussian police is indispensable wherever one wants to maintain security and order. (Laughter.) Most honorable public! It was only after I got the news that our district meeting office is being blessed with such a generous level of police protection that I could rest absolutely assured that we'll all be able to leave the hall with our noses, ears, eyes, and other body parts intact. (Laughter.) I have to tell you that it appears I possess quite a special attraction for the police. (Laughter.) I must admit to experiencing a certain joy each time, and,

---

* This speech is translated by Henry Holland from Luxemburg's *Gesammelte Werke,* Vol. 2, pp. 463–83.

† Luxemburg uses "*Obrigkeit*," a term that can be translated as "highest ruling instance." In combining this with "*auf Erden*" (on earth) Luxemburg is satirizing the authorities by using religious language.

‡ *Kommissar*, a specific rank in the German police.

§ Members of the *Schutzpolizei*. Also known as the *Schutzmannschaft*, these were uniformed police units in operation from the mid-nineteenth century and classified until 1919 as part of the military. On an organizational level, they had been separated from the *Kriminalpolizei* (criminal police force) in the Kingdom of Prussia in 1872, a restructuring that spread to other parts of Germany in the following years.

¶ "Moabit" refers to the massive criminal court located in the Berlin district of that name, evoking formidable state power.

as a speaker, a certain gratitude toward the praiseworthy police. I have to say to you that the presence of these gentlemen with their helmeted pates lends a certain spice to the whole thing. ("Very good!") And today, the very presence of the praiseworthy police provides a pretty foil for the subject that I wish to deal with tonight.

In the course of this evening, I hope to have an opportunity to illuminate the special connection between the proletariat's actions and demonstrations of the masses, and the praiseworthy police force. I reckon it's a good thing that these gentlemen get the opportunity of hearing for once what we think about them. ("Quite right!") I never lose hope that they could learn something too, and that's why we shouldn't be so mean with our words and with our lessons. For once, we want to throw our pearls to the—Prussian police.*

Party comrades and honorable public! There is indeed no subject more topical at a German union meeting at present than the subject of the mass strike and the unions. We have gathered here to discuss this subject, to reflect, as we could put it, in the lull between two giant battles. Only a few weeks ago, we fought an exemplary and magnificent battle here in Hagen and Schwelm,† worthy of the attention and the admiration of the entire class-conscious working class in Germany. And in no time at all, honorable public, you will perhaps be forced, you and countless colleagues and comrades, to join in a colossal struggle throughout Germany, of a kind that this country has never experienced before. You all know that, in a few days, the day after tomorrow, the representatives of the organized working class will enter into negotiations with the great capital magnates from the shipbuilding yards; these negotiations should decide whether 400,000 German metalworkers are to be thrown out into the cold.‡

Party comrades! Should this happen and should the consequence of this be—as is highly likely to be expected, considering the solidarity, the class consciousness, and the battle energy of all organized metalworkers—then we would witness a struggle right across Germany of a kind that the world has perhaps never seen before. Because then perhaps a million people would find

---

* Playing on the biblical reference (Matthew 7:6), common in German and English, "Das ist Perlen vor den Säuen werfen!" (throwing pearls before swine).

† In the middle of 1910, plant owners locked out around 20,000 metalworkers at Hagen, Schwelm, and other Westphalian localities. In response, 2,790 workers—from the German Metal Workers' Union, the Hirsch-Duncker Association, the Christian trade unions, and the Union of Smiths—joined forces with around 17,000 non-organized workers against the industrialists' attempts to split the workers' front, which was tightly welded despite manifold difficulties.

‡ The Association of German Metal Industrialists had threatened to lock out 60 percent of the metalworkers in Germany—approximately 400,000 people—in order to repress the waterside workers' strike that had been running since August 4, 1910. In negotiations at the start of October 1910, the shipyard owners were prepared to make partial concessions which were accepted by workers at the urging of the union leaders. The negotiating parties agreed that work would resume on October 10.

themselves in a struggle, together with their neighbors and their families, which comes down to a question of to be or not to be, between the strongest trade union organizations, and overly powerful, swanky capital.

Party comrades! In such a moment, as I have said, between two huge battles, it is pertinent for us to speak about this subject here and to reflect on what this most current of questions, both yesterday and tomorrow, means to us. So, party comrades and honorable public, learn to catch a glimpse of the fighting, organized working class in Germany and elsewhere in mid-battle, amid the fire of the struggle, in order to reflect, to analyze, and to accentuate one's awareness—in order to evaluate which weapons the working class should be using in its struggle.

And this is utterly natural; it arises out of the essence of the workers' struggle itself. The modern proletarian class does not direct its struggle according to a scheme, which has been laid down finished in some book or theory. The modern working class is, rather, an element inside of history, a dimension of social development, and it's in the midst of history, in the midst of its development and struggle that we learn how we have to fight. Party comrades and honorable public! It's precisely this which is admirable and epoch-making in this mammoth cultural work that lies within the modern workers' movement: that, for the first time, the mighty masses of the working people themselves are forging the weapon for their own liberation out of their own consciousness, their own conviction and their own understanding. And that's why it's extraordinarily important that we fully utilize such short moments of standstill between battles as we're experiencing here. In order to contemplate war, to analyze, and to examine all sides of the problems and questions that life presents to us.

One of the most important problems that both the union and the socialist organizations are currently engaging in, not merely in Germany but in all modern countries, is the problem of the mass strike. And now you see how an interesting phenomenon emerges. As so often, here it becomes obvious that history does not stand still, that development moves onward, and that Mephistopheles' statement from Goethe's *Faust* becomes utterly appropriate for our social-political life and work: "Reason becomes sham, beneficence a blight."* Everything changes with time.

The first commandment for political fighters like us is to move with the development of time, and to provide a constant account of changes, both in the modern world and in our battle strategy. Party comrades and honorable public! In the history of the idea of mass strike, the eternal law of historical development has confirmed its own validity, in an illustrious and striking manner. You

---

* Johann Wolfgang von Goethe, *Faust: A Tragedy*, Part I, Scene IV (trans. Bayard Taylor, 1870; Random House, 1950), p. 67.

all know very well that the idea of the mass strike, or the general strike as it was formerly known, has not just been invented in the last few days or years. Quite the contrary, for decades there have been people who have made propagating the idea of the general strike their specialty, their life's work. You will all have heard of Domela Nieuwenhuis,* who showcased himself particularly through propagating the idea of the general strike at international socialist congresses. You will all know that particularly in the Romance language countries, in Spain, in France, large entire sections of the trade unions, the so-called syndicalists, consider and propagate the general strike as the salvationist and unifying idea. And we've all seen earlier how those workers who stand on the soil of modern scientific socialism—those workers who have comprehended the necessity and importance of union organization and the struggle—have put all their energy into defending themselves against the ideas of the general strike as propagated by the anarchists. And they were completely right to do so. Party comrades! At both the socialist international congress in Brussels in 1891 and the congress in Zurich in 1893, the representatives of the working class of all countries rejected with a huge majority the idea of Domela Nieuwenhuis and friends. In France, however, we have relatively recently been witness to an interesting chapter in these reveries about the general strike. I myself had the pleasure of taking part in the International Socialist Congress in Paris in 1900.† And you will remember how strongly the French socialists were split back then in the course of what became known as the Millerand Crisis,‡ because of the great dithering regarding a socialist taking on the job of a minister. Back then, at the socialist congress in Paris, a gentleman by the name of Aristide Briand took to the podium. This is the same gentleman who now represents the bourgeois government as French prime minister and who now persecutes socialists and organized workers in some cases, much worse than any other bourgeois minister. This gentleman was no minister in 1900, but, rather, a furious and grimly determined supporter of the idea of the general strike. And I had to listen to his resounding speech in Paris, in which he abused us and all other Marxists who didn't want to believe in the true and exclusively liberating art of the general strike as utterly backward representatives of socialism. Party comrades and honorable public! As I have said, the socialists who stand on the

---

* A majority of the delegates at the International Workers' Congress in Brussels, August 16–22, 1891, had rejected Nieuwenhuis' motion to respond to every war with the general strike. At the International Socialist Workers' Congress in Zurich August 6–12, 1893, Wilhelm Liebknecht, Eleanor Aveling and Georgi Plekhanov also refused Nieuwenhuis' reintroduced motion.

† The International Socialist Congress in Paris was held September 23–27, 1900.

‡ Alexandre Millerand, who represented opportunistic politics in the French socialist movement, was the trade minister in Waldeck-Rousseau's reactionary bourgeois cabinet from June 22, 1899, to May 28, 1902. This first practical step by a social reformer to integrate the French workers' movement into the bourgeois state led to substantial conflicts between the revolutionary forces and the opportunists.

soil of Marxism, the trade unionists who are serious about union organization, all had nothing more than an empathetic smile at best, or just an indignant shrug of the shoulders for this idea at that time. And they were right, because what should happen? Precisely in those countries where the idea of the world-liberating watchword of the general strike was seen as the only means of getting out of the hell of capitalism overnight, precisely where this idea was so rife, the workers' organizations are now as low as can be, and remain until the present day the weakest of all countries. And it was now someone from the ranks of German Social Democracy, our old, unfortunately deceased and unforgettable Ignaz Auer* ("Bravo!") who, with his knack of coining pointed, epigrammatic catchphrases, refuted anarchism's favorite idea with just two words, by clearly and crisply declaring: "General strike—general nonsense."

Party comrades! This was the way things were until recently, and what do we see today? If we look at the bare facts, at the results of the last decade, from 1900 until now, looking at all the countries in which capitalist development is taking place, then we are forced to verify that huge general strikes and mass strikes are breaking out in one country after the other! I would simply like to remind you of the most important of these. In 1900, we had the massive miners' strike in Pennsylvania, about which the American party comrades claimed, and also explained, that it did more to disseminate socialist class consciousness than ten years of agitation would otherwise have done. In 1902 we had the great mass strike of the miners in Austria, which appeared to yield no results at first, but which subsequently, through the swing in public opinion and pressure on government and parliament, won the nine-hour working day for the miners. We experienced the mass strike of the miners in France in 1903, in the further course of which won the eight-hour working day for the French miners. There was the big mass strike in Belgium in 1902, the political strike, the struggle for universal suffrage. Right at the start of 1904, in January, we had the momentous general strike of the Dutch railroaders, which made the most colossal impression on the world. This also spread the shocking tidings that in Holland the complete transport network, and with that all economic life, had suddenly been paralyzed, and could be brought to a standstill through the will of a particular category of workers. And then, party comrades, came the year 1905. In January 1905 news reached Europe that appeared to come from a country in a fairy tale. The news was that in the northern capital of the Tsar of All the Russians—in Petersburg—100,000 to 200,000 proletarians had suddenly declared the mass strike, and had proceeded immediately to the palace, to demand political freedom and the eight-hour day. Now, party comrades, after that day, no month or day passed in Russia without local general strikes and mass strikes breaking out. In a country about which it had until then been

* Ignaz Auer, a member of the SPD's Party executive, had died on April 10, 1907, in Berlin.

assumed that it was a complete exception in the group of old cultured countries. In a country about which it was assumed that the laws of historical development break impotently at its borders and on its doorstep. A country which the wielders of power in Germany and especially in Prussia looked to with longing. Because those power-wielders believed that, in that country, lived the father of the only country in which the children don't cause him any trouble. Party comrades! In this very country, things started with a huge mass of proletarians rising up and utilizing the tool of the mass strike, the weapon of the mass strike, which is simultaneously political and trade union in nature, in the struggle against the exploiter class and to win political freedom. And as a lively echo, as a ringing out of the notes of this stormy period, we had a series of very large mass strikes in the autumn in Austria, as a demonstration and as a means of struggle for the general right to vote for the Imperial Council parliament, and for the regional parliaments in Bohemia, Galicia and Trieste. In the year 1905, we also had a gigantic railroaders' strike in Italy, and the mass strike in Galicia of 200,000 farm laborers, that category of worker which lives in the deepest possible deprivation and humiliation. Since then, no year has passed without a tremendous mass strike in this country or the other. Last year, in 1909, we had the unforgotten general strike in Sweden, which is still fresh in all your memories. At this moment, in this year we have had—I won't need to remind those of you who have experienced these things themselves—two brilliantly executed and victorious mass strikes in America. The first began in March and ended in April, the mass strike in Philadelphia, the second one, only recently ended, was the general strike of 70,000 male and female workers in the textile industry for women's clothes in New York. This forced through its demand that the only valid law—in the whole industry and in countless workshops—is that which the workers' union determines. ("Bravo!")

Party comrades! That is a short overview, shall we say, of the naked facts of the history of the mass strike in the last decade. And establishing these facts suffices, in order to draw a conclusion from them: the conditions in which mass strikes are realized have changed enormously over time. Do we therefore have any reason to assume or to think that all these mass strikes and general strikes that I have listed are, shall we say, a delayed triumph of the anarchistic idea? No certainly not, honorable public, it is certainly not our guests [i.e., the police] who have reason to be triumphant, or any reason to demonstrate to us that we've arrived at our destination after what could be called a delay. Please note well that it's precisely in all those countries where the most effective and powerful mass strikes have come about recently that anarchism has died out completely. And please also note the interesting fact that, during the Russian Revolution, in that country in which the mass strike as a political means of struggle was virtually baptized and applied, as it were, as an epoch-making and brilliant example, that in this country—which as it happens is the cradle of the well-known theoretician and anarchist Mikhail Bakunin, with whom Marx and Engels had hefty conflicts in the International—that, in Russia itself, during the whole big revolution, not only did anarchism play no part, it was even stamped down completely by the victorious throngs of the organized proletariat. ("Bravo!") Because, party comrades, this fact must be stressed in a historical manner: the sole form in which the name of anarchism allowed itself to be seen from behind its mask in the Russian Revolution, was as the store sign of the lumpenproletariat. Of the thieves, bandits, and hucksters, who, so as to clothe themselves in any possible idealistic cloak, called themselves anarchistic communists, and who were recognized by the entire socialist working class for what they are—representatives of the lumpenproletariat. Party comrades! Thus we see complete separation, virtually right at the beginning of our current period of development, of the idea of the mass strike from the anarchist foster fathers and propagandists of the general strike. The idea of the mass strike takes the stage in direct opposition to the madness of anarchism. Because, party comrades and honorable guests, while, for the anarchists, the idea of the general strike should be a cure-all remedy—virtually at the stroke of wand, overnight and without much effort—to suddenly leap over into a socialist paradise; while, for the anarchists, the idea of the mass strike was in direct opposition to political engagement and to political struggle, we now, on the contrary, view the mass strike as a political weapon, primarily used to serve the people in their quest to win political rights.

So this, distinguished audience, is what the facts look like, and now we all have good reason as thinking fighters to pose this question: What has happened, how has it become possible that an idea which for so long seemed impractical to execute and unrealizable, that this idea has now virtually become a daily manifestation, that it stands today on every agenda of the political and union movement? If you want to engage with the answer to this question with the thoroughness becoming to any serious politician, then you have to take a look at the economic development of recent decades, and specifically over the last decade. Honorable public and party comrades, those of you who live in one of the most important points in the western industrial region* know yourselves what you have experienced with your own bodies. The outstanding trait in Germany's development recently has been the tremendous concentration of capital, the concentration and clustering of large industry in all its power against the proletariat! Party comrades, remember how around twelve years ago in our own ranks, the ranks of Social Democracy, very loud, doubting voices could be heard, demanding that all Marxist tenets be revised that claimed that what Marx had said—regarding the thread and direction of the organized development of capital—must all be thrown on the scrap heap, because

* Hagen, where Luxemburg is speaking.

German capitalism was not actually developing as Marx had prophesized. It was said that the concentration of capital is not really moving forward, and that many small businesses are still keeping themselves above water. Party comrades—barely had this opinion been articulated, barely had the great work of revising Marxist tenets begun, when life itself came along and showed us—in such an obvious way that even a blind man must be able to see—that capitalist development in Germany had confirmed in a brilliant manner and according to Marxist preconditions just what our teachings had predicted. Nowhere more so than in Germany, more precisely in the last few years, has the power of capital become immensely concentrated, at the expense of the proletariat.

Nowhere more so than in Germany, and especially here in this western industrial region. Simply take a look at the most important branches of industry. Almost all of capital, and the combined power over the means of production, is concentrated everywhere in such few hands, in cartels that rule complete regions with omnipotence. The same applies to the coal industry, the iron industry, and, recently, the textile industry. What does the development of cartels against the working class mean? Several years ago, the German Reichstag established a special commission to investigate the essence and nature of the German cartels. The large magnates representing the various cartels were called together and had to respond to various questions asked them by Reichstag and imperial government representatives. One of these questions ran as follows: How do the cartels of large-scale industry in Germany position themselves regarding the labor question, what influence do you have on structuring working conditions? The gentlemen representatives of the cartels, and particularly Herr Kirdorf from Gelsenkirchen, grew outraged when answering, claiming that they never got involved in worker relations. The workers' conditions have nothing at all to do with the cartels, claimed the cartels' representatives. Our representative in the Reichstag, [Hermann] Molkenbuhr, responded by telling the gentleman to his face that such an answer displays a rather slack approach to the truth. And even Professor [Gustav] Schmoller, certainly a conservative, declared that he could not believe the cartels did not use their power to exert some sort of pressure on working conditions. But, party comrades, if any proof were still needed that the cartels are a direct enemy power against the working class and specifically against workers' organizations, then the most recent lockout of construction workers* provided brilliant proof of this. ("Quite right!") And it's utterly necessary that each of you note this fact, as fighters for and representatives of these workers' organizations, so you can hold it up in the face of our opponent. During the

* On April 15, 1910, around 160,000 construction workers began a struggle against the mass lockouts in the building industry. They pushed for their demands for wage rises and a reduction of working time through regional collective bargaining and political agitation. In some big cities, the strike lasted until the start of July.

construction worker lockouts—when hundreds of thousands of working-class families were staring hunger in the face, not knowing how they would still their children's hunger tomorrow and were on the breadline.* That is because of a single powerful word spoken by a clique of Hamburg capitalists—cartels, more specifically the Steel Works Association, and the Building Material Dealers—who declared as with one voice: our task now is to support the construction industrialists. Those construction entrepreneurs who refused to follow their association's orders, and who didn't want to lock out their workers, suffered attempts by local suppliers to force them to go through with the lockout, by refusing to deliver building supplies, a step aimed at increasing pressure on the workers. ("Boo!") This fact remains historical proof that the German cartels' representatives lied shamelessly when confronted by those representing the Reichstag and the government concerning the question of workers' conditions ("Quite right!"), just as they lied about using pressure in a way that has a negative impact on workers' conditions. But, party comrades, alongside cartels and syndicates, which are not merely there to concern themselves with the organization of production, we've also been blessed with an entire series of [so-called] workers' organizations during the last decade, which don't attempt to hide their aim of pursuing a deadly battle against the unions. We now have employers' associations in almost every branch which, through pushing down wages and coercively introducing forced labor documentation, attempt to rob the workers of the fruits of years of arduous union work, and which also try to dispute the right to collective bargaining. Party comrades! All these employers' associations are centralized at two points, at the Headquarters of the Employers' Associations, and at the Organization of Employers' Associations.† And according to the *Statistical Almanac for the German Empire* for 1910,‡ there are almost 270,000 workers organized under their sphere of influence. Now, party comrades, the real powers of these employers are actually much wider, because we all know that these gentlemen love to work mostly in the dark, and certainly don't rush to exhibit their organizations and their practices in broad, public daylight. In reality, the interrelations and connections of the class of capitalist industrialists—directed against the working class for example—are infinitely larger than the public knows. But now, party comrades, after we've seen how this type of economic development during the last decade has led directly to a gargantuan mass of capital, which is like, as it were, a sanctified power with a united will and a united hate initiating battle against the proletariat, let us

* In the original German text, Luxemburg says "*am Hungertuche nagen*," which translates as "to gnaw at a Lenten cloth," a long-standing phrase—derived from medieval Catholic practice—that suggests hunger, ostracization, and marginalization.

† These two distinct organizations—*die Hauptstelle der Arbeitgeberverbände* and *der Verein der Arbeitgeberverbände*—merged in 1913 to form *die Vereinigung Deutscher Arbeitgeberverbände* (the Union of German Employers' Associations).

‡ *Statistische Jahrbuch für das Deutsche Reich* (Statistical Yearbook for the German Reich).

turn to the political side of developments. What have we seen recently on Germany's political stage? The interrelations between economic, business, and political developments reveal themselves in a characteristic fashion. And we all know that the renowned Central Association of German Industrialists is, in a sense, the center, the pinnacle of the entire class of provocative entrepreneurs. This organization is led by [Henry] Bueck, about whom you've all heard the scandalous affair of how he offered the government 12,000 marks for purposes that have little to do with the well-being of the workers' movement.* But now this Central Association of German Industrialists—the greatest agitator against all workers' organizations and concurrently the highest instance pushing for protectionist, import duty politics, as well as being the biggest backer of reactionary measures and the largest obstacle to all social reforms in the German Empire—is also a supporter of all of the Conservative Party's measures.† My honorable public, there is nothing whatsoever and no phenomenon that reveals in such a typical way the social damages incurred by the development of our people—a phenomenon that must be discernible for the dimmest of observers—than that stage play that has been acted out recently in Germany, and especially in Prussia, in the struggle over the franchise.‡ And what has this struggle made clear? It's been made evident that the people have to reach for the means that are necessary for the working class, in order to win the most elementary of political-democratic rights, which a real liberalism should have already won for us. The matter in question is still the struggle for the general right of both sexes to vote in the elections to the Prussian bicameral legislature.

Party comrades and honorable public! It is a highly significant fact that we already had the general right to vote in Prussia, which now has to be fought for so laboriously. The point of time at which we had already won this right to vote was March 18, 1848. Party comrades, remember what then occurred in Germany! On that memorable day, the people of Berlin went onto the streets. They organized troops, they engaged the King's troops in street battles, and they beat those troops. The next day, on March 19, the people of Berlin lifted up their

* Henry Axel Bueck, general secretary of the Central Association of German Industrialists, offered the Imperial Ministry of the Interior 12,000 marks in 1898 to finance the campaign for the so-called Penitentiary Bill, introduced into the Reichstag on June 20, 1899. The bill was entitled "For the Protection of Trade-based Working Conditions" but was commonly known as the *Zuchthausvorlage*, or Penitentiary Bill, because of the penal sanctions it would have introduced against workers conducting collective action. The draft law was directed against the growing strike movement and was aimed at removing workers' right to strike and collectively bargain. Due to the mass actions that were taking place nationwide, it was possible to vote the law down in the Reichstag on November 20, 1899, although the Conservatives voted in favor.

† The German Conservative Party was founded in 1876 and had its nucleus of political power in the Prussian bicameral legislature.

‡ From mid-January 1910, mass movements continued to arise in all parts of Germany: hundreds of thousands of demonstrators demanded general, equal, direct, and secret suffrage for all persons over twenty in Prussia.

dead and carried them to the palace, forcing King Friedrich Wilhelm—who once had spoken so proudly about never tolerating a piece of written paper, called a constitution, to be pushed between himself and his subjects—the people forced this proud gentleman to take off his hat in front of them, in front of the fire of the battle of the barricades, and to lay this written paper at the feet of the victors of the barricades. Party comrades! In that age, on this piece of paper that you forced tenaciously from the king, was a text concerning the general right to vote for all Prussians who have completed the twentieth year of their lives. But, honorable public, this freedom of the day was still a piece of paper, and the task was to introduce this freedom into everyday life, and the working people of Prussia and Germany of the time were not yet ripe for this task. We did not have, back then, the enormous capitalist development that we do today, and it wasn't the workers, the class-conscious proletariat, but the liberal bourgeoisie. Power was passed into their hands. It was namely the industrial representatives of that age in Westphalia and in Rhineland, Messieurs Camphausen and Hansemann, who were made ministers after the confrontation of March 18, 1848. What could the liberal bourgeoisie of the time have achieved, thanks to the bloodletting and the sacrifices in terms of lives of the working people, if they had actually taken their political and liberal program seriously? Party comrades! It is strikingly evident that the liberal bourgeoisie of the day, if they had taken their program seriously, would have started with crushing the whole rotten *Vormärz** state machinery, and by proclaiming the republic in the whole of Germany. ("Bravo!") Party comrades! Bourgeois liberalism didn't do that back then, it failed to consolidate and safeguard the people's freshly won freedom. On the contrary, the bourgeoisie made peace with the crown and with feudalism of its own accord, as quickly as possible and behind the proletariat's back, and defrauded the people out of the fruits of their struggle. And why? Because they were more scared of the people, even back then, and hated them more than they did the complete Prussian reaction! Party comrades! Since then, we've experienced an even more profound decay of liberalism. Please note the following interesting point. Where is the big, current backlash within the Liberal Party coming from? From this very western industrial region [where the speech is being given]! While, in the Prussian franchise struggle, the proletariat, led by Social Democracy, must pay off the old debts of the bourgeois liberals in order to win the equal and general right to vote, which the fathers of our liberals stole from us in 1848, the most reactionary current within national liberalism is flowing from the Rhenish-Westphalian liberals. Precisely now, it is being revealed that the colossus of capital, which labors as an agitator against its own workers, is simultaneously the solid bulwark of

* *Vormärz* (pre-March), also known as the Age of Metternich, refers to the period prior to the 1848 March Revolution, considered by historians to begin either with the establishment of the German Confederation in 1815 or the French July Revolution of 1830.

reaction in political life. And so, we see in all fields—the well-known financial reforms, protectionist import-duty politics and the ever increasing spending on militarism in geopolitical adventures—an expansive trail, so that we must conclude that today the working class and Social Democracy may rely solely upon themselves, in the defense of the interests of freedom and the interests of democracy. All bourgeois parties confront us in a united camp of reaction.

Thus it follows, party comrades, that even on political territory, each step forward, each new political right can be acquired by none other than the working masses themselves, through a bold action, or more accurately through many long actions of the masses on the streets. We have already taken some steps forward, we have experienced, party comrades, in this struggle for the Prussian franchise, that the existing ruling order does not shy away from brutal interventions in our civil rights, in order to make it harder for us to triumph. Let's all think about that lovely experience that we had on March 6 in the Tiergarten in Berlin, where we, a crowd several thousand strong, stood utterly calm and peaceful in the spring sunshine, and did nothing more than repeatedly cry: "Long live general and equal suffrage!" Suddenly, a troop of mounted police appeared on the square and stormed at us, waving their sabers like a wild horde. That showed why the police carry sabers, and for whose security. Party comrades! We can tell this story now with serenity and equanimity because we forced these gentlemen to put their sabers back in their scabbards. Party comrades! We demonstrated more than this, we forced the Berlin chief of police—after he'd made massive proclamations against us, the revolutionary party, and had billboards stuck up, stating that the street is for transport and that demonstrations will not be tolerated—we forced him to leave the streets free for us, and taught him that the streets belong to us, the mass of the workers. ("Bravo!") Thus, party comrades, the masses' movement until now has proven to us that every step forward must be won forcibly by the pressure of the enormous masses of workers outside on the streets. And precisely as we've wrung the first victories out of the police's bloody fists up to now, it is solely on the streets and in great proletarian mass demonstrations that we'll smash the injustice of the three-class voting law. ("Quite right!) Party comrades! It's especially in the struggle over the Prussian franchise that we can—or almost must—make use of the most extreme and sharpened weapon, sooner or later, that is available to the organized proletariat: the political mass strike. Let the ruling authorities in Prussia wave their sabers about to their hearts' content. Perhaps all of you have heard which new secrets from that side were revealed at our latest Magdeburg Party Congress,* how, for example, a gentleman from Westphalia, the former Commanding General [Mortiz] von Bissing, has drafted

* The party conference of the Social Democratic Party of Germany took place September 18–24, 1910, in Magdeburg.

a whole campaign plan against the proletariat that's demonstrating in the streets. Let the gentlemen aim their cannons laden with live ammunition against the masses, as they did in Berlin on March 6. No amount of cannons or sharp sabers will help against the weapons that we've got in reserve. ("Bravo!" "Quite right!") All our experience so far has already shown that. Can any state, even if it surpasses the Prussian state's blindness and brutality—deploy cannons against hundreds of thousands of calmly and peacefully striking workers? Any state that wanted to butcher such a mighty mass of workers would have to be foolish and blind. For it would murder with its own hand the worker-bees, from whose honey it lives as a drone. ("Bravo!" "Quite right!") And, party comrades, can any state—and even if it has amassed its cannons against us—can that state compel peacefully striking workers to get the machines moving again? No! Even the most despotic state is not capable of that, and so it becomes evident that it's precisely the calm and peaceful weapon of the political mass strike that is the keenest weapon. Which we may have to reach for if the ruling reactionary forces continue to cling to their pigheadedness and illusions. Party comrades, while political developments almost compel us to reach increasingly toward mass strike in order to win the most elementary political rights, we continue to lead such politics in exactly the same direction in the trade union movement.

Honorable guests! Which conditions are we to thank for the large, recent mass strikes in the economic field, and which lessons should we draw from the storm brewing over your flourishing Metal Workers' Union? It's the capitalists who maliciously plan to provoke a massive trial of strength. Reflecting on the experience of the construction workers' lockout, it's well-nigh proven through documented evidence that the assault against the construction workers' organization was prepared by a long arm, proof that the industrialists executed this move in a planned fashion to force the proletarians into a desperate struggle through lockouts. It is exactly this same plan that the current plan of the shipbuilding capitalists is based on—as is also the case with the capitalists of the metal industry. When the capitalists and industrialists themselves have their hands on the means of forcing us into a mass strike through a lockout, thanks to the protection of a united authority capable of violence, our industrial organization is confronted with the urgent necessity of readying itself for the weapon of the mass strike to be used at a later point in time, as an inevitable part of the future struggle to defend the right to collective bargaining. From this emerges the most practical thing possible to look the future clearly in the eye, to say: the more the masses of the proletariat are prepared for this through a clear conception of the whole situation and through becoming conscious of their great tasks that lie before them, the more they are prepared to fight out this large battle, then the higher are our chances of emerging as a victor from this battle.

Honorable guests! Several arguments show up that are most frequently brought into play against the use of the mass strike. First, we are told that a mass strike, more specifically a political mass strike, means running a huge risk, as it entails exposing the trade union organization to a huge danger. Such a large clash could smash our trade union organization to pieces. Yes, it is true that in this or that tumultuous mass strike our organization could perhaps be damaged at first. But there are circumstances where a battle has to be commenced even under unfavorable conditions, if the honor of the organized workers' movement is to be saved at all.

Party comrades! The trade union organizations are principally created to serve us in our struggles—namely to defend our very first right, the right to collective bargaining, that is now so threatened—to serve us as a weapon in our struggles. Our trade union organizations are our artillery in the fight for a better future. What would your take be on a military state that declared that it couldn't go to war for fear that its artillery could be blown to bits? For what reason do we have artillery other than to fire at the enemy when the situation demands it? To see it from another angle, our weapons are not so crudely made as the weapons of military states. The cannons of military states really can be blown to pieces and rendered useless in a battle. Our organizations, on the other hand, acquit themselves successfully, and can only exist, in battle; they grow solely through battle. Think back to the time of the [Anti-]Socialist Law.* Was that not the toughest time that the German unions and German Social Democracy have experienced together? What did our organization look like immediately after the [Anti-] Socialist Law came into force? Our unions were smashed, and our press brought to a standstill, our organization was wiped out; but what impression did we make twelve years later, when the [Anti-] Socialist Law had to be rescinded? We stood there ten times stronger than before, and the Socialist Law lay there in shards. (Tremendous applause.) And this is how things will always go in the big struggle that our opponent is going to force upon us.

Party comrades! What do recent experiences show us? They demonstrate that there's no more advantageous time to build union organization than in a large mass struggle, which stirs up the ambivalent masses of the proletariat and makes them receptive to joining organizations. ("Quite right!") You saw this here in Hagen, where your Metal Workers' Union has made growth manifest in such a brilliant way since the last lockout. This very same trend is confirmed elsewhere. Take the example of Russia, as earlier mentioned. Until 1905, there were almost no trade union organizations in Russia. In the wake of the huge action of the striking masses that we observed there in 1905, they

---

* After two unsuccessful assassination attempts on Kaiser Wilhelm I in 1878, Chancellor Otto von Bismarck used these events as a pretext to introduce a law banning the Social Democratic Party. The Law against the Public Danger of Social Democratic Endeavors (known as the Anti-Socialist Laws) lasted until 1890. Although it did not explicitly ban the Social Democratic Party, it banned newspapers, public events, and trade unions that the government considered "subversive."

started sprouting like mushrooms in one administrative district after the other. Strong, young trade-unions organizations. The same thing happened back then in Belgium. Up until 1886, there was not a trace of trade union organization in Belgium. The first sign there of a general awakening came after the storm of mass strikes in the iron works. These mass strikes gave birth to the political movement, the struggle for general and equal suffrage, and concurrently Belgium's first trade union organizations. And from this perspective, the most recent occurrences in Philadelphia in America provide very instructional examples for us.

I have two testimonies from these that I'd like to read to you, because we have no better proof of how such elemental mass strikes potently strengthen the trade unions than the example of Philadelphia right now. It was at the start of spring of this year, on March 5, that the organized streetcar employees were fired in Philadelphia, precisely because they were organized. To defend their comrades, first a large number of streetcar employees declared the general strike, followed by individuals from many other professions in the city. The general strike closed with a magnificent victory. Moreover, trade union organizations have grown massively since then. We read, for example, in the German-American bakers' newspaper how Philadelphia had barely 350 bakery workers organized before the general strike was put into force. None of the large bread factories—and Philadelphia has a large number of these, like any other big city—had workers' organizations, but a bakery worker for each of the largest establishments in Philadelphia was present at this mass assembly [for the general strike], and there they declared that the factory had to be unionized before they would return to work: "The hour to act has arrived for our union, we cannot allow anything to remain undone. A comrade with organizational ability will be called to Philadelphia, to be available to help our comrades at all times in utilizing the situation to the greatest possible extent. The time has come and our army could grow sizably through the influx of Philadelphia's bakery workers. Until now, Philadelphia has slept. It has been shaken out of its sleep brutally and suddenly. The proletariat of Philadelphia is now aroused and full of energy." All that refers to a profession which had nothing to do with the original cause of the strike. The bakery workers organized in the wake of the mass strike that was generated in sympathy for the streetcar employees.

And here is another testimony from Philadelphia's textile industry. Mr. John Golden, the leader of the men and women who work in the branch, declared:

> This strike created the opening for us to reach more people with our organization than we would have reached in five years at a cost of 10,000 dollars. It signifies the complete organization of Philadelphia's textile workers. We have already registered 5,000 new members, and we expect that by the end of the week we'll have won the

> same number again. Educating and awakening wage laborers to an understanding of the necessity of self-organization is worth every sacrifice that this large struggle may demand. Irrespective of the result of the current struggle, the workers will emerge from it as victors, as they will be more strongly organized than previously.

So, honorable guests, it is becoming evident everywhere that it's precisely the Herculean mass strikes that are shaking up a large mass of what until now was an ambivalent working class, and that these strikes function as an illustrious form of agitation for the task of organizing the trade unions.

And now to deal with a further objection against the mass strike. Party comrades! People point out to us—and this played a big part regarding the promise of the mass strike in the Prussian franchise struggle—that we still have a large challenge in front of us in the form of a large mass of colleagues organized in opposition to us. We still have to engage with the workers organized in Christian unions and associations who do not share our standpoint, and are we able to undertake an action as large as the political mass strike if such large throngs of proletarians possessing other opinions are against us? Party comrades, those who articulate this anxiety must recognize that history takes effect in exactly the opposite way to what they claim. It's not the Christian organizations that could function as a serious obstacle in a mass strike action, but, rather, the other way around. There is no surer way of tearing the great throngs of the working class—currently aimed against us—away from their bourgeois leaders in Christian-Social unions, and other unions of that type, and winning them over to our side, than a big, bold mass action. Because, comrades, the more mass movements arise, and the more large questions and problems of the proletariat's basic interests are addressed in the struggle, so, correspondingly, more must the masses—which include members of the Christian unions and the Hirsch-Duncker Association—belong with us together. And the more it becomes clear that the whole of their associations' leaders' politics amounts to no more than leading the unions up the garden path. Party comrades! That's why we have to be happy each time a big mass movement means that supporters of the Christian unions and of the Hirsch-Duncker Association march together. We admit that this marching only fulfills its purpose if we direct the full glare of the public onto these proceedings, and we can exploit them; and when we can enlighten the masses who walk behind their bourgeois leaders regarding the actual essence of their interests and tasks.

Party comrades! We also have to deal with a further argument, which appears to be very plausible and a very dangerous weapon against the political mass strike, and the argument is this: we are putting to the test not only the principal factor behind the power of the trade union organizations, but also our funds, our financial means. There is no trade union that can declare in advance a mighty mass movement or mass strike: our union has insufficient financial means to pay the living costs of countless hundreds of thousands over long months to come. But, comrades, this whole understanding of the matter is wrong. In such cases, we must learn to count on something else besides coins ringing out in our funds and in our cashbooks. We have to count on the inexhaustible wellspring of idealism for the execution of our task. In the future, we won't be able to win the gigantic battles that stand before us merely by using finances. The greatest commitment must be tied fast to our great aims and tasks, and every single person among the masses has to understand that what's at stake are tasks for which one may not only suffer hunger for months on end, but for which one can, if necessary, give one's life. ("Bravo!") Party comrades! So far in history, counting on the ideals of the masses has never failed. Do we not have sufficient examples of this during the modern proletarian struggle for liberation, that the masses know how to put up with the very worst of conditions? As long as they've got their aim clearly in sight, which can lead them to throwing off the yoke of capitalism. Party comrades! This is what 1848 was like, not just in Germany, but also in France during the famous February Revolution. The proletarians of that age deceived themselves with the lovely madness that they merely had to put in a huge effort full of sacrifices, in order to realize a socialist ordering of society a short time after. After they forced the provisional government in France to proclaim the republic on February 24, 1871, they immediately voiced their claim: we demand that this time a social republic be constructed in France, in which there should be enough beans and bread for everyone. And, party comrades, the French proletarians back then marched on the streets of Paris with a black flag on which was written: "Workers! Live or welcome death!" The provisional government of the day, which was utterly scared of the proletariat assembled on the street, promised to construct a socialist republic and to guarantee everyone bread and work: but they needed some time to achieve these aims. These gentlemen knew however that the field of play would look very different three months later; they had to win time to gather together enough "blue beans"* for them to "feed" the starving! The proletarians of the time issued their memorable, historical words through the mouth of one of their own, one of the first and best workers of Paris. In front of the assembled provisional government, they declared: good, gentlemen, we'll give you time, we, the proletariat of Paris will starve for three months, but we want to have a social republic. Three months of the most horrible want followed, and they held out, believing that they would receive the famous social republic, with bread and work for everyone. When the three months were up, it wasn't the bread and work of the social republic that appeared on the streets, but, rather, the National Guard, the army, and the infamous battles of the June Days and the June massacres that followed, three

* *Blaue Bohnen* (blue beans) is an archaic German colloquialism for bullets.

days and three nights that were aimed at drowning the madness of the social republic in blood.

But, party comrades, even back then, the mass demonstrated that they would not shy away from any sacrifice. Back then there were no funds to maintain proletarians for three months, there were no trade unions, and no organization to keep up battle morale. How much today we must direct our vision toward bringing forth the sacrifices that may prove necessary, in light of the fact that we have such substantial cultural works of the German unions and of German Social Democracy behind us! To generate this intellectual spirit and this idealism from the masses, we need do nothing more than to regularly illuminate the fact that all struggles that we conduct, all mass strikes that lie in front of us, are nothing other than a necessary historical stage toward the ultimate liberation from capitalism, on the way to a socialist order.

Party comrades! Is not every lockout that we experience today a grand act of propaganda for socialism? Is not the mere fact that we stand facing a decision today–and need to ask ourselves whether a single power-statement made by a handful of capitalists will suffice to throw hundreds of thousands of men and women onto the street—does this not prove even to the blind that a societal order of this kind deserves to be chased to the devil? (Lively applause.)

Party comrades! Each lockout is one new nail in the coffin of the capitalist order, because it's precisely the lockout method currently preferred—which fails to conquer the proletariat—that provides the best proof that the current ordering of society is no longer possible, but has indeed become untenable, and that it has to make way for a new ordering. And is not every mass strike a step forward to overcoming this old order? Party comrades, the famous *Communist Manifesto* of Marx and Engels concludes with the words: "The proletarians have nothing to lose but their chains. They have a world to win." We will only be armed for the great battle—which we'll have to fight in the coming period—when every proletarian organized in a union has understood that their vocation is in the Social Democratic Party, when every socialist proletarian has understood that they have a duty to internalize socialist educational literature, and when every worker active in and organized through a union is simultaneously a steadfast warrior for socialist liberation, conscious of their goals. It is only under this battle cry that we'll be able to prove victorious in the coming battles, when the last proletarian has understood that they have not only their chains to lose, but a whole world to win. (Sustained and thunderous applause!)

The Political Mass Strike and the Unions*

Speech on October 1, 1910, at the General Assembly of the German Metal Workers' Union in Hagen in Westphalia

ACCORDING TO A NEWSPAPER REPORT

Comrade Luxemburg began her one-and-a-half-hour lecture by using biting satire to criticize the behavior of the Hagen Police Department. Contradicting the law governing associations, the police used violence to break into the general assembly. Moving onto her main theme, the speaker proceeded to present a historical review of the idea of the political mass strike and reflected on the activities of the international congresses that have addressed the issue. In a rigorous and informed manner, the speaker rejected all attempts to identify the idea of the socialist mass strike with anarchism. The speaker argued that where anarchism is practiced, it lacks any kind of organizational cohesiveness. Further, the speaker discussed the transformation in the image of the mass strike and the successes of such strikes in specific countries during the last decade. "We can only grow through struggle, and it's in the middle of the struggle where we learn how to fight"—said Luxemburg. The behavior of the liberal bourgeoisie in 1848 was accurately characterized as being hostile to the people.† Through longer contributions, often interrupted by thunderous applause, Comrade Luxemburg then discussed how the mass strike is propagated in our own ranks and how its opponents move against this propagation. It was, she said, precisely the trade unions which would have to engage with the idea of the mass strike more deeply than before, particularly in light of the entrepreneurial class's tactic of lockouts.

Comrade Luxemburg concluded her lecture by appealing to the workers' idealism, whereby she reminded her audience that the working class in other

---

* This article first appeared in *Arbeiter-Zeitung* (Dortmund), No. 233, October 5, 1910. It is translated by Henry Holland from Luxemburg's *Gesammelte Werke*, Vol. 7 (Berlin: Dietz Verlag, 2017), pp. 661–2.

† On March 18, 1848, Berlin workers, petty-bourgeois and students erected barricades and confronted and inflicted a defeat on the Prussian military. Friedrich Wilhelm IV was forced to withdraw troops from the city. Government power passed over into the hands of the liberal bourgeoisie. On November 8, 1848, a counterrevolutionary *coup d'état* was launched in Prussia. Under the direction of General Friedrich von Wrangel, the military marched into Berlin. Despite the military dispersal of the National Assembly, the disarming of the citizens' guards, and the declaration of a state of siege, the liberal bourgeoisie did not call upon the revolutionary masses of the people, who were standing ready, to engage in active resistance. By giving up the positions that they had battled for in March earlier that year, the bourgeoisie betrayed the revolution. Rosa Luxemburg discussed this failure of liberalism on several occasions, critically and at length.

countries had already fought hard battles without any support. She called upon the workers to unite in their organizations, and closed with the words from the *Communist Manifesto*: "The workers have nothing to lose but their chains. They have a world to win."*

When the working class has become conscious of its great task, and when even the last proletarian has understood this slogan of our great, fighting predecessor, then the time will have come to realize the *ideas of a socialism to liberate all peoples.*†

* Karl Marx and Friedrich Engels, *The Communist Manifesto, in Marx-Engels Collected Works*, Vol. 6, p. 519.

† The general assembly was attended by around 2,000 people, who, at the end of the speech, broke into applause, "of a kind that has rarely been recorded at a trade union meeting in Hagen. Comrade Luxemburg even received enthusiastic ovations out on the street and her walk back to the hotel was truly akin to a victory parade." Taken from the *Arbeiter-Zeitung* (Dortmund) of October 5, 1910.

1911

Stolypin's Regime*

The vengeful hand has now struck down the man who has directed the executioner's labor of the tsarist regime for the past *lustrum*.† The ancient sagas tell us about Attila, King of the Huns, and his pyramid of skulls. If we were to pile up the skulls of those murdered on Stolypin's orders into a heap, the world would see with outrage that the Hun regiment is still alive and well today. Thinking of the abomination of the St. Bartholomew's Day Massacre‡ can only make us shudder, yet under Stolypin's regime the mass murder lasted for years. Thus the shot fired during the gala performance in Kiev should hardly astonish anyone.§

The first phase of the Russian Revolution¶ ended in December 1905, when the armed uprising in Moscow was brought down. The first Duma sat on May 10, 1906. With teeth clenched, the tsarist government had to admit that the fake concessions had achieved nothing, and that the people would not allow themselves to be fobbed off with empty phrases. On May 21, the Duma was dissolved: Prime Minister [Ivan] Goremykin left, and Stolypin took the helm. A "new man" among the Russian dignitaries—a *parvenu*. Just as the Muscovite tsar Ivan the Terrible had once sidelined his boyars and put his trust in Malyuta

---

* This article first appeared in *Leipziger Volkszeitung*, No. 215, September 16, 1911. It was published anonymously, but we can assume that Luxemburg wrote it. She was thoroughly knowledgeable about Russian events, particularly the revolution of 1905–06 and its defeat by the counterrevolution. In September she had been involved in debates with friends about Russian problems, hosted a Russian guest again on the day the article was published, and met Lenin at the International Socialist Bureau meeting about the Morocco question on September 23–24, 1911, in Zurich. She had written recently directly about [Pyotr] Stolypin, for example in "Die Nationaldemokraten erklären die Revolutionäre für vogelfrei" (The National-Democrats Outlaw the Revolutionaries) in *Czerwony Sztandar* (Red Flag), August 30, 1906, and in "Artikel Lehren aus den drei Dumas" (Lessons from the Three Dumas) in *Przegląd Socjaldemokratyczny* (Social Democratic Review), April 1908. See Rosa Luxemburg, *Arbeiterrevolution 1905/06. Polnische Texte,* edited and translated by Holger Politt (Berlin: Dietz Verlag, 2015), pp. 228–32 and *The Complete Works of Rosa Luxemburg*, Vol. 4, pp. 375–94. It is translated by Henry Holland from Luxemburg's *Gesammelte Werke*, Vol. 7, pp. 691–4.

† Latin for a period of five years, originally denoting a purificatory sacrifice after a quinquennial census, suggesting an analogy regarding the assassination of Stolypin.

‡ During the St. Bartholomew's Day Massacre on August 24, 1572, Admiral Gaspard de Coligny and other leaders of the French Protestants (Huguenots) were ordered to be put to death alongside thousands of their co-religionists on the order of Queen Catherine de'Medici, mother of King Charles IX.

§ The assassination of Piotr Stolypin on September 14, 1911, in the Kiev opera house was carried out, according to some accounts, with the tsar's knowledge, although there is controversy about this. The wounds Stolypin incurred resulted in his death on September 18, 1911.

¶ In January 1905, 140,000 St. Petersburg workers paraded to the Winter Palace with a petition to entreat the tsar to improve their living conditions. The tsar gave the order for his troops to shoot rifle salvos at the demonstrators, who included women and children. Over 1,000 people were killed and around 5,000 wounded. This bloodletting triggered a wave of protest strikes and peasant uprisings throughout Russia and was the starting point of the 1905–06 Russian Revolution.

the executioner,* Tsar Nicholas now sidelined the highest echelon of his bureaucracy and put his trust in a man who successfully carried out the blood-soaked executioner's work in Saratov. The regime of terror commenced. Following Stolypin's orders, the self-styled "punishment expeditions" laid entire districts to waste. Martial law [*Standrecht*]† was proclaimed. The whole of Russia was handed over to the secret police's pack of hounds. From the Black Sea to the White Sea, from the Amur River to the Vistula, a forest of gallows arose. But the executioners played into the hands of the traitors, the group centered around Azef‡ and his consorts. The system was already in place when Stolypin took the helm, but never before had the plague of provocation been pushed to these limits, never had the system been utilized more impudently than it was under his regime. And because, even with "shortened trials," the murdering wasn't happening quickly enough and because even the military courts worked too slowly for the blood-hounds at the head of government, he built up another system, which had already been conceived during the government of his predecessor, Plehve.§ Working with the tsar's fullest possible cooperation, Stolypin organized the "Black Hundreds," those bands of hired, murdering blackguards who, while enjoying police protection, battered down anyone even suspected of being an "enemy of order"—of Stolypin's order. It was on his order that the terrible "pogroms," the massacre of the Jews, were staged, the aim of which was to excite the lumpenproletariat's most basic instincts, i.e., to contain the population in a condition of fear and shock. This is how Stolypin creates "peace" in Russia.

As regards administration, Stolypin's government knew as much as how to hurl Russia back to the level of a Mongolian barbarian state. The western Europeans believed the fairy tale about the Russian constitution. In reality, Russia today has been dissolved into a number of satrapies,¶ in which the "war governors" are given *carte blanche*. The rule of law has been suspended for five years now, and a state of emergency prevails in which the administrative authorities can do, and also not do, what they choose. The human material that has been handed over into working for this administrative power consists of those *chinovniks*,** about whom the man on the street says: the only reason

---

* Mayluta Skuratov, also known as Grigory Lukyanovich Skuratov-Belskiy, was one of the most sadistic leaders of the oprichnina during the rule of Ivan the Terrible.

† Luxemburg uses the term "*Standrecht*," which connotes a subsection of military law (*Wehrrecht*) whereby jurisdiction of the courts and other public legal authorities is transferred to the highest-ranking military commander within a specified geographical area. This military commander is assisted by a court-martial (*Standgericht*).

‡ In 1909, it was publicly revealed that Yevno Azef was a double agent.

§ Vyacheslav Konstantinovich von Plehve was assassinated on July 28, 1904, by Yegor Sazonov of the Socialist Revolutionary Combat Organization.

¶ A satrapy was a province in the ancient Persian empire governed by a satrap, a provincial governor, a powerful and sometimes semi-autonomous henchman of the central ruler.

** A pejorative term for high-ranking government bureaucrats.

they don't steal the stars from the sky is that the stars are too high to reach. The revolution gave this caste of thieving bureaucrats a curative shock, and it was only under Stolypin that they could breathe out again, and rush to recreate the system of most shameless and impudent plundering—and to compensate themselves for the shock they had received. Corruption has reached sheerly unbelievable levels again, everything is venal, contaminated and gone to the bad, the state is moving toward utter dissolution. As regards laws passed, Stolypin's laurels are no less formidable. It was not possible to simply abolish the Duma in 1906, because the revolutionary agitation of the masses was still too great. So, the second Duma was convened, because the powers that be were certain that the bourgeoisie, which the electoral law had "delivered up" to this new body, would never form itself into a powerful factor in political life. When this prediction was proven correct, and when the Cadets had blathered away any merit they may have possessed, the second Duma, convened in March 1907, was dissolved on June 16, by way of a cheeky *coup de main* that altered the electoral law, and which also convened the third Duma: the Duma in which the overt betrayers of the people have the oppressive majority. Now it fulfils its purpose of being a fig leaf of counterrevolutionary absolutism. Under the cover of the mendacious pretext of "first pacification, then reforms," Stolypin and his creatures play fast and loose with the people. Just as before, a single, legal guarantee of the most elementary civic freedom still doesn't exist, without which a constitutional state* is unthinkable, and not one of the most urgently needed reforms is even attempted. Yet when it comes to procuring means for the state for the army, navy and the bureaucracy, the Duma demonstrates its utterly inexhaustible generosity all the better. Revealing a quite grotesque absence of shame, a gigantic raid was carried out against the people, across the terrain of peasant society. The new Agrarian Law hands the peasantry's hereditary possession of common land over to bourgeois and aristocratic usurers—this measure proletarianized millions of people who had farmed the land until then. And, using the pretext of "social insurance," new burdens are dumped on the shoulders of the working class. Until now, factory owners were obliged, on the basis of current law, to provide medical help to ill workers, to maintain hospitals, and to compensate accidents fully. Now, the Duma is discussing a law to introduce compulsory sickness and accident insurance, but to introduce it at the workers' own expense.

The conflict that took place in March of this year rounded off the parody of a body that represents the people. This was not a conflict about the rights of peoples, but rather about the persecutory measures against the Poles and the Lithuanians, about which the reactionaries were divided among themselves,

* The term "*Verfassungsstaat*" that Luxemburg uses here can incorporate absolutist or theocratic as well as liberal (but not necessarily democratic) constitutional states.

because each group wanted to extract more profit from the situation. The Duma and the State Council refused to give their support, and Stolypin gave the "law-making bodies" a temporary boot by simply sending the Duma [representatives] home for three days, during which time he passed the law using "regulatory law channels"—the government has the right to pass provisional laws when the Duma is not sitting. The taunt was blatant, this was a crude and evil act of violence, a crasser kind cannot be imagined, but the hero of the "hemp neckties"* ended up being in the right: the Duma knuckled under.

In foreign politics, Stolypin's era was marked by two episodes: the Russian government had to silently stand by and watch while Austria seized Bosnia and Herzegovina with a lightning strike; in Persia however, the Russian government took action to support the counterrevolution through public violence and scurrilous maneuvering.† While, in Europe, tsardom is no longer permitted to join in the conversation, in Asia, it's more Asian than the Asians.

The revolutionary's bullet has inserted a period in the course of time. The shot that reverberated in the Kiev opera house proves one thing only: conditions in Russia continue to be of the kind that mad pressure induces a countering pressure, which expresses itself in assassinations. Like [Stepan] Balmashov, who shot dead Minister [Dimitry] Sipyagin,‡ the lawyer Bogrov, when asked about his accomplices, can answer: "My accomplices are those that rule, with the tsar at their head! They should be placed in the dock beside me."

Assessing this act in political terms is a different matter. Stolypin has a bullet in his body, but the system is intact! This desperate act of a single person, its impact on another single person, changes nothing, it won't even serve to scare off the bloodhounds—a truth that the last three decades of Russia's history provides ample evidence in support. The liberation of the proletariat can only be the work of the proletariat themselves, and this will also be the case in Russia.

---

* In 1907, liberal Cadet politician Fedor Rodichev (1854–1933) publicly criticized Stolypin for his predilection for "hemp neckties" that were used to "strangle the people's freedom."

† This refers to the invasion of the Russian military that suppressed Iran's Constitutional Revolution of 1907–11.

‡ The assassination of Ministry of the Interior Dmitry Sipyagin by the student Stepan Balmashov took place on April 15, 1902. Luxemburg's account of these events is in *The Complete Works of Rosa Luxemburg*, Vol. 3, ed. Peter Hudis, Axel Fair-Schulz, and William A. Pelz (London: Verso, 2018), pp. 17, 20, and 377.

The Reichstag Debates on the Mass Strike*

The conclusion of the Morocco debates in the Reichstag has taken the form of the bourgeois parties launching a concentrated attack against Social Democracy. The colonial contract between Germany and France has suddenly been forgotten about, as has the [German] imperial government's rejection of nationalistic pro-war agitation; forgotten too are the grievances of the chastised Junkers, of the disappointed supporters of the centrist parties, and the dissatisfied progressive liberals.† The bourgeois parties' *katzenjammer* [caterwauling] vented itself in an attack on the only truly common enemy—the representatives of the working class. Day three of proceedings thus confirms what has been surfacing, with a pleasing clarity, increasingly often: whichever spin you put on the parliamentary situation, the current rifts inside the bourgeois camp—and what occasionally seems to be a shared political line between Social Democracy and a part of that camp—are apparently vanishing this very moment in a hall of mirrors. This is what happens when circumstances confront that bourgeois camp with the elementary fact of an all-encompassing contradiction between the classes. Admittedly, it's difficult to draw any gratification from the ways and means with which our parliamentary group dealt with the attack this time. Looked at more closely, the bourgeois side chose a pretty unfortunate excuse for the assault. Which crime was Social Democracy accused of? Of intending to challenge the troops to refuse their duty to serve, in the event of mobilization for war, or of blocking such a war by use of a mass strike? Such an intention, if transformed into a tangible motion, would indeed be a highly reprehensible deed in the eyes of any Prussian state attorney. The eyes of the bourgeois "patriots paid by commission" would also see it as a crime worthy of damnation, as would all strata of the people still dumbed down by them. Yet the way a Prussian state attorney thinks—or the way national-liberal industrialists producing armor-plates for the ironclads think, or how peasants stirred up by "Christian" agitation think—is luckily not a yardstick for judging political questions in the rest of the world. In the eyes of the masses capable of judgment among the working population in the city and the country, the declaration that Social Democracy harbored this dreadful intention could only be taken as proof that this party is bitterly serious in its opposition to war. And

---

* Although the original was not signed, Luxemburg's letter of November 14, 1911, to Kostja Zetkin establishes its authorship. See Rosa Luxemburg, *Gesammelte Briefe*, Vol. 4 (Berlin: Dietz Verlag, 2001), p. 123. This article is translated by Henry Holland from Luxemburg's *Gesammelte Werke*, Vol. 7, pp. 707–11.

† Luxemburg is referring here to supporters of parties which, until 1910, had been known as the Free Minded Association (*Freisinnige Vereinigung*) (rightwing liberals) and the Free Minded People's Party (Freisinnige Volkspartei) (leftwing liberals) respectively. In 1910, these two groups merged into the Progressive People's Party (Fortschrittliche Volkspartei).

such a proof could only accentuate the sympathy that the broadest classes of the people have for Social Democracy, and could never cool or weaken these affinities. Now already, in the people's assemblies of our parties, in all parts of the empire without demur, there is no more tumultuous and passionate approval of the masses than for every word that is directed against war, and against the criminal and anti-human tendencies of contemporary militarism. Imperialism's latest adventure, the echo coming from the warmongering, glory-seeking state of Italy,* and our worst reactionaries' rattling of sabers, is all ideally suited to strengthen the steely disgust of the thinking working masses with regard to the idea of a war.

In this light, how our opponents' slanderous intentions should add up to anything at all in this case remains a mystery for [Mattthias] Erzberger and [Conrad] Haussmann.† For now, it remains only for us to value the honest intention behind their slander; following through on it would have certainly been an attempt using ineligible means directed against an ineligible object. In all of this, it was possible to present Social Democracy's real position calmly and in all clarity in the Reichstag—and not the tendentious, falsified position as portrayed by the staid patriots. There are two points of the opponents' libel campaign that require differentiation. When they claim that Social Democracy had decided to call upon the troops to refuse to serve in the case of war, that is obviously a flat lie, which cannot be traced to any resolution or even any motion put before a Social-Democratic conference or an international socialist congress. The reasons for this are very simple. As little as we believe that the blind obedience of proletarians, stuffed into soldiers' uniforms, will hold forever, and as little as we hide the fact that the cumulative development [of history] pushes us toward the day on which the masses of the people, herded into the rigid body of militarism, will rebel against the conductor's baton and refuse to comply with the butchery of humans—equally little should we or could we provoke such a refusal to obey using the road of party motions. A party demand to the soldiers to refuse to obey would be stupid, not because of potential conflict with the state attorney, but because it would be ineffective and superfluous, and because it would artificially anticipate a historical situation which we cannot by ourselves determine to be ripe.

Regarding the entirely different question of the mass strike in case of war however—as a means of protest or of struggle of the working class, industrial and otherwise—Social Democracy has not in any setting, as we already

---

* In September 1911, Italy had provoked a war against the Ottoman Empire. On September 29, 1911, the first day of the Turco-Italian War, the leaders of the Socialist Party called a twenty-four-hour limited general strike in Italy, building from demonstrations and rallies against the war in many Italian cities. Exploiting tensions between the imperialist powers concerning Morocco, Italy annexed Tripoli and Cyrenaica (the eastern region of modern Libya).

† Matthias Erzberger was a prominent member of the Catholic Center Party. Conrad Haussmann was a prominent Left Liberal politician.

demonstrated yesterday,* rejected its utilization in advance. Certainly, international Social Democracy already threw out Domela Nieuwenhuis's anarchistic pipe dream at the start of the nineties, repeatedly and pointedly, and for good reasons. But as we well know, the idea of the mass strike has undergone a major transformation since then, from being an anarchistic conjuror's trick, a wonderful and sudden means to overcoming militarism and capitalism, to being a Social Democratic means in the daily economic and political struggle.

And as such, it means this version of the idea of the mass strike has become accepted explicitly by German Social Democracy; indeed, there is perhaps no other country at present in which this idea arouses so much sympathy and interest than among the masses of enlightened German proletarians. When the resolution of the last Party Congress in Jena,† like the resolution of the publicized protest assemblies in Berlin, promised to fight war "by *all* means," then the mass strike as a means is self-evidently included in principle, and no grouping at the Jena Party Congress said anything to indicate that the mass strike should be excluded from these means. It is quite true that German Social Democracy and several other sections of the International refused, at the congresses in both Stuttgart and Copenhagen, to commit themselves in advance

---

* See "The Morocco Agreement in the Reichstag," in Luxemburg's *Gesammelte Werke,* Vol. 3 (Berlin: Dietz Verlag, 2003 [Sixth Edition], pp. 66–9. Originally published in *Leipziger Volkszeitung,* No. 263, November 13, 1911.

† The motion unanimously adopted by the party executive at the Jena Party Congress in 1911 reads as follows: "The Party Congress of German Social Democracy in Jena raises the most emphatic protest against every attempt to initiate a murderous war between cultured peoples, which the French, the English and the Germans are; this would by necessity be a world war, and would end in a general crisis. The efforts of a powerful capitalist clique to gain a foothold in Morocco, to exploit it more effectively using colonial-political means, and to claim thereby the blood and property of the German people, on the fraudulent precept that the honor and interests of the nation demand this, are refuted by the Party Congress as a deliberate falsification of the facts, and as a shameless hypocrisy. The only individuals, both here at home and abroad, who have a stake in agitation of the various cultured peoples are, alongside the colonial pirates, the bigots on land and at sea whose handicraft is war, who thirst after advancement and accolades, and the factory owners and suppliers of all sorts of war materiel, who could, through war, line their pockets with phenomenal profits—with the danger that hundreds of thousands of people could perish in these battles, and millions be plunged into destitution and misfortune. The only activity that can be thanked for the fact that central and western Europe have again been transformed into a condition of war-like unrest, is the pro-war agitation that has been conducted for years now among circles with a vested interest. This included attempts by these bounty hunters to push the imperial government into the role of the deferential underling, so that the nation's strength in terms of defense and its people could be sacrificed to the bounty hunters' interests. The degree to which these attempts were successful demonstrates the extent to which today's governments are merely the administrative committee for the property-owning classes. With outrage, the Party Congress rejects these impositions that have been made upon the people and expects that especially the German working class will use every possible means to prevent a world war. The Party Congress demands the immediate convening of the Reichstag, so that the representatives of the people be given the opportunity to articulate their opinions and to stand up against these inhumane machinations." Translated from *Parteitagsprotokoll* (Jena 1911), pp. 160 and 350.

to a mass strike in the event of war.* A commitment of this kind contradicts the complete Social Democratic concept of the political mass strike as a historical occurrence, the proximity of which can be predicted and prepared for through political education of the masses, but the commencement of which cannot be resolved in advance down to the last minute, and of our own free will. Whether in the event of war we'll be able to set a political mass strike moving is something impossible for a mortal to *affirm* in advance, because all specific circumstances of the next war and the total situation connected to it are unknown to us. It would be even less possible for a mortal to *negate* this possibility in advance. To do so, Social Democracy would, of course, have to resort to the means of mass strike in the event of war, if conditions, the general situation, the mood of the masses, and the interests and honor of the country threatened by the danger of war demanded this. Comrade [Richard] *Fischer* has hinted at the strict differentiation of tactics for before and after the outbreak of war.† This apparently places an obligation upon Social Democracy, as soon as war has finally broken out, to place itself in God's hands and to desist from the fight against the crime of militarism and is certainly not the prevailing position in either the party or in the International. On the contrary, the Stuttgart Resolution, the concluding passage of which the ISB sent as a reminder to socialists of all countries, explicitly recommends the following: "In case war should break out despite everything, all possible means should be applied to exploit the social crisis caused by the war in order to accelerate the overthrow of the existing order, i.e., to utilize the crisis in revolutionary terms."‡ Social Democracy's unrelenting animosity toward militarism and war, and the obligations that stem from this, doesn't allow us to take a break, to admit interruptions, to stop either before the beginning or the end of war. Its revolutionary activities to rally the masses against the abomination of war can only gain depth and breadth after a war has actually begun. Social Democracy cannot shrink from using any means that seems strong enough to suit the needs of the situation created, and that can strengthen the proletariat's position of power and accelerate its liberation.

---

* The reference is to the debates on antiwar resolutions at the international socialist congresses in Stuttgart, August 18–24, 1907, and in Copenhagen, August 28 –September 3, 1910.

† Discussing the indignation of revolutionary figures in Rosa Luxemburg's grouping—their complaint that an international conference wasn't convened immediately during the Morocco crisis—Richard Fischer comments: "But the first question to be asked is this: Have not the reasons that prompted the party executive and Comrade Bebel to have the conference postponed been justified by the course of events and by the facts [that war did not result]? No sooner raised, this question has of course already been answered." Lebedour responded: "Thwarting of the international action to arrive at mutual understanding." See *Parteitagsprotokoll* (Jena 1911), p. 238.

‡ See *Gesammelte Werke*, Vol. 7, p. 697, footnote 3, which refers to the ISB resolution from its meeting in Zurich September 23, 1911, on the Morocco crisis.

1913

Łódź*

Locked-out by the factory owners, 40,000 textile workers have been marooned outside of their workplaces because—after seven years of the cruelest misery, and after half a year of oppressive unemployment followed by an economic upswing—they have declared: It can't go on like this!† In the next few days, they could be joined by thousands more who will quit their jobs if they don't get their wages raised. Then 60,000 workers from a total of 83,000 would be participating in the labor struggle, i.e., three-quarters of the proletariat in the Polish Manchester.

Europe has seen bigger lockouts than the one that is currently stopping work in Łódź. But Europe does not have a second Łódź, and Europe has no second textile industry that can be measured against this capitalist hell in terms of rampant exploitation. This is why the struggle in Łódź is expanding far beyond the limits of a normal trade union battle for improved wage relations. We reflect on the role that Łódź played in the Russian Revolution,‡ the blood that the working class spilled on that field of battle, and the stamina with which they fought, until a regime of blood defeated them. This is all to an extent comparable, at least within the tsar's empire, only to events in the Baltic Sea provinces. In this context, the wrestling match in Łódź acquires the largest political significance.

Łódź is a city without a past. *German capital* conjured it out of the ground, during a period in which Saxony's textile industry was threatened with the loss of its export market because of political upheavals at the start of the nineteenth century. German capital, German managers,§ *and indeed thousands of German*

---

* This article first appeared in *Bremer Bürger-Zeitung*, No. 160, July 11, 1913. It was published anonymously, but Luxemburg is likely the author. Her renewed engagement with Łódź is evident from her letters to Leo Jogiches prior to July 1913. See *Gesammelte Briefe*, Vol. 4, pp. 281ff. The article was reprinted in *Der Textil-Arbeiter* (The Textile Worker) (Berlin), No. 30, July 25, 1913, under the heading "Der Riesenkampf der Textilsklaven in Łódź" (The Huge Battle of the Textile Slaves in Łódź). See also *Gesammelte Werke*, Vol. 3, pp. 291–5, in which two further articles about Łódź from *Der Textil-Arbeiter* of August 1 and August 29, 1913, appear. It is translated by Henry Holland from Luxemburg's *Gesammelte Werke*, Vol. 7, pp. 741–6.

† In the summer of 1913, primarily in June and July, the textile workers of Łódź and its environs fought for higher wages. As of August 8, 80,000 workers had taken part in the struggle. Military forces were held at the ready against strikers, and many workers were arrested.

‡ See the articles "Eine Riesendemonstration in Łódź; Streikrevolution in Łódz" (A Huge Demonstration in Łódź) and "Die Straßenschlacht in Łódź" (Street Battle in Łódź), in *Gesammelte Werke*, Vol. 6 (Berlin: Dietz Verlag, 2014), pp. 543–52. Originally published in *Vorwärts*, No. 126 (May 31, 1905) and No. 145 (June 24, 1905).

§ "*Meister*" in nineteenth- and early twentieth-century German connotes not only a high professional qualification, but also a specific legal status with major economic rights relative to other workers—principally the right to run an independent business in whichever trade the individual gained the title.

workers came to Poland during that period, and one workshop after the other started to spring up in this region, which lacks both rivers and woods. Later, when the advent of machines started to destroy the livelihood of home-working weavers and spinners, and one factory after the other was built—which the numbers of trained spinners and weavers could not meet the needs of—proletarianized peasants and manual workers streamed from far and wide into the city, and one block of "barracks to rent"* sprang up beside the next. A godforsaken factory-city took shape out of this small nest, filled with machine noise and smoke, without water, without sewers, and without even the simplest of cultural organizations and institutions. A mass of people squeezed into the workers' districts, who drank their dog's wages in the liquor stores, after their twelve- to fourteen-hour shifts. While in the millionaires' villas that shot up like mushrooms, in the variety shows and in the hotels, people blew their money Californian style.† And between these two extremes were the assiduous "people of Łódź," the small capitalists, the travelers and speculators, who, equipped with but limited means, sought to pull themselves up, through fraud and boundless exploitation, to the heights on which those "made men" like Poznan'ski, Scheibler, Geyer, Grohman and Kneitzer already walked.

The factory-owning type of this "promised land"—as one great Polish novelist called Łódź‡—was, according to this version of the narrative, a scrupulous hyena of original accumulation,§ who was not above either stealing gas out of the municipal gas pipes or destroying a complete generation of workers. However, the mass of workers in Łódź was, in contrast to the cultured tribe of the Warsaw workforce, one of the most uneducated in all of Poland, and continually reinforced in this by elements migrating from the villages. It's obvious that socialist agitation, starting in Warsaw and attempting to penetrate into Łódź, would struggle to gain a foothold, not solely because of the ignorance and dullness of the worker masses, but also because it received so little response from "intelligentsia" circles in the city, which were only interested in panting after profit. This despite the fact that socialist pioneers, ready for sacrifice, had grown out of such circles everywhere in Russia. While Łódź had only

* *Mietskaserne* literally translates as "barracks to rent," or "blocks of primitive apartments to rent." Luxemburg's use of this pejorative term suggests a comparison between the proletariat, "commandeered" into a city, and an enlisted army.

† The Wild West boomtowns were settlements that sprang up suddenly in mid to late nineteenth-century California with the Gold Rush. Boomtowns are associated with rapid population/economic growth and concomitant social disruption.

‡ The reference here is to Władysław Reymont's *Ziemia obiecana* (Łódź, 1897); the English title is *The Promised Land*. Andrzej Wajda's film of the book was released in 1975.

§ Luxemburg here uses the term *Ursprüngliche Akkumulation,* which is often translated into English as "primitive accumulation." Since Luxemburg almost never uses the term *primitive Akkumulation* in her works, "original accumulation" best captures her meaning. On the occasions in which Marx used the term "*primitive Akkumulation,*" he generally prefaced it with the adjective "so-called."

experienced the very tentative beginnings of secret socialist organizations in the years up until the year of revolution, in 1905, *it was nonetheless the first city in which the masses stirred themselves in the face of the revolution, and it was the city of the revolutionary mass movement during the revolution.* In 1892, news about the May Day festivities in Europe combined with the factory owners' and government's brutal behavior sparked a *mass strike lasting several days* by over 50,000 workers.* Yet although this was a boundless testimony to the workforce's revolutionary class instinct, the progress of the strike demonstrated that the workers did not possess a class consciousness worthy of the name. Simultaneously, the worker masses demanded the eight-hour day and "a Polish king"—[whereupon] a tailor was proclaimed as such—and then staged a massacre of the Jews, to which the government reacted by releasing the slogan: "Don't spare on the lead." One hundred men were [gunned down and left] by the wayside. After this explosion [of activity], which aroused hope among one part of Polish socialist circles that there would be an immediate surge in the Polish workers' movement, the Łódź volcano remained dormant for twelve years, only betraying the existence of the lava which glowed in its inner core through occasional tremors. The Łódź workforce was severely chastened. According to the statistics, the average annual wage of a factory worker in Russian Poland was 480 marks in 1897, while the average wage of a Łódź textile worker was only 440 marks. That said, specific categories, for example workers in the linen and jute factories, didn't earn much more than 300 marks annually. One could write a book about the tyrannical despotism of the managers and the factory owners, and the prostitution of the female workers, compared to which Octave Mirabeau's *The Torture Garden*† sounds like light reading for upper-class girls. It is hardly surprising that news of tsarism's defeat in Manchuria‡ and Russian working-class struggle transformed the working masses of Łódź into a torrential river of strikes. These were the working masses that unemployment had already mobilized in 1904, with Social Democracy organizing worker demonstrations during this period. In 1905, the working masses in Łódź rose up in a manner only previously seen in the history of Chartism in England. They took revenge for the fifty-year infamy of inhuman exploitation and humiliation. Shorter working shifts, better wages, but primarily revenge! Those were the slogans of the Łódź workers. Capital's worst bloodhounds, the

---

* The strike movement grew rapidly from May 1, 1890, encompassing the Łódź textile industry and peaking in the uprising of the Łódź workers on May 5, 1892, of around 80,000 strikers.

† Octave Mirabeau's *Le Jardin des supplices* (*The Torture Garden*) was first published in 1899. This scandalously violent and graphic novel presented an allegorical attack on European "civilization" and the hypocrisy, corrupt morality, and violence of bourgeois society.

‡ This refers to the Russo-Japanese War, fought from January 1904 to September 1905, for hegemony in the Far East. The war ended in a heavy defeat for Russian troops, which exacerbated the revolutionary crisis in Russia.

engineers and managers, were transported out of the factories on dung carts, sacks over their heads. The trade unions and socialist organizations grew by the day, and the suffering workers listened in silence to the tidings of socialism as if in religious rapture. Whoever experienced one of those mass meetings in the huge factories, at which the agitators of Social Democracy, alongside hundreds of unknown speakers, preached socialism in Polish and German to the masses hanging on their words—it is now possible to say that our Paris colleagues, Comrade *Zdzisaw Leder* and Comrade [Aleksander] Malecki took part in the historical formation of the Polish workers' movement in this period—will never forget this fantastic and towering image of the regeneration of a working class through the resuscitating breath of revolution and socialism.

The Łódź working class marched with revolutionary vigor, and with heroic stamina at the head of the whole Polish proletariat, and it created the largest of organizations—the illegal organizations of both the socialist parties* numbered over 30,000 members during the two years of the revolution. But the Łódź factory owners then plucked up courage† and resorted to *lockouts*. They started using the weapon of hunger against the revolutionary army as early as summer 1906, yet these were merely small beginnings in a few factories. But when the government had forced the first Duma to scatter, and when it became clear that the mass of workers no longer had any power to protest this step with stronger means, the directors of the largest factories of Łódź decreed the mass lockout of 40,000 workers from their safe Berlin hideout in December 1906. The proletariat of Poland understood the significance of this wrestling match. And the capitalists also didn't conceal the aim of this exercise. The lockout is a terrible device, as the factory owner said at the time to workers' representatives who had come to negotiate with him in Berlin, but it is an educational device: "Through experiencing absolute want, the workers should learn that only the factory owner can be lord of the factory." The workers of Poland collected 800,000 marks to demonstrate to the capital magnates that Łódź workers would not bow down to capital's gentlemanly point of view. But after three months of long battle, the Łódź working class laid down their weapons, with the Polish workers' press at the time describing this as a ceasefire. It turned out that this "ceasefire" would claim more working-class victims than the [previous period of armed] struggle and would last a very long time. Tsarism won the upper hand throughout Russia, with the property-owning classes backing tsarism because of fear of the proletariat. A reign of terror began across the empire, and the gallows were operated as never before anywhere in the world. In Łódź, the gallows were set up in a prison courtyard, so that they could be seen from the city. On the streets, the *soldateska*‡ rampaged daily, torture was

* The SDKPiL and the PPS.

† Luxemburg's use of "*sich ermannen*" is unusual, ironic, and sarcastic.

‡ An unleashed and lawless mob of soldiers. Luxemburg repeatedly uses the German

administered in police stations, those who resisted were martyred or driven to madness, and those who were weak were turned into Judases. The images from Łódź's prisons, about which Comrade *Feliks Kon** published in his book on military courts in Poland, will take their place among the worst horrors of counterrevolution. And that tsarist thug General Kasnakov, who directed this devil's work, was celebrated by the Łódź bourgeoisie in a revelry of champagne.

The years 1907 to 1912 were much tougher for the Łódź working class than those prior to the revolution. Capital took revenge. Wages were forced down to such an extent that men and women often earned only ten marks a week. The managers and the engineers went on a rampage. All workers' organizations were smashed and attempts to build them up again were consistently undermined, thanks to the oppressed condition of the working class and to "the spy business."† This means that Social Democratic organizations are still very weak today in Łódź compared to Warsaw, with its thousands of workers influenced by Social Democratic organizations that function regularly, as the election campaign and the insurance campaign show in an exemplary manner. But even the exploitation and suppression of the working class has its limits, and these were reached in the winter of this year. Thanks to the bad harvest of 1911, and the flooding of the money market, an economic crisis took shape in Łódź—in its turn influenced by the Balkan Crisis‡—in contrast to the general economic upturn in Russia. One-third of the workers had not a crust of bread to eat, the second third only worked a part of the week, and an enormous army of the unemployed was pushing down the wages of the other third. People were dropping like flies in the streets, and twelve-year old daughters of workers sold their bodies. Every attempt at organized aid to the workers' effort was thwarted by the government. In contrast, the city council obtained permission from the government to spend 200,000 marks on emergency works, and a committee of factory owners distributed 160,000 marks among 30,000 unemployed—a sum of money that was largely taken out of the mouths of the working section of the Łódź proletariat.

---

spelling of the Italian word "*soldatesca*," which was popularized and became pejorative in Germany especially through Schiller's accounts of the Thirty Years' War.

* See *Sądy wojenne w Królestwie Polskim* (War Courts in the Kingdom of Poland) (Kraków, 1909.) This pamphlet was published with the initials F. K. (Feliks Kon) as a publication of *Mys´l Socjalistyczny*, the PPS-Left's theoretical journal. Rosa Luxemburg wrote a comprehensive review of Feliks Kon's pamphlet under the title of "*Ein Denkmal der Schande*" (A Memorial to Shame), in *Pomnik han´by, Przegla˛d Socjaldemokratyczny*, No. 13 (July 1909), pp. 228–52.

† Luxemburg uses "*Spitzelwirtschaft*" here, which translates as "spy business" or "spy industry." This emphasizes the extent of spying—and the fact that significant sums of money could be made from it.

‡ Luxemburg is referring to the First Balkan War (October 1912–May 1913), which pitted Greece, Bulgaria, Serbia, and Montenegro against the Ottoman Empire. The Second Balkan War, in which Bulgaria battled its former Balkan allies as well as the Ottomans, began several weeks before the composition of this article.

And then the economic cycle improved again. The army of the unemployed began to go down in number. An electric shock passed through the masses. Not one single day had passed on which they felt sated—they had not yet properly warmed their limbs, stiff from the winter—and yet they moved into battle. After the hunger of unemployment, they could not bear to go back into the starving yoke of labor. They stated their demands for a 30 percent increase in wages across the board, as this was the same percentage by which wages had been reduced in recent years. Only a small section of the factory owners has given in. The larger section wants to "train" the workers to get used to starvation wages. Strikes followed on from the factory owners' refusal, and the strikes were followed by lockouts. Today 40,000 workers are already marooned outside their workplaces, and in the next few days this number could rise to 60,000.

A heavy silence dominates the city. Even among the bourgeoisie that feels so secure under the Cossacks' protection, fear begins to creep in. The press asks what the workers' unanimity conceals, and what their calm suggests. Isn't this the calm before the storm, like the one that raged in Łódź in 1905? Who can be sure? The government has strengthened the Cossack detachments in Łódź, for every eventuality.

If the international proletariat ever needed to help a movement of the foreign working class, and if the German working class ever had good reason to dig deep into their pockets, then it is now, in the case of the battle of the Łódź proletariat—a third of which consists of *German* workers.

Łódź's Huge Struggle

*40,000 textile workers locked out**

In Łódź, the Russian-Polish Manchester, one of those desperate battles between capital and labor has been underway for two weeks, like a horrific fire that leaps as fast as lightning, and spreads catastrophe across economic and social life.

The torment of the Łódź textile workforce stretches back several years and is almost indescribable. During 1905–06, Łódź workers built their trade unions with ardor—the Łódź Association of Textile Workers, for example, had 11,000 members. Their exemplary solidarity and discipline in the struggle led to a wage rise worthy of the name, and a general improvement in their working conditions. But in 1907, the industrialists took their revenge! Backed by the blood-soaked activities of the tsarist *soldateska* and their system of gallows justice, the industrialists prepared to deliver the terminal blow: a massive lockout of 40,000 workers, lasting six weeks, intended to cure the "covetous" workers of their fighting spirit by starving them. The workforce, terrorized by the tsarist bloodhounds, and oppressed by the long torment of hunger, had no choice but to grit their teeth and return to the loathed yoke. This is when a systematic suppression of wages started, and steadily pushed to the level of real starvation wages. It suffices to say that the wages of less well-situated workers in recent years in, for example, Scheibler's factory, Łódź's largest, amounted to no more than between 3.5 and 5 rubles, the equivalent of between 7.5 and 11 Reichsmark, weekly. And families with several members are supposed to be able to survive on that, despite exorbitant price rises in essential groceries!

But the best is yet to come. Last winter the scourge of unemployment was added to the whip of starvation wages. A severe crisis shook the Łódź textile industry. According to the newspapers, the unemployed numbered between 30,000 and 50,000. The privation in Łódź was abominable. People literally fell down dead in the street from starvation.

On March 9 of this year, the Society for Rapid Medical Aid was asked by the Łódź Chief of Police how many incidents had occurred, and they replied with the following: We are honored to be able to communicate the following

* This article first appeared in the SPD's central party newspaper, *Vorwärts*, No. 175, July 12, 1913. It was published anonymously but most likely written by Rosa Luxemburg. Her renewed engagement with Łódź is evident from her letters to Leo Jogiches prior to July 1913. See *Gesammelte Briefe*, Vol. 4, pp. 281ff. This article was reprinted in *Der Textil-Arbeiter* (The Textile Worker), Berlin, No. 30, July 25, 1913, under the heading *Der Riesenkampf der Textilsklaven in Łódź* (The Huge Battle of the Textile Slaves in Łódź). See also *Gesammelte Werke*, Vol. 3, pp. 291–5. It is translated by Henry Holland from Luxemburg's *Gesammelte Werke*, Vol. 7, pp. 747–9.

statistics, as registered by the society's first-aid station in Łódź. In January (of 1913), first aid was given at the scene of 419 incidents, in February at 332, in March there were 300 incidents up until the nineth of the month, i.e., in the space of nine days. *One group of incidents was related to people starting to die, the other group to people absolutely exhausted because of starvation, and all of these various phenomena combined can be related to unemployment.*

In May, the Social Democratic faction raised questions within the Petersburg Duma concerning this emergency and unemployment generally in Łódź.

At last, in the spring, things started to get better. The turning point was precipitated by a strong and general surge of textile-industry business. Not surprisingly, the workers decided to make use of this period of economic growth to win back at least a part of the improvements in wages that had been ripped away from them in 1907, and to ward off the most extreme form of poverty. In June, they made a general demand that was focused on a 20 to 25 percent wage increase, and after the industrialists responded with a categorical no, one section of the workers went out on strike. But then the capital magnates of Łódź got ready, just as they had done in 1907, to deliver a sledgehammer blow: they reacted to the strike with a *massive lockout*. At present, all well-known factories are closed: *Scheibler, Geyer, Poznański, Kunitzer, Krusche, Ender, Bennich, Kindler,* the *Steigert* brothers, *Findeisen, Eisert, Kestenberg*, etc. (The names show that the industrialists are mostly *German*.) In total, 40,000 workers are currently locked out.

It's obvious what the industrialists' plan is: the workers should be taught a lesson, right from their first attempt to get out of penury. They should immediately feel the boot of authority pressing down on their necks, so that they don't start fantasizing that they're allowed to start organizing again and recommence the trade union struggle. The boom period should only be allowed to serve the capitalist obsession with making profit, while for the workers the old misery of the period of economic crisis should go on just as before! That's the honest plan of the Łódź textile barons, a result of their secret meetings and desire to show solidarity with each other in moving against the workers, as they did in 1907.

The industrialists' brutal tactics have understandably produced the greatest possible bitterness among the Łódź workforce. These raised hackles are exacerbated by the use of legions of Cossacks, who have swamped Łódź to terrorize the workers just as the industrialists wished. The situation is so tense that we cannot rule out the [strike] movement extending to encompass all other trades and professions in Łódź. The modesty of the Łódź textile workers' demands—and their heroic stamina in the long years of struggle and want—has prompted strong sympathies among Poland's entire workforce. This is opposed to the insidious malice of the capitalist braggarts, which can only prompt feelings of utter outrage.

And so, we await a gigantic trial of strength for capital against some of its longest-suffering victims. Despite all the industrialists' brutality, the workers' prospects do not look so bad. The peak of the economic cycle is within sight, and the low reserves of finished goods are rapidly running out; it's an urgent situation for the industrialists. The workers have already forced concessions in a series of smaller factories. It all comes down to the great mass of those locked out being able to hold out, to sheer hunger not forcing them into a humiliating defeat.

On the Political Mass Strike: A Police Report*

Speech held on July 22, 1913, in the Social Democratic electoral association for the fourth Berlin Reichstag constituency

Comrade Dr. Rosa Luxemburg spoke on the political mass strike.† She began her deliberations by voicing vehement support for the mass strike. As her speech proceeded, however, she commented that one will have to reckon with the fact that the broad masses of the people won't participate in such a strike, because there are thousands of unorganized workers. Continuing, she touched upon the strike in Belgium,‡ and directed sharp criticism toward the capitalists who desire a war simply to line their own pockets. She concluded her speech with further criticism about the conduct of the Prussian government and of the imperial chancellor.

In the discussion, various members spoke both for and against Comrade Luxemburg's explication. Such a racket was stirred up among those present in the hall that one couldn't understand a word [...]

Rosa Luxemburg felt very offended by the criticism that her deliberations were subjected to.

---

* This speech is translated by Henry Holland from Luxemburg's *Gesammelte Werke*, Vol. 7, p. 754.

† For the comprehensive press report about this speech and its conclusion on July 22, 1913, see *Gesammelte Werke*, Vol. 3, pp. 259–66. See also Luxemburg's speech in Rummelsburg on August 10, 1913, in *Gesammelte Werke*, Vol. 7, pp. 760ff.

‡ On April 14, 1913, a political mass strike for universal suffrage had begun, which was carefully planned—organizationally, financially, and ideologically—by a special committee working in the whole country from June 1912. 450,000 workers took part. On April 24, 1913, the party conference of the Belgian Workers' Party decided to break off the strike after the Belgian parliament had decided in favor of a commission to consider reform of the voting law.

On Łódź's Huge Struggle*

The movement continues, and it continues to have an impact on ever wider circles of people. Other professions are already joining the textile workers. Influenced by them, the Łódź streetcar employees have also initiated a movement for wage improvements, and only the police's violent, last-minute intervention prevented a strike. So, too, have some workers on the railroad downed their tools. Others are also joining the strike without articulating their own wage demands, simply to express their protest against the textile barons' attitude, and their fraternal solidarity with those engaged in the battle. To sum up, the textile workers' struggle has again become the focal point of all passions in Łódź, as it has so often in recent years.

The textile workers unquestionably play a special role in the workers' movement in the tsar's empire. The history of the entire class struggle of Russia is locked into the textile workers' spontaneous movements, which constitute the most important milestones of the combined proletariat. It was the textile workers in the central Vladimir District of Moscow who first charted a course for the mass stirring of the Russian proletariat, through their sudden and vehement eruption at the start of the eighties that flared up dramatically like a torch.

This was, initially, a rather chaotic and confused movement, in which machines were smashed up and factories demolished. Social Democratic organization and agitation had not yet set to work in the tsarist empire, clarifying issues and showing the way forward. Yet even this first instinctive eruption of class struggle had important consequences for the Russian workers' movement: it provided the impetus for the introduction of laws protecting workers and for factory inspections in Russia. Around fifteen years later, in 1896 and 1897, workers from the two most important districts of the textile industry in Petersburg, a total of 40,000, conducted the first mass strike to achieve better wages and shorter working hours—an unheard-of event in Russia at that time—with unforeseeable consequences. Through this conflict, thoroughly trade union focused in its nature, the textile workers in the tsar's capital won an eleven-and-a-half-hour working day for the entire empire. Much more importantly, they opened up the period of systematic trade union struggle for the entire Russian workforce, and initiated the building of a combative organization, even if this was done in secret. The year 1896 also marked the start of a Social Democratic Party organization in Russia itself, which, building on the

---

* This article first appeared in *Der Textil-Arbeiter* (Berlin), August 1, 1913. It is unsigned but we can deduce that Luxemburg authored it from letters she wrote to Leo Jogiches in July 1913. See Luxemburg's *Gesammelte Briefe*, Vol. 4, pp. 281ff. It is translated by Henry Holland from Luxemburg's *Gessamelte Werke*, Vol. 3, pp. 291–5.

Petersburg textile strike, increasingly stoked, led, and organized the trade union and political movement in the whole empire.

The struggle in one of the largest centers of the textile industry in the tsar's empire, the Łódź district, played a similarly decisive role in the history of the workers' movement of Russian [occupied] Poland. For a long period in this locality, various social and national movements caused special problems for the work of establishing a deep-rooted trade union and Social Democratic form of agitation. Largely after Russia's protectionist tariff reform of 1877, spinning and weaving mills relocated in their entirety from Saxony (from Werdau, Crimmitschau, etc.) to the neighboring Russian-Polish region as foreign heavy industry. A class of entrepreneurs emerged in Łódź composed of Germans and Jews, thrown together with all sorts of upstarts on the make, and soldiers of fortune, unscrupulous and brutal by nature. Analogous to this were the workers, half immigrant Germans, half the lowly Polish proletariat of the surrounding villages, a linguistically and socially divided mix. And it has nonetheless been possible to achieve tough Social Democratic agitation in response to rapacious, large-scale capital development. Despite all the difficulties of an absolutist regime, it has been possible to transform these elements over time into a firmly established, disciplined workforce, the Germans and the Poles together in complete unity with each other and fighting on the front lines for the aims of the modern workers' movement.

The first spark that woke the Łódź proletarian mass out of its gloomy sleep was, at that time, the idea of *the May Day celebration*. In Russia proper, this global public holiday of labor could not establish roots until recently—in part due to the difference in calendars—and only in this last year, by means of an impressive cessation of work, did it find its way into the Russian mass movement. The opposite was the case for Russian [occupied] Poland, where workers greeted the holiday enthusiastically from the start, and where it was celebrated in Warsaw by tens of thousands stopping work. In 1892, Łódź suddenly stepped into the limelight: on May 1, 60,000 textile workers downed tools to demand the eight-hour working day. Once the movement had started to flow, it poured itself into a ten-day, tempestuous mass strike, which was only finally stemmed by the tsarist *soldateska's* bloody means.

Since then, a systematic and quiet, small-scale way of working has started and continued in Łódź, to educate the proletariat about the aims and significance of Social Democratic and trade union organization. Alongside Petersburg, Moscow, and Warsaw, Łódź is one of the most important hot spots of the revolutionary movement in the tsar's empire, lighting the way in both the tempestuous verve of individual encounters with tsarism and in long-term and disciplined trade union actions against the class of industrialists. In June 1905, Łódź workers put up the first barricades in the tsarist empire. But even in the middle of these revolutionary storms, the Łódź textile workers had constructed a trade union entirely matching the German model, which, in the course of time, grew to 11,000 paying members. Led by this union, the Łódź textile workers succeeded—over the course of a tough conflict lasting until 1907—in achieving a very significant general increase in wages, a shortening of working time, and the abolition of an exhaustive series of workplace abuses. At the beginning of the year 1907, the wage level of the Łódź workers far exceeded that of the German textile workers, specifically the Vogtland textile workers.

Then came the backlash. Revolutionary action collapsing in Moscow in December 1906 meant that the revolution's forward-pressing frontline had been broken, that the proletariat's campaign of political action throughout the empire had turned into a shambles, and that the power of absolutism, shaken but not yet toppled, had begun to recover. It was against this backdrop that Łódź's entrepreneurial class began to take revenge. The horrific suffering of the Łódź textile workers that now set in under the dual assault of tsarist punitive expeditions coupled with capitalist starvation measures mocks every attempt at description. Future historians, should they ever find out about the history of the Łódź proletariat from 1907 until now in all its gruesome detail, will hardly believe that any working class could endure such hellish agonies over years without betraying, for a single moment, the ideals of the worker's cause and the flag of socialism. Countless arrests, prison sentences, exiling, military courts and gallows, amid all that a simple lockout intended as a punishment, leaving 40,000 workers and their families without bread for six weeks, followed by a general wage reduction on top of previous reductions, down to one-third of previous wages, i.e., down to starvation level. An ongoing rise in grocery prices, as general as the reduction in wages, and finally a severe crisis in the Łódź textile industry, which meant that one section of the workers could receive earnings only for a couple of working days per week, while the majority were starving to death: all this is linked in an uninterrupted chain from 1907 until today. All parts of the proletariat in the tsar's empire have had to suffer heavily under the counterrevolution, but it is the Łódź proletariat that has suffered worst and most consistently. During last year, wages sank from 11 marks to 7.5 marks a week for the best-paid workers, while average wages sank from 8 to 7 marks a week. From January to March of this year, unemployment reached 50,000. According to police reports for these same months, ten people a day were picked up on the streets of Łódź who had collapsed and died of starvation, while in March the figure went up to thirty people a day!

And all this nightmarish misery is incapable of breaking the fighting spirit of the Łódź textile workers, or of degrading them to willing slaves of capital, as the industrialists hoped. No sooner had the crisis finally been followed by a period of economic upturn in May and June, accompanied by a reanimation of employment, than workers in one factory after the next demanded wage increases. In the cotton branch, these were generally at a level of 20 to 30 percent, while in the wool industry they averaged 25 to 40 percent. The favorable economic cycle should be exploited to make at least partial amends, and to recuperate achievements that have been lost. When the industrialists rejected these natural demands with a brusque "no!" without any negotiations, thousands walked out on strike immediately. Workers who had only just managed to come through outrageous starvation "treatment" lasting for years went into the new conflict without hesitation, ready to perform every sacrifice, exclusively for the sake of beating back the brutal domination of the entrepreneurial class, and of achieving sound foundations for a better future. But this was precisely what sent Scheibler, Geyer, Poznański, Ender, Krusche, and whatever all the other capital magnates are called, into a heightened state of frenzy. So the weavers and spinners of Łódź had not been cured of their "covetousness"? All of tsarism's inhuman oppressions and all its starvation remedies had not managed to draw them away from the ideas of the "firebrands"? Has the Łódź textile worker still not given up thoughts of a battle for a humane condition of being? An example must be set to punish this sacrilege! Whereupon a lockout followed at the largest factories. At others, the workers left factories themselves, without waiting for the ukase to arrive. At this very moment, around 63,000 workers—making with their families around 200,000 people in total—are marooned outside their workplaces. Łódź, at present, poses the question of to be or not to be for the whole workforce, the question of their right to struggle in trade union organizations, and questions about their entire future. Various smaller factories have already made concessions. The larger ones will have soon disposed of their stockpiles of finished goods, and will presumably have to yield, if the workers manage to hold on to some degree.

But in any case, a workforce that holds up the flag of the workers' struggle at such exposed posts and with heroism under such difficult circumstances deserves the sympathy and the respect of the entire international proletariat.

Donations should be sent by post, with a note that the contribution is specifically for Łódź, and should be addressed to the international shop steward, our colleague Paul Wagener, Berlin O 27, Andreasstr. 61 III.

On the Political Mass Strike [August 1913]*

Speech given as a contribution to the extended meeting of the party executive with trade unionists at the start of August 1913†

A POLICE REPORT FROM AUGUST 7, 1913

After this,‡ the platform was handed over to Rosa Luxemburg. She began by criticizing the behavior of the central executives of the different unions regarding

---

* This speech is translated by Henry Holland from Luxemburg's *Gesammelte Werke*, Vol. 7, pp. 756–9. Excerpts appear in Ottokar Luban, "Rosa Luxemburgs Engagement für den politischen Massenstreik. Zwei bisher unveröffentlichte parteiinterne Ansprachen vom Sommer 1913," in *Rosa-Luxemburg-Forschungsberichte*, Vol. 6, Leipzig 2008, pp. 118–22.

† The exact date cannot be discerned from the sources. The meeting probably took place before August 2 because Rosa Luxemburg was with Clara Zetkin in Sillenbuch, near Stuttgart, from August 2 to 8, 1913. See *Gesammelte Briefe*, Vol. 4, pp. 289–96. In addition to the members of the party executive and trade unionists, who were opposed to the political mass strike, prominent party members were also invited, including Karl Kautsky, Eduard Bernstein, Emil Eichhorn, the director of the SPD press office, and members of the Reichstag Paul Lensch, Richard Fischer and Daniel Stücklen. From the Berlin organizations of the party, Boeske, Max Groger, Davidsohn, Paul Hoffmann, Ritter and Max Cohen participated. In the Prussian Parliament (i.e., the state parliament for Prussia inside the German Reich, known in German as the Preussische Landtag), the party was represented by Konrad Haenisch, Adolph Hoffmann and Heinrich Ströbel. In light of the escalating and ever more vehement debates on the mass strike, this sitting of the executive was intended to prevent radical motions being passed at the upcoming party conference.

‡ Luxemburg's speech was preceded by lengthy explications by Heinrich Cunow, organized in advance by the party executive, about the historical beginnings of the idea of the mass strike/general strike. Heinrich Schulz pleaded for the mass strike not merely as a way to defend the right to vote for the Reichstag and the right to collectively bargain, but also as a means of winning new political rights. Arthur Stadthagen spoke about the mass strike as an unconditional necessity: "We have to negotiate," he argued; ceaseless discussions and deliberations would not enthuse the masses. Blum spoke against the mass strike as a means to win the democratic right to vote: it would lead to the collapse of both the party and the trade unions. Heinrich Stühmer argued that it was impossible to conduct a political mass strike without economic demands. Hermann Müller maintained that a mass strike, in light of the current stagnation of party and union life, would ruin everything that had been achieved so far. The Prussian franchise campaign had to be transformed into a struggle against the reaction in the whole of Germany. The priority was building up the organizational work and propagating the mass strike. According to Dr. Erdmann, it would be impossible to execute a mass strike in the West. The opponents would be the industrialists and the Catholic Center Party. In addition, Catholicism would prevent many workers from participating. According to Scheidemann, the existence and the influence of the Christian organizations meant that the mass strike would be excluded as an option for a long time. Too many people were indifferent, "unmanned" by capital, because the chain of welfare benefits for long-term workers over the previous twenty years, housing programs near the works and other factors held people back from participating in the struggle. There was no point calling a mass strike for demonstrations that would only last a couple of days. If a mass strike were to be organized, there was the additional problem that the moment would be missing in which to surprise the enemy, meaning that it would be possible to mobilize the military among the confusion.

the mass strike, and condemned the behavior of the executives in the current shipyard workers' movement.* The union leaders have lost touch with how the union members are feeling and thinking, claimed Luxemburg. The efforts of the executives of the central unions have been directed for some time now toward claiming the sole right to determine whether a strike is "justified," i.e., whether it's worthy of financial support. In so doing, the unions' executives argue thus: "As the executives of the unions are mainly responsible for generating financial means, they therefore have the right to decide." This is the message contained in the *Corresponding Paper of the German Unions*, issue twenty-eight, year seven.† This makes it seem as though the poor union functionaries had to cover the costs of the fights for wages out of their own pockets and as if the funds were the principal points, with the wage struggles appearing as vexatious side effects of the trade union movement. It is always the same old song of the backward and passive masses who must be whipped into shape from above.

This is the same song which the *Corresponding Paper of the German Unions*‡ has set to the following tune: "With its limited knowledge and

---

* From July 14 to the middle of August 1913, shipyard workers in Germany struck. After weeks of negotiations with the industrialists—around demands including reduced work time, higher wages and guaranteed paid holidays—brought no results, the provocative sacking of a number of the Hamburg shipyard workers' shop stewards provided the final trigger for the strike to break out. The action began in Hamburg and spread to Bremen, Flensburg, Kiel, Stettin and Vegesack. By the end of July, around 35,000 workers were on strike. The union leaders of the German Metal Workers' Union declared the action to be a "wildcat strike" and did not give any financial support. Despite the protests of around 10,000 strikers in many assemblies in Hamburg on August 14, 1913, against the union leaders' suffocation of the strike, the workers were forced to return to work without imposing any further conditions.

† See "Die Aufgaben der Gewerkschaftskartelle" (Tasks of the Trade Union Cartels), in *Correspondenzblatt der Generalkommission der Gewerkschaften Deutschlands* (Hamburg) (Corresponding Paper of the General Commission of the German Unions), Year 7, No. 28, July 12, 1897, p. 154.

‡ After speeches given by Adolf von Elm in front of trade union representatives, particularly the speech given at a party meeting in Hamburg on November 26, 1910—about which the *Correspondenzblatt der Generalkommission der Gewerkschaften Deutschlands* (Corresponding Paper of the General Commission of the German Unions in Germany) reported at length in January and February 1911—Gustav Stengele wrote the following to Karl Kautsky: "[Elm launched himself] against the well-known warning, pronounced by Bebel in Magdeburg, with all possible anger, and in so doing preached the gospel of the unconditional trust in their leaders, that the blind and inarticulate masses must have … At a party meeting of Hamburg's second electoral constituency, at which v. Elm participated as a member, all speakers, including Dr. Laufenberg and myself, took a hard line against the negation of democracy, contained in Von Elm's explications." See *IISG, Amsterdam Kautsky Archives, D XXI* 395. As Von Elm's arguments in this form were not printed in either the *Hamburger Echo* or in *Vorwärts* (Berlin), he dominated in the *Correspondenzblatt der Generalkommission der Gewerkschaften Deutschlands* in issue No. 1 on January 7, 1911; with his lecture "Massen und Führer" (Masses and Leaders) in issue No. 8, February 25, 1911; with his article "Massen und Führer. 1. Stimmungsmache gegen die Gewerkschaftsführer" (Masses and Leaders. I. Agitation Against the Union Leaders) and in issue No. 9, March 4, 1911, with "Massen und Führer. II. Die Bedeutung der ständigen Vertreter-Körperschaft für die Gewerkschaften" (Masses and Leaders. II. The Significance of a Standing Body of Representatives for the Unions). The last article contains the following: "*The mass mood can be turned around:* hosanna today,

know-how, not only does the 'mass' feel very good, it also thinks itself unusually clever." The article goes on to explain that, in the struggle with this dumbed-down mass, progressive union leaders are repeatedly condemned to a downright sad existence. They often have "to say things against their own convictions that the mass" can cope with, their only comfort being that the mass can only become clever by suffering harm, so that they can spin things in favor of their own wise insights, and against the motion passed by their comrades in the struggle and the principal party. Anyone who knows the peculiar conceptions that prevail in some trade union circles, about the essence of socialism itself, about the class struggle, and about class contradictions, will no longer be surprised by anything.

The chair [Hermann Molkenbuhr] interrupts at this point and requests the speaker return to the actual subject. None of this has anything to do with the mass strike, says Molkenbuhr.

Rosa Luxemburg responds that she is still going to deliver her comments on that subject. She merely wants to illustrate with what distance and superiority our union leaders stand in opposition to the mass and their actions. She then polemicizes against *Vorwärts,* delivering roughly the following comments: *Vorwärts* is absolutely not fulfilling its task of also achieving a theoretical schooling for its readers. It's becoming ever rarer to find a truly valuable scientific article in its pages. The extent to which *Vorwärts* is not fulfilling its task in the most internal party questions is demonstrated by the unending complaints that it cannot be prevailed upon to take up a clear position. Even in internal party struggles and discussions, *Vorwärts* talks about the "impartial press" in order to not veer to either the right or the left—and thus reinforces confusion and uncertainty. In the matter of propagating the mass strike, *Vorwärts* has so far achieved nothing. Above all else, a political mass strike demands determined leaders who are ready for action. And nothing can be discerned of such determination and readiness for action. It will be the duty of the mass to place itself at the head in the given moment. The Jena Party Congress* must demand the immediate convening of a Prussian Party Congress.† We need to

---

tomorrow: Crucify him! The *glorification* of the masses, which is trending today, is *just as deplorable as Byzantinism.* Virtues are attributed poetically to the masses, which they don't possess in the slightest. Above all, they're lacking knowledge about *economic relations.* Feelings in themselves will not suffice. Democratic mistrust against the leaders will only cause us to *endure failures.* The genuinely capable and honest people will not be overly pleased at figuring as the unskilled laborer serving the mass will, leaving the incapable free in all fields to lead the political, union-based and cooperative workers' movement into the quagmire and into anarchy ... And we have to put a stop to the *democratic drives* of some individuals, *who with their glorification of the masses are leading these masses to an absence of discipline and thereby to an absence of power.*" See *Correspondenzblatt der Generalkommission der Gewerkschaften Deutschlands,* No. 1, January 7, 1911, pp. 9–10.

* The Jena Party conference of the Social Democratic Party of Germany was planned for September 14–20.

† This refers to the convening of a party conference for the Social Democratic Party of

re-examine and forge new methods of struggle for this occasion. The masses are pushing for action, they are looking for a fight. Recognize that the fire that has taken hold of the masses amounts to something more than a flash in the pan. Do not allow the working class's desire to fight to fall asleep, as we would find it difficult to shake the masses back to life.*

Prussia to strengthen the struggle for a democratic voting law for Prussia. The fourth party conference took place from January 6 to 8, 1913.

* Eduard Bernstein spoke after Luxemburg had finished, evaluating the demonstrations of recent years as a positive omen for the will and the energy of the German workers for the mass strike. The determination of demonstrating and striking workers had pulled unorganized workers into the fray, argued Bernstein. The timid were becoming bold, the doubting optimists, and the slow and deliberative were becoming people of action. H. Krätzig urged consideration of the situation in Germany. The strongest party leading a mass strike against the strongest government and most steeled military organization in the world would have to reckon with the fiercest resistance. The mass strike would have to end with the victory of the proletariat; otherwise, it would suffer a heavy defeat. The mass strike would have to be the last possible means with which to determine political hegemony. That was the big difference from other countries, in which all sides were weaker and it wasn't a case of all or nothing.

On the Political Mass Strike [August 12, 1913]*

Speech and closing words given† at the general meeting of the electoral association for the district of Niederbarnim in Rummelsburg

---

* This piece was originally published in *Vorwärts*, No. 206, August 12, 1913. It is translated by Henry Holland from Luxemburg's *Gesammelte Werke*, Vol. 7, pp. 760–3.

† The following day, August 11, 1913, an unusually large number of bourgeois and conservative papers reported on the meeting, including the *Vossische Zeitung* [Voss Newspaper], No. 403, the *Deutsche Tageszeitung* [German Daily Paper], No. 402, the *Berliner Allgemeine Zeitung* [Berlin General Paper], No. 218, the *Zeit am Montag* [Monday Times], No. 32, the *Welt am Montag* [Monday World], No. 32, *Berliner Morgenpost* [Berlin Morning Post], No. 218, *Die Post* [The Post], No. 372 and the *Neue Reichscorrespondenz* [New Imperial Correspondence], No. 184. The meeting passed the resolution that Rosa Luxemburg had introduced. It reads as follows:

"The Party Congress welcomes the newly awaked interest of broad circles in the party for the question of the mass strike as a sign of the masses' mood for battle, and for the correctness of their feeling for the fact Social Democracy cannot dispense with extra-parliamentary means in the long run. However, instances within the party or the unions cannot artificially initiate the mass strike on command. It can only result from an escalation of the economic and political situation, as a cumulation of a mass action that's already flowing. Such a situation is unavoidable in Germany in the near future. A situation in which the cause of the equal right to vote in Prussia has got stuck in the bog, in which imperialism advances with the constant danger of war that brings, the stalemate on social reform, the ever more urgent necessity to defend the right to collective bargaining and to seize this right for rural proletarians and for workers and employees in state enterprises" [Luxemburg is using the differentiation common in German-language literature of this period, including much bourgeois literature, between *Arbeiter* (worker) and *Angestellte* (employee). An employee had access to specific social benefits that a worker did not. This is similar to the English-language distinction between "blue-collar" and "white-collar" workers] "and, finally, the full-scale collapse of the bourgeois parties, all transform a strong intervention by the working masses into a peremptory duty, if the reaction is not to triumph down the whole line. As a response to the reaction's harassment, and as a first precondition for successful mass actions, open and more decisive tactics by the party in all areas are absolutely necessary at present, as they are in the Reichstag and in the current struggle for the right to vote in Prussia. It is only strident revolutionary tactics of this kind, which consciously transfer the key points of the struggle over to the actions of the masses, and which do not shrink from any consequences of doing this, which are suited for keeping alive the energy for the struggle and idealism among the ranks of the politically organized; for carrying along the unorganized at the right moments; and for winning over these unorganized individuals long-term for the unions and for the political organizations." See *Vorwärts*, No. 11, August 11, 1913. The First State Attorney for the III Köngliche Landgericht (Third Royal Country Court) confidentially informed the chief of police, Division 7, that the demands articulated by the press organs could not be complied with. On October 14, 1913, the First State Attorney wrote as follows:

ACCORDING TO A NEWSPAPER REPORT

Summarized briefly, the essential aspects of her [Rosa Luxemburg's] speech were roughly as follows: As we appear currently to be in the middle of a conversation about the mass strike, we have to keep our eyes open for the practices used in other countries to apply it. We shouldn't allow the question of the mass strike to be separated from a consideration of the overall situation and of our party's political tactics. The mass strike cannot be utilized as a most extreme means of struggle if the party's parliamentary tactics have already led us into a cul-de-sac. As the masses are now discussing the question of the mass strike with such enthusiasm, even though this discussion has not been artificially whipped up, this suggests the masses have become clearly conscious that the means of struggle used hitherto will no longer suffice, in light of the advancing escalation of class contradictions. Because we're not moving forward on parliamentary terrain, the masses must find a way to express their will directly. We should not wait to apply the mass strike until the last proletarian has become politically organized. The organizations are strong enough to take on the leadership of the masses, and to pull those not yet politically organized along with them, when such an action starts. It is precisely this kind of mass struggle that would contribute to strengthening political and trade union organizations. We also have to raise the question here as to whether mass organizations can be retained at all in the long run, if nothing is done to put to the test the masses' devotion, readiness for sacrifice, and willingness to take risks. Nothing is healthier for the German working class than tumultuous battle. Fears that we here in Germany aren't ripe for these battles, or that we shouldn't be allowed to put the organizations on the line, are unfounded. However, a mass strike cannot be created by motions passed by the party executive and the general commission [of the German trade unions], but must develop out of the total situation instead, through the will of the masses. That said, the party's tactics must be directed toward reflecting the increasing bitterness of the masses. If

---

"I am musing over criminal prosecution measures against the author Rosa Luxemburg and other supporters of the resolution passed at the general meeting of the Social Democratic Association for the Reichstag constituency of Niederbarnim on August 10, 1913, because the specifics of criminal law that I have been considering do not appear to be applicable to the facts as ascertained… [ellipsis in original] I have therefore come to the conclusion that the existing criminal laws do not provide a handle for statements about the political mass strike, as have been made this year. With particular regard to the behavior of Rosa Luxemburg and her comrades at the assembly of the Niederbarnim electoral association, there appears to me to be no particular state interest in the prosecution of this individual case, in light of the fact that the same statements have been uttered in the press and subsequently at the Party Congress in Jena in the broadest public sphere, without, to the best of our knowledge, any intervention based on criminal law. Further, the question of the political mass strike at the Party Congress in Jena was shelved until further notice, and finally [we should note the fact] that the far more acrimonious remarks made by Rosa Luxemburg in the *Leipziger Volkszeitung* [Leipzig People's Paper] on June 28, 1913, have not led to any consequences." See "Taktische Fragen," in *Gesammelte Werke,* Vol. 3, pp. 246–58.

the vehemence of the masses leaves something to be desired, this is not least caused by the party pursuing politics that are not resolute enough. It suffices in this regard to remind listeners of the politics of restraint.* Other individuals refer to the example of the miners' strike in order to demonstrate that the unorganized masses cannot be won over to support an action [that they've had no hand in creating]: the unorganized masses didn't even want to support the miners' strike, they argue, even though this was merely concerned with immediate economic demands: if it came to a political strike, the unorganized sections of the masses would be the first to leave us in the lurch! These objections can be countered with the following: whoever knows about the miners' movement of 1905† must ask themselves whether the movement wasn't mucked up by the leaders making use of blurry tactics. Had not Kautsky also written in *Neue Zeit* about the 1905 miners' movement that one wouldn't get anywhere with the miners through a struggle for purely economic demands, and that the only option considered valid by them was a combination of trade union and political action?‡ The speaker states that she mentions this because Kautsky has been waving the lessons of the miners' strike in her face. The current debate on the mass strike should be greeted with joy, Luxemburg continued, as an expression of the mood and the situation in which the masses find themselves. "Our tactics have to move toward steering the ship of the party onto the waves of a strong, sharp and brave action." (Lively applause.)

Rosa Luxemburg's closing words included the statement that we had no cause to see conditions in the party as hopeless. "We have to face up to and overcome the deficiencies in the party with a clear awareness. As to the question of which type of mass strike I recommend," said the speaker, "I cannot propose a recipe. One cannot make a mass strike according to specific rules, one cannot regulate in advance for it, but one can foresee it and ready oneself for it, so that the situation can be exploited when it's favorable for the mass

---

* For the two-round election of January 1912, the party executive concluded a secret pact covering mutual tactical voting with the Progressive People's Party. This stated that the Progressives had to support Social Democratic candidates in thirty-one imperial constituencies, while the party executive committed itself to restricting its own activities in sixteen imperial constituencies: "Until the second round, no assemblies shall be held, no pamphlets shall be distributed, no ballots shall be delivered to the voters, and, on voting day itself, no transports shall be organized to bring people to the polls." See *Dokumente und Materialien zur Geschichte der deutschen Arbeiterbewegung* (Documents and Materials on the History of the German Workers' Movement), Vol. 4, (Berlin: 1967): pp. 395ff.

† From January 7 to February 19, 1905, around 215,000 miners struck in the Ruhr region for the eight-hour day, higher wages, and precautionary safety measures at work. The German and international working class supported them through solidarity strikes. This significant strike was supported by unaffiliated, unionized workers, the Christian unions, the Hirsch-Duncker Miners' Associations, the Polish Professional Union and also non-unionized workers.

‡ See Karl Kautsky, "Die Lehren des Bergarbeiterstreiks" (Lessons of the Miners' Strike), in *Die Neue Zeit (Stuttgart),* Year 23, 1904/05, Volume 1, p. 780ff.

strike. As the *Metalworkers' Paper* allows itself to criticize party motions,* so may we criticize the motion passed by the trade union congress on the shipyard workers' strike. (Applause.) The shipyard workers' movement, which came up from below, smashed itself to pieces on the statutes' impotent paragraphs.† A great struggle was throttled, simply to fulfil these statutes to the letter.

"The masses have to be told that the organization does not exist for its own sake, but as a means to an end," continued Luxemburg. "We should not allow everything to be done from above—the masses must be enthused with such a spirit that they are at their posts when the appointed hour comes, and so that the leaders, too, do not fail." (Strong applause.)

---

* See "Die außerordentliche Generalversammlung," in *Metallarbeiter-Zeitung* (Stuttgart), Year 31, No. 34, August 28, 1913, p. 272, and "Kopf klar und Pulver trocken!" in the *Metallarbeiter-Zeitung* (Stuttgart), Year 31, No. 32, August 9, 1913, p. 253. "If one closely studies the recent meetings in Berlin," argues the latter article, "which have focused on the question of the mass strike, then one will recognize, with no small measure of astonishment, that neither did any of the prophets nor did the well-known prophetess know how to say unambiguously *what* they actually *understood* under the concept of the mass strike, and *what* they wanted to *achieve* by utilizing it. Everything vanishes in the fog of the cloudiest of phrases. There was, admittedly, no shortage of thunderous speech. If the sound of trumpets could demolish the walls of the Prussian state or of the capitalist economic order, as that sound once burst open the walls of Jericho—then no stone in Prussia would be left standing by now. But it doesn't work like that. The only real tangible result is a *new seed of mistrust against the trade union civil servants,* who are truly plagued with enough problems. But that could have been achieved at a much cheaper price."

† "The statutes of the central executives of the trade unions refuse to grant [financial] support to their members in all cases, in which strikes are initiated without the approval of the executives. According to the statutes of the German Metal Workers' Union, whose members were the primary actors in the work stoppages, the members renounce all forms of support in such cases." See the "*Erklärung der Hauptvorstände der Verbände der Metall-, Holz-, Fabrikarbeiter, der Kupferschmiede, Schiffszimmerer, Maschinisten und Heizer und der Maler*" (Declaration of the Chief Executives of the Unions of Metal, Wood and Factory Workers, and of the Coppersmiths, Ships-joiners, Machinists, Stokers and Painters) issued on July 21, 1913. In *Zur Werftarbeiterbewegung. Correspondenzblatt der Generalkommission der Gewerkschaften Deutschlands* (Berlin), Year, 23, No. 30, July 26, 1913. See also, "Zur Lohnbewegung der Arbeiter auf den Seeschiffswerften" (On the Wage Movement of the Shipbuilders in the Shipyards), in *Metallarbeiter-Zeitung* (Stuttgart), Year 31, No. 31, August 2, 1913.

Łódź's Huge Struggle*

The majority of those who were locked out and on strike in Łódź have gone back to work. Yet 20,000 workers remain on strike at this very moment. In the category of large factories employing thousands, the strike is continuing only at the Ender and Krusche factories, while work has restarted at Scheibler, at Poznański and at Geyer under the old conditions. Despite this, the conflict has definitely not been fruitless. Workers have achieved wage increases comparable to smaller factories. And there are wage increases of between 10 and 15 percent in the following companies: Goldberg and Co., Rothenberg and Chodoroff, Oskar Preessak, Kroß and Co., the Seibert Brothers, B. Etkin, H. Wislizki, Kres, Asterblum, Diamant and Co., J. Rapaport, Moniz, Bermann and Silber, Tykoziner, Rosenblatt, Bauer, Steigert, Weicht, Leonhardt, Roussau and Co., Martin and Semek, Lubowski, Jakobowiz, Lebdiner and Gofran, Lichtenstein, Wyseranski, Ramisch, the Dobranizki Brothers, Wiener, Großmann, Chwat, Jarozinski, Muehle, Kanel, Motte and Co., Finkelkraut and Katz, Heinzel, Einsenbraun, Silberstein, Glaeser, Schochet, Teitelbaum, Danziger, Reichmann and Halpern. At Peiß's factory, wages have been raised by 18 percent, at Rothschild's by 20 percent, and at A. Prussak's works by between 20 and 30 percent. In all productive textile factories, wage rises of between 20 and 40 percent have been achieved. Further, strikers have won significant concessions in the neighboring settlement of Zgierz—which also has a textile industry and a labor struggle to match it—and in Konstantynów and Neurokit. Other groups of workers with rewards to show for their efforts include the workers at the Łódź gasworks, who joined the movement in sympathy with the textile workers, the Jewish and German typesetters, and the streetcar employees, all of whom have won concessions.

Generally, the workers are in a very fresh and combative mood. Most of them have returned to work with a strong resolve to take up the struggle again at the next favorable moment: it would have been simply physically impossible for the tens of thousands of strikers to have continued the strike in light of the meager support they have been receiving. It was only possible for most of the strikers to keep going for as long as they did by looking for accommodation with relatives in the surrounding villages, or by earning money bringing in the harvest. After years of the worst penury, and without any prospect of reliable support, tens of thousands have kept this labor struggle going for weeks. The highest officially registered tally of those locked out and on strike came in at

* This article first appeared in *Der Textil-Arbeiter* (The Textile Worker), No. 35, August 29, 1913, p. 277. It is translated by Henry Holland from Luxemburg's *Gesammelte Werke* Vol. 3, pp. 298–9.

69,000 people, of whom a substantial number contributed to the strike movement for over seven weeks. And now 20,000 remain on strike, or, if you include their families, c. 80,000 people suffering from sheer starvation, who still refuse to obey the commands of corporate power. Considering these circumstances, it is impossible not to admire the courage and tenacity of the Łódź workforce. Even if wage increases had not been achieved in some areas, this huge struggle would still demonstrate that we are dealing here not with wildfire, not with a heedless, desperate outbreak of activity, but rather with tenacious energy and steadfast courage for the struggle. We are dealing with a joy in sacrifice that knows no boundaries, whose authority has to be respected by friend and foe alike.

Jena Party Congress*

I. MOTION FOR A RESOLUTION ON THE POLITICAL MASS STRIKE†

Motion 94 (mass strike)‡ to replace paragraphs 2 to 4 with:

The sharpening of economic and political antagonisms in Germany compels the proletariat to develop ever greater power to defend itself against insidious attacks by the ruling classes, to improve its economic situation and extend its political rights. In the struggle against political disenfranchisement, the proletariat is increasingly forced to display the highest energy. This struggle culminates in the fight for universal, equal, and direct suffrage in all representative bodies, the conquest of which is a precondition for the proletariat's struggle for emancipation. The current state of the proletariat's lack of political rights, as can be seen most clearly in Prussia with its three-class franchise system, hinders the proletariat in all its efforts to improve its standard of living. It makes the worst enemies of trade union activity and social progress into the rulers of legislation, not only in Prussia but in the whole Empire.

This disgraceful voting law can only give way to a storm of suffrage by the great masses, as envisaged by the Prussian Party Congress of January 1910.§

The Party Congress welcomes the renewed interest from wide circles of the party on the question of the political mass strike. The prerequisite for the successful execution of a political mass strike is the most complete possible organization of the proletariat in political and economic terms and the infusion of these organizations with revolutionary enthusiasm for struggle and the willingness to make sacrifices. The Party Congress, therefore, makes it the duty of party comrades to work tirelessly for the expansion of political and trade union organization and the dissemination of the party and trade union press. The mass strike, however, cannot be artificially brought about on command from the party or union authorities. It can only arise as escalation of a mass action already flowing from the worsening of the economic and political situation.

In response to the attacks of reaction, and as the first prerequisite of successful mass action, an aggressive, determined, and consistent tactic of the

---

* These minutes/proceedings from the Jena Congress of the Social Democratic Party of Germany, September 14 to 20, 1913, were first published in *Parteitagsprotokoll über die Verhandlungen des Parteitags der Sozialdemokratischen Partei Deutschlands. Abgehalten zu Jena vom 14. bis 18. September 1913* (Protocols of the of the Party Congress of the Social Democratic Party of Germany, held at Jena from September 14 to 18, 1913) (Berlin: Buchhandlung Vorwärts 1913). It is translated by Jacob Blumenfeld from Luxemburg's *Gesammelte Werke*, Vol 3, pp. 328–37.

† This motion, introduced by Rosa Luxemburg and other Social Democrats, was rejected.

‡ Motion 94 was the resolution of the party Executive Committee.

§ The Congress of Prussian Social Democracy took place from January 3 to 5, 1910, in Berlin.

party is required in all areas. Only such a tactic, which deliberately shifts the center of the struggle to the action of the masses, can keep the fighting energy and idealism alive in the ranks of the organized, and carry the unorganized along at important moments and win them over permanently to trade-union and political organization.

The Party Congress calls on the party comrades and party officials to take all measures to ensure that the German proletariat is prepared for all contingencies in the coming struggles.

II. SPEECH ON THE TACTICS OF SOCIAL DEMOCRACY

When I heard Comrade Scheidemann's big speech yesterday, I wistfully thought of our opening ceremony on Sunday and the welcoming speeches of our foreign guests. The representatives of our fraternal parties came from Holland, Belgium, and Switzerland, and they explained to us one by one: what seems to us to be the most important thing in your meeting is the debate on the mass strike; for all of us in Holland, Belgium, Switzerland, and other countries, this was already a burning question. Even though the question of the mass strike is already practical for us, we know that to achieve a profound, serious theoretical treatment of this question, one must go to German Social Democracy, the vanguard of the International. Then came Scheidemann's speech about the mass strike.

I am afraid that if our out-of-town guests expected a generous, deeply penetrating, objective treatment of this highly important problem from the top leadership of our party, if they hoped to hear from the representative of the party's Executive Committee a far-sighted analysis of the political and economic situation in Germany and within the party, which must be considered in connection with the mass strike, if they expected to see firm, clear guidelines drawn up concerning our tactical responsibilities for the near future, then I am afraid they did not get their money's worth. For Scheidemann's speech about the mass strike was anything but a serious, objective treatment of this problem. This whole speech was tuned to two notes: Firstly, to the tone of Faust's assistant, Wagner, see how wonderfully far we have come in all areas.* And secondly, to a fight against the complainers, against the dissatisfied critics in our own party. If one listens to Scheidemann's remarks, then the party leadership is highly satisfied with everything in the party, everything is completely splendid.

I believe that the first condition for serious political leaders worthy of the name, leaders of a party of millions, a mass party like ours, is a highly sensitive ear for everything that stirs in the soul of the masses. ("That's right!") Now there is no doubt that we currently have a profound dissatisfaction in the ranks of the organized party comrades. ("That's right!") You need only go to the assemblies

---

* Reference to Goethe's *Faust,* Part I.

to hear this. One need only follow the reports from the party meetings before the Party Congress in all parts of Germany to see that speakers arise from the masses and declare that the organized masses are literally longing for a breath of fresh air in party life, that they want to have a fresh, sharp tone brought into our struggle, that they are tired of seeing nothing but parliamentarism always hailed as the sole means of salvation. But the party leadership knows nothing of any of this, and Scheidemann says: You speak of dissatisfaction? Where is the proof of the masses' lack of confidence in their leaders? Only naysayers can see such dissatisfaction, and the party leadership does not tolerate naysayers. (Laughter.) The party leadership was forced to affirm a whole series of distressing facts in its official report and in Scheidemann's speech. Our membership is not growing at the desired rate, we have a partial standstill and even a decline in the number of subscribers to our papers. Scheidemann told us that in view of the conditions in Prussia, the Prussian voting law, and the shameful failure of the last Prussian Landtag elections,* every reasonable person had to expect that the masses would now rise up in tremendous anger and come out to fight. And Scheidemann said: we should be surprised that the masses do not. And finally, Scheidemann himself noted an unfortunate slowdown in the movement within our party against the military bill.†

To all these facts, which should give every serious party leader an occasion to seriously analyze the situation, to discuss how and where the real roots of these phenomena should be sought and how to remedy them—to all these facts the party leadership finds only the easiest and most convenient explanation: a standstill of the organization and the press? Well, blame the crisis! At the same time, we should reassure ourselves that every crisis again shakes the walls that we so painstakingly built in the time of prosperity.

The Prussian suffrage struggle did not flare up after the shameful election defeat as Scheidemann took for granted. Yet the only thing the Executive Committee, our highest authority, has to say is that Scheidemann must be surprised about this. It would make more sense to ask whether our tactics themselves had not contributed a little to this, whether we have any reason to be surprised, and instead to ask ourselves what we should do to push back such phenomena. And finally, concerning the slowdown of the mass movement against the

* In the elections for the Prussian *Abgeordnetenhaus* (lower house of parliament), the Social Democrats gained 775,171 votes (28.38 percent of votes cast) but won only 10 seats, while the Conservative Party won 147 seats with 402, 988 votes (14.75 percent), as a result of the Prussian three-class franchise.

† In March 1913, the government introduced an army and spending bill [*Militär- und Deckungsvorlage*] into the Reichstag that was to enable a significant expansion in the size of the army. The SPD opposed the bill but was divided on approving the financial support for the army's expansion as it was partially funded by a new wealth tax. The revisionist wing of the party supported the finance measures and gained a majority of the SPD caucus, as a result of which the party's Reichstag members approved the so-called "Defense Contribution."

military bill, against the most outrageous imposition of imperialism we have experienced, for this, too, our highest authority has very sufficient reasons for explanation: first, the approval of the military bill was certain, and second, after the property taxes had already been fixed, then masses had to tell themselves —as Scheidemann literally said—that the worst was over! I was amazed that our highest party authority could express such a view here. If it were true, if the masses could tell themselves that after the approval of property taxes, the worst of the military bill was over, then we should be ashamed of the results of our agitation and our educational work. ("That's right!") If this were true, then the party leadership was the first to be obliged to alert and arouse the whole party with the question; if we have achieved so little, then it is high time that we look for ways and means to finally educate the masses to a socialist viewpoint. ("That's right!") Instead, we get rationalizations for calm in all areas.

So much for conditions within the party. There are, however, quite a few factors in the political and economic situation that really are suited to making the leaders of a 4-million-member party think seriously about tactics and review our previous ones.* Now imperialism is making a huge push with the latest military bill, the likes of which we have not seen in decades. Here we can see the behavior of the bourgeois parties—a new constellation against us. For what have we experienced? During the struggles against the defense and funding bills, those liberals who aroused so much hope in our ranks during the last Reichstag elections did not join our struggle to push through a thorough financial reform and fight against the Black-Blue Bloc,† but rather joined forces with the splendid Black-Blue Bloc. They stabbed us in the back and joined with the Center Party. Serious politicians had to follow this new situation in the coalition of the parties.

I would like to point out what an editorial from the *Vossische Zeitung* recently said about the Prussian election reform: the only hope for electoral reform—this is what a liberal newspaper writes—lies now with the Center. The liberals should now instigate electoral reform together with them. And what kind of electoral reform? Not the abolition of the three-class franchise system, but a better distribution of the divisions in this three-class franchise system. What does this new coalition mean? It shows that liberalism, after completely embarrassing itself a few years ago by joining with the conservatives, now wants to seize the latest opportunity offered by history to degenerate even more, in order to join with the Center against us. ("That's right!") What is this, Comrade Scheidemann, other than the shameful collapse of all your moderating tactics since the last Reichstag elections. (Shouting from the party leadership: "Oh, nonsense!")

---

* The Social Democratic Party won 4.25 million votes in the January 1912 Reichstag elections.

† The antisocialist, pro-government coalition of the Catholic Center Party and the Conservatives.

Party comrades, if our highest party authority does not take such facts as an occasion to pursue a serious examination of the previous tactical guidelines, then it is depressing to see the certainty in the preliminary drawing of the lines upon which politics should be conducted. In addition, there are also extremely worrying economic factors. We are at the beginning of a crisis, unemployment is rising, and there is every reason for us, as far-sighted politicians, to tell ourselves that our politics, our tactics, must be designed in such a way that we can direct the inevitable discouragement and despair that always takes hold of the masses in times of crisis, that we can guide this ferment, this dissatisfaction, into the foundation of a determined fighting spirit and not let it degenerate into dull stagnation.

Party comrades, only a determined, sharp, revolutionary tactic can steel the courage of the masses ("That's right!"), who are oppressed by the crisis. Instead of all this, Comrade Scheidemann thought that the most urgent task at this Party Congress was to fight against complainers in his own ranks, against the critics who supposedly artificially stir up dissatisfaction and imagine the worst. And Comrade Scheidemann made this fight against the internal enemy truly easy. He did not actually fight against the criticisms and views put forth; he preferred to be a second knight of St. George, who victoriously slayed the dragon he had only just hatched himself. (Great laughter.) What Comrade Scheidemann opposed here as the alleged view of the defenders of the mass strike is a distortion of the real views we hold. ("That's right!") Especially as concerns yours truly, if Comrade Scheidemann thinks he caught me many times with his criticism, even without mentioning my name, then I can shout back to him with Goethe: *You are like the spirit you understand, not me.* (Great laughter, restlessness, and partial agreement.)*

Party comrades, here are some examples of the distortion of views being attacked. When we point out, in the press and at assemblies, the omissions in our recent policies, when we emphasize that, for example, a party of our strength and our oppositional, revolutionary position should not stand quietly by and watch such first-class political events as the kaiser's silver jubilee† or the visit of the tsar to Germany but must call for some kind of protest action, then Comrade Scheidemann comes and says: What, do you want to drive people into the streets, do you want to endanger thousands of lives? And you could literally see a puddle of red blood forming on the streets of Berlin at the mere suggestion of a demonstration against the tsar's visit,‡ as befits Social Democracy. As if we hadn't already seen massive street demonstrations in Berlin itself

* Johann Wolfgang von Goethe, *Faust: A Tragedy*, Part I, Scene I: "Thou Art like the Spirit which thou comprehendest, / Not me." (Trans. Bayard Taylor, 1870; Random House, 1950), p. 20.

† The twenty-fifth anniversary of Kaiser Wilhelm II's accession to the throne was celebrated in June 2013 with a flurry of monarchical and militaristic commemorative activities.

‡ In May 1913.

and in Germany three years ago, in which thousands of lives were not lost, as if we hadn't already seen a completely peaceful mass strike in various countries, most recently in Belgium, as Comrade Scheidemann so beautifully described ten minutes later! Party comrades! If you want to make it easy for yourself to apologize for the fact that nothing at all was done, not even ordinary meetings about the tsar's visit, not even a decent editorial in the central organ *Vorwärts* (Laughter), then your rationalizations are terrible.

A second example: when we say that in Germany, as in all other countries, we need not wait to eventually use the mass strike until the last man and woman have paid their dues as organized members of a party branch, when we point out that, in a revolutionary situation, where great historical tasks lie before us, the organization of the party will probably have the strength and intellectual influence to carry along even the unorganized masses, when we say that it is backward and wrong to regard the membership booklet as the sufficient legitimation for class struggle, for a revolutionary action of the proletariat, when we declare that the politics and tactics of the party must be ready to arouse the necessary enthusiasm and feeling of self-sacrifice in the great popular masses also outside those who are organized, because only in this way can we bring along the enormous crowd of the unorganized and win them over to the organization—then Comrade Scheidemann comes along and says: Indeed, that means tearing down the organization. ("That's right!") That means lack of discipline, that means arousing the distrust of the functionaries. In his attacks on us, Comrade Scheidemann spoke a few times about a lack of responsibility and unscrupulousness. ("Very true!") I do not wish to use such expressions but allow me to say that this way of challenging the views of an opponent borders very sharply on demagoguery. (Müller [party leader]: "You are one to talk!")

Here's a third example of the complete ignorance from our highest authority concerning what we really strive for and demand. We are told: If you forcibly provoke and lead a discussion about the mass strike and the conditions of its application in Germany, then you are only forcing us to say that we are not yet able to do this today. You are thus forcing us to reveal the weakness of our position to the enemy ("Very true!"), and how wrong is the policy of someone who says: I have a mighty sword against you in my pocket, but I cannot use it today.

Well, party comrades, these are the viewpoints with which one wants to master the greatest popular movement in the history of the world! Do not say too loudly, I pray you, that we still have an enormous crowd of unorganized people, otherwise our enemies may find out; do not say too loudly that we have yellow unions,* for that is our secret. (Cheerfulness and laughter.) Party

---

* The "yellow" unions that arose after 1880 were employer-supported strike-breaking organizations that fought against the revolutionary workers. The "yellow" designation comes from France, where the members of the strike-breaker organizations wore the gorse blossom as a club badge.

comrades! The weaknesses of our position are no secret to our opponents. ("That's right!") It is ridiculous to imagine that the pros and cons, that the whole situation which must be discussed and considered from the standpoint of the mass strike, should be handled secretly in a closed room hidden from the authorities. We are accused, both in the *Neue Zeit* and here in Comrade Scheidemann's speech, of almost being putschists ("That's right!"), of being conspirators. This is what people say who want to apply the typical conspiratorial tactics to the modern mass strike by imagining that the outbreak of the mass strike must be a surprise, it must be worked out in secret, in a closed room by a handful of authorities. (Laughter.)

This question was already settled here on the same platform in 1905 with all the desired clarity. I quote the corresponding words of Comrade Bebel, the speaker for the mass strike at the Party Congress in Jena.* He said: "This brings us to the proposition of the political mass strike. We are told: one makes the political mass strike, but one does not speak of it!" And to this Bebel replied: "It will be foolish to attempt to avoid this discussion and to act as if we did not hear it. That is ostrich politics. Even if this question is limited on all points, as many would desire, nevertheless every thinking man, and especially every leader of the party who deserves this name, must ask himself if the time is not here for the party to discuss this proposition." ("That's right!") "Lively approval" it says in the minutes. (Scheidemann: "That happened back then too!") "When large masses come into question, one cannot leave measures in which the masses have a role to play undiscussed before the masses." ("That's right!") "If the masses are to enthusiastically champion a certain action, then they demand to know the effect and purpose of the measure." ("That's right!") "That is their right. Besides, enlightened masses do not blindly follow given orders ... That would be a pathetic party which lets itself be intimidated by the public prosecutor and the criminal laws into defending its human and civil rights."† Of course, in response to the words Bebel spoke, you must shout: "That's right!" (Unrest)

Chairman Ebert: "I cannot allow such insinuations to be made to the members of the Party Congress. (Shouting: "A handful doesn't matter!")

That was not an insinuation at all. Anyone who shouts "That's right!" to the words of Bebel does so with full conviction. (Lively agreement.)

I believe indeed that you endorse Bebel's words. You just forget—and here you interrupted me—that these words still have the exact same meaning today as they did in 1905. For it is completely incorrect to think that simply because a mass strike is accepted in principle at a party congress, it is over for the masses outside. Yes, how do you see the matter? You shout "that's right" when I read that Bebel said that if the mass strike is to come about, the masses must take

---

* This speech is available in English at the Marxist Internet Archive, marxists.org.

† Protocol of the negotiations of the Party Congress of the Social Democratic Party of Germany. Held in Jena from September 17 to 23, 1905.

care of it. Yes, do you think it was already over for the masses, for the millions, when you passed a resolution at the 1905 Party Congress? ("Very good!") Don't you understand that the masses as such must deal with it in mass assemblies? ("That's right!") Because we are not speaking to the masses here, we are only formulating things that have to be thought through, digested and accepted by the comrades outside.

So when you shout "that's right!" to what Bebel said in 1905, then it is inconsistent and wrong if you also think of the mass strike tactic as such: *Roma locuta, causa finita!* [Rome has spoken, the case is closed!] A party congress has spoken, that settles it. Certainly, the mass strike in Germany, as everywhere, if it is to have any chance of success, must come from the masses. And that is why we say in our resolution that the mass strike cannot be ordered overnight by the leaders of the trade unions and the party, as some authorities imagine today. ("That's right!") Neither can it be commandeered by the leaders when it has become historically ripe. ("That's right!") Yet our task is not exhausted with this realization, if we want the mass strike to be successful when it comes about, to bring us the maximum amount of positive results and benefits, political and socialist education, and the awakening of the masses. For this, it is necessary that the masses and the party stand tall when the historical situation comes; that is, we must consciously prepare ourselves for these historical events and educate the masses. Certainly, the party must stand at the front of the movement, but in order to stand at the front it must not wait quietly for the revolutionary situation to be pulled by the masses. Rather, it must prepare the masses to follow us in full confidence by shaping all tactics and methods of struggle in a sharp offensive toward the revolutionary side.

And when Scheidemann recommended his resolution with a raised voice, saying that there are authorities behind it, I believe that the Party Congress is not there to shout hurrah for the will and views of the authorities, but rather it is there so that the authorities learn what the masses want. ("That's right!") And what they want can be summed up in one sentence: We respond to all the attacks of reaction by saying, clearly and openly, at the Party Congress: we are sharpening our weapons, and we are ready! (Roaring applause.)

On the Political Mass Strike [September 19–20, 1913]*

Speech held at an internal sitting of delegates and foreign guests at the Jena Party Congress of German Social Democracy†

ACCORDING TO A POLICE REPORT

The general strike is the political strike: the strike against the state. Not the strike of a single trade union against one or more employers or an employers' association, not the strike of many trade unions in support of a strike that broke out against the employers in another trade union, but any strike, of whatever scope, directed against the state for defense or attack, as a demonstration or as a means of coercion. Therefore, the name *political strike* is more fitting. The political strike directly affects Social Democracy as a political entity. The other strike is a matter for the trade unions alone, although it is indisputable that any major economic strike also affects state life and can therefore easily turn into a political strike. For Social Democracy, the political strike is no substitute for parliamentary or political action. We do not believe in a tactic that, without constant practice, propaganda, and organization by and for the parliamentary struggle, could call the workers united in free groups to defensive or offensive action against the government, over and over again. We are convinced that, through this, the proletariat would be defeated every time. (Agreement.) Socialist organization in associations that are unyielding, well-trained and remain disciplined for as long as possible is, in our opinion, the only means of defeating the bourgeoisie at all times and everywhere, or of defense against it, if there are to be good chances of success. (Applause.) Nor do we believe that a general or political strike is capable of casting capitalism to the ground. The organization of capitalism, with its economic and intellectual

* This account of Rosa Luxemburg's speech is translated by Henry Holland and Manuela Kölke from Luxemburg's *Gesammelte Werke*, Vol. 7, pp. 784–8. It was previously published as excerpts from a lecture by Ottokar Luban, "Rosa Luxemburgs Engagement für den politischen Massenstreik. Zwei bisher unveröffentlichte parteiinterne Ansprachen im Sommer 1913" (Rosa Luxemburg's Commitment to the Political Mass Strike. Two previously unpublished internal party speeches from the summer of 1913) in *Rosa-Luxemburg-Forschungsberichte* (Rosa Luxemburg Research Reports), Vol. 6, Leipzig, 2008, pp. 122–6.

† One hundred delegates and numerous foreign guests participated in this session chaired by Hermann Molkenbuhr, which aimed to clarify the applicability of the mass strike in Germany. Rosa Luxemburg and Friedrich Ebert were the two main speakers.

production and its political means of power, is too vast, too comprehensive to be revolutionized with a single simple means, to be murdered with a single blow. ("Quite right.") If anyone believes this, then they underestimate its power and lead the working class astray with such propaganda. (Lively approval.) First, the power of the organization must rise in the proletariat itself. The bourgeois revolution was a struggle of possessors against possessors, of economically powerful against economically powerful. Moreover, it aimed only at producing a society of individuals. The proletarians are, each for themselves, powerless—and so they instead set themselves the goal of a society of organizations. It follows that they cannot achieve victory until organizations within the proletarian class have grown. The dismantling of capitalism cannot be arrived at without distinctive organizations. People who want to disorganize the old do not, however, want absolute disorganization. Rather, these people want to organize the new. The trade union struggle, the political struggle, and the cooperatives are the means to do this. They create new organs inside the old organism, whose growth is capable of blowing up the old body. That said, who claims to know the path of development and the future so exactly that they would dare to say, "These are the radical means, and the only radical means, for arriving at socialism"? The syndicalists dare to say this when they argue that trade union action suffices, or the general strike and the refusal of military duty are the only means. But when we look at corporate trusts, we learn that such a position leads to the destruction of trade union action and makes strikes impossible. Social Democracy does not predict the future in such a utopian manner, with all details worked out, as do the syndicalists. It looks for the means it will use on the road of its own development, without therefore declaring these to be the only and eternally viable means. (Agreement.) Social Democracy condemns in equal measure such positions: neither the cooperative by itself, nor union action on its own, nor parliamentary action [in isolation] can overcome capitalism. We don't believe in a deification of the cooperatives, of the mass strike, or of the parliamentary majority. We recognize all too clearly that our opponent's massive power will enable it to take our weapons from us, or to destroy them. That is why, on each occasion, we make use of the means that seems to us best suited to its purpose in the given context. We are prepared for and reckon with the possibility that we will have to swap our current weapons for other ones. (Applause.) In that section of the *Communist Manifesto* entitled "Bourgeois and Proletarians," Marx describes the development of the class struggle: "At first the contest is carried on by individual laborers, then by the working people of a factory, then by the operatives of one trade, in one locality."*

---

* Marx and Engels, *Manifesto of the Communist Party*, in *Marx-Engels Collected Works*, Vol. 6, p. 492.

Since that time, the extent and the strength of the struggle have grown. The industrialists' associations and the workers' associations are battling it out across the territory of the entire country. Because of the connections between industry and the transport sector, strikes break out simultaneously among various occupational groups. Now and again, people have been thinking about international strikes. There is in fact no alternative to all these developments. Wherever production and transportation concentrate themselves and the division of labor increases, wherever production takes place for the needs of the world market, and the production process forms the entire world into one whole, even if it is still badly joined together, the battle between capital and labor must encompass entire peoples. But this is not only the case in the field of economics. The clashes between the state and the working class will become ever more weighty. To the same extent that capitalism grows, the state—welded by bureaucracy and militarism into an independent power and guard of bourgeois society—demands ever more for itself. The burdens placed on the working people, that part of surplus value that the state claims for itself, will grow increasingly. These burdens will overtake the small amount the workers are given back in the form of health, unemployment, and other insurance schemes and pensions, etc. The claims that the workers lodge with the state will multiply in relation to the growth of their self-confidence and their organization. Militarism and imperialism, import duties, the decline of liberalism, the rejuvenation of reactionary forces on the one hand, and the stagnation or snail's progress of laws for workers on the other, all this can do nothing but goad workers on to a struggle that incorporates ever widening fields, including political terrain. We note simultaneously how the working class, conscious of the increasing size and power of its opponent as it is also of its own strengths, looks around for new means with which to fight on a wider playing field, with possibly greater success and perhaps even victory. Of these various means, the mass strike is the one that has been most discussed, and the one that has been applied in various countries. Independent of our own judgment regarding such means, the fact that the growth of the struggle forces us to consider its application must fill everyone with joy. The growth of the struggle can only be taken as a sign of decisive blows to come, of victory drawing near. (Lively applause.) We immediately see that the political strike is an extreme means, a *dangerous means in the current period.* Why is this? Because it is a means that attacks capitalist society in its general and highest form of organization, the state. When the general interest of the whole bourgeoisie is thus attacked, each and every concession awarded to this means of violence would be understood by the bourgeoisie as a partial betrayal of its total power, and as a first admission: the proletariat is more powerful than the property-owning class. Do other means of force exist that the working class might make use of that offer more guarantees of success than the mass strike? Reflecting on history, we can find:

1. *The armed struggle.* We cannot consider this option *as long as* the army is a tool without a will in the hands of the government. (Assent.)

2. *Refusing to pay taxes.* But the proletariat pays *too little direct taxation* for this means to have any purchase. (Both assent and dissent.)

3. *Refusing military duty.* In the initial stages, this will lead to prison sentences at least, and, during periods of unrest, to the death penalty for the individuals who refuse to serve. (Assent.)

The *only means that is left to us is the political strike.* The proletariat doesn't have another means of force, at least not in the coming period. This is the main point and it's to this that I wish to direct the comrades' attention. Because the consequence is that those who reject this means of extreme struggle, used either for attack or defense, without further consideration, reject the proletariat using forceful resistance from the start, even when the proletariat has no other options open to it. Trade unions, the right to vote, and cooperatives can all be abolished in one go by legal means; the *gradual growth that Social Democracy wishes for, in accordance with abstract rules*, can be hamstrung at a stroke. *What should happen then, if there are no means of force?* We are not arguing for the mass strike here. It is far too clear that it's still a very dangerous means for the time being. But I present the question to the comrades: *What are you accomplishing*, if you *reject* this means *absolutely?*

If anyone believes that a pivotal section of the bourgeoisie will gradually come over to our side, that the liberals and the progressives will gradually be forced into compromises and pacts with us, *in which we're the stronger party*, and which not only serve to weaken the whole proletariat by making minor concessions to one part of the proletariat, so that later, as soon as it comes to our real interests, they'll turn their backs on us; if anyone, put briefly, does not believe that the chasm between the owning and the non-owning classes is so deep that the bourgeoisie will ultimately need to use violence against us, *as soon as we attack their private property—which we are compelled to do because of the facts of historical development*—if anyone holds this conviction, then they can say: I reject the political strike because a much more reliable path exists. But there are no signs at all of such a pacification among a really large part of the bourgeoisie. On the contrary, the forces of reaction have seized the platform in all countries. The bourgeoisie is using the means of import duties, militarism and imperialism everywhere to extend its power and to oppress the workers still further. Compared to this, the small amount of legislation for workers is scraps from the table compared to a feast. (Lively assent.) One cannot claim that class contradictions are diminishing. They're at an impasse at best, standing still. Comrades present here today must understand that I don't negate the possibility that one part of the bourgeoisie might change their thinking and adopt socialism as the only way out of the increasing destitution of capitalism. We could name this or that sign that makes the chances of such a possibility dimly visible.* (From the audience: "The living dead!" Great and sustained amusement.) But I can merely state: at present, we see the opposite, or, in more general terms, we see the bourgeoisie's political and economic power increasing faster than that of the proletariat, and we note particularly the growth in reactionary ideas.

In the context of the current proliferation of the power of large-scale industry and large-scale finance, we believe that these contradictions will be ratcheted up still further. As far as I can judge, the proletariat will have to use violent means more often, to confront violent means. I therefore recommend that we prioritize our old tactic of using our deliberations to be prepared for the worst case—which would mean the class struggle's intensification—and therefore not reject the political strike as a means. For the very reason that economic development is going to drive us to that place that we wanted to arrive at anyway. (Lively applause.)

(Comrade Luxemburg's lecture, which was sometimes greeted with vigorous applause, lasted for one hour and fifteen minutes.)†

---

* For the two-round election of January 1912 the party executive concluded a secret pact covering mutual tactical voting with the Progressive People's Party. This involved the understanding that the Social Democrats would limit the extent of their campaigning against some Progressive candidates.

† In his comments, Friedrich Ebert regarded the political mass strike as expedient in countries where the proletariat still has nothing to lose. In Germany, on the other hand, great caution was called for, he argued, because the stakes were higher for the proletariat. In times of great tension and spontaneous upheaval of the proletariat, Ebert was in favor neither of a ban nor of unconditional support for this the mass strike. He saw the most important prerequisite as the strengthening of the party, the trade unions and the cooperatives. The core point of his comments was: "We do not believe in the miracle power of the political mass strike as the sole means. At this moment, we still perceive the overwhelming supremacy of the ruling class, against which the proletariat is too fragmented to dare a decisive struggle. That is why we need to strengthen the organizations so that we can become stronger. If the trade union organizations come to full strength, if they are filled with socialist consciousness and intimately linked to a strong political party, then the political strike can become a means that must be used, that can inflict shocking blows on the ruling class and that in this way can contribute to an ultimate general victory. Then perhaps this means can even become the form in which the final battles between the proletariat and the bourgeoisie are fought out. (Applause.)" Engelbert Pernerstorfer and Erhard Auer spoke after Ebert, and Karl Kautsky then had his say. His remarks lasted almost an hour, after which Ebert emphasized the position of the party executive: "The organizations must be trained and educated. Everything must be tightly intertwined and function smoothly. The consumer associations must be able to supply the ammunition. Voluntary discipline must become a reflex, so that if all leaders were to be arrested—something we must reckon with happening first—the fight could still continue with calm and determination. It is precisely because the resolution of the party executive emphasizes the organization, that the strike against the state will be successful." He concluded by saying that "if the opportunity presents itself to strike a blow against the present form of government through our economic power, we won't let it go. (Loud applause.)" See also Luxemburg's "Zur Massenstreikresolution des Parteivorstandes" (The Mass Strike Resolution of the Party Executive), in *Gesammelte Werke*, Vol. 3, pp. 322–7.

Mass Strike and the Taxation Question*

Talk given on September 29, 1913, to the members meeting of the Social Democratic association in Hanau

ACCORDING TO A NEWSPAPER REPORT

Our position on the Party Congress that just ended† demands that we make discussion of the mass strike and the taxation question in party and trade union meetings one of our most important tasks. Of course, we will approach the questions of the May Day celebration, of unemployment benefits, etc. with the same enthusiasm. I must firmly reject the accusation that we have dealt with that last issue in an offhand fashion. It is completely understandable that these two new problems, the mass strike and the tax question, have shifted into the center of public interest. The entire course of events we're experiencing compels us to choose: either we admit to our impotence or we reach for new weapons. Although the majority at the Party Congress decided in favor of the executive's resolution on the mass strike question,‡ and on the taxation issue

---

* This account of Luxemburg's talk was first published in *Volksstimme* (People's Voice) (Frankfurt am Main), No. 229, September 29, 1913. It is translated by Henry Holland and Manuela Kölke from Luxemburg's *Gesammelte Werke* Vol. 7, pp. 794–6.

† The Party Congress of the Social Democratic Party of Germany took place September 14–20, 1913, in Jena. See pp. 83–90, above.

‡ The party executive's resolution reads as follows: "With regard to the motion passed at the Mannheim Party Congress (1906) confirming the Jena Party Congress motion of 1905, the most encompassing application of the mass work stoppage should be considered as one of the most effective political means, not only to fend off attacks on the people's existing rights, but also in order to win new rights for the people. Winning general, equal, direct and secret suffrage to all representative bodies is one of the preconditions for the proletariat's liberation battle. The three-class voting law not only strips non-owners of their rights but also holds them back in all their efforts to improve how they earn their living, it turns trade union activism and social progress into the worst of enemies and transforms the caste of Junkers into the rulers of law-making authorities. That is why the Party Congress calls upon the disenfranchised to harness all their energies in the fight against the three-class voting law, in the knowledge that we cannot conduct this fight victoriously without major sacrifices. In rejecting the mass strike as a means to banish social detriment according to an anarchistic conception of the term—an infallible political means, which can be applied at any moment of time—the Party Congress simultaneously articulates its conviction that the working class must engage with all its strength to achieve equal political rights. The masses can only execute the mass strike in a situation where all organs of the workers' movement are in complete unity, and through masses that are class conscious, passionate about the ultimate goals of socialism, and ready to accept every sacrifice. This is why the Party Congress imposes the duty on party comrades to work tirelessly for the construction and expansion of the political and trade union organizations." Congress passed this resolution by only two votes. A number of delegates abstained, because they considered the Social Democratic motion from the

in favor of the Wurm-Südekum resolution,* this in no way means a defeat for the radicals. These radicals have, on the contrary, battled their way to a fine victory, by awakening interest in these two important questions. People have been forced to show their true colors. You have already heard how a trade union leader thinks about this question. We have achieved what we wanted to achieve in that we have swayed the majority in the direction that we wish for. This process enabled us to notch up two large victories for ourselves: firstly, the public and clear statement made by the trade union leader Bauer,† and secondly the concluding speech by Comrade Scheidemann.‡ We must carry the ideals of the mass strike more and more into the masses, so that we finally get a party congress that agrees with our view.

Unfortunately, the debates on the tax question did not rise up to the task at hand. The plan was that Wurm would deal with the fundamentals of the question, while Südekum would discuss its practical side. Both were speakers for the majority; the executive didn't plan for any speaker for the minority. We retain our standpoint precisely as before: we won't give a single man or a single penny to this system. Unfortunately, a significant section of the radical comrades at the Party Congress underwent a change, which we regret. In 1909, Wurm and Kautsky were still of our opinion. The majority of the parliamentary group's support for the property tax§ will incentivize the military to keep on demanding new direct and indirect taxes. The touchstone in important questions of this kind is always the principles of our party program and our efforts to achieve

---

Niederbarnim electoral district, not yet voted on, to be more important. However, after Congress adopted the party executive's resolution, the Niederbarnim motion was declared to have been already dealt with.

* A large majority adopted the resolution. In so doing, Congress positioned itself behind the declaration already made by the SPD in the Reichstag on budget limits and condoned the parliamentary group's approval of both property tax laws.

† Gustav Bauer, vice chairman of the General Commission of the Trade Unions, took the podium directly after Luxemburg. He disputed that Luxemburg had in fact given an analysis of the conditions of the political mass strike and stated that all discussions of the political mass strike would discredit him. "If we continue with our tactics up until now, work on building up the organization and push back the enemy step-by-step, the point in time will come at which the fulfilment of our wishes will become inevitable."

‡ In his closing words, Scheidemann characterized the mass strike debate as poorly timed, polemicized against Luxemburg's positions, and pleaded for the retention of the well-worn tactics of the last forty years. "We want to hold our fire for now, so in that moment in which things become serious, we are able to do that which we consider right and necessary."

§ In March 1913, the government introduced an army and spending bill [*Militär- und Deckungsvorlage*] into the Reichstag that was to enable a significant expansion in the size of the army. The Social Democratic Party opposed the bill but was divided on approving the financial support for the army's expansion as it was partially funded by a new wealth tax. The revisionist wing of the party supported the finance measures and gained a majority of the Social Democratic Party caucus, as a result of which the party's Reichstag members approved the so-called "Defense Contribution."

our final goal. In this matter Belgium* and Holland† were actually our best teachers. In the future, the ruling class will always separate the regular plans to cover general Reichstag spending [*Deckungsvorlage*] from the military budget: those same rulers will win a bourgeois majority for the military budget, while our comrades help cover the Reichstag's spending budget through supporting property taxes. We must respond to this fatal error that the majority in our parliamentary group are making, and to the Wurm resolution, by subjecting it to a fresh and vibrant critique. A new field of work has presented itself; if we stir the masses, then success is inevitable. Seen from this perspective, we're satisfied with the Jena Party Congress. (Lively applause.)

* On April 14, 1913, a political mass strike for universal suffrage began which had been carefully planned by a special committee working in the whole country since June 1912—planned in an organizational, financial and ideological sense. About 450,000 workers took part in the strike. On April 24, 1913, the party conference of the Belgian Workers' Party decided to break off the strike, after the Belgian parliament had decided in favor of a commission to consider the reform of the voting law.

† Demonstrations for suffrage reform for the election campaign had taken place on June 2, 1913, in the Netherlands; the Social Democratic Workers' Party (SDAP) had originally planned these as a one-day general strike action. Around 8,000 people participated in marches in Amsterdam, 5,000 in Rotterdam, 2,500 in Leeuwarden, 2,000 in Arnheim and 1,500 in Groningen; on June 5, 1913, several thousand people participated in evening events in Utrecht and other cities. There were, however, no signs of work stoppages. See *Vorwärts* (Berlin), June 5–20, 1913.

1914

Can the Mass Strike Be Considered a Means of Defense for the Proletariat in a Changed Political Constellation?*

The thought of the political strike, *the strike against state power*, lives in the head and heart of all socialist workers. The political strike will be influenced by the development of society and social power relations. Will the future bring us gradual, peaceful growth into democracy and socialism? I don't think so. Everywhere we see the opposite: increasing reaction and intensification of the class struggle. Now, after all this, the working class has no other means than the strike. They say this weapon is dangerous to us. But that does not mean it is also fatal for us. I will not downplay the risk. The more rights the workers have won, the more they have to lose, the more cautious they will be in using this means. But the danger does not lie solely in the political character of the strike. The danger of coming into conflict with state power and its means of violence lies in every large or widespread strike that deeply affects economic life, even those for higher wages, etc. (Agreement.) Every large strike by miners, transport workers, etc., brings confusion into social life and gives the state cause to intervene. But none of these giant strikes has crushed the organizations or the state's power. None ended with the complete victory of the workers. The success was mostly partial and indirect. The giant miners' strikes† usually ended in immediate defeat, but as a further consequence, they realized important social reforms through their pressure. The mass strikes in other countries teach us the same lesson. The Swedish mass strike‡ formally ended with a compromise, but it basically fended off a general attack of the business coalition on the Swedish unions. The Austrian demonstration strikes resulted in winning the right to vote. The mass strikes of the farm workers, with their formal partial inconclusiveness, have strengthened organization among the farm workers in Italy. And I do not need to say a word about the success of the last mass strikes

---

* This speech was given January 14, 1914, in the Social Democratic parliamentary group. It is translated by Jacob Blumenfeld from Luxemburg's *Gesammelte Werke* Vol. 7, pp. 806–9.

† In the spring of 1912, millions of miners in several European countries went on strike for higher wages and better working and living conditions. The struggle took on greater proportions in England and Germany, where one million and 250,000 workers respectively were involved. In some cases, police and military forces were deployed but they did not succeed in breaking through the frontline. In England, the government was forced to compromise and within an unusually short time passed a minimum wage law for miners; in the Ruhr district in Germany, however, the strike ended in defeat, as the union leaders broke off the strike against the will of the miners.

‡ In Sweden, by resolution of the Social Democratic Party, a mass political strike was carried out from May 15 to 17, 1902, to add pressure to the demand for electoral reform. The strike, in which 116,000 workers took part, was broken off after the parliament urged the government to introduce a new suffrage bill by 1904.

in Belgium. All mass strikes, whether economic or political, demonstration or combat strikes, have upheld what we can call Bebel's testament. The achievements of the political strike are incalculable, their value changes according to the degree of proletarian class consciousness. A political strike carried out with strength and solidarity is never lost because it is what it aims at—a proletarian show of force in which the combatants steel their strength and sense of responsibility and the ruling classes become aware of the strength of the adversary. But if every mass strike until now, without exception, has brought neither total victory nor defeat of the proletariat, but, on the contrary, almost always a strengthening of workers' organizations, class consciousness and sense of power, then the question arises: How can that great and final mass strike ever come about in Germany if the mass of the proletariat is not first prepared, trained and roused by a long period of mass strikes, of economic and political mass struggles? But how can the Prussian state employees, the railroad workers, postal workers, etc., who today are frozen in blind obedience, the farm workers who have no right to organize, the broad strata of workers who are still stuck in opposing organizations, in Christian, Hirsch-Duncker, or yellow unions,* and the mass of the German proletariat, who are neither open to union organization nor Social Democratic agitation, suddenly be ready for a final mass strike, for a life-and-death struggle? Surely this would include a preceding period of stormy mass struggles, demonstration strikes, huge economic struggles, etc., so that they may gradually be freed from their rigidity, their blind obedience, their fragmentation, and join the ranks of Social Democracy.

The suffrage and demonstration movements are an excellent opportunity for rousing and enlightening the indifferent masses, for winning over opposed working class circles, as regular agitation is not remotely able to do. (Agreement.) It is extremely short-sighted to separate the question of the Prussian electoral reform from the question of the Reichstag voting law. For the Prussian suffrage struggle, we are told, our fiercest means should not be used; we want to save them in case the right to organize or the right to vote in the Reichstag is robbed. Surely, we must finally understand that in the present situation, the struggle for Prussian electoral reform is basically nothing other than the struggle for the right to vote in the Reichstag. It is clear that a strong and victorious campaign for Prussian suffrage is the surest way to parry a blow against Reichstag suffrage in advance. A real mass action on a grand scale can only be sustained if it is treated not as a dry exercise following the baton of the party leadership, but as a great class struggle in which all major economic conflicts are utilized, all moments that arouse the masses channeled into the maelstrom of the movement, not avoiding the increasing escalation of the situation and

* In 1913, the Christian trade unions had over 340,000 members in 4,915 local groups; the Hirsh-Duncker trade unions had 106,618 members in 2,153 local groups.

decisive battles but meeting them with resolute and consistent tactics. I conclude with Kautsky's words:* Happy are those who are called to share in this sublime struggle and glorious victory (Loud applause.)†

---

* See Karl Kautsky, *The Road to Power*, trans. A. M. Simons (Chicago: Block, 1909), p. 127.

† The discussion on Rosa Luxemburg's speech was scheduled for the following session on the same day. After fierce debate Bernstein proposed entrusting a fifteen-member commission with the further examination of the question of the mass strike. The motion was approved by 52 votes to 37 with 11 abstentions. The following members were selected: Ledebour, Hoch, Bernstein, Peus, Vogtherr, Keil, Büchner, Zubeil, R. Fischer, Noske, David, Schumann, Spiegel, Haberland, Rühle.

On the Prussian Suffrage Struggle*

The declaration by the minister of the interior in the Prussian House of Representatives that the government would not even dream of a voting bill once again presents our party with a serious choice.† The outright no, which has now been directly countered by the masses' commanding call for abolishing the three-class franchise disgrace, is a brash provocation, a gauntlet thrown down to the working class, and at the same time an official, definitive confirmation that the universal right to vote in Prussia can only be won from the streets and in the streets alone. Parliamentary action along these lines has long since gone bankrupt, which could not be otherwise given the betrayal of bourgeois liberalism. The government's current position shows that not even sham fights are to be expected in the parliamentary sphere concerning the electoral law, that the masses are no longer even allowed the slightest illusions, as if they could expect a turn of events from any side but themselves, under their own determined action.

Official declarations like Loebell's are political acts that demand an appropriate response. A party of millions, which has proclaimed innumerable times that the abolition of the Prussian three-class franchise system is one of its most important and urgent political tasks, a goal to which all forces and the utmost measures must be devoted, such a party cannot silently accept a challenge like this. In the proletarian class struggle, as in any political struggle, blow for blow is the best tactic, which of course does not mean a senseless blow into the air, but the most fitting and effective "blow," in each case, as an answer. After all, in the present situation, even a further wait-and-see silence, as we had already seen for four years with the Prussian electoral law, would be definitely preferable to a new endeavor with half measures that breaks off after a few attempts and is then given up.

Of course, serious mass action cannot be provoked as simply and easily as the shrill call for the mass strike that suddenly resounded in our Leipzig newspaper.‡ It sounds very firm when, as in the Leipzig article, one rejects all assemblies, even street demonstrations and discussions about the mass strike, and then calls directly for a mass strike in Prussia. It is time, however, for those in our ranks to learn that mass strikes are not "made," they are not suddenly

---

* This article first appeared in *Sozialdemokratische Korrespondenz* (Social Democratic Correspondence) (Berlin), No. 58, May 23, 1914. It is translated by Jacob Blumenfeld from Luxemburg's *Gesammelte Werke,* Vol. 3, pp. 452–5.

† On May 18, 1914, the Prussian minister of the interior, Friedrich Wilhelm von Loebell, provocatively stated in the Prussian House of Representatives that the government did not intend to increase the influence of the masses and democratize the right to vote.

‡ See "Out with the Political Mass Strike in Prussia!" *Leipziger Volkszeitung*, No. 113, May 19, 1914.

staged one fine morning by orders of the party leadership, following their baton, like a military parade. Even in countries where the political mass strike has already become a trusted, tried and true weapon, such as Italy or Russia, the call for a mass strike can only be issued by the party in each individual case with a prospect of success if the masses have already been brought to a high degree of agitation and combativeness by some political event or the economic situation. In Germany, however, where until now the masses have been raised by party and trade union discipline mainly to wait, and trained only in parliamentary election actions, and where the Prussian suffrage movement in particular has been at a standstill for years, the fighting spirit and the passionate élan that are absolutely necessary for a first serious mass strike movement cannot be artificially conjured up overnight by the party leadership. Large mass movements have their psychology and their laws that serious leaders must reckon with.

But precisely this psychology also suggests that, today, it would be more harmful than useful to once again take a few timid steps in the Prussian electoral campaign only to stop halfway and return to business as usual as soon as possible. The Berlin party leadership has issued the call for mass protest assemblies against the declarations of the Prussian minister, and it is true that, in the present situation, mass assemblies throughout Prussia seem to be the first step to spur the masses to activity. But these assemblies would only have real purpose and significance if they were conceived as the *beginning* and not the *end* of the action, if the momentum, the rallying cries, the whole tone of these assemblies were consciously designed from the outset to initiate further, larger actions that would increase with the mood of the masses. At the same time, the call for an energetic militant action should be carried into the dues-paying nights, into the local meetings, the *workshops* and *factories*, and thrown to the masses seriously and emphatically at *every* opportunity. One can never promise with certainty in advance specific actions in the name of the masses for a specific case. But what a party of our size is definitely obliged to do, once it begins an action, is to do its utmost to bring the masses onto the scene and unleash their combativeness. However, the difficulties of this task in the present situation should not be underestimated. After the fierce battle cries that our party has already announced several times in the Prussian suffrage campaign, especially after the mass movement was called off in 1910 halfway through its course while it was in full swing, it might not be so easy now to get the masses back on their feet again and make them believe that we are deadly serious this time about the threat of a rousing popular movement against the three-class parliament.

In any case, we may call on the masses to protest *only* if we ourselves are deadly serious about it, only if we are prepared, as far as possible, to advance the masses to the utmost consequences. If, however, protest gatherings are to remain only a weak sham action, then it is decidedly better to refrain from them. The authority of the party with the masses as well as with the opponents suffers more when we create the misleading impression of our own indecision through half actions and paper resolutions than if we continue to wait and see. The events, the challenging position of the reaction, and the threat to the right to organize are forcibly driving the masses in Prussia to sooner or later lose their patience, and, at the first opportunity—with or without the initiative of the party—to kick up a holy thunderstorm in response to the present reactionary misconduct. For a party historically called upon to lead large masses of the people, it is of course seldom advisable to allow the elementary movements of the masses to overtake it. But at least it is better to wait for the inevitable thunderstorm, as we have done up to now, than to discourage the masses by weak half measures and thus weaken their fighting spirit instead of enhancing it.

Once Again the Prussian Suffrage Struggle*

The Berlin protest assemblies on May 26 set the ball rolling in the Prussian suffrage struggle. The Berlin workers, for their part, gave a worthy response to Loebell's challenge by kicking off the struggle throughout Prussia in seventeen brilliantly attended assemblies in the best fighting mood. In some electoral districts, they expressed their conviction in sharply pointed resolutions that the May 26 assemblies can only be the first step in a renewed struggle for Prussian suffrage, which, naturally, must grow until it reaches the only effective and highest display of power by the proletarian masses in the political mass strike. And in exactly the same sense, the central organ, *Vorwärts*, called out in its appeal to those Berlin assemblies: "*The second stage of the suffrage movement begins! Form the storm columns for the suffrage struggle!*"† Both the party's central organ, which, of course, must be in touch with the leading authorities on such important matters, as well as the Berlin working class, who are just as naturally called to lead the Prussian suffrage struggle, have unequivocally appealed to the entire party in Prussia to enter the fight across the board. This action by the central organ and the Berlin leadership has placed a serious duty before the entire party. Clearly, an organization of our size and importance cannot lightly throw threats and battle cries into the world without taking appropriate action. Clearly, a party of 4 million people cannot officially declare that "the second stage of the suffrage movement begins" without lifting a finger to realize this announced "second stage."

We would make fools of ourselves to friend and foe and seriously jeopardize the prospects of the Prussian suffrage struggle for the long term if we were to arouse false suspicions in the masses, as if there was no serious will to act behind our slogans, as if we were capable, like the liberals, of pairing roaring overtures with pitiful failures of militancy. And finally, let us not forget that the eyes of the entire International are fixed on German Social Democracy. The Berlin protest rallies and the refreshing battle cry of *Vorwärts* have found the most joyful echo abroad. Thus Comrade Bracke wrote in the Parisian *Humanité* on May 31 at the end of a detailed article about the nascent "second stage of the suffrage movement": "From now on, German Social Democracy will resume the struggle for equal voting rights. At several party congresses, they decided to tirelessly lead the struggle, and, if it does not work in Parliament, then to conquer the right to vote in the streets. They also declared that, if necessary, the weapon of the mass strike would be used in this struggle … The meetings

* This article first appeared in *Sozialdemokratische Korrespondenz* (Social Democratic Correspondence) (Berlin), No. 64, June 6, 1914. It is translated by Jacob Blumenfeld from Luxemburg's *Gesammelte Werke*, Vol. 3, pp. 456–58.

† "Volkstrutz gegen Junkertrutz" (*Volkstrutz* against *Junkertrutz*), *Vorwärts* (Berlin), No. 139, May 14, 1914.

are now underway, the party press is doing its part, the leaflets are being distributed. The German working class can be relied upon to carry the fight to the end. They are not fighting for themselves alone, but for the proletariat of the whole world." The Prussian struggle is being followed just as seriously and attentively in the rest of the world.

In the meantime, the Prussian party headquarters seem to be somewhat hesitant about taking the necessary initiative for action throughout the country. The usual underestimation of the masses' fighting spirit may play a large role in this. In ordinary times, it is always a more or less difficult decision for the responsible organs of a large mass party to give the first call for major actions without having the certainty that the call will be followed by actions worthy of its scale and force. But a mass party can never have such complete certainty in advance, and it certainly cannot be won if the leading organs are immobilized by reservations. Anyone who experienced the unforgettable demonstration movement of 1910 in Prussia could hear from the leading authorities, in all parts of the country without exception, that they never dared to expect the magnitude and impact of those actions. The actual fighting mood and discipline of the masses at that time had far exceeded all calculations of the leading comrades. And we will often have the same experience, provided, of course, that the party itself does not approach the matter hesitantly and unsteadily, without enthusiasm and faith, provided, in particular, that we do not mislead the masses by announcing actions that we do not follow up on at all.

The times in which we live carry so many provocations each day to arouse the masses that it would be a miracle if the masses, with proper, consistent, and persistent agitation, did not muster up the required fighting spirit. After all, what matters is not an artificially puffed-up action, not a one-time decision brought about by force, but to give expression to the exasperation and indignation stored up in the masses for all kinds of causes, to deliver the necessary answer to the brazen challenge of the Prussian Junkers, and—to take the party's own words seriously. Whether and to what extent the mood of the masses will allow the action to unfold in each individual stage of the movement cannot be determined with certainty in advance and even less ordered from above with the baton. But what can be foreseen with deadly certainty is that no mood and no action at all will be achieved in the foreseeable future if the party, after a timid half step, continues to do nothing at all following the strong trumpet blast of the beginning "second stage" and the forming of "storm columns," if the press, the voting associations, and the local organs of the party do not do what is necessary to rouse the masses.

It is the direct duty of a fighting party like ours to trigger the masses' maximum capacity for action at every moment. And if the initiative is lacking from the center, then, in a true democratic party like ours, the initiative must come from below, from the provinces.

The Establishment of a Mass Strike Fund*

Explanation of the resolution of the Greater Berlin Social Democratic General Assembly of June 14, 1914†

It is to be expected that the significant advance made by the collection of a mass strike fund will be greeted with jubilation by the broadest sections of the enlightened workers in Germany, as a clear and tangible sign that the will to act in the party is not an empty phrase, that we are moving from the phase of threats to the phase of fulfilment.‡

The "struggle fund" should be understood only in this sense. Under no circumstances should we, by collecting funds for the future mass strike, give the workers the impression that the money now collected is the actual preparation

---

* This article first appeared in *Volksstimme* (Chemnitz), No. 138, June 19, 1914. It is translated by Jacob Blumenfeld from Luxemburg's *Gesammelte Werke*, Vol. 7, pp. 880–1.

† According to *Volksstimme* (Chemnitz), Rosa Luxemburg is the author. The *Schwäbische Tagwacht* (Stuttgart), No. 137, June 17, 1914, reported only what was said about the suffrage struggle: "Comrade *Luxemburg* regretted that in 1910, when the suffrage struggle was in full swing, when we had well-attended meetings and brilliant street demonstrations in ever-increasing numbers, it was broken off by a sign from above. Now the second stage of the suffrage struggle is announced with the strongest words from different sides. But if nothing really happens, the discouragement of the masses will spread even further. Of course, if one is not determined to carry the movement to its final consequences, if it is rather to be expected that the movement will be crushed again at a certain level, then it is better to do nothing at all. It is extraordinarily dangerous to let loose blaring battle cries that are not meant seriously." In particular, the representative of the trade unions spoke against her proposed resolution. For the June 14, 1914, speech at the Third General Assembly of the Federation of Social Democratic Electoral Associations of Berlin and Surroundings, and the resolution based on the report from *Vorwärts* (Berlin), No. 160 June 15, 1914, see Luxemburg's *Gesammelte Werke*, Vol. 3, pp. 464ff.

‡ On June 19, 1914, a state secretary of the Imperial Justice Office sent a letter to the Reich Chancellor commenting on the mass strike meetings of the Social Democrats in connection with changes in the criminal code. Among other things the letter said: "Whoever calls for a mass strike and expects—which will regularly be the case—that his call will lead to a breach of contract in more or less numerous cases, is liable to prosecution under §110 [...] If the mass strike, as is the case here, is to serve political purposes, the penal provision against high treason is also applicable. According to §82 No. 2, anyone who shall try to violently change the constitution of a federal state is guilty of high treason. The right to vote for parliament is part of the constitution. Any act preparing a violent change in the right to vote is therefore punishable under §86 with imprisonment in a correctional house or penitentiary for one to three years, in mitigating circumstances with imprisonment for six months to three years. In preparing the new Criminal Code, the question of combating the mass strike through criminal law was the subject of extensive discussion. The Criminal Law Commission has approved [...] a new regulation criminalizing ceasing work in breach of contract and passive resistance in a number of companies important for supplying the general public (§271, §272). In order to combat the mass strike, it is also important that, following the decisions of the commission, §110 of the Criminal Code has been expanded to include not only the call to break a contract but also the mere incentive to do so (§210)."

for the act of struggle, one whose success depends on the amount of money collected, whose beginning is tied to a certain minimum of that amount. The only example among the countless political mass strikes abroad in which the collection of funds was made a condition of action was the last Belgian suffrage strike, which, in terms of its political effect, achieved far less than the earlier Belgian strikes and many others that were carried out with no collected funds. *The effectiveness of mass action does not primarily depend on the size of the fighter's wallet*, but on the boldness and consistency of the political tactics that accompany and guide the mass strike. We also saw from the fate of the May Day celebrations how the question of support can become a fatal obstacle to the action itself. All the more reason for clearly and sharply impressing upon the workers as we collect funds for the mass strike that the focus of preparation is not in the coffers, but in the willingness of the masses to make any sacrifices for the struggle, including hunger. The real "struggle fund" of every great historical movement is *not ready money, but the idealism of the masses and the forward-looking, consistent policies of their leaders.**

* The editors of *Volksstimme* (Chemnitz) added an epilogue to the explanation, stating that Luxemburg would certainly be right, but that the earnings of a collection also testify to how far the masses are really willing to "at least make a financial sacrifice for now." Moreover, the practical importance of the purse should not be underestimated. In the police files of June 24, 1914, there is a note that, at the suggestion of the Party's Executive Committee, the "mass strike fund" should be renamed a "suffrage fund" in order to prevent "any possible intervention by the authorities." "As is well known, the party executive does not at all agree with the establishment of a mass strike fund, but nothing would stand in the way of establishing a 'suffrage fund' that involves not only Greater Berlin but all Prussia."

1915

What's with Liebknecht?*

> 3. The core of the proletariat's organization as a class lies in the International…
> 4. The duty to execute the resolutions of the International takes precedence over all other organizational duties.
>
> (Principles)†

Workers! Party comrades! The saber dictatorship is about to take down its most implacable enemy. The military "trial" against Karl Liebknecht is imminent.

This trial is a brazen comedy. It takes place behind closed doors. The defense is utterly restricted. As "judges," the key chair is held by high military officers, i.e., the very representatives of the same saber rule against which Liebknecht undauntedly fought.

The summit of the infamy is the indictment. It reads: attempted war treason in the field! Although Liebknecht was not in the field on May 1, but in Berlin at Potsdamer Platz, he is to be persuaded that he joined the May Day demonstration "in the field." Although he was in Berlin as a member of the Reichstag, as an elected representative of the people, he is to be tried as a soldier. Although he demonstrated on May 1 as a flag-bearer of international socialism, to rally the popular masses in all countries to fight against the massacre of the people, he is accused of committing "war treason" against the German army.

It is clear that the government and its henchmen are planning a judicial murder of Karl Liebknecht! The hated champion of socialism, the indomitable defender of the working class, is to be assassinated by his mortal enemies; removed from the public stage, the troublemaker is to disappear into oblivion!

And this tidy plan is prepared by all clever means. The military justice system, which otherwise works swiftly as a guillotine, is so strangely slow this time that the splendid indictment was only finished five weeks after Liebknecht's arrest. Why? Because they wanted to get rid of the Reichstag and the Landtag first!‡ As doggedly as the two chambers behaved, the henchmen of the saber dictatorship feared that this monstrous indictment and this bloody farce of a trial would find a certain echo in the tribunes of the Reichstag or the Landtag, and the people may get agitated as a result.

---

* This article initially appeared as an illegal leaflet of the Spartacus group in June 1916. It is translated by Jacob Blumenfeld from Luxemburg's *Gesammelte Werke,* Vol. 4 (Berlin: Dietz Verlag, 2000 [Sixth Edition]), pp. 194–7.

† These are taken from the "guiding principles" that follow twelve theses in the "Draft Junius-Theses," consisting of amendments made by Karl Liebknecht to the Gruppe Internationale conference on January 1, 1916. The complete text may be found in Luxemburg's *Gesammelte Werke,* Vol. 4, pp. 43–7.

‡ On June 8, 1916, the Reichstag was adjourned by imperial decree until September 25, and, on June 20, the Landtag was adjourned until November 14, 1916.

Even better! On June 9, the mouthpiece of the German government, Wolff's Telegraphic Bureau, spread the news that Liebknecht had been charged under Section §89 of the Criminal Code.*

This was a deliberate lie. The government shamelessly lied to the public! Section §89 of the Criminal Code identifies imprisonment as the minimum penalty. The charge against Liebknecht, however, comes under §57 of the Military Criminal Code, and this paragraph dictates a minimum sentence of ten years in jail!†

Only in the best-case scenario can a quarter of this sentence, i.e., two and a half years in jail, be given. Liebknecht will thus be sentenced to prison in any case, and since it involves the stripping of all civil rights, it also includes the loss of his parliamentary mandate!

This is the purpose of the whole judicial comedy! The counterfeiting trick of Wolff's Telegraphic Bureau is supposed to mask this prepared hoax, to lull public opinion at home and abroad to sleep so that the unforeseen hoax is met with complete silence!

But now the crowning of the sham! Two weeks ago in Braunschweig, a delegation of the General Command from Hannover, headed by a captain, made the following remarks in the "Nutrition Committee":

> The General Command was aware that the Braunschweig workers were in a ferment, that the excitement was growing. If we do not prevent it, the general strike will break out and spread like a fuse to Hanover, Magdeburg, Leipzig, Berlin, and other cities. And then the war would be over! This disaster must be prevented! For this purpose, mass food banks are to be set up in Braunschweig to appease the workers. If the city authorities fail at this, then the General Command itself will intervene. The people must be reassured at all costs!

This is how they want to butter up the workers, to throw them a bone, like a dog, so that the judicial murder of Karl Liebknecht can be carried out unhindered.

Workers, party comrades, and you, women of the people! Will you let

---

* Paragraph 89 of the Reich Criminal Code reads: "A German who intentionally aids an enemy power during a war that has broken out against the German Reich, or who causes disadvantage to the military power of the German Reich or its allies, shall be punished for treason by imprisonment in a correctional house for up to ten years or in a penitentiary for equal duration. If there are mitigating circumstances, imprisonment for up to ten years is possible. In addition to imprisonment, the loss of public office and the loss of rights resulting from public elections can be recognized."

† Paragraph 57 of the Military Criminal Code reads: "Anyone who commits treason in the field shall be punished for war treason with imprisonment for not less than ten years or with life imprisonment."

yourselves be caught by this infamous trick? Will you tolerate the assassination of your most loyal leader?

Liebknecht fought for all of us. He sacrificed himself for the proletariat, for international socialism. He has shown that, also in Germany, one stands for one's socialist convictions with the whole person. Liebknecht is always ready to give the last drop of blood for the liberation of the working class. Will you now calmly leave him to the vengeance of the capitalists, the Junkers, the Krupp clan, the military camarilla?

Workers! Liebknecht's cause is your cause. In Liebknecht they want to strike you, assassinate you, silence you, so that the massacre of the people continues unhindered. In Liebknecht, the revolt of the German proletariat against the crime of war is to be crushed. Will you tolerate this?

No and a thousand times no!

The tidy plan of judicial murder behind the scenes, in the quiet closet, should be shamed. Raise your voice! Show that behind Liebknecht stand hundreds of thousands, millions, who feel and think like him. Let the henchmen try to sentence Liebknecht to prison! Let them dare! The verdict will arouse such an echo in the empire and in the trenches that the war makers won't know what hit them!

From millions of throats shall Liebknecht's cry ring in their ears:

Down with the war! Down with the government!

1916

Liebknecht*

The unbelievable has happened: the government has dared to make the shameful sentence against Liebknecht even more severe and to add alongside imprisonment the stripping of his political rights, i.e., the loss of his parliamentary mandate! Revenge is sweet, especially when so easy, when the enemy is tied hand and foot and the duel is disguised in the comedy of a "trial" behind closed doors. For it is clear: the awful verdict is not "punishment" for Liebknecht's participation in the May Day demonstration alone, it is retribution for his entire appearance in the Reichstag and Landtag, where he was the only one to tear the mask off the face of the bloody farce of the civil truce in front of the whole world; retribution also for his attitude in the detention cell and in the courtroom, where the man in chains defied his henchmen, morally chastised them and stood firm and unshakable as an oak to the revolutionary faith, to international socialism.

Yet the authorities would never have dared to pass such a disgraceful sentence if they had not been accustomed to German Social Democrats kowtowing to them since the outbreak of the war. Because they regarded the Social Democrats as the government's protection force and henchmen for the last two years, they pounced with seething fury upon anyone who remained upright.

For what did Liebknecht do? He only did what the resolutions of the international congresses, what the program, the Party Congress decisions, the principles, and the traditions obligate all socialists to do. Liebknecht acted in the spirit and sense of these principles, these resolutions. If what he did was "treason," then all the German delegates at the congresses and party conventions who voted for those resolutions, the entire party, which subsequently recognized those resolutions as binding, made themselves liable to prosecution for preparing, inciting, and instigating treason. And yet the state prosecutors did not dare dream of bothering the Social Democrats for their resolutions. Until August 4, 1914, friend and foe alike took it for granted that Social Democracy would resist the war with all its might, and relentlessly oppose its continuation. Today, Liebknecht is sent to prison for fulfilling this self-evident duty. Why? Only because official Social Democracy has abandoned the revolutionary class struggle, because it has transformed itself from a party of international proletarian class struggle into a party of government, a footstool of imperialist class rule.

Liebknecht's prison sentence is thus a mark of Cain on the forehead of the

---

* This unsigned article first appeared in *Spartacus*, No. 1, September 20, 1916, and was later published in *Spartakusbriefe* (Spartacus Letters), Berlin, 1958, pp. 217–20, where Rosa Luxemburg is named as the author. It is translated by Jacob Blumenfeld from Luxemburg's *Gesammelte Werke* Vol. 4, pp. 215–8.

official German Social Democracy, a seal of their betrayal of the duties of international socialism and the historical tasks of the proletariat.

As a victim of the bankruptcy of Social Democracy during wartime, Liebknecht in his personal fate embodies the fate of the German proletariat as a class, and he takes that with him to his prison cell. Liebknecht's "treason" consists in *fighting* for peace. But the whole further fate of German and international socialism depends on whether the proletariat will understand how to *fight* for and dictate peace.

With the outbreak of the World War, socialism dropped out as a factor of history. The war thus brought with it a tremendous strengthening of capitalist class rule, political and social reaction, and militarism. What will happen *after* the war, what conditions and what role awaits the working class depends entirely on the manner in which peace is achieved. If it only comes through the eventual exhaustion of the military powers on all sides, or even—which would be the worst—by the military victory of one of the warring parties, in short, without the intervention of the proletariat, with complete tranquility within the state, then such a peace means only the sealing of the world-historical defeat of socialism in war. The most radical party congress and congress resolutions cannot later replace what was lacking in deeds and actions at the right time. Then imperialism will remain the absolute master of the situation even after the war, and Social Democracy will no longer count as a powerful factor in social life, either in peace or in war.

After the bankruptcy of August 4, 1914, the second decisive test for the historic vocation of the working class is thus whether it will understand how to *end* the war, the outbreak of which it did not prevent—not to welcome peace from the hands of the imperialist bourgeoisie as the deed of cabinet diplomacy, but to force it on the bourgeoisie, to fight for it.

Yet fighting for peace does not mean trying to persuade Bethmann-Hollweg in the Reichstag that he has the duty to enter into peace negotiations with Grey. Fighting for peace does not mean signing submissive petitions to the government. Fighting for peace also does not mean applauding in police-approved assemblies and raising hands for peace resolutions, only to quietly continue preparing ammunition for the war with one's own hands the next day, enabling "perseverance" and patiently enduring the military dictatorship on an empty stomach.

Fighting for peace means ruthlessly using all the weapons of the working class to stop the continuation of massacres in the country as well as in the field. It means, like Liebknecht, not running away from any sacrifice or danger, so as to break the civil truce and stop the saber dictatorship.

Only when such a determined mass struggle puts an end to the war can peace lead to a powerful new upswing of socialism and to the rebirth of the International as a living power.

And only the same determined mass struggle for peace can free Liebknecht from his cell.

When the English people rose up in the seventeenth century to fight for political freedom, their first step was to liberate the martyrs of freedom. The dark gates of the Tower of London opened, and the people cheered their champions through the streets, sprinkling rosemary at their feet.

In Paris, when the bells of the great revolution rang, putting an end to the feudal Middle Ages in Europe, the first gesture of the popular masses was—storming the Bastille. Parisian women tore down with their own hands the hated stronghold where French absolutism let the heroes of liberty languish.

In Russia, too, in 1905, when the popular masses celebrated their first triumph over tsarist absolutism and the war with Japan, they immediately rushed to the gates of the prisons, and under their commanding onslaught, the dungeons spewed out their longtime victims.

Liebknecht, too, can be freed from his prison by the masses of the German proletariat only when they have regained their duty, their honor, and thus their true power.

Liebknecht's henchmen know very well the love that hundreds of thousands in the country and in the trenches have for him. The military dictatorship wanted to show just this to the workers and soldiers: "We do not respect your pain and your anger, we can offer you everything, but you will not dare anything for Liebknecht's liberation, you are and remain cannon fodder!" Now it is up to the proletarians in work overalls and soldiers' uniforms to give the answer.

When the High Court of Justice announced the harsher sentence on July 23, Liebknecht shouted with his head held high: "And yet I repeat: Down with the war! Down with the government!"

Liebknecht's chains will fall when German Social Democracy wipes from their foreheads the mark of Cain for betraying international socialism, when millions of women and men in the country and in the trenches find the courage to call out as fearlessly as Liebknecht:

Down with the war!
Down with the government!

1917

The Russian Revolution*

To write about the Russian Revolution is somewhat difficult, given the uncertainty and confusion of the news that has reached foreign countries about it so far. It is particularly difficult for a weekly paper containing positions that may have to be qualified, or even refuted, based on new reports arriving daily.

There are, however, some aspects that can be established today, without fearing that they will appear irrelevant tomorrow. These aspects are essential to the historical nature of this revolution. Questions as to where the tsar and tsarina are currently to be found, and which member of the tsar's family deigns to do a deal with the revolution—or not, as the case may be—and more queries of that kind may be very interesting for philistines, but they are no matter for politicians, especially since, at this particular moment, it is evident that the Russian Revolution is definitely not aiming for the jugular of tsardom as such.

According to its historical nature, this revolution is a revolt of the bourgeoisie against tsarism's inability to successfully battle its way through a world war. It is commonly understood that the Russian bourgeoisie passionately longed for this world war and fueled it: the depiction of the Russian war as a penetration of thieving barbaric hordes into western European culture, based on long-lost ways of speaking from years back, counts as one of the most infuriating con-tricks pulled by the German-Government Socialists. Just before the outbreak of war, Professor [Paul von] Mitrofanov, a respected historian, educated at German universities, and, on a personal level, certainly a Germanophile, elucidated in a very convincing manner how "property and education" in Russia—that is, the Russian bourgeoisie—were dying for a war with Germany. He went on to explain how the bourgeoisie, with that desire, were encountering resistance wherever they stretched out their capitalist tentacles.†

Against this background, we must see that the attempt to greet the Russian Revolution as a herald of peace is utterly invalid. Quite the opposite: the current wielders of power in Russia want to conduct the war with doubled energy and, they hope, with doubled successes. Indeed, some signs seem to indicate that their worry about the tsar potentially signing sign a separate peace with Germany might indicate that such fears are more than bad nerves in the impetuous course of events. This would also explain why part of the aristocracy,

* This article was first published in *Der Kampf* (The Fight) (Duisburg), No. 42, March 24, 1917, and signed with the symbol ♂, which Luxemburg had earlier used (in 1898) for some of her journalistic articles. See *Gesammelte Werke*, Vol. 6, pp. 129. The article is translated by Henry Holland and Manuela Kölke from Luxemburg's *Gesammelte Werke*, Vol. 7, pp. 1024–6.

† See Paul von Mitrofanov's "Offener Brief über das Verhältnis von Rußland und Deutschland vom 12. April 1914" (Open Letter on the Relationship between Russia and Germany), in *Preußische Jahrbücher* (Prussian Yearbook), ed. Hans Delbrück, April–June 1914, Vol. 156, pp. 386ff.

and in particular, a section of the armed forces, has joined the Russian Revolution.

Thus this revolution confirms Lassalle's famous words: it is impossible to make the bourgeoisie truly excited about the ideals of liberty, equality and fraternity, but when it comes to defending their capitalist interests, they're ready to fight tooth and nail.* We could even give the Russian bourgeoisie proportionate praise for the fact that they are able to draw on greater strength for their noble altars than many others are who live farther west. But ultimately, the bourgeoisie always remains the bourgeoisie, and they are unable to make a revolution without leaning on the masses of the people who have been steeled into being a revolutionary force by the exacting school of misery and hunger. This is how it was in France in 1789, in France and in Germany in 1848—and this is how it still is in Russia in 1917.

Which is why the words of the Roman poet† are applicable to every victorious revolution: behind the horseman, however gloriously he returns from battle, sits black Care. Enough is known about how the bourgeoisie managed to rid themselves of this care in 1789 and 1848. The very day after victory, the warriors who had fought for victory with their blood and their muscles were paid off with the vilest ingratitude! And there's not the least reason to doubt that the Russian bourgeoisie will keep to this same, trusted method. Although its program does contain a series of relatively far-reaching demands, it must be noted that these are political and not social in nature. And the Prussian example of 1848 has taught us what can result from the convocation of an elected National Assembly, voted for by means of general, equal, secret, and direct suffrage—an assembly that is intended to discuss the empire's new constitution. The workers of Berlin had fought to win this very same "success" in 1848, but, barely a year later, the "three-class" voting system had arrived, which we are still stuck with today.

Will the Russian workers let themselves be duped once again? For German workers, this is the decisive and principal question of the Russian Revolution that will decide everything. We're not scared of this question, but rather trust confidently that they have learned from the painful experiences of their class and are unwilling to hand over the fruits of the victory, which they have won through their fight, to the bourgeoisie—whatever tough, drawn-out battles it might cost to secure these fruits for themselves. Only then will our [Ferdinand] Freiligrath's prophecy be fulfilled, which, in the present honeymoon of the Russian Revolution, only seems like tangible irony:

---

* See Luxemburg's writings "Lassalle und die Revolution" (Lassalle and the Revolution) in *Gesammelte Werke*, Vol. 1, p. 417ff. and "Lassalles Erbschaft" (Lassalle's Inheritance) in *Gesammelte Werke*, Vol. 3, p. 220.

† Luxemburg is referring to the line by Horace: "Behind the horseman sits black Care." (*Odes*, 3.1.40)

Look here, each western nation!
One people still can feel
Rebellion's bold salvation
In its gauntlet-grasp of steel!
In dim far eastern regions—
Outpost of freedom's legions—
The tides of battle swell,
Whose waves, their reflux taking,
And every fetter breaking,
Shall make you free as well!*

* Ferdinand Freiligrath, from "Ungarn 1848" (Hungary 1848), translation in *Poems: From the German,* ed. Kate Freiligrath-Kroeker, trans. Ernest Jones (Leipzig: Tauchnitz, 1871), pp. 224–6.

The Revolution in Russia*

Although postponed for several years, war could not prevent what was palpably approaching before its outbreak—the resurgence of the revolution. After 1911, the Russian proletariat had overcome the leaden weight of the counterrevolutionary period, and year after year unfurled the revolutionary banner of 1905 through economic and political mass strikes and protests, but then was thrown into chaos by the imperialist war for two and a half years, repressed by the saber dictatorship and disoriented by nationalism. It rose again to shake off the yoke of absolutism and force the Russian bourgeoisie to rapidly march forward.

If, today, the revolution in Russia has so swiftly triumphed in just a few days, it is solely and exclusively due to its historic significance as the continuation of the great revolution of 1905 to 1907. The counterrevolution could only put it down for a short period of time, but the unfinished work of the revolution demanded a definitive solution, and the inexhaustible class power of the Russian proletariat flared up just now under the most difficult circumstances. It was the fresh memories of the years 1905/1906, of the partial, unrestricted political rule of the proletariat in Russia, of its bold advances, its extreme revolutionary program, which today has led the Russian bourgeoisie to decide so rapidly to get ahead of the movement. It was fear of the unrestrained unfolding of the people's revolution, as it had shown its Medusa head to the bourgeois ruling class in the years 1905–07, that immediately made the [Mikhail] Rodziankos, [Pavel] Milyukovs, and [Alexander] Guchkovs† side with the revolution and, for their part, advocate for a decidedly liberal program. This is an attempt by the propertied Russian bourgeoisie, grown wise over the course of ten years, to seize hold of the people's movement and carry out its political tasks in bourgeois-liberal fashion in order to eliminate its openly democratic and social tendencies.

Here—despite all the know-it-alls, prudent cautionary councils, and skeptical pessimists—it becomes clear that the work of the 1905 revolution has not been lost, that the sacrifices it cost at that time were not made in vain, and that the bold revolutionary character of the demands advocated by the socialist workers represented a very "practical" policy. The present courage and energy

---

* This article first appeared in *Spartacus*, No. 4, April 1917. It is translated by Manuela Kölke from Luxemburg's *Gesammelte Werke*, Vol. 4, pp. 242–5.

† M. V. Rodzianko was the chairman of the Provisional Committee of the Duma formed on February 27, 1917. He acknowledged the revolution but was anxious to halt further revolutionary development and to restore the previous order. Pavel N. Milyukov was a leader of the liberal Cadet Party (constitutional democrats), A. I. Guchkov was a member of the moderate reformist Octobrist group of constitutional monarchists.

of the Russian liberal bourgeoisie are nothing but a faint reflection of the conflagrations of 1905 to 1907. The same unfolding of the power of the proletariat, which previously had thrown [the liberal bourgeoisie] into the arms of counterrevolution after just a short period of time, immediately pushed them to the front of the movement this time, precisely to prevent repetition of the previous developments.

Thus the revolution in Russia has today defeated bureaucratic absolutism at the first attempt. However, this victory is not the end, but only a weak beginning. For, on the one hand, the retrograde movement of the bourgeoisie from its present ostensible position of confident liberalism must sooner or later, with inevitable logic, given its general reactionary character, culminate in its class opposition to the proletariat. On the other hand, the once-awakened revolutionary energy of the Russian proletariat must, with equally inevitable historical logic, regain the path of radical democratic and social action and resume the program of 1905: a democratic republic, the eight-hour day, expropriation of large estates, etc. Above all, however, for the socialist proletariat in Russia this is the most urgent slogan that is inextricably linked to all the others: end the imperialist war!

Here the program of the Russian revolutionary proletariat is transformed in the sharpest contrast to the Russian imperialist bourgeoisie, which is enthused about Constantinople and makes a profit from the war. Action for peace can only be developed in one form in Russia and elsewhere: as revolutionary class struggle against one's own bourgeoisie, as a struggle for political power in the state.

These are the irrefutable perspectives of the further development of the Russian revolution. Far from having finished its work, it has only made a brief prologue that will be followed by the most powerful class struggles for peace and the radical program of the proletariat.

The great historical drama on the Neva River does not lack its cute satyr play on the Spree. If memory does not deceive us, the slogan on August 4, 1914, was the liberation of Russia from tsarist despotism. This was supposedly the noble aim of the mass slaughter, and for the sake of this "old program of Marx and Engels," the men of the Social Democratic faction decided to support the war.

And now—where is the rejoicing about the achieved goal of German warfare? Where is the triumph in the government press: "We've achieved it, hooray!"? The German "liberators" look at the work of the Russian Revolution like drowned rats. They can't even put a decent façade, a good face, on this terrible story. The comedy of the first months of the war, the farce staged by and *for* German Social Democracy for the purpose of giving the masses the runaround, is already forgotten to such an extent that the actors do not even try to conceal their bad mood by bringing out the dusty masks.

The pallid fear of Russia strengthening itself through an inner restoration, the scornful comparison between a Russia that freed itself through revolution and an "independent Poland" liberated by "German fists," and, most of all, the fear that the unfortunate Russian example might spoil the good manners of the German proletariat, show themselves like an involuntary twitch that is evident everywhere. In Mosse's newspaper, a luminary of German liberalism is quite naively trying to provide comforting and soothing proof that the splendid "liberation of Russia," which was the noble goal of the war, will nevertheless be shattered by internal difficulties and anarchy.*

But the German proletariat is also faced with a question of honor and a question of fate by the events in Russia.

As long as the silence of the graveyard and blind obedience prevail in all the belligerent countries, the collapse of the proletariat results from the failure of international solidarity, a common global disaster that is, albeit unevenly, distributed to all parts. However, as soon as the proletariat in Russia denounced the "truce" [*Burgfrieden*] through open revolution, it was stabbed in the back by the German proletariat that is quietly continuing to support the war. Now the German troops in the East are no longer fighting against "tsarism," but the revolution. And while the Russian proletariat picks up the struggle for peace at home—this has surely already begun and will increase with each passing day—the persistence of the German proletariat in its attitude of obedient cannon fodder turns into an open betrayal of their Russian brothers.

"The first shot fell in Russia." Russia freed itself. Who would free *Germany* from the saber dictatorship, East Elbian† reaction, and imperialist slaughter?

---

* A reference to Rudolf Mosse's liberal newspaper *Berliner Tageblatt*.

† *Ostelbien* or East Elbia refers to the German territories to the east of the Elbe river, especially the Prussian lands of Brandenburg, Pomerania, and Silesia, which had been shaped by a long history of conservatism, serfdom, and Protestantism.

Russian Problems*

Now that the image of the Russian Revolution and its work has become clear and distinct, despite all the obscuring and mystifying efforts of the self-interested bourgeois rapporteurs, some of the main features of the mighty events can be highlighted and grasped from the tangled mass of details.

At this moment, Russia once again confirms the old historical lesson: there is nothing more improbable, impossible, and fantastic than a revolution the hour before it breaks out, and there is nothing simpler, more natural, and self-evident than a revolution after it has fought its first battle and won its first victory. As diligently as the German press has been reporting on civil unrest, crises, and fermentation in the tsarist empire for years, the German public, like the whole world, is visibly breathless at this moment before the sudden, mighty spectacle of the Russian Revolution. A thousand reasons could have been given against its possibility a week before its outbreak. The people were oppressed by the terrible war, misery, and suffering. The bourgeois classes were forever cured of their dream of freedom by the memories of the revolution ten years ago, and, above all, were chained to tsarism by imperialist plans for conquest. The broad circles of the working class were demoralized by the nationalist fury triggered by the war, its best socialist core group decimated by the bloodletting of combat, crushed by the saber dictatorship and left without organization, without a press, without leaders. As two times two is four, so it could be proven, down to the last detail, that in Russia today desperate outbursts and anarchy were plausible, whereas a modern, purposeful, ideal-oriented political revolution was naturally unthinkable. And now? All lies, words, chatter! The revolution has legitimized itself in the only way that every necessary movement legitimates itself in history: through struggle and victory.

Two aspects of the Russian events are most surprising to the European public: their rapid triumph and the radicalism they showed from the very first moment. The Provisional Government, consisting entirely of lame bourgeois elements, has already declared itself in favor of the democratic republic! But these two aspects can only be astonishing to the superficial glance of the philistine, who never notices the deeper historical connections between today and yesterday. Those, however, who keep in mind that the revolution of March 1917 is a continuation of the revolution of 1905 to 1907, only interrupted by the counterrevolution and then the World War, cannot be surprised either by its rapid victory or its resolute action. Now it simply emerges from the lap of Russian society as the ripe fruit of the troubles, struggles, and sacrifices of the

* This article appeared first in *Der Kampf* (The Fight) (Duisburg), No. 44, April 7, 1917, under Luxemburg's pseudonym "Gracchus." It is translated by Manuela Kölke from Luxemburg's *Gesammelte Werke*, Vol. 4, pp. 255–7.

last ten years, and is comforting proof that not a drop of blood shed by our Russian brothers over the past decade for the cause of freedom, and not a day of anguish in dungeons and prisons endured by so many Russian comrades, had been sacrificed in vain. The freedom they now enjoy, they have amply earned and paid for.

The striking radicalism of the Russian liberals, who have suddenly developed their republican program from the most wishy-washy constitutionalism, as well as the violent shift to the left of the Russian national liberals and even the conservatives, is in itself a surprise only to the philistine, for whom the slogans, programs, and outward show of parliamentary life count as eternal truths. The historically educated, on the other hand, can only smile and see in this a mere repetition of the experiences of the English, the French, and the March [1848] revolutions: namely that in stormy times, the attitude of all classes and parties depends on the power and attitude of the most radical, that is the working class. The more boldly it sets its goals, and the more readily it puts all its power behind these goals, the further to the left the whole bourgeois phalanx follows it.

Sure enough, the Russian workers have no organizations, no voter associations, virtually no trade unions, no press. But they have what is decisive for their power and influence: fresh fighting spirit, determined will, and boundless readiness to make sacrifices for the ideals of socialism. They have those qualities without which the most beautiful organizational apparatus is just worthless rubbish and a dead weight at the feet of the proletarian masses. Admittedly, without organization, the working class cannot be actionable for long. We are therefore as sure as if we saw it with our own eyes that, at this moment, in Petersburg, Moscow, and in all of Russia, the workers are feverishly engaged in creating those organizations, political associations, trade unions, educational institutes, newspapers, the whole apparatus. As was the case ten years ago, the first gesture of the revolutionary Russian proletariat will be to make up for all the shortcomings of its organization in the shortest possible time. And such an organization, born out of struggle and steeled in its fire, will surely prove to be a true armor of power, not a straitjacket of powerlessness.

The Russian proletariat has clearly marked out its course in the present situation. Strong and radical, each of its political and social demands, like the work of the revolution as a whole, must above all advance the slogan "End the war!" The Russian workers must naturally marry the achievement of peace with the whole of their actions, even prioritize it, and they certainly are already doing so now. In this way, however, they will enter into the first great conflict with their own bourgeoisie, a sharp class struggle against the enemy in their own country.

It remains to be seen whether the Russian proletariat, which is sure to spare no sacrifice, will bleed, and perhaps bleed to death, alone in this struggle for the cause of peace, which is at the same time the cause of international socialism.

The Old Mole*

The outbreak of the Russian Revolution has broken the stalemate in the historical situation that had arisen with the continuation of the World War and the simultaneous failure of the proletarian class struggle. In a Europe filled with the air of decay stifling everyone for almost three years, a window has suddenly been opened, and a fresh, invigorating gust of air blows in, to which everything turns, breathing a deep sigh of relief. In particular, the "German liberators" are anxiously watching the spectacle of the Russian Revolution. Both the whimpering tributes of the German and Austro-Hungarian governments for the "parasites and conspirators," and the nervous tension with which every utterance by [Nikolai] Chkheidze† and the workers' and soldiers' council is received concerning the question of war and peace, now palpably confirm the truth of what only yesterday was unthinkingly dismissed by the socialists from the *Arbeitsgemeinschaft*.‡ This was namely the fact that no diplomatic "agreements" and no messages from Wilson but solely and exclusively the revolutionary action of the proletariat offers the way out of the deadlock of world war. The victors of Tannenberg and Warsaw§ are now trembling, looking to the Russian proletarians, the "mob in the street," for their "liberation" from the choking noose of war!

Of course, even with the greatest heroism, the proletariat of one single country cannot loosen this noose. The Russian Revolution is itself growing into an international problem. The Russian workers, with their aspirations for peace, come into the harshest conflict not only with their own bourgeoisie, which they already know how to tame, but also with the English, French, and Italian bourgeoisie. The rumblings of the bourgeois press in all the Entente countries—of the *Times*, *Matin*, *Corriere della Sera*—show that the capitalists of the West, these brave campaigners for "democracy" and the rights of "small nations," are watching with gnashing teeth and hourly mounting rage the advances made by the progress of the proletarian revolution that has put an end to the glorious era of undivided imperialist rule in Europe. These capitalists

---

* This article first appeared in *Spartacus*, No. 5, May 1917. The article is not signed. It was republished in *Spartakus im Kriege. Die Illegalen Flugblätter des Spartakusbundes im Kriege* (Spartakus in War. The Illegal Pamphlets of the Spartakusbund), edited and introduced by Ernst Meyer (Berlin: Kommunistische Partei Deutschlands, 1927), which names Luxemburg as the author. It is translated by Manuela Kölke from Luxemburg's *Gesammelte Werke*, Vol. 4, pp. 258–64.

† Nikolai S. Chkeidze, leader of the Mensheviks in the Russian State Duma and chairman of the Petrograd Soviet after the outbreak of the February Revolution in Russia.

‡ *Arbeitsgemeinschaft* (working group) was the initial name of the center-left and antiwar opposition within the SPD that soon became the USPD.

§ In the battle of Tannenberg, August 23–31, 1914, German troops decisively defeated the Russian army; they occupied Warsaw on August 5 during the summer offensive of the Central Powers in 1915.

of the Entente now provide the strongest support for the Russian bourgeoisie, against whom the Russian proletariat revolts in its struggle for peace. They can exert the greatest pressure on Russia in every way—diplomatically, financially, commercially—and they surely do so already. A liberal revolution? Provisional government of the bourgeoisie? Beautiful! They would immediately be officially recognized and welcomed as guarantors of Russia's military fitness, and obedient instruments of international imperialism. But not one step further! If the Russian revolution were to show its proletarian core—and turn logically against war and imperialism—then its dearest allies would immediately bare their teeth and attempt to curb it by any means necessary. This now imposes on the socialist proletariat of England, France, and Italy the indispensable duty of raising the banner of revolt against that war. Only by means of emphatic mass actions at home against their own ruling classes can they avoid openly betraying the revolutionary Russian proletariat and stop it from bleeding to death in an unequal struggle against not only the Russian bourgeoisie but also the Western bourgeoisie. The interference of the Entente powers with the internal affairs of the Russian Revolution that has already taken place demands, as a matter of honor, that the workers of these countries protect the Russian Revolution by attacking the flank of their own ruling classes in order to compel them to make peace.

But now the German bourgeoisie! With a sour smile and a bitterly weeping eye, they observe the actions and the growing power of the Russian proletariat. Lulled by their customary view of the working masses at home as mere military and political cannon fodder, they might well prefer to utilize the Russian proletariat to get themselves out of the war as soon as possible. German imperialism in distress, which is currently in deep trouble in the West as well as in Asia Minor, and at its wits end due to famine at home, would like to extricate itself from the affair as quickly as possible and with some semblance of decorum in order to quietly patch itself up and arm itself for further wars. They imagine that the Russian Revolution will serve this end by means of its proletarian-socialist tendency for peace. It is in the same spirit of speculation that imperialism hopes to do business with the help of the Russian Revolution, just as it did with the Entente powers, though now from the opposite side. The Western powers want to put the bourgeois-liberal tendency of the revolution in front of the chariot of imperialism in order to continue the war until the defeat of its German rival. German imperialism would like to avail itself of the proletarian tendency of the revolution in order to escape the imminent threat of military defeat. Well, why not, ladies and gentlemen? German Social Democracy had served so well in passing off your unrestrained mass slaughter [*Völkermord*]* as an "act of liberation" against Russian tsarism. Now Russian

---

* "Völkermord" literally means the mass killing or slaughter of entire peoples. Its contemporary English translation often connotes genocide—the intentional destruction of an ethnic,

Social Democracy is supposed to help free the trapped "liberators" from the thorny situation of the war gone wrong. The German workers helped to wage war when it suited imperialism, while the Russian workers are supposed to make peace for the same reason.

Meanwhile, it is not quite as easy to deal with Chkheidze as with little Scheidemann. With a hasty "rally" of the "*Norddeutsche Allgemeine*"* and a speedy dispatch of little Scheidemann to "negotiations"† in Stockholm, one can expect at best to get a kick from the Russian socialists of all stripes. As a poorly "rigged" separate peace negotiated with Russia only in passing—which the German "liberators" would like since it is a burning issue for them—the matter is definitely not going to be arranged. For the Russian proletariat to see its peaceful tendency succeed, it must acquire an increasingly decisive position in the country as a whole, so that its class action grows to gigantic proportions in scope, momentum, diligence, and radicalism so that Social Democracy can sweep along with or cast aside all the remaining undecided classes duped by bourgeois nationalism. With barely concealed horror, the German "liberators" now find themselves face to face with this clearly visible and inevitable, but also repellent, flip side of the peace tendency in Russia. They fear—and with good reason—that the Russian Moor,‡ unlike his German counterpart, will not want

---

national, racial, or religious group. This sense of the term did not exist in Luxemburg's time. *Genocide* was first coined by Raphael Lemkin in 1944, combining the Greek word γένος (genos, "race, people") with the Latin suffix *caedo* ("act of killing"), and officially defined by the United Nations Genocide Convention in 1948 as any of five "acts committed with intent to destroy, in whole or in part, a national, ethnic, racial or religious group, as such." These five acts were: killing members of the group, causing them serious bodily or mental harm, imposing living conditions intended to destroy the group, preventing births, and forcibly transferring children out of the group.

* *Norddeutsche Allgemeine Zeitung* was a newspaper commonly viewed as a mouthpiece for the German government.

† A Dutch-Scandinavian Committee of the International Socialist Office invited all the socialist workers' parties and organizations of the belligerent countries to Stockholm for a conference in May 1917 "to examine the international situation." While the parties of the Entente countries declined, the SPD in June (with the endorsement and active support of German government agencies) sent a delegation including, among others, the party chairman Friedrich Ebert, Hermann Müller and Scheidemann. The Petrograd Soviet of the Workers' and Soldiers' Deputies, who had also been invited, did not take up the proposal of the Dutch-Scandinavian committee. It instead invited socialists of all countries who were against the war and for a democratic peace without annexations and contributions to a conference in Stockholm in July 1917. After discussions between the Russian representatives and the Dutch-Scandinavian committee, which had had to postpone its conference, a decision was made to organize a joint so-called peace conference. The Zimmerwald left, especially the Bolsheviks and the Spartacus group, protested against a conference with the participation of right Social Democrats, and the International Socialist Commission, as an organ of the Zimmerwald movement, rejected the signing of the invitation call. As the English and French governments refused to allow the delegates from their countries to leave for Stockholm, the conference did not take place.

‡ *Moor* was a term initially used by Europeans to refer to the Muslim inhabitants of Spain and the Maghreb in North Africa, and was often used in a derogatory manner in Luxemburg's time to justify discrimination against Muslims and people of color. This was not universally the case—Marx, for instance, was affectionately called by his family and close friends "the Moor" due

to "leave" after having done his work, and they fear the sparks that could fly from neighboring fires to the barns east of the Elbe. They may have realized that only the unfolding of the utmost revolutionary energy in a comprehensive class struggle for the political power in Russia is capable of effectively carrying forward the struggle for peace. But at the same time, they long for the good old days of tsarism, for the "century-old faithful friendship with the Eastern neighbor," Romanov absolutism. *Tua res agitur!* Your interests are at stake! This warning cry from a Prussian minister against the Russian Revolution endures in the soul of the German ruling classes, and the heroes of the Königsberg trial are all still "as glorious as on the first day."* To have a republic, namely one that is freshly built and controlled by the revolutionary socialist proletariat, existing right on its flank—that is really more than the police and military state east of the Elbe can be expected to handle. And on top of that, this East Elbian police spirit is obliged to confess their secret aversion right out in the open. The German "liberators" today must publicly swear with their raised hand that they do *not* intend to strangle the revolution and put the dear snub-nosed Nikolai back on the tsarist throne! The Russian revolution forced the German "liberators" before the whole world to give themselves this resounding slap in the face that suddenly wiped from the slate of history the completely infamous lie that the German Social Democracy and the official mythology of German militarism had lived on for three years. In the same way, the storm of a revolution has a cleansing, antiseptic effect: eliminating all lies, it suddenly sweeps away with a merciless broom all the dung heaps of official hypocrisy that have been accumulating in Europe since the outbreak of the World War and the silencing of the class struggle. The Russian Revolution tore away the mask of "democracy" from the face of the Entente bourgeoisie, and from German militarism it tore away the mask of the liberator from tsarist despotism.

Nevertheless, the question of peace is not quite as simple for the Russian proletarian as would suit the beliefs of Hindenburg and Bethmann. The victory of the revolution as well as its further tasks for the future requires more secure backing. The outbreak of the revolution and the commanding position of the proletariat immediately reduced the imperialist war in Russia to what, according to the mendacious phrase of the ruling classes, it allegedly is in all countries: a national defense. The beautiful dreams of Constantinople and "democratic-national" plans for reallocation of people to different areas [*Umteilungspläne*], which were to make the world so much happier, were immediately shoved back down the throats of Milyukov and associates by the masses of workers and

---

to his swarthy appearance. Luxemburg is using the term here to illustrate the German bourgeoisie's condescending view of the Russian proletariat as mere servants or slaves to their ends.

* In July 1904, nine German Social Democrats were put on trial in Königsberg for subversion against tsarist Russia, insulting the tsar, and conspiracy for transporting revolutionary literature into Russia. Karl Liebknecht was one of the defense lawyers.

soldiers, and the slogan of national defense was put into practice. However, the Russian proletarians can end the war and make peace with a clear conscience only if their work—the achievements of the revolution and their continued unhindered progress—has been secured! *They*, the Russian proletarians, are today the only ones who *really* must defend the cause of freedom, progress, and democracy. And these things must be secured today not only against the harassment, pressure, and warfare of the Entente bourgeoisie but tomorrow, above all—against the "fists" of the German "liberators." A semi-absolutist police and military state is not a good neighbor for a young republic shaken by internal struggles, and an imperialist soldiery bound in blind obedience is not a good neighbor for a revolutionary proletariat which is readying itself for the most intrepid class struggles of unforeseeable scope and duration.

The German occupation of the unfortunate "independent Poland" is already a heavy blow against the Russian Revolution. The operational basis of the revolution is indeed compromised when a country that was always one of the most blazing hearths of the revolutionary movement, that, in 1905, politically marched at the head of the Russian Revolution, is now completely neutralized, socially transformed into a graveyard, and politically transformed into a German barrack. Who can now guarantee that tomorrow, when peace has been concluded and once German militarism has pried itself loose from the burden of war and sharpened its claws, it will not strike at the flank of the Russian proletariat in order to prevent German semi-absolutism from being dangerously shaken?

The wretched "assurances" of yesterday's heroes of the Königsberg trial do not suffice to reassure us. The example of the Paris Commune is still too fresh in our memories. After all, the cat cannot leave the mouse alone. The World War has unleashed such an orgy of reaction in Germany, revealed such a degree of military omnipotence, stripped away the façade of the greatness of the German working class, and revealed the foundations of so-called "political freedom" in Germany to be so void and brittle that its prospects from this point of view have become a tragic and serious problem. The "danger of German militarism" to imperialist England or France is, of course, humbug, war mythology, competitive clamor. The danger of German militarism to revolutionary republican Russia, on the other hand, is a very real fact. The Russian proletariat would be very careless politicians if they failed to ask themselves whether the German cannon fodder that allows imperialism to lead it to the slaughterhouse on every battlefield today would not tomorrow obey the command to fight against the Russian Revolution. Scheidemann, Heilmann, and Lensch will already have procured a "Marxist" theory for it, and Legien and Schlicke will surely prepare a treaty for this slave trade, all in keeping with the patriotic tradition of the German princes who sold the children of their country as cannon fodder abroad.

There is only one serious guarantee against these genuine concerns for the future of the Russian Revolution: the awakening of the German proletariat, a position of power for the *German* "workers and soldiers" in their own country, and a revolutionary action for peace by the *German* people. Concluding peace with Bethmann and Hindenburg is a damned difficult venture and an ambiguous suggestion for the Russian revolutionary soldiers. Peace with the German "workers and soldiers" would be concluded immediately and would rest on a solid foundation.

Thus the question of peace is, in reality, dependent upon the most unhindered, most radical unfolding of the Russian Revolution. The latter, however, is in turn bound up with the revolutionary parallel action for peace on the part of the French, the English, the Italian, and, especially, the German proletariat.

Will the international proletariat shift the responsibility for the struggle against the European bourgeoisie onto the Russian workers alone, thereby surrendering it to the imperialist fury of the English, French and Italian bourgeoisies and the lurking and threatening reaction of the German bourgeoisie? This is how the question of peace should really be formulated at the moment.

The conflict between the international bourgeoisie and the Russian proletariat thus reveals the dilemma of the last phase of the global situation: either world war to the point of being bled white, or proletarian revolution—imperialism or socialism.

And here we are again confronted by our old betrayed slogan of socialist revolution, which we have repeated a thousand times in our propaganda, and which we failed to put into practice just when, at the outbreak of the World War, it was supposed to come alive. Then again, it appeared logical to every thinking socialist as the long and hopeless mass slaughter dragged on. It once again emerged tangibly in the negative form as the result of the wretched fiasco of attempted diplomatic understanding and bourgeois pacifism. Today, it again stands before us in a positive light; it has come to life in the work, the destinies and the future of the Russian Revolution. Despite the betrayal, despite the general failure of the working masses, despite the disintegration of the Socialist International, the great historical law is making headway: like a mountain stream that had been diverted from its course and plunged into the depths, it comes to light again as a clear wellspring in an unexpected place.

History, old mole, you worked well! At this very moment, the slogan, the warning cry, such as can be raised only in a great period of global change, resounds through the International, through the German proletariat: Imperialism or socialism! War or *revolution*! There is no third way!

Two Easter Messages*

The grandiose world-historical drama on the Neva River does not lack its grotesquely cheerful sideshow on the Spree. Under the impact of the Russian Revolution, Prussian Germany begins to "modernize" itself. And what kind of "reorientation" is brought to light here? A residue of the Jesuit Law† and the famous language clause of the Law on Association‡ are abolished! One is a legacy from the blessed times of Bismarck's Exceptional Laws of 1872 and the other from the beautiful times of the Bülowian "Hottentot" bloc.§ That's the way Germany today tidies up with pride! Yes, and let's not forget, the Imperial Easter message¶ has also promised that after the war, God willing—and if the German people continue to behave—it will even bestow some kind of plural suffrage** to the Prussian House of Representatives and "reform" the Prussian House of Lords! Keep your nose on your face, said Uncle Bräsig.†† *These* are the reforms to which Germany has already bestirred itself in the aftermath of the Russian events. Now, are we not appropriately rewarded for the roughly 2 million human lives that were consumed in the mass slaughter, for the misery and hunger of the masses, for the terrible tax burden that looms in the future, for the state of siege, and for the saber dictatorship, patiently endured for three years? Do not the German people conduct their business best when they obediently dance to the tune of the ruling classes and keep their mouths shut? Only a rogue doesn't get this by now.

---

* This article first appeared in *Spartacus*, No. 5, May 1917. This article is not signed. The editors of the *Gesammelte Werke* attribute the article to Luxemburg on the advice of the veteran and founding member of the German Communist Party, Rudolf Lindau. It is translated by Manuela Kölke from Luxemburg's *Gesammelte Werke*, Vol. 4, pp. 265–9.

† The Law of Exception, adopted in June 1872 by the Reichstag, forbade the activities of the Jesuit Order and related orders and congregations in the domain of the German Reich. The so-called Jesuit Law was abolished on April 13, 1917, by the Federal Council (Bundesrat).

‡ By the resolution of the Federal Council (Bundesrat) of April 19, 1917, Paragraph 12 of the Law of Association (Reichsvereingesetz) of 1908—which prohibited the use of non-German languages in public meetings—was repealed.

§ After the Reichstag elections of 1907 (the so-called "Hottentot Elections," named for their link with the German war in South-West Africa) the conservatives, the national liberals, and the left liberals joined together to form the Bülow bloc. Based on this bloc, Reichskanzler Bernhard von Bülow was able to implement a series of reactionary laws and measures in the Reichstag. "Hottentot" was a derogatory description used by Europeans at the time to refer to the Khoekhoe people of southern Africa.

¶ In a decree of April 7, 1917, Wilhelm II had announced a reform of Prussian suffrage for the postwar period and some other constitutional changes in an attempt to appease growing mass discontent.

** Plural suffrage is an undemocratic system in which voters with higher income, higher education, or other special conditions can cast more than one vote.

†† Literal translation of: "*Daß du die Nas' ins Gesicht behältst*"—a Low German idiom calling on someone who is utterly surprised, flustered and agitated to pull themselves together; coined by Fritz Reuter (1810–74) in his novel *Ut mine Stromtid* by his character Inspector Bräsig.

All joking aside, nothing so abruptly and glaringly illustrates the frightening, rigid reaction to which Germany had sunk in the light of the Russian fire as these grotesque attempts at "reform." Who wouldn't be reminded of some old auntie, who, upon hearing news of a comet's impending collision with the earth, rushes to fetch her oldest shawls out of a chest in order to knock out the moths? Today all make pilgrimages to Russia, that "Cossack land" of yesteryear, like the three holy kings of the Orient toward Bethlehem and the cradle of the savior; meanwhile Germany—the land of "constitutional freedoms"—uncovers its East Elbian compost heap, stirs it a little and appears in its infernal stench like a scarecrow from the Middle Ages. Such heaving of the political tectonics will bring about revolutionary eruptions within twenty-four hours!

Yet the German proletariat, too, is still quite bewildered and thinks that the revolution taking place in Russia is just a pleasant and edifying spectacle in its own neighborhood. It doesn't understand that this is *its own cause*, the cause of the one and indivisible international proletariat, which is here making the first attempt at world-historical confrontation with the class rule of capital. Those "leaders" of the German proletariat, who to their misfortune have grown up—or more correctly, regressed—within the school of the old German Social Democracy understand this even less. The working group* has responded to the Russian Revolution by establishing a completely new "action program,"† meaning thereby a long list of terribly radical proposals that it intends to present to *the Reichstag*. So much to be found in there! Nearly the entire party program is copied, ready to be tabled before the delegates of the Reichstag. One really does not know what to say to this tragicomic geriatric "revitalization" [*Johannistrieb*]. *That* is what's most important in this hour: to submit motions to the Reichstag?! To *this* Reichstag of an imperialist Guard of Mameluks!‡ And precisely *now*, when a world finally wants to make it clear to the German masses that they can expect *nothing* from parliamentarianism, but everything

---

* That is, the center-left faction of the SPD (which included Kautsky), the Sozialdemokratische Arbeitsgemeinschaft, which several weeks earlier had become the Unabhängige Sozialdemokratische Partei Deutschlands (Independent Social-Democratic Party of Germany), or USPD.

† On March 29, 1917, the Social Democratic working group presented to the Reichstag an action program in which it demanded, among other things, the speedy conclusion of a peace without annexations, suffrage reform, the right of the Reichstag to vote on war and peace, the dismissal of the Reichskanzler on the decision of the Reichstag, and the abrogation of exemptions. The conclusion of a peace and the abrogation of the exemptions were rejected by the Reichstag on March 30, 1917. The other proposals were passed to a constitutional committee.

‡ The German phrase "imperialistische Mamelukengarde" specifically refers to the Mameluks of the Imperial Guard (French: Mamelouks de la Garde Impériale), a cavalry unit that served in Napoleon I's Imperial Guard during the Napoleonic Wars. Originally made up of Mameluks, an Arab class of slave soldiers, the unit eventually was mostly recruited from an ethnically diverse mixture of mostly Turkic, Caucasian, eastern European and southeastern European soldiers. The literal translation of Mamelukes, Mamluks and Mamelouks is "those who are owned," meaning "enslaved people."

only from their own initiative, energy, and capacity for action; *now*, when Russia palpably shows to even the blindest what "action program" and "action" really mean—it is *now* that the working group comes before the Reichstag with a load of oh-so radical demands. And banging their heads against the wall about these motions is supposed to be an "action!"

But hold on! Maybe we are wrong. Perhaps the "action program" of the working group was not at all to be taken seriously as a parliamentary action; perhaps it was only meant as a conventional aid to remind the masses of the Social Democratic program. Perhaps it was a way of proclaiming from the rostrum of the Reichstag that nothing could be achieved there, in the Reichstag, that everything can only be achieved by the mob "in the street?" Well, we have a clear commentary on the actual view of the working group on this question, namely in the Berlin "Bulletin" (*Mitteilungs-Blatt*)* of the working group that wrote in its Easter article on April 8:

> It is an old truism that no revolutions can be artificially made. This applies to our time more than ever. It is possible to stage coups, but they are *condemned to futility in the face of the magnificently organized might of today's military state, just as significantly erupting hunger riots can be quickly repressed.* In a revolution, as in a modern war, a great number of factors must coalesce before an entire nation is struck by violent convulsions. That's why it is also wrong *to attempt to schematically transfer the revolutionary phenomena and revolutionary means of one country to another*, where the economic foundations, the political and social conditions, the historical development, and the character of the people are quite different ...
>
> *We have to reckon with circumstances different from over there in Russia; therefore, the struggle for our inner freedom must take on different forms.* This struggle has begun these days *on parliamentary grounds* under the moral impression of the events in Russia. [Emphasis R. L.]

Thus an unambiguous avowal of wisdom: in Russia, revolutions are made; in Germany, on the other hand, one "fights" in the Reichstag. Literally the very same was stated by Theodor Wolff and the ambitious lawyer W. Heine in Mosse's *Freisinnsblatt* [Free Thinker's Bulletin]!† Here we have, once again, an oh-so classical flowering of the unadulterated, unscathed, incorruptible, incorrigible parliamentary cretinism for which no beating would be too severe. Here is preached precisely the impossibility of a mass revolution in Germany, and

* *Mitteilungs-Blatt des Verbandes der sozialdemokratischen Wahlvereine Berlins und Umgegend* (Newsletter of the Organization of Social Democratic Electoral Associations in Berlin and Surrounding Area).

† German newspaper mogul Rudolf Mosse, who was allied with the liberal Free Thinkers, founded the *Berliner Tageblatt* (Berlin Daily) in 1871, and in 1891, also in Berlin, the *Volks-Zeitung* (People's Paper), which openly expressed agreement with the liberal Free Minded Association (Freisinnige Vereinigung) on domestic issues.

tasteless chatter about the "magnificently organized means of power of the modern state" is rehashed. All this, even though the Russian workers' and soldiers' council shows just how aptly these means become the means of power of the people, of the revolution, if—just if—the proletariat is revolutionary!

In Germany the working group knows how to assign a different role to the proletarian masses. Since "the power of our parliamentarians" "alone is too weak," the same article continues, they should remain "in close contact" with the masses and ensure their "participation" in the parliamentary actions of the chosen ones in the Reichstag. "Only then will our parliamentarians be able to enforce their demands for freedom." And this *Mitteilungs-Blatt* claims to have drawn this profound insight from the experiences of Russia—the same Russia in which the masses have just established the republic in *direct, self-reliant, revolutionary action*, not only against absolutism but also *against a monarchist, reactionary parliament*—the Russian Duma. They needed to thoroughly suppress the Russian Duma, and more, completely cast it aside in order "to be able to enforce the demands for freedom!" Truly—here the world presents itself quite differently compared to one as viewed by others! Therefore, in Germany, the masses are supposed at most to form only the chorus, accompanying the great deeds of the representatives of the Reichstag with a "supporting" melody. The parliamentarians still remain the people of action, *they* have to enforce the "demands for freedom," and the Mamluk-Reichstag of imperialism is called on to become the birthplace of German freedom! Thus the "action program" of the working group appears as a worthy counterpart to the Prussian-German "reforms" noted above—both of which make a mockery [*Eulenspiegeleien*] of the mighty global turning point of the Russian Revolution. But what is most interesting in the pretty avowal of this "newspaper" is its basic conception of the events in Russia.

Wholly in the spirit of bland liberalism, the leaders of the "working group" thus consider the Russian Revolution merely as a bourgeois-liberal correction of antiquated tsarism. They have no idea that it is, at the same time, a proletarian *transitional* revolution of world-historical significance, which *must* have an effect on all capitalist countries, and that, precisely as a proletarian-socialist struggle for power, it can only be carried out by revolutionary means—in Germany as much as anywhere else! And this consumptive theory of the "awesome might of the state" and the replacement of the revolution by parliamentary "struggle" is preached to the German workers at the very moment when the question of peace, as the whole future of international socialism, depends on the German working class finally getting rid of its fatal delusion that it was taught by official German Social Democracy for decades: namely, the dogma that everything that is achieved elsewhere by revolutionary means, can be achieved in Germany "on parliamentary grounds," by the chattering of the representatives of the Reichstag! Truly, the Easter message of the Berlin working group splendidly matches the Imperial Easter message concerning Prussian electoral reform: both are products of a musty, insipid political wisdom, which, in spite of world war and global upheaval, is positively proud to have learned nothing, and to have forgotten nothing.

Burning Issues of Our Time*

I. WAR AND PEACE

The Russian Revolution was the first conspicuous expression of proletarian class politics since the bankruptcy of international socialism at the outbreak of the World War, and thus the first advance for peace of world-historical significance. On the very next day, after the victory over the old regime, the Russian proletariat began to take action against the war. It was initially directed at depriving the imperialist war of its character, as it was led by the tsarist regime and the Russian bourgeoisie. Yet after some fierce struggles, the masses of Russian workers were so victorious that the Provisional Government officially recognized the formula for the aims of the war: no annexations, no reparations, a peace based on the self-determination of nations.† At first glance, proletarian politics had thus achieved a full and decisive victory. It seemed to have made way for peace and revolution. But in reality, this victory only confronted the Russian proletariat with new difficulties and problems.

The peace formula has been identified, but it is still a long way to attain peace. *How* can peace be achieved?—that is the question now. A separate peace [*Sonderfriede*], as all the socialist tendencies in Russia seem to have realized, would not be an end to the World War, but only a renewed outbreak. Every separate peace is, for that reason, not a proletarian policy, but a purely bourgeois policy, because it amounts to a one-sided national solution to the problem of war; because it disregards the fate of the European proletariat as a whole, in order to free, only one single country from the claws of war. In this case, a separate peace would be even worse: It would be an invaluable aid to German imperialism, thus to the worst enemy of the German proletariat, to the strongest bulwark of reaction in Europe and—to the most dangerous enemy of the Russian Revolution on the day after the end of the war.

But a general peace cannot be brought about by Russia alone. The Russian proletariat can suppress the resistance of its own ruling classes, but it is unable to exert decisive influence on the imperialist governments of England, France, and Italy, since, here, the decisive pressure could naturally, as in Russia itself,

* This article first appeared in *Spartacus*, No. 6, August 1917. It was not signed. It was reprinted in *Spartakus im Kriege. Die Illegalen Flugblätter des Spartakusbundes im Kriege* (Spartakus in War: The Illegal Pamphlets of the Spartakusbund), edited and introduced by Ernst Meyer (Berlin: Kommunistische Partei Deutschlands, 1927), which names Luxemburg as the author. It is translated by Manuela Kölke from Luxemburg's *Gesammelte Werke*, Vol. 4, pp. 275–90.

† On March 28, 1917, the Provisional Government, in an appeal to the citizens of Russia, declared that the object of Russia was not rule over other peoples and the conquest of foreign territories, but the right of self-determination of the nations. At the same time, however, it was emphasized that Russia would obey all the commitments undertaken by tsarism toward the imperialist states of England and France.

only come from within, from the English, French, and Italian proletariat. Thus, in reality, despite the powerful and victorious peace action of the Russian masses, neither a separate nor a general peace can be achieved in practice for now. As long as this situation persists, the war will continue, and the Russian proletariat will face the inevitable question: how to act in this war.

The officially recognized peace formula of the workers' and soldiers' council in Russia seemingly deprives the war of its character as an imperialist war of annexation—at least for Russia. It reduces it to pure national defense in the only true sense of the word, for, in this case, it is the defense of the achievements of the revolution under the sovereign guidance of the revolutionary masses. Yet political defense alone cannot be *militarily* separated from the offensive. Whoever wages war at all must, whatever the aims of the war may be, place it militarily as far as possible on the offensive, bearing in mind the old tried and tested principle of every struggle that a powerful attack has always been the best form of defense. Obviously compelled by this logic, the Russian minister of war, Kerensky, as well as the majority of workers and soldiers, decided to take the offensive.

However, all active warfare and every military offensive by the Russians at present, do not—by virtue of the objective state of affairs and its current logic—serve the defense of the Russian Revolution, but rather the interests of Entente imperialism. No peace formula, however radical and democratic it may be, can obliterate the patent fact that every military operation undertaken by Russia benefits the imperialist war aims of England, France, and Italy, that, in proclaiming to be fighting a purely defensive war, the Russian Republic actually participates in an imperialist war, and while appealing to the right of nations to self-determination as a principle, in practice it promotes the rule of imperialism over foreign nations.

But what if Russia refuses to undertake any offensive and—as in the first months after the outbreak of revolution—limits itself militarily to a passive wait-and-see attitude, merely on standby to ward off, for better or worse, any possible German attacks? With this passivity, which is, in itself, only a half measure, a way of avoiding the war and not of ending it, Russia renders invaluable services to German imperialism by allowing it to use its main forces only against the Western front, and, by having its back, so to speak, in the East. Thus the Russian Republic finds itself between Scylla and Charybdis. If, for example, it wants to pull itself out of the noose of mass slaughter through a separate peace, it betrays the international proletariat and its own fate to German imperialism. But if it is unable to enforce a general peace alone, then it has only the choice between active warfare, with which it serves the interests of the Entente imperialism, and passive warfare by means of military inactivity, with which it—as surely as death—promotes the enterprise of German imperialism.

This is the actual state of affairs of the Russian Republic—a tragic situation in which the beautiful formula of peace, which has been greeted like a redeeming magic word by all, does not change in the least. And this state of affairs necessitates that the Russian proletariat, in spite of all its heroic struggles and victories, in spite of its unfolding of power against war and imperialism, is, in fact, today condemned to remain a plaything of imperialism and any tactic it may adopt will ultimately benefit imperialism. There is simply—as paradoxical as that may sound—no right tactic to be followed by the Russian proletariat today: whichever it may choose, it will be wrong. And this has a very sound, deep-seated reason. Because of its objective causes and its historical character, the present World War is an international contest between imperialist powers, and not even the best will in the world, in any corner of the world, in any one country, by any participant, or by any stretch of the imagination, can turn it into its opposite, namely a democratic war of national defense. Caught on the wheel of the world imperialist catastrophe, the Russian Republic, for its own part, cannot evade the consequences of this catastrophe by itself; it can neither extricate itself from the wheel nor bring the wheel to a standstill by itself. The international catastrophe can only be stemmed by the international proletariat. Only a proletarian world revolution can liquidate the imperialist world war. The contradictions in which the Russian Revolution is inextricably involved are nothing but the practical manifestations of the fundamental contradiction between the revolutionary policy of the Russian proletariat and the craven policies [*Kadaverpolitik*] of the European proletariat, between the class action of the masses in Russia and the betrayal of the German, English, French working masses of their own class interests and of socialism.

Those who reassure themselves with the formation of oppositional minority groups or parties, or with equally individual advances in the parliaments, and thus behave as though the honor of international socialism has been saved, always forget that the real fate of socialism cannot be decided in conventicles and in chattering parliamentary booths, but only in large actions of the masses. As long as the masses do not move, as has been the case until now, all "independent" conventicles, together with their resolutions, conferences, and memoranda, weigh as much as chaff in the wind.

II. THE DICTATORSHIP OF THE PROLETARIAT

However, the fate of the Russian Revolution is even more fatally linked to the World War than the surface of things nowadays suggests. The overthrow of the tsarist regime, which the liberals view as the real and final subject matter of the Russian Revolution, is, of course, only its brief prologue. As the fruit of all capitalist development, the revolution does not think of stopping in its further logical progression at those achievements that the cretinism of "public opinion" in Europe, including so-called Social Democratic opinion, would like it to stop at. Its natural tendency leads to a general confrontation of the classes at the heart of Russian society, with the main role naturally falling to the most advanced and radical class, the industrial proletariat. The goal toward which this development is headed is inevitably the dictatorship of the socialist proletariat. Precisely because the struggle against imperialism and for peace became, from the first moment on, the axis of the political revolution, the standard-bearer of this struggle—the socialist working class—immediately came to the fore and has already taken control over half of the government in the coalition ministry.*

Yet the coalition ministry is, in itself, a half measure that imposes all responsibility on socialism, without remotely granting it the full opportunity to develop its program. It is a compromise that, like all compromises, is condemned to ultimate fiasco. The new coalition ministry will, by virtue of internal logical development, sooner or later have to give way to a purely socialist government, that is to say, the actual and formal dictatorship of the proletariat. But here the fate of the Russian Revolution begins. If an international proletarian revolution does not support it soon enough, the dictatorship of the proletariat in Russia is condemned to a stupefying defeat, against which the fate of the Paris Commune seems like child's play.

Most notably, the Russian Revolution reveals social and political problems that can only be solved on an international scale. The inevitable shattering of bourgeois forms of property by the imminent solution of the agrarian question, the shattering of capitalist forms of exploitation by a radical transformation of working conditions, which the Russian working class must strive for, the shattering of the bourgeois state by a truly popular rule—none of this is possible in the current European framework, in the framework of the crassest militaristic reaction, which has unrestrainedly and unrestrictedly taken over rule in all countries since the outbreak of the World War.

The more the dictatorship of the proletariat approaches Russia, the more the likelihood increases of the inevitable flight of the Russian bourgeoisie into the arms of counterrevolution. Now, the Russian bourgeoisie bears the yoke of popular rule only with deeply hidden resentment and hatred, and only as long as the war lasts, which means as long as the masses are armed and hold the fate of the country in their hands. Once the war is over, then all the Milyukovs, Rodziankos, and their associates will immediately move from the left to the far right, and there is no doubt that the two classes—the petty bourgeoisie and the peasantry—that today follow the urban proletariat will most likely stab

* The provisional government reached a crisis in April 1917, when it faced large demonstrations of workers and soldiers. A coalition government was formed in May 1917 that, in addition to representatives of the bourgeoisie, contained representatives of the Socialist Revolutionaries (SRs) and the Mensheviks.

it in its back, helped by the lumpenproletariat and all the elements cowed by the deposed tsarist regime. The readiness with which the liberal bourgeoisie accepted the dominant position of the socialists and demanded their participation in the government did not correspond merely to their predicament, but also to the calculation and the intent to burden the socialists with part of the responsibility and soon the entire responsibility for government affairs with all their insurmountable difficulties, so as to compromise socialism and summon all counterrevolutionary elements to resist it.

Finally, however, the more the dictatorship of the proletariat advances in Russia, the more the entire European bourgeoisie prepares its crusade against the Russian Republic. It is already in full swing in the Entente countries and finds expression in the mudslinging against the revolution that runs through all the bourgeois press of those countries, through the *Matin*, the *Morning Post*, the *Stampa*, the *Corriere della Sera*, reporting tall tales about murder, arson, looting, anarchy, bankruptcy, and dissolution on a daily basis. The campaign of slander, which is quite reminiscent of the behavior of the European bourgeois press toward the Paris Commune, systematically incites European public opinion against the Russian Revolution, mobilizes all bourgeois instincts, and prepares them for the crusade against Russia.

For the time being, the German and Austrian states are exceptions that react with reserved sympathy—for very transparent reasons: for them, the Russian Revolution is the most important card in the present state of war. The Central Powers regard it as a convenient object of exploitation and speculation, both because of Russia's own military inhibitions and the pressure that Russia exerts on the Entente countries with regard to peace and the reduction of the war aims. But this means that the benevolently reserved attitude of official Germany toward the revolution will continue just as long as the war lasts. As soon as the war, whatever its outcome, comes to an end—and especially in the case of a somewhat favorable outcome for Germany's position of power—the natural contrast between the Prussian-German military and police state and the Russian Republic with all its hitherto restrained violence will break through. The Central Powers have much better reasons for the war of extermination against revolutionary Russia than England, France, or Italy. Above all because Germany and Austria, the most reactionary states in Europe, have to protect the greatest inventory of the reaction against revolutionary dangers; moreover, because they are in the immediate vicinity of the center of the revolution, at the outbreak of a European revolution, Germany—as its ruling classes would instinctively realize—would become, given its leading capitalist position, the center of the international uprising.

It follows from this that the period of unhindered development of the Russian Revolution is as long as the war lasts. The duration of the war is its [the Russian Revolution's] historical period of grace, and the Russian proletariat, in fighting for a general peace, is actually fighting for the rope around its own neck. If peace is achieved as a concoction, as a result of an understanding of the capitalist governments, and not as the work of the European uprising of the proletariat, then it will enable the Russian bourgeoisie, the Entente countries, and Germany in particular to immediately collectively attack the Russian revolutionary proletariat and choke the common enemy of European "order" in rivers of blood. The Entente press already prepares the excuses, slogans, and psychological climate for this turnaround. The Stockholm Socialist International, however, which, as a negotiator of the imperialist governments, prepares a "negotiated peace" [*Verständigungsfrieden*] between them, is acting, without the slightest inkling, as the accomplice of the future Black International, which will deliver the death blow to the Russian Revolution on the day after the peace agreement.

III. STOCKHOLM

If the first precondition for the resurrection of international socialism is the reckoning in all countries with the policy of August 4 [1914] and the return to active class struggle, the Stockholm Conference with all its trappings is the surest way to prevent this. The renunciation of governmental socialism* presupposes a thorough and far-reaching process of self-criticism, the clarification and demarcation of the genuine socialist elements from the bourgeois politics pursued under a socialist guise. This process, already underway and making progress in every country, is still largely only in its initial stages and now once more completely halted by the Stockholm "deliberations." Here, the most heterogeneous elements and tendencies come together under a common slogan of peace and in joint work on its preparation. Social-imperialists of Scheidemann's orientation and the opposition of Haase-Ledebour's persuasion, warmongers and supporters of unrestricted submarine warfare by the German General Commission of the trade unions and representatives of the Russian workers' and soldiers' council, socialist ministers in bourgeois and imperialist governments à la [Thorvald] Stauning and Albert Thomas† and socialist ministers in the revolutionary committee, minority socialists of the Entente countries and majority socialists of the Central powers, speculations of the German government and elemental slogans of the Russian Revolution meet here in utter confusion in a big mess, where any clarification and differentiation is hopelessly lost [*untergeht*] in the humbug of "preparation for peace." What is actually prepared by this confusion is not peace, but mutual reconciliation between the "neutral" and "warring" socialists, mutual absolution and a general

* That is, socialists becoming members of a bourgeois government.

† Thomas was a leading French socialist who served as Minister of Armament during World War I. Stauning was a Danish socialist who was Minister Without Portfolio in the cabinet of Carl Theodor Zahle, leader of the Social Liberals.

amnesty for sins committed, and the restoration of the former International as a hotbed [*Toleranzhaus*] of socialist betrayal. The opposition of the Haase-Kautsky orientation, which here, as always, is prepared to sacrifice the lasting fundamental interests of socialism to the next opportunity, now blindly chases after the fascinating phantom of "peace" and for its sake is ready to "participate in each and every conference," to make "peace" with both the devil and Beelzebub. This opposition is well versed in verbose "caveats" and "reservations" against government socialism, which have as much meaning as the famous "reservations" of a principled character who at the same time votes for the budget or war credits. The fact that governmental socialists of all countries, that is the people who actually wage war, are admitted to a joint "peace action" transforms all this into a worthy continuation of the prostitution of socialism which has been practiced for the last three years in accordance with the war policy of August 4 [1914]. The immediate result of Stockholm's humbug, however, is a fatal new misleading of the masses, who, instead of recognizing their own revolutionary action in all countries as the only true factor of peace, again and again are fobbed off with false hopes and waiting for the idle chatter of their so-called leaders in Stockholm, and for the "memoranda," "negotiations," and "understandings" of just a few dozen tricksters who, in reality, represent nothing but the howling misery of political bankruptcy in their own countries. Thus the working masses of Europe are once again distracted from their sense of responsibility and initiative and lulled into passivity.

But that's not all. In terms of content, the Stockholm peace farce—and this is its focus—has evolved to voluntary preparatory work for the future diplomatic congress of governments. The socialist work for peace will here consist of negotiations on the future map of Europe's nations, on the question of annexations, war indemnities, and so on. Instead of discussing the tasks of the class struggle, the ways and means to bring about peace through proletarian self-activity, instead of creating a program by which the revolutionary proletariat shapes social and political conditions according to socialism, representatives of the proletariat end up doing the dirty work for the bourgeoisie. Socialists are here to prepare by the sweat of their brow the understanding between capitalist governments, in complete blindness to the fact that every "negotiated peace" of today's governments must be a peace and an agreement against the proletariat and at its expense, a trade in which its own hide is brought to market.

What helps to make the Stockholm dealings outwardly appear as socialist policy, and thus contributes most to the misleading of the masses, is the formula put forward by the Russian workers' and soldiers' council: peace without annexations and compensation on the basis of the right of a people to self-determination.

With the Russian proletariat, the emphasis is, of course, not on this formula, but on the fact that it has imposed its own peace policy on the bourgeoisie of its country in general. In Russia, the real peace factor is the revolution that has taken place and the socialist workers' position of power behind that formula of peace.

As for the magic formula that the socialists in the rest of Europe have happily taken up, it has nothing to do with socialist policy. It is the formula of a negative result of the World War, a failed, undecided test of imperialism. It is the formula of a decision postponed for later, a pause for recovery of the military powers until the next dance. In fact, this formula corresponds first and foremost to the present situation and needs of German imperialism, which has already realized that, this time, it will not be able to implement its plans for world domination and is only anxious to get out of trouble as soon as possible. The governments of the Entente, which still hope for decisive military success, do not want to know anything about this formula for the time being. Given the actual insolubility of the bloody conflict by military means, however, the formula "no annexations, no compensation" objectively corresponds to the interests of the ruling classes of all countries and leads in its positive content to the restoration of the status quo. But what does the return to the pre-war state mean? It is the restoration of the balance of power before the outbreak of the World War; that is, the restoration of the old state borders, the *old* annexations, the former colonial possessions, the former hegemony of the great military states, their former economic rule over the "spheres of interest," in short, the restoration of all the conditions created by a long chain of earlier wars and recent imperialist developments. And this status quo, together with old state borders and old external power relations, naturally includes the old internal power relations: bourgeois class rule, the capitalist state, and imperialism as an all-dominating power, as a general basis.

This is the positive content of the enchanting negative formula. The matter of course with which the socialist parties here put a formula of peace on their flags in their writing, which means nothing other than the simple preservation and reinstatement of capitalist class rule, as the creation of a *modus vivendi* for an imperialism gone wild, this matter, of course, is characteristic of the blatant conceptual confusion that has taken place in socialist circles of all countries since the outbreak of the war. In reality, the Stockholm "preparation for peace" under the slogan "no annexations, no compensations" is a direct continuation of the policy of August 4, that is, the abdication of the proletariat as a class with its own politics and action, its continuation as a tool of the ruling classes and imperialism.

Admittedly, this slogan is wrapped up by the Russians in a very radical and socialist sounding principle: the right to self-determination of nations.* This is

* A reference to the two wings of the RSDRP—Mensheviks and Bolsheviks—most of whom supported the right of the subject nations of the former Russian Empire to national self-determination.

supposed to be the new, the democratic aspect of the order to be restored. But it will suffice to ask the simple question about the practical feasibility of this principle to expose it as a hollow phrase. How and for whom should the self-determination of the nations be realized in the conclusion of peace? Only for the peoples of the territories currently under military occupation? That would mean to sanctify the entire *former* land theft under the rule of capitalism, its entire haggling and colonial policy, to exclude its victims from the principle of self-determination! Or should all oppressed, annexed nations and countries of the world in all the states now be questioned about the fates desired by them and led to the ballot box? Whoever expects or asks this from today's governments would first have to be examined for their mental capacity—apart from the fact that the whole idea of the "votes" of nations on the question of their nationality is a pipe dream that does not reckon with class differences and a thousand other real facts.

Here, socialists fool around just as much with the principle of the self-determination of the nations as the capitalist governments with the "liberation of the nations" and the "national defense." Just as imperialist war is not national defense or liberation of nations, the right of self-determination of nations cannot be realized within the framework and under the rule of capitalist states. The only real condition for the self-determination of the nations is the socialist revolution, that is, the political and economic self-determination of the working classes as the real mass in every nation. As long, however, as the rule of the capitalist class exists—and the core of the formula for peace, "no annexations, no compensation," proceeds precisely from the steadfastness of this class rule—the self-determination of nations remains a crude mystification that is just good enough to mislead the proletarian masses of all nations.

In fact, in the fog of this phrase, the Entente governments meet up, pretending to protect "small nations" only to continue the slaughter for their sake: President Wilson, who took the United States to war on behalf of its capitalist magnates exclusively for the rights of nations, Milyukov, the liberal enthusiast and poet of Russian imperialism, Kautsky, the substitute theorist of the Haaseian substitute opposition, Scheidemann, former errand boy of Bethmann-Hollweg, and all the terrible musicians of socialism in the neutral countries.

Indeed, likewise, the Russian workers' and soldiers' council, and the Russian Socialist parties! But if ever, the principle applies here: if two do the same, it is not the same. The Russian proletariat has done its duty and continues to do so. It has put its peace policy into practice by making revolution and is in the process of taking things into its own hands. That's all it can do for peace because now the proletarian masses of other countries have a say. As long as they do not move, but rather stubbornly continue to starve, murder, and allow themselves to be murdered under the command of imperialism, the Russian proletariat has no choice but to turn around in the circle of irreconcilable contradictions and cling to the straws of an iridescent socialist phraseology. The first call of the workers' and soldiers' council "to the peoples of the world" from March 27 is tantamount to the first real socialist peace policy.* The current peace formula is only the concession of the Russian working class to the sad fact that this call has so far fallen on deaf ears.

IV. THE ALTERNATIVE

The peace action in the style of Stockholm, which consists in bringing about an understanding between belligerent governments and forging a common formula of war aims to prevent a shift in the position of power of the imperialist states, is purely bourgeois politics. Proletarian class policy must push the peace action on to a completely different track.

It is not for international socialism to ensure that the imperialist governments reach an agreement with one another and make peace on their own initiative, but, conversely, to use all its power to prevent that peace being achieved in *such a way*; that is, as *the work of capitalist governments*. The principal task and vital interest of international socialism at present is to ensure that peace is a *work of the international proletariat and its revolutionary action*, that it is achieved in the struggle *against* the capitalist governments, that it flows from the proletariat's position of power, and that it brings about a radical shift in the social and political conditions of the capitalist states. From the proletarian class point of view, there are no other means to end the imperialist mass slaughter than the open resistance of the masses, which, at the same time, must grow into the struggle for political power in the state. It is just the same alternative that international socialism faced on August 4, 1914. And only when one has recognized and grasped the full inevitability of this world-historical decision will the tragic fate of socialism in the World War cease to be an incomprehensible riddle.

Only political naivete of the Haaseian type of opposition could assume that the whole problem of socialism on August 4 would have been exhausted in the question of whether or not Social Democratic parliamentarians voted for war credits. According to this view, peculiar to parliamentary cretinism, socialism would be saved if the 110 men in the Reichstag refused the credits while recommending that the masses of the working class fulfil their "civic duty," that is, calmly play the role of cannon fodder for the imperialist mass slaughter. Thereby, socialist virtue was to be safeguarded at minimal cost, and

---

* In an appeal on March 27, 1917, the Petrograd Soviet of Workers' and Soldiers' Councils had asked the peoples of the world to take the decision on war and peace into their own hands and to carry out joint actions for peace. The German proletariat, in particular, was invited to shake off the yoke of absolutism and not be used as an instrument for war.

at the same time, any risk was to be avoided. But history does not make things so convenient for socialism, and the problem was not the vote of a handful of Social Democratic parliamentarians in the once-leading country of socialism, Germany. The vote of the parliamentarians for or against war credits was important only as a signal for the masses to adopt this or that tactic; as a prelude to the unfolding of a positive program of the class struggle in war. Refusing the war credits on August 4 would have made sense only as a declaration of war against the war and imperialism across the board—in conjunction with the overt reopening of a revolutionary program of action and an appeal to the masses to take into their own hands the organization of national defense, and thus political power, through their uprising. There is no way of seriously opposing the outbreak of the war—except by actions, and not by phrases—not back then, and not today.

But if one was afraid of this as the only viable path of struggle, then there was nothing left but complete renunciation of every struggle and every policy of one's own—that is, political abdication. Approving the war credits and the policy of August 4 were, thus, only logical consequences, which imposed themselves by force since there was no middle ground in that world-historical situation. International socialism was faced with an either/or. Either struggle for political power, or bankruptcy and co-optation to prevailing governmental policies. The same situation has lasted since the outbreak of the war, and today, in view of the problem of peace, the history of the European working class holds up the same promissory note like a relentless usurer: "Ay, his breast, So says the bond."* Only through the great open power struggle of the proletarian masses can socialism do away with the World War. If it does not do this, it will remain nothing more than idle chatter about a peace that, yes, precisely through the chatter, seeks a balance between belligerent powers, henchmen of imperialism, and footstools of bourgeois class rule. And in this way, socialism becomes the exact opposite of itself, and can then, after a peace thus achieved, abdicate as a historical factor.

The apparent sore point of real socialist politics in times of war is that revolutions cannot be made on command. This argument is supposed to serve as an excuse and cover, both for its attitude regarding the outbreak of proletarian mass slaughter and for its current position on the peace question. But the seemingly obvious "practical" objection is nothing but an evasion. Of course, revolutions cannot be made on command. Yet this is not the task of the socialist party either. There is only the duty to bravely "tell it like it is" at any time; that is, to clearly and explicitly present to the masses their tasks at the given historical moment, to put forth a political program for action and the slogans which flow

* William Shakespeare, *The Merchant of Venice* IV.1.252–3. This is Shylock's line demanding the promised "pound of flesh" before Portia annuls the transaction by pointing out that the bond does not allow any blood to be shed.

from the situation. Whether and when the revolutionary mass uprising follows from this is something the socialist movement must confidently leave to history itself. If the movement fulfils its duty in this sense, it acts as a powerful factor in unleashing the revolutionary elements of the situation and contributes to the acceleration of the outbreak of mass actions. But even in the worst case, when it first appears as a voice in the wilderness to whom the masses deny their allegiance, it establishes—as it will always and unavoidably turn out on the final account—a moral and political position, the fruits of which it will later reap with accrued interest when the hour of historical fulfilment strikes. Today's Russian Revolution, in which the socialists occupy an unprecedented position of power, is but a result of the decades-long, unwavering call of Russian Social Democracy in the wilderness of a seemingly hopeless situation—the call for a mass revolution under the banner of proletarian class politics as the only way to break the chains of absolutism.

Conversely, if the socialist parties deny the class struggle, as they have done from August 4 to the present day, they become the most effective means of paralyzing the masses, that is, a counterrevolutionary factor. International socialism has indeed been the most reliable guardian of bourgeois class rule since the outbreak of the World War. And it remains faithful to this function, especially at this moment, by using all its strength in the quest of the Stockholm conference for an understanding with the imperialist governments—that is, for the reinstatement of imperialism in its pre-war position of power.

In reality, international socialism is not preparing the end of the war, but rather burial shrouds for peace, first for the Russian Revolution and then for itself as a factor of modern world history. Today, as three years ago, there is only the alternative: War or revolution! Imperialism or socialism! To proclaim this loud and clear—for everyone to draw the revolutionary consequences in their country—this is the only proletarian-socialist work for peace that is possible today.

1918–19

Historical Responsibility*

After the truce, the separate peace between Germany and Russia is only a matter of time.† In the future, history will undoubtedly, among other moments from the World War, capture the grimaces of German semi-absolutism, with which it acknowledges the "spongers and conspirators" as legal rulers, solemnly proclaiming the principle of non-interference in foreign national affairs, and protects the revolutionaries at the Neva River from the "defamation of the Entente." The Königsberg trial, the rally of spies on the Russians, the military service to tsarism—all of it forgotten. Why wouldn't it be? If German Social Democracy has forgotten the Erfurt Program, why should the German government not forget trivialities such as the Königsberg trial? One thing conditions the other.

It was only with rock-solid trust in the unshakable dullness of the German masses that the German reaction could afford the daring experiment, to shake "heinous" hands with the St. Petersburg "murderous arsonists," who have just tossed throne, altar, interest payments on foreign bonds, status, titles, and various other sacrosanct matters onto the garbage heap, who hang refractory commanders-in-chief out the window of the railroad car, and put burdensome aristocratic princes in the dungeon. This by Prussian-German semi-absolutism in confidential negotiations with Lenin and Trotsky, who, only a few years ago, had to stay clear of the Berlin police department! Who does not remember the delicious scene in *My Uncle Benjamin*,‡ where the proud and arrogant count, who has a fishbone stuck in his throat, kisses the despised bourgeois doctor on

---

* This article first appeared in *Spartacus*, No. 8, January 1918. It is not signed. It appears in *Spartakus im Kriege. Die Illegalen Flugblätter des Spartakusbundes im Kriege* (Spartakus in War. The Illegal Pamphlets of the Spartakusbund), edited and introduced by Ernst Meyer (Berlin: Kommunistische Partei Deutschlands, 1927), which names Luxemburg as the author. It is translated by Henry Holland and Manuela Kölke from Luxemburg's *Gesammelte Werke*, Vol. 4, pp. 374–9.

† In accordance with the Decree on Peace adopted by the Second All-Russian Soviet Congress on November 8, 1917, in which negotiations were to be proposed for a just and democratic peace and the immediate conclusion of a truce on all the belligerent countries, negotiations began with the German high command at Brest-Litovsk, after the governments of the Western powers rejected negotiations. The German government pursued the goal of securing a separate peace, safeguarding the theft of areas in the East and freeing its resources for an increased war effort on the Western Front. The masses that were rising up in Germany were to be deceived by this apparent willingness of the government to attain peace. On December 15, the truce was signed and the opening of peace talks was agreed upon on December 22. In signing the treaty of Brest-Litovsk on March 3, 1918, Soviet Russia lost a territory of about 1 million square kilometers, in order to create breathing space to consolidate Soviet power and build an army that could defend against both internal counterrevolution and imperialist interventions.

‡ Satirical novel by Claude Tillier, originally published in France in 1843. There were a number of German translations in the early 1900s, testifying to its popularity in Germany at that time.

a usually covered part of the body just to secure his help. "Distress knows no commandment," said Reichskanzler Bethmann-Hollweg. How much would Hindenburg and Ludendorff prefer to make their "Big Bertha" talk with the "gang" in Petersburg!* But hush! Such heart's desires must be reserved for a future opportunity. For the time being, the Petersburg "gang" is highly convenient, and its subversive peace gospel sounds like heavenly music to German imperialism.

According to press reports, Trotsky has given several speeches in the Central Committee of the Soviets about the international situation, wherein he describes the effects of the Russian offer of peace on all countries in the rosiest of tones. Western Europe is demonstrating, apparently, that the "boldest hopes" of the Russian Soviet have been fulfilled and a general peace is on the best possible road to being realized.

If these press reports are correct, then a lot of water must be poured into Trotsky's foamy wine. It is psychologically understandable that, in their situation, the Bolsheviks—when it comes to the decisive question of peace—now have the need to consider their policy a success, and to present it as such to the Russian people. Sober contemplation brings different things to light.

The immediate effect of the ceasefire in the East will merely be that German troops will be ordered to the West. Or, to put it more precisely, this has already occurred. Still, Trotsky and his comrades have comforted themselves and the Soviet by stating that they wanted to enforce, as a ceasefire condition, the obligation that no redeployments of troops would take place, so as not to stab the Western powers in the back. The German military no doubt laughed up their sleeves at this announcement, as they also know in which baskets they should keep their eggs. Even before the ceasefire was signed, hundreds of thousands of German troops had been redeployed to Italy and to Flanders. The latest bloody German advances near Cambrai, and, in the South, the recent "dazzling" successes in Italy, are already repercussions of the Bolshevik toppling-of-power in November in Petersburg.

Still warm from fraternal scenes with Russian revolutionary soldiers, from shared group photographs, songs, and toasts to the International, the German "comrades" are already diving into the fire of heroic mass actions, their sleeves rolled up, in order, for their part, to slaughter French, English and Italian proletarians. Due to the fresh mass input of German cannon fodder, the butchery on the entire Western and Southern Fronts will flare up tenfold. It goes without saying that France, England, and America will be pushed, through this, into the most extreme and desperate efforts. And so the immediate effects to ensue from the Russian ceasefire, and the separate peace in the East that is founded upon

* *Dicke Berta* refers to the super-heavy howitzer developed by the armaments manufacturer Krupp in Germany on the eve of World War I.

it, are not the acceleration of a general peace, but instead, at first, the extension of the murdering of peoples, and a monstrous rise in the bloody character of this murder, which will demand casualties on both sides, making the number of casualties to date look pale by comparison. Secondly, the ceasefire will result in an enormous strengthening of Germany's military position and its most daring annexation plans and appetites.

In the East, the annexation of Poland, Lithuania, and Courland,* whether initially in an open or veiled form, is already a done deal between the Central Powers. Bearing in mind the actual position of Russia, German imperialism is naturally no longer assuming it will mount any serious resistance as regards the negotiations for a separate peace.

Free from all cares in the East and with fresh reserves of troops, it is now considering putting on a quite different display in the West from previously. Soon, it will laughingly toss the mask of virtuous impartiality that the precarious situation has forced it to wear into the lap of Scheidemann, and if God—who's known to take sides with the strongest battalion—wills it so, German imperialism will proceed to dictate a "*German* peace." In their most recent speeches, Czernin† and his consorts are already singing to a quite different tune from the one currently being hummed from the papal notes on peace.‡

This is the way things are and the Bolsheviks are committing an act of self-deception if, in the light of their separate peace, they choose to see the heavens of a general peace sung by choirs of angels. Those "having the last laugh" regarding the Russian Revolution are until now only Hindenburg and the Pan-Germans.§

If, however, matters and their repercussions head in the opposite direction, then this is in no way primarily the Russians' fault. From the word go, they have been in the fatal situation of having to choose between two different punishments: of yoking themselves either to the Entente's plough or to the machine of German imperialism. But the first would have meant the continuation of the war, while the second means reaching a peace agreement. No wonder that they finally chose the latter!

---

* Courland was a duchy in the Baltic region (West Latvia) until annexed by Russia in 1795. Despite its size, it had overseas colonies for a brief period in Tobago (in the Caribbean) and Gambia (in West Africa). After the Russian retreat in World War I (1915), Courland came under German administration.

† Ottokar Graf [Count] Czernin von und zu Chudenitz, the Austrian foreign minister since 1916, led the Austrian delegation at the Brest-Litovsk peace talks.

‡ Pope Benedict XV challenged the governments of the warring states on August 1, 1917, to bring about a just and lasting peace. He recommended the following points as a foundation for the peace talks: reduction of the arms industry; the creation of a neutral court of arbitration; freedom of the seas; the withdrawal of all demands for war reparations; the return of currently occupied territories; and peaceful agreement over contested territories.

§ The Pan-German League of 1891–1939 advocated German world hegemony and had the nationalist goal of political unification of all German-speaking people.

The whole calculation behind the Russian fight for freedom is based on the tacit presumption that the revolution in Russia ought to become the signal for the revolutionary rising of the proletariat in the West: in France, England, and Italy, but above all in Germany. Only in this case, no doubt, would the Russian Revolution have become the start of a general peace. This has not happened up to now. With the exception of the courageous efforts of the Italian proletariat, the Russian Revolution has been left in the lurch by proletarians from all countries. But the class politics of the proletariat, innately and in its core-being international, can only be realized on the international level. If they now remain limited to one country, while the working class in other countries pursues bourgeois politics, then even the subsequent consequences of the revolutionary vanguard's action will be reversed. And this is why the sole international impact of the Russian Revolution to date is a massive increase in strength of German imperialism and a general intensification of the World War. The guilt for this tragic, historical *quid pro quo* lies primarily with the German proletariat. This is the group that must bear the main responsibility in the court of history for the monstrous streams of blood that have now been allowed to flow, as well as for the social and political consequences of a possible wrestling-to-the-ground of the Western powers by triumphant German imperialism. It is only the immobile, corpse-like attitude of the German proletariat that has forced the Russian Revolution into concluding a peace deal with German imperialism as the sole ruling power in Germany. And it is only this same corpse-like attitude that has made it *possible* for German imperialism to use the Russian Revolution for its own purposes.

Don't the German workers feel the slap in the face of their rulers unabashedly saluting the red Jacobin bonnets in Petersburg at the same moment in which those rulers—if I may say so—dismiss the German people's representatives like dogs to their kennel and muzzle the German people again?* But the German "workers' leaders" don't even seem to notice such a caress. Instead, they, including the "Independents,"† insist on strongly advising the German government not to miss out on this good opportunity, and not to act in an aloof way—they shouldn't refuse to shake the "Russian hand of peace." No need to worry, you good people—German imperialism won't pass up the opportunity of letting the Petersburg Jacobins pull their chestnuts out of the fire. In this

* On December 1, 1917, the Imperial President of the Reichstag (equivalent to speaker of the house of parliament) was empowered by the Reichstag to determine the date and agenda of the next parliamentary session.

† The Independent Social-Democratic Party of Germany (USPD) broke away from the Majority Social Democrats primarily over policies regarding continuation of the war or seeking peace and was founded as a separate party in April 1917. The Majority Social Democratic Party of Germany (German: Mehrheitssozialdemokratische Partei Deutschlands, MSPD) was the name officially used by the Social Democratic Party of Germany (SPD) during the period 1917–22.

business, the "workers' leaders" don't need to even bother incurring their own expenses.

And in view of this turn of events, in which a conclusion of peace becomes the extension of war, the revolutionary victory of the Russian proletariat is transformed into the greatest strengthening of power for German half-absolutism, and the "Working Group"* can find nothing more urgent to do than demand that the German government announce their war aims! "Where have the German war aims got to?" shouts the *Leipziger Volkszeitung*. The gramophone of the "Independents" has only this one scratched record, and all they can do is keep repeating it, time and again. "If the German government insists on following their previous political course, this danger threatens (the continuation of the war until it has been bled out, until Europe's total catastrophe [R. L.])†—despite the Russian's readiness for peace!"‡ In this threatening fashion, the Leipzig Party organ concludes its hundredth warning to the German government.

Oh, for heaven's sake, of course the German government will continue to cling to "its politics to date." We cannot see any reason for it, the "Executive Committee of the ruling classes," to change its politics in the least. It is the German working class that has every reason to change its politics to date. It is up to it—if we don't want the war to lead to a general collapse or to the triumph of the crassest kind of German reaction—to shake off its "previous politics," i.e., the politics of cannon fodder, and to announce its own "war aims" against imperialism in public.

A general peace cannot be reached in Germany without bringing down the ruling power. Only with the torch of revolution, and in open mass struggles for political power, for the rule of the people and for the republic in Germany, can we prevent a renewed resurgence of mass murder and German annexationist triumph in both East and West. The German workers are now called upon to carry the tidings of the revolution and of peace from East to West. Here, no pursing of the lips will do—here, you have to blow the whistle.

---

* The Sozialdemokratische Arbeitsgemeinschaft (Social Democratic Working Community) was a grouping of Social Democrats excluded from the party for their antiwar views who subsequently founded the USPD.

† The phrase in parentheses is an interpolation by Luxemburg.

‡ "Wo bleiben die deutschen Kriegsziele?" (Where Are the German War Aims?) in *Leipziger Volkszeitung*, No. 282, December 4, 1917.

Fragment Concerning War, the National Question and Revolution*

In the period in which class hatred against the proletariat and its immediately imminent social revolution has become absolutely decisive for everything the bourgeois classes have done and have neglected to do—for their program for peace and their future politics—how has the international proletariat been acting? Utterly blind to the lessons of the Russian Revolution, and forgetting even the basic ABCs of socialism, it pursues the peace program of the bourgeoisie,† elevating it to its own program! Cheers for Wilson and the League of Nations! Cheers for national self-determination and disarmament! This is now the banner under which socialists of all countries are suddenly uniting—together with the Entente's imperialistic governments with the most reactionary parties; with government-socialist windbags; with "sticklers-for-principles," oppositional socialists of the swamp; bourgeois pacifists; petty bourgeois utopians; nationalistic *parvenu* states; bankrupt German imperialists; the Pope; the Finnish hangmen of the revolutionary proletariat; and the Ukrainian scholarship students, clinging to the apron strings of German militarism.

In Poland, the Daszyńskis are now in trusting league with Galician noblemen and Warsaw's bourgeoisie; in German Austria, [Victor] Adler, [Karl] Renner, Otto Bauer and Julius Deutsch walk arm in arm with the Christian Socialists,‡ with large landowners and German nationalists; in Bohemia, Soukup and Němec march in a closed phalanx with all the bourgeois parties—a touching and general reconciliation of the classes. And flying over all the national drunkenness, the international banner of peace. Everywhere, the socialists are pulling the chestnuts of the bourgeoisie out of the fire, are helping, with their good reputation and their ideology, to cover up and to save morally bankrupt bourgeois society, and to renovate and consolidate the building of bourgeois class rule.

And what are the first practical laurels reaped by these unctuous politics? Undermining the Russian Revolution and the partition of Russia.

These are the same politics employed on August 4, 1914, only turned on their head in the concave mirror of freedom. The capitulation of the class

---

* This piece is translated by Henry Holland and Manuela Kölke from Luxemburg's *Gesammelte Werke*, Vol. 4, pp. 366–73.

† On January 8, 1918, Woodrow Wilson, president of the United States, presented a fourteen-point program in a keynote address to the U.S. Congress, calling for arms limitation, compensation of colonial claims, the restoration of the independence of Belgium, the eviction of foreign troops from Serbia, Montenegro and Romania, the independence of the nationalities under Turkish rule, and the formation of a League of Nations.

‡ A reference to the Christian Social Party, a right-wing formation that sought to attract disaffected social democrats—often with anti-Semitic demagoguery.

struggle, the union with each national bourgeoisie for the purpose of mutual slaughter, transformed into an international unification of the entire world in a "peace based on an agreement." They all fall for the crudest, most tasteless fairy tale, a melodrama: capital has suddenly disappeared, class oppositions are now null and void. Disarmament, peace, democracy, harmony of the nations. Power bows down before the law and the weak straighten themselves up. Krupp will produce—Christmas lights instead of cannons,* and the American city of Gary† will get turned into a Fröbel kindergarten.‡ A Noah's Ark, where the lamb grazes peacefully beside the wolf, the tiger purrs, blinking like a huge house cat, because the antelope scratches behind its ear, while the lion and the goat play blindman's bluff together. And all this resulting from the magic formula of Wilson, the president of the American billionaires, all this with the help of Clemenceau, Lloyd George, and Prince Max of Baden. Disarmament, on the heels of England and America developing new militarisms—with Japan as the supplier—and military technology expanding immeasurably. After all states are, thanks to state debts, now in the clutches of military-and-finance-capital! After colonies—ah, colonies remain. This is the point at which the concept of class struggle formally capitulates to the concept of the nation. The harmony of the classes in each nation appears to be the precondition for and complementary to the harmony of those nations that, it is presumed, should rise out of the World War to join the "League of Nations."§ For the moment, nationalism triumphs. Nations and mini-nations are petitioning from all sides for their right to create a state. Moldering corpses are rising out of century-old graves, filled with the vigor of spring, and people "without history," who have never created independent states, now feel a strong urge to do so.¶ Poles, Ukrainians, Belarusians, Lithuanians, Czechs, Yugoslavians, ten new nations in the Caucasus. Zionists are already constructing their Palestine Ghetto, for the time being in Philadelphia. Tonight is Walpurgis Night. On top of the nationalistic Blocksberg:

---

* The Krupp family business is one of the oldest and largest arms manufacturers in Europe. It produced steel and weapons in Germany in both world wars.

† Gary, Indiana, developed by US Steel in 1906 as a site for steel production and a major supplier of armaments in World War 1. Luxemburg writes "Gari" in the original.

‡ In 1837, the early childhood educator Friedrich Fröbel founded the first school for children under the age of seven. He called his school a "Kindergarten." His pedagogical innovations included an emphasis on play and activity.

§ Luxemburg often places the German word for the League of Nations, "*Völkerbund*," inside scare quotes. This demonstrates both the novelty of the body and Luxemburg's skepticism toward it.

¶ Luxemburg is using the phrase used in some of Engels's writings—wrongly attributed at the time to Marx—that dismissed the national demands of Czechs, Slovenes, and others in the Balkans as "peoples without a history."

> Broom will bear and stick will lift …
> She's damned who cannot fly tonight.*

But nationalism is merely the rhetorical shell. The core, the historical content that is located beneath it, is as many-sided and as rich with connections as the phrase "national self-determination"—which it hides itself under—is hollow and inadequate.

As in every great revolutionary period, various unsettled accounts and oppositions, old and new, are coming to the table to be settled: antiquated remains of the past along with the most relevant questions of the present and problems of the future, yet barely born, all mixed up colorfully together. The decline of Austria and Turkey is the final liquidation of the feudal Middle Ages, a postscript to the work of Napoleon. With regard to the collapse and shrinking of Germany, however, the moot point is the bankruptcy of the most recent and strongest form of imperialism and its plans for world domination, which were only formed during the war. At the same time, it is merely the bankruptcy of a special method of imperialistic rule: rule by the East Elbian Reaction and military dictatorship, by the methods of state of siege and extermination; it is the collapse of the Trotha strategy, transferred from the Herreros and the Kalahari Desert onto Europe.† The decline of Russia, outwardly but also formally in terms of its results: the creation of new, smaller, nation states—the decline of Austria and Turkey analogous to this contains an opposing problem: on the one hand the capitulation of proletarian politics, using the nationalist yardstick at the feet of imperialism; on the other hand capitalist counterrevolution against proletarian seizure of power.

In his pedantic, schoolmasterly schematism, a K[autsky] sees in this the triumph of "democracy," the simple equipment/accessory and representational form of the nation state. The dry petty-bourgeois formalist naturally forgets to peer into the inner historical core, forgets, as one called to be the guardian of the temple of historical materialism, that "nation state" and "nationalism" are per se empty shells, into which each historical epoch and class relations in each country pour their own specific material content. The German and Italian "nation state in the 60s" was both the slogan and the program of the bourgeois state, of bourgeois class rule, the thrust of which directed itself against the medieval-feudal past, the patriarchal-bureaucratic state, and the fragmentation of economic life. In Poland, the "nation state" was the traditional slogan

---

* Johann Wolfgang von Goethe, *Faust: A Tragedy*, Part I, Scene 21: "Bears the broom and bears the stock, / Bears the fork and bears the buck: / Who cannot raise himself tonight, / Is ever more a ruined wight." (Trans. Bayard Taylor, 1870; Random House, 1950), p. 153.

† A reference to the notorious war of annihilation conducted by German General Lothar von Trotha against the Herero and Nama peoples during the war in German South-West Africa, 1904–07. He later served as an important influence on the young Adolf Hitler.

of the agrarian-aristocratic and petty-bourgeois opposition against modern capitalist development, the thrust of which was directed against the modern phenomena of life: both against bourgeois liberalism and against its opposite number, the socialist workers' movement. In the Balkans, as in Bulgaria, Serbia and Romania, nationalism—whose powerful outbreak was marked by the two bloody Balkan Wars as prelude to the World War—was, on the one hand, the expression of rising capitalist development and bourgeois class rule in all these states, an expression of the conflicting interests of these bourgeoisies among themselves as well as the clash of their developmental tendencies with Austrian imperialism. At the same time, given the general atmosphere of imperialistic development, nationalism in these states—even if, at its core, it is merely the expression of a very recent, still germinal form of capitalism—has been and still continues to be colored by clear German imperialistic tendencies. In Italy, nationalism has already become the company sign for purely imperialistic-colonial appetites, in a quite thorough and exclusive way; this nationalism of the Turco-Italian War* and the appetite for Albania has as little in common with Italian nationalism of the 1850s and 1860s as Mr. Sonnino has with Giuseppe Garibaldi.†

In Russian Ukraine, nationalism, until the October overthrow in Petersburg in 1917, was a nothing, a soap bubble, the pomposity of a few dozen professors and advocates, most of whom can't even speak Ukrainian.‡ Since the Bolshevik Revolution, this nationalism has become one of the petty-bourgeois counterrevolution's very real interests, the thrust of which is directed against the socialist workers' movement. In India, nationalism is the expression of the aspiring native bourgeoisie, who aspire to independently exploit the country on their own account, instead of serving only as an object for the exploitation of English capital; this nationalism is comparable, in terms of its social content and its historical level, to the emancipation struggles of the United States of America at the end of the eighteenth century.

Thus nationalism reflects all conceivable interests, nuances, and historical situations. It glimmers in all possible colors. It is nothing and everything, it is merely the ideological husk, everything comes down to determining its specific, social core.

Thus the current general global explosion of nationalism conceals in its midst the most colorful mishmash of the most varied special interests and tendencies. But through all these special interests runs, like an axle, a general

---

* The Turco-Italian War of 1911 to 1912 centered on Italy's (ultimately successful) effort to seize eastern Libya from the Ottoman Empire. Italy at the time also had colonial ambitions on Albania, still under Ottoman control.

† The conservative-liberal politician Sidney Sonnino was Italian foreign minister from October 1917 to January 1919.

‡ In reality, Ukrainian independence—temporarily achieved only a few months later—had considerable popular support.

interest, created by this particular historical situation: fierce opposition to the proletariat's imminent world revolution.

The Russian Revolution, with the Bolshevik rule that it has created, has placed social revolution on the agenda of history. It has, in quite general terms, driven forward the class opposition between labor and capital to the utmost degree. Suddenly, it has opened a gaping chasm between the two classes, out of which volcanic vapors pour and fiery flames blaze. Just as, in its time, the Parisian proletariat's June rising and the June massacre [of 1848] practically split bourgeois society into two opposed camps for the first time, between which only one law can exist—a fight for life or death—Bolshevik rule in Russia has effectively positioned bourgeois society into this final face-to-face battle for life or death. Bolshevik rule has destroyed and dispersed the fiction of the tame working class with which one reaches and settles for peaceful legalistic agreements; the fiction of a type of socialism that swaggers with harmless theoretical phrases, but, in practical terms, worships the principle of "live and let live"—in short, it has destroyed that very illusion that grew in practice in the last thirty years of German Social Democracy and, in its footsteps, in the whole International—the type of socialism that reaches peaceful legalistic agreements. Suddenly, the Russian Revolution has destroyed, with its bare fists, the *modus vivendi* that was constructed between socialism and capitalism during the last half-century of parliamentarism, and that turned socialism into a harmless phrase for electoral agitation, the blue horizon in the distance compared to the bloody, serious problems of the present, of this very day. The Russian Revolution has brutally torn open the terrible scar that bourgeois society has carried since the June Days in Paris in the year 1848.

All this, admittedly, happened at first only in the consciousness of the ruling classes. Just as the June Days, with the power of an electric shock, had instantly impressed upon the consciousness of the bourgeoisie of all countries their irreconcilable class opposition to the working class, with a deadly hatred of the proletariat—whereas the workers of all countries needed decades to absorb the lessons of the June Days, their consciousness of class struggle—so now the Russian Revolution has awakened in the propertied classes of all countries a seething, volatile fear and hatred against the imminent specter of the proletarian dictatorship, which is comparable only to the feelings of the Parisian bourgeoisie during the June [1871] slaughter and the butchery of the Commune. "Bolshevism" has become the call for practical, revolutionary socialism, for the aspirations of all of the working class to seize power. It is in this obliteration of the social abyss at the heart of bourgeois society, in this international deepening and accentuation of class opposition, that Bolshevism's service to history lies. And in this work—as always in the case of large historical interconnections—all the specific mistakes and errors of Bolshevism disappear as inessential.

These feelings are today the essence of the nationalistic delirium into which the capitalist world appears to have fallen, they are the objective historical content to which the motley nationalisms now registering themselves can, in reality, be reduced. The small, young bourgeoisies that aspire now to an independent existence quiver not merely with the desire to win unrestrained and undemeaned class rule, but also with the long-denied wish to throttle, with their own hands, the deadly enemy—the revolutionary proletariat; a role that, up until now, they had to leave up to the clumsy state apparatus of a foreign power. One doesn't like leaving it up to a third party to practice love or hate. The bloody orgies carried out by Mannerheim, the Gallifet of Finland,* show how much hate has arisen in the glowing heat of recent years in the hearts of all these "little nations," of all these Poles, Lithuanians, Ukrainians, Czechs, Croatians, etc., waiting simply for the chance to tear into the entrails of the revolutionary proletariat, using "nationalist" means. In all these "young nations," who frolic like lambs, white and innocent, on the grassy meadow of world history, already lurks the fierce, snarling tiger waiting to "pounce" at the first tremor of Bolshevism. Behind all these idyllic banquets and the fraternization at dazzling parties in Vienna, Prague, Zagreb and Warsaw, Mannerheim's open graves, which Red Guards must dig themselves, are already gaping, and the murky silhouettes of gallows loom in Kharkiv, created when the Lubinskis and the [Vsevolod] Holubovychs invited the German "liberators" into Ukraine.†

And the same basic thought dominates Wilson's entire democratic peace program. The "League of Nations" in the atmosphere of the drunkenness of the victory for Anglo-American imperialism and of Bolshevism, cast as a bogeyman on the world stage, can lead to only one thing: a bourgeois world league to keep down the proletariat. The first fresh victim that High Priest Wilson will place at the head of his auguries, in front of the Ark of the Covenant of the "League of Nations," will be Bolshevik Russia, upon which the "self-determined nations," conquerors and conquered, will leap.

Here the ruling classes once again demonstrate their unerring instinct for their own class interests, their wonderful, fine sensibility for dangers that threaten them. While outwardly the bourgeoisie are enjoying lovely weather, and proletarians of all countries are getting high on the nationalist and League-of-Nations tremors of spring, bourgeois society feels a reverberation in all its limbs, announcing the historical swing on the barometer and a sudden change of weather. While the socialists, with doltish diligence as "national ministers," look to fetch their chestnuts of peace out of the fire of world war,

---

* In May 1918, White Guard troops led by Carl Gustav Mannerheim in concert with German troops crushed the Finnish Revolution that had begun in January 1918. Revolutionaries fell in the tens of thousands.

† Holubovych was prime minister of the independent Ukrainian Peoples Republic from January to March 1918.

the bourgeoisie already sees behind its back the inescapable calamity drawing near: the giant specter of social revolution, straightening itself up, which has silently entered the stage in the background.

It is this, the objective insolubility of the tasks facing bourgeois society, that turns socialism into a historical necessity and makes the world revolution unavoidable.

No one can predict how long this final period will last and which forms it will take. History has departed from worn-out rails and a comfortable pace, and each new step, each new turn on the path, opens up new perspectives and new horizons.

What matters is grasping the real *problem* of this period. The problem is the dictatorship of the proletariat, the realization of socialism. The difficulties of the task do not lie in the strength of the opponent, or in the resistance of bourgeois society. The war has rendered its force of last resort*—the army—useless for the purpose of keeping down the proletariat: it has become revolutionary itself. The material basis of its [the boureoisie's] existence—the preservation of society—has been wrecked by the war. The moral basis for its existence—tradition, slow regularity, authority—is gone with the wind. The entire mechanism has loosened itself up, has become fluid and movable. The conditions of the fight for power for an aspiring class are more favorable than ever before in world history. Power is ready to drop into the lap of the proletariat like a ripe fruit. The difficulty lies within the proletariat itself, in its immaturity, or rather in the immaturity of its leaders, the socialist parties. The working class balks, recoiling repeatedly from the undetermined enormity of its task. But it *must*, it *must*—history is cutting off all its escape routes—lead tortured humanity out of night and horror and into the light of liberation.†

---

* In the original, Luxemburg uses "ultima ratio" (from Latin *ultimus*, "last, utmost" and *ratio*, "means, possibility"). It generally refers to the last resort, the last means or the last way out in a conflict of interests when all other proposed solutions have previously been rejected because (allegedly) no agreement could be reached with them.

† The manuscript had a final sentence that is illegible.

Not Following the Script*

Russia is certainly not following the script. Kautsky, the theoretician, can't find proof of Russia's economic ripeness for social revolution in the occupational statistics for that predominantly agricultural country.† He forgets that, if we were to make judgments exclusively on occupational statistics, neither the great revolution in France nor the March Revolution in Germany would have been allowed to take place at all.

What's the real story then, regarding statistics and historical materialism? In Germany, where, according to the statistics, the proletariat could present a full certificate of maturity for the seizure of power, medieval half-absolutism is enjoying a lovely upsurge. In Russia, economically and socially backward according to the statistics, the urban proletariat, supported by the peasantry, has already seized the rudder of the state.

The greatest theoretician of the swamp,‡ and all who gaze at the upheaval in Russia full of good wishes and yet full of heart-felt pessimism, might possibly be right, if Russia were located on the moon. But, both economically and politically, Russia is merely a part of Europe. In the rarefied air of abstraction, Marxist theoreticians of Kautsky's ilk love ruminating about the global economy, international developments, and their interrelations. However, as soon as they're thrown on their faces down onto the flat earth, together with these interconnections, they unconsciously fall back into a purely bourgeois way of thinking: state boundaries also constitute the boundaries of all social forces and effects; Russia takes the stage as an isolated world in itself, Germany also for itself, and so on.

But is Russia ripe for the social revolution? What a brilliant question! As if the social revolution were a "national" matter that discovers its driving forces, but also its own conclusion, within Russia's borders.

What these well-wishing proponents of the complete transformation in Russia forget is that this revolution, with its specific course, is not a product made possible merely by Russian developments, but, rather, by the global development of capitalism and its class contradictions.

---

* This article first appeared in *Spartacus*, January 8, 1918. It was republished by the KPD (Spartakusbund) in *Spartakusbriefe* (new printing), Berlin, 1920, pp. 153–6 and in *Spartakusbriefe* (Berlin: Institute for Marxism-Leninism at the SED Central Committee, 1958), pp. 414–17. It is translated by Henry Holland from a photocopy of the original.

† See Karl Kaustky, "Die Erhebung der Bolschewiki" (The Rising of the Bolsheviks) in *Sozialistische Auslandspolitik. Korrespondenz* (*Socialist Foreign Policy Correspondence*), ed. Dr. Rudolf Breitscheid et al., Year 3, No. 46, (Berlin, November 14, 1917). Republished in Marga Voigt, ed. *Clara Zetkin, Die Kriegsbriefe* (Berlin, 2016), pp. 447–51; Jörn Schütrumpf ed., *Diktatur statt Sozialismus. Die russische Revolution und die deutsche Linke 1917/18*, pp. 98–102.

‡ Luxemburg often uses this phrase to refer to the centrist USDP, in which Kautsky was the best-known figure.

It continues to be more or less a matter of so-called coincidence, i.e., the combined causation of many historical circumstances, hidden from outside view, that determines which country seizes the initiative and leadership in each of the epochs that are moving toward revolution. From the final third of the eighteenth century until the middle of the nineteenth century, it was England that, exactly like today, was much more developed in capitalistic terms than France. And yet it wasn't England, but rather France that assumed the political leadership of Europe in this period, transmitting new impulses to it through each of France's tremors.

Now Russia has taken the initiative for the social regeneration of Europe, in part precisely because it has been trotting along significantly behind Europe in terms of its social development. In Russia, modern capitalist class-contradictions were bound to each other for too long, its revolutionary energy dammed up under the oppression of absolutism: on the one hand, the huge tension of the unsolved—and, inside the frame of the bourgeois state, unsolvable—agricultural question; on the other hand, the most mature proletarian ideology that the West has yet produced—with the aid of scientific socialism.

And just at the very moment when this ideology presents itself as mere dead words—in Germany, the country that cradled it—without any enlivening effect on the thought and leadership of the masses, the same ideology blazes up over there like columns of fire* in one of the mightiest deeds of world history. Thus, bearing a flaming witness precisely to its foundational concept: its *internationalism*.

The Russian proletariat can only be comprehended as the global proletariat's vanguard, which expresses the degree of maturity of international class contradictions through its movements. What is now raising its voice in Petersburg involves developments in Germany, England, and France.

Therein lies the fate of the Russian Revolution, both its fortune and its outcome. It can only reach its goal as a prologue to the *European* revolution of the proletariat. But if, however, the European and the German workers should continue merely to watch the exciting performance, as sympathetic guests sitting on the fence, then Russian Soviet rule is in for a fate no different from the fate of the Paris Commune.

These inner interconnections are now finding expression in all sorts of visible restraints on Bolshevik politics. The only way to explain—which doesn't mean excuse—the fact that the Bolsheviks managed so much as a flirtation

---

* The word *Feuersäule* was not common in Luxemburg's time. It appears in Luther's translation of the Bible at the point in the Old Testament when the Israelites are leaving Egypt (Exodus 13: 21): "1. *Und der HERR zog vor ihnen her, am Tage in einer Wolkensäule, um sie den rechten Weg zu führen, und bei Nacht in einer Feuersäule, um ihnen zu leuchten, damit sie Tag und Nacht wandern konnten. Niemals wich die Wolkensäule von dem Volk bei Tage noch die Feuersäule bei Nacht.*"

with the German government-Socialists recently, is to view it as a desperate grasping for any kind of starting point for proletarian action in Germany. The fact that they negotiate with Hindenburg and [Georg] Hertling* may, in their eyes, seem to be no more than a sad necessity: one that casts a lurid light on German conditions, but not even a shadow on those in power in Petersburg. However, the fact that they attempted to infect the German masses with revolution through channels as dirty as Parvus†–Scheidemann should signify, even to the Bolsheviks, a scatterbrained ambiguity, which doesn't at all fit with the Bolsheviks' high moral standards and intolerance.‡

But a further deviation shows itself to be more important and to bear a heavier burden: "the right of nations to self-determination" brandished by the Soviet government.

In reality, there is only *one* form of self-determination of nations that does not scorn this "right"—and that is the revolution of the proletariat of the mass of the people in every nation. Excepting this while [operating] in the framework of the bourgeois state renders the "the right of nations to self-determination" a hollow phrase—in practice it consistently surrenders up the masses of people to the ruling classes.

Obviously, it is a task of the revolutionary proletariat to introduce the most far-reaching political democracy and equality of rights for the nationalities, but anointing the world with newly baked national class-states should be the least of its worries. The bourgeoisie in every nation is the only group interested in the apparatus of state independence directed toward the outside world—which has nothing whatsoever to do with democracy. We know state independence itself to be a dubious thing, and it has been used often enough as a disguise for horse-trading in peoples.

Similarly, the annexation of Poland, Lithuania, and Courland by the Central Powers, whether carried out in the course of the peace negotiations or at a later point, will certainly be portrayed as the wish of the nations concerned. There is nothing easier than finding the necessary "minister" in every nation of the [Jan] Kucharzewski type,§ or other Krapülinkis¶ like him, who behave like the

* Georg Graf (Count) von Hertling was Chancellor of the German Reich from November 1, 1917, to September 30, 1918.

† Parvus (aka Alexander Helphand) had been among Luxemburg's closest colleagues and collaborators in the fight against revisionism and for the mass strike, until he swung to the right and supported the German war effort during World War I.

‡ Although Parvus offered Lenin his support following the Bolshevik seizure of power, Lenin rebuffed his offer, stating, "The revolution needs good minds, but above all clean hands." Parvus had conducted secret negotiations with Philipp Scheidemann and other German Social Democrats in Copenhagen and Stockholm, sounding them out about possible support for the Bolsheviks. Luxemburg could not have known of Lenin's response at the time.

§ Jan Kucharzewski was forcibly imposed as prime minister of Poland between November 1917 and February 1918 by the German occupying forces.

¶ A figure in Heinrich Heine's poem *Two Knights* who is also referred to by Marx in *The*

obedient slaves of German militarism while they hope to construct thorough class domination over their own people with its help.

This is what makes it likely that as events proceed the Bolsheviks will be frequently caught on thorns that they themselves have so thoughtlessly propagated.

Yes, they have made several mistakes and will probably make many more. But this is the way things unravel in the process of great historical upheavals. Things are faultless and run like clockwork only in conventicles, or in mass parties, like the late German Social Democracy that only led a fake political existence and conducted fake battles. As regards the unforgettable and huge demonstrations for Prussian suffrage in Treptow Park and in the Tiergarten,* everything functioned in an obviously glorious way, when, under Eugen Ernst's† brilliant leadership, a dozen of the Berlin constabulary [*Schutzleute*] were so cleverly tricked. Leaving aside the small detail that the huge masses, also under Eugen Ernst's leadership, when confronted by the same dozen mounted *Schutzleute,* so quickly took to their heels—at least when these had unsheathed their swords—that the police nags couldn't stop choking for the clouds of dust. Other than that, it all went off brilliantly.

But real mass historical confrontations do not proceed in such an impeccable way. It may well be that the Bolsheviks are certain to make many more mistakes. But they are aptly captured by the words of Lessing about the noble horse that never knocks more sparks out of the stones than when it trips up. And posterity will certainly judge them in the way old [Franz] Ziegler‡ passed judgment at Lassalle's grave: "He was a human with thousands of errors, yes even vices, but he was a complete human being."

How will history judge the Russian working class?

Eighteenth Brumaire of Louis Bonaparte at the end of Chapter 1: "Finally, the scum of bourgeois society forms the holy phalanx of order and the hero Krapülinki [a dissolute aristocrat] installs himself in the Tuileries as the 'savior of society.'" See *The Eighteenth Brumaire of Louis Bonaparte*, in *Marx-Engels Collected Works*, Vol. 11 (New York: International Publishers, 1979), p. 112.

* "The Social Democratic Party of Germany issued a call for a large assembly for democratic voting laws, the so-called *Wahlrechtsspaziergang* (Suffrage Stroll) for March 6, 1910. In order to trick the Prussian authorities, Berlin's Treptow Park was announced as the assembly point. The Berlin chief of police banned the assembly and filled Treptow Park with a strong police presence. In the meantime, around 150,000 people had gathered in the Tiergarten and marched toward the Brandenburg Gate. Mounted police moved against the demonstrators, using sabers, causing several injuries. On the same day, numerous and powerful demonstrations took place in other Prussian cities and German states for general, equal, secret and direct suffrage." See *Spartakusbriefe* (Berlin: Institute for Marxism-Leninism at the SED Central Committee, 1958), p. 417, note 1.

† Eugen Ernst (1864–1954) was a functionary of the Social Democratic Party in Prussia. In 1910, at the time of the Prussian franchise campaign, he was chairman of the party in Prussia, and he had a particular interest in outwitting the Berlin Political Police. He was later aligned with the right wing of the Social Democratic Party and became Berlin Police President during the suppression of the Spartacist uprising in January 1919, when he replaced the USPD's Emil Eichhorn in that office.

‡ Franz Ziegler, a left-liberal veteran of the 1848 Revolution, served a period of imprisonment for high treason "for advocating resistance to the Prussian government's taxation laws."

Toward the Catastrophe*

World-historical destiny takes place with relentless logic. The German proletariat, neglecting to grab the wheels of imperialism's vehicle of assault by the spokes, is now being dragged around by it to defeat socialism and democracy throughout the whole of Europe. The German worker marches forward, up to his knees in blood, over the bones of the Russian and Ukrainian, Baltic, Finnish revolutionary proletarians, over the national existence of the Belgians, Poles, Lithuanians, Romanians, over the economic ruin of France, to plant the victory banner of German imperialism everywhere.

But every military victory won outside by way of German cannon fodder means a new political and social triumph of the reactionaries within the Empire. With every storming of the Red Guard in Finland and South Russia, the power of the East Elbian Junkerdom and Pan-German capitalism is rising. With every shattered city in Flanders, a position of German democracy is lost.

Already now, in the middle of the war, the German working class, as it deserves, is chastised with whips and scorpions. The miserable fiasco of the Prussian electoral reform† and the most outrageous proposed tax legislation in German history are the first receipts for the willing executioners of foreign freedom.

The government socialists, who presume to retrieve treasures from the morass of their political prostitution, do not even find earthworms anymore. After having played out their only policy trophy in the splendid July resolution of the Reichstag,‡ they just wait with resignation for the "German peace" from the hands of Hindenburg, which shall bury the revolution and socialism forever.

The historical speculation of the political moles will once again prove to be wrong. Although the mass slaughter has taken on horrible dimensions in

---

* This article first appeared in *Spartacus*, No. 9, June 1918, and was republished in *Spartakusbriefe* (Spartacus Letters), (Berlin: Institute for Marxism-Leninism at the SED Central Committee, 1958), pp. 422–6. It is translated by Manuela Kölke from Luxemburg's *Gesammelte Werke*, Vol. 4, pp. 380–4.

† The electoral reform proposal submitted to the Prussian Ministry of State on November 24, 1917, provided the right to vote for men over twenty-five years of age. This draft was rejected in the Prussian Chamber of Deputies on May 2, 1918, by a majority consisting of conservatives, some national liberals, and the Center Party. Instead, a proposal by the parliamentary commission of the House of Deputies was adopted, according to which the Prussian three-class franchise system was merely revised, and every man over twenty-five years, in addition to his basic vote, received as many as five more votes, depending on his wealth and income. The reactionary character of electoral law had not changed.

‡ On July 19, 1917, the Reichstag, with the votes of the SPD, the Progressive People's Party, and the Center, had decided on a so-called peace resolution, calling for an imperialist negotiated peace, acknowledging the current conquests. This maneuver of the German bourgeoisie, supported by the right-wing leaders of the Social Democracy, was designed to weaken the revolutionary antiwar movement in Germany.

the West, a decisive military outcome is still as far afield as it was a year or two ago. The more German militarism lashes out, the more the Western states are naturally whipped to the utmost resistance by the warning example of the peace agreements in the East. The end of the bloody orgy, which the Scheidemanns and [Ernest] Heilmanns fatally await with their eyes closed, may still be a long time coming.

But one thing becomes clearer with each passing day: the *German* victory can, in any case, mean nothing other than the catastrophe of bourgeois society.

In any military decision of today's World War, imperialism would be the actual victor, the international proletariat the actual vanquished. In a *German* victory, however, imperialism would take hold in its most reactionary, violent, and provocative form. A series of purely historical circumstances requires this with compelling logic.

English and French imperialism are rooted in the old colonial policy, based on traditional lines. German [imperialism], which was in an embryonic state before the outbreak of the World War, has grown to immense dimensions in the course of it; it is still growing with every passing day and fills itself with the bloodshed of millions slaughtered; it fills its urge for world conquest, which knows of no traditions, no fetters, no respect.

English and French imperialism have their territories of power and expansion overseas, while German [imperialism] has set up its tents in the heart of Europe; the whole of Eastern Europe has been groaning under the German yoke since the dictated peace of Brest-Litovsk.

English imperialism is, for historical reasons, tied to certain democratic forms; while the French is, for economic reasons, accustomed to a slow pace and a stagnating character. German imperialism unites the brutal agitation of the Prussian Junker and police state with the impetuous greed of modern financial capital, which has reached its greatest concentration directly in the bloody christening of this war.

While, therefore, Anglo-French imperialism overthrew all pre-capitalist conditions in Asia and Africa during the last century, its own policy in Europe has been and remains essentially conservative. German imperialism itself now throws the firebrand of revolution and anarchy into European capitalist conditions. In the few months of its unscrupulous economy, according to the methods in East Elbia, it has, in Poland, Lithuania, Estonia, Courland, Livonia, Ukraine, in Romania, in the Caucasus turned everything upside down. From Finland to the Black Sea, it has created misery, ruin, inextricable confusion, an exacerbation of national and class antagonisms, and a deadly hatred that transforms all of Eastern Europe into a seething volcano. Outwardly contained only with great effort, the explosion in the East is only a matter of time.

But everything announced in pangs of anarchy in the lightning storms in the East is child's play compared to what is rising on the horizon in the *West*, in the event that Hindenburg's "Big Bertha" is to be sent to create "order" there too—and, if France, like Poland, is to have pieces of living flesh torn off its flanks, if Belgium and Ukraine are to be constantly strangled, if Flanders like the Baltic is to be delighted with German "liberation"!

Precisely because every German victory in the West immeasurably increases the East Elbian reaction and imperialist lunacy at its core, a new order in Western Europe of some permanence—as well as the production of some barely tolerable equilibrium for all peoples even in bourgeois-capitalist forms under German dictates—become no less than impossible.

The world domination of "Big Bertha," with Europe under the yoke of Prussia-Germany—that is simply an unworldly fantasy, which only the [Ernst] Reventlows* in their naïve cannibalism, in their political jungle nakedness, or only the lackeys of governmental socialism can seriously believe in. German saber rule over Europe is a fever dream of bloodlust and the call for European revolution is the awakening.

Toward this and no other goal do the "victorious" Germans stagger, as they now ruthlessly plunder nations, ruin countries, strangle revolutions, "free" nations, torture and mutilate foreign lands, transform flowering fields into gruesome wastelands and spread human blood like manure.

And what would it look like in Germany after a "German victory?" Germany being transformed into a permanent war camp in order to hold down defeated Europe with blood and iron—that means nothing other than grinding state bankruptcy, economic ruin under the burden of dizzying war debt and further armament. In its wake—that is, after the starvation of war from patriotic enthusiasm—comes the cat-o'-nine-tails of indirect taxes and monopolies, in other words: after the starvation of war from patriotic enthusiasm comes the peace with an empty stomach [*Friedenshungertuch*] as the only remuneration for the masses of people!

That is how the thousand-year-old empire of German imperialism looks; anarchy on the outside, collapse on the inside, they are one and the same. The "German victory"—if and whenever it arrives—is built on sand; more precisely on a hurricane; it is a house of cards that cannot last a day, under which the foundations begin to tremble and split on the very next day.

The German worker, therefore—very soon, and even more so after a "German victory"—will have to resort to the revolution, even if he still struggles against it and plays dead, not wanting to hear the voice of the times. The executioner of foreign freedom, the *gendarme* of the European reaction, will soon have to rebel against his own work, because iron historical laws won't allow themselves to be mocked. With his own hands, by his own blind

---

* Ernst Graf (Count) zu Reventlow advocated reckless warfare by any means during the First World War. He was one of the main supporters of an annexationist peace.

obedience, by his own "victories" in the service of the reaction, the German proletarian prepares in these days for the European and thus the German revolution.

And when the hour strikes, those who have now turned away from Russia to slither on their bellies before Hindenburg will turn back to the East to borrow a bit of sacred ember from the fire that today they attempt to stamp out with their blood-stained army boots at the behest of imperialism.

Handwritten Fragments* on the History of the International, German Social Democracy, War, Revolution, and Postwar Perspectives†

[The] Intern[ational] & its History

1‡

1. 1864.
2. 1889. *May Day Commemoration.*

Authorities

Concept that the "Party Congress" decides. "Authorities." "Statute." Legality (civil process based).

2

Authorities or party congresses cannot make a decision, but only the mass of the people & the people as a movement, & that means on an *international* basis.§ *Peace*. The Party Congress "after the war."

---

* These handwritten fragments were written mostly in 1918. This text matches as accurately as possible Luxemburg's extremely fragmentary original. All cross outs are by Luxemburg. Excerpts were published in Annelies Laschitza, *Im Lebensrausch, trotz alledem. Rosa Luxemburg. Eine Biographie* (Zest for Life, Despite Everything. Rosa Luxemburg. A Biography) (Berlin: Aufbau Verlag, 1996), pp. 580–4, and in Theodor Bergmann and Wolfgang Haible, eds., *Reform–Demokratie–Revolution. Zur Aktualität von Rosa Luxemburg* (Reform–Democracy–Revolution. On the Relevance of Rosa Luxemburg), supplement to *Sozialismus*, Vol. 4, No. 97, Hamburg, 1997, pp. 42ff. It is translated by Henry Holland from Luxemburg's *Gesammelte Werke*, Vol. 7.2, pp. 1088–1114

† The fragments were written partly in pencil and partly in ink, on three different sorts of paper. Luxemburg marked the ordering of the key points in several different ways and made considerable changes to the notes. This makes it impossible to reach definitive conclusions about their immediate occasion and purpose. They were probably intended both to further Luxemburg's own understanding and to serve as ideas for planned future writings. Mathilde Jacob wrote to Clara Zetkin on January 25, 1919: "She wanted to publish a second part of the *Junius Pamphlet*, and in spirit she wrote the structure for that herewith." See also *Gesammelte Werke*, Vol. 7, pp. 1107ff.

‡ The numbers that the editors of the German-language edition printed in bold were inserted by Luxemburg, presumably at a later date to the text they are found beside.

§ In these fragments "u" is used as an abbreviation for "*und*" (and). In the English text the ampersand (&) is used at all the corresponding points in the German.

Perspectives of Soc[ial] D[emocracy] after the war, the ruin of Christen[dom] and of Liberalism
(Ideology o.[f] the *Center),* of *Militarism,* of War Socialism.
(no decision despite victory) com[parison] with 1871.

3

The First International, founded by Marx & Engels in the y[ear] 1864,* couldn't yet function as a bringing together of the European workers' movement, it was itself the cradle of such [a movement]. The intention was that the first ~~spli~~ shoots of modern socialism in individual countries should be planted out of & through the Marxist International. The shared trunk was established boldly here ~~etc~~ in a world historical deed, it was now an ~~imperative now is for its roots~~ imperative for socialism to put down roots in ~~several~~ all capitalist countries. The work was accomplished, but ~~first~~ in serving this task the historical vocation of the First International exhausted itself, after barely ten years of being, it dissolved, to make way for the slow process of founding socialist worker parties in the individual states.

4

After the bloodletting of the Paris Commune in the y[ear] 1871,† the French workers' movement of the [18]80s got itself together again, followed by the socialist] party ~~parties~~ in Italy, Belgium and in England; in this period in Germany, Social Democracy passed its test of maturity before the panel of history in its ~~battles~~ unyielding wrestling with Bismarck's state of emergency legislation.‡ By the end of the [18]80s the modern worker's movement had been erected on solid foundations in Europe, & as soon as this had been achieved,

---

* The International Workingmen's Association, later known as the First International, was founded on September 28, 1864, in London. Present were German, English, French, Italian, Polish, and Swiss workers and political exiles. The association's programmatic documents, such as the inaugural address and the provisional statues, were composed by Karl Marx.

† The "Bloody Week" in Paris, May 21–28, 1871, ended with counterrevolutionary forces crushing the Paris Commune, which was the first attempt in global history to establish working-class hegemony beginning March 17, 1871. Government troops killed around 30,000 communards and arrested approximately 85,000 who were subject to deportation, forced labor and prison sentences.

‡ On October 21, 1878, the law "Against Social Democracy's Commonweal Endangering Aspirations" was proclaimed and enacted. This had been passed in the Reichstag on October 19, 1878, with the help of pressure applied by Otto von Bismarck, by 221 votes to 149. This new legal measure outlawed German Social Democracy, left its members open to persecution and harassment, and made the Party's work considerably harder. Under pressure from the masses and in the face of divisions inside the ruling classes (reflected in the results of the Reichstag elections of February 20, 1890), the Reichstag refused to extend the Socialist Law.

~~there~~ a natural urge sprang out of that to connect with the maternal soil from which ~~those~~ this movement drew its energy: toward international unification.

The Paris Congress of the y[ear] 1889, which launched the Second International,* consisted this time of representations of younger but already more solidly rooted ~~soci~~ workers' parties of various countries; the imperative now, in contrast with the First International, was to establish ~~and connect with~~ the shared trunk [of political work] *from below*. The motions passed by the Paris Congress demonstrate that with the right instinct, ~~z~~ people choose the only path capable of building up the power of the International.

5

The incongruous motion about the May Day commemoration† articulated the Second International's actual ~~P~~ historical problem in an offhand way: the International will either become a mass movement for the worker masses' own activities in all countries, or it will not exist at all. The May Day commemoration was the *sole* form of immediate activation of the proletarian masses in the spirit of international solidarity; what else was left over ~~remained~~ from the Second International was congresses & manifestos, i.e., demonstrations of a small heap of representatives *in the name* of the masses, and words, authorities & ceremonies. The May Day was intended as the single international deed, *individual* deed of millions of people. And ~~concerning~~ in the fate of May Day, the fate of the Second International was to be ~~could be~~ sealed.

6

~~Born~~ Born out of a fresh and bold longing for deeds, May Day was degraded in the leading countries of the Second International, at first in Germany through the political leaders who turned it into an empty demonstration, and finally through the trade union leaders, who throttled it in the noose of the clause that made support [compulsory]. In the debates about May Day in the German Party Congress in the final years before the war, the breakdown of German &

---

* The Second International's founding Congress took place in Paris in 1889. In attendance were representatives from Finland, France, the Netherlands, Italy, Norway, Austria, Poland, Romania, Russia, Sweden, Switzerland, Spain, Hungary, and the United States. Germany was represented by eighty-one participants. Alongside reports on the situation of labor and the socialist movement in the various countries, the following issues were discussed: abolition of the army and standing army and general arming of the people; ways and means of realizing the demands of labor protection; international legislation regarding labor protection; legal regulation of the working day and of daytime and night-time labor and labor on Sundays and public holidays; working time for youth and women; child labor; evaluation of large industry and small-scale businesses, including labor carried out by homeworkers; and international demonstrations for May 1.

† The 1889 Paris Congress's resolution to hold demonstrations for the eight-hour day in all countries on May 1, 1890, marked the birth of the modern May Day celebration.

international Social Democracy had already been ~~sealed~~ revealed in draft form;[*] the motions passed regarding the May Day commemorations were already a form of fiery writing, an omen, on the wall of the International. ~~While~~ When the sole mass action with an international character was stalled in a coldblooded manner because of a public and pronounced ~~angs~~ fear of incurring sacrifices, ~~became~~ the International was already inherently a corpse, ~~the ostentatious questions about mass action~~

7

the ostentatious Basel Congress[†] was already unconsciously a wake.

I

The game draws near to its end, the orgy wheezes its final breaths. From the tip of its head to its toes ~~wit~~ dripping with dirt & blood, the bourg[eois] world emerges from the World War. The turnaround came overnight. ~~The transformation came over night. Suddenly the stiff iron ring gave way, which had locked~~

---

* The pivotal point of the debates about May Day was how it should be defended in the face of increasing regulation by capitalist entrepreneurs and trade union leaders. At the Nuremberg Party Congress in 1908, the party board was commissioned to resume negotiations with the General Commission of the Trade Unions, regarding the question of financial support for May Day commemorations. See the *Parteitagsprotokoll* (Minutes to the Party Congress), Nuremberg, 1908, p. 550. A motion spelling out the May Day agreement was passed at the SPD Congress in Leipzig in 1909. It stated, "A commission to prepare the May Day commemoration should be set up in all localities, if possible, at the beginning of the year; this commission will be made up of representatives from the Trade Union Alliance and the party organization in equal measure. The chair of each local commission is to be voted for by the commission itself. The commission has the task of taking responsibility for a respectable commemoration … The planned commemoration may not take place on any other day than May 1. In the case of lockouts resulting from May Day, the workers affected can be granted support; the workers organized through the party and the unionized workers have a right to such support. To support locked out workers, municipal funds should be created for larger areas … The financial means necessary for this support should be raised through the party organization and the trade unions in the municipality where the lockout takes place, through means of voluntary donations and collections." See *Parteitagsprotokoll* (Leipzig: 1909), p. 511. The party conference in Jena in 1913 added to this, "From those Party comrades employed in the offices and editorial teams of the Party and of the trade union, the Party conference expects that they contribute their daily wage for May 1 to the May Day fund, with thoughts for the sacrifices that the workers offer in the struggle for the May Day commemoration." See *Parteitagsprotokoll* (Jena, 1913), p. 557. See also Luxemburg's "*Die Begräbnis der Maifeier*" (The Burial of May Day) and "*Die Maifeier vor der Entscheidung*" (May Day Faces Difficult Decisions) in *Gesammelte Werke*, Vol. 2, p. 269–73 and 274–8.

† An International Socialist Congress took place in Basel on November 24–25, 1912, in response to the First Balkan War. The sole point on the agenda was the international situation and the common action against war. See: Luxemburg, "*Diskussionsbeitrag zum Balkankrieg in der Sitzung des ISB am 28. Oktober 1912 in Brüssel*" (Contribution to Discussion on the Balkan War in the Meeting of the International Socialist Bureau, Brussels, on October 28, 1912) (*Gesammelte Werke*, Vol. 7, pp. 736–7).

~~us in like an Esk~~ The transformation came overnight. Suddenly the rigid iron ring gave way, which had locked us in like a ~~Esk~~ long Eskimo winter, as if a spring storm had suddenly swept along in the night. Things started cracking and bursting all over the place. An atmosphere of hope, a movement in the air, a general push, slide and disturbance.[*]

These are the jokes history places on us. Well dug, old mole! Despite the failure of socialism, despite ~~all highly heape~~ the total victory of brutal violence, ~~of~~ despite the highest triumphs of Imper[ialism]. Any kind of hesitation and pessimism would be ludicrous. The laws of hist[orical] ~~e~~ dialectic don't allow themselves to be mocked. They are suddenly finding ways out on that very same broad road, on which they had seemed to have lost themselves in Europe. ~~sud~~ They first allowed the Tower of Babel ~~where to be heaped up~~ to grow up to the sky, only to then make it tumble down, as if it had been the stupid toy of a child.

[The following paragraph is crossed out.]

Re. 7. The time has now arrived to do the ~~bi~~ accounts & pay the bills.

Above all, the prol[etariat] has to settle up with itself, make an inventory, and review & preview things to come.

Thoughts turn in three directions:

1. To the past, to answer the question about the *Why*.

2. ~~In the~~ After the Russian Revolution, to sift through its lessons.

3. To the future, to look at ~~the situat~~ the new situation that has been created by the war, & at the perspectives & tasks for socialism resulting from it.

[End of the deletion.]

II

As soon as we look back on the past, the paths diverge into three directions.

The Gov[erment]-Soci[ialists] consider their current politics to be a direct continuation of the old "proven" tactics of G[erman] Soc-D[emocracy] ~~in the Intern.~~ & can discern an uninterrupted ~~thr~~ and non-contradictory thread of devel[opment].

The Haase-Kautskys regard *their* politics ~~d~~ as the direct continuation of the old G[erman] Soc-D[emocracy].

Both are right. The old G[erman] Soc-D[emocracy] was a two-headed beast. Its two elements: a radical turn of phrase & opport[unistic] practice. A revolutionary theory & a purely parliam[entary] kind of politics.

According to Haase-K[arl] K[autsky], everything in the past was good & right. In other words, their entire politics during the war ~~has~~ was directed toward *Restoration*. *Status quo ante* in the party ~~socialism~~ just as *Status quo ante* in bourg[eois] socie[ty] & in the Intern[ational].

---

* Reference to the February Revolution in Russia, 1917.

As such, ~~the~~ their historical understanding is already judged in advance. The world-hist[orical] bankruptcy of soc[ialism] in the war, which even they do not deny, appears in this interpretation to be an accidental work of a leader's personal renegadism, an act of weak-mindedness, of confusion of the masses.

But "accident" ~~& personal guilt or error have been~~ as an explanation in world history is nothing more than a ~~c~~ cover-up for our ignorance & ~~lack~~ incomprehension, just as it is in our understanding of nature.

~~The first condition~~ This sort of "historical interpretation" is doubly shameful for dedicated supporters of Marxist ~~mater~~ historical materialism. Further evidence that Marxism, ~~with~~ especially with regard to ~~its~~ its official ~~mandarins~~ temple guardians, the so-called Central Marxists, was not an assimilated, lively and fruitful perspective, but was rather dead apologetics.

K[arl] K.[autsky] The Intern[ational] instrument of peace![*]

~~The~~ This is how Soc-D[emocracy] & the trad[unions] have, through a half cent[ury] of training, prepared the troops—for Hindenburg & Ludendorff, *Schutztruppen*[†] for *Mannerheim*[‡] for the Hetman & for the Baltic barons.[§]

This abomination, this depth of dishonor, this wicked self-prostitution appeared at first to be incomprehensible. One was tempted to believe in a particular villainy among the mass of German people. But there wouldn't be anything as natural as that! Regarding large decisions, history knows no middle paths of the sort spun out across the still water of parliament[arism]. In G[er]m[a]ny as everywhere the prol[etariat] was confronted with an either/or. The options were either revolutionary class s[truggle] or—in forgoing this—the savoring of all possible levels of humiliation & of betrayal. The heroic deeds in Finland etc. represent the line through the past of the *old G[erman]*

---

* See Kautsky's "Die Sozialdemokratie im Kriege" (Social Democracy in the War), *Die Neue Zeit*, Vol. 33. 1914/1915, Vol. 1, pp. 1–8.) and "Die Internationalität und der Krieg" (Internationalism and War), p. 240). In these essays, Kautsky defends the thesis that the International "is not an effective tool in war, it is essentially a tool of peace." See also Luxemburg's "*Der Wiederaufbau der Internationale*" (The Reconstruction of the International) in *Gesammelte Werke* Vol. 4, p. 21. Luxemburg concludes: "Kautsky, as the representative of the so-called 'Marxist center,'—or, articulated in political terms, as the theorist of the swamp, who has degraded theory for years, turning it into the compliant maid of the official practice of the 'party authorities,' thereby contributing substantially to the current breakdown of the party—has now even cobbled together a new theory precisely to justify and to whitewash this breakdown."

† "*Schutztruppe*" (protection force) were the special forces established in the 1890s used to conquer and control Germany's colonies in Africa. Bismarck had intended the trading companies to police themselves, but in response to powerful anti-colonial resistance he created a colonial wing of the military in addition to the standing army and navy.

‡ In May 1918, White Guard troops led by Carl Gustav Mannerheim together with German troops crushed the Finnish Revolution that had begun in January 1918. Tens of thousands of revolutionaries fell victim to the counterrevolution.

§ *Hetman* is a historical term for a Ukrainian military commander. Pavlo Skoropadskyi used the title when he took power in Ukraine in April 1918, with the backing of the German army, deposing the socialist-led government of the Ukrainian People's Republic, the Central Rada (Council – national assembly).

Soc-D[emocracy] & the Second Intern[ational]. They obliterate the old authority & the tactics from Engels—K[arl] K[autsky].

G[erman] Soc-D[emocracy] wanted to ~~immo~~ immortalize Engels' tactical program (1895),* which had served it well for a stretch. It was imposed onto new conditions—onto the imperialistic ~~per~~ era that ~~Engels~~ Marx & Engels didn't get to know, of which Engels experienced the first weak beginnings, but could no longer integrate into the calculation—common sense became non-sense, good deed—a blight.† G[erman] Soc-D[emocracy] & to an even greater extent the trad[e unions] had become, seen in historical terms, a conservative party, their ideology contradicting their practice to an ever ~~sharp~~ greater extent. And as ever in such cases, the symptoms of 1) corruption, 2) confusion & paralysis crept in.

[Written in the left-hand margin:]

Everyone else followed in the footsteps of G[erman] Soc-D[emocracy].—With social[ism] in this condition in all countries, the International could only hang in the air. It had become a phrase, a showpiece.

"Idealism" immunizing the masses, just as small children are immunized against smallpox. A revolutionary *tactic* that keeps pace with deve[lopment] is the only means of creating idealism.

The split personality of German Soc-D[emocracy] ~~was~~ is accurately mirrored in its official theorist Kautsky. ~~Shortly before~~ A few years before the war he wrote his pamphlet "The Road to Power," in which he, with a light rod in the fog of theor[etical] abstraction, heaved the breakdown of capit[alist] soc[iety] & the realization of soci[ialism] immediately before us. With the outbreak of war, which immediately previous had been seen as building the practical ~~condition for~~ foundation under that theoretical horizon, Kautsky's road to power transformed into a road to powerlessness, in the classical admission, that the International i.e., socialism, is not a method against war, but is merely an "instrument of peace," a declaration of soc[ialism]'s bankruptcy as practical politics.

~~Ad 2 9~~

3

What is decisive in the conclusion of the war & the further unfolding of developments is the breakdown of *German* imp[erialism]. With its fall, the bourg[eois] world is starting to slide—proof that it wasn't Russian tsarism but rather the

---

* This is a reference to Friedrich Engels's "Introduction to Karl Marx's "Class Struggles in France from 1848 to 1850" (1895). In: *Marx-Engels Collected Works*, Vol. 27 (New York: International Publishers, 1990), pp. 506–25.—See also Luxemburg's "Ermattung oder Kampf" (Fatigue or Struggle), *Gesammelte Werke*, Vol. 2, pp. 344–77 which contains a detailed discussion of this issue.

† Johann Wolfgang von Goethe, *Faust: A Tragedy*, Part I, Scene IV (Trans. Bayard Taylor, 1870; Random House, 1950), p. 67.

German forces of reaction that were the ~~keyst~~ cornerstone & the bulwark of intern[ational] reaction. This is where the contradictoriness of both camps of imperialism finds its expression.

~~It would be~~ Nothing would be or & less historical, than to explain both camps—because we've got imperialism here & imperialism there—as being one & the same.

There are only two modes in which ~~soc~~ proletarian-soc[ialist] politics can act in relation to the bourg[eois] wars, which correspond to two stages in socie[tal] development.

Either the ~~soc~~ prol[etariat] is not yet mature enough to take the stage as an autonomous factor in politics. Then ~~the soc.~~ its leaders & ideologues are left no other option than to

4

weigh up both warmongering ~~?~~ parties against each other, to assess each of their motivations & the consequences of their victories from the standpoint of gener[al] progr[essive] development, and to join one or the other side. This was the situation & also the politics of Marx & Engels, and of Lassalle ~~not to menti.~~ in the war periods of the [18]50s & [18]60s. ~~until the Franco-Prussian War, in which socialists took an active role for the first time, naturally as opponents of their warmong[ering] bourgeoisie on both sides.~~

Or if socialism assumed an autonomous form of politics during periods of war, then it was naturally against the war itself, i.e., against *both* parties in the war.

5

In the Fran[co]-Prussian War? …*

In the current world war, the proletariat was called upon to rise up against both imperialist camps & ~~both toget~~ to battle against imper[ialism] as a system in both of them together. Because it did not do this & what's more now faces the task of first working out an autonomous role for itself—out of the ~~situ~~ state of affairs the war has created and during the liquidation of the war—one of its first tasks is to ~~objectiv~~ account for the objective ~~consequences of the~~ tendencies of both of the ~~war~~ imperialist camps.

All cats ~~of the dull & part. crude form of radicalism~~ are gray in the dark—& ~~*so*~~ can one form of imperialism ~~so~~ be confused with another.

---

* On July 19, 1870, France declared war on Prussia with the aim of preventing the unification of Germany. On February 26, 1871, the German Reich and France concluded a preliminary peace treaty at Versailles, which accepted the Prussian-German aims: France was compelled to concede Alsace and a large part of Lorraine (with rich reserves of iron ore) to Germany, and to pay reparations of 5 billion francs within three years.

In dialectical perceptions drawn from history, without which all soc[ialist] politics are merely blown on the breeze, the inner contradictions & differences ~~within the~~ in the womb of

6

Imperialism ~~of the highest~~ very important & of a high level of practical significance.

~~That~~ The war being concluded through a military decision, as is currently in process, means a defeat for the intern[ational] proletariat in every case, by every possible conclusion. It is always at the cost of & on sufferance of the work[ing] cl[ass] that peace is made, by every type of peace agreement and settlement. ~~Imp~~ Bourg[eois] gov[ernments] concluding a peace agreement would definitely mean the victory of imp[erialism]

~~Just~~ But~~,~~ for soc[ialism]'s future prospects, everything depends on which methods are used to reach peace, & which tendency inside imper[ialism] wins the upper hand at first.

~~The Germ~~ It would be a slap in the face to every histor[ical] ability to differentiate, if one wanted to ignore the insight that the ~~Germa~~ imp[erialism] of the Central Powers

7

& of the Entente does not express two different tendencies.
1. ~~Whoever the~~ It is of decisive importance for the Central Power, that *German* im[perialism] ruled completely here. Over there a coalition, in which equally powerful capitalist[ic] states—Engl. & America—are in rivalry with each other. In addition: a young up and coming Japan.

The Germans were allied to Austr[ia], a collapsing ruin, a rotting corpse carcass,

Turkish m[ilitary] state, a corpse & an *object* of imperialism.

~~Bulgar~~

2. German imp[erialism] combines East Elbian methods with the daredevilry of strong capit[al].

[In the left-hand margin]:

Absolute failure of pub[lic] opinion, worst possible censor, absolute disappearance of the trade un[ion] move[ment].

The English have ~~trad~~ democr[atic] traditions & world imper[ialism] ~~d~~ in full blossom, using freer methods (against Austr[alia], Canada and the Dominions).

America—Democracy.

8

3. In G[er]m[a]ny militarism has predominated since 1870, being the cement of the G[erman Empire]. Imperial const[itution] as Bismarck's present. In Engl[and] & Amer[ica], militarism was first born in this world war, meaning it couldn't play any role in the life of the country.

~~Resulting from this~~

4. Engl., Amer., Fr[ance], Italien Imper[ialism] abroad. Gmny—in Europe itself. ~~Because~~ The old *Kulturnationen** turned into the object of investigation.

[Written in the left-hand margin:]

5. The complete ~~failure~~ bankruptcy of *Germ[a]n* Soc-D[emocracy] if Germany would have won ~~concerning~~ would have sealed the fates of the intern[ational] for decades.

Resulting from this, G[er]m[a]ny's supremacy would have built a ~~Thr~~ strong iron ring of reaction—whole of Austria, ~~& the west~~ Balkans, & the West deep into Flanders & France.

G[er]m[a]ny's world supremacy would have meant a yoke for Europe & that's why, in the long run, it was a *utopia*, which only the primeval jungle-nature & the cannibalism of the German imp[erialists]—the Reventlows & Rohrbachs—could believe in. And that's why one year of G[er]m[a]ny's trial supremacy over eastern & western Euro[pe] is enough.

9

Anglo-Fren[ch]-Amer[ican] Imper[ialism] does not spurn such methods in any way. It is merely that ~~u~~ until now, ~~it~~ it has only had ~~the~~ the opportunity to ~~try them~~ successfully apply them on ~~negroes~~ Kaffir, Basothos, Indians, Arabs, Redskins, Australian Aborigines & Tasmanians. German Imp[erialism] came into the situation & had the primitive naivety to try them out on Russians, Poles, Finns, Belgians, French & Romanians.

Its supremacy in Ukraine & in Russ[ia], upsetting everything & making everything start to slide, sweeping the undermost on high, fanning the resistance ~~to~~ of the West into a bright flame.

The ~~democr.~~ opposite to German imp[erialism], the character of coalition, the democr[atic] traditions of countries have led to a situation in which the Entente has had to counter the German method of the brutal fist with the demagogy of the democr[atic] phrase. Right of nations, moral right of the weak,

* "*Kulturnation*" is the idea of a shared national culture, used variously to justify chauvinism and imperialism.

10

~~See~~ peace, disarmament & courts of arbitration. All phrases that inexpiably belong to the essential nature of the practice & the possibilities of Entente Imp[erialism], as to every imp[erialism]. But its exactly this contradiction, which would have stayed ~~&~~ covered up had G[e]rm[a]ny been victorious, that ~~no~~ now ~~has~~ after the Entente victory has to be ~~pla~~ put to the test, has to take on form in reality, & the ~~su~~ inescapable fate of Entente Imp[erialism] & all of bourg[eois] society starts to fulfil itself.

[Written in the left-hand side of the page, without classification]

Disheveled capit[alist] socie[ty] has to have an ideology. All old forms are used up, sullied, trampled down: God's mercy, Christianity (church), the deep & ~~etern~~ secret wisdom of diplomacy, before which the limited under[standing] of subjects had to bow down etc., all arts of government, "historical rights," alliances etc., all gone to the devil. A renovation is unavoidable. Pacification after the atrocity of the war!! Militarism made savor[y].

~~With the~~ Out of its overall character, out of its situation in the four years of war, the Entente has to pretend that this is a peace reached in the light of an overwhelming democr[atic]-pacifistic ideology. It must reflect back to the peoples that this is a peace of the moral & legal renewal of the world.

In that moment in which it was victorious, the Entente became a prisoner of its own phraseology. In that moment

11

where the Entente sits at the conference table, to make a peace of renewal, the crisis of bourg[eois] society begins.

During the few years of its milit[ary] march to victory, German imp[erialism] shook up, shocked & revolutionized all of Europe & in turn the whole world ~~from~~[.] Entente imp[erialism], which countered the German variety with phraseology as the ~~strongest~~ weapon of necessity, as ~~like~~ a means of waging war, is forced now to use its victory for the realization of phraseology & completes thereby *nolens volens* the revolutionary work begun by the Germans. ~~Both together~~

a,b,c

ad ~~11~~ a

In order that both can ~~clearly~~ tangibly be expressed, so that the special tendency & the spec[ial] char[acter] of both imp[erialist] camps can break through in full maturity, ~~it was necessary~~ & can unfold, it was necessary, that ~~each camp in due course~~ first the G[erman] imp[erialism] attained full victory. ~~Was only through~~ Therefore 1) the capitulation of the G[erman] prolet[ariat]. 2) the capit[ulation] of the Russ[ian] Revol[ution] ~~that became possible~~ effects things.

How the military breakdown of Russia ~~under the rule~~ ensued after the October Revol[ution] in 1917 & which lessons can be drawn from that, is a matter for another chapter.* At this stage merely the objective consequence of this fact.

~~The Brest-Litovsk peace transformed the outbreak of the Russ[ian] Revol[ution] in~~ The utter polit[ical] failure of the intern[ational] & more explicitly of the German prol[etariat], &, on the other hand, the utter milit[ary] failure of the Russ[ian] prolet[ariat] transforms the outbreak of the Russ[ian] Revol[ution] into an outrageous ~~much desired~~ biggest stroke of luck for G[erman] imp[erialism]. The capitulation of Brest-Lit[ovsk]† started G[erman] imp[erialism]'s march to victory, ~~i.e., facilitated~~ securing absolute supremacy for it over Central & Eastern Europe

b

& gave it the possibility, ~~its~~ of unfolding to the full range of its inner tendencies & prospects of world supremacy.

The behavior of the German prol[etariat] and of German Soc-D[emocracy] made the untrammeled breakthrough of these tendencies possible, in its core, in the ~~most brutal~~ centauresque, curt, and most heroic forms.

If this world supremacy has not resulted, yes, even if the plans for this world supremacy today have ultimately broken down and have been buried, then neither the German prol[etariat] nor the Russ[ian] Revol[ution] is responsible for this. It has happened *despite* the failure of the Russ[ian] prol[etariat] in their battle against German imp[erialism], just as it happened despite the failure of the German ~~& the intern[ational]~~ prolet[ariat] in these struggles. The ~~trium~~ complete victory, the dictatorship of German imp[erialism] over Russia & ~~its~~ the prospect of its world supremacy being tangibly close where the factors that first whipped the countries of the West up to carry out those utmost efforts, which have led to the defeat of G[erman] imp[erialism] & ~~the~~ the World War being decided on a military

c

level—decided by Entente imp[erialism], which carries the final crisis of bourg[eois] socie[ty] in its womb.

This is how the interconnectedness of cause & effect, of the political behavior of the German prol[etariat], of the Russian Revol[ution], of the German victory, of the defense of the West & of ultimate victory for the Entente are

---

* See Luxemburg's "On the Russian Revolution," pp. 215–46, below.

† On December 15, 1917, an armistice was signed between Russia and the Central Powers, and an agreement was reached to commence peace negotiations on December 22, 1917. When the "stolen peace" was then signed at Brest-Litovsk on March 3, 1918, Soviet Russia lost around 1 million square kilometers worth of territory.

joined together to make an uninterrupted chain. Via all possible detours & serpentine lanes, and via all unforeseeable incidents, hist[orical] devel[opment] leads back to the foundational problem: the global antagonism between capital & labor, between imper[ialism] & soc[ialism].

That implies: *historical nec[essity]*. That creature won't allow herself to be duped or to be corrupted, ~~not~~ and she doesn't allow people to do deals with her. Like Shylock, she demands her pound [of flesh]. This is a classical proof for the power of social[ism]. ~~Despite~~

Even German imp[erialism], if it had won, would ultimately simply have unleashed the Social Rev[olution]. But between these two events, an undefined period of time of strict reaction would have resulted. The Entente's victory

12

pushed bourg[eois] societ[ty] straight into the maelstrom of revolution. ~~Because s~~ Regarding the role of socialism, it is especially important to note that a victory for German imp[erialism] ~~an uprising of~~ would have destroyed the chances for a revol[ution] in G[erman]y for an incalculable period ~~in the future~~ of time. [German imperialism's] defeat, its breakdown ~~open up the~~ pull the prospects for that revolution into the immediate foreground, and make these prospects ineluctable. The ~~game~~ of fate of the Entente & of bourg[eois] soc[iety] on a large scale repeats itself inside G[er]m[a]ny on a small scale. The defeat has brought a democr[atic] phraseology onto the political stage, but this phraseology will become a material factor in the ~~storm~~ urgency of events. Now G[er]m[a]ny can neither go back to the East Elbian reaction, nor can it go forward to a serious realization of these phrases. ~~Their~~ This contradiction brings about an unavoidable solution:

13

The *German Revolution*. The same applies to Austria: victory would have artificially conserved the carcass, defeat lets loose the process of decay, ~~of hour~~ in full flow & considering the insolvability of the problem—revolution. Further: G[erman] victory would have led to the conservation of Turkey, while the Entente leads to its Dissolution, & revolution in the Balkans. ~~The oppos~~ With regard to the decisive role played by the German prol[etariat], the *German* revol[ution] means the signal for the int[ernational revolution.] ~~The French working cl., which through the milit. defeat~~ The Fren[ch] working cl[ass]—who would have been inhibited in taking revolut[ionary] action because of fears for the French Republic in the event of victory for the half-absolutism of the Hohenzollerns—will now be free in their ability to act & the German example will have to be imitated by the French working class.

14

~~Above all it is clearly~~

This is how bourgeois society ~~has~~ has suddenly started to slide, through the war & its conclusion. Its class rel[ations], its national ~~relat., its~~ problems, its state borders, the economic & technical conditions for its existence, its complete range of ideologies—all suddenly in sheer upheaval, ~~in~~ all has started to flow, all has been sucked into the whirl & tide ~~of contra~~ of renewal. The oldest relat[ions], which have become historic, honorable and covered with moss, ~~movement~~ have started to shake. Inertia has been overcome, the impasse surmounted.

By stirring up problems everywhere, bourg[eois] society is unavoidably driving itself toward the abyss. ~~All problems~~ There is not one problem that this society brings to the surface which it is also in a position to solve.

Nationalities problem

Peace problem

[Written in the right-hand margin:]

Philippines (since when: 1870 or since the partition of Poland? Colonies?!)

9 15

Food supply problem

~~Nutrition problem~~

~~Costs of the war Ta~~

Financial Problem (Tax, cost of the war)

Democracy

Regarding each of these problems, bourgeois society hits its own limits.

Additionally, ~~experiment about~~ a further ~~incong~~ contradiction: the problems of war push bourgeois society into finding democratic & social solutions. They must create ~~the Soc-Dem~~ a broad basis on all sides in order to save themselves, in order to call upon Soc-D[emocracy] to help with the effort. Simultaneously, bourgeois society pushes the image of the Russian Revolution as the bogeyman, in the most fierce opposition against the proletariat & against socialism. ~~The Holy Alliance & the League of Nations~~

Through ~~this~~ the start of this period of sliding & ferment, bourg[eois] society has delivered itself up to its own fate. It no longer has a choice, it has handed over the reins. There is no way back for it. The *status quo ante*, ~~the ideal of the Independent Soc-D[emocratic]~~ is as impossible as

16

returning to the earth of the Carboniferous Era or of the ~~Trias~~ antediluvial period. But if bourgeois society decides to go forward, then it's groping in the dark. Its own phrases will trap it more thoroughly, transforming it into an acrimonious earnestness. ~~With~~ Whatever it plays with will grow more ~~bitterly~~ terribly serious by the day & the near future stares at it with a stony, Sphinx-like countenance.

There *is* no solution for the problems that have been exposed, there is no safe foothold in the sliding movement that has been started—other than the social world revolution, ~~toward~~ into the bottomless pit of which [bourgeois] society is driving itself.

[The following paragraphs have been scored through several times.]

That things have turned out thus cannot be credited to the intern. proletariat. Until now,

17

it has been the work of imperialism, the work of objective societ[al] development.

With merciless resolve & with an iron fist, this development drags the prolet[riat], like one of the *Moirai** toward socialism, regardless of whether it kicks back or whether it plays dead. While ~~polit~~ Marxism as a political form in the war suffered a numbing bankruptcy—as a historical apprehension, it is celebrating the highest possible triumph. And ~~while~~ through raising up the conclusion of the war—with its hist. insight, illuminating certainty & dazzling luster—out even from out of the political bankruptcy of the prolet[ariat]—[Marxism] orders the Prol[etariat] back onto the rails of soc[ialist] politics.

18

Now it's time to settle accounts. p. 2)

The first is—self-criticism. Already regarding this point, ways of dealing with the situation differ sharply. The *Haasen*† of this world & the Social government.

[End of deletion.]

Emerging from the war, the ~~socialist.~~ proletariat appears at first to be every bit as torn & split, as full of ferment & adjournment, as the bourg[eois] socie[ty] itself. Its ideology is every bit as fissured, torn into national troops, & split into different camps in each individual state. Because the proletariat has not grasped

* In ancient Greek religion the Moirai were the personifications of Fate.

† A pun on [Hugo] Haase and *Hasen*, the German word for hares.

how to oppose bourg[eois] socie[ty] in the World War, it must at first share that society's fate: ideology, politics, its tasks ~~in~~ vacillating, postponement, starting to ferment. But out of this ferment & deferral, the will & the insight still has to form & crystalize—for the liquidation of bourg[eois] soc[iety], for taking on all the problems that it has exposed—problems which, in trying to solve, bourg[eois] soc[iety] is

19

compelled to come to grief & end up in its death throes.

[Written in the left-hand margin, without classification marks:]

In this situation, months can achieve things as regards polit[ical] education & maturity, which full prior decades were not able to impart.

II

[The following sentences have been crossed out.]

Already in the process of reviewing the past & its evaluation, paths of opinion diverge:

The Gov[ernment]-Soc[ialists] consider their current politics to be a direct continuation of the old G[erman] Soc-D[emocracy] & the intern[ational] & can discern a lo[ng] and uninterrupted and non-contradictory line of devel[opment].

The Haase-Kautskys regard their politics of opposition to be the direct continuation of the old G[erman] Soc-D[emocracy] & of the Intern[ational].

Both are right. The old G[erman] Soc-D[emocracy] was a two-headed beast. Its two elements: a radical turn of phrase & opportunistic practice. A revolutionary theory & a purely parliamentary group kind of politics.

According to Haase-Kautsky, everything in the past was good & just. Their

[End of the deletion.]*

1. The economic problem. An incredible quantity of means of production have been destroyed in the war: iron & steel, copper, complete raw materials ~~forests~~ motors, ~~finished parts~~ ships, forests, huge stretches of cropland & meadows, & in the highest prod. [sic.] The main stem of Europe's educated & technically trained workforce, the product of decades of culture—along with their ~~whole~~ offspring—the next generation; ~~through the substitution of many inferior~~ a large part of those remaining disabled. That means, the workforce attacked down to its roots. The peasant economy everywhere ~~through rundo~~ neglected & run down.

* This deleted material was incorporated into an earlier section of these notes. See p. 191 above.

[In the left-hand margin:]

After every earlier war, an econ[omic] upswing started. That—something different!

The first things we will notice: shortage of trained labor power, shortage of raw materials & simultaneously unemployment for the masses that are flooding back [home] as a result of the shortage of raw materials, and the dissolution of the ~~arms~~ war industry. A terrible general ~~industry & trade~~ economic crisis & a global famine are immediate threats. Further: appalling downturn in public health, an increase in the mortality rate, ~~urgent~~ the threat of a severe decrease in population, physical degeneration, epidemics! ~~Hunger revolts, loot[ing], anarchy~~ To ~~preve~~ control these horrors, ~~(Government-Socialist wisdom only knows one method, at least to start with: continuation of the forced economy, i.e., bread coupons, conserves, swedes & illicit trade & the state of siege!~~

Capitalist anarchy is in no condition to get rid of these things. In the shortest possible period of time, it will lead to anarchy & to a gener[al] fall. The "state economy" showed its true colors during the war: 1) Eternal perpetuation of the state of siege. 2) ~~breeding gr.~~ A classically fertile culture for illicit trade & profiteering on basic foodstuffs. 3) Starvation of the masses. The one & only thing that could save socie[ty] are radical socie[tal] measures on a large scale, which are not impeded by private property & interest in profits, & which do not stop at "national" borders.

~~radical~~ Cultivating stretches of land that until now have not been used, ~~the immediate~~ the utmost increase in agricult[ural] productivity.

Drawing on all ~~pow~~ labor abilities for the purposes of productive work.

[Left-hand margin:]

through the abolition ~~of tax favors* for private~~ large-scale landowner[s].

Transformation into general use of the large private forests, hunting grounds & estates of the ~~magnates,~~ dynasties, churches & monasteries. Introduction of cooperative-based organization into peasant ~~economy~~ production, ~~generous, comprehensive utilization of the forces of water~~ Immediate, fundamental restructuring of labor conditions, in order to utilize female powers of labor without damaging their health & to take account of the reduced capability of the male members of the workforce left over from the war. Housing reform because of epidemics!, the entire rebuilding of cities; making a unification of the urban & the rural economy necessary! Nationalization of sanitation in the case of threats of epidemics! Abolition of the production of luxuries in ~~military provision~~ arms production.

---

* The word in the original is "*Liebesgaben*" (gifts of love), which Social Democrats used ironically when referring to the Imperial government's tax gifts to Junker landowners.

2. The Financial Problem. All states, ~~whether warring or neutral~~ emerge from the war with debt burdens at as yet unheard-of levels—the victors and the defeated, warring and neutral states. Finance & Arms capital, Banking Capital has got the cap[italist] state wrapped round its little fingers; in G[er]m[a]ny, the domestic, in Fr[ance] & Eng[land], foreign capital. What is going to become of this debt burden? Taxation of the masses? They can't pay. Taxation of capital? The cap[italist] state will never bring itself to do that. In England only one—part, but to balance that, compensation in India etc. ~~With this. publ[ic] debt. With this~~ This publ[ic] debt will gobble up all forms of income from now on. And the rebuilding of the economy? At now of all times, when the state is facing the largest possible expenditure. On top of that provision for war inval[ids], for widows & orphans! ~~Only~~ Canceling the debt is the first precondition for the maintenance of states, but it's precisely this sole path of escape that is impossible.

3. The Problem of Nationalities. To which year do we backdate the restitution of right. To 1871? But Poles refer back to 1772! But what about Ireland? And India? The Philippines? The Chinese "leases"? Algeria & Tunisia? And the whole colonial problem?

Further: How can one reconcile the nationalities with each other? What will happen with China & Persia, will they now be left in peace? And with the *negroes?* in the U[nited] States?

4. Problem of peace and disarmament. It is precisely armament's capital that has become the most powerful during the war. All the wealth wasted during the war has accumulated there! England & America, ~~Jap.~~ have now really created milit[arism] for the first time. Japan, as supplier, has grown enormously. The technology of militarism no longer tolerates any "small businesses." "A wee bit of militarism" is just as impossible[*] as "a little bit of anarchy" in the context of production. This same armament capital is now (directly & through the banks) the main creditor in the States. And politically too, militarism has trumped, in no place more so than in the Uni[ted] States, in Wilson's [White] House.

Partition of Turkey
" of the German colonies
~~Viol~~ Compensation for Japan.
Gigantic realignment of power rel[ations]. New ~~oppon~~ competitors.
Engl[and] & Amer[ica], Engl[and], Amer[ica] & Jpan.
Only one way out of all this: socialism!

It's like a landslide, unstoppable, one boulder pulls the next down with it.

---

* In the source text, "possible."

The old Europe is shaking at its joints & cracking in upon itself ~~&.~~, and with it the old bourg[eois] world. ~~From this~~ Nothing can remain from this apart from rubble, and out of this rubble nothing can emerge apart from—soc[ialist] soc[iety].

~~North~~ East & West & North tremble,

Kingdoms burst, thrones split …[*]

[The following sentences are crossed out.]

Karl without a country

~~G~~ A never-existing performance about a kingdom that has disappeared, because one fine day, when a ~~gardener's tool chest~~ creel had fallen over, its peoples crept away in all directions, like ~~worms~~ crabs.

To IV

The new nation states (K[arl] K[autsky's] theory: Nat[ion state]-democracy) The cloven hoof that is hidden behind this democracy has been shown in Ukraine, Finland, the Baltic countries, and Poland. We have to wring this chick's neck, before it starts growing feathers.

[End of the deletion]

Fruits of the education ~~products~~ of G[erman] Soc-D[emocracy] & Legiens:

The German workers as butchers of the communes in Finland, in Riga, in Ukraine.

[In left-hand margin.]

Mannerheim,[†] the Gallifet[‡] of Finland. ~~The Swede~~n

In the breaks ~~in the sch~~ between sentry duty they probably read the trade union official organ ~~or~~ & in the local party newspaper.

The great-grandchildren of those German *landsknechts*[§]—who were sold, ~~as cannon fodder~~ like cattle, into foreign parts by ~~the~~ their Duodez despots[¶]—did not deny their true selves, the tradition of the servant nations ~~& nations~~ is deep in their veins.

The German worker as the scourge of intern[ational] socialism & the revol[ution].

---

* The allusion is to Goethe's *West-östlicher Divan,* (Stuttgart: Cotta, 1819): "Nord und West und Süd zersplittern, / Throne bersten, Reiche zittern."

† Several decades aftr crushing of Finland's short-lived socialist republic, Mannerheim allied Finland with Nazi Germany during World War II.

‡ Gaston Alexandre Auguste, Marquis de Galliffet was the French general who directed the brutal crushing of the Paris Commune.

§ The *Landsknechts* (often translated as "servants of the earth") were German mercenary soldiers of the late fifteenth and early sixteenth centuries who fought in phalanxes with pikes. They were a formidable military force with a reputation for independence, ferocity, and discipline.

¶ "*Duodezstaat*" can be translated as "microstate." The word was popularized in Luxemburg's lifetime by the satire *Duodez,* published in 1906 by Hermann Löns.

The horror of the Finnish counterrev[olution], the German occupation of Ukraine & in the Baltic States will only come to light bit by bit. The atrocity of the June ~~Days~~ massacre of the y. 1848 & of the Commune butchery carried out by Gallifet will pale in comparison. And each of these atrocities, every sentence of blood, every slaughtered ~~yes~~ Finnish Red Guardist, ~~the~~ Latvian prol[et], & Ukrainian peasant will rise up out of the grave ~~again~~ as a witness against the German working class, & against G[erman] Soc-D[emocracy]. ~~Like the curse~~

The sign of Cain on their foreheads, the repressive forces of the reaction,[*] backbone of the most reactionary gover[nment] of the world.

"That was the war of the German unionist."

Nothing has yet happened. As yet, we thank Wilson & the English tanks for the beginnings of the "new ordering." The G[erman] prol[etariat] has not yet done anything, to wash off its blood-guilt and to ~~wash~~ prove it's become human.

I

Decay Process in S[ocial] D[emocracy & the Int[ernational] since August 4, 1914[†]
party & soc[ialist] org[anizations] are no product of art, but rather of history. Function: rev[olutionary] cl[ass] struggle.—As soon as this stops happening, the apparatus starts to collapse in on itself. The war concludes the second period in the history of social[ism]. The first period ~~up to the Com~~ from the [18]30s to the Paris Commune: spontaneous risings of revolution with utopian attempts at the immediate realiz[ation] of soc[ialism] (48). Second period from the start of the [18]60s (Lassalle & Intern[ationals] first & second) up to the outbreak of the World War: parliamentarianism & continual organization regarding the daily struggle. The first period served the purpose of splitting up bourg[eois] society into classes & to carve out the clear outline of cl[ass] opposition. The second period served the purpose of ~~creating~~ organizing this ready-made & recognized opposition ~~of an organization~~ of class opposition as an ongoing daily phenomenon. The fall of the Commune was the critique & the conclusion ~~bankruptcy~~ of the first period. The World War is the critique & the conclusion ~~bankruptcy~~ of the second period. Hegel's dialectic triumphs: now a return to the tasks of the first period: ~~in order to~~ realiz[ation] of soci[ialism], but with a higher basis.

* *Gendarme-Pandurs* in the original. This seems to be a reference to Trenck's *Panduren*, a light infantry unit of the Habsburg Monarchy, raised by Baron Franz von der Trenck under a charter issued by Maria Theresa of Austria in 1741.

† The following thoughts, listed as I–III, are in ink, and presumably written in one sitting.

II

~~P Sch~~ Inner Weaknesses (Contradictions) of the Second Period

1.

Outwardly, the bankruptcy occurred on August 4. Internally, for decades.

The International was a phrase & a performance of spectacles. Proof: the fates of the May Day commemorations.

National politics of S[ocial] D[emocracy] was: parliamentarism. (Organization, press, funds, party conferences, literature, sign[ificance] of the elections & of the factions.)

High point: the "put-a-damper-on" election [of 1912.][*]

Products & foundations of the period: passivity of the masses, lack of critique coming from the masses. (Now revealed in the fates of the party press: Hamburg, Chemnitz, Kiel etc.) Role of the masses merely to function as a pedestal for a dozen politicians, just like in the bourg[eois] parties. Hand to mouth politics, without any of [their] own politics.

The organization [got] tangled up in a diametrical contradiction to serve its own purpose. Mass-org[anization] as a method to turn the masses into an unconscious tool of a handful of functionaries.

The cleft in the entity of the workers' movem[ent]: theory, revolutionary; practice, purely bourgeois. That's why possibility in the party for both extreme revol[utionaries] and for purely bourg[eois] elements (revisionists). Both were in the right. Between them quagmire as the natural ~~u S~~ product of contradiction. Hegemonic tactic embodied in Bebel: bringing the diverging extremes into one boat, conserving the inner contradiction, papering over the oppositions. In this, the inner party tactics have exhausted themselves & culminated for the last fifteen–twenty years.

[In left-hand margin]

Engels' preface to the KiK!![†] Parliamentarism as the only form of politics.

All this forced to the point of becoming an ideal in G[er]m[a]ny. All other countries eager to follow in G[ermany's] footsteps.

That the origin of the guerrilla war with Revisionism & the pyrrhic victory over it.

Symptoms before August 4, 1918: failure in the Morocco affair, the fiasco

---

* The 1912 election to the Reichstag, with a reference to the covert electoral deals made between the SPD and progressive liberals.

† A reference to his 1895 preface to Marx's *Class Struggles in France, 1848–1850*.

concerning the right to vote in Prussia, vote in favor of ~~armed for~~ contribution for the army (complete désarroi in 1913 already, just before the outbreak [of war]), the fear of the mass strike.

2.

Role & the devel[opment] of the trade un[ions] in the last twenty years. Gaining autonomy out of a branch of the soc[ialist] mov[ement], bureaucracy above the masses. Tra[de Union] tactic: avoiding all big conflicts. Purely defensive. Return to the tactics of the Engl[ish] trade unions of the 60s & 70s but [this time]—in the era of cartels, banks, imperialism, militarism, inflation, indir[ect] taxation, import duties! The German tra[de unions] have gone backward in terms of their deve[lopment] & now, marked by the imper[ialistic] orgy, they have reached the stage of using the tactics the Engl[ish] t[rade unions] used at the start of heavy ind[ustry], & from the heyday of liberalism. (Symptoms: dock workers strike, Ruhr miners' str[ike], May Day stifled, Bömelburg's statements.)*

III

The question's knotted center

Imperialism forces a decision, a trial of strength, a battle for polit[ical] power. For decades, S[ocial Democracy] has not fought any form of battle for polit[ical] power. It merely limits us to certain methods of struggle: organized mass demonstrations, methods of parliamentary agitation. But as they are not taken to the next level, both of these are turned into ends in themselves & thereby into methods of polit[ical] powerlessness.

~~The pretense could~~ The existence of socialism was thus built upon a pretense. The outbreak of World War put this to the test. Power struggle between Imp[erialism] & Soc[ialism] had to decide things. The refusal of the war credits

---

* This refers to the speech about the political mass strike given by Theodor Bömelburg at the Fifth Congress of German Trade Unions, which took place from May 22 to 27, 1905, in Cologne: "All in all, one will have to say to oneself, that the political mass strike can of course be discussed, but one will have to consider very carefully if it should be enacted. Our job in the German trade union movement is to ensure that the discussion disappears, and that solutions for the future are left up to each individual moment. (Quite right!) We all know what effort it cost us for the trade unions to climb to the level they now have. That work was not achieved in a single year, no, the work of three or four decades is contained in that achievement. It has been a huge sacrifice to reach the level the organization currently has, and we will have to pay an even greater sacrifice to raise the organization up to a still higher rung of power." The Congress strongly rejected the use of the mass strike and even prohibited (by a vote of 200 to 17) any discussion of it. Bömelburg headed the General Commission that issued these rulings. See John A. Moses, *Trade Unionism in Germany from Bismarck to Hitler, 1869–1933, Volume I: 1869–1918* (London: George Prior, 1985), p. 152: "Bömelburg's ideas on the mass strike were identical to those being expressed in circles about May Day. Both meant incurring unnecessary risks to union organization."

[i.e., without accompanying measures] is nonsense. It would have been necessary to call for ~~Ka~~ resistance right down the line. That is what the one hundred and ten [SPD representatives in the Reichstag] felt & were therefore *consistent* in their U-turn, as they shied away from a power struggle. The rej[ection] of the loan could only have been significant if it had been understood as a signal for the resistance of the masses. ~~The starting point for theft~~

This development faced a dilemma: imperialist world war or proletarian revol[ution].

And more precisely

1) either Soc[ial] Democracy's increasingly attacking politics should have led to a revol[utionary] situation years ago & prevented the outbreak of the World War. Or the other way round, the outbreak of war should have given the signal for the outbreak of revol[ution].

This was the logic of the situation that led to the politics of August 4, 1914. The notion that merely rejecting a loan would be enough is, in itself, an expression of parliament[ary] cretinism.

[The following paragraphs are crossed out.]

4.

Further Perspectives

The Russ[ian] Rev[olution] remains the first link in the chain of Europ[ean] transition [to] revol[ution], however short or long the interruption that precedes it might be. The social & polit[ical] balance of bourg[eois] soc[iety] has been destroyed, destroyed precisely because of the World War. A peaceful period of parliament[iary] c[lass] ru[le] by the bourgeoisie is no longer possible—

The collapse of Soc-D[emocracy] now unchains & liberates the energy of the masses, wakes again its critique & in so doing performs an educational role. The only thing still possible is a series of catastrophes: either revolutionary or ~~cri~~ imperialist or both jumbled up together.

5. [END OF THE DELETION.]

What were the causes.

What caused Soc-D[emocracy] to take the wrong road in terms of its deve[lopment]? It wanted to take tactics that had served it well only for a few decades, and eternalize them & stretch them out, even to cover the era of imperialism. It simply shrank back from the open cl[ass] st[ruggle] for soc[ialism], it did not take its final goal seriously & didn't want to refrain from bourg[eois] parliamentarism, although it was already out of date, in histori[cal] terms, and bankrupt when the war broke out.

5

Directions?

Quagmire. ~~wants~~ its role before August 4.

It now wants to go back to all of the above; restoration. Meaning it utterly does not understand what has occurred. It wants to resume all the mistakes that led to August 4.

Stand

The German prol[etariat] was on the road to establishing world supremacy for German imp[erialism].

~~NB On foreign politics. To point I 3.~~

Only two types of standpoint are possible:

1. either the prol[etariat] ~~play~~ claims the role of an autonomous, active factor in politics. In this case, it can only push for an intern[ational] kind of politics, i.e., one that is relevant & realizable in all countries. From the standpoint of this form of politics, *every possible* conclusion of the war *without* the prol[etariat's] *active participation* will appear to be a defeat for the proletariat's class & ~~ev~~ the milit[ary] victory of any of the warring camps will appear as a triumph for imperialism.

2. or the prol[etariat] plays as yet *no* auton[omous] role & is merely a suffering participant of bourg[eois] ~~pl~~ class politics. It would then be imperative for thinkers to weigh up & estimate the eventualities of this [non-autonomous] kind of politics ~~not~~ in case of victory ~~or~~ for one or ~~or~~ the other imper[ialist] camps, from the standpoint of gener[al] interests & perspectives for the *further* develop[ment] of bourg[eois] socie[ty] & the cl[ass]-s[truggle]. *This* was the st[andpoint] from which Marx saw things in 1848, as he had no alternative.

~~On~~ Seen from this st[andpoint] in the World War today, ~~is~~ the victory of G[erman] imp[erialism] would be the most fatal outcome, ~~w~~ and its defe[at] the only prospect for the awakening of the G[erman] prol[etariat]. The Russ[ian] Revol[ution] & its military capitulation to Germany appears in this light—~~as an intern. disaster, a factor that international socialism~~, i.e., under the precondition of the actual political failure of the intern[ational] prol[etariat]—as a factor, which temporarily places the prospects for soci[ialism] in Europe in the gravest danger.

[The following sentences are crossed out.]

Analysis of the economic impetus behind the World War.

According to Parvus, the Entente defends England's position of world power, which ~~its~~ was already nearing its end before the war; ~~it~~ thus, the Entente [shows itself to be] the representative of econom. & polit. back~~ward~~wardness!

[End of the deletion.]

Regarding Social Dem[ocracy] before 1914

G[erman] Soc-D[emocracy]—& to a lesser extent the Intern[ational]—had some old general orientation, in terms of its politics. It lived from hand to mouth, from election to election. It chatted about the forthcoming world war, without really thinking about it (Basel!) & deliberately avoided all controversial questions. (The case both for the intern[ational] congresses & for the G[erman] party congresses.)

(About Revolutions 8)

1. Str. 12.

Historical materialism perceived as an utterly undeveloped theory, still in its first stages. (In opposition to this, see Kautsky & Mehring against Bernstein)

2. Str. 29

Chapters I. and III. Böhm-Baw[erk] & Conrad Schmidt

3. Labriola's Lectures 32.

4. *Charakteristika Neokantianismus** 8

5. 0 metaphyce 23

6. 0 Comcie 88

LOOSE NOTES†

3. What should the workers do now?

a) ~~Intern~~ The same interests in the states that are *not* at war as in the belligerents.

Destitution, *Increase in the forces of reaction* (Switzerland, Holland, Italy, Uni[ted] States)

b) The blossoming of One country at the cost of another is impossible.

fundam[ental] contradiction:

The largest Grmn. Expo[rt] ~~& Engl.~~ to Gr. Brit. and its colonies

Imp[ort] is largest *from* " "

almost ¼ in 1912 out of 6.7 bill. *exp[ort]* 1.5 bill.

over 1/3 in 1912 out of 6.0 bill. imp[ort] 2.1. bill.

---

* An attack on the "characteristic neo-Kantianism" that characterized many leading theorists of the Second International; Hegel was treated as a virtual "dead dog" by the Marxists of the Second International.

† These loose notes are to be found at the end of the handwritten fragments regarding the emergence and development of capitalism, including economic and global historical comparisons. Due to the thematic connections to the fragments about the history of the Internationals and of the German workers' movement, they have been inserted here.

c) Strengthening the work[ing] cl[ass] through trade union means, and at the cost of other means, has already become impossible.

d) The battle against imper[ialism] is only possible on the *international* level, and only through political means.

5

But what if other countries are not yet ready for this. Now Moscow, the June Days, [the Paris] Commune, Berlin, Vienna.

The difficulties that would result for a country in this category would only be: that it would have to seek peace as soon as possible. And other workers would follow this example. Our ~~Pol~~ true, prol[etarian] politics in war is, for this very reason, *international* from the start.

[The following sentences have been crossed out.]

On the Main Question (Defense)

The fundamental mistake ~~in Rus~~ in Gmny as elsewhere was the slogan of "*Peace!*" That is no social[istic] slogan, but rather bourg[eois] pacifism. The only soc[ialist]-prol[etarian] slogan possible can only be: *"Revolution"* instead of *war.* And revolution is the opposite of peace. (In this point, the Indep[endents] are exactly the same as the Scheidem[en].)

NB War of the Soviet Republ[ic] against Germany is every bit as much *class struggle* as the war against Kaledin—Kornilov—Dutov—Semenov! (Despite the fact that the Entente is party to this, *Sertius gaudius.**

[End of the deletion.]

Regarding Soc-D[emocracy] before 1914

In the manner character[istic] of all *conservative* ~~parties~~ institutions, it [Social Democracy] was bound, as if by oath, to *tradition.* Every ~~deed~~ utterance about life, every proposal had to legitimize itself by going under the label of "so-called old and trusted tactics" & there was no more annihilating rebuke than the label "new tactics." That was how this "revol[utionary]" party had settled down, psychologically speaking, into the principle of conservatism! What was revolutionary in the movement had to first legitimize itself ~~as~~ through its origin in the *past.*

(NB And that's exactly what the Indep[endents] are pushing forward: in literal terms, in the pa[m]phl[et] by Ledeb[our]-Ad.[olph] Hoffm[ann] about the International!)

---

* The editors of *Gesammelte Werke,* Vol. 7, corrected this to *Serius gaudeum,* "on late joy."

"Nation State" & national politics.

World economy. *"Nationality"*
[Additionally, the following dates and notes are to be found on the sheets:]
Vorw. 3.11.
Vorw. 25. 11.
Sunday, from 9. Duncker [?] Julek
December 2, Andreassäle*
Wednesday street [house number] 21.
Youth Section II. Kr.
Tsarist Empire.

* The *Andreassäle* were meeting venues in Berlin-Friedrichshain, in Berlin's East End, sometimes used for events by the Social Democrats of Berlin's 4th Electoral District.

On the Russian Revolution*

I.

The Russian Revolution represents the most tremendous event to have occurred during the World War. Its outbreak, its unprecedented radicalism and the effect that it continues to exert give the lie to the rhetoric employed zealously by official German Social Democracy as an ideological cover for German imperialism's campaign of conquest when this campaign was initiated—i.e., the rhetoric according to which it was the mission of German bayonets to overthrow Russian tsarism and to liberate its oppressed peoples. The revolution in Russia has assumed an enormous scale; its far-reaching effects have convulsed all class relations; it has enveloped all social and economic problems; and it has made consistent progress since the initial stage of the bourgeois republic, such that the overthrow of tsarism remains a mere brief episode and is virtually reduced to a trifling significance. All these circumstances clearly demonstrate that the liberation of Russia was not the work of the war and the military defeat of tsarism, that it was not to be credited to "German bayonets in German fists"—contrary to the pledge thus formulated in a leading article in *Die Neue Zeit* under Kautsky's editorship. Instead they show that the liberation of Russia had deep roots in Russia itself, and that internally it was fully ripe. The military adventure of German imperialism under the ideological cover provided by German Social Democracy did not bring about the revolution in Russia—on the contrary, this military adventure initially interrupted the revolution for a period following the latter's first storm surge in the years from 1911 to 1913, and served to create the most adverse, abnormal conditions for the revolution following its subsequent eruption.

Moreover, for any thinking observer this course of events also constitutes a powerful refutation of the doctrinaire theory to which both Kautsky and the government-Social-Democrats† subscribe—namely that Russia, as an economically backward, predominantly agrarian country, is not yet ripe for social revolution and a dictatorship of the proletariat. This theory, which holds that the only feasible revolution in Russia is a *bourgeois* one, is simultaneously

---

* This unfinished manuscript from 1918 was first published in 1922 by Paul Levi, according to a handwritten manuscript from Rosa Luxemburg's literary estate. It is translated here by Nicholas Gray from Luxemburg's *Gesammelte Werke*, Vol. 4, pp. 332–65. Some of the notes are adapted from the original English language edition (Workers' Age Publishers, New York: 1940).

† During the war, German Social Democracy divided into three factions: the majority leadership, which openly supported and entered into the Imperial government; the Kautsky section, which declined responsibility for the conduct of the war but supplied many of the theoretical arguments for those who accepted such responsibility; and the section led by Rosa Luxemburg and Karl Liebknecht, which openly argued against war and for international solidarity and proletarian revolution.

shared by the opportunistic wing of the Russian workers' movement, the so-called Mensheviks under the seasoned leadership of Axelrod and Dan; it is from such a conception that socialists in Russia derive their tactic of forming a coalition with bourgeois liberalism. Both the Russian and the German opportunists concur completely with the German government-Social-Democrats in this fundamental conception of the Russian Revolution—a conception that automatically entails the position taken with regard to the detailed questions of tactics: in the opinion of all three factions, the Russian Revolution ought to have come to a halt at the stage corresponding to the noble task that, according to the mythology propagated by German Social Democracy, the war waged by German imperialism had set itself, namely the overthrow of tsarism. If the revolution went beyond this stage, if it set itself the task of establishing a dictatorship of the proletariat, then this corresponded, according to the above doctrine, to a simple error on the part of the radical wing of the Russian workers' movement (i.e., on the part of the Bolsheviks); likewise, on this view, all the harsh storms that have come down on the revolution and all the turmoil that has afflicted it in its subsequent trajectory present themselves as the result of this fateful error. *Theoretically*, this doctrine, which is recommended as the fruit of "Marxist thought" by the *Vorwärts* of Stampfer and by Kautsky alike, boils down to the original "Marxist" discovery that the socialist revolution is a national, domestic affair, so to speak, for each modern state in itself. Of course someone such as Kautsky knows very well how to outline within the ether of an abstract schema the world-economic connections of capital that turn all modern countries into a single integrated organism.

Russia's revolution, which is the fruit both of an *international* development and of the agrarian question, cannot be resolved within the constraints of bourgeois society.

Practically, this doctrine tends toward a denial of the responsibility of the international—and first and foremost the German—proletariat in regard to the history of the Russian Revolution, thus abnegating the international context of this revolution. It is not the immaturity of Russia that has been demonstrated through the course taken by the war and the Russian Revolution, but rather that of the German proletariat relative to what is required in order for it to fulfil its historical mission; it is the primary task of any critical appraisal of the Russian Revolution to bring this to the fore as explicitly as possible. The fate of the Russian Revolution depended entirely on *international* events. That the Bolsheviks have based their policy completely on the world revolution of the proletariat is the most brilliant testament to their political far-sightedness and fundamental steadfastness, and to the audacious sweep of their policy. It is in this context that the tremendous leap taken by capitalist development in the last decade becomes manifest. The revolution of 1905–07 evoked no more than a feeble resonance in Europe. As such it necessarily remained a mere opening chapter. The continuation and resolution of what had been thus initiated were bound up with European development.

Clearly, not uncritical apologetics but thorough and considered criticism alone is capable of salvaging the wealth of experiences and drawing the lessons from what has occurred. It would indeed be a ludicrous notion to claim that absolutely everything that those undertaking the first world-historical experiment with the dictatorship of the working class have done—or have omitted to do—represents the pinnacle of perfection, especially given that this experiment has taken place under the most difficult conditions imaginable: it has been attempted in the midst of a worldwide conflagration and the chaos of an imperialist mass slaughter, within the iron grip of the most reactionary military power in Europe, and despite being confronted by the complete failure of the international proletariat. Conversely, the elementary concepts of socialist politics, and an insight into the necessary historical preconditions for such a politics, render unavoidable the assumption that, under such fatal conditions, even the greatest idealism and steadfast revolutionary energy are incapable of realizing democracy or socialism, and can engender nothing more than impotent, distorted attempts at either.

It is the absolutely elementary duty of socialists in all countries to clarify for themselves these issues, along with their profound interconnections and far-reaching effects, since it is only by means of such bitter realization that the entire extent of the international proletariat's own responsibility for the fate of the Russian Revolution can be gauged. Furthermore, it is along this path alone that the decisive importance of the concerted international advance of the proletarian revolution is thrown into sharp relief—i.e., as a fundamental condition, in the absence of which even the greatest proficiency and sacrifices on the part of the proletariat in a single country will inevitably become embroiled in a confusion of contradictions and errors.

Nor can there be any doubt that it has only been with the greatest internal misgivings and extreme inner reluctance that the gifted figures at the vanguard of the Russian Revolution—i.e., Lenin and Trotsky—have taken certain decisive steps on the thorny path they navigate, with snares of all kinds on either side. Lenin and Trotsky have acted under conditions of bitter compulsion and exigency amid the swirling maelstrom of events; nothing could be more alien to these leading figures than to see everything that they have done in these conditions—and everything that they have failed to do—meet with acquiescence on the part of the International and be held up as the prototype for socialist policy, a paradigm to be uncritically acclaimed and eagerly imitated.

It would be equally inappropriate to fear that a critical appraisal of the road taken thus far by the Russian Revolution might serve to dangerously undermine the esteem in which Russian proletarians are held or the fascination they attract as paragons—a role that is, so the argument runs, supposedly necessary in order to overcome the fatal inertia of the German masses. Nothing could be more perverse than such a point of view. An awakening of the revolutionary drive of the working class in Germany cannot be conjured up by appealing to an immaculate authority in the spirit of the paternalistic methods employed by the German Social Democracy of blessed memory, whether such authority be that of the party's own "executive bodies" or that of the "Russian paradigm." It is not the generation of a mood of revolutionary euphoria that can engender the historic capacity for action within the German proletariat—on the contrary, this can only be achieved through insight into the dreadful seriousness and extreme complexity of the tasks at hand; it can only emerge from political maturity and intellectual independence, from a capacity for critical judgment on the part of the masses (a faculty systematically obliterated over decades by German Social Democracy under various pretexts). For German and international workers alike, to engage critically with the Russian Revolution in all its historical connections represents the best possible schooling for the tasks confronting them as a result of the present situation.

II.

In its general course, the first period of the Russian Revolution, from its outbreak in March to the overthrow of the Provisional Government in October, corresponds precisely to the schema of development that characterizes both the Great English Revolution and the Great French Revolution. It is the typical initial trajectory of every major general confrontation between the revolutionary forces engendered within the womb of bourgeois society and the fetters of the old society.

Its development naturally travels along an ascending line: from moderate beginnings toward an ever-greater radicalization of aims and, in parallel, from a coalition between parties and classes toward the autocracy of the radical party.

Initially, in March 1917, the "Cadets"—i.e., the liberal bourgeoisie—stood at the head of the revolution. The first general swell of the revolutionary high tide swept everyone and everything along with it: the Fourth Duma, the most reactionary product of the four-class suffrage* that had ensued from the *coup d'état*,† was suddenly transformed into an organ of the revolution. All the

* In the electoral law of December 1905, the electorate was divided into three *curiae* (constituencies) according to estate and property, whereby landowners were accorded particular privileges and the number of members of parliament representing workers and peasants was restricted. After the *coup d'état* of 1907, further restrictions were added, effectively guaranteeing domination of the Duma by large-scale landowners and the high bourgeoisie and ensuring that the peoples of the peripheral regions of Russia were either disenfranchised altogether or enfranchised only to an extremely restricted extent.

† On June 3, 1907, the tsarist government dissolved the second imperial State Duma and ordered the arrest of the members of the parliamentary group of the Social Democratic Party.

bourgeois parties, including those of the nationalist right, suddenly formed a phalanx against absolutism. The latter was toppled by the first assault virtually without any struggle, like a deceased organ that merely needed to be touched in order for it to fall away from the body. The brief attempt by the liberal bourgeoisie to salvage at least the dynasty and the throne was likewise crushed within a few hours. In a matter of days, or even hours, the torrential surge of this development raced over distances that it had previously taken decades to cover in France. Here it was evident that Russia was realizing the results of a century-long European development, and above all that the 1917 revolution was a direct continuation of that of 1905–7 rather than a gift bestowed by German "liberators." The movement of March 1917 immediately resumed at the very point where it had interrupted its work ten years previously. The democratic republic was the finished product of the revolution's very first assault.

Now, however, began the second and more difficult task. From the outset, the masses of the urban proletariat had been the driving force of the revolution. Their demands were not limited to political democracy, however; they were also oriented toward the burning question of international policy, the question of an immediate peace. The revolution simultaneously gripped the mass of the army, which raised the same demand for an immediate peace, and the mass of the peasantry, which pushed the agrarian question—the pivot of the revolution since 1905—into the foreground. An immediate peace on the one hand, and land on the other: the co-existence of these two goals entailed an internal split in the revolutionary phalanx. The demand for an immediate peace stood in sharp contradiction to the imperialist tendency of the liberal bourgeoisie, whose spokesperson was Milyukov;* the land question was initially a bugbear for the other wing of the bourgeoisie (i.e., for the squirearchy),† but it was subsequently to become a sore point for the entire bourgeois class as it represented an attack on the sanctity of private property in general.

Thus on the day following the revolution's first victory there began an internal struggle within its fold over these two burning issues: peace and the land question. The liberal bourgeoisie initiated a tactic of filibustering and evasion. The masses of workers, the army, and the peasantry surged forward ever more tumultuously. There can be no doubt that the fate of the political democracy of the republic was bound up with the questions of peace and land. The bourgeois

It simultaneously issued a new electoral law without the approval of the imperial State Duma. This *coup d'état* allowed the government to claim a right-wing oriented majority and to turn the imperial State Duma that was elected in 1912 into an organ of power of "the reactionary strata, the tsarist bureaucracy allied to the feudal landowners and the top bourgeoisie." (Lenin *Collected Works*, Vol. 19 [Moscow: Progress Publishers, 1974], p. 4.)

* The leader of the Cadets, P.N. Milyukov, was Foreign Minister in the Provisional Government.

† *Landjunkertum* in the original.

classes, which had been inundated by the first storm surge of the revolution and had allowed themselves to be swept along to the point where the republican form of the state was established, began at once to search for support bases in the rear and set about the clandestine organization of the counterrevolution. [A. M.] Kaledin's Cossack campaign against Petersburg* was a clear expression of this tendency. Had this offensive met with success, it would not only have set the seal on the peace question and the agrarian question: it would have sealed the fate of the republic itself. A military dictatorship with a reign of terror over the proletariat and the subsequent restoration of the monarchy would have formed the inexorable sequence of events.

Against this background, it is possible to gauge the utopian—and at core reactionary—tactic by which the Russian Kautskyite socialists (the Mensheviks) have allowed themselves to be guided.

It has been nothing less than astonishing to observe how this diligent man† has, through his tireless labor of writing during the four years that the World War has lasted, calmly and methodically ripped one theoretical hole after the other in the fabric of socialism, such that the latter emerges from this labor like a sieve, with not a single part of it intact. The uncritical indifference with which Kautsky's followers regard this assiduous endeavor by their official theoretician, swallowing each of his new discoveries without so much as batting an eyelid, can be matched only by the indifference with which the followers of Scheidemann and Co. witness how the latter proceed to rip holes in socialism *in practice*, step by step. Indeed, these two endeavors complement each other perfectly; since the outbreak of the war, Kautsky, the official guardian of the temple of Marxism, has, in reality, merely elaborated theoretically what the Scheidemanns have accomplished in practice: firstly, the establishment of the International as an instrument of peace; secondly, disarmament, the League of Nations and nationalism; and, finally, democracy, *as opposed to* socialism.‡

Holding tenaciously to the fiction of the bourgeois character of the Russian Revolution on the grounds that Russia was allegedly not yet ripe for social revolution, they clung desperately to the coalition with the bourgeois liberals—i.e.,

---

* The Cossack ataman A. M. Kaledin had mobilized the Don Cossacks in support of the counterrevolutionary troops that marched on Petrograd under the leadership of L. G. Kornilov with the aim of crushing the revolution and establishing a military dictatorship. Led by the Bolsheviks, the workers and soldiers confronted the counterrevolutionaries and defeated them.

† Luxemburg refers here to Karl Kautsky.

‡ The expression, "the International an instrument of peace" refers to the excuses Kautsky gave for its bankruptcy during the war ("an instrument of peace is not suited to times of war"). It probably refers also to the theory that the International, being peaceful, is not an instrument for revolutionary struggle. Kautsky substituted talk of disarmament (without the removal of the causes and roots of war) for a revolutionary struggle against war. When the struggle for socialism began in earnest, Scheidemann defended capitalism against socialism in practice, while Kautsky, according to Luxemburg, did so in theory.

to the forcible alliance between those elements that had been so divided by the natural internal course of revolutionary development that they now stood in a relation of utter contradiction with one another. These Axelrods and Dans aimed to cooperate at any price with the very classes and parties that represented the greatest threat to the revolution and to democracy—the latter representing the revolution's first achievement.

Given this situation, it is to the historic credit of the Bolshevik tendency that it has, from the outset, proclaimed and pursued with iron consistency the only tactic that could rescue democracy and drive the revolution forward. All power was to be held exclusively by the masses of workers and peasants, by the soviets: this was effectively the only way out of the difficulty in which the revolution had become embroiled—this was the sword stroke with which the Gordian knot was cut. This was the means by which the revolution was led through the narrow mountain pass and the way was opened toward the open country in which it could continue to unfold without inhibition.

Lenin's party was thus the only one in Russia that had a grasp of the true interests of the revolution in this initial period—it was the element that drove the revolution forward, being in this sense the only party to pursue a socialist politics.

This also explains how the Bolsheviks, who, at the beginning of the revolution, constituted a minority that was ostracized, slandered and hounded on all sides, were led within the briefest period of time to the forefront of the revolution and were able to rally under their banner all the genuinely popular masses—the urban proletariat, the army, the peasantry—alongside the revolutionary elements within democracy (i.e., the left wing of the Socialist Revolutionaries).

The actual situation in which the Russian Revolution found itself came down within a few months to the following alternative: victory of the counterrevolution or dictatorship of the proletariat—i.e., Kaledin or Lenin. Such was the objective situation that, very soon, arises in every revolution once the first intoxication has evaporated; in the Russian case, this situation resulted from those concrete, burning questions—the question of peace and that of land—for which no solution was to be found within the framework of the "bourgeois" revolution.

Here the Russian Revolution has merely confirmed the basic lesson of every great revolution, whose vital law can be formulated as follows: the revolution must either press forward very rapidly and decisively, tearing down all obstacles with an iron hand and setting its goals ever further ahead, or else it will very soon be cast back behind its weaker starting point and crushed by the counterrevolution. In revolution there can be no standing still, no running in place, no settling for the first goal that happens to be achieved. And those who attempt to apply the homespun wisdoms gleaned from the parliamentary battles of frogs and mice* to revolutionary tactics merely demonstrate that the psychology of the revolution and its very vital law are utterly alien to them, and that all historical experience is to them a book with seven seals.

Consider the course of the English Revolution following its outbreak in 1642.† Here the logic of events entailed that it was only the feeble vacillations of the Presbyterians and the halting war against the royalist army—the Presbyterian leaders deliberately avoiding a decisive battle with, and victory over, Charles I—that rendered decisive action on the part of the Independents an incontrovertible necessity: the latter had no alternative but to drive the Presbyterians out of Parliament and to seize power themselves. And furthermore, within the army of the Independents it was likewise the lower petty-bourgeois mass of the soldiers, the Lilburnian "Levellers," that formed the driving force of the entire Independent movement, just as it was ultimately the proletarian elements of the mass of soldiers—those that found expression in the Digger movement—that constituted the leaven of the democratic party of the "Levellers."

Without the intellectual influence of revolutionary proletarian elements on the mass of soldiers, and without the pressure exerted by the democratic mass of soldiers on the bourgeois upper stratum of the party of the Independents, there would have been no "purging" of Presbyterians from the Long Parliament, nor any victorious end to the war against the army of the Cavaliers and the Scots, nor the trial and execution of Charles I, nor the abolition of the House of Lords and the proclamation of the republic.

And how did events unfold in the French Revolution? The seizure of power by the Jacobins proved, after four years of struggle, to be the only means of salvaging the gains of the revolution, of realizing the republic, of smashing feudalism, of organizing the defense of the revolution both internally and externally, of suppressing the conspiracy of counterrevolution, and of spreading the revolutionary wave from France to all of Europe.

Kautsky and his Russian kindred spirits, who were at pains to uphold the "bourgeois character" of the Russian Revolution in its first phase, represent the direct counterpart to those German and English liberals of the preceding century who distinguished two phases in the Great French Revolution: the "good" revolution of the initial, Girondin phase and the "bad" one initiated by the Jacobin coup. The shallowness of the liberal conception of history naturally required no understanding of the fact that without the coup by the "immoderate" Jacobins, the initial, tentative half-gains of the first, Girondin phase would

* *Batrachomyomachia*, or the Battle of Frogs and Mice, is an ancient parody of the *Iliad* (a work traditionally attributed to Homer); its authorship has not been conclusively established. Marx often used the term to describe the infighting among exiled revolutionaries.

† Luxemburg is here drawing on her "Notes on the English Revolution," which is found in *The Complete Works of Rosa Luxemburg*, Vol. 4, pp. 449–78.

have been immediately buried underneath the ruins of the revolution; likewise, this conception simply ignored the fact that, in 1793, the real alternative posed to the Jacobin dictatorship by the iron course of historical development did not consist in "moderate" democracy, but rather in the restoration of the Bourbons! The "happy medium" cannot be maintained in any revolution, for the natural law of revolution demands a swift decision: either the locomotive is driven full steam ahead to the furthest point of its historical ascent, or else its own gravitational force will cause it to roll back down to its point of departure at the bottom, plunging irredeemably into the abyss all those who, during its ascent, had attempted to stop it halfway up because their energy was depleted.

This explains how it is that, in every revolution, only the party that has the courage to issue the call to surge forward and is willing to assume responsibility for the consequences will be capable of taking leadership and seizing power. This also explains the deplorable role played by the Mensheviks—the Dans, the [Irakli] Tseretelis and others—who, having initially exerted an immense influence on the masses, were then given to protracted vacillations, and, having resisted tooth and nail the seizure of power and the taking of responsibility, were then swept ignominiously from the stage.

Lenin's party was the only one to understand what is required of a truly revolutionary party and wherein its duty consists; it was the only one to ensure the progress of the revolution by issuing the slogan "all power to the proletariat and peasantry."

It was thus that the Bolsheviks solved the famous question of winning "the majority of the people"—a question that has long weighed upon the German Social Democrats like a nightmare. As inveterate acolytes of parliamentary cretinism* they simply apply the homespun wisdoms of the parliamentary nursery to the revolution: in order to carry anything through, it is first necessary to have a majority—so the argument runs. The same supposedly applies to a revolution: first a "majority" has to be formed. The actual dialectic of revolutions, however, turns this wisdom of parliamentary moles on its head: the path runs not from the formation of a majority to revolutionary tactics, but rather in the opposite direction—from revolutionary tactics to the formation of a majority. Only a party that understands how to lead—how to drive things forward—gains support in the midst of the storm. The resoluteness with which, at the decisive moment, Lenin and his comrades issued the only slogan that could propel events forward—"all power to the proletariat and peasantry"—transformed them almost overnight from a persecuted and much-maligned minority, whose leaders were obliged like Marat to hide in basements, into the absolute masters of the situation.

* A term first applied by Marx to those parliamentarians who think that all history is decided by motions, votes, and points of parliamentary debate.

Furthermore, the Bolsheviks immediately established as the goal of this seizure of power a complete and extremely far-reaching revolutionary program: this program consisted not in the securing of bourgeois democracy, but in the dictatorship of the proletariat for the purpose of realizing socialism. In historic terms, it is thereby to their eternal credit that they were the first to proclaim the ultimate goals of socialism as the immediate program of practical politics.

Lenin, Trotsky, and their comrades have fully accomplished all that a party could possibly muster in the hour of revolution in the way of courage, forcefulness of action, revolutionary far-sightedness and consistency. The Bolsheviks evinced the revolutionary honor and capacity for action that was so entirely lacking in western Social Democracy. Their October uprising not only salvaged the Russian Revolution, it also salvaged the honor of international socialism.

III.

The Bolsheviks are the historical heirs of the English Levellers and the French Jacobins. Yet the concrete task that confronted them following their seizure of power was incomparably more difficult than that of their historical predecessors.* The slogan of the immediate and instantaneous seizure and distribution of land by the peasants† was undoubtedly the most succinct, the simplest and most clean-cut formula for achieving two goals: the smashing of large-scale landed property and the immediate binding of the peasants to the revolutionary government. As a political measure to reinforce the proletarian-socialist government, this was indeed a superb tactic. Unfortunately, however, it had two sides: the reverse side was that the immediate seizure of the land by the peasants had, for the most part, nothing in common with a socialist economy.

The socialist reconfiguration of economic relations presupposes two conditions that must obtain concerning to agrarian relations: firstly, only the nationalization of large-scale landed property, as this represents the most technically advanced concentration of agrarian means of production and

* A note added by Rosa Luxemburg in the top margin of the manuscript, without any indication as to where it was to be included in the text, reads as follows: "(Significance of the agrarian question. Already in 1905. Then, in the third Duma, the right-wing peasants! The peasant question and defense, the army.)"

† Through the land decree issued on 8 November 1917 by the Second All-Russian Congress of Soviets of Workers' and Soldiers' Deputies, and according to the "peasant mandate" contained in this decree, private ownership of the land was abolished and the property of landowners and lands owned through appanages [royal grants], by monasteries and by the Church were expropriated without compensation. Land was distributed to working people according to the principle of equality in the use of the land—i.e., according to determinate standards regarding labor and usage. The form that the use of the land could take—whether to be undertaken by individual households, the commune or the *artels* (cooperative associations)—was left for each individual village to determine. Lands where agriculture operated in a highly developed form were not distributed; these passed over instead into the hands of the commune (the *mir*) or of the state.

methods, can be the point of departure for the socialist mode of economy in the countryside. It is, of course, not necessary to deprive the small-scale peasant of his parcel of land, and it is not a problem to suggest to him that he might allow himself, of his own free will, to be won over by the advantages of social production, first to cooperative association and ultimately to inclusion within overall social production. In view of these considerations, it is self-evident that every socialist economic reform in the countryside must begin with large- and medium-scale land ownership. Such a reform must transfer the right of property above all to the nation, or rather—and this amounts to the same thing under a socialist government—to the state, for this alone will afford the possibility of organizing agricultural production according to a range of important and interlocking socialist considerations.

Secondly, moreover, one of the preconditions of this reconfiguration is the elimination of the separation between agriculture and industry that is characteristic of bourgeois society in order to make room for a reciprocal permeation between, and a fusing of, these two spheres, and in order to permit an arrangement of both agricultural and industrial production according to a unified standpoint. However productive operations might be organized at the individual level (whether through urban communities as suggested by some, or centrally by the state), a uniformly implemented and centrally initiated reform is a precondition in any case; and a precondition for such a reform is the nationalization of the land. The nationalization of large- and medium-scale landed property and the unification of industry and agriculture—these are two fundamental facets of any socialist economic reform: without them, there can be no socialism.

Who can reproach the Soviet government in Russia for not having implemented these colossal reforms? Lenin and his comrades have held power for no more than a brief period and have found themselves in the midst of the powerful vortex of internal and external struggles, besieged on all sides by countless enemies and opponents. It would be a jest in poor taste to demand or to expect of Lenin and his comrades that, in these conditions, they should have solved, or even begun to tackle, one of the most difficult problems of the socialist revolution—in fact it would be no exaggeration to say *the* most difficult problem! Once we too have taken power in the west, we will, even in the most favorable of conditions, lose some teeth in our attempts to crack this tough nut before we have overcome the worst of the innumerable complicated difficulties of this enormous task!

Once it has taken power, a socialist government must, in any case, do one thing: it must take measures that are oriented toward fulfilling the above-mentioned preconditions for a subsequent socialist reform of agrarian relations, or it must at least avoid anything that could bar the way to taking such measures.

Yet the slogan issued by the Bolsheviks calling for the immediate seizure and distribution of landed property by the peasants necessarily had an effect in virtually the opposite direction. Not only does this fail to constitute a socialist measure, it also blocks the route to any such measure: it piles up insurmountable difficulties in the path of the reconfiguration of agrarian relations along socialist lines.

The seizure of landed estates by the peasants on hearing the short and precise slogan of Lenin and his friends—"go and seize the land!"—merely led to the sudden, chaotic transfer of large-scale land ownership to peasant land ownership. What this created was not social property, but new private property, namely, the breaking up of large-scale property into medium- and small-scale property, and the fragmentation of the relatively advanced large-scale agricultural enterprise into the primitive, small-scale holding, the latter operating with technical means from the time of the pharaohs. Worse still: not only did this measure and the chaotic and purely arbitrary form of its implementation fail to eliminate property disparities in the countryside, these were, in fact, intensified. Although the Bolsheviks called on the peasantry to form peasant committees in order to somehow turn the seizure of the landed property of the nobility into collective action, it is clear that this general guidance could alter nothing in relation to the actual practice and the actual power relations in the countryside. With or without committees, the rich peasants and usurers who formed the village bourgeoisie and who hold actual local power have been, without doubt, the main beneficiaries of the agrarian revolution. As anyone can tell without a moment's hesitation by merely reckoning on their fingers, social and economic inequality within the peasantry has not been eliminated as a result of the distribution of the land—on the contrary, it has increased, and class antagonisms within this sphere have been intensified. This shift in power, however, has occurred to the *detriment* of proletarian and socialist interests.

Lenin's speech on necessary centralization in industry, nationalization of the banks, commerce, and industry. Why not of the land?

Lenin's own agrarian program was different before the revolution. The slogan was taken over from the much-maligned Socialist Revolutionaries, or more accurately, from the spontaneous movement of the peasantry.

In order to introduce socialist principles into agrarian relations, the Soviet government now sought to create agrarian communes made up of proletarians—mostly urban, unemployed elements. Nevertheless, as might easily be anticipated, the results of these efforts necessarily remained microscopically slight when measured against the entire scale of agrarian relations, and do not represent a significant factor when assessing this question.* (Having broken

---

* A note added by Rosa Luxemburg in the left-hand margin of the manuscript, without an indication as to where it was to be included in the text, reads as follows: "Grain monopoly with premiums. *Now, post festum*, they are attempting to introduce class struggle into the village!"

up large-scale landed property—the most suitable starting point for a socialist economy—into small-scale holdings, the attempt is now made to build up model communist productive facilities from small beginnings). Under the given relations, these communes merely have the value of an experiment, and not that of a comprehensive social reform.

Previously, any socialist reform in the countryside faced resistance from at most a small caste of aristocratic and capitalist large-scale landowners and a small minority of rich village bourgeoisie; the expropriation of these strata by a revolutionary mass of the people would be child's play. Now, by contrast, following the "seizure of landed property," any attempted socialist reform of agriculture will be confronted by an adversary consisting of an enormously expanded and powerful mass of property-owning peasantry, which will fight tooth and nail to defend its newly acquired property from any socialist attacks. Now the question of the future socialization of agriculture and thus of production generally in Russia has become a matter of antagonism and struggle between the urban proletariat on the one hand and the mass of peasants on the other. How sharp this antagonism has already become is demonstrated by the peasants' boycott of the cities, whereby the former withheld foodstuffs from the latter in order to engage in speculation with these means of existence, in precisely the same way as practiced by the Prussian Junkers.

The French peasant of the small-scale holding became the most valiant defender of the Great French Revolution that had provided him with the land confiscated from the émigrés. As a Napoleonic soldier, he carried the French flag to victory, traversing the whole of Europe and crushing feudalism in one country after the other. It might be that Lenin and his friends expected their agrarian slogan to have a similar effect. Yet the Russian peasant, having seized possession of the land on his own initiative, would not dream of defending Russia and the revolution to which he owes his land. Instead, he clings to his new possessions, abandoning the revolution to its enemies, the state to its downfall, and the urban population to starvation.

Lenin's agrarian reform has engendered in the countryside a new and powerful popular stratum of adversaries of socialism, whose resistance will be much more dangerous and tenacious than that previously offered by the aristocratic owners of large estates.

The Bolsheviks are, in part, to blame for the fact that military defeat has turned into the collapse and disintegration of Russia. To a great extent, the Bolsheviks have themselves aggravated these objective difficulties in the situation through a slogan* that they have brought to the fore of their policy—namely the so-called right of self-determination of nations. What such a slogan implied, in reality, was the disintegration of the Russian state. The right

* In the original manuscript, policy.

of the various nationalities of the Russian Empire to determine their own fate independently, "including through separation from the Russian state," was a formula repeated time and again with doctrinaire obstinacy by Lenin and his comrades and it formed a particular battle cry of theirs during their opposition to the war waged by Milyukov and then by Kerensky;* this formula formed the axis of their domestic policy after the October Revolution, and it constituted the entire platform of the Bolsheviks in Brest-Litovsk,† being the only weapon that they could bring to bear against the dominant position of German imperialism.

The most striking thing about the tenacity and unbending consistency with which Lenin and his comrades adhered to this slogan is that it stands in sharp contradiction both to their otherwise outspoken centralism in politics and to the stance that they have taken vis-à-vis other democratic principles. On the one hand, they have displayed their profound disdain for the Constituent Assembly, for universal suffrage, for freedom of the press and freedom of assembly—in short, for the entire apparatus of basic democratic freedoms of the popular masses that, taken together, formed the "right of self-determination" in Russia itself. On the other hand, however, they have treated the right of self-determination of nations as a jewel of democratic politics, for the sake of which all practical considerations of real critique were to be silenced. Whereas they had remained utterly unimpressed by the plebiscite for the Constituent Assembly—a plebiscite held on the basis of the most democratic franchise in the world and in the complete freedom of a people's republic—and had simply declared its results to be null and void on the basis of sober and critical deliberations,‡ in Brest they advocated the holding of plebiscites among

---

* The Provisional Government, after the downfall of the tsar during the earlier months of 1917, attempted to continue the war and denied the right of the national minorities to separation from Russia. P. N. Milyukov as Foreign Minister had assured the Entente countries that it would fulfil all its obligations as a member of this alliance in order to bring the war to a "victorious conclusion." This led to protests and demonstrations by workers and soldiers, resulting in the formation of a governmental coalition in which representatives of the Socialist Revolutionaries and the Mensheviks participated alongside representatives of the bourgeoisie. A. F. Kerensky (serving first as minister of justice, then minister of war, and finally prime minister), continuing the pro-war policy, ordered an offensive in July 1917 with 60,000 casualties.

† During the peace negotiations in Brest-Litovsk, the Soviet government insisted on one of its fundamental principles, namely the right of self-determination of all belligerent countries, including the right of every nation to secede and form an independent state. This right was to be realized by means of a referendum conducted under specific conditions among the entire population of a given territory.

‡ The slogan calling for a constituent assembly to be convened—a constituent assembly representing the highest form of democracy within a bourgeois-democratic republic—had been central to the agitation of all currents in the Russian revolutionary movement. Following the October Revolution, the demand was deemed by the Bolsheviks and their Left Socialist Revolutionary allies to be politically and practically obsolete. However, since a large proportion of workers and peasants continued to support the demand, the Council of People's Commissars decided to hold elections on the date previously set by the Provisional Government.

Russia's foreign nationalities over the latters' state allegiance, and upheld such referendums as the true palladium of any freedom and democracy, as the unadulterated quintessence of the will of peoples and as the highest adjudicating authority in questions of the political destiny of nations.

The blatant contradiction here is all the more incomprehensible given that, as we shall see later, the democratic forms of political life in every country in actual fact represent highly valuable—or indeed indispensable—foundations of socialist politics, whereas the celebrated "right of self-determination of nations" is nothing other than hollow, petty-bourgeois phraseology and humbug.

Indeed, what is such a right supposed to signify? It belongs to the ABCs of socialist politics that socialism opposes every form of oppression, including that of one nation by another.

If, despite all this, Lenin and Trotsky and their friends—being otherwise such sober and critical politicians who have nothing but an ironic shrug of the shoulders for every kind of utopian phraseology such as "disarmament," "League of Nations," etc.—made just such a hollow phrase their own virtual hobbyhorse on this occasion, then it would seem that this occurred as a consequence of an opportunistic type of politics. Lenin and his comrades obviously made the calculation that the only secure means of binding the many disparate nationalities that coexisted within the Russian Empire to the cause of the revolution, to the cause of the socialist proletariat, would be to grant them, in the name of the revolution and socialism, the utmost and most unrestricted freedom to decide their own destinies. This was analogous to the Bolsheviks' policy vis-à-vis the Russian peasants, whose hunger for land was to be satiated by the slogan in favor of the direct seizure of the landed property of the nobility, thus binding them to the banner of the revolution and the proletarian government. Unfortunately, however, in both cases, the calculation went completely awry. Lenin and his comrades evidently expected that as proponents of national liberation—even to the point of "secession from the state"—they would turn Finland, Ukraine, Poland, Lithuania, the Baltic countries, the Caucasian countries, etc., into just as many loyal allies of the Russian Revolution; instead we witnessed a spectacle that was the reverse of these expectations: one after the other, these "nations" took advantage of their freshly bestowed freedom in order to ally themselves with German imperialism as mortal enemies of the Russian Revolution and to carry the banner of counterrevolution to Russia itself under protection of their new ally. The brief episode involving Ukraine in Brest—a vignette that engendered a decisive turnaround in those negotiations and in the entire domestic and foreign political situation of the Bolsheviks—serves as a prime example of this tendency.*

* The Ukrainian Tsentralna Rada (Central Council of Ukraine – national assembly) had signed a treaty with the Central Powers on January 27, 1918, even though its regime had already collapsed by this point and Soviet power had conquered nearly all of Ukraine. Germany gained

The conduct of Finland, Poland, Lithuania, the Baltic countries and the nations of the Caucasus demonstrates in the most compelling terms that the Ukrainian case does not represent a random exception—instead it typifies the choice that is made in these instances.

Admittedly, in all these cases, it is not in actual fact the respective "nations" that engage in such reactionary policies, but only the bourgeois and petty-bourgeois classes, who—in sharpest opposition to their own proletarian masses—pervert the "national right of self-determination" into an instrument for their counterrevolutionary class politics. Yet—and this brings us to the very nub of the question—precisely therein lies the utopian, petty-bourgeois character of this nationalist slogan: within the harsh reality of class society, particularly in times when class antagonisms are extremely intensified, it simply transforms itself into a means of bourgeois class domination. The Bolsheviks have been taught a lesson, one that has caused them and the revolution a great deal of damage, namely that under the rule of capitalism there is no self-determination of the nation, that in a class society each class of the nation strives to "determine itself" in a different way, and that for the bourgeois classes considerations of national freedom are completely subordinated to those of class domination. Like the Ukrainian petty bourgeoisie, the Finnish bourgeoisie was completely unanimous in preferring German despotism to national freedom if the latter was associated with the dangers of "Bolshevism."

If Lenin and Trotsky seriously hoped that these actual class relations could be transformed into their opposite through the "plebiscites" that formed the central focus in Brest, and that a majority vote in favor of alignment with the Russian Revolution could be achieved by relying on the revolutionary popular masses, this represented an incomprehensible optimism on the part of the Bolshevik leaders; if, on the other hand, this was merely a tactical feint in the duel with German despotism, then it was a perilous one that was tantamount to playing with fire. Even in the absence of German military occupation, the celebrated "plebiscite"—if ever such had been held in the peripheral countries—would in all probability have everywhere produced results that disappointed the Bolsheviks, given the state of mind of the mass of peasants and that of a broad stratum of proletarians (the latter displaying even more indifference than the former), and given the reactionary tendencies of the petty bourgeoisie and the innumerable means of influencing the ballot that the bourgeoisie had at its disposal. Indeed, the following is an inviolable rule when it comes to such plebiscites on the national question: the ruling classes will either manage to prevent them from being held when they do not suit them, or, in the case where a plebiscite is actually held, they know how to influence its outcome through a

the right to occupy Ukraine through the terms of the treaty and made claims for the ultimate annexation of Ukraine during the Brest-Litovsk negotiations on January 27 and 28, 1918.

panoply of measures. The upshot of such measures is that socialism cannot be introduced by means of plebiscites.

That the question of national aspirations and separatist tendencies was ever interpolated into revolutionary struggles at all was surely a grave error, one that was compounded by the fact that this question was foregrounded as a result of the Brest peace and, even more critically, by the fact that it was stamped as a shibboleth of socialist and revolutionary politics. All this has served to sow extreme confusion within socialist ranks and to shake the position of the proletariat particularly in the peripheral countries. In Finland, the socialist proletariat occupied a position of power for as long as it fought as part of the closed ranks of the Russian revolutionary phalanx: it held a majority in the Finnish parliament and in the army, it had reduced its own bourgeoisie to complete impotence, and it was master of the situation within the country. At the beginning of the century, at a time when the follies of "Ukrainian nationalism"—with its currency of *karbovanets* and its "Universals"*—and Lenin's hobbyhorse of an "independent Ukraine" had not yet been devised, Russian Ukraine was a stronghold of the Russian revolutionary movement. It was from there—from Rostov, Odessa, and the Donetsk region—that the first lava streams of the revolution flowed in 1902–04, igniting the whole of southern Russia and turning it into a sea of flames, thus preparing the way for the 1905 eruption; the same thing occurred in the present revolution, in which the southern Russian proletariat furnished the elite troops of the proletarian phalanx. Since 1905, Poland and the Baltic countries have constituted the most powerful and reliable forges of the revolution, and the socialist proletariat has played a prominent role within them.

How could it come to pass that the counterrevolution suddenly triumphed in all these countries? The nationalist movement tore the proletariat away from Russia, and it was precisely this that left the proletariat disabled and at the mercy of the national bourgeoisie in the peripheral countries. Contrary to the spirit of the genuine international class politics that they otherwise advocated, the Bolsheviks failed to strive for the most compact alignment and consolidation of revolutionary forces across the entire territory of the Empire; they failed to defend tooth and nail the integrity of the Russian Empire as a territory of revolution; they failed to confront nationalist separatist endeavors by counterposing to these the common bond and inseparability of proletarians of all nations within the ambit of the Russian Revolution. Instead, the Bolsheviks have done the exact reverse: through their droning nationalist phraseology of the "right of self-determination, including that of secession from the state," they have provided the bourgeoisie in all countries of the periphery with the most

---

* The manuscript speaks of *Karbowentzen*, which appears to be a Germanization of the Russian word for "silver roble," probably referring to a special Ukrainian coinage, and of "*Universals*," the name applied to certain manifestoes or declarations of the Ukrainian Rada (national assembly).

welcome and brilliant pretext for its counterrevolutionary campaigns and furnished the very banner under which these campaigns could be fought. Instead of warning proletarians in the countries of the periphery that any separatism is a bourgeois trap and suppressing separatist endeavors with an iron fist (the use of which would, in this case, have been truly in the spirit—and to the benefit—of proletarian dictatorship), they instead confused the masses in the peripheral countries with their slogan, leaving them vulnerable to the demagoguery of the bourgeois classes. Through this nationalist demand they paved the way for, and induced, the disintegration of Russia itself, thus pressing into the hands of their enemies the very knife that the latter would subsequently drive into the heart of the Russian Revolution.

Admittedly, without the help of German imperialism (without the "rifle butts in German fists" as Kautsky's *Neue Zeit* put it), the Lubinskys and other *Schufterles** of Ukraine, the Erichs and Mannerheims of Finland and the Baltic barons would never have been able to overpower the socialist masses of proletarians in their respective countries. Yet national separatism was the Trojan horse by means of which German "comrades" with bayonets in their fists were able to enter all these countries. Real class antagonisms and the military relations of power brought about the intervention by Germany. However, it was the Bolsheviks that furnished the *ideology* that provided cover for this campaign of counterrevolution, and in so doing they have reinforced the position of the bourgeoisie and weakened that of proletarians. The best evidence of this is Ukraine, which was to play such a fatal role in the destiny of the Russian Revolution. Ukrainian nationalism in Russia was very different from, for instance, the Czech, Polish or Finnish varieties: it was nothing but a mere whim, a folly of a few dozen petty bourgeois members of the intelligentsia, without the slightest roots in the economic, political or intellectual relations of the country, without any historical tradition (given that Ukraine had never formed a nation or a state), without any national culture apart from the reactionary romantic poems of Shevchenko. It is literally as if one fine morning, the inhabitants of the coastal regions of the North European Plain in which Low German is spoken were inspired by Fritz Reuter† to attempt to found a new Low German nation and state! And this derisory farce involving a few university professors and students was artificially inflated into a political factor by Lenin and comrades through their doctrinaire agitation around the "right of self-determination, including that of ... etc." They accorded such an importance to what was initially nothing more than a farce that it eventually became a deadly serious matter—not as a serious national movement (since such a movement lacked any roots), but as a figurehead and rallying banner for the counterrevolution. At Brest, this *fata morgana* [mirage] provided the cover for the creeping advance of German bayonets.

---

* *Schufterles* means scoundrels.

† Fritz Reuter (1810–1874), novelist who wrote in *Plattdeutsch* (Low German) dialect.

There are times in the history of class struggles when such slogans take on a very real significance. The lot of socialism is a fatal one in that, in this world war, it fell to it to supply ideological pretexts for counterrevolutionary policy. At the outbreak of war, German Social Democracy hastened to bedeck the predatory expedition of German imperialism with an ideological shield retrieved from the lumber room of Marxism, by declaring this campaign to be what our doyens had yearned for in 1848—i.e., an expedition to liberate Russia (and other territories of the Russian Empire) from tsarism. It fell to the lot of the Bolsheviks—the very antipodes of the government-Socialists in Germany—to bring grist to the mill of the counterrevolution with their slogan in favor of the self-determination of nations, thus supplying an ideology not only for the strangulation of the Russian Revolution itself, but also for the planned counterrevolutionary liquidation of the World War as a whole. We have every reason to scrutinize the policy of the Bolsheviks in this regard very thoroughly. The "right of self-determination of nations," coupled with the League of Nations and disarmament by the grace of Wilson,* constitutes the battle-cry under which the coming confrontation between international socialism and the bourgeois world will be played out. It is evident that both the slogan in favor of self-determination and the nationalist movement as a whole—this latter currently posing the greatest threat to international socialism—have been extraordinarily reinforced precisely by the Russian Revolution and by the negotiations in Brest. It will be necessary to tackle this platform exhaustively. The Bolsheviks were caught on the barbs of this phraseology, bloodily lacerating themselves in the process: its tragic destiny within the Russian Revolution must serve the international proletariat as a cautionary example.

The result of all of this was German dictatorship, which endured from the Brest peace treaty to the "supplementary treaty"!† The 200 expiatory sacrifices in Moscow.‡ This situation resulted in terror and the crushing of democracy.[441]

---

* Luxemburg refers to US President Woodrow Wilson here.

† The Treaty of Brest-Litovsk March 3, 1918, with German-Russian Supplementary Treaty of August 27, 1918, stipulated that once the eastern borders of Estonia and Livonia had been determined, Germany would evacuate the territories occupied by it eastward of these borders. Germany was to undertake a progressive evacuation of the territory east of the Berezina in proportion with Soviet Russian compliance with the terms of the Financial Agreement, which determined the schedule of compensation payments that Soviet Russia was to make. Soviet Russia renounced sovereignty over Estonia, Livonia and Georgia. Under the terms of the German-Russian Financial Agreement of August 27, 1918, Russia was obliged to pay 6 billion marks to Germany.

‡ The "two hundred expiatory sacrifices" may refer to the execution of persons charged with complicity in the assassination of the German ambassador to Russia, Count Wilhelm of Mirbach-Harff on July 6, 1918—an event that resulted in hundreds of arrests, although actually many fewer executions. Mirbach had been shot by members of the Russian Left Socialist Revolutionary Party, which had cooperated with the Bolsheviks until the signing of the Brest treaty and then went into violent opposition. From this time forward, the Russian government was a dictatorship of the Bolshevik Party (soon renamed the Communist Party), which launched what came to be known as "the Red Terror," designed to intimidate and defeat those seeking its overthrow.

IV.

These matters can now be examined more closely by means of a few examples.

The famous dissolution of the Constituent Assembly in November 1917 played a prominent role in the policy of the Bolsheviks. This measure determined their further position, and, to a certain extent, marked a turning point in their tactics.

It is a fact that Lenin and his comrades had vociferously called for a Constituent Assembly to be convened, right up to their victory in October, and that Kerensky's government's policy of using delaying tactics in this matter constituted one of the charges leveled by the Bolsheviks against this government—in fact, this policy formed the basis for some of their most violent attacks upon it. Indeed, Trotsky remarks in his interesting pamphlet, *From October to Brest-Litovsk*, that the October Revolution represented the "salvation of the Constituent Assembly" and of the revolution generally. "When we said," he continues, "that the road to the Constituent Assembly was not by way of Tsereteli's Preliminary Parliament, but by way of the seizure of the reins of government by the soviets, we were quite sincere."*

And yet, following these declarations, Lenin's first step after the October Revolution was none other than … to dissolve the very same Constituent Assembly that the revolution was to have ushered in. What reasons dictated such a perplexing about-face? Trotsky comments upon this issue extensively in the aforementioned text, and his arguments can be cited here:†

> [If the months preceding the October Revolution were months of continuous gain in popular support for the left—of a general increase in Bolshevik following among workers, soldiers, and peasants—then this process was reflected within the Socialist Revolutionary Party in an increase of the left wing at the expense of the right. Nevertheless, on the party lists of the Social Revolutionists there was a predominance of three to one of old leaders of the right wing (…). To this should be added also the fact that the elections themselves were held during the first weeks after the October Revolution. The news of the change traveled rather slowly from the capital to the provinces, from the cities to the villages. The peasantry in many places had but a very vague idea of what was taking place in Petrograd and Moscow. They voted for "Land and Liberty" for their representatives in the land committees, who in most cases gathered under the banner of populism: but thereby they were voting for Kerensky and [Nikolai] Avksentiev, who were dissolving the land committees and arresting their members (…). This state of affairs should give a very clear idea of the extent to which the Constituent Assembly lagged behind the development of political events and party groupings.]

* Leon Trotsky, *From October to Brest-Litovsk* (Project Gutenberg, 2004), p. 153.

† This quotation and references to Trotsky's text are missing in the original manuscript. These have been included here within square brackets.

This is all absolutely sound and most compelling. Yet one cannot help wondering how it could be that people as clever as Lenin and Trotsky failed to arrive at the most obvious conclusion from the above facts. Since the Constituent Assembly was elected long before the decisive turning point—the October Revolution*—and its composition did not reflect the new state of affairs but was rather an image of a past that had been superseded, it necessarily followed that the course of action to be taken was to dissolve the obsolete—and thus stillborn—assembly and to call fresh elections for a new Constituent Assembly without delay! The Bolsheviks did not wish to entrust the fate of the revolution to an assembly that reflected Kerenksy's Russia of yesterday, the period of vacillations and coalition with the bourgeoisie—nor should they have done so. The only course open to them, then, was to replace the old assembly by immediately convening a new one that emanated from the renewed, progressive Russia.

By contrast, from the particular inadequacy of the Constituent Assembly that was convened in October, Trotsky infers that any popular representation whatsoever issuing from general elections during the revolution will be inadequate—he thus makes a generalization concerning popular representation from a particular instance:

> Owing to the open and direct struggle for power, the working people acquire much political experience in a short time and pass rapidly from one stage to the next in their development. The ponderous machinery of democratic institutions lags behind this evolution all the more, the bigger the country and the less perfect its technical apparatus.†

Here Trotsky refers to the "machinery of democratic institutions" per se. The first point to raise is that this evaluation of representative institutions expresses a somewhat schematic, rigid conception, one that is emphatically contradicted by the historical experience of all revolutionary epochs. According to Trotsky's theory, any elected assembly is nothing other than a static reflection of the intellectual constitution, political maturity, and disposition of its electorate at the precise moment at which the latter went to the polls. The democratic body is thus the permanent mirror image of the masses on the day of the election, in the same way that Herschel's night sky never shows us celestial bodies as they are, but rather as they were at the precise moment at which, from an immeasurable distance, they dispatched their emissaries of light toward Earth. Any living, intellectual connection, any lasting interaction between those elected and the electorate is hereby denied.

Yet all historical experience utterly contradicts this! Such experience demonstrates the contrary, namely that the vibrant atmosphere of the popular

---

* Elections for the Constituent Assembly were mostly *arranged* prior to the October Revolution, but the elections *took place* after October.

† Trotsky, *From October to Brest-Litovsk*, p. 158.

mood continuously radiates around representative bodies, permeates them and gives them direction. How else could it be that in every bourgeois parliament there are times—whenever there are rumblings in the factories, workshops and streets—when we witness the most amusing capers by "the people's representatives," who, suddenly inspired by a new "spirit," strike completely unexpected chords, the most desiccated mummies occasionally behaving like youngsters, and the various little Scheidemanns* promptly discovering revolutionary tones resonating in their breasts?

And yet are we supposed to believe that the enduring influence that the mood and political maturity of the masses exerts upon elected bodies would, in the very midst of revolution, dissipate when confronted by the rigid schema of party insignia and electoral lists? The very opposite is true! It is precisely the revolution whose scorching heat engenders that rarefied, vibrant, receptive political atmosphere in which the waves of popular mood and the pulsing beat of popular vitality have an instantaneous and most marvelous effect on representative bodies. It is precisely this phenomenon that gives rise to the familiar dramatic scenes from the initial stage of all revolutions, in which old, reactionary or extremely moderate parliaments elected through limited suffrage under the *ancien régime* suddenly become heroic advocates of the revolution, the embodiment of its *Sturm und Drang*.† The classic example of this is of course the famous Long Parliament in England, which, having been elected and convened in 1642, sat for seven years and reflected in its inner life all the swings in the popular mood, in political maturity, in class differentiation and in the progress of the revolution toward its climax, from the initial submissive skirmishes with the crown under a "Speaker" who remained on his knees, right up to the abolition of the House of Lords, the execution of Charles I and the proclamation of the Republic.

And was not the same wonderful transformation repeated in the French Estates General,‡ in the parliament elected by census suffrage under Louis Philippe? Indeed—to cite a striking recent example that is so close to Trotsky—was it not also repeated in the Fourth Russian Duma, which, having been elected under the most draconian rule of the counterrevolution in the year of salvation 1912,§ suddenly sensed the glowing heat of the coming insurrection in February 1917, and became the point of departure for the revolution?¶

* "*Scheidemännchen*" (Little Scheidemen), a variant on Luxemburg's habitual play on the name of the pro-war, government Social Democrat Phillip Scheidemann.

† *Sturm und Drang*, conventionally translated as "storm and stress" but perhaps better rendered as "storm and drive," was a proto-Romantic movement in German literature and music in the latter part of the eighteenth century, with a particular focus on individual subjectivity and the free expression of extremes of emotion.

‡ In the original manuscript: [*Generalstaaten*] "General States."

§ In the original manuscript: 1909 (see Section II, first footnote).

¶ It was this Fourth Duma that, after popular demonstrations in February 1917, sent two emissaries to the tsar to request his abdication.

All of this demonstrates that there is a powerful corrective to the "ponderous machinery of democratic institutions;"[*] namely in the living movement of the masses, and the unrelenting pressure that this movement exerts. Furthermore, the more democratic the institution, and the more vibrant and powerful the pulse of the political life of the masses, the more immediate and precise is their influence—despite rigid party insignias, outdated electoral lists, etc. To be sure, every democratic institution has its constraints and inadequacies, which it undoubtedly shares with all human institutions. Yet the remedy that Trotsky and Lenin have discovered—the elimination of democracy as such—is worse than the evil that it is supposed to prevent, for it occludes the very living source alone from which any correction of all the deficiencies inherent within social institutions can emanate. That source is none other than the active, uninhibited, vigorous political life of the broadest masses of the people.[†]

Let us take another striking example, namely the right of suffrage developed by the Soviet government.[‡] It is not completely clear what practical significance is attached to this right of suffrage. From the critique of democratic institutions by Lenin and Trotsky, it can be seen that, on principle, they reject popular representation on the basis of general elections, preferring instead a system founded upon the soviets alone. This being so, it is in fact unclear why a system of universal suffrage should have been developed at all. To my knowledge, this system of suffrage has not been implemented in any way; there has been no mention of elections to any kind of popular representative body on such a basis. A more likely hypothesis is that it has remained a mere theoretical product of the conference room, as it were. Yet, in itself, it constitutes a remarkable product of the Bolshevik theory of dictatorship. Each system of suffrage, in common with all political rights as such, is not to be measured against any given abstract schemas of "justice" or similar bourgeois democratic phraseology but should rather be evaluated with regard to the social and economic relations to which it is tailored. The system of franchise elaborated by the Soviet government was, in fact, devised for the purposes of the period of transition from bourgeois-capitalist society to the socialist form of society—i.e.,

---

* "Institutions" replaced by ellipsis in the original manuscript. The quotation reads: "the ponderous machinery of democratic institutions" (Trotsky, *From October to Brest-Litovsk* p. 158).

† In other versions of this text there is a break here and a subheading: V. The Question of Suffrage.

‡ The constitution that was adopted on July 10, 1917, stipulated that the following citizens over the age of eighteen years would have the right to vote and to stand as a candidate in elections irrespective of their creed, nationality or residential status: "All who have acquired the means of livelihood through labor that is productive and useful to society, and also persons engaged in housekeeping that enables the former to do productive work, i.e., laborers and employees of all classes who are employed in industry, trade, agriculture, etc., and peasants and Cossack agricultural laborers who employ no help for the purpose of making profits." Soldiers of the Soviet army and citizens that had lost their capacity to work also had the right to vote. The franchise was denied to those who employed wage laborers or who lived from an income without doing any work, such as private merchants, members of the clergy, and former police officers.

the period of the proletarian dictatorship. In accordance with the interpretation of this dictatorship advocated by Lenin and Trotsky, the right to vote is granted only to those who live by their own labor, being denied to everyone else.

Now, it is clear that such a franchise only makes sense in a society that is also economically capable of granting all who wish to work an adequate standard of living—one that is worthy of civilization—on the basis of their own labor. Is this true of contemporary Russia? Given the tremendous difficulties with which Soviet Russia has to contend, cut off as it is from the world market and from its most important sources of raw materials, and given the dreadful general disruption to economic life and the abrupt upheaval in relations of production as a result of the revolution in property relations in agriculture, industry and commerce—given all these circumstances, it is obvious that innumerable livelihoods have been suddenly uprooted and catapulted from their normal course, the individuals concerned having no objective possibility of finding any use for their labor power within the economic mechanism. This obtains not only for the class of capitalists and large-scale landowners, but also for the broad stratum of the middle classes* and even for the working class itself. It is a fact that the contraction in industry has caused a massive exodus of the urban proletariat to the countryside in order to search for employment in agriculture. In such circumstances, a political franchise that has the general compulsion to work as an economic precondition is an utterly incomprehensible provision. It is supposed to tend toward disenfranchising the exploiters alone. And while productive labor power is being uprooted en masse, the Soviet government conversely finds itself compelled in many cases to cede national industry to former capitalist proprietors on lease, as it were. Likewise, the Soviet government also found itself obliged in April 1918 to strike a compromise with bourgeois consumer cooperative societies. Furthermore, the Soviet government has had no option but to engage bourgeois experts as consultants. Another consequence of this situation is that increasing strata of the proletariat are maintained by the state, out of public funds, as Red Guards, etc. In reality, the system of franchise elaborated by the Soviet government has left broad and increasing strata of the petty bourgeoisie and the proletariat, for whom the economic organism provides no means to comply with the compulsion to work, without any political rights.

This is an incongruity that qualifies the Soviet franchise as a utopian product of fantasy, one that is detached from social reality. And precisely for this reason it fails to constitute a serious instrument for proletarian dictatorship.†

---

* "*Mittelstand*" is used in two different senses: 1) as a collective noun grouping small- and medium-scale enterprises (usually in Germany); 2) in a sociological sense, denoting the middle classes. Here it would seem that the latter is indicated.

† A note added by Luxemburg in the left-hand margin, without an indication as to where it was to be included in the text, reads: "An anachronism, an anticipation of the legal situation

When, in what was a rebellion against the workers' government, the entire middle class, the bourgeois and petty-bourgeois intelligentsia boycotted the Soviet government for months on end following the October Revolution, disabling railway, postal and telegraph communications as well as the education system and the administrative apparatus, it was, of course, necessary to use all manner of measures to exert pressure upon this class and to smash its resistance with an iron fist. Such measures included the withdrawal of political rights and of economic means of existence. This simply represented an expression of socialist dictatorship, which cannot shirk from deploying its power in order to enforce or prevent determinate measures in the interests of the whole. By contrast, a system of franchise that pronounces a general disenfranchisement upon broad strata of society and places them outside the framework of society *politically*, while it is incapable of accommodating them within this framework *economically* (i.e., a system of franchise that enacts disenfranchisement not as a concrete measure for a concrete purpose, but rather as a general rule of lasting effect)—such a system of franchise is no necessary feature of dictatorship: on the contrary, it represents an unviable improvisation.*

Yet the question is not exhausted by the Constituent Assembly and the system of franchise: also at issue was the abolition of further important democratic guarantees, such as the guarantees of a healthy public sphere and the political activity of the working masses. These guarantees consisted in the freedom of the press, the right of association and of assembly; now that these have been abolished, all opposition to the Soviet government has effectively been outlawed.† Trotsky's line of argument (referred to above) regarding the

---

that will only obtain when the socialist economic basis for it is already given—this is not the case in the period of transition corresponding to proletarian dictatorship."

* A note added by Luxemburg in the left-hand margin, without an indication as to where it was to be included in the text, reads as follows: "Both Soviets and a Constituent Assembly based on *universal suffrage* as backbone." A note found on a loose, unnumbered sheet of paper reads as follows: "The Bolsheviks labeled the soviets as reactionary, because peasants (peasants' and soldiers' delegates) constituted a majority within them. Once the soviets had placed themselves on the side of the Bolsheviks, they then became the true representatives of popular opinion. Yet this sudden reversal was bound up only with *peace* and the agrarian question." The following passage was found crossed out on an unnumbered loose sheet of paper in the manuscript: "The Bolsheviks designated the soviets as reactionary because their majority consisted of peasants (peasant and soldier delegates). After the soviets went over to them, they became correct representatives of public opinion. But this sudden change was connected only with peace and land questions."

† Freedom of the press, assembly and association was formally guaranteed only to the working class in the new Soviet constitution: "Proletarian democracy suppresses the exploiters, the bourgeoisie—and is therefore not hypocritical, *does not promise them* freedom and democracy—and gives the working people *genuine democracy. Only* Soviet Russia has given the proletariat and the whole vast laboring majority of Russia a *freedom and democracy* unprecedented, impossible and inconceivable in any bourgeois democratic republic, by, for example, taking the palaces and mansions away from the bourgeoisie (without which freedom of assembly is sheer hypocrisy), by taking the printshops and stocks of paper away from the capitalists (without which freedom of the press for the nation's laboring majority is a lie)."

unwieldiness of democratic electorates is far from satisfactory as justification for these infringements. On the contrary, it is a patent and indisputable fact that without a free, untrammeled press, without an unimpeded right of association and assembly, rule by broad masses of the people is completely unthinkable.*

Lenin states that the bourgeois state is an instrument for the oppression of the working class, and the socialist state an instrument for the suppression of the bourgeoisie. He argues that the socialist state is, to a certain extent, merely the inversion of the capitalist state. This simplified conception disregards what is most essential here: bourgeois class rule requires no political training or education of the entire mass of the people, or at least not beyond certain narrowly drawn boundaries. For proletarian dictatorship, in contrast, such education is its very life element, the air without which it would not be able to exist.

"Owing to the open and direct struggle for power …"† Here Trotsky contradicts himself and his own friends in the party. Precisely because Trotsky's statement holds true, the Bolsheviks have, by stifling public life, occluded the source of political experience and rising development. Alternatively, it would have to be surmised that such experience and development were necessary up to the seizure of power by the Bolsheviks, by which point they had reached their zenith, and that they have become superfluous from that point on. (Lenin's speech: Russia is won for socialism!!!)

In reality, the reverse is true! It was precisely the colossal tasks that the Bolsheviks took on with such courage and resolve that required the most intensive political training of the masses and the greatest accumulation of experience.‡

The tacit presupposition underlying the theory of dictatorship as formulated by Lenin and Trotsky is that the revolutionary party has, in its pocket, a ready-made formula for socialist transformation, and that this formula merely needs to be assiduously implemented. This is unfortunately—or perhaps, fortunately—not the case. Far from being an aggregation of ready-made prescriptions that have merely to be applied, the practical realization of socialism as an economic, social, and legal system is something that lies in the mists of the future. What we possess in our program amounts to no more than a few major signposts that indicate the general direction in which to look for the measures that are to be taken, and these indications are predominantly of a negative

* In other versions of this text there is a section break and a subheading: Section VI.

† Ellipsis in the original manuscript. The full quotation reads as follows: "Owing to the open and direct struggle for power, the working people acquire much political experience in a short time and pass rapidly from one stage to the next in their development" (Trotsky *From October to Brest-Litovsk*, p. 158).

‡ A note added by Luxemburg in the left-hand margin, without an indication as to where it was to be included in the text, reads as follows: "Freedom only for the supporters of the government, only for members of the party—however numerous these may be—is no freedom at all. Freedom is always only freedom for those who think differently. Not on account of a fanaticism that upholds 'justice'; rather because all that is invigorating, wholesome and purifying in political freedom depends on this essence, whose effect is negated when 'freedom' becomes a 'privilege.'"

character at that. We know approximately what we have to eliminate at the very outset in order to clear the path for the socialist economy; by contrast, there is no socialist party program nor any socialist textbook that can instruct us as to the quality of the innumerable concrete measures, both major and minor, that are needed in order to introduce basic socialist features into the economy, the legal system and all social relations. This constitutes no defect; on the contrary, it is precisely herein that the advantage of scientific vis-à-vis utopian socialism consists. The socialist system of society shall—and *can* only—be a historical product: it is born of its own school of experience, in the hour of fulfilment; it emerges from the becoming of living history. Furthermore, just like organic nature (of which it ultimately forms a part), this living history has the alluring habit of always producing, alongside any real social need that it engenders, the means to satisfy such need: it generates problems and their solution simultaneously. Yet if this is the case, then it is evident that, by its very *nature*, socialism *cannot* be imposed—it *cannot* be introduced by *ukase*.* It has as its prerequisite a series of coercive measures—against property, etc. The negative—the dismantling of what exists—can be decreed; the positive cannot. It is a *terra incognita*. A thousand problems. Experience alone is capable of making corrections and opening up new paths. Only uninhibited, effervescent life fashions a thousand new forms and improvisations, contains *creative power*, and corrects all mistakes. The public life of states where freedom is restricted is so meager, so miserable, so schematic and so sterile precisely because by excluding democracy, the living source of all intellectual wealth and progress is occluded. (Proof of this: the year 1905 and the period from February to October 1917.) In these cases, this occurred on a political level; the same applies to the economic and social spheres. The entire mass of the people must participate in public life. Otherwise, socialism is merely decreed, imposed from the conference table of a dozen intellectuals.

Public control is indispensable. Otherwise, the exchange of experiences remains restricted to the closed circle of officials in the new government. Corruption is then inevitable. (Lenin's words, *Bulletin* no. 36.)† Socialism in practice requires a complete intellectual revolution in the masses who have been degraded by centuries of bourgeois class domination. Social instincts in

* A *ukase* was a decree issued by the tsar in Imperial Russia.

† In the original manuscript Luxemburg gives an erroneous reference here (*Bulletin* no. 29). The article "Nach der Russischen Revolution" (After the Russian Revolution) was published in *Mitteilungs-Blatt des Verbandes der sozialdemokratischen Wahlvereine Berlins und Umgegend* (Bulletin of the Federation of the Social-Democratic Electoral Associations of Berlin and Environs), No. 36, December 8, 1918. It contains an exhaustive reproduction—sometimes word for word—of "The Immediate Tasks of the Soviet Government (see Lenin, *Collected Works*, Vol. 27, pp. 235–77), in which Lenin expounds the difficulties of development in Soviet Russia after the victory of the October Revolution; sets out the tasks for the period of transition from the capitalist to the socialist social order; and explains the function of the new state power in the struggle for the development of the economy and for protection against counterrevolution, corruption and sabotage.

place of egoistic ones, mass initiative in place of lethargy, idealism that provides sustenance through all kinds of suffering, etc., etc. No one knows this better, describes it more penetratingly, or repeats it more persistently than Lenin.* He errs completely in the means that he employs, however. Decrees, the dictatorial powers of factory supervisors, draconian punishments, the reign of terror—these are all mere palliatives. The only way to a renaissance is the school of public life itself, the most unrestricted and broadest democracy, public *opinion*. In contrast, the very reign of terror itself has a demoralizing effect.

If all this ceases to exist, what remains in reality? In place of representative bodies constituted by general popular elections, Lenin and Trotsky have installed the soviets as the only true representation of the working masses. Yet

---

* A note added by Luxemburg in the left-hand margin, without an indication as to where it was to be included in the text, reads as follows: "Lenin's speech on discipline and corruption. Anarchy will also be inevitable here and everywhere else. A lumpenproletarian element is inherent within bourgeois society and cannot be separated from it. Evidence: 1) East Prussia, the 'Cossack' depredations; 2) The general outbreak of robbery and theft in Germany ('racketeering', postal and railway personnel, police, complete blurring of the boundaries between the well-ordered society and the penitentiary); 3) The rapid lumpenization of labor union leaders. Draconian measures of terror are powerless against this. On the contrary, they corrupt further. The only antidote: idealism and social *activity* of the masses, unrestricted *political* freedom." Luxemburg added the following elaborations on a loose sheet of paper, without an indication as to where they were to be included in the text: "The struggle against the lumpenproletariat forms a highly important problem in its own right in every revolution. In Germany and elsewhere we will also have to confront this problem. The lumpenproletarian element is deeply inherent in bourgeois society, not only as a particular stratum (as a social waste-product that swells to enormous proportions particularly in times when the walls of the social order are collapsing), but also as an integrating element within society as a whole. Events in Germany—and to a greater or lesser degree in all other states—have demonstrated how all strata of bourgeois society succumb to lumpenization. The gradations between commercial price gouging, *szlachta*-style racketeering [the *szlachta* was a class of Polish minor nobility, its members often without means], fraudulent commercial operations, adulteration of foodstuffs, swindling, embezzlement by officials, theft, burglary, and robbery have become so fluid that the boundary between the respectable citizenry and the penitentiary has vanished. This is a repetition of the same phenomenon whereby bourgeois dignitaries regularly undergo a rapid lumpenization when they are transplanted to an alien social soil in an overseas colonial setting. When conventional constraints and the pillars of morality and right are stripped away, bourgeois society, whose innermost vital law represents the most profound immorality (i.e., the exploitation of human beings by human beings), succumbs immediately and unrestrainedly to simple lumpenization. The proletarian revolution will have to struggle everywhere against this enemy, this instrument of counterrevolution. And yet, in this relation, too, terror is a blunt, or indeed a double-edged, sword. The most draconian martial law is impotent against outbreaks of lumpenproletarian malignancy. Indeed, each lasting state of emergency leads inexorably to despotism, and each despotism has a depraving effect on society. Here too, the only effective means at the disposal of the proletarian revolution consist in radical measures of a political and social nature, the most rapid transformation of the social guarantees of the livelihoods of the masses and the fomenting of revolutionary idealism, which can only be sustained by the intensively active life of the masses within a context of unrestricted political freedom. Just as the free action of sunrays constitutes the most effective, purifying and healing remedy against infectious illnesses and pathogens, so too the only healing and purifying sun is the revolution itself, its principle of renewal. This principle consists in the intellectual life, the activity and the self-responsibility of the masses, such that the form taken by the revolution consists in the broadest political freedom."

with the stifling of political life in the country as a whole, vitality within the soviets will also necessarily tend to wane. Without general elections, without unrestricted freedom of the press and of assembly, without a free struggle of opinions, vitality withers away in each public institution—it becomes a pseudo-vitality in which bureaucracy is the only remaining active element. Public life gradually falls into a slumber, a few dozen party leaders with inexhaustible energy and boundless idealism direct and govern; among the latter, a dozen outstanding minds are, in reality, the ones that lead, and an elite from within the working class is occasionally mustered in order to applaud the speeches of the leaders and to show unanimous approval for the resolutions drafted by them. This is basically a clique economy—a dictatorship to be sure, but not the dictatorship of the proletariat: instead, it is the dictatorship of a handful of politicians, i.e., dictatorship in the bourgeois sense, in the sense of Jacobin rule (as exemplified by the extension of the interval between each Congress of Soviets from three to six months!). Worse still: such conditions will necessarily lead to a barbarization of public life: attempted assassinations, the execution of hostages, etc. This is an all-powerful, objective law that no party can circumvent.

The basic error within Lenin and Trotsky's theory is that, just like Kautsky, they counterpose dictatorship to democracy. Both the Bolsheviks and Kautsky pose the question in terms of "dictatorship *or* democracy." Kautsky naturally decides in favor of democracy—more accurately, in favor of *bourgeois* democracy, precisely because he presents this as the alternative to socialist revolution. Conversely, Lenin and Trotsky resolve in favor of dictatorship in contradistinction to democracy, and thus in favor of the dictatorship of a handful of persons—i.e., *bourgeois* dictatorship. These are two opposing poles that are equally far removed from genuine socialist politics. When it seizes power, the proletariat must ignore Kautsky's advice: it cannot renounce socialist revolution in order merely to commit to democracy under the pretext of the "country's immaturity": to do so would be to betray itself, the International and the revolution. It ought to—or rather, it *must*—begin immediately to take socialist measures in the most vigorous, unrelenting, and ruthless fashion: it must exercise dictatorship, but dictatorship of the class, not of a party or clique, where dictatorship of the class signifies a dictatorship exercised within the broadest public sphere, with the most active, uninhibited participation of the popular masses, and within unrestricted democracy. "As Marxists, we have never been idol-worshippers of formal democracy," writes Trotsky.* It is certainly true that we have never been idol-worshippers of formal democracy. Nor have we ever been idol-worshippers of socialism or Marxism. Does it follow from this that we can also, à la Cunow, Lensch and Parvus, cast socialism or Marxism into the lumber room when it becomes inconvenient for us? Trotsky and Lenin are the

* Trotsky, *From October to Brest-Litovsk*, p. 157.

living negation of such an option. That we have never been idol-worshippers of formal democracy merely means that we always distinguish the social core from the political form of *bourgeois* democracy, we have always revealed the bitter core of social inequality and lack of freedom beneath the sweet shell of formal equality and freedom—not, however, in order to discard this shell; instead we have done so in order to spur the working class not to content itself with this mere husk, but, rather, to conquer political power so as to fill it with a new social content. It is the historic task of the proletariat when it comes to power to create socialist democracy in place of bourgeois democracy—not to eliminate democracy altogether. Yet socialist democracy is not something that only begins in the Promised Land, once the substructure—the socialist economy—has been established; it does not come as a ready-made Christmas present for the obedient populace who, in the interim, have loyally supported the handful of socialist dictators. Socialist democracy commences simultaneously with the dismantling of class domination and the construction of socialism. It begins at the very moment of the seizure of power by the socialist party. It is nothing other than the dictatorship of the proletariat.

Yes, indeed, dictatorship! However, this dictatorship consists in the manner in which democracy is *applied*, not in its elimination; it consists in vigorous, resolute interventions that impinge upon the vested rights and economic relations of bourgeois society: the socialist revolution cannot be realized without such interventions. Yet such a dictatorship must be the work of the *class*, and not of a small leading minority acting in the name of the class—that is, it must proceed at every step from the active participation of the masses; it must remain under the immediate influence of the latter, under the control of the entire public sphere; it must emanate from the burgeoning political schooling of the popular masses.

The Bolsheviks would also have proceeded precisely in this way, had they not been afflicted by the dreadful compulsion of the World War, German occupation and all the abnormal associated difficulties that were inevitably bound to distort any socialist policy, no matter how imbued it might be with the best intentions and finest principles.

This is glaringly demonstrated by the Soviet government's abundant use of terror, particularly in the most recent period prior to the collapse of German imperialism and following the assassination of the German ambassador. The truism that revolutions are not baptized with rose water* is in itself somewhat inadequate.

Everything that is occurring in Russia is comprehensible and constitutes an inevitable chain of causes and effects, the point of departure and keystone

* "On either side harm must be done before good can accrue—revolutions are not to be made with rose water." Lord Byron, letter of October 3, 1819, *Byron's Letters and Journals: A New Selection*, ed. Richard Lansdown (Oxford: Oxford University Press, 2015), p. 338.

of which is the failure of the German proletariat and the occupation of Russia by German imperialism. To expect that Lenin and his comrades should have conjured up the finest democracy, the most exemplary dictatorship of the proletariat and a flourishing socialist economy in such conditions would be to demand superhuman feats from them. Through their resolute revolutionary stance, their exemplary drive and the force of their action, and their unswerving loyalty to international socialism, they have genuinely achieved all that was possible under such devilishly difficult conditions. The danger begins only where they make a virtue out of necessity by establishing a theory that sets in stone every detail of the tactics imposed upon them by such fatal conditions, and where they attempt to recommend to the international proletariat that it should emulate these as the paradigm of socialist tactics *per se*. In so doing, they cast a shadow over themselves quite unnecessarily, and conceal their genuine, undeniable historical achievements under a bushel of unavoidable missteps. Likewise, having fought and suffered for international socialism, they do it a disservice by attempting to store as new discoveries in its cumulative memory all the distortions perpetrated under duress in a situation of emergency in Russia—distortions that in the final analysis merely reflected the bankruptcy of international socialism in the present world war.

Let German Government-Socialists cry that the rule of the Bolsheviks in Russia is a travesty of the dictatorship of the proletariat! This was, or is, true only because it was a product of the stance of the German proletariat, which itself was a travesty of socialist class struggle. We are all subject to the law of history, and it is only internationally that the socialist order of society can be realized. The Bolsheviks demonstrated that they could achieve everything that a genuine revolutionary party is capable of accomplishing within the limits of historical possibilities. They should not attempt to perform miracles. An exemplary and flawless proletarian revolution would be a miracle in a country that is isolated, exhausted by World War, throttled by imperialism and betrayed by the international proletariat. What is crucial is to distinguish the essential from the inessential, the core from the merely contingent in the politics of the Bolsheviks. In this last period, in which we face decisive, final struggles all over the world, the most important problem of socialism remains the burning question of the times. This is not a mere question of tactical detail: what is at issue is the proletariat's capacity for action, the drive of the masses, and the will to power of socialism as such. In this context, Lenin and Trotsky and their friends were the first to lead the way, and to set an example for the proletariat—they remain to date the only ones who can proclaim, in the words of Hutten, "I dared!"*

* Ulrich von Hutten's 1520 *Aufwecker der teutschen Nation* (Arouser of the German Nation), which proclaimed his support for Martin Luther, opens with the motto "*Ich hab's gewagt*" (I have dared to do it).

This is what is essential and *enduring* in the politics of the Bolsheviks. In *this* sense it is historically to their eternal credit that they have led the way for the international proletariat with the conquest of political power and by posing the realization of socialism as a practical problem, and that they have given a powerful impetus to the conflict between labor and capital throughout the world. In Russia, the problem could only be posed; it could not be solved there. And in *this* sense, the future everywhere belongs to "Bolshevism."

The Russian Tragedy*

Since the Treaty of Brest-Litovsk, the Russian Revolution has found itself in a very awkward position. The policy that has guided the Bolsheviks' action is obvious: peace at all costs in order to gain a respite during which they can expand and consolidate the dictatorship of the proletariat in Russia and realize as many socialist reforms as possible. In this way, they plan to await the outbreak of the international proletarian revolution and, at the same time, to expedite it by the Russian example. Since the utter war-weariness of the Russian masses and the simultaneous military disorganization left behind by tsarism appeared, in any case, to make the continuation of war a futile shedding of Russian blood, there was no other way out but to conclude peace as quickly as possible. This is how Lenin and comrades assessed the situation.

This was dictated by two purely revolutionary viewpoints: by the unshakable faith in the European revolution of the proletariat as the only solution and the inevitable consequence of the World War; and by their equally unshakable resolve to defend by any means possible the power they had gained in Russia, in order to use it for the most vigorous and radical transformations.

And yet this assessment largely overlooked the most crucial factor, namely German militarism, to which Russia surrendered unconditionally through the separate peace (*Separatfrieden*). The Treaty of Brest-Litovsk was in reality nothing but the capitulation of the revolutionary Russian proletariat to German imperialism. Admittedly Lenin and his friends deluded neither themselves nor others about the facts. They candidly admitted their capitulation. Unfortunately, they did deceive themselves in hoping to purchase a genuine respite for the price of this capitulation that would allow them to truly save themselves from the hellfire of the World War by means of a separate peace. They did not reckon with the fact that the capitulation of Russia at Brest-Litovsk meant a tremendous strengthening of the imperialist Pan-German policy and thus, precisely, a lessening of the chances for a revolutionary uprising in Germany. Instead of the end of the war against Germany, it would merely bring about the beginning of a new chapter of this war.

---

* This article first appeared in *Spartacus*, No. 11, September 1918, and was republished in *Spartakus im Kriege. Die Illegalen Flugblätter des Spartakusbundes im Kriege* (Spartakus in War. The Illegal Pamphlets of the Spartakusbund), edited and introduced by Ernst Meyer (Berlin: Kommunistische Partei Deutschlands, 1927), which names Luxemburg as the author. The editor of *Spartacus* published it with the following footnote: "The article expresses fears, which are often prevalent among our circles—fears arising from the *objective situation* of the Bolsheviks, and not from their *subjective* behavior. We publish the article chiefly because of its conclusion that without the German revolution there would be no salvation of the Russian Revolution, no hope for socialism in this World War. The *only* solution is the mass uprising of the German proletariat." The article is translated by Manuela Kölke from Luxemburg's *Gesammelte Werke*, Vol. 4, pp. 385–92.

In fact, the "peace" of Brest-Litovsk is an illusion. Not for a moment was there peace between Russia and Germany. War has continued from Brest-Litovsk up to the present day, but a peculiar war waged by only one side: systematic German advance and tacit Bolshevik retreat, step by step. The occupation of Ukraine, Finland, Livonia, Estonia, the Crimea, the Caucasus, larger and larger tracts of southern Russia—this is the result of the "state of peace" since Brest-Litovsk.

And this meant, in the first place, the strangulation of the revolution and the victory of the counterrevolution in all the revolutionary strongholds of Russia. Because Finland, the Baltic States, Ukraine, Caucasus, the Black Sea—this is all *Russia*, namely the territory of the *Russian Revolution*, no matter what the hollow, petty-bourgeois phrase-mongers may babble about the "right of national self-determination."

Secondly, this means the isolation of the Greater Russian part of the revolutionary terrain from the grain-growing and coal-mining regions and from the sources of ore and naphtha, that is, from the most important and vital economic sources of the revolution.

Thirdly, the encouragement and strengthening of all counterrevolutionary elements within Russia, enabling them to offer the strongest resistance against the Bolsheviks and their measures.

Fourthly, Germany will take on the role of arbiter in Russia's political and economic relations with all its provinces—Finland, Poland, Lithuania, Ukraine, and the Caucasus—as well as the neighboring countries such as Romania.

The overall result of this unrestricted German reign in Russia was, naturally, a tremendous strengthening of German imperialism, both internally and externally, and thus, of course, a white-hot intensification of the resistance and war-readiness of the Entente countries, that is, the prolongation and intensification of the World War. And more: Russia's defenselessness, as revealed by the advancing German occupation, must naturally tempt the Entente and Japan into a counterattack on Russian territory in order to combat Germany's huge predominance and simultaneously to satisfy their imperialist appetites at the expense of the defenseless colossus. Now the north and east of European Russia, as well as the whole of Siberia, are cut off, and the Bolsheviks are isolated from their last sources of essential supplies.*

The end result of the Treaty of Brest-Litovsk is that the Russian Revolution is thus encircled, starved, and strangled from all sides.

But within the country as well, in the territory that the Germans left to

* With the landing of English and American troops in Murmansk as well as Japanese and American troops in Vladivostok in the spring of 1918, foreign military intervention had begun in Soviet Russia. The interventionists united with the local counterrevolutionaries to destroy Soviet power. By the end of 1920, the Red Army succeeded in crushing the main forces of the interventionists and White Guards. The war against the Japanese and White Guards lasted until 1922.

the Bolsheviks, the power and the politics of the revolution were forced into dire straits. The assassinations of [Wilhelm von] Mirbach and [Hermann von] Eichhorn* are a tangible response to German imperialism's reign of terror in Russia. Social Democracy, to be sure, has always rejected terror as an individual act, but only because it considered the mass struggle to be a more effective means, not because it preferred passive toleration of reactionary despotism. It is, of course, only one of the W.T.B.'s [Wolff's Telegraphic Bureau's] official falsifications that claims the Left Socialist Revolutionaries carried out these assassinations at the instigation or on the orders of the Entente. Either these assassinations were intended as a signal for a mass uprising against German rule, or they were only impulsive acts of revenge born of despair and hatred of bloody German rule. Whatever their intention, they gravely endangered the cause of the revolution in Russia, namely by creating divisions within the hitherto ruling socialist groups. They drove a wedge between the Bolsheviks and the Left Socialist Revolutionaries, and, indeed, they created an abyss and mortal enmity between the two wings of the revolutionary army.†

Certainly, social differences—the antagonism between the property-owning peasantry and the peasant-proletariat, among other things—would sooner or later have led to the split between the Bolsheviks and the Left Socialist Revolutionaries. Until the Mirbach assassination, however, events did not appear to have progressed so far. In any case, it is a fact that the Left Socialist Revolutionaries lent their support to the Bolsheviks. The October Revolution that brought the Bolsheviks to the helm, the dispersal of the Constituent Assembly, the Bolsheviks' reforms until now, would hardly have been possible without the cooperation of the Left Socialist Revolutionaries. Only Brest-Litovsk and its aftermath drove the wedge between the two wings. German imperialism now appears as the arbiter between the Bolsheviks and their former revolutionary allies, just as it is the arbiter of their (the Bolsheviks') relations with the Russian border provinces and neighboring states. It is obvious that, because of this, the resistance to the Bolsheviks' rule and reform measures, already enormous in any case, will increase, and the basis upon which their rule rests has been significantly diminished. Probably this internal falling-out and division of the heterogeneous elements of the revolution were inevitable, just as it is inevitable in the progressive radicalization of every developing revolution. *Now*, however, a controversy has occurred over Germany's brutal dictatorship

---

* On July 6, 1918, in Moscow, the German Ambassador, Wilhelm Count von Mirbach-Harff, and on July 30, 1918, in Kiev, the General Field Marshal Hermann von Eichhorn, commander in chief of German troops in Ukraine, were assassinated by Left Socialist Revolutionaries. These assassinations were supposed to provoke a war with Germany. The Soviet government, which condemned these individual terrorist acts, successfully blocked the intention of the Socialist Revolutionaries and averted the threat of war.

† The Left Socialist Revolutionaries, which had been a dominant force in the soviets, were expelled from it in July 1918.

over the Russian Revolution. German imperialism is the thorn in the flesh of the Russian Revolution.

But this is not the full extent of the danger! The iron circle of the World War, which seemed to have been broken in the east, once again relentlessly encompasses Russia and the whole world: The Entente is advancing with Czech* and Japanese troops from the north and east as a natural and inevitable consequence of the German offensive from the west and south. The inferno of the World War is leaping across Russian soil, and, at any moment, may engulf the Russian Revolution. To withdraw from the World War—even at the price of the greatest sacrifices—is something that, in the final analysis, is simply impossible for Russia to do.

And now, the most dreadful prospect looms like an eerie ghost ahead of the Bolsheviks at the final stage of their thorny path—an alliance between the Bolsheviks and Germany! This, to be sure, would forge the final link in that disastrous chain that the World War has hung around the neck of the Russian Revolution: first retreat, then capitulation, and finally an alliance with German imperialism. In this way, the Russian Revolution would be dragged by the World War, from which it sought to withdraw at any cost, over to the opposite camp—from the side of the Entente while under the tsar to the German side under the Bolsheviks.

It is to the everlasting credit of the Russian revolutionary proletariat that its first gesture following the outbreak of the revolution was the renunciation of allegiance to the army of Franco-English imperialism. In view of the international situation, however, to render military service to German imperialism is even worse.

Trotsky is supposed to have said that if Russia had to choose between Japanese and German occupation, it would choose the latter since Germany was much more ready for revolution than Japan. The agonizing aspect of this speculation is obvious. For Japan is not Germany's only opponent; so, too, are England and France, and of these, no one is able to say whether their internal situations are more favorable than Germany's to the proletarian revolution. Trotsky's reasoning is completely wrong, however, since the prospects and possibilities of revolution in Germany are dimmed each time German militarism is strengthened or gains a victory.

But then other considerations, quite different from these apparently realistic ones, must be taken into account. An alliance between the Bolsheviks and German imperialism would be the most terrible moral blow that could be

---

* At the end of May 1918, a revolt broke out among the Czechoslovak Legion, which had been formed from prisoners of war and was to move through Siberia and the Far East to France. The Legionnaires, who were joined by thousands of White Guards, occupied a large part of Siberia and the Urals, as well as areas on the Volga. The Red Army smashed the insurrection at the end of 1919.

delivered against international socialism. Russia was the one last corner where revolutionary socialism, purity of principles, and ideals still held sway. It was a place to which all sincere socialist elements in Germany and Europe could look in order to find relief from the disgust they felt at the practice of the Western European workers' movement, in order to arm themselves with the courage to persevere with faith in pure actions and sacred words. The grotesque "coupling" of Lenin and Hindenburg would extinguish the source of moral light in the East. It is obvious that the German rulers are holding a gun to the Soviet government's head and are exploiting its desperate situation in order to force this monstrous alliance upon them. But we hope that Lenin and his friends will not surrender at any price and that they will oppose this unreasonable demand with a categorical "This far but no further!"

A socialist revolution supported by German bayonets, the dictatorship of the proletariat under the patronage of German imperialism—that would be the most monstrous event we could ever hope to witness. And what is more, it would be pure *utopianism*. Not to mention the fact that the moral prestige of the Bolsheviks would be destroyed in the country, that they would lose all freedom of movement and independence, even in domestic policy, and within the shortest possible time would disappear from the scene altogether. Any child can see that Germany is only waiting for an opportunity to combine with a Milyukov, a Hetman or God knows what other obscure gentlemen and political dabblers, to put an end to Bolshevik splendor and strangle Lenin and comrades with their own hands, after they have played their part as Trojan Horses, as they did with the Ukrainians, the Lubinskys and the rest.

If this were to happen, all previous sacrifices, including the great sacrifice of Brest-Litovsk, would have been completely in vain; for their price would ultimately be moral bankruptcy. Any political downfall of the Bolsheviks in an honest struggle against the overwhelming forces and hostile pressures of the historical situation would be preferable to this moral downfall.

The Bolsheviks have certainly made a number of mistakes in their policies, and perhaps are still making them—but name one revolution in which no mistakes have been made! The notion of a revolutionary policy without mistakes, especially in this completely unprecedented situation, is so absurd that it is worthy only of a German schoolmaster. If the so-called leaders of German socialism lose their so-called heads in such an unusual situation as a simple vote of the Reichstag, and, if their hearts sink into their boots and they forget the whole of socialism like a badly learned lesson, even though the ABCs of socialism are clearly drawn out—how could one expect a party caught up in a truly thorny and outrageous historical situation, in which it would show the world new wonders, not to make mistakes?

The fatal situation in which the Bolsheviks find themselves today, however, is, together with most of their mistakes, a result of the fundamental insolubility of the problem posed to them by the international, above all the German, proletariat. To carry out the dictatorship of the proletariat and socialist revolution in a single country surrounded by rigid reactionary imperialist rule and ravaged by the bloodiest World War of human history—that is a squaring of the circle. *Any* socialist party would have to fail in this task and perish—whether it chooses the will to victory and belief in international socialism, or self-renunciation as the guiding star of its policies.

We would like to see those spineless jellyfish, the Axelrods, Dans, [A.] Grigorjanz,* and all the others, who are now foaming at the mouth over the Bolsheviks and lamenting their misery abroad—and, guess what? They have found a sympathetic ear with such heroes as [Heinrich] Ströbel, Bernstein, and Kautsky—we would like to see these Germans in the Bolsheviks' place! Their whole superior attitude, of course, would rapidly exhaust itself in an alliance with the Milyukovs in domestic policy, and with the Entente in foreign policy. Add to this a conscious renunciation of all socialist reforms, or even attempts in this direction—so much for their consciously insipid wisdom that says Russia is an agrarian country and Russian capitalism is just not adequately cooked yet!

Such is the false logic of the objective situation: *any* socialist party that came to power in Russia today *must* pursue the wrong tactics so long as it, as part of the international proletarian army, is left in the lurch by the majority of this army.

Blame for the failures of the Bolsheviks lies ultimately with the international proletariat, and above all with the unprecedented and persistent baseness of German Social Democracy. This party which in peacetime pretended to march at the head of the world proletariat, which presumed to instruct and guide the whole world, which in its own country counted at least 10 million supporters of both sexes—this is the party that has nailed socialism to the cross twenty-four hours a day for the past four years at the bidding of the ruling class like venal mercenaries of the Middle Ages.

The news arriving from Russia today about the situation of the Bolsheviks is a moving appeal to what vestiges of honor remain in the masses of German workers and soldiers. In cold blood they have left the Russian Revolution to be torn to pieces, encircled, and starved out. May they, even in the eleventh hour, save the revolution from the most terrible fate: from moral suicide, from an alliance with German imperialism.

There is only one solution to the tragedy entangling Russia: an uprising at the rear of German imperialism, the German mass rising as a signal for the international revolutionary end of the mass slaughter. Saving the honor of the Russian Revolution at this fateful hour is identical with vindicating that of the German proletariat and of international socialism.

---

* After the Bolshevik Revolution, Mensheviks such as Axelrod, F. I. Gurwitsch (pseudonym: Dan) and Grigorjanz were expelled or emigrated from Russia.

The Little Lafayettes*

The old familiar game of history duly repeats itself in Germany. Just when the foundations of the old class rule start to shake and tremble, a "reform ministry" appears on the scene at the eleventh hour. In 1789, when the thunderous rumble of the great revolution in France could be heard, Louis XVI decided with a heavy heart for the Necker Ministry. On the eve of the July Revolution in 1830, the Bourbon restoration tried out a momentary allegiance with the Martignac Ministry, which was to make concessions to the opposition. And in 1848, when the first barricades of the February Revolution were already built by the Parisians, the one-day ministry of Thiers and Odilon Barrot appeared on the scene.†

The historical purpose of such "reform ministries," formed at the last hour with a full storm approaching, is always the same: the "renewal" of the old class state "by peaceful means." That is, changes of formalities and trifles in order to preserve the essence and core of the old class rule and thus prevent the genuine radical renewal of society through the mass uprising.

The historical fate of these eleventh-hour ministries is always the same —they are burdened with the curse of powerlessness due to their inner contradictions and half-heartedness. The people instinctively perceive them as an attempt by the old powers to remain at the helm. The old powers mistrust them as unreliable servants of their interests. The driving forces of history, which have led to the reform ministry in the first place, will soon sweep past it. It does not save or prevent anything, but only unleashes and accelerates the revolution it was supposed to prevent.

That is also the purpose and will be the fate of the Prince Max–[Adolph] Gröber–Scheidemann–[Friedrich von] Payer reform ministry.‡

The novelty of this historic game, however, is this: Up to now, only the most lame and wishy-washy of liberals—a Necker, a Martignac, an Odilon Barrot—have offered themselves up to playing such a lightning rod role in the last hour. No resolute radical, no leader of the bourgeois opposition, no republican has yet adopted such a miserable role. Now, for the first time in history, a party that

---

* This article first appeared in *Spartacus*, No. 12, October 1918. It is not signed, but in *Illustrierte Geschichte der Deutschen Revolution* (Illustrated History of the German Revolution) (Berlin: Internationaler Arbeiter-Verlag, 1929), pp. 172–3, Luxemburg is named as the author. The article is translated by Manuela Kölke from Luxemburg's *Gesammelte Werke*, Vol. 4, pp. 393–6.

† Adolphe Thiers and Camille Odilon Barrot are being referred to here.

‡ On October 1, 1918, Prince Max of Baden was appointed Chancellor of the Reich. He formed a so-called parliamentary government that was supposed to stop the revolutionary movement in Germany, save imperialist class rule and negotiate with the Entente. This government included the leader of the Center Party group of the Reichstag, Adolf Gröber, as representative of the Progressive People's Party, Friedrich von Payer, and Philipp Scheidemann and Gustav Bauer as representatives of Social Democracy.

calls itself Social Democratic is offering itself up to play the savior in distress as the catastrophe of existing class rule visibly approaches, to take the wind out of the sails of the approaching storm of the people with pseudo-reforms and pseudo-renewal, to keep the masses in check.

And already *Vorwärts*, that political prostitute, is shouting out to the German workers:

> The goal of a German democracy will soon be achieved by peaceful revolution. Then the enormous question of a new world economic order will approach us, and socialism will make its advance. What matters now is that nothing of what remains is gratuitously ruined and unnecessarily destroyed. We must not be guided by emotions, but only by a clear understanding of what is needed by our severely tested people—*they need to avoid anything that brings new misfortune to old misfortune.*

So the matter is clear. Democracy has been achieved "by peaceful means." For an heir to the throne of Baden becomes chancellor of the Reich, and Scheidemann and Bauer take ministerial chairs—this is "democracy." And then "socialism" begins. Gröber on the right, Payer on the left, Scheidemann in the middle, a national liberal in the back and Prince Max at the head—this is how "socialism will make its advance." In the *Communist Manifesto*, Marx and Engels said, in their naivety, that the liberation of the working class must be the act of the working class. Those fools! In Germany, the liberation of the working class will be the act of the national liberals, the centrists, the liberals [*Freisinnige*] and their government socialist servants!

And the purpose of this political dissipation? "Order! Silence!" Above all, no attacks against private property and the rule of capital! You working masses who hunger and freeze, you who resent and rebel, do not move, do not "ruin" anything, do not "destroy" anything, do not add "new misfortune" to "old misfortune." The collapse of the Hindenburg dictatorship and German imperialism—that is "old misfortune"—and proletarian revolution in Germany—that is "new misfortune." No wonder the Mosse-paper* says of this call by *Vorwärts*: "These prudent guidelines will find decisive approval in the broadest circles of the liberal bourgeoisie." They sure as hell will!

At this moment, the program of government socialism is thus clearly expressed with all the cynicism of those who have been tried and tested in political prostitution.

And that is the core difference between today's German ministerial socialism† and its French and Belgian versions. When [Jules] Guesde and [Marcel]

---

* The liberal newspaper *Berliner Tageblatt*.

† In what became known as the "Millerand Crisis" in the Second International, the French Socialist, Alexandre Millerand entered the bourgeois government of Waldeck-Rousseau in 1899

Sembat and [Emile] Vandervelde entered the bourgeois ministry, it was not the proletarian revolution that was approaching in their countries, but the German invasion.* It was the first massive tidal wave of unleashed imperialism that swept them away from their class position and pushed them into collaboration with the bourgeoisie in the name of "national defense."

The German government socialists entered the ministry to cooperate with the bourgeoisie not at the beginning but at the end of the war, after the ministerialist experiment in France and Belgium had completely worn itself out, torn itself apart and corrupted itself; after the disillusionment of the proletarian masses, and their return to class struggle, had already begun; after the Russian Revolution had shaken the fabric of bourgeois society throughout the world; after imperialism had taken off militarily, politically and morally; after the existence of the class state in Austria had fallen into a hopeless crisis; after the dissolution of discipline and the revolutionization of the masses of soldiers was already in full swing in the German army; after the popular masses in Germany, in Austria, in Bulgaria were already in the most violent fermentation. In short, after the dialectic of the four-year war made the international revolution of the proletariat inevitable! Guesde and Vandervelde deserted their class position in the first moment of the war, before the advance of the German military battalions—Scheidemann and Bauer entered the government of the bourgeoisie at the end of the war, before the impending advance of the revolutionary battalions of the socialist proletariat. Guesde and Vandervelde served the puppet of "national defense"—Scheidemann and Bauer serve the bloody seriousness of "capitalist defense."

Therefore, it is all too visibly symbolic that they take their ministerial chairs next to a princely heir to the throne, that they inaugurate their "democracy" with a solemn demonstrative homage to the *monarchy*.

When the mass revolution broke out in Paris on 5 October 1789, and the Parisian women's procession with drumrolls and the cry for "Bread! Bread!" went to Versailles where the royal family with their courtiers sat, pale with fright and hidden in the castle—there, at that moment, Lafayette, the revolutionary Tomfool of Two Worlds,† performed his famous balcony scene in Versailles. He persuaded the shaking Marie Antoinette to step onto the balcony with him, and here, in front of the swaying crowd, he solemnly kissed the queen's hand. This touching monarchical homage confused the crowd for a

---

alongside the Marquis de Galliffet, who was responsible for the repression of the 1871 Paris Commune (the "Commune's executioner").

* At the outbreak of the First World War, Marcel Sembat and Jules Guesde, leaders of the French Socialist Party, and Emile Vandervelde, representative of the Belgian Workers' Party, entered the bourgeois governments of their respective countries.

† Lafayette had volunteered in the North American War of Independence and was promoted to general. During the French Revolution, after the republicans took power in 1792, he joined the camp of the counterrevolution.

moment, and even spurred them on to applause. But the farce did not prevent the drama from continuing: it did not prevent Marie Antoinette from following her husband to the guillotine, or Lafayette from escaping the rancor of the revolution by fleeing abroad. The Scheidemanns and Bauers, who begin by kissing the hand of the German monarchy, will end up using blue beans* against striking and demonstrating German workers. With its current entry into power, government socialism, ultimately playing the role of the savior of capitalism, stands in the way of the coming proletarian revolution. The proletarian revolution will walk over its corpse. Its first call, its first stage, must be the *German Republic.*

* *Blaue Bohnen* (blue beans) is an archaic German colloquialism for bullets.

The Beginning*

The revolution has begun. What is called for now is not glee over what has been achieved, not triumph over the defeated enemy, but the strictest self-criticism and iron preservation of energy to continue the work that has begun. For our accomplishments are small, and the enemy is *not* defeated.

What has been achieved? The monarchy has been swept away; the supreme governing power has been transferred into the hands of the workers' and soldiers' representatives. But the monarchy was never the real enemy: it was only a façade; it was the figurehead of imperialism. It was not the Hohenzollerns who unleashed the World War, set all corners of the globe on fire and brought Germany to the brink of the abyss. The monarchy, like every bourgeois government, was the executive of the ruling classes. The imperialist bourgeoisie, the capitalist class rule—that is the criminal that must be held accountable for the mass slaughter.

The abolition of the rule of capital, the realization of the social order of socialism—this and nothing less is the historical theme of the present revolution. This is a tremendous work that cannot be accomplished in the twinkling of an eye by a few decrees from above: it can only be borne by the conscious action of the mass of workers in cities and in the country, and brought safely across heavy seas by the highest intellectual maturity and unflagging idealism of the masses of people.

The path of the revolution follows clearly from its ends; its method follows from its task. *All power in the hands of the working masses, in the hands of the workers' and soldiers' councils, protection of the work of the revolution against its lurking enemies*—this is the guiding principle behind all measures to be taken by the revolutionary government.

Every step, every action of the government ought to point like a compass in this direction:

- Expansion and re-election of the local workers' and soldiers' councils so that the first chaotic and impulsive gesture of their formation will be replaced by a conscious process of coming to understand the aims, tasks, and methods of the revolution;
- regular meetings of these representatives of the masses and the transfer of real political power from the small committee of the Executive Council to the broader base of the workers' and soldiers' councils;

* This article first appeared in *Die Rote Fahne* (Berlin), No. 3, November 18, 1918. It is one of the first writings composed by Luxemburg upon her release from prison, where she had spent most of the war. It is translated by Manuela Kölke from Luxemburg's *Gesammelte Werke*, Vol. 4, pp. 397–400.

- immediate convocation of the National Council (*Reichsparlament*) of workers and soldiers as soon as possible to establish the proletariat of all of Germany as a class, as a compact political power, and to make them the bulwark and impetus of the revolution;
- the immediate organization not of the "*peasants*," but of the rural proletariat and smallholders who, as a class, so far have not engaged in the revolution;
- formation of a proletarian Red Guard for the permanent protection of the revolution and training of the workers' militia, to keep the entire proletariat on watch at all times;
- suppression of the organs of administration, justice, and the army that have been taken over from the absolutist military police state;
- immediate confiscation of dynastic property and possessions as well as large-scale land holdings as an initial temporary measure to secure the food supply of the people, since hunger is the most dangerous ally of the counterrevolution;
- the immediate convocation of the World Labor Congress in Germany in order to emphasize clearly and distinctly the socialist and international character of the revolution—for the future of the German revolution is anchored in the International, in the world revolution of the proletariat alone.

We have enumerated only the first necessary steps. What is the current revolutionary government doing?

- It leaves the state as an administrative organism from top to bottom calmly in the hands of yesterday's pillars of Hohenzollern absolutism and tomorrow's tools of counterrevolution;
- it convenes the constituent National Assembly, thereby creating a bourgeois counterweight to the workers' and soldiers' representatives, diverting the revolution onto the tracks of bourgeois revolution, and spinning the socialist goals of the revolution into oblivion;
- it does nothing to destroy the continued power of capitalist class rule;
- it does everything to placate the bourgeoisie, to proclaim the sacrosanctity of property, to safeguard the inviolability of capital relations;
- it allows the counterrevolution to continue at every turn, without appealing to the masses, without loudly warning the people.

Peace! Order! Peace! Order! So it echoes from all sides, in all proclamations of the government, and so rejoices the echo from all bourgeois camps. The clamor against the specter of "anarchy" and "putschism"—the well-known infernal music of the bourgeois concerned about its safety deposit boxes, its property, and its profits—is the loudest note of the day, and the revolutionary workers' and soldiers' government placidly tolerates this general march to mount an assault on socialism; indeed, it participates in word and deed.

This is the result of the first week of the revolution: in the Hohenzollern state basically nothing has changed; the workers' and soldiers' government acts as the deputy to the imperialist government that has gone bankrupt. All its actions are carried out through fear of the working masses. Even before the revolution gains momentum, its only vital force, namely its socialist and proletarian character, will have been spirited away.

Everything is in order. The reactionary state of the civilized world will not become a revolutionary people's state within twenty-four hours. Soldiers who yesterday, as gendarmes of reaction, murdered revolutionary proletarians in Finland, Russia, Ukraine, and the Baltic States, and workers who calmly allowed this to happen, have not in twenty-four hours become clear, goal-oriented supporters of socialism.

The picture of the German Revolution corresponds to the inner maturity of the German situation. The government of the German Revolution at its present stage is in the hands of Scheidemann and Ebert. And the independents who solemnly attest in *Die Freiheit* that one can form a "purely socialist government"* with them, thus qualify themselves as the appropriate partners in the firm at this initial provisional stage.

But revolutions do not stand still. Their vital law is to advance rapidly, to outgrow themselves. It is already being driven forward by its inner contradictions from this initial stage. The situation can be understood as a beginning, as a condition not sustainable in the long run. If the counterrevolution is not to gain the upper hand all along the line, the masses must be on their guard.

A beginning has been made. What happens next is not in the hands of the gnomes who want to stop the course of the revolution and put a spoke in the wheel of world history. It is the realization of the ultimate goal of socialism that is on the agenda of world history today. The German Revolution has now hit upon the path illuminated by this shining star. Step by step, through storm and stress, through battle and torment and misery and victory, it will reach its goal.

It must!

---

* See "An die Partei I" (To the Party I) in *Die Freiheit* (Berlin), No. 1, November 15, 1918.

The Old Game*

Liebknecht murdered two hundred officers in Spandau.
Liebknecht was murdered in Spandau.
The Spartacus people have stormed the Royal Stables.
The Spartacus people wanted to invade the *Berliner Tageblatt* with machine guns.
Liebknecht is looting the shops.
Liebknecht distributes money among the soldiers, to incite them to counter-revolution.

The Spartacists advanced against the House of Representatives. In light of this news, panic arose at the Progressive People's Party's parliamentary group held there and the honorable assembly scattered, leaving behind hats, umbrellas and the like, precious and nowadays almost irreplaceable objects at the scene of the expected gruesome deeds.

For a week now, the wildest rumors about our direction have been buzzing around in Berlin. If a windowpane clinks somewhere in the street, or a tire bursts at the corner with a loud bang, the Philistine looks around with ruffled hair and goosebumps on his back: Aha, surely "the Spartacists are coming!"

Various people have turned to Liebknecht with a touching personal request to exempt their husbands, nephews, or aunts from the intended Massacre of the Holy Innocents planned by the Spartacists. This really and truly happened in the first year and month of the glorious German Revolution.

Who doesn't think of the delicious scene in *The Magic Flute*, where the little rascal Monostatos, frightened by Papageno's shadow, trembling with fear, sings:

I think it is the devil,
Yes, yes, it's the devil,
Oh, if I were a mouse,
How I would hide!
Oh, if I were a snail,
I would crawl into my house!†

Beneath all these buzzing rumors, ridiculous fantasies, unlikely robbery stories, and shameless lies, a very serious process is underfoot. It is systematic.

---

* This article first appeared in *Die Rote Fahne* (Berlin), No. 3, November 18, 1918. It is translated by Manuela Kölke from Luxemburg's *Gesammelte Werke*, Vol. 4, pp. 401–3.

† These lines are from two scenes in Act One of Mozart's *The Magic Flute*. The first lines are from the Trio when Monostatos and Papageno see each other and take fright: "Aah! That must be the devil!" The subsequent lines are from Papageno in the Finale: "Oh, if I were a mouse / How I would hide! / If I were as little as a snail, / I would crawl into my house!"

The agitation is moving according to plan. The rumors are purposefully fabricated and then launched into the public: it is a matter of using these phantasmagorias to put the Philistines in a panic-stricken mood, to confuse public opinion, to intimidate and mislead the workers and soldiers, to create a pogrom atmosphere and to politically assassinate the Spartacist tendency before it has the chance to bring its politics and goals to the broad masses.

This is an old game. Remember just four years ago, at the outbreak of war, when the great fairy tales of golden cars, French planes, poisoned wells, and gouged eyes were deliberately and purposefully put into circulation by the warmongers' agents to provoke blind military furor and use the workers as cannon fodder? So too, now, work is being done to mislead the masses and sow blind hatred among them, so that they may be used unconsciously and uncritically against the Spartacists.

We know the method, and we know the text and the authors as well.* The dependent Social Democrats,† Scheidemann, Ebert, Otto Braun, Bauer, Legien, and Baumeister—these are the circles who deliberately poison public opinion with shameless lies; they incite the people against us because they fear our criticism, and they have every reason to fear it.

These people, who one week before its outbreak denounced every thought of revolution in Germany as a crime, "putschism," adventurism, who declared that Germany had already achieved democracy because Prince Max was Chancellor of the Reich, and Scheidemann, together with Erzberger, was walking around in a minister's tailcoat. These people today want to persuade the nation that revolution is complete, that the main goals have already been achieved. *They want to halt further progress of the revolution; they want to salvage bourgeois property and capitalist exploitation!* That is the "peace" and "order" that are supposed to be protected from the revolution.

Therein lies the rub. And this is also the reason why the gentlemen cultivate such mortal fear and deadly hatred against us. They know perfectly well that we do not want to plunder shops, but we do want to abolish capitalist private property; that we do not want to storm the Royal Stables or the House of Representatives, but we do want to smash the class rule of the bourgeoisie; that we

---

* Adapted from Heinrich Heine, "Deutschland. Ein Wintermärchen" (Caput I): "Ich kenne die Weise, ich kenne den Text, / Ich kenn auch die Herren Verfasser / Ich weiß, sie tranken heimlich Wein/ Und predigten öffentlich Wasser." ("I know the tune, I know the words, / I also know every author ;/ I know they secretly drank wine, / While publicly preaching water." Translated by Joseph Massaad, heinrich-heine.net.

† By "dependent Social Democrats," Luxemburg means the members of the Majority Social Democratic Party of Germany (Mehrheitssozialdemokratische Partei Deutschlands, MSPD) which was the name officially used by the Social Democratic Party of Germany (SPD) during the period 1917–22. It is a play on the name of the more left-wing Independent Social Democratic Party of Germany (Unabhängige Sozialdemokratische Partei Deutschlands, or USPD), which split from the SPD in 1917.

do not want to murder anyone, but we do want to push the revolution forward relentlessly in the interests of the workers.

With full consciousness and clear intent, they distort our socialist goals into lumpenproletarian adventures in order to mislead the masses. People cry out against coups, murders, and similar nonsense, but they mean socialism. By trying to assassinate the Spartacist tendency, they want to strike at the heart of the proletarian revolution itself!

But the game won't work. We are not going to be silenced. Let them incite undecided classes of workers and soldiers against us. Let a momentary return of the counterrevolutionary force once more clap us up in the irons we have just escaped. The relentless course of the revolution cannot be stopped. We will raise our voices loudly; the masses will hear us, and then they will turn all the more vehemently against the agitators and manufacturers of the rumor of pogroms. The storm will not break over stables, bakeries, and fearful Philistines, but it will sweep you away, you reactionary bourgeois cronies of Prince Max and yesteryear, you guardian troops of capitalist exploitation, you lurking outposts of the counterrevolution, you wolves in sheep's clothing!

The National Assembly*

From the *Deutsche Tageszeitung, Die Vossische*† and *Vorwärts* to the independent *Freiheit*, from Reventlow, [Mattias] Erzberger, Scheidemann to Haase and Kautsky, comes a unanimous call for a National Assembly. At the same time, there is a unanimous cry of fear at the idea of power being in the hands of the working class.

All the "people," the whole "nation," are to be called upon to decide by majority resolution on the further fate of the revolution.

This slogan is taken for granted by the open and insidious agents of the ruling classes. We discuss neither *in* the national assembly nor *about* the national assembly with the warders of the capitalists' safes.

But even independent leaders are in line with the warders of capital on this crucial question.

In this way, as [Rudolph] Hilferding states in *Freiheit*,‡ they want to spare the revolution any recourse to violence, or civil war with all its horrors. Petty-bourgeois illusions! They imagine that the most powerful social revolution since the beginning of humankind will develop in such a form that various social classes will come together, engage in a pleasant, calm and "dignified" discussion with each other, and will afterwards hold a vote—perhaps even with the famous "division of the assembly."§ Subsequently, when the capitalist class sees that it is in the minority, it, as a well-disciplined parliamentary party, will declare with a sigh: "There's nothing we can do! We see that we are outvoted. Well, we shall submit and hand over all our lands, factories, mines, all our fireproof safes and nice profits to the workers."

Indeed, the houses of Lamartine, Garnier Pagès, Ledru-Rollin, the petty-bourgeois illusionists and chatterers of 1848, are not extinct; they have arisen again—without the luster and talent and allure of novelty—in the boring-pedantic scholarly German edition of Kautsky, Hilferding, and Haase.

These profound Marxists have forgotten the ABCs of socialism.

They have forgotten that the bourgeoisie is not a parliamentary party, but a ruling class in possession of all economic and social means of power.

---

* This article first appeared in *Die Rote Fahne* (Berlin), No. 5, November 20, 1918. It is translated by Manuela Kölke from Luxemburg's *Gesammelte Werke*, Vol. 4, pp. 407–10.

† The *Vossische Zeitung* was a well-known liberal newspaper published in Berlin from 1721. It was considered the national newspaper of record until it was shut down by the Nazi Party in 1934.

‡ See Hilderding's "Revolutionäres Vertrauen!" (Revolutionary Confidence) in *Die Freiheit* (Berlin), No. 6, November 18, 1918.

§ The so-called "*Hammelsprung*" (mutton jump or sheep run) was a voting procedure in Parliament in which voters had to leave the room and enter it again through three different doors—for yes, no and abstention, respectively—to be counted. This procedure is better known as *division of the assembly*.

These gentlemen Junkers and capitalists will remain quiet only so long as the revolutionary government is content to put little beauty patches on the capitalist wage relationship. They are good only so long as the revolution is good, that is, so long as the vital nerve, the artery of bourgeois class rule—capitalist private property, the wage relationship, profit—is left undisturbed.

As soon as profit is at stake, when private property is to be done away with, then the goodwill is over.

Today's idyll, in which wolves and sheep, tigers and lambs graze peacefully side by side, as in Noah's Ark, lasts just until the minute socialism begins to be put into practice.

As soon as the famous National Assembly really decides to fully realize socialism, to eradicate the rule of capitalism root and branch, then the struggle begins. Once the bourgeoisie is struck at the very heart—and its heart beats in a safe-deposit box—it will fight a life and death battle for its rule, amassing a thousand open and covert methods of resistance against the socialist measures.

All this is inevitable. All this must be fought through, warded off, beaten down—with or without the National Assembly. The "civil war," which some have anxiously tried to banish from the revolution, cannot be banished. For civil war is just another name for class struggle, and the idea of implementing socialism without a class struggle, by means of majority parliamentary decision, is a ridiculous petty-bourgeois illusion.

So, what is gained, then, with this cowardly detour called the National Assembly? The bourgeoisie's position is strengthened; the proletariat is weakened and confused by empty illusions; time and energy are dissipated and lost in "discussions" between the wolf and the lamb. In a word, one plays into the hands of all those elements whose purpose and intention are to defraud the proletarian revolution of its socialist goals and to reduce it to a bourgeois-democratic revolution.

But the question of the National Assembly is not a question of opportunity, not of greater "convenience." It is a question of principle, a question of the revolution's self-knowledge of its socialist character and its limitations.

The first decisive step in the Great French Revolution was taken in July 1789, when the three separate Estates combined in a joint National Assembly. This decision left its stamp upon the whole future course of events; it was the symbol of the victory of a new bourgeois social order over the medieval-feudal society of Estates.

Likewise, the symbol of the new socialist social order borne by the present proletarian revolution arises from the class character of its true task, and from the class character of the political organ that is to execute this task: the workers' council, representative of the urban and rural proletariat.

The National Assembly is an outmoded legacy of bourgeois revolutions, an empty shell, a stage-prop from the times of petty-bourgeois illusions of a "united people," of the "liberty, equality and fraternity" of the bourgeois state.

To resort to the National Assembly today is consciously or unconsciously to turn the revolution back to the historical stage of bourgeois revolutions; anyone advocating that is a secret agent of the bourgeoisie or unconscious spokesman of petty bourgeois ideology.

The struggle for the National Assembly is fought under the battle cry of "democracy or dictatorship." Even socialist leaders obediently adopt these slogans of counterrevolutionary demagogues without noticing that this alternative is a demagogic falsification.

Today it is not a question of democracy or dictatorship. The question that history has put on the agenda is: *Bourgeois* democracy or *socialist* democracy? The dictatorship of the proletariat is democracy in a socialist sense. This is not a question of bombs, coups, riots, "anarchy," as the agents of capitalist profit dishonestly claim, but rather, of the use of all means of political power for the realization of socialism, for the expropriation of the capitalist class—in the interests of and by the will of the revolutionary majority of the proletariat, that is, in the spirit of socialist democracy.

There can be no socialism without the conscious will and action of the majority of the proletariat! In order to intensify this consciousness, to steel this will, to organize this action, a class organ is necessary: a national council of the urban and rural proletarians.

The convocation of such a workers' representative body in place of the traditional National Assembly of the bourgeois revolutions is, in itself, an act of the class struggle, a break with the historical past of bourgeois society, a powerful means of arousing the proletarian masses, a first open and abrupt declaration of war against capitalism.

No evasions, no ambiguities—the die must be cast. Yesterday parliamentary cretinism was a weakness; today it is an ambiguity; tomorrow it will be a betrayal of socialism.

A Daring Game*

From the *Kreuz-Zeitung*† to *Vorwärts*, the German press echoes defamations against "terror," "putschism," "anarchy," "dictatorship."

Quis tulerit Gracchos de seditione querentes?‡ Who is not moved when the chief guardians of bourgeois anarchy, those who in four years have turned Europe into a heap of rubble, create an outcry about the "anarchy" of the proletarian dictatorship?

In order to protect the palladium of "order," private property, and class rule, the propertied classes—who in a thousand years of history, at the slightest hint of rebellion from their slaves, did not once shy away from any act of violence or infamy—are now crying out over the threat of violence and terror—from the slaves themselves. The Thiers and Cavaignacs, who murdered tens of thousands of Parisian proletarian men, women, and children in the June slaughter of 1848, also filled the world with howls about the alleged "atrocities" of the Paris Commune.

The Reventlows, Friedbergs, Erzbergers, who, without batting an eyelid, drove one and a half million German men and youth to the slaughterhouse—for Longwy and Briey,§ for the sake of new colonies; the Scheidemann-Eberts, who, for four years, made all means available to fund the greatest bloodletting humanity has experienced: they all now shout in a hoarse chorus about "terror," about the alleged "tyranny" threatened by the dictatorship of the proletariat!

The gentlemen may take a leaf from their own history books.

Terror and tyranny played a very specific role in the bourgeois revolutions. In both the Great French Revolution and the Great English Revolution, the execution of the king signified a world-historical break from feudalism, a necessary act of self-understanding [*Selbstverständigung*] for the aspiring bourgeois society, which only worked its way up to an abrasive opposition to the old regime spontaneously during the course of the revolution. Only when the executioner's axe flashed over Charles Stuart's head and the guillotine over the Bourbon's fat head, did bourgeois society itself, having entered into the revolution unknowingly, recognize its own irreconcilable opposition to the old feudal rule.

---

* This article first appeared in *Die Rote Fahne* (Berlin), No. 9, November 24, 1918. It is translated by Manuela Kölke from Luxemburg's *Gesammelte Werke*, Vol. 4, pp. 411–4.

† The *Kreuz-Zeitung* (official title *Neue Preussische Zeitung*, nicknamed for the Iron Cross on its masthead) was the paper of Prussian conservatives, founded during the 1848 revolution.

‡ The Latin phrase is from the satires of Juvenal and roughly translates as "Who would tolerate the Gracchis railing about sedition?"

§ Longwy and Briey are communes in northeastern France, where much of the fighting during World War I occurred.

The Jacobin reign of terror in France was nothing more than a desperate attempt by the radical petty bourgeoisie to take up and assert its permanent rule in France at a time when, historically, it was only the upper bourgeoisie that was called to rule throughout Europe. It was an attempt to nail the great revolution to its ideological phrasing—that is, to formal freedom, equality, and fraternity—against the real content of this phrasing, namely the takeover of industry and finance capital. It was an attempt by the masses of the petty bourgeoisie to cling to power, after their role as battering rams had long played out: to secure the necessary minimum gains of the bourgeois revolution, and to make a transitional phase of revolution their ultimate goal; to make their phrasing their content, and their means their purpose. Jacobin terror was thus also a means of self-understanding for the classes in bourgeois society, and of distinguishing one class from another.

In a word: in the bourgeois revolutions, terror and tyranny were the means to destroy historical illusions and defend hopeless interests against the course of history.

The socialist proletariat, thanks to the theory of scientific socialism, enters into its revolution without any illusions, with complete insight into the final consequences of its historical mission; it enters into irreconcilable opposition and mortal hostility toward bourgeois society as a whole. It enters the revolution not to chase utopian fantasies against the course of history, but to accomplish, supported by the iron engine of development, what is the historical imperative of the hour: to make socialism a reality. The socialist proletariat is to fulfil its historic mission as a mass, and as the vast majority of the working class.

It therefore does not need to start with destroying its own illusions through bloody acts of violence, with digging an abyss between itself and bourgeois society. What it needs is the entire political power of the state, the use of this power to ruthlessly abolish capitalist private property, wage slavery, bourgeois class rule, to build a new, socialist social order.

But there are others today who urgently need terror, tyranny, anarchy: the bourgeois gentlemen, all the parasites of the capitalist economy who fear for their possessions and privileges, their profits, and sovereign rights. They are the ones who blame the socialist proletariat for the fictitious anarchy, for false coups; and they do so in order to unleash real coups, to unleash real anarchy through their agents at the right moment to strangle the proletarian revolution, to let the socialist dictatorship drown in chaos, and to establish forever the class dictatorship of capital on the ruins of the revolution.

The heart and mind of today's agitation against the revolutionary vanguard of the proletariat is capital and its struggle for existence. Its hand, its tool, is with the dependent Social Democracy.* Their terms of service have outlived

* That is, the majority Social Democrats; see footnote † on page 262, above.

the revolution; the rulers, as well as the servants, have simply put red badges on their clothes.

The central organ of the dependent Social Democracy, *Vorwärts*, is now the central organ of the counterrevolutionary campaign against the Spartacists.

The military commander of Berlin* is arming the security guards with real bullets against fictitious "attacks" by the Spartacists. The sycophants of [Otto] Wels and comrades incite the most indecisive elements among the soldiers against Liebknecht and his friends. We repeatedly receive threatening letters and warnings.

We watch the spectacle from a historical perspective with a cold-blooded smile. We see through the play, the actors, the directors, and the roles.

But what, one might ask, would the masses of revolutionary proletarians do if the agitation achieved its purpose—if, for example, one hair were to be harmed on the head of the one whom they had carried from prison to their arms, and recognized as the appointed leader? Who would then have the power to preach cold-bloodedness to these masses?

You bourgeois gentlemen and servants of capital that has been condemned to extinction at *Vorwärts*, you speculate on the ignorance and the political inexperience of the masses like bankrupts speculating on the last card. You lurk in wait for your moment; you crave the laurels of Thiers, Cavaignac, Galliffet and Co.

It's a daring game. The day and hour belong to the dictatorship of the proletariat, to socialism. Whoever resists the assault vehicles [*Sturmwagen*] of the socialist revolution will be left on the ground with broken limbs.

* Otto Wels, a member of the majority SPD, had been appointed city commander of Berlin.

To the Proletarians of All Countries*

Proletarians! Working men and women! Comrades!

The revolution has found its way into Germany. The masses of soldiers who, for four years, were driven to the slaughterhouse for the sake of capitalist profits, the masses of workers who for four years were drained, squeezed dry and starved out—they have risen. The terrible tool of oppression, Prussian militarism, that scourge of humanity, lies broken on the ground. Its most visible representatives, and thus the most visible culprits of this war, the emperor and the crown prince, have fled the country. Workers' and soldiers' councils have been formed everywhere.

Proletarians of all countries, we are not saying that, in Germany, the working people now hold all power in their hands, that the full victory of the proletarian revolution has already been achieved. All those socialists who in August 1914 abandoned our most precious possession, the International, and who for four years betrayed both the German working class and the International, are still sitting in the government.

But, proletarians of all countries, the German proletariat now speaks to you. We believe we have the right to appear before your tribunal in its name. From the first day of this war, we have endeavored to fulfil our international duties by fighting that criminal government with all our might, and by branding it as the culprit truly responsible for the war.

Now, at this hour, we are vindicated before history, before the International and before the German proletariat. The masses enthusiastically agree with us; ever-broadening circles of the proletariat share the realization that the hour of reckoning with capitalist class rule has come.

But the German proletariat cannot accomplish this great work alone. It can only fight and win by calling on the solidarity of the proletariat of the whole world.

Comrades of the belligerent countries, we know your situation. We are well aware that your governments, having achieved victory, are now dazzling certain sections of the people with the outward splendor of victory. We know that, in this way, they manage to exploit their success in the slaughter to eliminate all memory of its causes and objectives.

But we also know something else. We know that in your countries, too, the proletariat has made the most terrible sacrifices of flesh and goods, that it is tired of the horrible bloodbath, that the proletariat now returns home and finds poverty and misery, while billions have been amassed in the hands of a

* This article, written as a call from the *Spartakusbund* (Spartacus League), first appeared in *Die Rote Fahne* (Berlin), No. 10, November 25, 1918, and was also distributed as a flyer. It is translated by Manuela Kölke from Luxemburg's *Gesammelte Werke*, Vol. 4, pp. 415–18.

few capitalists. They have recognized and will continue to recognize that your governments have also waged war for the sake of the great moneybags. And they will further recognize that your government, when it spoke of "law and order" and "the protection of the rights of small nations," actually meant [the protection of] capitalist profits, just as ours did when it spoke of the "defense of the homeland." And they will see that the "just" peace and the "League of Nations" amount to the same vile robbery as the Treaty of Brest-Litovsk. In both cases, we find the same shameless rapacity, the same will to oppress, the same resolution to exploit to the utmost the brutal superiority of their weapons of murder.

Imperialism of all countries knows no "negotiation." It knows only one right: capitalist profit; only one language: the sword; only one means: violence. And when it now speaks in all countries, in yours as well as ours, of the "League of Nations," "disarmament," the "rights of the small nations," the "self-determination of peoples," this is only the usual false jargon of the rulers deployed to put to sleep the vigilance of the proletariat.

Proletarians of all countries! This war must be the last! That is what we owe to the 12 million murdered victims, to our children, to humanity.

Europe is ruined by this heinous mass slaughter. Twelve million corpses litter the gruesome scenes of imperialist crime.

The flower of youth and the vigor of the people are mowed down. Immeasurable forces of production have been immeasurably depleted. Humanity is close to bleeding to death in this bloodletting, unprecedented in world history. Winners and losers alike stand on the edge of the abyss. Humanity is threatened by the most terrible famine, the stagnation of the entire processes of production, by epidemics and degeneration.

Those great criminals responsible for this terrible anarchy, this unleashed chaos, namely the ruling classes, are incapable of controlling their own creations. The beast of capital that conjured up the hell of World War is unable to banish it, to restore real order, to secure bread and work, peace and culture, justice and freedom for a tortured humanity.

What is being prepared by the ruling classes in the name of peace and justice is only a new work of brutal violence, from which the hydra of oppression, hatred, and new bloody wars raises its thousand heads.

Socialism alone is capable of accomplishing the great work of lasting peace; of healing the thousand bleeding wounds of humanity; of transforming the fields of Europe, which have been stamped down by the apocalyptic horsemen of war, transforming them into flourishing gardens; of conjuring up tenfold new productive forces in place of those that have been destroyed; of awakening all physical and moral energies of mankind; of replacing hatred and discord with fraternal solidarity, harmony and respect for all who wear a human face.

If representatives of the proletarians of all countries join hands under the banner of socialism to make peace, that peace would be secured in a matter of a few hours. Then there would be no disputes over the left bank of the Rhine, Mesopotamia, Egypt, or the colonies. Then there would be one people only—the working people of all races and tongues. Then there would be only one right—the equality of all people. Then there would be only one goal—welfare and progress for all.

Humanity faces this alternative: dissolution and destruction into capitalist anarchy, or rebirth through social revolution. The moment of decision has come. If you believe in socialism, now is the time to show it through your deeds. If you are socialists, now is the time to act.

Proletarians of all countries, if we now call upon you to fight together, it is not for the sake of the German capitalists who, in the name of the "German Nation" seek to escape the consequences of their own crimes; it is for our own sake as well as yours. Remember that your victorious capitalists stand ready to bloodily suppress our revolution, which they fear as though it were in their own country. You yourselves have not become more "free" because of "victory," but only more enslaved. If your ruling classes succeed in stalling the proletarian revolution in Germany and in Russia, next they will turn against you with twice as much force. Your capitalists hope that victory over us and over revolutionary Russia will give them the power to chastise you with scorpions and to build a thousand-year reign of exploitation upon the grave of international socialism.

That is why the German proletariat looks to you at this hour. Germany is pregnant with the social revolution, but only the world proletariat can realize socialism.

And that's why we call out to you: Rise to the struggle! Rise to the deed! The time of empty manifestos, platonic resolutions, and resounding words is over. The hour of action has come for the International. We call on you: Elect everywhere workers' and soldiers' councils that will seize political power and work with us to establish peace.

Not Lloyd George and Poincaré, not Sonnino, Wilson and Erzberger or Scheidemann shall make peace. Peace is to be made under the flying banner of the world socialist revolution.

Proletarians of all countries! We call upon you to accomplish the work of socialist liberation, to restore human dignity to the disgraced world and to make true the pledge with which in the old days we often welcomed each other and with which we bid farewell to each other:

The International will be all humanity!
Long live the world revolution of the proletariat!
Proletarians of all countries, unite!

In the name of the Spartacus League
Karl Liebknecht, Rosa Luxemburg, Franz Mehring, Clara Zetkin

The Acheron in Motion*

The nice little plan for a well-behaved, peaceable, "constitutional" German Revolution, which preserves "peace and order," and which regards the protection of capitalist private property as its primary and most urgent task—these little plans are going to hell: *Acheron has been set in motion!*† While up there in government circles an amicable arrangement with the bourgeoisie is being maintained by all means, the mass of the proletariat down below is rising and shaking a threatening fist: *The strikes have begun!* There are strikes in Upper Silesia, at the Daimler Works, etc., but this is only a beginning. The movement will naturally surge forward with ever-increasing power and intensity.

How could it be otherwise? A revolution has taken place. Workers, proletarians—in uniform or in overalls—made it. Socialists, representatives of the workers, are sitting in the government.

And what has changed in the wages and living conditions for the mass of workers? Nothing at all or virtually nothing at all! Scarcely had a few miserable concessions been made here and there when the bosses attempted to spirit away even that little scrap from the proletariat.

The masses are consoled with the prospect of the future golden fruits that are supposed to fall into their laps from the National Assembly. By means of long debates, talk, and resolutions of parliamentary majorities, we are supposed to slide softly and "calmly" into the promised land of socialism.

The healthy class instinct of the proletariat rebels against the schema of parliamentary cretinism. "The liberation of the working class must be the work of the working class itself," says the *Communist Manifesto*. And the "working class" is neither the few hundred elected representatives who control the destiny of society through speeches and arguments, nor the two or three dozen leaders who occupy government offices. The working class—that is the broadest mass itself. Only its active participation in overthrowing the capital relation can prepare for the socialization of the economy.

Instead of waiting for the government's exhilarating decrees or the resolutions of the "great" National Assembly, the mass instinctively resorts to the only real path leading to socialism: *the struggle against capital*. The government has so far gone to great lengths to reduce the revolution to a political one and,

---

* This article first appeared in *Die Rote Fahne* (Berlin), No. 12, November 27, 1918. It was not signed, but in *Um Rosa Luxemburgs Stellung zur russischen Revolution* (On Rosa Luxemburg's Position on the Russian Revolution) (Hamburg: Press of the Communist International, 1922), Clara Zetkin names Luxemburg as the author. It is translated by Manuela Kölke from Luxemburg's *Gesammelte Werke*, Vol. 4, pp. 419–22.

† In Greek mythology, Acheron is the river of pain and woe that forms the border with Hades, the underworld.

crying out against any threat to "peace and order," to establish harmony among the classes.

The mass of the proletariat is calmly toppling the house of cards that is revolutionary class harmony and waving the feared banner of class struggle.

The incipient strike movement is proof that the political revolution has burst into the social foundation of society. The revolution is recalling its own original purpose; it casts aside the stage props of personnel changes and decrees which that not changed the social relation between capital and labor in the least and is itself entering on to the stage of events.

The bourgeoisie may well feel that this has touched its Achilles heel, that here the joke of the government's harmlessness has gone too far, and the terrible face-to-face confrontation of two deadly enemies is beginning in terrifying earnest. Hence the bourgeoisie's pallid fear of and hoarse rage at the strikes. Hence the feverish efforts by their lackeys among the trade union leaders to catch the approaching hurricane in the nets of their old bureaucratic-official methods and thereby to paralyze and enchain the masses.

Futile efforts! The petty fetters of trade union diplomacy in the service of capitalist rule proved their worth admirably in the period of political stagnation that preceded the World War. In the period of revolution, they will fail miserably. Every bourgeois revolution of modern times has been accompanied by a turbulent strike movement—in France at the end of the eighteenth century and in the July and February Revolutions, and also in Germany, Austria-Hungary, and Italy. Every great social upheaval naturally produces fierce class struggles in a society founded upon exploitation and oppression. So long as bourgeois class society persists in the equilibrium of its everyday parliamentary routine, the proletariat also patiently continues to walk the treadmill of the wage system, and its strikes will have only the character of weak correctives to a system of wage slavery that is generally considered to be unshakable.

As soon as a revolutionary storm dislocates the equilibrium of the classes, the strikes change suddenly from a gently lapping surf into tidal waves; the very depths begin to move; the slave does not merely protest against the pressure of the chain that is too painful, but rebels against the chain itself.

So it has been in all previous *bourgeois* revolutions. As these revolutions, which always led to the entrenchment of bourgeois class society, subsided, the proletarian slave rebellion usually collapsed, and the worker returned, head bowed, to his treadmill.

In the present revolution, the strikes that have just broken out are not a "trade-union" dispute about trifles, about the trimmings of the wage system. They are the natural response of the masses to the tremendous convulsion that capitalism underwent upon the collapse of German imperialism and in the brief political revolution of the workers and soldiers. They are the beginning of a general confrontation between capital and labor in Germany; they herald the onset of the mighty class struggle, the outcome of which can be nothing less than the elimination of the capitalist wage system and the creation of the socialist economy. They are releasing the living social force of the present revolution: the revolutionary class energy of the proletarian masses. They are inaugurating the period of direct activity of the broadest masses, an activity for which the socialization decrees of, and measures taken by, any representative body or the government can provide only an accompaniment.

This incipient strike movement involves at the same time the masses' most succinct criticism of the chimera of their so-called "leaders" concerning the "National Assembly." They already *have* the "majority," the striking proletarians in the factories and mines! The dolts! Why don't they invite their bosses to a small "debate" so that they can outvote them with an "overwhelming majority" and realize all their demands smoothly and "according to order"? For the time being it is, after all, formally a question of genuine trifles, of purely superficial features of the wage system!

Let Mr. Ebert or Haase try to approach the striking coal miners of Upper Silesia with this ridiculous plan—they are sure to receive a striking answer. But what bursts like soap bubbles when it comes to trifles is supposed to hold fast when the entire social edifice is overthrown!

By its mere appearance on the scene of the social class struggle, the proletarian mass has passed over all the previous shortcomings, half measures and cowardice of the revolution and gone to the matters at hand. The Acheron is in motion, and the toddlers who carry on their little game at the head of the revolution will either tumble head over heels or finally learn to understand the colossal importance of the world historical drama in which they are cast.

Party Congress of the Independent Socialist Party*

The flow of the revolutionary period draws people, things, and circumstances into its critical vortex, sifting through them, reshaping them, and forcing them to make decisions. Names, programs, and parties must prove themselves with the touchstone of deeds. Nothing half done and ambiguous will last. Whoever is not with me is against me, that is the principle of revolution.

Independent Social Democracy is inherently a child of weakness, and compromise is the essence of its existence. Its thread of life began with the compromise of Haase, who—while an opponent of war credits—read the memorable declaration of the Socialist Group on August 4, 1914, and tied his name to the world-historical collapse of German socialism and the International.

Its further history includes granting war credits three times for two years—thus supporting Scheidemann and comrades in their betrayal of the working class by word and deed—contrary to their own verbal criticism of the politics of the majority.

Its official birth as an independent party was not an act of decisive resolution, not a clear decision on its own initiative, not an historical act, but the forced result of expulsion by Scheidemann and Co. in an episode of pathetic bickering over "party discipline" with the desecrators of the socialist banner.

The party's life story corresponds with its origin. It always trotted behind events and developments; it never took the lead. It never managed to draw a fundamental line between itself and the majority Social Democrats. All forms of bedazzling ambiguity that led to confusion among the masses—negotiated peace, the League of Nations, disarmament, the Wilson cult, all the phrases of bourgeois demagogy that spread veils of darkness over the naked, rugged facts of the revolutionary alternative during the war—all these things found keen support. The whole attitude of the party oscillated helplessly around the cardinal contradiction of, on the one hand, seeking to continue to retain the bourgeois governments as the appointed powers most likely to conclusively achieve peace, while on the other hand speaking out for the mass action of the proletariat.

A faithful mirror of this contradictory practice is eclectic theory—the hodgepodge of radical formulas that leads to the irretrievable abandonment

* This article first appeared in *Die Rote Fahne* (Berlin), No. 14, November 29,1918. It was not signed, but in *Um Rosa Luxemburgs Stellung zur russischen Revolution* (On Rosa Luxemburg's Position on the Russian Revolution) (Hamburg: Press of the Communist International, 1922), Clara Zetkin names Luxemburg as the author. It is translated by Manuela Kölke from Luxemburg's *Gesammelte Werke*, Vol. 4, pp. 423–6.

of the socialist spirit. The slogan of national defense in the purely bourgeois sense, paired with the discovery by the theoretical leader of the party* that the International would only be an instrument of peace, and not a weapon against war, amounted to an empty justification of the politics of Scheidemann and Co.

Until the outbreak of the revolution, it was an ad hoc policy, lacking a unifying worldview that could illuminate the past and the future of German Social Democracy from a point of view that could shed some light on its broad lines of development.

Such a party, suddenly confronted with the historical decisions of the revolution, was destined to fail miserably. A granite foundation that withstands storms just as steadfastly as periods of tepid calm, the steel of decision that in great moments generates the spark of action—such things did not exist. A drifting sand dune—that is all the Independent Social Democrats [the USPD] had to offer in the onslaught of events.

And their policies, tactics, and principles scattered like wind-borne sand. After sitting out four years of war and benefitting from the branding of Scheidemann-Ebert as traitors of socialism and the International—to the disgrace and corruption of the workers' movement—their first act after the outbreak of the revolution was to join forces with Scheidemann-Ebert to form a common government and proclaim this prostitution of its own principles as "purely socialist" policy.† In that hour when the ultimate socialist goals were finally the practical task of the day, when the supreme duty was to enact the sharpest, most relentless divorce between the camp of the revolutionary proletariat and the enemies—open as well as covert—of revolution and socialism: in that hour, the Independent Party instead hastened to enter into a political partnership with the most dangerous bases of counterrevolution, to confuse the masses and to facilitate treachery.

Its real mission as a partner in the Scheidemann-Ebert company is to mystify, through a system of ambiguities and cowardice, its clear and unambiguous character as a protective force of bourgeois class rule.

The most classic expression of this role of Haase and comrades is their attitude to the most important slogan of the day, the *National Assembly*.

Two positions alone are possible on this issue, as on all others. Either one wants the National Assembly as a means to stunt the proletariat in its power, to paralyze its class energy, to dissolve its ultimate socialist goals into a cloud of smoke—or one wants to put all power into the hands of the proletariat, to allow the revolution already begun to unfold into a tremendous class struggle for the new socialist order, and for this purpose, to establish the political rule

* A reference to Karl Kautsky.

† On November 10, 1918, the Council of People's Representatives, which Friedrich Ebert, Otto Landsberg and Philipp Scheidemann of the SPD, and Emil Barth, Wilhelm Dittmann and Hugo Haase of the USPD had joined, was confirmed as a provisional government by the General Assembly of the Berlin Workers' and Soldiers' Councils.

of the great mass of the workers—the dictatorship of the workers' and soldiers' councils. For or against socialism, for or against the National Assembly, there is no third way.

Here too, the Independent [Social Democratic] Party is making a desperate effort to unite hill and valley, fire and water, in the name of "unity." It wants the National Assembly to be the highest adjudicative and decisive authority, but it also wants to postpone this National Assembly as long as possible and to realize the main features of socialization *beforehand* through the dictatorial measures of the present government.

The tortuous middle position, as always, amounts to ambiguity, indeed to political dishonesty. Either one is serious about the National Assembly as the appointed and decisive representative of the people, in which case one would not tolerate putting this supreme authority before finished facts, and thus, *behind* the cart of the most important social upheavals. Or one is serious about the socialist dictatorship of the proletariat, in which case, one would not treat it as a fleeting, provisional erasure of revolutionary history and hand over its barely started work to the final judgment of a bourgeois-democratic assembly.

A party that, in the hour that needs great, clear, bold decisions of world-historical significance, only reveals ambiguities, fluctuations and half measures, that wants to make foreign policy with the imperialist, annexationist David, culture and elementary education with the German-national chauvinist Haenisch, socialism with the executioner of the revolution, Ebert; a party that, following Barth, admonishes the striking masses to passivity and supine obedience under the bosses' whip—such a party is judged and sentenced by its every word and every deed. This party was a product of decades of mire in the German workers' movement. Today, the German proletariat needs a socialist party at its head that is up to the task. There is no place in the revolution for a party of half measure and ambiguity.

The party's ambivalent politics corresponds to ambivalence in its ranks. Growing numbers of the party's supporters stand in sharp opposition to the backward elements of Hasse-Kautsky's leading group who make up the dead weight of the Independent [Social Democratic] Party. The current state of the party has become untenable. It must be held to account.

The most expeditious convening of the Party Congress, which will bring clarification and decision, has become an undeniable demand! The revolution needs sharpened weapons. The vast majority of the Independent [Social Democratic] Party will have to answer whether it is itself a Damascus blade or a "sword of cardboard."

"And what she is, that should she dare to appear."*

---

* "Und was sie *ist*, *das* wage sie zu scheinen!" A quotation from Friedrich Schiller, *Maria Stuart*, Act I, Scene 7.

The "Immature" Mass*

Last Thursday† a meeting of the soldiers' councils took place in the Reichstag building in Berlin. The atmosphere was stormy. A counterrevolutionary clique gathering around Lieutenant Waltz had been established only the day before—Lieutenant Waltz himself confessed that he had participated in the preparations of the revolution in order to be able to inform the general command—and acted in unison with a single purpose, seeking to kill the revolution with a loud voice. They did not succeed. After long, noisy scenes, the assembly dissolved with an almost unanimous motion for compromise—perhaps the only disgrace in the entire meeting.

For there is nothing more natural than the fact that, in times of revolution, political excitement and emotion express themselves in vociferous forms. Hotheads may not be the highest product of the political education of the people, but they are a higher product than the "old and deserving party comrade" who slumbers blissfully with half-closed eyelids over the annual report of the superior party secretary on dues nights [*Zahlabend*].

We, therefore, said nothing against the excitement and the wild emotions of the masses, not even when, in that first plenary meeting of the workers' and soldiers' councils in the Circus Busch, all the excitement turned against us and the soldiers turned their guns on Comrade Liebknecht. We fought those whose shabby demagogy misdirected the zealous will of the masses along the wrong tracks; we have tried and still try to give the masses a clear understanding of their situation and their goals, while retaining their enthusiasm and stormy passion for the enormous tasks they are to complete. We hold that great things can only be accomplished with enthusiasm.

Vorwärts sees it differently. An editor is sitting somewhere in a writing chair of the *Vorwärts* editorial office asking in the tone of the petty bourgeois [*Biedermann*], which is peculiar to all con men: "Hand on your heart! Do you believe that an assembly like yesterday's has call to—and is capable of—making decisions about the fate of our people?"‡

After its verdict on the assembly has been passed by this rhetorical question, *Vorwärts* does not forget to remind us of its old midwifery remedies. First, there is law and order. And after all the gifts of this blessed Daughter of

* This article first appeared in *Die Rote Fahne* (Berlin), No. 18, December 3, 1918. It was not signed, but in *Um Rosa Luxemburgs Stellung zur russischen Revolution* (On Rosa Luxemburg's Position on the Russian Revolution) (Hamburg: Press of the Communist International, 1922), Clara Zetkin names Luxemburg as the author. It is translated by Manuela Kölke from Luxemburg's *Gesammelte Werke*, Vol. 4, pp. 427–30.

† November 28, 1918.

‡ See "Nur die Demokratie kann uns retten!" (Only Democracy Can Save Us!) in *Abend-Vorwärts* (Berlin), No. 328a, November 29, 1918.

Heaven have been duly praised, the second recipe is delivered: political and parliamentary training.

Too often have we represented the fruits of political and parliamentary training as a virtue for the working class. Today we don't want to depict them that way again. Just look at the "revolutionary" achievements of this socialist government after three weeks of revolution; look at the deeds accomplished by the "politically and parliamentary trained" Mr. Ebert, in his dealings with Wilson.* We have had enough of such "political and parliamentary training."

But *Vorwärts* has not had enough. The meeting of the soldiers' councils in Berlin, which doesn't appeal to its "politically and parliamentary trained" taste, provides it with further reason to generalize, and to conclude that:

> Had one experienced yesterday's events, one would sincerely understand what a vile deception of the people the *Russian Soviet government*, praised by fools, is. Our workers and soldiers—and this can probably be said without a trace of nationalist superiority—are superior by far to the Russian in terms of general education and political training. If the system of the Council Constitution fails in our country, it is the best proof that even for the most educated and intelligent of people, this system is impracticable because it is an "*inner impossibility*."†

Thus "without nationalist superiority," two statements have been made: First, that the German workers and soldiers are far superior to the Russians in terms of general education and political training; second, that the whole system is not feasible—it suffers from an inner impossibility because even the most educated and intelligent of people do not have sufficient education and intelligence. And all this then leads to a third observation: "Only the Constituent National Assembly can save us from this hullabaloo."

There is one truth in all of this. On average, the German people attended school longer, learned to write better, and do mental arithmetic better than the Russian people. In addition—one of the bases for "political and parliamentary training"—they enjoyed education in religious and patriotic history for longer than the Russians, and then attended German Social Democracy's university of "political-parliamentary education." This teacher told us to consider the world's most shameless war of robbery as a defense against a "shameful raid," that the threatened safety deposit boxes of the capitalists were our "hearth and home," that the robbery of Belgium and northern France was "our just cause"; and that the murder of our proletarian brothers in Finland, Ukraine, Livonia, Estonia, in the Crimea, was a struggle for "law and order."

* Friedrich Ebert secured a promise from the U.S. government for American food supplies on the condition that the power of the workers' and soldiers' councils would be abolished, and the capitalist social order would remain secure.

† "Nur die Demokratie kann uns retten!" (Only Democracy Can Save Us!) in *Abend-Vorwärts*, No. 328a, November 29, 1918.

The whole purpose of this revolution is the fierce rebellion of the masses against the consequences of this "parliamentary and political education," against the school as well as the schoolmaster, but nonetheless, *Vorwärts* stands at the ready to take the masses back to school with the "Constituent National Assembly."

Certainly, they would all stand in line here, the "politically and parliamentary trained" gentlemen, the [Kuno von] Westarps and the Erzbergers, the Stresemanns and the Gröbers, the Payers and Haussmanns, all heirs to a bourgeois art acquired through centuries and designed to deceive the people. And with them would come the Scheidemanns and the Eberts, the Davids and Lensches, who have copied this art from those who clear their throat and spit. They would all come back together and continue their profession of popular deception, which they have practiced over four years of war with a horrible virtuosity, and which culminated in the bloody battlefields in France and the first mass action of German workers and soldiers.

With the prank that it has performed here, *Vorwärts* stands worthily side by side with its master Friedrich Ebert: If he, hand in hand with Mr. Wilson, has attempted to physically kill the revolution by hunger, then *Vorwärts* seeks to assassinate it spiritually by once more erecting before the masses that brazen tablet that the bourgeoisie and every ruling class have held up against the oppressed for millennia and on which is written: "You are not mature and you will never be—this is an 'inner impossibility.' You need leaders—we are the leaders."

This has now happily developed into the state philosophy of reactionaries of all epochs and countries. This spectacle does not become more pleasing because the same *Vorwärts*, just twelve hours after it declared in an editorial the spiritual backwardness of the masses to be "philosophically" an eternal phenomenon, then, in a spate of demagogic bickering against a member of the Executive Council, appealed to shame, honor and conscience because this member also spoke of "the masses not being ripe yet;"* and then *Vorwärts*, a day later, declared the maturity of the same soldiers' council, because it has taken a decision that suits the *Vorwärts*' books.† The *Vorwärts*' shamelessness is not improved by hypocrisy.

No proletariat in the world, not even the German one, can eradicate from one day to the next the traces of thousands of years of subjugation, the traces of the shackles laid on them by Scheidemann and his ilk. Neither the political

---

* See Friedrich Stampfer: "Die Wahlen zur Nationalversammlung" (Elections for the National Assembly), in *Abend-Vorwärts* (Evening Forward), No. 329a, November 30, 1918.

† See "Die Soldaten für die Nationalversammlung" (The Soldiers for the National Assembly) in *Vorwärts*, No. 330, December 1, 1918. On November 29, 1918, the meeting of Greater Berlin's Soldiers' Councils voted for the National Assembly and for its convening on February 16, 1919, by a two-vote majority.

constitution nor the intellectual constitution of the proletariat reaches its peak on the first day of the revolution. Only revolutionary struggle will raise the proletariat to full maturity in every sense.

The beginning of the revolution was the sign that this process of maturing will start. It will progress rapidly, and *Vorwärts* has a good yardstick with which it might measure the onset of full maturity. On the day when its editors are thrown from their seats, and along with our gentlemen Scheidemann, Ebert, David and the like, are sent to where the Hohenzollerns and Ludendorffs are—on that day full maturity has arrived.

The Socialization* of Society†

The proletarian revolution that has just begun can have no other goal and no other outcome than the realization of socialism. The working class must seek above all else to take the entirety of the state's political power into its own hands. But for us socialists, political power is only a tool. The goal for which we must use this power is the transformation of all economic conditions from the ground up.

Today, all the wealth belongs to a few Junkers and private capitalists: all the largest and the best estates as well as the mines, plants, and factories. For their hard work, the great mass of the workers receives only a meager living wage from the Junkers and capitalists. The purpose of today's economy is the enrichment of a small number of idlers.

This situation should be done away with. All social wealth, the ground and soil with all the treasures stored in its depths and on its surface, all the factories and plants must be taken out of the control of the exploiters as the common property of the people. The first duty of a real worker's government is to declare, through a series of decrees, the most important means of production to be national property and to put it under social control.

Only then, however, will the actual and most difficult task begin: the construction of the economy on an entirely new basis.

Today, production in every enterprise is run according to the initiative of the individual capitalist. The entrepreneur determines what is to be produced and how, or where, when and how the goods produced should be sold. The

* The German Revolution of 1918 gave rise to a series of intense debates concerning the socialization of society. For many, socialization meant the nationalization of heavy industry and agriculture by the state, while more radical currents argued that workers' and soldiers' councils should obtain direct co-management and control over enterprises and that their role be officially incorporated into any new constitutional arrangement. According to Julius Braunthal, *History of the International Volume II: 1914–1943* (London: Nelson and Sons, 1967), p. 214: "The government of People's Commissars issued a solemn proclamation on November 12, 1918, promising to carry through a Socialist program. This was what the people expected. No one now doubted that Socialism was going to be achieved in Germany in real earnest. No one dreamed of opposing it. The peasants would have been glad to see the big estates split up and distributed among them; they were in no way worried about the nationalization of heavy industry in the Ruhr, and indeed they had never opposed it. The Junkers and the big industrialists did fear the change, but it seemed inevitable to them, for they had lost their control over the armed forces. The workers were absolutely determined to obtain a new social order, and a new social order now seemed an inexorable necessity to all classes of the population." After the establishment of the National Assembly in January 1919, the SPD and its coalition partners dropped the promise of socialization, which, all along, had been for them merely a concession to derail the demands of revolutionary workers and peasants.

† This article first appeared as "Die Sozialisierung der Gesellschaft" in *The Young Guard* (Berlin), December 2 and 4, 1918. It is translated by Zachary King from Luxemburg's *Gesammelte Werke*, Vol. 4, pp. 431–4.

workers do not have anything to do with this, since, after all, they are merely living machines tasked with carrying out their work.

All this must be different in the socialist economy! The private entrepreneur will disappear. Production will no longer be aimed toward the enrichment of individuals, but toward providing the community with the means of satisfying its every need. Accordingly, the factories, works, and agricultural enterprises must be reorganized along completely new lines.

First, if production is to have the goal of ensuring a humane and dignified life for everyone, generously providing nourishment, clothing, and other cultural means of existence to all, then the productivity of labor will have to be much greater than it is today. The fields must produce a much bigger harvest, the most advanced technology must be used in the factories, only the richest coal and ore mines must be exploited, etc. It follows from this that socialization will spread above all in the large enterprises of industry and agriculture. We do not need and do not want to take that bit of property away from small-scale farmers and craftsmen who eke out a living by their own labor, on a small piece of land or in their workshop. In time, they will all come to us voluntarily and learn to recognize the advantages of socialism over private property.

Second, in order for everyone in society to be prosperous, everyone must work. Only those who perform useful labor for the community, be it manual or mental labor, may demand that society provide them with the means of satisfying their needs. A life of idleness, the kind usually led by the rich exploiters today, will end. *A general work requirement* for everyone able to work will be a matter of course in the socialist economy, with the exception, of course, of young children, the aged and the sick. The community must readily provide care for those unable to work—not, as is the case today, with miserable handouts, but with abundant food, education for children, comfortable accommodation for the elderly, public healthcare for the sick and so on.

Third, the means of production, like the workforce, must be used frugally and economically according to the same considerations—that is, for the sake of the general welfare. The waste we see at every turn today must stop. We must therefore abolish the *industry of war and armaments* entirely, because a socialist society does not need any murder weapons, and the precious materials and labor used in their production must be spent on useful production instead. The *luxury industries,* which produce all kinds of extravagances for wealthy do-nothings, will also need to come to an end, as will the keeping of personal servants. All the people employed in these industries will find a more useful and dignified occupation.

If we thus create a nation of workers, where everyone works for everyone, for the general welfare and benefit of all, then, fourthly, work itself must be organized in a completely different way. Work today, whether in industry or in agriculture or in an office, is usually an agony and a burden for the proletariat.

One goes to work only because one has to, as otherwise one will not obtain the means to live. When working in socialist society, where everyone will work for their own well-being, it will naturally be crucial to make the greatest allowance for *health* and the *desire to work*. We must introduce healthy working spaces, short working hours that do not exceed one's normal capacity, and all the means of recreation and variety at work that allow everyone to do his part with pleasure and love.

But there is a *corresponding human material* that is part of all these great reforms. Today, the capitalist stands behind the worker with his whip—be it the capitalist himself, or his foremen or supervisors. Hunger drives the proletarian into the factory, to work for the Junker or the industrial farmer, or into the office. The entrepreneur then makes sure that no one wastes time, or wastes the materials, and that good and competent work is done.

In the socialist economy, the entrepreneur and his whip will fall by the wayside. Here, workers are free and equal people who work for their own well-being and benefit. That means, simply, to work for oneself, to work diligently on one's own initiative, without wasting the wealth of society and while yielding realistic and punctual work. Every socialist enterprise will, of course, need its technical managers who understand the business with precision, who can arrange what is necessary for everything to run smoothly, in order to reach the most appropriate division of labor and the highest performance. That means following these directions willingly and completely, maintaining discipline and order without provoking conflict or confusion.

In a word: The worker in the socialist economy must prove that he can work in a diligent and orderly manner, maintain discipline and do his best without the lash of hunger, without the capitalist and his lackeys standing behind him. This calls for self-discipline, mental maturity, and moral seriousness. This requires a sense of dignity and responsibility, a whole new inner rebirth for the proletarian.

No socialism can be created with people who are lazy, careless, egoistic, ungrateful, and indifferent. A socialist society requires people who are all full of enthusiasm and fervor for the common good, full of compassion and a willingness to make sacrifices for fellow human beings, full of the courage and determination to dare to do the most difficult tasks.

But we do not need to wait centuries or decades for such a race of human beings to develop. Right at this very moment, in the struggle and in the revolution, the proletarian masses are absorbing the idealism they need and acquiring this mental maturity. And in order to lead the revolution on to victory, we also still need courage and endurance, inner clarity and a will to sacrifice. By recruiting capable fighters for today's revolution, we are creating the socialist workers of the future as they are needed for the foundation of a new order.

The working youth are called on especially for these great tasks. As the next generation, they will form the true foundation of the socialist economy. It is now up to them to show that they can rise to meet the great task as the bearers of the future of humanity. There still remains an entire old world to overturn and a completely new one to build. But we will do it, my young friends, won't we? We will do it! As the song goes:

> We lack for nothing, my wife, my child,
> as everything that through us thrives,
> in order to be free as birds:
> we just need time!

Fourteen Dead—One Woman Murdered*

Yesterday, December 6, Berlin became the scene of a bloody onslaught from the counterrevolution.† At five o'clock several troop detachments positioned themselves under the leadership of officers loyal to Scheidemann: the Franzers,‡ flamethrowers, sappers, radio operators marched in a demonstration through the streets and occupied the house of parliament where the Executive Council of the workers' and soldiers' councils was in session; a group of the soldiers with a noncommissioned officer at their head forced their way into the meeting and declared *the Executive Council was under arrest*, on the alleged *order of the Ebert-Haase government*. The leaders of the coup went on to declare that they had come *to eliminate the Executive Council and proclaim Ebert as the president of the German Republic*.§

Comrade *Hedrich*, who was present at the meeting as a representative of the *Bavarian* Workers' and Soldiers' Councils, managed to explain to the soldiers what an unheard-of assault they were committing on behalf of their commanding officers. The soldiers declared they had no idea against whom and for what purpose they had been mobilized. *They only knew they had been promised five marks per person!* After the infamy of the coup had been made clear to them, they agreed to arrest their commanders and withdrew.

---

* This article first appeared in *Die Rote Fahne* (Berlin), No. 22, December 7, 1918. It was unsigned, but Paul Levi, Luxemburg's close colleague and collaborator, confirmed her authorship. It is translated from the original by Zachary King and appears here for the first time in English.

† Paul Levi later reported, "On the morning after December 6, 1918, after the bloodbath on Chausseestraße, the arrest of the Executive Council, the proclamation of Ebert as president, the occupation of the *Rote Fahne* by mobs of soldiers, Rosa Luxemburg said outright to the Scheidemann-Ebert clique, in *Die Rote Fahne*, that this performance was a pre-arranged, planned Bonapartist *coup*." See Levi, "*Der Blutpakt*," in *Die Rote Fahne. Zentralorgan der Kommunistischen Partei Deutschlands* (*Spartakusbund*), Vol. 3, No. 82, May 20, 1920.

‡ "*Franzers*" refers to the air force.

§ Philipp Scheidemann, working cheek by jowl with Friedrich Ebert at the time, reported in his 1928 memoirs: "There was a great scare on the evening of December 6, 1918. A mob of armed workers and soldiers marched up to the Reichskanzlei, led by a man named Spiro and with the participation of some men from the Foreign Office—Barons von Stumm and Rochus von Rheinbaben, Count Matuschka and others—to call up Ebert to become president … Ebert refused pensively … In the circles of the men involved in this business, especially that of Baron Rochus von Rheinbaben, it is thought to this day that the operation was undertaken with Ebert's agreement. Ebert, supposedly, had gone back on his word in the decisive moment, to the surprised dismay of the plotters who had put their lives at stake. This was probably because he had received notice of the unrest in the north not long before the arrival of the crowd. Baron von Rheinbaben reported to me that it was originally not Spiro but a certain Marten who had called on Ebert to take up the presidency. And further: 'There were only soldiers on our side.' On the day before the operation, he—Baron von Rheinbaben—had been given 100,000 Marks by Erzberger, in Erzberger's own office. He then, according to the source, passed the sum on to a precise location." Phillipp Scheidemann, *Memoiren eines Sozialdemokraten*, Vol. 2. (Dresden: C. Reissner, 1928), pp. 332–4.

Simultaneously, *the offices* of *Rote Fahne* were occupied by another group of troops, specifically, the Kaiser Franz Guard-Grenadier regiment. They locked the editorial rooms, stairs, courtyard, and entrance, stopped the machines, broke cabinets, searched tables and drawers. They were looking for Liebknecht, and "the whole group of the Spartacists" were to be arrested. Here, too, the coup leaders referred to an order from the Ebert-Haase government.

Here, too, the Bavarian representative, Hederich, appeared and explained the lie to the soldiers, at which point they withdrew in dejection.

Blood has flowed in the streets of Berlin! Machine guns, which stood prepared well in advance, were fired on peaceful demonstrators, unarmed soldiers coming down Chausseestraße after a meeting in the Germania-Säle. The chief of police had been informed of their demonstration the day before. *Fourteen dead lay on the pavement*, including one woman! The number of wounded is still unknown.

Workers! Soldiers! Comrades! Now you see who is organizing coups, who is sowing anarchy, who wants to choke the revolution with blood! Now you see who is instigating fratricidal war, and who wants to establish a dictatorship—a saber dictatorship of the counterrevolution!

Now you see who wants to stifle freedom of public opinion in Germany!

The soldiers who let themselves be misused for this criminal assault on the Executive Council of workers' and soldiers' councils and the *Rote Fahne* are not the guilty ones. They are sad, pitiful victims of the slanderous campaign which used them as executioners against the revolution just as Hindenburg and the Hollenzollerns used them as cannon fodder for four years.

The true criminals are the instigators who stand behind them, who organized the assault in secret.

These criminals are Wels and comrades, the Scheidemann-Ebert clique and their fellow travelers, who have stirred the soldiers up for weeks, who have taken all the counterrevolutionary elements under their protection, who have led a systematic smear campaign against the Spartacus League, who have formed a white guard of noncommissioned officers, who have created a real atmosphere of pogroms in Berlin with the bogeyman of "Bolshevism."

Workers! Soldiers! Comrades! The revolution is in serious danger! Save, save, save your work of November 9! Save the revolution, freedom, socialism! Raise your thunderous voices and your millions of arms against the criminal gangs arranging coups, anarchy, and murder!

Workers! Soldiers! Comrades! Fourteen corpses lie on the pavement of Berlin! Defenseless, peaceful soldiers, laid low by cowardly, insidious murder! Bring in those guilty to answer for this bloody crime! Sweep the true criminals from the government, the disgraceful instigators, the tempters of the unenlightened masses of soldiers: Wels, Ebert and Scheidemann and their comrades!

Their names have now become the slaughter call of the counterrevolution, the field markers of anarchy and fratricide, the banner of high treason to the revolution!

Energy! Resolve! Determination! It is time to act! The bloody crime must be punished, the conspiracy of Wels, Ebert, Scheidemann must be put down with an iron fist, and the revolution must be saved.

Down with Wels, Ebert, Scheidemann and their comrades!
All power to the workers' and soldiers' councils!
To work! To the barricades! To the fight!
Down with the blood-covered, cowardly organizers of the coup!
On with the revolution!

On the Executive Council*

Amid the chaos of mutually colliding counterrevolutionary assaults, smear campaigns, and conspiracies, an event of utmost importance for the fate of the revolution is taking place: *the elimination of the Executive Council of the workers' and soldiers' councils and its consignment to complete powerlessness and insignificance.*

We remember well how things stood at the beginning of the revolution. The revolution of November 9 was brought about by workers and soldiers. The formation of the workers' and soldiers' councils was the first act of the revolution, its first lasting product, its first observable victory. The workers' and soldiers' councils embodied the fact that the dominance of the imperial bourgeoisie had been destroyed, and that a new political and social order could begin, defined by the great masses of the people and comprised of workers and soldiers.

The workers' and soldiers' councils were thus the organs of the revolution, the bearers of the newly created order, the executors of the will of the working masses, whether dressed in a worker's overalls or a soldier's uniform. A vast expanse of work opened up before the workers' and soldiers' councils. The task fell to them to set the will of the revolutionary masses to work and to build the whole social and political machinery of the state from scratch and in line with the social interests of the proletariat.

In order to tackle this work, the workers' and soldiers' councils, which are scattered all over the German Reich, need a central organ to express their will and their actions in a single voice, and the Executive Council of the workers' and soldiers' councils was elected to act as such an organ on November 10 at the Circus Busch in Berlin.

Of course, it was first put to a vote by the Berlin Workers' and Soldiers' Council. The Reich parliament of the workers' and soldiers' councils could not be convened immediately, and so the Executive Council had to be elected by the Berlin Workers' and Soldiers' Council to act *provisionally* as the central organ for German workers and soldiers.

Therefore, while awaiting the convention of the Central Council of the workers' and soldiers' councils, the Executive Council had to be the highest authority in the German Reich, the bearer of the sovereignty of all working people, the uppermost organ of power in the socialist republic.

---

* This article first appeared in *Die Rote Fahne* (Berlin), No. 26, December 11, 1918. It was not signed, but in *Um Rosa Luxemburgs Stellung zur russischen Revolution* (On Rosa Luxemburg's Position on the Russian Revolution) (Hamburg: Press of the Communist International, 1922), Clara Zetkin names Luxemburg as the author. It is translated by Zachary King from Luxemburg's *Gesammelte Werke* Vol. 4, pp. 435–9.

Thus reads the first declaration with which the Executive Council introduced itself on the day following its constitution on November 11:

> "To the Inhabitants and Soldiers of Greater Berlin!"
>
> The Executive Council of the workers' and soldiers' councils has been elected by the workers' and soldiers' councils of greater Berlin and has commenced operation.
>
> All communal, regional, state and military departments are to continue with their work. *All orders and actions of these departments shall be carried out under the authority of the Executive Council of the workers' and soldiers' council*." [emphasis R. L.]

Here the self-evident fact is stated in no uncertain terms, without the slightest dissension from any quarter, that the Executive Council represents the full array of political power in the republic, and that *all* organs and departments of the state are its subordinates, only vehicles for its will.

What has become of this sovereign position of power in the four short weeks that have passed since then?

From the beginning, a "Council of the People's Deputies" was simultaneously put in place alongside the Executive Council, which acted as the "political cabinet" of Ebert and Haase.

Arising initially out of a parity agreement between the Majority and the Independent Social Democrats, this Council of People's Deputies was notoriously *confirmed* in Circus Busch on November 10 by the same plenary meeting of the greater Berlin workers' and soldiers' councils that elected the Executive Council.

What was the relationship between these two organs supposed to be? As the workers' and soldiers' councils intended, and as the yet-unchallenged declaration of the Executive Committee on November 11 made clear, if the Executive Council was to be the *highest* authority of the republic, then it should also be apparent that the "Council of People's Deputies, i.e., Ebert, Haase and others, would be *subordinate* to the Executive Council, like all other organs and departments of the state. The Ebert-Haase cabinet could solely and exclusively be an organ for carrying out the will of the Executive Council.

This, and nothing else, was also the view *of all parties concerned* in the first moments after the formation of these two bodies.

That did not last long, however. On the very next day, Scheidemann's people began their undisguised efforts to turn Ebert's cabinet into an independent body, first *alongside* the Executive Council and then, step by step, *above* it. The old line from Lassalle* on the written constitution and actual relations of

* Ferdinand Lassalle's 1862 speech "On the Essence of Constitutions" exposes the illusory character of written constitutions and how they disguise the real class relations underlying them.

power was to prove true once again. The right of sovereignty was, according to the will of the workers' and soldiers' councils, on the side of the Executive Council, while Ebert and Co. knew how to bring *de facto* power to their own side.

They knew how to stall the Executive Council through endless commission meetings, consultations on proper authority, and delaying tactics, and, through this, to hold the question of their mutual relationship in abeyance. But while this was debated on the public stage, Ebert's people *handled it* behind the scenes. They mobilized the counterrevolutionary elements, leaned on the reactionary officer corps for support, created a base for themselves in the bourgeoisie and the military, and pushed the Executive Council l against the wall with ruthless cynicism.

The ripe fruit of this bustling activity, the operation they were to carry out, was the coup of December 6,* which, in order to proclaim the Ebert dictatorship, had to eliminate the Executive Council, and the completion of this operation was the entry of troops into Berlin.

To characterize the current state of the Executive Council it is enough simply to state that an act of such enormous significance transpired in the first place, not just the incursion of troops, but their non-disarmament *without the approval, indeed against the objections of the Executive Council.*

Crowning it all is the *oath* that the Guard Troops rendered to Ebert:

> We vow, in the name of the troops which we represent, to use all our power both for the sake of the united German Republic and its provisional government, the Council of the People's Commissars.

The Guard Troops were also urged to back only the Council of the People's Commissars in their oath. "The government" is only the Ebert cabinet; the Executive Council is not even mentioned, it *does not exist!* It is treated like air.

The whole operation of deploying troops, not disarming them, and the swearing of oaths is obviously done *without* the Executive Council and behind its back. We are steadfast in our conviction that the Executive Council first found out about the entire affair from the papers, like the rest of the public.

Yes, this operation, this oath, from which the Executive Council is completely excluded, even seems to be aimed directly *against* the Executive Council! Marching the troops in, arming them, having them swear an oath—this was

* Units led by reactionary officers undertook an attempt at a coup, organized by Otto Wels, the Berlin Social Democratic city commandant, the general command of the Guard Corps, the Ministry of War, and the Foreign Office. They arrested the Executive Council of the Berlin Workers' and Soldiers' Councils, occupied the offices of *Die Rote Fahne*, called for Friedrich Ebert to be made president, and opened fire on an unarmed demonstration on Chausseestraße, killing fourteen people and wounding thirty.

a demonstration by Ebert's cabinet, a show of power, a threat, and, above all, a provocation against the Executive Council of the workers' and soldiers' councils!

The Executive Council is a shadow, it is nothing—this is what Ebert's march should have said before the whole world as it welcomed the guards.

And this audacity, this self-confidence on the part of the counterrevolution, came four weeks after the revolution was made by workers and soldiers!

Clearly, the intention was for the workers' and soldiers' councils in the Executive Council to be affected, and, in the councils, the masses of the workers and soldiers themselves. *Their* organ, the organ of the proletarian revolution, has been condemned to total powerlessness; power has been wrenched from their hands and turned over to the counterrevolutionary bourgeoisie.

Of course, no political force allows power to slip out of its hands, unless it brings it on itself. Only the Executive Council's inability to act and its own indolence made it possible for Ebert and Scheidemann's people to play this game.

The victim, however, is the working class itself. At the upcoming meeting of the state parliament of the workers' and soldiers' councils, it will be the duty of the working class to create an Executive Council that will be capable of leading more than a shadow existence, capable of wresting this stolen power back from Ebert and Co. with a strong hand. If the workers' and soldiers' councils of all Germany do not ruthlessly crush Ebert and Scheidemann's gang, they will soon see themselves, just like today's Executive Council, immobilized and throttled by the victorious counterrevolution.

What Does the Spartacus League Want?*

I.

On November 9, workers and soldiers smashed the old German regime to pieces. The Prussian saber's bloody delusion of world domination has melted away on the battlefields of France. The criminal gang that sparked this worldwide conflagration and drove Germany into a sea of blood has finally reached its wits' end. Deceived for four years, the people who had forgotten their cultural duty, their sense of honor and their humanity in service to this Moloch, who let themselves be abused in the service of every abomination, awoke from four years of torpor to find themselves at the abyss.

On November 9, the German proletariat rose up to cast off their shameful yoke. The Hohenzollerns were driven away, and the workers' and soldiers' councils were elected.

But the Hohenzollerns had long ceased to be the representatives of the imperialist bourgeoisie and the Junkers. It is the class rule of the bourgeoisie that is truly to blame for the World War—in Germany as in France, in Russia as in England, in Europe as in America. It is the capitalists of the world who are the real instigators of this mass slaughter. International capital is the insatiable Baal whose bloody maw has swallowed millions upon millions of living human victims.

The World War has presented society with an alternative: either the continuation of capitalism, new wars and the quick descent into chaos and anarchy, or the abolition of capitalist exploitation.

With the end of the World War, bourgeois class rule has forfeited its right to exist. It is no longer capable of bringing society out of the terrible economic collapse left in the wake of the orgy of imperialism.

The means of production have been destroyed on a massive scale. Millions of workers, the best and the most skilled core of the working class, have been slaughtered. Those still alive will return home to the sneering misery of unemployment. Famine and disease threaten to destroy people's strength at its root. Due to the enormous burden of war debts, the financial bankruptcy of the state is inevitable.

There is no help for this, no way out of this bloody tangle and yawning abyss, no salvation other than through socialism. Only the world revolution of the proletariat can bring order to this chaos, only it can provide everyone with work and bread, only it can bring an end to the mutual human butchery

---

* This manifesto for the Spartacus League was written by Rosa Luxemburg and, with slight modifications, was chosen as the party manifesto on the day of the founding of the Communist Party of Germany. It was published in *Die Rote Fahne* (Berlin), No. 29, December 14, 1918. It is translated by Zachary King from Luxemburg's *Gesammelte Werke*, Vol. 4, pp. 440–9.

of the war, only it can bring peace, freedom, and true culture to an overworked humanity. Down with the wage system! This is the cry of the hour. We need cooperative labor instead of wage labor and class rule. Materials and the means of labor can no longer remain the monopoly of one class—they must become the common property of all. No more exploiters and exploited! Production must be organized and products must be distributed in the interests of the general public. We must abolish the current mode of production, exploitation, and robbery; that contemporary commerce that is only a fraud.

Instead of employers and wage slaves, free comrades in work! Work that is no one's anguish because it is everyone's duty! A humane, dignified existence for everyone who does his duty to society. Henceforth, hunger shall no longer be the curse of work, but the punishment of the idler!

Only in that society can hatred between peoples and servitude be uprooted. Only when that society is realized will the Earth no longer be defiled by the murder of human beings. Only then can we say:

This war was the last.

At this hour, socialism is the only lifeline for humanity. The words of the *Communist Manifesto* blaze like a fiery omen over the crumbling walls of capitalist society:

*Socialism or descent into barbarism!**

II.

The realization of the socialist organization of society is the most tremendous task ever to fall on the shoulders of a class or a revolution in world history. This task requires the complete reconstruction of the state and a radical upheaval in the economic and social foundations of society.

This reconstruction and this upheaval cannot be decreed by any government agency, commission, or parliament—they can only be taken up and carried out by the people themselves.

* This quotation cannot be directly traced to the *Communist Manifesto*, though comparable images positing such alternative historical outcomes do exist. In Luxemburg's speech to the "Founding Congress of the Communist Party of Germany," (see p. 352, below) she posits either "salvation through socialism" or a "descent into anarchy" as compared to the *Communist Manifesto*, where the possibility is either "revolutionary reconstitution" or the "common ruin of the contending classes." In *The Junius Pamphlet* (1915) Luxemburg wrongly attributes the phrase to Engels; in fact, it derives from Karl Kautsky. See Ian Angus, "The Origin of Rosa Luxemburg's slogan 'Socialism or Barbarism,'" johnriddell.com. For Luxemburg, while socialism is historically necessary (an "objective possibility"), only capitalism's cataclysmic demise is inevitable. The question for Luxemburg is, what will replace it? While "salvation through socialism" may be urgently necessary, "barbarism" (a failed society) is equally possible: This view influenced followers of Luxemburg who subscribe to a radical, disjunctive view of history. Luxemburg's anti-evolutionism may be seen in Georg Lukács's messianic positing of the "realm of freedom" versus the "abyss" in *History and Class Consciousness* as well as Walter Benjamin's positing of "salvation" (socialism) or "annihilation" in *One-Way Street*.

In all previous revolutions, it was only a small minority of the people who led the revolutionary fight, who set its goals and direction and used the masses only as a tool to lead its own interests, the interests of the minority, to victory. The socialist revolution is the first one capable of achieving victory in the interest of the vast majority, and only through the vast majority of the workers can it achieve victory.

The calling of the proletarian masses is not merely to set the goals and direction of the revolution with a clear vision. They must also, through their own action, bring socialism, step by step, to life.

The essence of socialist society lies in the fact that the great working mass of the people will cease to be a mass that is governed. Rather, the entirety of political and economic life will involve the activity of the people, animated by conscious and free self-determination.

Thus the proletarian masses must take all the traditional institutions of bourgeois class rule, from the uppermost tip of the state to the smallest community: the federal councils, the parliament, the municipal councils, and replace them with the institutions of their own class: the workers' and soldiers' councils. They must occupy all the posts, supervise all operations, judge all needs of the state according to their own class interests and the tasks of socialism. And only in the constant, living interaction between the people and their institutions, the workers' and soldiers' councils, can their work fill the state with the spirit of socialism.

Even the radical reorganization of the economy can only be consummated as a process carried out by the mass action of the proletariat. In socialization, the naked decrees of the highest revolutionary agencies are only empty words. Only the working class can turn word into flesh through its own deeds. The workers can take control over production and, finally, over actual management and leadership, in dogged struggle with capital, shoulder to shoulder in every workplace, through the unmediated pressure of the masses, through strikes, through the creation of their own permanent institutions of representation.

Instead of dead machines that the capitalist puts to use in the production process, the proletarian masses must learn to become thinking, free, independent directors of this process. They need to acquire the sense of responsibility of functioning members of the whole people who are the sole possessor of social wealth. They need to develop diligence without the stick of the entrepreneur, supreme achievement without capitalist slave-drivers, discipline without subjugation and order without domination. The highest idealism in the interest of the whole, the most rigorous self-discipline, and the true civic sense of the masses are the moral foundations of the socialist society, just as mindlessness, egoism and corruption are the moral foundations of the capitalist society.

The working masses can only acquire all of these socialist civic virtues together with knowledge and capabilities for the direction of socialist concerns through their own activity and their own experience.

The socialization of the society can only be realized through the tenacious, indefatigable struggle of the working masses in all their breadth, at every point at which labor and capital, the people and bourgeois class rule, come face to face.* The liberation of the working class must be the work of the working class itself.

III.

In the bourgeois revolutions, bloodshed, terror, and political assassination were the indispensable weapons in the hands of the rising classes.

The proletarian revolution does not require any terror for its aims—it despises and abhors the killing of human beings. It has no need of this weapon because its battle is not with individuals but with institutions, because it does not enter the arena with naive illusions whose disappointment would lead it to bloody revenge. The proletarian revolution is not the desperate attempt of a minority to shape the world according to its ideals: it is the action of the great mass of the people in their millions, called to fulfil their historical mission and to translate historical necessity into reality.

But the proletarian revolution is also the death knell for all forms of servitude and oppression. This is why all the capitalists have risen up against the revolution like a man fighting for his very life, all the Junkers, the petty bourgeois, officers, all those who benefit and live as parasites from exploitation and class rule.

It is a mad delusion to believe that the capitalists will obey the verdict of any parliament or of any national congress in good faith, that they will peacefully give up their property, their profit, or their privilege to exploit. All ruling classes have doggedly clung to their privileges until the very end. Whether the Roman patriarchs or the feudal barons of the Middle Ages, the English cavaliers, or the American slaveholders, "the boyars" of Walachia or the silk manufacturers of Lyon—they all shed rivers of blood, they made their way through corpses, murder and fire, they incited civil war and treason, all in order to defend their privileges and their power.

The imperialist capitalist class, as the last scion of the exploiting class, surpasses all its forebears in brutality, in unveiled cynicism, in malice. It will defend its Holy of Holies, its profit and its privilege of exploitation, with tooth and nail and with every means of cold cruelty displayed in the entire history of

---

* Literally: look into the whites of each other's eyes (*einander ins Weisse des Auges blicken*). It is clear from this passage that Luxemburg meant more by "socialization" than the nationalization of property by the state.

colonialism and in the last World War. It will move heaven and earth against the proletariat. It will mobilize the peasantry against the cities, it will foment backward sections of the workers against the socialist avant-garde, it will attempt to hinder every step of socialism by a thousand means of passive resistance, it will set a score of Vendées on the throat of the revolution, it will invite foreign enemies, the murder weapons of Clemenceau, Lloyd George and Wilson, as its saviors, it will turn the country into a smoking heap of rubble rather than give up wage-slavery of its own free will.

All this opposition must be broken, step by step, with an iron fist and with ruthless energy. The violence of the bourgeois counterrevolution must be countered by the revolutionary violence of the proletariat. The attacks, intrigues and subversions of the bourgeoisie must be countered by the unbending clarity of purpose, wakefulness, and ever-active preparedness of the proletarian masses. Against the imminent dangers of the counterrevolution, [there must be] the arming of the people and the disarming of the ruling classes. Against the bourgeoisie's obstructive parliamentary maneuvers, [there must be] the active, productive organization of the masses of workers and soldiers. Against the omnipresence and thousand means of power of bourgeois society, the concentrated, compact, and fully developed power of the working class. There must be a unified front of the entire German proletariat: the South and the North, the cities and the country, the worker and the soldier, the living, intellectual leadership of the German revolution and the International. Only the expansion of the German proletarian revolution can create the granite foundation on which the edifice of the future can be built.

The fight for socialism is the most colossal civil war seen in world history, and the proletarian revolution must prepare the necessary equipment for itself. It must learn to use it—to fight and to win.

To thus equip the concrete working mass of the people with all political power for the tasks of the revolution—that is the dictatorship of the proletariat, and therefore true democracy. True democracy is not in the false equality of debating life's questions in parliament, where the wage slave sits next to the capitalist, where the country proletarian sits next to the Junker. It is only there, where the million-headed mass of the proletariat seizes all the power of the state in its own weathered fist, in order to, like the god Thor with his hammer, smash the head of the ruling class—only this is a democracy that is not a betrayal of the people.

In order to enable the proletariat to fulfil these tasks, the Spartacus League demands:

For the Immediate Safeguarding of the Revolution

- The disarmament of the entire police, all officers and non-proletarian soldiers, the disarmament of all members of the ruling classes;

- the confiscation of all weapons and ammunition stockpiles and arms factories by the workers' and soldiers' councils;
- the arming of the entire adult male proletarian population as a *Workers' Militia*, the formation of a *Red Guard* from the proletariat as an active part of the militia for the constant protection of the revolution from counter-revolutionary attacks and subversion;
- the abolition of the right of command for officers and noncommissioned officers, the replacement of blind military obedience with the voluntary discipline of soldiers, the election of superiors within their units with the right of recall at any time, and the abolition of military jurisdiction;
- the removal of officers and capitulators from all the soldiers' councils;
- the replacement of all the former regime's political institutions and agencies with representatives of the workers' and soldiers' councils;
- the appointment of a revolutionary tribunal for the conviction of those most responsible for the war and its continuation, the Hohenzollerns, Ludendorff, Hindenburg, Tirpitz and their comrades in crime, as well as all counterrevolutionary conspirators;
- the immediate appropriation of all food supplies for the provision of the people.

In the Political and Social Spheres

- The abolition of all individual states, a unified German socialist republic;
- the elimination of all parliaments and municipal councils and the assumption of all their functions by the workers' and soldiers' councils and their committees and institutions;
- the election of workers' councils from across Germany by the adult working population of both sexes, in the city and in the country, according to workplace, as well as the election of soldiers' councils within their units with the exception of officers and long-serving professional soldiers, the right of workers and soldiers to recall their representatives at any time;
- the election of delegates from the workers' and soldiers' councils from all of Germany for the *Central Council* of workers' and soldiers' councils, for the election of the *Executive* Council as the highest organ of legislative and executive authority;
- the convening of the Central Council at least every three months in the interim—under the condition of the new election of its delegates each time—for the constant supervision of the operations of the Executive Council and the establishment of living contact between the masses of the workers' and soldiers' councils in the Reich and their highest governmental authority. The right of local workers' and soldiers' councils to recall and replace their representatives in the Central Council at any time, if they do

not act according to the intentions of those who entrusted them with their roles, the right of the Executive Council to appoint and to remove People's Commissioners, the central state authorities and civil servants;
• the abolition of all differences in social position, all decorations and titles, the complete legal and social equality of the sexes;
• far-reaching social legislation, the shortening of the working day for the control of unemployment and with consideration of the physical exhaustion of the workers in the World War, a workday of no more than six hours;
• the immediate and fundamental reorganization of the provision of food, housing, healthcare, and education according to the sense and spirit of the proletarian revolution.

Immediate Economic Demands
• The confiscation of all dynastic wealth and income for the public;
• the annulment of governmental and other public debts as well as all war loans, with the exception of subscriptions of an amount to be defined by the workers' and soldiers' councils;
• the dispossession of the grounds and soil of all large- and middle-scale agricultural firms, the formation of socialist agricultural cooperatives under unified central management for all of Germany, peasant farms to remain in the possession of their owners until the point of their voluntary affiliation with the socialist cooperatives;
• the appropriation by the Council Republic of all banks, mines, industrial works and all big businesses in industry and trade;
• the confiscation of all wealth over an amount to be defined by the Central workers' and soldiers' council;
• the takeover of all public transport by the Council Republic;
• the election of works councils in all workplaces, who shall manage the internal affairs of the workplace by mutual agreement with the workers' councils, regulate working conditions, monitor production and take over the management of the workplace;
• the establishment of a central strike commission, which, in constant cooperation with the works councils, shall ensure the uniform management, the socialist orientation and the strongest support from the political power of the workers' and soldiers' councils.

International Tasks
• The immediate establishment of relations with fraternal parties abroad in order to provide the socialist revolution with an international foundation and arrange and secure the establishment of peace through the international fraternity and revolutionary rise of the world proletariat;

This Is What the Spartacus League Wants!

And because this is what it wants, because it is a warning and an urging on, because it is the socialist conscience of the revolution, it is hated, persecuted, and slandered by all open and secret enemies of the revolution and of the proletariat.

Crucify it! cry the capitalists, trembling for their cash registers.

Crucify it! cry the petty bourgeois, the officers, the anti-Semites, the press lackeys of the bourgeoisie, trembling for the fleshpots of bourgeois class rule.

Crucify it! cry the Scheidemanns, having sold the workers to the bourgeoisie, like Judas Iscariot, trembling for their pieces of silver, their political power.

Crucify it! repeat the voices of deceived, betrayed, abused strata of the workers and soldiers, like an echo, not knowing that they are raging against their own flesh and blood when they rage against the Spartacus League.

All the counterrevolutionaries, enemies of the people, antisocialists, equivocating, shadow-dwelling, indistinct opponents of the Spartacus League are united in hatred and slander. This is proof that the heart of the revolution beats in the Spartacus League, that the future belongs to it.

The Spartacus League is not a party that will assume power over the working masses or through the working masses. The Spartacus League is only the most purposeful, conscious part of the proletariat, directing the whole wide mass of the workers toward their historical tasks at every step, supporting the ultimate socialist goal at every individual stage of the revolution and representing the interests of the proletarian world revolution in all national issues.

The Spartacus League refuses to share governing power with the stooges of the bourgeoisie, with the Scheidemanns and the Eberts, because it sees that this cooperation would betray the principles of socialism, strengthen the counterrevolution, and disable the revolution.

The Spartacus League will likewise refuse to take power if only because the Scheidemann-Ebert government has discredited itself, and the independents, by working with them, have found themselves at a dead end.

The Spartacus League will never take governing power by any other means than through the clear, unambiguous will of the vast majority of the proletarian masses from all of Germany, never if not by virtue of their conscious affirmation to the Spartacus League's views, goals and methods of struggle.

The proletarian revolution can only reach full clarity and maturity at last by making its way, gradually through defeats and victories, step by step, along the way to the Golgotha of its own bitter experience.

The victory of the Spartacus League lies not at the beginning, but at the end of the revolution: its victory is identical with that of the great millions of the proletarian socialist mass.

Proletarians, arise! To the struggle! There is a world to conquer and a world to battle against. In this last class struggle in world history, where the highest aims of humanity are at stake, these are our words for the enemy: Thumbs to your eyes and knees to your chest!*

The Spartacus League

---

* The German phrase "*Daumen aufs Auge und das Knie auf die Brust*" is from Lassalle, in an 1863 appeal for solidarity between the working class and the bourgeoisie against absolutism: "*Dann also kein neues Kompromiss mit ihm, sondern: den Daumen aufs Auge und die Knie auf die Brust*!" (So no new compromise with him, but thumb on eye and knee on chest!). Ferdinand Lassalle, *Was Nun? Zweiter Vortrag über Verfassungswesen* (What Now? Second Lecture on Constitutional Affairs) (Zurich: Meyer and Zeller, 1863), pp. 40–2.

To the Barricades*

Tomorrow, the Central Council of the workers' and soldiers' councils will gather from all over Germany;† in the meeting of this body, at least in organizational terms, the revolutionary proletariat from all over Germany, be they workers or soldiers, will glimpse the finest fruits of the maturing tree of the revolution.

One would like to have imagined this gathering differently. One would like to think that, as soon as the first rising wave of the proletarian movement brought us the Central Council, the stars of the revolution would have shone brightly from that very first hour of its birth, so that, on November 9, it would have brought light to the proletariat in its terrible night of war and bondage.

In those first hours, the Central Council was not to be found. In its place came a replacement: The Executive Council of the Berlin Workers' and Soldiers' Council took the duties of the Central Council in its own hands—in its all-too-weak hands.

And so the Central Council convened at an hour when the revolution had lost its first meteoric gleam, that gleam that was dampened by all the revolution's opponents in those first days and—unfortunately—by its supporters as well. Even they had so often believed that, with the miracle brought by November 9, the business of the revolution would be over. Now all of them have recovered their sight. Those who believed that the old historical powers, the ruling classes who had reigned a thousand years, would be terrified by cheering crowds, waving soldiers and the fluttering of red flags under the linden trees—today they all see how the counterrevolution and capitalism are coming back to life. Capitalism had only feigned death for a few days, like a bedbug. But it already seems to have found the moment and the opportunity to suck new blood.

The machinations of the counterrevolution are perfectly obvious. Even at that hour they managed to appoint Ebert-Scheidemann to act as their agents in the government, and from there to block the energy of the revolution and to redirect it onto the path of the counterrevolution.

---

* This article was first published in *Die Rote Fahne* (Berlin), No. 30, December 15, 1918. It was not signed, but in *Um Rosa Luxemburgs Stellung zur russischen Revolution* (On Rosa Luxemburg's Position on the Russian Revolution) (Hamburg: Press of the Communist International, 1922), Clara Zetkin names Luxemburg as the author. It is translated by Zachary King from Luxemburg's *Gesammelte Werke*, Vol. 4, pp. 450–4.

† The First General Congress of the Workers' and Soldiers' Councils of Germany met in Berlin from December 16 to 21, 1918. Representatives from the SPD dominated. On January 19, the congress approved a plan to carry out the election of a National Assembly which would maintain legislative control, and the election of a Central Council of the Workers' and Soldiers' Councils that would be granted only the power of advising on important legislative proposals.

What hasn't this "socialist" government accomplished? Every day, a new decree: a decree restoring the old state authorities; a decree that attempted to restore the scattered, cowering, hunted rural councils, police chiefs and mayors; a decree declaring private property to be untouchable; a decree declaring the courts, the institution of "class justice," to be "independent," giving them *carte blanche* for maintaining justice for the sake of a single class; a decree ordering taxes to be paid as before. *Nulla dies sine linea*,* not a day without a decree putting another little brick back into the rotten edifice of capitalist rule, another brick that was threatening to fall out.

Who would hold it against the bourgeoisie, under such inviting circumstances, for thinking itself strong enough to cast aside its agents and the Ebert-Scheidemann-Haase government and take the lost reins back into its own hands? It is moving forward at a leisurely pace, step by step. First, it convinced its agents to transfer power back to it through the detour of the National Assembly. The Ebert-Scheidemann government pounced on their task with the zeal of renegades: working toward the National Assembly day and night, on every street and every square, striving with all its power for the sake of the bourgeoisie, organizing *coups d'état* and allowing proletarians to be shot down, bowing and scraping for the military and saluting the black, white and red flag†—and even after all this they still haven't earned the thanks of their patrons, of capitalism.

Their master has grown impatient, he tires of his servant, time is short, and he believes his moment has come again and he doesn't give a damn about the National Assembly: he wants the old Reichstag back.

So, the hour has arrived when the Central Committee convenes for Germany. Renewed, fortified, capitalism stands ready to act.

And the revolution? There is no doubt about it: if the revolution were to take place in those revolutionary organs that the first days created, in the workers' and soldiers' councils, and if their status and importance were to be a measure of the status and importance of the revolution, then the revolution would be in a bad way.

A massive smear campaign was launched against the workers' and soldiers' councils. All small errors—that inevitably crop up in such troubled times, errors that were the most everyday occurrence and practice under the old regime, and that today result from inexperience—were exaggerated into capital crimes and used as conclusive evidence of the unsuitability of the council system.

And then the shadow of the Entente was evoked to finally bring the councils to an end. Mister *Ebert* was the first: he was the one who *voluntarily* offered

---

* Literally translated as "not a day without a line," this comment by Pliny the Elder (about the hardworking artist Appelles) is comparable to the contemporary idiom "another day, another dollar."

† The German imperial flag.

up the councils' heads on a silver platter to America in exchange for food supplies, he *begged* that the food only be delivered in exchange for the workers' and soldiers' councils. *Ebert, Scheidemann and Haase's* government raised the specter of famine in Germany; they hammered their message into everyone's head: either the councils—or bread.

Then the news came that, supposedly, the Entente powers were threatening to march into Germany—every day a new report on this: the Entente is closing in, the Entente threatens, a diplomatic note is imminent, Clemenceau has declared—Lloyd George has declared—every day a new report and every day a new lie.

For everything was a lie. Not a word of it was true. Every printed word had been invented by the Foreign Office and in the Reichskanzlei [Reich Chancellery]. Here, it even outdid the old regime: not even it had deceived the people with such impudence, determination, shamelessness and contempt as this new government.

And the councils did not understand the need to oppose this. They left the entire apparatus for influencing "public opinion" in the hands of the government, of the counterrevolution, and they merely watched in silence as this government, this counterrevolutionary club, attempted to set fire to their house on a daily basis.

But the councils' weakness is not the weakness of the revolution. *It* cannot be trapped or eliminated by such paltry measures. *It* continues to grow and will soon become what it is: the proletarian revolution. Strikes are spreading across the country like wildfire. The proletariat is rising up: yesterday Upper Silesia, today Berlin, tomorrow in the Rhineland and Westphalia, in Stuttgart, in Hamburg; proletarians are breaking all the chains forged to bind them by the government, the party and the trade unions, they are meeting face to face with their enemy, capitalism. The noise about "democracy," made so exquisitely for many a pseudo-socialist in the first days of the revolution, is behind us, and the revolution is rising up in its naked, massive form and is flexing its muscles: for smashing the old world and building the new.

These are the forces in which the assembled Central Councils can find support, which they must simultaneously serve and dynamically lead. This is the only spring from which their strength and vital energy can flow.

The revolution will live on without the councils. The councils will die without the revolution.

Much has been neglected. The councils have made their way gropingly and timidly, self-conscious amid a flood of slogans from the party, its gaze artificially limited by clichés and catchphrases that work to obscure the significance of its role in what took place—the power of what took place.

The Central Council can make up for all these omissions by taking the four most urgent measures and thus securing the position it deserves:

• It must clear the nest of the counterrevolution, the place where all the threads of the counterrevolutionary conspiracy converge: it must eliminate the Ebert-Scheidemann-Haase cabinet.

• It must demand the disarming of all the frontline troops who do not recognize the workers' and soldiers' councils unconditionally as the highest authority and who will become the personal bodyguards of the Ebert-Haase cabinet.

• It must demand the disarming of all officers and the White Guard formed by the Ebert-Haase government and create a Red Guard.

• It must reject the National Assembly as an attempt on the life of the revolution and the workers' and soldiers' councils.

By taking action on these four steps immediately, the workers' and soldiers' councils can still take command of the revolution: the proletariat wants them to lead; as long as the councils are willing to take a strong lead against capitalism, the proletariat is ready to give the councils its all and to lift them to the highest height, shouting:

All power to the workers' and soldiers' councils!

Extraordinary General Assembly of the German Independent Social Democratic Party of Greater Berlin—On December 15, 1918*

According to a newspaper report

I. SUPPLEMENTARY PRESENTATION ON THE POLICIES OF THE USPD

Comrade Haase has just delivered an indictment of his very own policy and defended the policy of the Ebert-Scheidemann government.† He claimed that Liebknecht was prepared to join the government, but he has forgotten to mention the condition Liebknecht had named. This condition was that the new government take a fundamentally socialist direction in its policy. We are still prepared to join the government even today, provided this condition is met. Regarding what happened with Schwartzkopff, a comrade will tell you that every appeal to unity is essentially an attempt at fraud.‡

Five weeks have passed since November 9. Since then, the scenario has completely changed. Reaction is much stronger now than it was in the first days. And Haase tells us: see how marvelously far we've come. His duty should have been to show us the progress made by the counterrevolution, which has been helped along by the government in which Haase sits. Instead of preventing the counterrevolution, this government has strengthened the bourgeoisie and reaction. The bourgeoisie could hardly wish for a more favorable government, a government that is a mere fig leaf for its counterrevolutionary goals.

The current government has not even attempted to take the most elementary measures. Has it annulled the war debts? Has it armed the people to defend the revolution? It banned the Red Guard and recognized Wels's White

---

* This article first appeared in two parts in *Die Freiheit* (Berlin): Part I, in No. 57, December 16, 1918, and Part II, in No. 59, December 17, 1918. It is translated by Zachary King from Luxemburg's *Gesammelte Werke*, Vol. 4, pp. 455–9

† Hugo Haase had attempted to justify the USPD's participation in the government, the policies of the Council of the People's Commissioners, and the necessity of a vote on the National Assembly.

‡ The slogans "unity," "parity," and "no infighting," taken up by the Social Democrats and centrists, had found resonance among many workers and soldiers. During strikes in Berlin in January 1919, Schwartzkopff machinists carried red flags with the caption "Spartacus Gesellschaft" (Spartacus Company). They also carried placards with the slogan: "Schwartzkopff workers of Berlin: come to an understanding, if not with, then against your leaders." They called for the unification of workers despite party leadership.

Guard. During the coup on December 6 all the counterrevolutionary threads led back into Ebert and Wels's hands. [Arnold] Lequis and Hindenburg and all the officers and generals took their place in the government, and Haase tells us that this is a socialist government. It is precisely these government methods that confuse the proletariat. All the independents should have left the government after December 6; they should have rejected responsibility for what had occurred in order to rouse the masses and inform them that the revolution was in danger. Since this did not happen, the masses had to be lulled back to sleep, and Haase's speech today was the continuation of this policy of distraction.

Haase listed the achievements of the new government—nothing but bourgeois reforms that prove how backward Germany had been; these are the obsolete debts of the bourgeoisie, and not the revolutionary conquests of the proletariat that they should have been.

Haase also said that we shouldn't slavishly copy the tactics of the Russians, since Germany's economy is more developed. We must, however, learn from them. At first, the Bolsheviks had to gain experience. We can benefit from the fruit of this experience.

Socialism is not a question of parliamentary elections, but a question of power. The proletariat must fight the bourgeoisie in class struggle, shoulder to shoulder and face to face. And to do so, the proletariat must be equipped. It is no longer a matter of discussions and majority votes. Haase has proposed to delay the National Assembly, but, at the same time, he sees it as an arena for political struggle. The party leadership of the Independents set April as the date for the National Assembly. Their representatives have discredited themselves by moving the date to February 16.

Haase has extolled the principle of democracy. Now, if the principle of democracy is to apply, it should certainly apply above all in our own party. But in that case, the Party Congress should be called immediately, so that the masses can say whether they still want this government.

If the USPD has just suffered an electoral defeat in Berlin,* then the real reason behind it is Haase's policy in the government. (Tumultuous interruption.) How absurd to blame the Spartacists when it was precisely we who shook the masses into revolutionary consciousness! Haase and his friends fought against the social patriots for four long years, only to make peace with the offenders. And for that reason, it is they who are truly guilty.

Haase wanted to accuse us of subordinating our opinion to that of the masses, since we refuse to take over the government without the approval of the masses. We do not subordinate ourselves, nor will we wait patiently. We

* The election of delegates to the First General Congress of the Workers' and Soldiers' Councils of Germany took place on December 14, 1918. The Majority Socialists obtained more delegates than the USPD.

want to denounce your half measures and your weaknesses. By leaving the government, Haase and his friends would awaken the masses and free them of their illusions. If they continue, however, to cover for the government, then the people will rise up and sweep them away. In the revolution today, there is no speech and no brochure that can do the work of informing the public. Today, the public must be informed through deeds.

Yes, the state of the USPD is unsustainable since there are elements at play that do not belong together. Either one is resolved to make joint efforts with the social patriots or one goes with the Spartacus League. The Party Congress must decide this question. But in demanding the Party Congress, we can tell that Haase's ears are just as clogged as Scheidemann's were when we made the same demand during the war.

I submit the following resolution to the association meeting: On December 15, 1918, the extraordinary association meeting of the USPD of greater Berlin demands:

- The immediate resignation of the representatives of the USPD from the Ebert-Scheidemann government;
- the association meeting rejects the convocation of the National Assembly, as it can only lead to the strengthening of the counterrevolution and the betrayal of the socialist goals of the revolution;
- the immediate assumption of all political power by the workers' and soldiers' councils, the disarming of the counterrevolution, the arming of the working population, the formation of the Red Guard for the defense of the revolution, the dissolution of the Ebert Council of People's Commissioners, the endowment of the Executive Committee of the workers' and soldiers' councils with the highest power of the state;
- the association meeting demands the immediate convocation of the Party Congress of the USPD.*

We stand at a moment of world-historical significance, shortly before the conference of the Central Council. The revolution has been brought almost to the edge of the abyss, and the proletariat must pull back with a firm hand. The government has done everything to divest the Central Council of its power in advance, it has disarmed the civilian population and the proletariat, it has taken measures that are contrary to the revolution and confuse the masses. This must be rigorously resisted. (Lively applause.)

* 195 votes were cast in favor of this resolution. Rudolf Hilferding's resolution, which proposed the organization of the election for the National Assembly as the most important political task of the USPD, received 485 votes.

II. CONCLUDING REMARKS

Our duty is to demolish every bridge with the current government. This is our demand, and it is a justified one. We know this because Comrade [Emil] Barth just stood up a moment ago to list off his heroic revolutionary deeds. If Comrade Barth is really such a revolutionary, then he has regressed very quickly in the last five weeks. Now Comrade Barth participates in all of the Ebert government's counterrevolutionary actions. Why did he join this government? Why didn't he stay in the ranks of the proletariat, where a true revolutionary belongs? No, comrades, individual people do not create a revolution; if the revolution does not come from the masses themselves it isn't worth anything at all. Ströbel argued that the representatives of the USPD should participate in the government through revolutionary collaboration. No, comrades, for us socialists, it is not a question of governing, but of overthrowing capitalism. It is still unshaken, it still persists; it is not a question of showing that we are a party capable of governing but cannot govern now, in this government—this has already been proven. We've been told that we must wait a long time before the majority of the proletariat makes up its mind according to our revolutionary views. Those who invoke this argument completely and totally misjudge the living and dynamic tempo of revolutionary development. We are not the ones who want to take power. We want the majority of the proletariat to take political power in their own hands. All those who have built up the *monstrosity of the National Assembly* have brought confusion to the masses and set back revolutionary development by months and years. Hilferding emphasized the democratic principle. But this formal democratic equality is a pack of lies as long as the economic power of capital persists. There can be no debate with the bourgeoisie and the Junkers as to whether socialism should be established. Socialism does not mean sitting together in parliament and passing laws. For us, socialism means the total, ruthless defeat of the ruling classes (general laughter), a ruthlessness that the proletariat is capable of developing in its struggle. The *National Assembly* is meant to serve as a bridge over the abyss between capital and labor. You now have to choose which road to take, either with us or with Scheidemann. There is no way of evading it, it is only either-or.

National Assembly or Council Government?*

Thus reads the second point of the agenda of the Reich Conference of workers' and soldiers' councils, posing what is, in reality, the primary question of the revolution in the present moment. Either a National Assembly or all power to the workers' and soldiers' councils, either the renunciation of socialism or the fiercest class struggle of the fully equipped proletariat against the bourgeoisie: this is the dilemma.

It is an idyllic plan, this: to realize socialism by way of parliament, through simple majority rule! What a shame that this dreamy fantasy plucked from the sky takes no account whatsoever of the historical experience of bourgeois revolution, let alone the specifics of proletarian revolution.

How did things fare in England? That is the cradle of bourgeois parliamentarianism, that is where it had its earliest and strongest development. When the hour of the first modern bourgeois revolution struck there in 1649, the English parliament could already look back on more than 300 years of history. Thus the parliament became the center, the bulwark, the headquarters of the revolution from its very outset. The celebrated Long Parliament, which bore and nurtured all the phases of the English Revolution, from the first skirmish between the opposition and the king's forces to the trial and execution of Charles Stuart, this parliament was an unrivalled compliant tool in the hands of the emerging bourgeoisie.

And what did it produce? This same parliament had to create a special "parliamentary army," selecting parliamentarian generals from its own womb to go into the field and defeat feudalism and the royalist army of the Cavaliers in a long, tough, and bloody civil war. The fate of the English Revolution was not decided in the debates of Westminster Abbey—though that may have contained the intellectual center of the revolution—but on the battlefields of Marston-Moor and Naseby; it was brought into being not by brilliant parliamentary speeches but by the farmer cavalry that made up Cromwell's Ironsides. And its path, starting in parliament and civil war, led to parliament being "purified" twice and, finally, to Cromwell's dictatorship.

And in France? That was where the idea of the National Assembly was first born. It was a world-historical intuition of genius on the part of Mirabeau and others when they declared in 1789: from now on, the three previously separate "estates" of the nobility, the clergy and "the third estate" will gather *together* as

---

* This article first appeared in *Die Rote Fahne* (Berlin), No. 32, December 17, 1918. It was not signed, but in *Um Rosa Luxemburgs Stellung zur russischen Revolution* (On Rosa Luxemburg's Position on the Russian Revolution) (Hamburg: Press of the Communist International, 1922), Clara Zetkin names Luxemburg as the author. The article is translated by Zachary King from Luxemburg's *Gesammelte Werke*, Vol. 4, pp. 460–3.

a National Assembly. This Assembly was, in fact, a tool in the class struggle of the bourgeoisie, precisely due to the fact that the estates met together. From the very beginning, the "third estate," that is, the revolutionary bourgeoisie, had a compact majority in the National Assembly alongside the strong minorities of the two upper classes.

And what did this produce? The Vendée, emigration, the treason of the generals, the intrigues of the clergy, the revolt of fifty departments, the coalition wars of feudal Europe, until, at last, the only means of securing the victory of the revolution: the dictatorship, and, as its final form, the reign of terror!

The parliamentary majority was hardly useful in the fight for the *bourgeois* revolution! And then indeed, what is the difference between the bourgeoisie and feudalism when measured against the yawning chasm separating labor and capital today! What was there in terms of class consciousness on either side of the opponents facing off in 1649 or 1789, in comparison with the deadly, unquenchable hatred raging today between the proletariat and the capitalist class! It was not without reason that Karl Marx held the light of his science up to the most hidden forces driving the economic and political gears of bourgeois society. It was not without reason that he illuminated its peculiar doings and affectations, right up to the finest veins of its feeling and thought, as products of the basic fact that it lives by feeding like a vampire on the blood of the proletariat.

It was not without reason that August Bebel concluded his celebrated speech at the Dresden Party Congress with the cry "I am and will remain the mortal enemy of bourgeois society!"

This is the last great battle, a matter of whether exploitation is to be or not to be, a turning point in the history of humanity, a fight in which there can be no excuses, no compromise, no mercy.

And this last battle, surpassing all its predecessors in the enormity of its mission, is supposed to complete what no other class struggle or revolution has ever completed: it is supposed to dispel the death struggle of two worlds in the gentle whisper of a parliamentary battle of words and majority votes!

Even parliamentarianism was an arena in the class struggle of the proletariat, as long as the quiet everyday life of bourgeois society continued: it was the tribune where the masses gathered around the flag of socialism to be trained for the fight. Today, we stand at the halfway point in the proletarian revolution, and today we must take the axe to the tree of capitalist exploitation ourselves. Bourgeois parliamentarianism, like the class rule of the bourgeoisie, which is its exclusive political goal, has forfeited its right to exist. Now the class struggle is coming to its limits in its undisguised, naked form. Capital and labor have nothing more to say to each other, they can only seize one another with an iron embrace in a final fight to determine who will be thrown to the ground.

Lassalle's words are more valid today than ever: The revolutionary act is always *to express what is*. And *what is* means: On the one side is labor—on the other, capital! Without any hypocrisy about amiable agreements when it is a question of life and death, without any victories of common ground where the only concern is that of "both sides." The proletariat, *constituted as a class*, must gather all political power in its own hands with clarity, openness, honesty, and, thanks to its clarity and honesty, force.

The greater and lesser prophets of bourgeois rule have chanted "political equality, democracy!" at us for decades.

And today, the stooges of the bourgeoisie, the Scheidemanns, are chanting "political equality, democracy!" in their wake, like an echo.

Yes, they just need to be made into reality first. For the words "political equality" will only become flesh when economic exploitation has been destroyed root and branch. And "democracy," government by the people, only begins with the seizure of political power by the working people.

It is essential to develop the practical critique of historical actions through the words misused by the bourgeois classes for centuries. We must make "*Liberté, Egalité, Fraternité*," proclaimed by the French bourgeoisie in 1789, into the truth for the very first time—by abolishing the class rule of the bourgeoisie. And it is essential, as the first act of this saving deed, to proclaim loudly before the whole world and before centuries of world history: What was considered equality and democracy until now: parliaments, national assemblies, equal ballots, was a pack of lies! Full power in the hands of the working masses, as a weapon for smashing capitalism to pieces—this is the only true equality, this is the only true democracy!

Ebert's Mamelukes*

The work of the Reich conference has reached a worthy culmination. After providing the strongest support to Ebert's counterrevolutionary headquarters, after cutting itself off from the street and from the revolutionary masses of the proletariat, it has ended by committing suicide and dealing the deathblow to the workers' and soldiers' councils!

How cynically, how brazenly did Ebert's people set the conference in motion, like a puppet, taking advantage of the parliamentary helplessness and guilelessness of the workers' and soldiers' delegates. Here are two pieces of evidence.

On Wednesday evening† a certain "Lüdemann Motion" suddenly appeared, in a completely unremarkable and incidental manner, demanding that, "until the further provision of the National Assembly," all legislative and executive power in directing the Reich should be transferred—that is, to Ebert's cabinet.‡ This motion was passed on Wednesday evening on the fly, without any debate! And the congress was not made aware that it had already anticipated the "further regulation" of the matter by the National Assembly, before the question of the National Assembly was even debated, let alone before any kind of decision had been reached! On Thursday, the question on the agenda was whether the National Assembly should be convened at all, and on Wednesday Ebert's clique let the congress decide that the National Assembly had the right to the final governing say in affairs and that all political power could be transferred without delay to the Ebert cabinet! The Congress was deceived into framing its own debates on the primary question of the revolution as a done deal, as a comedy.

A second example: On Thursday, after the presentations and the closing remarks on the subject of the "National Assembly," it came to a vote. Two decisive proposals were picked out from the multitude: [Ernest] Däumig's proposal, which posed the fundamental question of the National Assembly or council constitution, and a proposal from Ebert's camp, setting the date of the vote on the National Assembly for January 19.

---

* This article first appeared in *Die Rote Fahne* (Berlin), No. 35, December 20, 1918. It was not signed, but in *Um Rosa Luxemburgs Stellung zur russischen Revolution* (On Rosa Luxemburg's Position on the Russian Revolution) (Hamburg: Press of the Communist International, 1922), Clara Zetkin names Luxemburg as the author. The article is translated by Zachary King from Luxemburg's *Gesammelte Werke*, Vol. 4, pp. 464–7.

† December 18, 1918.

‡ Lüdemann's motion, which Ebert supported, passed by 290 to 115. See *Allgemeiner Kongreß der Arbeiter- und Soldatenräte Deutschlands. Vom 16. bis 21. Dezember 1918 im Abgeordnetenhause zu Berlin, Stenographische Berichte*, (General Congress of Workers' and Soldiers' Councils in Germany from December 16 to 21, 1918, in the Berlin House of Representatives, Stenographic Reports) (Berlin: Zentralrat der sozialistischen Republik Deutschlands, 1918), p. 88.

Every schoolchild understands that, first, before the *date* of the election can be decided, the basic question has to be resolved as to whether it should come to a vote *at all.* Before the date can be fixed for killing off the council constitution, one has to comment on the question of whether this prank should take place or not.

Leinert, however, presiding over this meeting, regards the workers' and soldiers' councils of this Congress as an old-style entrepreneur regarded his workers: "You can offer them anything." And it's correct! The Congress quietly allows it to happen: *first* a vote is taken on the election date, then Däumig's essential question is voted on, as if they could be manipulated by a simple trick!

Even with all that, on no account do we want to present the view that the congress allowed itself through pure carelessness and helplessness in external affairs to get entangled in this like an inexperienced girl brought to sin by a cunning seducer. The composition of this Congress and its behavior, from beginning to end, has certified its decided, untiring partisanship for the side of the Scheidemann counterrevolution. The Ebert clique's undisguised maneuvers only reveal that they are degrading the Council Congress to the level of Mameluke guards, that they have brought back all the old ruses and stage tricks at the first Congress of the revolution—and with such success!—that Scheidemann's legions used to corrupt and infantilize the "authorities" of the old party and trade unions in preparing the ground for the shambles of August 4.

The Council Congress then made one more last step as the willing tool of the counterrevolution: it expressly rejected any cooperation on the part of the executive committee in the legislative power of the Council of People's Commissioners, and endowed Ebert's government with dictatorial powers!

The Congress of the workers' and soldiers' councils crowned its work by stripping the councils of all their power and giving it to Ebert's clique, who have the coup of December 6 on their conscience, the fourteen corpses on Chausseestrasse and Marten and Lorenz's conspiracies!*

The starting point and the only tangible achievement of the Revolution of November 9 was the formation of the workers' and soldiers' councils. The first congress of these councils ends with the negation of its own unique achievement, by snatching power from the proletariat, by demolishing the work of November 9, and reversing the revolution!

Here, however, the powers of counterrevolution have cut off their nose to spite their face. The Mamelukes of the Ebert guard have taken their blind obedience too far. The bow, stretched beyond its limit, sends the arrow speeding back at the archer.

---

* Marten, who initiated the formation of the counterrevolutionary Association of German Women for the Welcome of the Troops, and Lorenz, responsible for the delivery of arms to the militias as head of the War Ministry, were among the plotters of the counterrevolutionary coup on December 6, 1918.

When the Council Congress condemned the workers' and soldiers' council, i.e., the very body from which it derives its authority, to a mere shadow existence, it thus also *overstepped its authority, betrayed the mandate it was handed by the councils, annulled the ground on which it based its existence and its authority.* By deciding to strip the councils of all their powers, the congress did not dissolve the *latter* as a political force, but itself, and, thinking it was dealing the councils their deathblow, made its own authority null and void.

The workers' and soldiers' councils *have not been* dissolved as a political force and *cannot* be dissolved. They do not exist at the mercy of any congress; they were born out of the revolutionary act of the masses on November 9. The revolutionary masses will *not* commit the suicide planned for them. The workers' and soldiers' councils will remain, they will now consolidate their power with ten times the energy and will defend the Revolution of November 9, their right to existence. They will declare the counterrevolutionary work of their unfaithful representatives to be null and void, and will find the strength and the courage to declare in this decisive hour, as Luther once did:

Here I stand, I can do no other!

TWO POSTSCRIPTS:

In consideration of the fact that the Executive Council has been deprived of any ability to cooperate in legislative power and thus turned into the shadow being of a "supervisory authority" condemned to lack either power or influence, the USPD faction declared that it could no longer participate in the Executive Council. *As a result of this, the Executive Council consists entirely of representatives voted in from Ebert's people.* Ebert's "supervision" over Ebert's government! The devil supervised by his mother-in-law! All the political power and all its institutions exclusively in the hands of the Scheidemanns!

And of course, even this humiliation has its fig leaf. For Haase will remain in the Council of the People's Commissioners, pinned on Ebert's loins like a girdle of shame. Yes, he's staying! And Dittmann and Barth are staying too. The left wing of the USPD is retreating from the Executive Council to save its honor, and its right wing is standing firm as the "principled" cover for political prostitution.

The Haase clique is ducking out of the Party Congress in order to avoid its responsibility, in order to avoid a clear verdict. The inner logic of the matter produces the verdict and clarity. The masses of the party will be directly *challenged* and *forced* to pass their judgement!

The congress's directors are giving it the treatment it deserves. After it had done and allowed everything needed by the counterrevolution, it had to be sent home. After the second item—the National Assembly—had been settled, they wanted to brazenly halt the rest of the agenda. What's the point of that useless chatter about socialization, about peace, when the main thing—the dictatorship of the Ebert government—had already been achieved? The Moor had done his work, the Moor had to go.*

The Moor was ready for that, too. But then "the street" intervened. Such a raging, elemental protest arose in the gallery at the unveiling of this pristine plan that even the Mamelukes in the hall below became scared. It was resolved to hold the hearing on the two presentations, on socialization and on peace.

In any case, it was an empty formality. Two platonic speaking exercises on the way out, heard out "for decency's sake" by men who had already put on their hats and overcoats.

Nonetheless, this last little glimmer of a sense of shame and propriety served to hold back the clenched fist of the masses.

* Quotation from Friedrich Schiller, *Die Verschwörung des Fiesco zu Genua*, Act III, Scene 4.

A Pyrrhic Victory*

The first conference of the Reich Congress of Councils is over. Surveying its accomplishments as externally presented in its debates and resolutions, we can see that they are a victory for the Ebert government and a victory for the counterrevolution in every respect. Locking out the revolutionary "street," nullifying the political power of the workers' and soldiers' councils, convening the National Assembly, giving dictatorial power to the clique of December 6—what more or better could the bourgeoisie desire in the current situation? "The dictators don't want to know anything about the dictatorship that has been thought up for them,"† rejoices *Freiheit*, that sad organ of political ambiguity.

Naturally, the self-proclaimed organ of the workers' and soldiers' councils has, instead of seizing political power for the business of the revolution, which was its mission, committed suicide and surrendered the political power entrusted to it.

This reflects not merely the general inadequacy of the first unripe stage of the revolution, but also the particular difficulty of this proletarian revolution, the specificity of its historical situation.

The fighters of all previous revolutions bore their colors openly when they went into battle: class against class, program against program, buckler against buckler. And while there have been intrigues, plots and tricks in every revolution, they were precisely the notorious intrigues, plots and tricks of the *counterrevolution*, the royalists, the aristocrats, the reactionary military. They were always the supporters of the overthrown or threatened system, taking counterrevolutionary measures for the sake of and to save this system. It was enough to drag the compromised shields and coats of arms out of the dark into the light—then the crowd, with a loud halloo, would pick the old scarecrows to pieces.

In today's revolution, the defensive troops of the old order do not go into battle under the shields and coats of arms of the ruling classes, but under the banner of a "social democratic party." If the Ebert-Haase government were to honestly and openly call themselves [Ernest von] Heydebrand, Gröber and

---

* This article first appeared in *Die Rote Fahne* (Berlin), No. 36, December 21, 1918. It was not signed, but in *Um Rosa Luxemburgs Stellung zur russischen Revolution* (On Rosa Luxemburg's Position on the Russian Revolution) (Hamburg: Press of the Communist International, 1922), Clara Zetkin names Luxemburg as the author. It is translated by Zachary King from Luxemburg's *Gesammelte Werke*, Vol. 4, pp. 468–71.

† The *Freiheit* continues: "and we have always emphasized that the fight for the dictatorship of the councils is irrelevant because the dictators have not wanted to know anything about the mission that has been thought up for them." ("*Ein heißer Tag*" [A Hot Day]. *Die Freiheit* [Berlin], No. 65, December 20, 1918.)

[Paul] Fuhrmann,* then not a single person from the workers' and soldiers' delegates would have risked following them. If the main question of the revolution was openly and honestly stated as *capitalism or socialism*, doubt and vacillation would be impossible today in the great mass of the proletariat.

History alone will not make it so simple or so easy for us. The class rule of the bourgeoisie is fighting its last world-historical fight today under another's flag, under the flag of the revolution itself. It is a socialist party, it is a creation of the workers' movement and the class struggle that has turned itself into the most forceful instrument of the bourgeois counterrevolution. Its core, tendency, politics, psychology, methods—all these are perfectly capitalist. Only its signs, its apparatus and phraseology are left over from socialism. And signs, apparatus and phraseology are enough to deceive the broad masses as to its political core and content, to degrade the delegate council of the revolutionary proletariat to a counterrevolutionary detachment of Mamelukes!

That is the school of German Social Democracy, that is the record from the last twenty-five years of its activity. The ghost of August 4, 1914, reigns over the conference hall of the Congress of Councils. The old pre-revolutionary Germany of the Hohenzollerns, of Hindenburg and Ludendorff, of martial law and mass executions in Finland, in the Baltic and Ukraine, was still intact in the hall of the Parliament—despite the collapse on the battlefields of France and despite November 9!

And even so, that Germany no longer exists. That is the miraculous secret of all inwardly ripened, historically necessary social revolutions, that a day of revolution changes the countenance of society and turns the old into the past for ever and ever.

The eruption of November 9—however weak, however inadequate, however convoluted it was—created a rift between yesterday and today that can no longer be bridged. As a little snowflake suffices to bring massive avalanches into motion and to bury boulders, valleys, and villages underneath them, so did the weak stimulus of November 9 suffice to throw the class conditions in Germany off balance and to cause a general swaying and shaking in its foundations.

The process of destabilizing and overthrowing bourgeois class rule can result in nothing other than the triumph of social revolution because there remains no way out of the bankruptcy of imperialism, no salvation other than in socialism.

The situation becomes more urgent every day, every day chisels away more directly and more mercilessly at the world-historical dilemma.

The mass of soldiers flooding back is transforming gradually into the mass of workers, taking off the livery of imperialism and putting on the overalls of

* All three were leading German conservative politicians at the time.

the proletariat—the soldiers are coming back into contact with the nurturing soil where their class consciousness is rooted, and tearing the threads that tied them temporarily to the ruling classes.

At the same time, we see the rise of the enormous problems of unemployment, economic struggles between capital and labor, and the financial bankruptcy of the state. The inward denouement of the capitalist economy is revealing its Medusa head. Its economic antithesis can be seen in the hot forge from which new embers flare up out of the class struggle every day.

And with this, it is assured that the revolutionary tension and the revolutionary consciousness of the masses are becoming more acute and sharper every day. The Council Congress has just done its best toward a clarification and training of the masses through the rough and abrupt contrast in which it faces their situation and spirit. In the few days of its deliberation, it has demonstrated to the proletariat and the soldiers that fighting tooth and nail against the counterrevolutionary government is an inevitable and vital issue.

Only a lack of clarity and half measures, only veils and fog are dangerous to the cause of the revolution. Every bit of clarity, every revelation adds fuel to the fire of the revolution.

The Congress of Councils has accomplished such a rigorous, complete labor in these few days, has so thoroughly cast aside all the veils from the heart of the counterrevolution, that its conference must rouse the conscience of the proletarian masses like a mine blast.

Starting from the moment when the council delegates finished speaking, the right to speak is with the workers' and soldiers' councils all over Germany and the working masses. They will speak, and they will *act*. The victory of the Ebert government will remain—like all the victories of the counterrevolution—a Pyrrhic victory.

The Election of the National Assembly*

Following their polished "victory" at the Council Congress, Ebert's people believe that they have succeeded in striking their major blow against the power of the workers' and soldiers' councils, against the proletarian revolution and socialism.

They are mistaken. They have ensured the ruin of this counterrevolutionary plan and [have ensured] that, through the revolutionary action of the masses, this move by the capitalist protection force will be thwarted.

Just as we exploited the infamous Prussian three-class franchise system in order to fight *against* the three-class parliament *from within* the three-class parliament, so will we exploit the election of the National Assembly for the struggle against the National Assembly.

At this point, of course, the analogy ends. Participation in the National Assembly, for real supporters of the revolution and socialism, cannot have anything in common with the conventional schema, with traditional "exploitation of the parliament" for so-called "positive achievements." Not in the old routine of parliamentarianism, nor in order to affix a patchwork of improvements and cosmetic changes to legislative proposals, nor to "gauge our strength," to review our supporters, or to bring out all the familiar phrases from the time of the bourgeois-parliamentarian treadmill and from the vocabulary of Haase and his comrades.

We are now standing in the middle of the revolution, and the National Assembly is a counterrevolutionary fortress being erected *in opposition to* the revolutionary proletariat. And thus, it is valid to storm this fortress and raze it. In order to mobilize the masses *against* the National Assembly and call them to join in the fiercest fight, we must exploit both the vote and the platform of the National Assembly.

This won't be in order to pass laws together with the bourgeoisie and its shield bearers, but to expel the bourgeoisie and its shield bearers from the temple, to storm the fortress of the counterrevolution and victoriously hoist up the flag of the proletarian revolution—this is why participating in the election is necessary.

Is a majority in the National Assembly required to do this? Only devoted followers of parliamentarian cretinism believe this, those who want to decide the revolution and socialism through parliamentary majorities. Even the fate of the National Assembly will not be decided by a parliamentary majority *within*

---

* This article first appeared in *Die Rote Fahne* (Berlin), No. 38, December 23, 1918. It is unsigned but was clearly written by Luxemburg. It is translated by Zachary King from Luxemburg's *Gesammelte Werke*, Vol. 4, pp. 472–4.

the National Assembly: this question will be resolved by the proletarian mass outside, on the shop floors and in the street.

It would suit the gentlemen of the Ebert-Haase cabinet, it would suit the Junkers, the capitalists and their retinue to slip by neatly and let the proletariat content themselves as quiet onlookers while, inside, it's their hide on the line!

Nothing will come of this scheme. They may have been quick enough, thanks to the rush of the Mameluke congress of the workers' and soldiers' councils, to have wrapped up their counterrevolutionary work—but nevertheless it was and remains nothing but a bill of goods they are trying to sell to themselves. The actual goods, however, belong to the proletarian mass, the real bearer of the revolution and its socialist tasks. They, the masses, can determine the fate and the course of the National Assembly. Their own revolutionary activity determines what will be *within* and what will be *outside of* the National Assembly. The balance hangs in the action that takes place outside, and that will come to knock wildly on the gate of the counterrevolutionary parliament. But of course, the election itself and the action of the revolutionary representatives of the masses inside must serve the business of the revolution. All the tricks and ploys of the worthy assembly must be denounced loudly and mercilessly, its counterrevolutionary work has to be revealed to the masses at every step, and the masses must be called to decide and to intervene—this is the task in participating in the National Assembly.

The bourgeois masters, headed by the Ebert government, want to ban and disable the class struggle through the National Assembly, and to use it to dodge its revolutionary decision. Despite this plan, the class struggle should charge into the National Assembly; it should exploit its election and its proceedings to accelerate the moment of the revolution.

We are approaching turbulent times. Unemployment and economic conflicts will grow steadily in the next weeks and months. The great conflict between capital and labor that carries the fate of the revolution in its breast and that, in its final outcome, allows for no other solution than the collapse of capitalist class rule and the triumph of socialism: this conflict will ensure that the masses' revolutionary spirit and activity will grow every day.

The National Assembly's purpose is, according to the plan of the Ebert clique, to raise a dam against this revolutionary tide. What's needed then is to direct the tide into, in the middle of and through the National Assembly, to sweep the dam away.

The electoral action, the platform of this counterrevolutionary parliament, must be a tool for the training, the organization and the mobilization of the revolutionary mass, a stage in the struggle to establish the proletarian dictatorship.

Our participation in the National Assembly means: to storm the gates of the National Assembly with the masses, to raise the clenched fist of the revolutionary proletariat in the midst of the assembly and to wave the flag bearing the fiery letters: *All power to the workers' and soldiers' councils!*

Proletarians, comrades, to work! There is no time to lose. Today the ruling classes are still gloating over the victory of the Ebert government in the Council Congress, they are waiting and hoping for January 19 as the day of return to unadulterated class rule. They should not rejoice so soon. The Ides of March are not yet through and those of January are not either. The future belongs to the proletarian revolution, everything must serve it, including the election of the National Assembly.

The Reich Conference of the Spartacus League*

Tomorrow, representatives from the most hated, the most slandered, the most hunted political movement, the Spartacus League, will gather together from all over Germany. Proud and confident, they will gather for brief counsel under their storm-tested flag to decide their aims and path going forward, with the hot breath of the revolution all around them.

Just as once upon a time in Flanders the word "*Geuzen*," or beggar, became the symbol of a merciless revolutionary fight, so has the name "Spartacist" become a symbol of unrelenting proletarian energy in Germany today, a symbol of unswerving adherence to the goals of socialism, of everything hated to death, as an abomination, by the ruling classes and capitalist society.

The league looks back over a brief but tumultuous past. The collapse of German Social Democracy on August 4, 1914, was the hour in which Spartacus was born. The crashing bankruptcy of conventional party tactics, the party's shameful betrayal of the most sacred duty and honored tasks of socialism in the great hour of decision, immediately brought the open and ruthless rebellion of the Spartacists against the plan. They held the first public protest against the official party's disgrace as early as August 1914, which was published in the Italian, English and Dutch press and called out loudly to the socialist International: Have hope and pull yourselves together! There are still socialists in Germany!

While the working masses, frozen in the hypnosis of war's frenzy, still watched the victorious onrush of imperialism passively or even jubilantly, and as a leaden cemetery silence lay over the party after its suicide on August 4, it was these same Spartacists who ran the first conferences in Stuttgart, Frankfurt am Main and Leipzig, who gave the first signals to gather against the official party, who sparked the first conflicts face to face with the traitors of socialism and the International.

The small flock fought tirelessly under a state of siege in the saber dictatorship, at the Reichstag's podium, in the newspaper *Internationale*, in the *Junius* brochure, in flyers, in order to save the honor of the German proletariat, to rouse the masses to kindle the sacred sparks of revolutionary idealism into a fire.†

---

* This unsigned article first appeared in *Die Rote Fahne* (Berlin), No. 43, December 29, 1918. In *Die Rote Fahne* (Berlin), No. 304, December 28, 1928, Luxemburg is named as the author. It is translated by Zachary King from Luxemburg's *Gesammelte Werke*, Vol. 4, pp. 475–8.

† "The Junius Brochure" is a name popularly given to *The Crisis of German Social Democracy*, written in 1915 by Luxemburg while she was in prison, and published in 1916. Luxemburg wrote it under the pseudonym "Junius," which had been utilized by a dissident political pamphleteer

Persecution fell on the troublemakers thickly, like hail. One after another they disappeared from the scene for years, filled up the prisons and the jails or were sent off from the shop floor into the trenches. But if only one remained free, the flock immediately began to form from scratch, and the underground work continued—the hard, subversive work to undermine the old edifice of imperialism.

And the gang integrated itself ever more broadly and closely with the proletarian masses. While the Independents, after two years of collaborating with the Judases of the labor movement, broke away from them, hesitant and vacillating, only to stubbornly take up the rotten and bankrupt traditions of the old Social Democracy and its parliamentary shadow life, the Spartacists paved the way for the new revolutionary tactics: for extra-parliamentary mass action, they tirelessly called for mass strikes until the first successes strengthened and raised their self-confidence and the workers' fighting courage.

After every attempt, the waves of the struggle, which had hardly been moved at all, fell and leveled out, and a leaden calm seemed to take hold of the spirit of the masses. This was the work of an iron will and a faith that moves mountains, one which wouldn't let up for a single day in these four-and-a-quarter-years, which wouldn't give up the unflagging work of mining and digging, which refused to fall into cozy pessimism toward the "German masses," which served as a cheap excuse for the Independents' own laziness.

The Spartacists never despaired, just as they never hesitated. They whistled cheerfully in their barred cells as they had at work, in the trenches as they had in the conspiratorial counseling quarters where informants were sniffing around and bloodhounds surrounded them. They sharpened their arrows, spread their flyers, tugged roughly at the conscience of the masses, boldly threw the gauntlet over and over in the face of the jubilant colossus of imperialism.

When the colossus fell crashing to the ground from its clay feet on November 9, the German proletariat finally stood up to its full height and the revolution began.

The bourgeoisie also began a crusade starting from the first day of the revolution—the petty bourgeoisie, the military brass, the Ebert and Scheidemann clique: all the counterrevolutionary elements opposed to the Spartacus League. That was what it [the Spartacus League] got for fulfilling its duty under the saber dictatorship of imperialism. At the same time, the reliable instinct of the guardians of a threatened capitalist social order caused it to aim all its poisoned arrows at the beating heart of the proletarian revolution.

---

in eighteenth-century England, a pseudonym probably derived from the anti-monarchist rebel of ancient Rome, Lucius Junius Brutus. Luxemburg's pamphlet combined a critique of the Social Democratic Party of Germany with an analysis of the imperialist causes and devastating military impacts of the First World War, famously warning that humanity stood at the crossroads of socialism or barbarism.

The mortal enemies of the proletariat and socialism have not been betrayed by their instincts. The Spartacus League has a special role to play in the German Revolution, a task of great responsibility, a high duty.

A yawning abyss separates the League from the stooges of the exploiters and the oppressors, from the blood-spattered Ebert-Scheidemann clique—the League has nothing to offer them but a clenched fist.

An abyss also separates it from the Independents [USPD] who have managed, in the five weeks of the revolution, to develop not forward but backward, from the wartime do-nothing critics of Scheidemann's prostitution into active participants in this prostitution, offering a hand to the Ebert-Scheidemann clique to work together in *coups d'état*, intrigues and graves, infamies and pools of blood. Even tomorrow, they may finally cut themselves from the shameful gang of the Ebert government under the pressure of general scorn and their own moral collapse. The word for them is: too late! They are finished as far as the Revolution and the proletariat are concerned. Their path leads off into the morass of the counterrevolution to which they have so long offered their helping hand.

But a boundary also separates us from the wavering, hesitant members of the USPD, who have been embittered by the long fall of Haase, Dittmann and comrades and yet never found the courage or the backbone to denounce them openly, or to begin their great reckoning with the masses, setting them against the alternative resolution of the counterrevolution or their expulsion from the ranks of the fighting proletariat.

Revolutions do not admit of any half measures, any compromises, any tiptoeing, or cowering. Revolutions require showing one's face, having clear principles, committed hearts and whole men.

Today's revolution, which is only in its first stage of development, which has enormous prospects before it and world-historical problems to overcome, must have an infallible compass to point unfailingly toward the same grand goals, in every stage of its fight, in every victory and defeat: toward the socialist world revolution, toward the relentless power struggle of the proletariat for humanity's liberation from the yoke of capital.

This compass, this wedge, pointing and pushing to be the socialist, proletarian yeast of the revolution—that is the specific task of the Spartacus League in the current struggle between two worlds.

History is the only true teacher of the proletariat and revolution is its best school. They will ensure that the "little flock" of the most slandered and most persecuted will, step by step, become what its worldview affirms in it: the fighting and triumphing masses of the revolutionary socialist proletariat.

Founding Congress of the Communist Party of Germany*

I. SPEECH IN SUPPORT OF KPD PARTICIPATION IN THE NATIONAL ASSEMBLY ELECTIONS

Every one of us, including Comrade Levi, is filled with joy by the source of the mood of fierce opposition that developed here during his speech.† We understand and value inordinately the revolutionary spirit and resolve that you display; when Comrade Rühle warns you all about opportunism,‡ we shall ignore this reproach. Perhaps our work has not been in vain, considering such resolute party comrades. The danger of opportunism is not as great as Comrade Rühle suggested here. I am convinced that it is our duty to speak loudly and clearly when we represent an opinion that opposes yours. We would be pitiful representatives of the Spartacus League, standing defiantly against the world, if we didn't have the courage to stand and face our own comrades.

The joy that I just expressed regarding the mood that you express so thunderously is not unambivalent. I don't know whether to laugh or cry when I think about this joy. I am convinced that you want to be a bit too comfortable and hasty in your radicalism, as your calls of "on with the vote!" demonstrate. That is not the kind of maturity and seriousness that belong in this hall. I am deeply convinced that we must contemplate and deal with this matter calmly. We are called to the greatest tasks of world history, and we cannot consider with too much thoroughness and maturity the steps that lie ahead of us if we are to be sure of reaching our goal. Such important decisions cannot be forced. We should take a contemplative and serious attitude that is not counter to revolutionary spirit but essential to it.

I want to give a short example of the lack of consideration you are giving to matters that demand mature scrutiny. One comrade here, calling vehemently from the side and spurred on by revolutionary impatience, demands that we waste no time. Discussing one of the most important questions is called wasting time! This comrade justifies himself by referring to Russia, an example that suggests a lack of care in searching for the correct arguments. The situation in Russia at the time when the National Assembly was rejected was somewhat

---

* This speech was given at the founding congress of the Communist Party of Germany (KPD), which was held from December 30, 1918, to January 1, 1919, in Berlin. It is translated by Henry Holland from Luxemburg's *Gesammelte Werke*, Vol. 4, pp. 479–511.

† Delegated to do so by Spartacus League's Central Committee, Paul Levi approved the newly formed KPD's participation in the elections to the National Assembly.

‡ In his speech, Otto Rühle rejected participation in the elections for the National Assembly and labeled such participation opportunistic.

similar to today's situation in Germany. But have you forgotten that, before the rejection of the National Assembly in November, something else occurred—the revolutionary proletariat's seizure of power? Have you perhaps already secured a socialist government today, a Trotsky-Lenin government? Russia has had a long history of revolution, which Germany has not. In Russia, the revolution begins not in March 1917, but in the year 1905. The most recent revolution is but merely the final chapter, behind which lies the full period from 1905 on. You have nothing backing you, apart from the miserable half-revolution on November 9 [1918]. We must persistently ask what would now benefit the revolution the most, what its next tactical tasks would look like, and how these should be articulated.

Don't be in such a hurry but be patient enough to hear me out. Some among us want to labor in parliament with slogans. But that is not what it comes down to. Which is the surest path to educating the masses in Germany about their tasks? Your tactics assume such a constellation of circumstances that, in fourteen days, when people are departing from Berlin, it will be possible to build a new government in the city. "We are going to build a new government here in fourteen days." I would be delighted if this were to turn out to be the case. But as a serious politician, I cannot construct my tactics based on speculation. Not all possibilities have been exhausted, however. I will need to expand upon those possibilities that will be brought about by the government's new course, the next phase of a very tough conflict. But I am duty bound to pursue those paths revealed to me through my consideration of the conditions in Germany. The tasks are extraordinary and concern the socialist world revolution. But what we have seen in Germany until now is the continuing immaturity of the masses. Our next task is to prepare the masses to fulfil these tasks. Some, apparently, want to achieve this through parliamentarism. The word should decide matters. I tell you* that, precisely thanks to the immaturity of the masses, who have, until now, not understood how they can lead the system of councils to victory, the counterrevolution has managed to erect the National Assembly as a bulwark against us. And now our road leads straight through the middle of this bulwark. It is my duty to direct all common sense against this, to enter into the National Assembly, to bang my fist on the table there, [and to state that] the people's will is the highest law. It is here that we must decide. When the mass has been won over to the level of maturity of the [revolutionary] minority, it will form itself into the ruling power, and its representatives will expel those groups from the temple who have no place there, our opponents, the bourgeoisie, the petty bourgeois, etc. But the mass has not [yet] reached this point.

---

* At this point in her speech Luxemburg switches to the polite and formal version of "you" in German, expressed as "*Ihnen*" and "*Sie*," in contrast to the informal, second person plural form, "*ihr*" and "*euch*," which she had been using.

You have to be consistent in your arguments. On the one hand, you speculate based on the outward appearance of such maturation, and count on such revolutionary power and consciousness among the masses that you promise to install a socialist government to replace the National Assembly within fourteen days. On the other hand, you state that, should a National Assembly be formed, the pressure from the street will sweep it away. Do not delude yourselves that, if we were to instruct the masses not to cast their ballots into the ballot boxes, then the elections would look different. The elections represent a new instrument in the revolutionary struggle. You, on the other hand, are still imprisoned in old mental structures. For you, the only thing that exists is the Imperial German Parliament. You cannot imagine using these means in a revolutionary spirit. You understand either machine guns or parliamentarism. We, however, want a more refined form of radicalism. Not merely this coarse-grained "either/or" variety. Yes, it's simpler and more comfortable, but it is a simplification that will not serve to educate and guide the masses.

From a purely practical viewpoint, would you really be able to say, with a clear conscience, if you were to agree upon the boycott that you are the primary core of the German working class? And that, as the representatives of the revolutionary class, you are able to assure people with a clear conscience that the mighty masses of the working class will in fact follow your calls for a boycott, and not take part? I am talking about the great masses and not about the groups that belong to us. Here we must consider millions of men, women, young people, and soldiers. I ask you clearly if you can say, with a good conscience, that these masses—if we were to agree here on boycotting the National Assembly—would turn their backs on the elections or, better still, raise their fists against the National Assembly? You cannot assert that with a clear conscience. We know about the circumstances that prevail among the masses, and how very unripe those masses still are. The fact remains that, at the very point at which we want to bring revolutionary spirit into these minds, you cut off the possibility of wrenching supremacy out of the hands of the counterrevolution. While we support activity in the revolutionary sense of the word, you make yourselves comfortable, ignore counterrevolutionary plots, and leave the masses exposed to counterrevolutionary influences. You yourselves surely feel that you can't do this.

How can you influence the elections if you declare, from the start, that we view them as null and void? We have to show the masses that there is no better answer to the counterrevolutionary motion against the system of councils than to achieve a massive demonstration of voters, who vote for precisely those people who oppose the National Assembly and support the system of councils. That is the active method of redirecting the firearm that is being aimed at us, by aiming it at our opponent's breast. You must understand that the individual who states that he suspects us of opportunism has not taken the time—under work and time constraints—to assess calmly and thoroughly both his and our position.

This can only be about which method is better suited to serving the common purpose of educating the masses. No one is talking about opportunism in this hall—Comrade Rühle, please note that! When you say, "I am concerned about the damaging consequences of parliamentarism for the masses," your argument contains a deep contradiction. On the one hand, you are so sure about the masses' revolutionary maturity that you start from the premise of constructing a socialist government here—i.e., reaching the definitive end of socialism—within just fourteen days. On the other hand, you are scared, on behalf of the same so-very-ripe masses, about the dangerous effects of voting. I have to say to you frankly that I am scared of nothing at all. I am convinced that the masses, right from the start, are born and created through the overall situation in such a way that they will understand our tactics correctly. We have to guide the masses in the spirit of our tactics so that they understand how to utilize the instrument of voting not as a weapon of the counterrevolution, but rather as one used by class-conscious, revolutionary masses to crush those people who have pressed it into our hands.

I will conclude by formulating a concept: in terms of our purpose and intention, nothing divides us at all, we stand on the same ground of fighting against the National Assembly as a counterrevolutionary bulwark, of mobilizing the masses and rousing them to destroy the National Assembly. It remains a question of expedience and method. Your methods are simpler and more comfortable, while ours are rather more complicated, and I value them for that very reason, because they will deepen the revolutionary consciousness of the masses. Moreover, your tactics involve speculation about the unstable circumstances of the coming weeks, while ours keep in sight the long path still ahead of us, in terms of guiding the masses. Our tactics calculate the immediate tasks in the context of all the tasks of the revolution that lie before us, up to the point where the German proletarian masses are mature enough to take the reins themselves. You tilt at windmills when you insinuate that I use opportunist arguments. We will have to utilize the street—after all, our tactics are based on developing our main activities on the street. What you say proves that you either want to use machine guns, or you want to get into the German Reichstag. It's exactly the opposite! The street should rise to a position of rule and of triumph everywhere. We want to plant a victorious banner inside the National Assembly, based on activity taking place outside. We want to blow up this bulwark from the inside. We want the stage in the National Assembly and at all electoral rallies. Whether or not you pass the motion in this way or another, you stand with us on common ground, on the ground of the revolutionary struggle against the National Assembly.

II. SPEECH AGAINST A UNITARY ECONOMIC-POLITICAL ORGANIZATION FOR THE WORKERS' MOVEMENT

Comrades! Far from regretting that a so-called debate on the trade unions has developed out of today's discussion, I actively welcome this. It was evident from the moment we approached the work of addressing our economic tasks that we would immediately confront the great wall that the trade unions have erected before us. The question of the struggle for liberation is identical with the question of combating the trade unions. There is ten times more justification for doing this in Germany than in other countries because Germany is the only country that has seen no wage movements in four years of world war, and this on trade union orders. Even if the unions hadn't done anything else, for that alone they deserve to perish tenfold. During the course of the war and the revolution, up to the present day, the official unions have shown themselves to be a bourgeois state institution, an organization of the capitalist ruling class. This is why it's obvious that the struggle concerning socialization in Germany has to prioritize considerations about the liquidation of these trade union obstacles that block socialization. Which methods should be used to achieve this liquidation? Which better structure should replace the trade unions?

I must position myself decidedly against the proposal of the comrade, who, in a Bremen motion,* proposes what is alleged to be a unitary organization. They have failed to notice one thing. We are in the process of expanding the workers' and soldiers' councils into the vehicles of all political and social needs and means of power of the working class. This perspective needs to be definitive for the organs of the economic struggle.

The guiding principles† elucidate a central point: the workers' councils are called upon to lead and to oversee economic battles from the standpoint of their companies. Works councils,‡ voted for by company representatives in cooperation with workers' councils that also emerged from the companies, are

* This refers to a motion from Felix Schmidt (Hannover), Ernst Rieger (Berlin) and others to make it obligatory for KPD members to resign from the trade unions. The motion was withdrawn. Schmidt and the others argued that belonging to trade union congresses was incompatible with the KPD's aims and tasks. They called for the creation of workers' organizations, geographically limited to local areas, that would take over production after a victorious revolution. These organizations were styled as "unitary organizations" *(Einheitsorganisationen)*.

† Luxemburg is referring to the "*Wirtschaftliche Übergangsforderungen für die Industrie- und Handelsarbeiter*" (Transitional Economic Demands for Industry and Trade Workers). Parts of this text were printed in the newspaper *Freiheit* (Berlin), No. 83, December 18, 1918, and in the *Deutsche Allgemeine Zeitung* (Berlin), No. 664, December 31, 1918, and distributed at the Party Congress.

‡ Here Luxemburg differentiates between the recently established workers' councils—in German, "*Arbeiterräte*," with strong similarities to the Russian soviets—and *works councils*, in German "*Betriebsräte*," a more traditional and conservative form of worker participation still found in many companies in Europe and North America today. She uses "*Betriebsräte*" at this point in her speech.

collaborating to lead the Imperial Economic Councils (*Reichswirtschaftsräte*).* You will have noted that the guiding principles are aimed at nothing less than the complete hollowing out of all functions of the unions. (Applause.) We expropriate those functions from the unions that the workers trusted, and that betrayed them. We replace the unions with a new system based on completely different foundations. The comrades who propagate a unitary organization appear to be entangled in thinking. [...]†

Those were the means and paths that could have been seized before the revolution. Today, we have to concentrate on the system of workers' councils; the organizations should not be tied together using a combination of the old form, union and party, but should rather be put on a completely new footing—works councils, workers' councils, and others rising up to form an entirely new structure that has nothing in common with the old, inherited tradition.

We should not unthinkingly accept a motion of this sort from Bremen and Berlin. For me, the slogan of withdrawing from the unions comes with a small snag. What's going to happen to the prodigious financial means currently in the hands of these union gentlemen? That is merely a small, practical question. I would not like us to forget all aspects of the process of liquidating the unions. And I do not want a separation in which perhaps part of the means of power remains in those union hands.

I conclude with this proposal: I would like to advance the motions that have been brought here to the same Economic Commission that worked on these headnotes. This commission has been voted in by those workers' and soldiers' councils that stand on the same ground as the Spartacus League, and the commission works through consultation with members of the Spartacus Central Committee. It does not feel that it has a mandate to formulate final decisions but has, instead, worked on these guiding principles to present them to comrades throughout the country. The various memberships should engage with this literature, so that everything can be placed on the widest possible democratic foundation, and so that every individual participates. Then we can be sure that what we have produced is a ripe fruit of the struggle. I ask you to consider your proposals simply as proposals, to forward them to the Economic Commission, and to present them in accordance with the guidelines of the various memberships.

---

* At the Second Congress of the Councils of Workers, Peasants and Soldiers, April 8–14, 1919, delegates voted for a motion brought by Max Cohen-Reuss of the SPD Majority, intended to create "chambers of work" (*Arbeitskammer*) as a counterpart to the chambers of commerce (*Handelskammer*) that had existed since the early 1800s. "Imperial Economic Councils" is a literal translation of *Reichswirtschafträte*. This body is referred to by politicians, economists and other contemporaries between the end of 1918 and the middle of 1919.

† Omission in the original.

III. OUR PROGRAM AND THE POLITICAL SITUATION

Comrades! As we approach the task today of discussing and adopting our program,* more lies behind this endeavor than the formal fact that we constituted a new, independent party yesterday, and that the new party has to officially adopt a program. Great historical processes lie behind today's deliberations: the time has come when the entire socialist program of the proletariat must be constructed on new foundations. Party comrades, this binds us together with the threads spun by Marx and Engels in the *Communist Manifesto* exactly seventy years ago. As you know, *The Communist Manifesto* treats socialism and the execution of socialist final goals as the immediate task of the proletarian revolution. This was the basic approach taken by Marx and Engels in the 1848 Revolution and also the approach they saw as the foundation for proletarian action in the international sphere. At that time, both of them, together with all leading minds of the proletarian movement, thought that they faced the immediate task of introducing socialism; all that was necessary was to carry out the political revolution, and seize the political authority of the state, in order to immediately constitute socialism in flesh and blood. The preface to the [new German edition of the] *Communist Manifesto* of 1872, signed jointly by Marx and Engels (reprinted in the edition of 1894), says:

> No special stress is to be laid on the revolutionary measures proposed at the end of Section II. That passage would, in many respects, be worded very differently today. In view of the gigantic strides of modern industry in the last twenty-five years, and of the accompanying improved and extended party organization of the working class, in view of the practical experience gained, first in the February Revolution, and then, still more, in the Paris Commune, where the proletariat for the first time held political power for two full months, this program has in some details become antiquated. One thing especially was proved by the Commune, viz., that "the working class cannot simply lay hold of the ready-made state machinery, and wield it for its own purposes."†

And how was that passage worded [in the original edition of 1847], which was declared out-of-date? It reads as follows that on page 23:‡

> The proletariat will use its political supremacy to wrest, by degrees, all capital from the bourgeoisie, to centralize all instruments of production in the hands of

* See *Gesammelte Werke*, Vol. 4, pp. 440–49.

† Marx and Engels. "Preface to the 1872 German Edition of the *Manifesto of the Communist Party*, in *Marx-Engels Collected Works*, Vol. 23 (New York: International Publishers, 1988), p. 175.

‡ Here, Luxemburg refers to the page numbering of the original 1872 German edition: Friedrich Engels and Karl Marx, "Vorwort [zur deutschen Ausgabe von 1872]," in *Werke*, Vol. 4, p. 573–4.

the state, i.e., of the proletariat organized as the ruling class; and to increase the total of productive forces as rapidly as possible.

Of course, in the beginning, this cannot be effected except by means of despotic inroads on the rights of property and on the conditions of bourgeois production; by measures, therefore, which appear economically insufficient and untenable, but which, in the course of the movement, outstrip themselves, necessitate further inroads upon the old social order, and are unavoidable as a means of entirely revolutionizing the mode of production.

These measures will, of course, be different in different countries.

Nevertheless, in most advanced countries however, the following will be pretty generally applicable.

1. Abolition of property in land and application of all rents of land to public purposes.

2. A heavy progressive or graduated income tax.

3. Abolition of all rights of inheritance.

4. Confiscation of the property of all emigrants and rebels.

5. Centralization of credit in the hands of the state, by means of a national bank with state capital and an exclusive monopoly.

6. Centralization of the means of communication and transport in the hands of the State.

7. Extension of factories and instruments of production owned by the State; the bringing into cultivation of wastelands, and the improvement of the soil generally in accordance with a common plan.

8. Equal liability of all to work. Establishment of industrial armies, especially for agriculture.

9. Combination of agriculture with manufacturing industries; gradual abolition of all the distinction between town and country by a more equable distribution of the populace over the country.

10. Free education for all children in public schools. Abolition of children's factory labor in its present form. Combination of education with industrial production, etc., etc.*

As you see, these are the same tasks, with some variations, that we are facing today: the introduction and realization of socialism. Seventy years of capitalist development lie between the time when the program was formulated and the present day, and the dialectics of history have led us to the point where we return today to the position Marx and Engels subsequently abandoned as erroneous. Back then, they had good reason for relinquishing it as an error. The development of capital in the intervening period has taken us to a point where what was error then has become truth today, and it is our immediate task today

---

* *Manifesto of the Communist Party*, in *Marx-Engels Collected Works*, Vol. 6, pp. 504–5.

to fulfil what Marx and Engels stood for in the year 1848. Between that point of development, the beginning, and our understanding and task today lies no less than the whole evolution not merely of capitalism, but also of the socialist workers' movement, and primarily that movement in Germany, as the leading country of the modern proletariat.

This development has taken a peculiar form. After Marx and Engels—affected by the disappointments of the 1848 Revolution—relinquished their view that the proletariat was immediately and directly capable of realizing socialism, in every country Social Democratic and socialist parties were formed that adopted a quite different standpoint. The daily petty struggle in political and economic fields was declared to be the immediate task, in order to train the army of the proletariat bit by bit, an army that would be called upon when capitalist development had ripened to the point where socialism could be realized. This substitution, this entirely different foundation for the socialist program, was given a very typical form particularly in Germany. As the authoritative source for Social Democracy in Germany up to its collapse on August 4 [1914], the Erfurt Program put immediate and so-called "minimum" tasks at the top of the agenda, with socialism itself, located merely as a guiding star in the distance, as the final goal. What is decisive, however, is not what was written in the program, but rather the living interpretation of the program; an important historical document of our workers' movement was definitive in how the program was understood—namely the preface which Friedrich Engels wrote in 1895 to *The Class Struggles in France, 1848 to 1850*. Party comrades! I do not reopen this question out of mere historical interest, but rather as an utterly current question and a historical duty that we will have to face by building our program today on the same foundations that served Marx and Engels in 1848. With respect to the changes that historical developments have brought about in the intervening period, we have a duty to undertake a revision, consciously and with utter clarity, in opposition to the views that guided German Social Democracy up until the collapse on August 4. This revision shall be officially undertaken here.

Party comrades, how did Engels formulate the question in that famous preface to Marx's *The Class Struggles in France*,* which he wrote in the year 1895, i.e., after Marx's death? First, reflecting right back to 1848, he demonstrated that the conviction that the socialist revolution is at hand is outdated. Then he continues with this description:

---

* Engels's 1895 introduction to *Class Struggles in France* (already toned down in recognition of the censorship laws) was watered down by reformists in an SPD reprint in *Vorwärts* that implied that he favored peaceful, legal change and believed barricade street fighting to be an outdated way to achieve power.

> History has proved us, and all who thought like us, wrong. It has made it clear that the state of economic development on the Continent at that time was not, by a long way, ripe for the removal of capitalist production; it has proved this by the economic revolution which, since 1848, has seized the entire Continent, has really caused big industry for the first time to take root in France, Austria, Hungary, Poland and, recently, in Russia, while it has made Germany positively an industrial country of the first rank—all on a capitalist basis, which in the year 1848, therefore, still had great capacity for expansion.*

He then lays out how everything has changed since that period, arriving at the question of what the tasks of the parties in Germany are now:

> The war of 1870–71 and the defeat of the Commune had transferred the center of gravity of the European workers' movement for the time being from France to Germany, as Marx foretold. In France, it naturally took years to recover from the bloodletting of May 1871. In Germany, on the other hand, where industry was, in addition, furthered (in positively hothouse fashion) by the blessings of the French milliards and developed more and more quickly, Social Democracy experienced a much more rapid and enduring growth. Thanks to the understanding with which the German workers made use of the universal suffrage introduced in 1866, the astonishing growth of the Party is made plain to all the world by incontestable figures.†

Then follows the famous account of how our vote grew from one Reichstag election to the next into the millions, from which Engels draws the following conclusion:

> With this successful utilization of universal suffrage, an entirely new mode of proletarian struggle came into force, and this quickly developed further. It was found that the state institutions, in which the rule of the bourgeoisie is organized, offer still further opportunities for the working class to fight these very state institutions. They took part in elections to individual diets, to municipal councils and to industrial courts; they contested every post against the bourgeoisie in the occupation of which a sufficient part of the proletariat had its say. And so it happened that the bourgeoisie and the government came to be much more afraid of the legal than of the illegal action of the workers' party, of the results of elections than of those of rebellion.‡

---

* Frederick Engels, "Introduction to Karl Marx's *The Class Struggles in France*, 1848 to 1850" [1895], in *Marx-Engels Collected Works*, Volume 27 (New York: International Publishers, 1990), p. 512.

† Frederick Engels, "Introduction to Karl Marx's *The Class Struggles in France*, 1848 to 1850" [1895], in *Marx-Engels Collected Works*, Volume 27, p. 512.

‡ Frederick Engels, "Introduction to Karl Marx's *The Class Struggles in France*, 1848 to 1850" [1895], in *Marx-Engels Collected Works*, Volume 27 pp. 514–15, 516.

And here Engels appends an extended critique of the illusion which suggests that under the modern relations of capitalism the proletariat can achieve anything at all on the street, through revolution. I believe that it is time, in light of where we stand today, in the middle of the revolution, a revolution characterized by street fighting, to confront the approach that was officially German Social Democracy's bread and butter down to the final hour, and which is responsible for the events of August 4, 1914. ("Quite right!")

I do not intend to say that Engels made himself personally complicit in the entire development of events in Germany. I am merely saying that this is a classic documentation of the position that was vitally alive in German Social Democracy—or rather of the position that killed it. This is the point, party comrades, at which Engels argues—with all his specialized knowledge in the realm of military science—that it is pure illusion to believe that the working people can carry out a revolution through street fighting, given the contemporary development of military technique and of industry. Counterposing the balance of forces in this way had two conclusions: Firstly, the parliamentary struggle came to be seen as the opposite of the proletariat's direct revolutionary action, and as being well-nigh the only means of class struggle. This critique issued into what we can call the pure form of "parliamentarism-only." Secondly, and in a remarkable fashion, that which is precisely the mightiest organization of the class state—militarism, the mass of proletarians stuffed into army uniforms—was perceived as, from the start, immune from and not accessible to any form of socialist influence. And when the preface says it's sheer foolishness to think the proletariat could ever successfully manage these machine guns and soldiers armed with the newest technical means of battle, given the developments today of huge armies, the preface is obviously working with the assumption that whoever is a soldier supports the ruling classes, from the beginning to forever. This mistake would be almost incomprehensible coming from a man who stood at the forefront of our movement, when judged from the standpoint of our experience today, if we did not know the circumstances under which the historical document was actually written. With all honor to our two great masters, and specifically to Engels, who died much later, and who honorably represented Marx's positions, we must make clear that it is known that Engels wrote this preface under direct pressure from the parliamentary group in the Reichstag of that day. That was in the period when in Germany—after the Antisocialist Laws had been dismantled at the start of the [18]90s—a strong left radical current had made itself felt inside the German workers' movement, which wanted to save the party from being absorbed into a purely parliamentary struggle. In order to smash the radical elements theoretically, and to keep them down practically, in order to prevent their views from gaining recognition among the wide masses through the authority of our great teachers, Bebel and his comrades urged Engels—it was characteristic of our situation back then, since the parliamentary group in the Reichstag decided, both intellectually and tactically, the party's tasks and destiny—to write that preface, it now being of the most the urgent necessity to save the German workers' movement from anarchistic derailments.* And from then on, this apprehension really did dominate the deeds, but also the non-deeds, of German Social Democracy, up until the lovely incident on August 4, 1914. This was the proclamation of "parliamentarism only." Engels did not live to experience the practical consequences of this application of his theory.

I am convinced—and anyone who knows the works of Marx and Engels and knows the vital and revolutionary, genuine, undistorted spirit that breathes in all their teachings and writings, must also be convinced—that Engels would have been the first to have protested against this dissipation and ruination of the workers' movement that had already taken hold in Germany decades before August 4. August 4 did not fall on us out of the blue as an unfortunate malfunction but was, rather, the logical consequence of that which we had experienced day by day and year by year. ("Quite right!") I am certain that Engels and Marx, if they had lived, would have been the first to protest this with all their power, and to haul the cart back with a mighty hand so that it did not roll down into the swamp. But Engels died in the same year in which he wrote the preface. We lost him in the year 1895; since then, unfortunately, the theoretical leadership has passed out of Engels' hands and into Kautsky's. We witnessed how every protest from the left against this "parliamentarism only" that occurred at every Party Congress—supported by a sometimes larger, sometimes smaller groups of comrades, who battled tenaciously against this spreading swamp, the perilous consequences of which must be clear to all—would be stigmatized as anarchism, anarcho-socialism, or at least anti-Marxism. Official Marxism was intended to serve as a cover for every settling of scores, every deviation from the real revolutionary class struggle, every half-baked measure that condemned German Social Democracy and the entire workers' movement—including the trade unions—to wasting away in the framework of and upon the soil of capitalist society without genuinely aspiring to shake up society and throw it off the rails.

Now, party comrades, we are experiencing a moment today in which we can say that we have returned to Marx and stand under his banner. When we declare in our program today that the proletariat's immediate task is nothing less than—summarized in a few words—transforming socialism into truth and deed, and destroying capitalism root and branch, we stand on the same ground occupied by Marx and Engels in 1848, terrain that we have never, in principle, deviated from. Now we'll see what true Marxism is and what this

---

* In 1895, the SPD was engaged in a bitter dispute within its ranks concerning *Der Jungen*, an anarchist current; by the end of the year, *Der Jungen* adherents were expelled from the party, at Bebel's insistence. Luxemburg often noted that, while the SPD took a hard line against the anarchists, it never sought to expel the Revisionists.

ersatz Marxism was ("Spot on!"), which for so long made itself at home in German Social Democracy. You can see where this kind of Marxism leads by today's representatives: the henchmen Ebert and David and their consorts. These are the official representatives of the doctrine that presented itself as the true and unadulterated form of Marxism for decades. No, Marxism does not lead to a place where we pursue counterrevolutionary politics alongside the "Scheidemen."* True Marxism fights against those who attempt to falsify it, it digs like a mole among the foundations of capitalist society and leads us to a situation where the best part of the German proletariat marches under our flag, under the revolution's coat of arms; even on the other side, where the counterrevolution seems to rule, we have our supporters and future comrades in battle.

Thus we stand here today, party comrades, led, as I mentioned before, through the dialectical process of history and enriched by seventy years of fully concluded capitalist development, on the spot where Marx and Engels stood in 1848 as they unfurled the banner of international socialism for the first time. Back then, while checking over the errors and illusions of the year 1848, it was thought that the proletariat had an everlasting journey ahead of them until socialism could become reality. Of course, serious theoreticians have never been content with positing any particular date for the breakdown of capitalism as obligatory and reliable. But roughly speaking, it was imagined that a very long journey still lay ahead, and that was expressed in every line of that very preface that Engels wrote in 1895. But now we can draw a conclusion about this calculation. Was it not, in comparison to the development of earlier class struggles, a very short period? Seventy years of large-scale capitalist development have sufficed to bring us to a point today where we can start getting serious about ridding the world of capitalism. And what's more, not only are we capable of carrying out this task today, it is not merely our duty to the proletariat to do so. Rather, meeting this challenge is the only way whatsoever of salvaging the existence of human society. (Vigorous applause.)

Because, party comrades, what of bourgeois society has this war left behind it, except a huge pile of ruins? Formally speaking, all means of production are still held in the hands of the ruling classes, with almost all decisive means of power. We're under no illusions about that. But what they're able to set in motion with these means—apart from convulsive attempts to re-establish exploitation through bloodbaths—is nothing other than anarchy. They have reached the point where the dilemma facing humankind today can be described as either descent into anarchy, or salvation through socialism. On the terrain of their class supremacy, and of capitalism, it is impossible for the bourgeois classes to use the results of the World War to find any kind of way out. And

* A pun on Scheidemann's name, the German word "*schiede*" meaning "divorced."

thus, it has come about that we have reached precisely the truth Marx and Engels first pronounced as the scientific basis of socialism in that great charter, *The Communist Manifesto*: socialism will become a historical necessity, which we can experience today in the most exact meaning of the word. Socialism has become a necessity, not merely because the proletariat is no longer willing to live under the conditions that the capitalist classes serve up to them, but also because, if the proletariat does not fulfil its class duties by realizing socialism, then we shall all face ruination together. (Vigorous applause.)

Now that, party comrades, is the general basis on which we construct the party program we are officially adopting today, the draft of which is in the pamphlet *What Does the Spartacus League Want?** This program stands in conscious opposition to the standpoint on which the Erfurt Program was based; it consciously opposes the distinction made between the immediate, self-styled "minimum demands" of the political and economic struggle on the one hand, and the socialist final goal, described as the maximum program, on the other. In conscious opposition to this, we choose to liquidate the results of the last seventy years of development, and especially the immediate results of the World War, by saying: there is no minimum and no maximum program for us, socialism is one and the same thing: that is the minimum we have to promote in today's world. ("Absolutely!")

I will not now go into details on individual measures that we have laid before you in our draft program, because you can take up positions on each of these individually, and it would be a step too far to discuss the details here. I see it as my task to merely trace out and articulate those general, essential features that differentiate our program from *so-called* official German Social Democracy. I consider it more important and urgent that we reach agreement about how to evaluate concrete circumstances, our tactical challenges, and the practical solutions given the political situation, about the course of the revolution until now, and about further, foreseeable directives. We intend to discuss the political situation in accordance with the understanding I have attempted to sketch—from the standpoint of the realization of socialism as the immediate task—which should light the way forward for every other measure, and every other commentary.

Comrades, our Party Congress today, which is, as I believe I may say with pride, the inaugural Party Congress of the only revolutionary socialist party of the German proletariat, is taking place, coincidentally—or rather, truth be told, not by coincidence—at the same time as a turning point in the development of the German Revolution itself. After the events of the last few days, we may say that the first act of the German Revolution has been concluded, that we now enter into a second, further stage of development, and that it is the duty

* See pp. 301–9, above.

of all of us—in order to gain a better, deeper understanding of the future—to practice self-criticism, to undertake a reflective, critical examination of what's been achieved, what we've done, and what we've failed to do, in order to get a handle on how we should proceed. Let us, then, carefully scrutinize the events of the first act of the revolution!

Its point of departure was November 9 [1918]. The Revolution of November 9 was full of shortcomings and weaknesses. This should not come as a surprise. The revolution followed four years of war, four years during which the German proletariat—schooled by Social Democracy and the trade unions—displayed a measure of ignominy and repudiation of their socialist vocations to an extent unparalleled in any other country. Standing on the ground of historical development, which is exactly what we do as Marxists and socialists, we cannot expect the same Germany that produced the terrible spectacle of August 4 and the following four years would experience a glorious revolution directed by class consciousness toward a clear aim. What we experienced on November 9 was the breakdown of three-quarters of existing imperialism, and only one-quarter the victory of a new principle. (Agreement.) The moment had simply arrived in which imperialism—a colossus with feet of clay, crumbling from within—had to fall apart; what came next was a more or less chaotic and aimless movement, with very little consciousness, in which the unifying thread and the constant, redemptive principle were summarized into one single slogan: build workers' and soldiers' councils. That's the watchword of this revolution that, despite all the shortcomings and weaknesses of the first moment, established its place among proletarian socialist revolutions. We should never forget, when they argue with us, using their calumnies against the Russian Bolsheviks, to answer with the question: Where did you learn the ABCs of your current revolution then? You learned of workers' and soldiers' councils from the Russians. (Agreement.) Those little folks who see themselves as authorized heads of the so-called German socialist government go hand in hand with the English imperialists in their murderous attack on the Russian Bolsheviks, who derive their power, at least formally, from the workers' and soldiers' councils. With that, they must admit that the Russian Revolution first created the watchwords for the world revolution. We can say with certainty—and this follows, as a matter of course, from the overall situation—that, in whichever country the proletarian revolution breaks out after Germany, the first step will be to build workers' and soldiers' councils. ("Quite right!")

It is precisely in this that we have the unifying international bond for our proceedings; this is the cue that distinguishes our revolution utterly from all earlier, bourgeois revolutions, and it is very characteristic of the dialectical contradictions among which this revolution—as do all revolutions—moves, that on November 9, as it emitted its first cry, its birth cry, as it were, it had already found the watchword that leads us forward to socialism: workers' and soldiers' councils. This was what rallied everything together. The revolution instinctively found this watchword, even though it was still so backward in terms of its shortcomings, weaknesses, lack of initiative and clarity of aims that it nearly managed to let half of the instruments of power that it had conquered on November 9 slip out of its hands on the second day after the revolution. This demonstrates that on the one hand, the revolution today is subject to the superior law of historical necessity, which guarantees that we will advance step by step toward our goal, despite all difficulties, entanglements, and our own errors. On the other hand, one must say, when one compares this clear slogan with the paucity of practical results attached to it, that these were simply the first childlike steps of the revolution, which still has more mighty things to achieve and a long way to go to mature into a complete realization of its first watchwords.

Party comrades, the first phase from November 9 until the last few days has been filled with illusions from all sides. The first illusion of the proletarians and soldiers who made this revolution was their belief in the possibility of unity under the banner of what passes by the name of socialism. What can be more characteristic of the revolution of November 9 than that its first result was leadership passing into the hands of those who only two hours before the outbreak of the revolution considered it their chief duty to agitate against it ("Absolutely!"), to make the revolution impossible—and place it into the hands of Ebert-Scheidemann, along with Haase! The motto of the Revolution of November 9 was the idea of uniting the various socialist currents under the general call for unity—an illusion that would be bloodily avenged. The events of the last few days have produced a bitter awakening from such illusions. But the self-deception was universal, affecting Ebert-Scheidemann and the bourgeoisie no less than ourselves. Another illusion held onto by the bourgeoisie in this current moment is believing that by means of the Ebert-Hasse combination, by means of the so-called socialist government, they would be able to control the proletarian masses and strangle the socialist revolution. Another illusion of the Ebert-Scheidemann government is that, with the aid of soldiers returning from the front, they would be able to hold down the working masses in their socialist class struggle.

These were the multifarious illusions which that the recent events—a full gamut of illusions that have now trickled away into nothingness. We have seen that Haase uniting with Ebert-Scheidemann under the sign of "socialism" is, in reality, nothing other than a fig leaf to cover up a purely counterrevolutionary policy; experience tells us that we will be cured of this self-deception. There is a particular revolutionary method of curing the people of its illusions, but this cure is unfortunately bought at the cost of the blood of the people. This was the case here, as in all previous revolutions. It was the blood of the victims in the Chausseestraße on December 6 and the blood of the murdered naval marines on December 24* that brought the truth home to the masses: that what you've glued together as a so-called socialist government is nothing other than a government of bourgeois counterrevolution, and whoever tolerates this state of affairs is working against the proletariat and against socialism. ("Spot on!")

But, party comrades, the Ebert-Scheidemann gentlemen's illusion that they were capable of permanently holding down the proletariat with the help of soldiers from the front has also trickled away. Because what has resulted from December 6 and from December 24? We've all been able to witness the soldiers' devastating disappointment, and the start of their critical stance against those same gentlemen who wanted to use them as cannon fodder against the socialist proletariat. This, too, is determined by the law of the necessary, objective development of the socialist revolution, that the individual battalions of the workers' movement can be guided to a place—step by step, and through their own bitter experience—wherein they can recognize the true path for the revolution. After Berlin, fresh masses of soldiers were introduced to the field as cannon fodder to suppress the stirrings of the socialist proletariat—and now we are seeing that in barrack after barrack, there comes a demand for the pamphlets of the Spartacus League. Party comrades, this marks the close of the first act. Ebert-Scheidemann's hopes of ruling over the proletariat with the help of backward soldiers have been largely smashed. What they can expect in the not-too-distant future is an ever clearer revolutionary understanding in the barracks, causing the army of the fighting proletariat to grow and the forces of counterrevolution to dwindle. From this it follows that another political actor still has to lose its illusions, and that is the bourgeoisie, the ruling class. If you read the newspapers of the last few days after the events of December 24, you will notice a very pronounced and clear tone of disappointment and outrage: the henchmen up at the top have proven themselves to be inept. ("Quite right!")

People expected that Ebert-Scheidemann would prove themselves to be strong men, capable of taming the beast. And what have they accomplished? They have enacted a couple of inadequate coups, and as a sequel the hydra of the revolution raises its head even more determinedly from the other side. This means a mutual disillusion on all sides! The proletariat has lost all illusions about the combined structure of Ebert-Scheidemann-Haase as a so-called socialist government. Ebert-Scheidemann have rid themselves of the illusion that they can permanently keep down proletarians in workers' clothing with the help of proletarians in uniform. And the bourgeoisie has lost its illusion that they can use Ebert-Scheidemann-Haase to defraud the whole socialist revolution in Germany of its goals. This is nothing but a negative balance, thousands

* On December 24, 1918, counterrevolutionary troops led by Lieutenant General Arnold Lequis attacked the People's Navy Division in the City Palace and the Royal Stables using artillery. In this clash, eleven marines, and fifty-six soldiers from Lequis' troops, lost their lives. The marines were aided by armed Berlin workers. Due to this assistance, the attack failed.

of rags from destroyed illusions. But it is, in truth, a great gain for the proletariat that only these torn shreds remain after the first phase of the revolution, for nothing is more destructive for revolution than illusions, and there is nothing that benefits it more than the clear and open truth. With this conviction, I appeal to a classic figure of German intellect, who was no proletarian revolutionary, but a bourgeois, intellectual revolutionary: I mean Lessing, who, in his final texts, as a librarian in Wolfenbüttel,* wrote the following passage, which I've always liked and found interesting:

> I do not know whether it be a duty to sacrifice fortune and life to the truth … But I know that it is a duty, if one does want to teach the truth, to teach all of it or none at all; to teach it clearly and roundly, without riddles or reserve, and without doubting its power and utility… For the greater the error, the shorter and straighter the way to the truth; refined error, by contrast, can keep the truth eternally distant to us, even as it steadily becomes clearer to us, that it is error … One who thinks merely of hawking truth masked and rouged may well be truth's procurer—but never truth's lover.†

Party comrades, Messieurs Hasse, Dittmann and so forth have wanted to hawk revolution as a socialist commodity, covered with a mask and smeared with rouge, and have proven themselves to be the procurers of the counterrevolution. Today, we are free of these ambiguities and the commodity stands and faces the mass of the German people in the form of the brutal and burly Messieurs Ebert and Scheidemann. Today, even the dullest person cannot fail to see that this is counterrevolution, pure and simple.

What presents itself as the next stage of development now that we have this first phase behind us? This obviously cannot be a question of prophesizing, but rather of drawing logical conclusions from what we've experienced up to now and applying them to likely future paths, in order to build our own tactics, our own way of fighting. Party comrades, where does the road now lead to? You've already received some hints about this in the most recent statements made by the new Ebert-Scheidemann government, in their pure, unadulterated tones. What can the course of this so-called socialist government lead to now that, as I have already shown, an entire set of illusions has disappeared? With each day that passes, this government steadily loses more support among the great mass of the proletariat; besides the petty bourgeoisie, there are only remnants, sad remnants of the proletariat, who stand behind it, but it is very unclear how long even they will remain with Ebert-Scheidemann. These two will lose

* Gotthold Ephraim Lessing held the role of librarian at the famous library of cultural history in Wolfenbüttel, now known as the Herzog August Bibliothek.

† This passage comes from Gotthold Ephraim Lessing, *Eine Duplik* (On Love of Truth), It is translated here by Henry Holland. Another translation may be found at bartleby.com.

increasingly more backing from the soldiers, as they have embarked down the road of critique and of self-reflection, a process that moves slowly at first, but which, however, will not stop for a rest until it has reached full socialist consciousness. They have lost all that was credited to them by the bourgeoisie, because they have shown themselves to be not strong enough. So where can this government's road lead to? Very soon, they will make a clean break with their travesty of socialist politics and, if you read the new political program of these gentlemen, you will see that they sail out into the second phase—the phase of counterrevolution unveiled, yes, what I would call the restoration of earlier pre-revolutionary relations—with full steam ahead. What is the new government's program? It includes the election of a president who will have a position somewhere between the king of England and the American president ("Quite right!"), or, in other words, something near to a King Ebert, and secondly, the reconstruction of the Federal Council Bundesrat. Today, you can read the independently stated demands of the governments of the south of Germany, which reinforce the federal state character of the German Empire.* The reintroduction of the dutiful old Federal Council and also, naturally, of its sidekick, the German Reichstag, is now only a matter of weeks away. Party comrades, Ebert-Scheidemann are simply following the path of restoring relations to the way they were before November 9. But in so doing, they have placed themselves on a slippery slope, which they will tumble down to end up lying with crushed limbs at the bottom of the abyss, because restoring social relations to the way they were before November 9 was already outdated on November 9, and today is far from being possible. The government will be forced into pushing an ever more intense form of counterrevolutionary politics, in order to strengthen the backing from their own class—the bourgeoisie—whose real class interests they represent, a backing that has been weakened by recent developments. A clear wish is expressed in these demands from the southern German states published today in the Berlin newspapers, to bring about what is known as "increased security" for the German Empire, or, to use good German terms for such things, to force through a state of emergency against "anarchistic," "putschist" and "Bolshevist"—i.e., socialist—elements. Circumstances will push Ebert-Scheidemann to resort to a dictatorship, with or without a state of emergency. The consequence of this, however, is that we will experience a much fiercer conflict and much tougher class struggles in this second phase of revolution

---

* Representatives of the governments of Baden, Bavaria, Hesse, and Württemberg had stated the following demands in Stuttgart on December 27–28, 1918: "1. A new structuring of the German Empire as a federal state; 2. the creation of an imperial government and national assembly, capable of political action; 3. speedy implementation of a peace for the German Empire." They spoke against the creation of an exclusively central government that would demote the governments of the individual federal states to provincial administrations. They also demanded to take part in negotiations with the U.S. about deliveries of basic foodstuffs through a delegation representing the shared interests of the southern German governments.

("Absolutely!"), precisely because of prior developments, the logic of the events themselves, and the violence that encumbers the Ebert-Scheidemann project. A much fiercer conflict is ahead, not merely because these political events have inevitably led to the start of combat between the revolution and the counter-revolution—without illusions, hand-to-hand, eye to eye—but also because a new fire, a new flame is increasingly spreading into everything, and that is the flame of economic struggle.

Party comrades, it is very characteristic of the first period of the revolution down to December 24 that—we have to be fully conscious about this—it was still an exclusively political revolution and this is what accounts for the beginner status, the shortcomings, the unfulfilled character and the unconscious aspect of this revolution. This was the first stage of a transformation, the main tasks of which actually involve economic territory, a transformation of economic relations. The revolution was ingenuous, with a child's lack of consciousness, groping its way forward without knowing where it was going, possessing, as we have said, a purely political character. It is only in the last few weeks that strikes have started to make their presence felt, in an utterly spontaneous fashion. We want, now, to come out and say it: it is the essence of this revolution that strikes are growing extensively, and that they will increasingly become the central point and the main cause of the revolution. ("Quite right!") This, then, is an economic revolution, and, as such, will become a socialist revolution. But the battle for socialism can only be fought through the masses, shoulder to shoulder against capitalism, in every workplace, with every proletarian against every employer. Only then can this become a socialist revolution.

From an uninformed perspective, needless to say, people imagined things proceeding differently. People thought it would suffice to merely overthrow the old government and install a socialist government in its place, which would then introduce socialism by decree. This, in its turn, was nothing other than an illusion. Socialism has not been made, and cannot be made, by decrees, and can also not be made by a socialist government, however excellent. Socialism has to be made by the masses, and by every proletarian. Where the chains of capitalism are forged, there must the chains be broken. That alone is socialism, and that is the only way of making socialism.

And what is the external form of this struggle for socialism? The strike, and that's why we are now seeing the economic phase of development coming to the fore in this second period of revolution. I also wish to emphasize here that we can be proud of the following indisputable statement: we in the Spartacus League, the Communist Party of Germany, are the only people in all of Germany who stand by the striking and battling workers. ("Absolutely right!") You will have read and witnessed how the Independent Party positions itself toward the strikes at any opportunity. There has been no difference between the outlook of the *Vörwarts* and that of the *Freiheit*. Both newspapers said the same thing: socialism means hard work and diligence. And they say that even while capital is still in charge! We cannot make socialism in that way, but rather only through carrying on an unremitting struggle against capitalism, the claims of which are defended by people from the most extreme troublemakers to the Independent Party to the *Freiheit*, with the only exception being the Communist Party. Thus we find that all forces that do not stand with us on revolutionary-communist soil are persistent enemies of the strikes.

We may conclude from this that in the forthcoming phase of the revolution, strikes will not only increase in number, but will rather become the central point, the decisive point of the revolution, pushing back the purely political questions. You will thus appreciate that a considerable intensification of the struggle in the economic field will occur. The revolution will come to the point where the bourgeoisie no longer finds it funny. The bourgeoisie can afford mystifications in the political field, where a masquerade is still possible, where people like Ebert-Scheidemann can still pose as socialists in public—but not where profit is at stake. Then the Ebert-Scheidemann government will be forced to choose between these alternatives: either put an end to the strikes and eradicate the movement that threatens to destroy their regime—or the Messieurs of the Ebert-Scheidemann lot will have played their last card. I also believe that their political measures alone will mean that they will have played their last card very soon. The Ebert-Scheidemann lot find it particularly painful that they have not received much trust from the bourgeoisie. The bourgeoisie will think long and hard about whether they will be able to lay the ermine cloak on the coarse upstart Ebert. If things get this far, they will end up saying, "It's not enough that he has blood on his hands—he has to have blue blood in his veins." ("Spot on!") If things get this far then people will say, "If we want to have a king, then we don't need a *parvenu* who can't even behave like a king." (Laughter.)

So, party comrades, Messieurs Ebert-Scheidemann are reaching the point that a counterrevolutionary movement will show itself. They will be unable to quench the blazing flames of the economic class struggle, and they will fail to satisfy the aspirations of the bourgeoisie. They will have to go underground, either in order to make way for an attempt at counterrevolution—which would perhaps take the form of a desperate fight under the command of a Mr. Groener* or an outright military dictatorship under Hindenburg—or they will have to yield to other counterrevolutionary forces.

We cannot predict exactly, nor can we make any clear positive statements about, what will come. But the decisive issue is not outer appearances, or the precise moment when this thing or that thing will occur. It is enough that

---

* The Ebert–Groener pact was the pledge of mutual support made between Ebert, as the head of government of Germany, and Wilhelm Groener, Quartermaster General of the German Army, on November 10, 1918. Ebert effectively placed the ruling SPD on the side of the counterrevolution.

we know the broad strokes of coming developments: after the first phase of revolution, which is one of predominantly political struggle, comes the phase characterized predominantly by an intensification of the economic struggle, during which, sooner or later, the Ebert-Scheidemann government will have to disappear into Hades.

It is equally difficult to predict what will happen to the National Assembly in the second phase of development. It is possible, if it comes into existence, that it will be a new school for the education of the working class. But it is equally possible that no National Assembly at all comes into being—we cannot predict anything. Let me say parenthetically, so that you understand the grounds from which we defended our position yesterday: we were against limiting our tactics to a single alternative. I do not want, at this point, to open up this discussion all over again, but rather to simply state this, so that none of you who are listening superficially can get the idea "Ah, now she's changed her tune." We are in complete accordance with the position we took up yesterday. We do not want to base our tactics in relation to the National Assembly on what is a possibility but not a certainty, that the National Assembly could be blown sky-high.* Rather, we want to base our tactics on all eventualities, should the National Assembly come into being, including its use for revolutionary purposes.

And what will then remain for the rundown Ebert-Scheidemann government, or for any other allegedly Social Democratic government which may get its hands on the tiller? As I have said, the proletariat as a mass has already slipped from their hands; the soldiers, equally, may no longer be used as counterrevolutionary cannon fodder. Which options are still open to these poor little people, to save their situation? They have only one chance left, and if you, party comrades, have read the press reports today, you will have learned where the last reserves are based, which the German counterrevolution will lead into the field against us, if worse comes to worse. You have all read that in Riga the German troops are already proceeding arm in arm with the English against the Russian Bolsheviks. Party comrades, I have documents in my hands here that provide an overview of what is currently being dealt out in Riga. The entire thing is emanating from the Eighth Army's High Command, hand in hand with Herr August Winnig, the German Social Democrat and union leader. It was always presented as a bare fact that the poor Ebert-Scheidemann cohort were the Entente's victims. In reality, *Vörwarts* has, for weeks, since the start of the revolution, been using the tactic of presenting things in such a way as if the Entente's sincere wish were throttling the Revolution in Russia, and it was only through this presentation that the Entente first warmed to the idea. We have proven here with documentary evidence that this plan was carried out at the cost of the Russian proletariat and of the German Revolution. In a telegram of

* Luxemburg uses the phrase "*das nähmlich die Nationalversammlung in die Luft fliegt.*"

December 26, Lieutenant Colonel Buerkner, Chief of the General Staff of the Eighth Army, reports on the negotiations that he traveled to Riga to conclude. The telegram in question reads as follows:

> On 23.12. talks took place between Winnig, delegate for the [German] Empire, and the English government representative, previously Consul General in Riga, Monsanquet, on board the English ship "Princess Margaret," to which the German commander in chief or his representative was requested to participate. It was determined that I participate. The purpose of the conversation was to specify armistice conditions. The conversation took the following course:
>
> From the English: the ships here at dock should supervise the execution of the conditions. Based on the ceasefire conditions, the following is demanded:
>
> 1. That the Germans maintain a military force in this district sufficient to keep the Bolsheviks in check and not allow them to penetrate forward from their current positions ...
>
> 3. A breakdown regarding the current dispositions of the troops that are combating the Bolsheviks, both the German and the Latvian, is to be sent to the British military staff officer, for the attention of the senior marine officer. All future questions regarding the troops, mustered for the purpose of fighting the Bolshevists, are to be communicated to the same officer.
>
> 4. A sufficient military force has to be maintained, armed, at the following points, to prevent them being taken by the Bolshevists, and to prevent the Bolshevists penetrating forward in a general line, which joins the following localities: Walk,* Wolmar,† Wenden, Friedrichstadt, Pensk, Mitau.
>
> 5. The railroad from Riga to Liepāja is to be protected against Bolshevist attacks, and all British provisions and post that are transported on this line are to receive priority treatment.

There then follows a series of demands. And here is the answer of the German delegate and trade union leader, Herr Winnig:

> While it is unusual to want to force a government to continue to occupy a foreign state, in this case that is our actual wish, a necessity in order to protect German blood. [Luxemburg interjects: "The Baltic Barons!"] We also consider ourselves morally obliged to help that country which we would have liberated from previous connections with other states. Our efforts would be made difficult, however, firstly due to the condition of our troops, who, affected by the ceasefire conditions, no longer want to fight but rather to go home, and who, besides that, consist of old war invalids; secondly, our efforts have been made difficult by the behavior of the

---

* Divided, from 1920 on, into Valga in Estonia and Valka in Latvia.

† German name for Valmiera in Latvia.

> Baltic governments of this locality, who regard the Germans as their oppressor. But we are anxious to create voluntary units ready to fight, which we have partly achieved already.

What they're doing here is counterrevolution. A while back, you read about the creation of the "Iron Division," explicitly constructed to combat the Bolsheviks in the Baltic States.* It wasn't clear at that point how the Ebert-Scheidemann government would position themselves toward this new entity. Now you know that it was the government itself that proposed its creation.

Party comrades, another brief remark about Winnig. We can calmly state the fact that the German union leaders—it is no coincidence that a union leader carries out such political services—and the German Social Democrats are the biggest, most infamous ne'er-do-wells that this world has ever seen. (Thunderous cheers of approval and applause.) Do you know where these people—Winnig, Ebert, Scheidemann—belong? According to the German criminal code, which they themselves declare to be fully valid, and according to which they allow legal judgments to be pronounced, these people belong in jail doing hard labor! (Thunderous cheers of approval and applause.) Because, according to the German criminal code, any individual who undertakes to solicit German soldiers to carry out foreign service is to be sentenced to hard labor. And today leading the "socialist government" we have—let's be clear about this—not merely people who are the Judases of the "socialist movement" and of the proletarian revolution, but jailbirds who have no place whatsoever in a decent society. (Thunderous cheers of approval.)

In connection with this point, I will read you a resolution at the end of my speech, for which I expect to receive your unanimous approval, that we should move with the requisite vigor against these people who as of now control the fate of Germany.

Comrades, to return to an earlier thread of my argument, it is obvious that these plots—the creation of Iron Divisions, and specifically the aforementioned deal with English imperialism—signify nothing less than the final efforts to throttle the German socialist movement, but this is linked to the cardinal question, the question of the prospects for peace. What can be observed in these agreements, apart from the rekindling of the war? While these ne'er-do-wells perform a comedy in Germany, claiming that they've got their hands completely full with creating peace—and that we are the people who are the

* From mid-November 1918, the Army Higher Command in Riga, in collaboration with the Imperial Commissar for the Baltic States, and the right-wing trade union leader August Winnig, organized the creation of counterrevolutionary voluntary units, similar to the *Eiserne Division* (Iron Division), intended for deployment against the Baltic and Finnish workers, and against the Poles. In Germany, these *Freikorps* became the decisive element among the civil-war troops against the revolution. They would murder Rosa Luxemburg and Karl Liebknecht two weeks later.

troublemakers, who make the Entente uneasy and delay the peace settlement—with their own hands they prepare to rekindle war, a war in the East that will be followed by war in Germany. Once more we have a situation leading to the fact that we have to steady ourselves for a period of intense conflict. We will have to defend not only the interests of socialism and the interests of the revolution, but also of world peace, and this is precisely the justification for the tactics that we of the Spartacus Group alone consistently pursued through four whole years of war. Peace means the world revolution of the proletariat! There is no other way to establish and safeguard peace than the victory of the socialist proletariat. (Vigorous approval.)

Party comrades, what general tactical considerations can we draw from this for the situation we face in the coming period? Your first conclusion may be the hope that the Ebert-Scheidemann government will be overthrown and replaced by a genuine socialist proletarian revolutionary government. However, I would draw your attention not toward the top, but rather toward the base. We must not simply repeat the illusion of the first phase of the revolution, that of November 9, that it is enough for the progress of the socialist revolution to overthrow the capitalist government and replace it with another one. The only way of ushering in the victory of the proletarian revolution is to start at a diametrically opposite point and undermine the Ebert-Scheidemann government at every turn with socialist, revolutionary, mass struggle of the proletariat. Moreover, let me remind you of a number of the German Revolution's shortcomings that have not been overcome with the end of the first stage; we have unfortunately not yet reached the point at which we can ensure the victory of socialism by toppling the government. I have attempted to show you that the revolution of November 9 was principally a political revolution, while it has to become essentially an economic revolution. It was also only an urban revolution, and the countryside has, until now, remained almost untouched. It would be madness to attempt to realize socialism without changing agriculture. From the standpoint of socialist economics, it is utterly impossible to restructure industry without also transforming agriculture. The most important idea of the socialist economic order is the abolition of the opposition and division between city and country. This separation, this contradiction, this conflict is a purely capitalist phenomenon, which will have to be addressed immediately when we have positioned ourselves according to the socialist standpoint. If we are serious about socialist restructuring, then we must direct attention just as much toward the countryside as to the industrial centers, and yet in this regard we still, unfortunately, have not even reached the beginning of a beginning. We have to treat this seriously, not merely because without agriculture we cannot socialize, but also because while we may think we have reckoned with the final reserves of the counterrevolution that stand against us and our endeavors, we have not yet reckoned with one other important reserve: the peasantry.

Precisely because they have been untouched until now, they still constitute a reserve for the counterrevolutionary bourgeoisie. And the first thing they will do when the flames of socialist strikes are burning at their heels is to mobilize the peasantry, who are fanatical devotees of private ownership. The only means of moving against this threatening counterrevolutionary power is to carry the class struggle into the country, by mobilizing the landless proletariat and the poorer peasants against the richer peasants.

From this, we can draw conclusions about what we have to do in order to ensure the preconditions for the success of the revolution and I want therefore to summarize our next tasks in this direction. Above all else, in the future, we have to extend in all directions the system of workers' and soldiers' councils, especially the workers' councils. What we undertook on November 9 are only weak beginnings, and not even that. You are aware that the counterrevolution plans to continue its destruction of the system of workers' and soldiers' councils. In Hesse, these councils have been completely suspended, and in other locations, power has been wrenched from their hands. We have not only to build up the system of workers' and soldiers' councils, but also to introduce rural laborers and small peasants into this council system. We have to seize power, and the prospect of seizing power raises this question: What, across Germany, can and should each workers' and soldiers' council do? ("Bravo!") That is where power lies, and we have to hollow out the bourgeois state from below, by ending the separation of legislative and executive powers and uniting them in the hands of the workers' and soldiers' councils.

Party comrades, this is the mighty field that we must till. We must prepare from the bottom up, until the workers' and soldiers' councils have such power that, when the Ebert-Scheidemann government, or anything similar, is overthrown, this will be no more than the final act. As such, the seizure of power will not be a single blow but rather an ongoing action, with us progressively occupying the bourgeois state until we are in control of all posts and defending them tooth and nail. My view and that of my party friends is that the workers' councils should likewise lead the economic struggle. The leadership of the economic confrontation, and its expansion down ever further reaching roads, should also be in the hands of the workers' councils. The workers' councils must possess all state power. This is what we have to work toward in the coming period, and it follows, if we face up to this task, we must reckon with a massive and immediate intensification of the struggle. It is imperative now to fight, step by step, hand to hand, in every state, in every city, in every village, in every municipality, for all the powers of the state must be torn away from the bourgeoisie bit by bit and transferred to the workers' and soldiers' councils.

But our party comrades and proletarians have first to be schooled for this task. Even in places where workers' and soldiers' councils already exist, people are still lacking consciousness about the purposes for which they exist.

("Quite right!") We have first to show the masses that the workers' and soldiers' council should function as the central lever for state machinery, that it has to take control of all forms of state authority and to guide all these forms into the fairway of socialist revolution. Even those working masses already organized into workers' and soldiers' councils are still miles away from this goal, with the exception, of course, of a few smaller minorities of proletarians who are clearly conscious of their task. This situation is not unsatisfactory, but rather normal for the present period. The masses have to learn how to exercise power through exercising power. There is no other way. We have advanced beyond the days when the watchword was to "educate the proletariat in a socialist way," though the Marxists of the Kautsky school still seem to be living in those days. Educating the proletarian masses in a socialist way meant holding lectures and distributing leaflets and pamphlets to them. No, the proletarians don't need any of that. They will be educated through their deeds. ("Quite right!") The motto here is: in the beginning was the deed. The deed is indispensable in order for the workers' and soldiers' councils to realize their mission to become the sole public authorities in the whole empire. This is the only way for us to prepare the ground so that it becomes ready for the upheaval that will crown our work. And that's why, party comrades, it was not without a clear calculation and a clear consciousness that we said to you yesterday, that I in particular said to you, "Don't imagine that this will be an easy struggle!" Several comrades took me the wrong way, as if I had assumed that you wanted to boycott the National Assembly while standing around, arms folded. I would never have dreamt of saying that. I just could not go into depth on that point; in today's framework and context, I have the chance to do so. I meant that history is not going to make things easy for us like the bourgeois revolutions, in which it was sufficient to overthrow the official authorities in the center, and to replace these with a couple, or with a couple of dozen, new men. We must work from below, and that reflects the mass character of our revolution, which aims to transform the very land and soil of society, and the character of the modern proletarian revolution, [reflects] that we have to seize political power not from above, but rather from below. November 9 was an attempt—a weak, half-hearted, half-conscious, and chaotic attempt—to overthrow public authority and class rule. It is now necessary to direct the entire consciousness of the combined power of the proletariat toward the foundational structures of capitalist society. Down below, where each employer faces his wage slaves, down below, where all the executive organs of political class supremacy face the objects of this supremacy—the masses—that is where we must tear the rulers' means of authority away from them, step by step, and take them into our own hands. When I describe it like this, the process appears more protracted, perhaps, than one would tend, at first, to imagine. I believe that it is healthy for us to gaze with utter clarity on all the difficulties and complications of this revolution. For I hope that this description of the major difficulties and the tasks piling up does not affect any of you so as to temper your mettle or your energy; it doesn't do this to me. The greater the task, the more we will draw together all our collective forces. We must not forget that the revolution knows how to complete its works with incredible speed. I shall not attempt to foretell how much time this process needs. Who among us cares about the timing, so long as our lives are long enough to bring it to pass! The only thing that matters is that we know clearly and exactly what is to be done; and to the best of my ability, I have attempted to sketch, in broad outline, what is to be done.

IV. PROTEST RESOLUTION AGAINST THE ACTIONS OF THE GERMAN GOVERNMENT IN THE EAST*

The Reich Conference is outraged about the actions of the German government in the East. The combination of German troops with Baltic barons and with English imperialists does not only signify the despicable betrayal of the Russian proletariat and of the Russian Revolution, it also signifies the seal on the world alliance of capitalists of all countries against the battling proletariat worldwide. In view of these enormities, the Party Congress again declares that the Ebert-Scheidemann government is the deadly enemy of the German proletariat. Down with the Ebert-Scheidemann government!

* The resolution referred to was adopted unanimously.

The First Party Congress*

The revolutionary vanguard of the German proletariat has joined up to form an independent political party. The founding of the German Communist Party has taken place in the manner desired and predicted by the Spartacus Group. It has taken place in the framework of the group's general approach, purposeful from the start, and it was neither a conventicle nor a handful of radical leaders acting on their own accord and "constructing" a splinter group by excluding the general public. The party has formed as a natural product of historical development, as a few lines in the career path of the German Revolution, and, as such, as the manifestation of the political life of the proletarian masses. The founding of the Communist Party is part of the turning point that concludes the first phase and commences the second phase of the German Revolution.

The illusions of November 9 have been destroyed; the shortcomings of that day have come, publicly, to light. Ebert-Scheidemann's veiled counterrevolution in the one political camp provokes the unbridled and ruthless unfurling of the revolutionary flag in the opposite camp; the sharp swing to the right in the empire's official leadership provokes a powerful move to the left in the worker- and soldier-masses of the base.

A clarification of the oppositions, an intensification of the struggle, the revolution's maturation and self-definition. These are the events that gave rise to the Communist Party of Germany and that it must respond to. Related phenomena include the groups of International Communists† joining the party, and the commencement of negotiations about organizational cooperation between the newly founded party and the Revolutionary Shop Stewards from the large Berlin workplaces. While these negotiations have not yet led to a positive result, they should be seen as only the start of an utterly self-evident and inexorable process of uniting all genuinely proletarian and revolutionary elements in a single organizational framework. The fact that Greater Berlin's Revolutionary Shop Stewards—the moral delegates of the Berlin proletariat's core troops—are working together with the Spartacus League has been underlined by the joint participation of both organizations in all of the revolutionary actions of the Berlin workforce to date. Such bonds, forged with deeds, are the only real and genuine basis for organizational union. They are born out of the

* This article first appeared in *Die Rote Fahne* (Berlin), No. 3, January 3, 1919. It was unsigned, but Luxemburg was identified as the author in *Die Rote Fahne* (Berlin), No. 306, December 30, 1928. It is translated by Henry Holland from Luxemburg's *Gesammelte Werke,* Vol. 4, pp. 512–5.

† It was principally the group of Bremen Leftists and a leftist group in Dresden who named themselves the International Communists of Germany in November 1918. They joined the Communist Party of Germany at the inaugural Party Congress.

class interests of the proletarian masses and the vitality of the revolution, and therein lies the guarantee that the inner logic of events will eventually lead the Revolutionary Shop Stewards into the only purely proletarian-revolutionary camp, the Communist Party of Germany. The inhibitions and indecisions that are blocking this step in the present hour are themselves a remnant of the process of dissolution in the USPD, of the destabilizing and paralyzing half measures on which this party is founded. But, that said, we can assume that the healthy and genuinely revolutionary elements in the USPD will clear away this final remnant. To achieve this, they will have to rescue themselves from the suffocating atmosphere of a party that is, in reality, no more than a corpse, and move to the place where the revolutionary struggle has found its clearest and most determined expression.

Indeed, the revolution calls for unified and immediate action, announced with a commanding voice. Through this transition to its second phase, it has raised immeasurably the tasks that it sets the proletariat; its frame of action has widened enormously, its revolutionary plough has dug deeper into the earth. The transformation of a revolution primarily of soldiers on November 9 into an out-and-out workers' revolution—the metamorphosis of a superficial, purely political revolution into the extensive process of general economic confrontation between labor and capital—demands a wholly different degree of political maturity, education and toughness from the revolutionary working class than had sufficed in the first, incipient phase.

The imperative now is to substitute the current revolutionary *mood* with an unyielding, revolutionary *conviction*, to substitute the systematic for the spontaneous. The imperative is to tackle the job of laying the foundations for the socialist structure, now enriched by the sum total of experiences from the first period. The imperative is to turn the system of workers' and soldiers' councils from an improvised contraption into a bold vehicle that will secure all public social power for the proletariat.

And one more thing! What we experienced from November 9 until now was not actually a *German* Revolution: it was a long series of fragmented local revolutions and mini-revolutions, at times not without the traits of an operetta, painting a confused and colorful picture that reflected both German disjointedness and backwardness and the disjointedness of the revolutionary army of the proletariat. The natural weaknesses of the initial phase must be overcome. The mass unified *German* Revolution has to be prepared by the political and social maturity of the proletarian masses in all of Germany, by going beyond local barriers and specifics to the common goal and shared battlefront.

In contrast to the traditional "milestone"-type praise of what the recently concluded Party Congress has achieved, we can admit openly that the Party Congress has only been able to complete bits of the enormous work put before it and to sketch outlines. Itself a fragment of the revolution, it also cannot claim to have been sufficiently thorough or to have completed an exhaustive work.

That said, essentially the most important thing seems to be what the revolution has achieved so far. It produced a *summa* as a line drawn under the historical lessons of previous revolutions, it indicated major guidelines for forthcoming developments, and it issued a strong call to Germany's undivided proletariat to ruthless battle.

The spirit of all delegates from all parts of the empire allows us to hope that industrious work has been achieved, that the appeal will resonate, and that the Communist Party of Germany, as shock troops, will become the gravedigger of bourgeois society.

The imperative now is to go to work with all possible power. As Liebknecht said in conclusion to his remarks:

> The cruel political and social disappointments and the collapse of the capitalist economy are the most eloquent propagandists for the social revolution.
>
> Our task is to support and direct this "propaganda of objective relations" with clarity, energy and enthusiasm. The historical mission of the Communist Party of Germany is to forge the German proletariat into a mighty hammer that will smash class supremacy.

What Are Our Leaders Doing?*

People and things mature with uncanny speed in the fiery atmosphere of the revolution. Only three weeks ago, as the Germany-wide conference of the workers' and soldiers' councils ended, Ebert-Scheidemann seemed to be at the zenith of their powers. The representatives of the masses of revolutionary soldiers and workers throughout Germany had blindly submitted to their leadership. The convocation of the National Assembly, which excluded the people on "the street," the downgrading of the Executive Committee [*Vollzugsrat*],† and with it the workers' and soldiers' councils, [reduced them] to the status of powerless puppets. What a triumph for the counterrevolution, right down the line! The fruits of November 9 appeared to have been squandered and gambled away, the bourgeoisie breathed a sigh of relief and the masses stood there baffled, disarmed, bitter, and yes, even desperate. Ebert-Scheidemann fancied themselves to be at the peak of their power.

The stupid fools! Not even twenty days have gone by since then, and their ostensible power has started to falter overnight. The masses are the genuine power, the real power, due to the force of their interests and of the iron laws of history. They can be put in chains temporarily or deprived of every formal power at an organizational level—yet these masses need only to stir, only to straighten up their spine, and then straight away the earth starts to shake under the feet of the counterrevolution.

Anyone who experienced the mass demonstration yesterday in the *Siegesallee*, who sensed this rock-solid revolutionary conviction, this glorious mood, this power of the deed that emanated from the masses, must conclude that the proletariat has grown enormously in political terms through the lessons of the last few weeks and the most recent events. It has become conscious of its power, and all that remains is to act on this power.

Ebert-Scheidemann and their clients, the bourgeoisie, who are clamoring constantly about "*coups*," are experiencing at this very moment the same disappointment once felt by the final Bourbon, who, in response to his outraged cry about the "rebellion" of the people of Paris, was answered with the words, *"Monsieur, this is no rebellion, this is a revolution!"*

---

* This article first appeared in *Die Rote Fahne* (Berlin), No. 7, January 7, 1919. It was not signed, but in *Um Rosa Luxemburgs Stellung zur russischen Revolution* (On Rosa Luxemburg's Position on the Russian Revolution) (Hamburg: Press of the Communist International, 1922), Clara Zetkin names Luxemburg as the author. It is translated by Henry Holland from Luxemburg's *Gesammelte Werke*, Vol. 4, pp. 516–18.

† During the Revolution, the Executive Committee (*Vollzugsrat*) took on the role of temporary central authority of the workers' and soldiers' councils of Greater Berlin, Prussia, and the whole German Empire. Its task until the nationwide Imperial Congress of the Councils in December 1918 was to check the work of the Council of People's Commissars under Friedrich Ebert (Germany), and Paul Hirsch (Prussia).

Yes, it is a *revolution* with all its externally confusing developments, with its alternating ebb and flow, with momentary surges toward seizing power, and equally momentary retreats of the revolutionary tide. And through all this apparent to-ing and fro-ing the revolution asserts itself victoriously, step by step, and marches forward relentlessly.

It is precisely in the struggle itself that the mass needs to learn how to fight and how to act. And today, we can sense that Berlin's working class *has* learned, to a large extent, how to act; it yearns for decisive deeds, for clear situations, for uncompromising measures. It is a different working class from what it was on November 9; it *knows* what it wants and what it should do.

But what about its leaders, the executive organs of its will? Have the Revolutionary Shop Stewards from the large workplaces and the radical elements in the USPD also grown during the same period in terms of power of the deed and determination? Has their capacity for action kept pace with the growing energy of the masses?

We're afraid that we can't answer this question with a simple yes. We fear that the leaders are still the same as they were on November 9, and that they've hardly learned anything new.

Twenty-four hours have passed since the Ebert government's attack on Eichhorn.* The masses responded impulsively to their leaders' appeal: Spontaneously and on their own strength they carried through Eichhorn's reinstatement. On their own initiative, they occupied *Vörwarts,* seized the bourgeois editorial offices and Wolff's Telegraph Office, [and] armed themselves as far as possible. They are waiting for further instructions and to see how their leaders act.

And what have these leaders done in the meantime? What decisions have they made? Which measures have they undertaken to secure victory for the revolution in this tense situation in which its fate is to be decided, at least in terms of its next phase? We see and hear nothing! It may well be that the delegates of the workers are *consulting* with each other thoroughly and at length. But the order of the day is *to act.*

We can bet that Ebert-Scheidemann are not tying themselves in knots with consultations. And they certainly aren't asleep. They are quietly preparing their intrigues with the usual energy and circumspection of the counterrevolutionary; they are sharpening their swords in order to ambush and slay the revolution.

* On January 4, 1919, the Social Democratic government declared that they had dismissed the Berlin chief of police Emil Eichhorn, who was a member of the left wing of the USPD. The Revolutionary Representatives, the Berlin leadership of the USPD and the Central Committee of the KPD issued a joint call to the working people and soldiers, to participate in actions aimed at the reversal of Emil Eichhorn's dismissal, the disarming of the counterrevolution, and the arming of the workers. Hundreds of thousands demonstrated in Berlin on January 5, gathered on the Siegesallee, and marched from there to the office of the chief of police.

Other lily-livered elements are no doubt already hard at work for "negotiations," bringing about compromises, throwing a bridge across the abyss that has opened up between the masses of workers and soldiers and Ebert's government, and trapping the revolution into a "settlement" with its deadly enemy.

There is no time to lose. Iron-willed steps must be taken immediately. The masses and the soldiers faithful to the revolution must be given clear and speedy directives; their energy and their desire for battle have to be pointed toward the correct goals. The vacillating elements among the troops can only be won for the sacred cause of the people by resolute and clear actions carried out by the revolutionary bodies.

Act! Act! Courageously, decisively and consistently—that's the accursed duty and obligation of the revolutionary representatives and the honest socialist party leaders. Disarm the counterrevolution, arm the masses, occupy all positions of power. Act *quickly*! The revolution obliges us. In world history, its hours count for months and its days for years. May the organs of the revolution be conscious of their higher duties!

Neglected Obligations*

Since November 9, the revolutionary wave crashes periodically against the same wall: the Ebert-Scheidemann government. The occasion, the form, and the load borne by the collision differ in each of the revolutionary crises that we have lived through in the last eight weeks. But the cry "down with Ebert-Scheidemann!" is both the *leitmotif* of *all* crises to date and also the demand with which each crisis fades away, the demand ringing out from the masses in an ever louder, more unanimous and more insistent way.

This is also entirely natural. The revolution's further development is afflicted by the fundamental mistake of November 9. People were placed at the head of the revolutionary government who had done everything within their powers, up to the last minute, to prevent the revolution breaking out, and who, after the outbreak, installed themselves at the head with the clear intention of preventing the revolution at the first appropriate opportunity.

If the revolution is to proceed on its course, if it is to develop, stage by stage, in order to fulfil its historic tasks of abolishing bourgeois class rule and of realizing socialism, then the wall that opposes it, the Ebert-Scheidemann government, has to be cleared out of the way.

The revolution won't be able to avoid addressing this special task, and it is into this task that all experiences from eight weeks of revolutionary history flow. The Ebert government's provocations—December 6: the oath of the guards;† December 24: the most recent attack against the chief of police—all push the revolutionary masses directly toward the brusque, naked, and implacable alternative: either the revolution has to abandon its proletarian character and its socialist mission, or Ebert-Scheidemann and its supporters have to be driven from power.

The broadest masses of the proletariat in Berlin and in the main revolutionary centers of the empire have comprehended this. This clear and sharp recognition—ringing in a passionate, mighty cry out of 100,000 throats in every single moment: down with Ebert-Scheidemann!—that is the benefit that recent events have brought us.

What, however, is *not at all* clear—and it is in this that the revolution's

---

* This article, entitled "Versäumte Pflichten," first appeared in *Die Rote Fahne*, No. 8, January 8, 1919. It was not signed, but in *Um Rosa Luxemburgs Stellung zur russischen Revolution* (On Rosa Luxemburg's Position on the Russian Revolution) (Hamburg: Press of the Communist International, 1922), Clara Zetkin names Luxemburg as author. It is translated by Henry Holland from Luxemburg's *Gesammelte Werke*, Vol. 4, pp. 519–22.

† On December 10, 1918, troops of guards led by counterrevolutionary officers entered Berlin and were greeted by Friedrich Ebert, Adolf Wermuth—the first mayor of Berlin—and Heinrich Scheüch, minister for war. They were sworn in for the "Republic," with Lieutenant General Arnold Lequis swearing the oath for the officers and soldiers.

weakness and immaturity come to light—is the question of *how* we are to conduct the struggle to clear out the Ebertian government, of *how* we translate the step of the revolution's inner maturity, which we have already reached, into deeds and power relations. Nothing has illustrated these weaknesses and deficits so crassly as the last three days have done.

Getting rid of the Ebert-Scheidemann government doesn't mean storming into the Reich Chancellery and hunting down or arresting a few people. Above all, it means seizing all real positions of power, and also *holding down* and *using* these positions.

What have we experienced in these three days? Everything that really was conquered—the reoccupation of the chief of police's office, the occupation of *Vörwarts*, the occupation of Wolff's Telegraphic Bueau and of the bourgeois editorial offices—all of that was the masses' spontaneous work. What have the bodies that stood (or pretended to stand) at the head of the masses in those days made of it: the Revolutionary Shop Stewards and the Central Executive Committee of the USPD of Greater Berlin? They have neglected the most elementary rules of revolutionary action that exist:

1. When the masses occupy [the office of] *Vowärts*, then it is the duty of the Revolutionary Shop Stewards and of the USPD's greater Berlin party executive to facilitate immediate editorial leadership in the interests of Berlin's revolutionary working class. But where then are the editors hiding? What are Däumig and Lebedour up to—journalists and editors by reputation and vocation—now, when the left in the USPD don't have any kind of party organ—why are they leaving the masses in the lurch? Was "consulting" a more urgent business than performing deeds?

2. When the masses occupy Wolff's Telegraphic Bureau, then the paramount duty of the revolutionary organs of the working class is to *make use of* the telegraphic bureau for the purpose of the revolution. To use it to relay news about what is happening in Berlin to the public, to the masses, to their comrades throughout the empire, and to inform them about the situation. This is the only way in which a spiritual connection can be created between the Berlin working class and the revolutionary movement in the whole empire, without which the revolution can triumph neither here nor there.

3. If one is opposing the Ebert-Scheidemann government in the toughest kind of struggle, one does not immediately commence "negotiations" with the same government. Let the Haase people—Oskar Cohn, the Zietz woman, Kautsky, Breitscheid, and whatever all these uncertain figures* are called—seize every opportunity to speedily spin threads to connect them again to the Ebert people, who they only broke from with a heavy heart. For their part, the

* In German, "*schwankende Gestalten*." This is a quotation from the first line of the dedication in Goethe's *Faust*, Part I: "Now you approach again, you uncertain figures." Johann Wolfgang von Goethe, *Faust: A Tragedy*, Part I (Translation by Bayard Taylor, 1870; Random House, 1950).

Revolutionary Shop Stewards, who do have empathy with the masses, know well that Ebert-Scheidemann is the revolution's deadly enemy. Do we negotiate with a deadly enemy? These negotiations can only lead to one of two things: either to a compromise, or—even more surely—merely to a delay, which will be used by the Ebert people to prepare the most brutal, violent measures.

4. If the masses on the street are to be called upon, [if they are] to be ready for the alarm, then they have to be told clearly and comprehensibly what they have to do, or at least what is happening, what both friend and enemy are doing and planning. Of course, the masses belong on the street in times of revolutionary crisis! They're the only stronghold and only security of the revolution. When the revolution is in danger—*as is the case now, to the highest degree!*—then it's the duty of the proletarian masses to keep watch at the location where they can express their power: on the street! Merely their presence and their contact with each other are a threat and a warning to all the revolution's open and concealed enemies: take cover!

But it's not enough merely to call out the masses, they also have to be politically active. They have to be called on to decide everything that should be done and that should be avoided. Did the Revolutionary Shop Stewards and the USPD's Greater Berlin party executive not consider it necessary to present their decision—to let themselves in for "negotiations" with Ebert-Scheidemann—in front of the masses gathered on the Siegesallee? They would have received such a threatening answer that they would have lost all desire for diplomacy!

The masses are prepared to support every revolutionary action, and to march to the ends of the earth, for the cause of socialism. One might issue them clear demands and show them a consistent and decisive attitude. The idealism of the working class, and the loyalty of the soldiers to the revolution, can only be strengthened through decisiveness and clarity in the leadership organs and in their politics. And that means a form of politics today that refuses all indecisiveness and half measures, committing itself instead to a single *leitmotif*: down with Ebert-Scheidemann! This lesson has yet to be learned.

Germany was the classic country of organization and, what's more, of fanaticism about organization, even being conceited about its organizational levels. The movement's spirit, aims and ability to act have been abandoned* for the sake of "organization." And what can we experience today? In the revolution's most important moments, the first thing that fails in a lamentable fashion is the famed "organizational talent." Organizing revolutionary actions is simply something quite different from following the script about how to "organize" empire-wide general elections, or elections to a court of commerce. The organization of revolutionary actions has to be and can only be learned

* The verb in the *Gesammelte Werke* is "*preisgegeben*" (disclosed) but this is footnoted: "*In der Quelle: freizugeben*," i.e., "in the original: *freizugeben*" (released). Translator's note.

during the revolution itself, just as swimming can only be learned in water. That's what historical experience is there to teach us. But it is also necessary to *learn* from that experience.

The experience of the last three days calls out to the leading organs of the working class with a loud voice: Don't talk! Don't consult endlessly! Don't negotiate! Act!

The Leaders' Failure*

Things in Berlin have taken a turn that demands the fiercest critique and the most serious consideration from the working masses.

In the course of the last few days, we have stated several times, openly and clearly, that the leadership of the Berlin mass movement is sorely lacking in terms of determination, power of the deed, and revolutionary spirit. We have said, with clarity, that the leadership lags far behind the masses in maturity and readiness to fight. We have done everything possible through critique, both inside the leading organizations, using initiative and persuasion, as well as outside—in the *Rote Fahne*—to drive the movement forward, to spur on the Revolutionary Shop Stewards from the large workplaces to act in a hard-hitting manner.

Yet all efforts and attempts have collapsed, ultimately because of the diffident and dithering behavior of that entity.

After the most splendid mood and fighting energy of the masses had been allowed to dissipate and fizzle out for four days through complete lack of direction (after the prospects of the revolutionary struggle had been most seriously shaken and the position of the government effectively strengthened by twice starting negotiations with the Ebert-Scheidemann government) the revolutionary leaders finally decided between Wednesday night and Thursday to break off the negotiations and resume the struggle all down the line. The *general strike* slogan was issued, and the call: *To arms!*

This was, however, the only action that the Revolutionary Shop Stewards could be bothered to carry out.

It is self-evident that the demands of general strike and of armament are thrown at the masses, but one has to do everything to ensure the energetic execution of these demands. The Revolutionary Shop Stewards have done nothing of the sort! They contented themselves with these bare phrases and by Thursday evening decided—to commence negotiations with Ebert-Scheidemann for the third time!

This time, the united movement—that has started to form among the workers at the Schwartzkopff works, and at several other large workplaces—provided the necessary excuse to break off the struggle that had just begun in all its forms. The workforces of Schwartzkopff, of AEG, and of the Knorr-Bremse are part of the core troops of the Berlin revolutionary proletariat, and

---

* This article first appeared in *Die Rote Fahne*, No. 11, January 11, 1919. It was not signed, but in *Um Rosa Luxemburgs Stellung zur russischen Revolution* (On Rosa Luxemburg's Position on the Russian Revolution) (Hamburg: Press of the Communist International, 1922), Clara Zetkin names Luxemburg as the author. It is translated by Henry Holland from Luxemburg's *Gesammelte Werke*, Vol. 4, pp. 523–6.

there can be no doubt at all about their best intentions. But in this case, they have become the object of a con trick pulled by the Haase people: Oskar Cohn, Dittmann and others. By working with favorite catchphrases like "unity" and "no bloodletting" in a demagogical fashion, these people intend to weaken the masses' energy for battle, to sow the seeds of confusion, and to reduce the decisive revolutionary crisis to an ugly compromise with the counterrevolution.

It is obvious to anybody who doesn't want to be duped that this razzmatazz about unity from the USPD does the greatest imaginable service for Ebert-Scheidemann in the present situation. Hanging in thin air, trembling from the risky trial of strength with the working class, only half supported, and unwillingly, by the wavering troops, and snarled at with suspicion by the bourgeoisie—the traitors of socialism have experienced the most encumbered hours of their brief government splendor during the last few days. The forceful performance of the masses on the streets, and the twist that the government's own brutal provocation took on in the Eichhorn case, became too much for these adventurers. They then admitted that they had already half lost, clearly demonstrating the utter indecision and fumbling uncertainty of their counter-revolutionary measures in the last few days.

The negotiations and, ultimately, the unity movement, then provided them with a brief reprieve. Again, the USPD proved itself the counterrevolution's guardian angel. Haase-Dittmann resigned from Ebert's government,* but on the streets they pursue the same fig leaf politics of the "Scheidemen."

And the left in the USPD supports and takes part in these politics! The conditions for the newly agreed negotiations with the government formulated by *Ledebour* have been accepted by the Revolutionary Shop Stewards. They are demanding in turn that Ebert, Scheidemann, Noske and Landsberg resign from the government, as the price for the workers' capitulation. As if this were about *individuals*, and not about a particular kind of politics! As if this was aimed at anything but confusing and deceiving the masses, at anything but moving the typical and appointed representatives of the "Scheidemen's" infamous politics out of the limelight. Merely in order to replace them with random colorless extras, who, acting as stooges, replicate the same politics while Ebert-Scheidemann work away pulling wires behind the stage, thus escaping being put on trial by the masses!

One way or another, the entire politics of negotiation—initiated by the USPD, supported by the Revolutionary Shop Stewards—is intended to make the revolutionary working class capitulate and to mask the inner oppositions and contradictions. It is the politics of November 9 to which the situation and political unity of the masses, which has been ripening for eight weeks, is to be scaled back!

---

* USPD People's Commissars Emil Barth, Wilhelm Dittmann, and Hugo Haase resigned from the government on December 29, 1918. The right-wing Social Democrats Gustav Noske and Rudolf Wissell replaced them in the cabinet.

The Communist Party is clearly not participating in these shameful politics and rejects every responsibility for them. We continue to see it as our duty to push forward the cause of the revolution, to oppose with relentless energy all attempts at confusion, and to warn the masses, by means of obdurate criticism, about the dangers of the Revolutionary Shop Stewards' politics of procrastination, and the USPD's politics of the swamp.

The crisis of the last few days broadcasts lessons of the highest importance and urgency to the masses. The ongoing situation of deficient leadership and lack of central organization in the Berlin working class has become untenable. If the revolution is to move forward, if the proletariat's victory, and socialism, is to become anything more than a dream, then the revolutionary working class must create leadership organs that are up to the task of directing and utilizing the battle energy of the masses. But above all the coming period must be dedicated to the liquidation of the USPD, that rotting corpse, the products of whose putrefaction are poisoning the revolution. The confrontation with the class of capitalists in Germany is primarily taking the shape of a settling of accounts with the Scheidemann-Ebert lot, who act as the bourgeoisie's battle ramparts.

The most urgent tasks in the coming period are clarity—and a tougher, more hardline struggle against all the attempted cover-ups and negotiations that are bogging us down—the building of the masses' revolutionary energy, and the creation of appropriate organs of leadership. These are also the most significant lessons to be drawn from the last five days, from the greatest efforts of the masses, and from the most lamentable failure of their leaders.

Houses of Cards*

On top of smoking ruins, and between the pools of blood and corpses of murdered "Spartacists," the heroes of "order" rush to strengthen their supremacy anew. The Ebert government frantically pulls itself together to consolidate its power: from now on, they will rule by bayonet. Like the Caesars before him, Ebert has the Guards parade in front of him and expresses to them in the face of the dead and wounded on the cobblestones of Berlin "the government's gratitude to the brave troops," and assigns to them the task of maintaining the safety of the *National Assembly* through force of arms. "Commander in Chief" Noske, in his daily bulletin from the 11th [of this month] reactivates the old, well-known register of Hindenburg, von Kessel, and all the other henchmen of the Hohenzollern regime: "In the East, with revolvers drawn, carloads of Spartacist gangs are plundering one house after the other … They have let slip their recent guise that they were a political movement, and theft and plundering are revealed to be the one and only aim of the revolt." The government's patience has been exhausted, and now the "heavy artillery" and machine guns shall have their say. "*The working class must unite against Spartacus,*" concludes this upstart with blood-stained hands.

This is how the "Scheidemen" want to reassert their authority to govern: on the corpses of Berlin's revolutionary workers, with the material assistance of the counterrevolutionary military, and with the moral support of the bourgeoisie.

But there is a flaw in this calculation. The military and the bourgeoisie who are helping Ebert-Scheidemann get off the hook today want to enjoy the fruits of this bloody harvest *themselves*. These elements will support the "socialist" government only as long as they believe that they can keep a tight rein on the proletarian masses by waving the false flag, and that they can choke the revolution and socialism by applying "moral" pressure. This last week has forced open the chasm that yawns between the Ebert government and the revolution. It is clear today that Ebert-Scheidemann can only rule by the bayonet. If this is true, however, then the bayonet will also rule *without* Ebert-Scheidemann. The bourgeoisie are going for broke and are screaming for a public proclamation of a dictatorship of the saber and a complete restoration of the old "order."

"The rebels deserve a summary court-martial, or prison hard labor," cries the *Tägliche Rundschau*, "and they do not deserve freedom … The reestablishment of peace and order must be carried out to the final degree; the

* This article first appeared in *Die Rote Fahne*, No. 13, January 13, 1919. It was not signed, but in *Um Rosa Luxemburgs Stellung zur russischen Revolution* (On Rosa Luxemburg's Position on the Russian Revolution) (Hamburg: Press of the Communist International, 1922), Clara Zetkin names Luxemburg as the author. It is translated by Henry Holland from Luxemburg's *Gesammelte Werke*, Vol. 4, pp. 527–30.

[regular] police force, which has virtually ceased to exist since November 9, must be restored to its former size and significance, and the *Schutzmannschaft* must be rearmed and given back all its previous powers."*

At the same time, the leader of the Noske Guard, *Colonel Reinhardt*, announces *that he will impose martial law; he is not taking orders from anyone, including the government, because he's a soldier and will make independent decisions.* And the 3rd Guard Regiment declares on its own that it is "determined to bring about the National Assembly, by force of arms." In Berlin and the suburbs, officers are arresting people on their own initiative.

This is how the counterrevolutionary officer corps rebels against the Ebert government, making it clearly understood that the whole thing was meant to be the other way around: Ebert-Scheidemann were meant to get their fingers burnt for the bourgeoisie—not the bourgeoisie for Ebert-Scheidemann. But if it comes to that, if the bourgeoisie have to save the "socialist" government from the revolutionary working class, then their game is up, and the bourgeoisie has every reason to think that there are more capable candidates for the saber dictatorship than the upstarts, Ebert and Noske.

From a third side, however, the Haase party is attempting to use the crisis to create a coalition government of "all socialist tendencies" in keeping with Haase's fig leaf politics, drowning all the inner contradictions of the revolution in an indiscriminate mélange, concealing all oppositions, and dissolving the fighting energy of the masses in a lazy compromise. The plan is that only the "compromised leaders"—Ebert, Scheidemann, Landsberg, Noske—leave the stage, that merely *individual persons* be swapped, but that Scheidemann-ism as a *political form* keeps its hands on the tiller, and "all socialist organizations" should form a shared government with it.

Considering the corpses of murdered proletarians and "Scheidemen's" bloody orgies, "Spartacists" today, tenfold more than previously, waste no more than a disgusted look and a clenched fist in response to these pathetic politics of compromise and betrayal of the revolutionary cause. The Haase people's catchphrase about the coalition of "all socialist tendencies" is, in reality, just a repetition of the former well-known combination of the "Scheidemen" and Independents. The only aim of the USPD's "unification" hype is to resurrect the Ebert-Haase government with new personnel. And the stronger the terms of the attacks on Ebert-Scheidemann in the *Freiheit* today, the greater the certainty of the preparation—under cover of this fake cannonade—for the shameful fall of the USPD, a party that despite all it has learned, despite the fact that it was forced to give up the joint venture with the "Scheidemen" on December 28, simply wants to return to these business arrangements—albeit under different company leaders.

* This is a reference to the Royal Constabulary, who were unable to restrain the revolutionaries.

Thus the current crisis gives rise to three combinations: Ebert-Scheidemann want to retain the *status quo* and its own supremacy with the support of the bayonets of the bourgeoisie; the USPD wants to rewind events back to the stage of November 9, with an Ebert-Haase government under different names; the bourgeoisie wants things to revert back to the situation *before* November 9, i.e., back to the naked saber dictatorship.

Because these combinations are based on obsolete historical stages that have been overcome, all three are houses of cards. The revolution won't allow itself to be reduced or revised back, neither back to November 9, nor—and even less so—back to the lovely times *before* November 9. It has just as little interest in allowing itself to be trapped in a deadlock under Ebert's scepter.

The entire political meaning and historical content of the crisis of these last few weeks lies precisely in the fact that the revolution gets driven forward by its own inner force and logical development in order to follow through on the proletariat's conquest of power and the realization of socialism, even while, at every turn today, obstructive factors are placed in its path. While these oppositional forces may win the upper hand for the present using crude force, they are completely powerless to hold back the further process of development and the victory parade of the revolution.

And this truth expresses itself best in the fact that not one of the combinations that can be created out of the ruins of this week can have any kind of permanence. Whatever comes into being tomorrow or the next day as a result, and as a solution to the crisis, it will be *a provisorium*—a house of cards. Whether the naked force of machine guns wins the upper hand, or the ambiguity of the USPD's plans for a cover-up, the revolution's elemental forces—*the economic struggles*—will thwart all these plans in the shortest time possible. Again and yet again, the revolution will place the fundamental problem on the agenda, the general settling of accounts between labor and capital. And this settling of accounts is a world-historical confrontation between two mortal enemies that can only be fought out in a long battle for power, eye to eye, hand to hand.

Barely have the rubble and the corpses of these most recent episodes been cleared away, and the revolution returns to its tireless daily work. The Spartacists proceed on their path with indomitable steadiness. The number of casualties demanded from it grows every week, but the number of its supporters grows a hundredfold. The prisons and hard labor penitentiaries filled up under the wartime state of emergency, and now the graves in Friedrichshain* fill up under Ebert-Scheidemann's "socialist" government. But the masses of the proletariat gather ever more thickly around the banner of relentless

---

* Revolutionaries who were killed in March 1848 in Berlin are buried in a cemetery in a park in Friedrichshain, a neighborhood in the east of Berlin. New graves were added for the fallen of the November 1918 Revolution.

revolutionary struggle. While some tiers of society for now allow themselves to be drugged and trapped by demagogy and the hollow phrase "unification," by tomorrow they will stand all the stronger and more loyal—after fresh disappointment and sobering experience—behind the only party that knows nothing of compromise and vacillation, which proceeds along its historically prescribed path, without looking to the left or to the right, and without counting either enemies or dangers. All the way to victory.

Order Prevails in Berlin*

"*Order prevails in Warsaw!*" announced cabinet minister Sébastiani to the Paris Chamber in 1831, as Suvorov's *soldateska*, after their atrocious storming of the suburb of Praga, pushed forward into the Polish capital to begin their hangman's work on the rebels.†

"*Order prevails in Berlin!*" proclaims the bourgeois press triumphantly, as do Ebert, Noske, and the officers of the "victorious troops," to whom the petty-bourgeois Berlin mob waves with handkerchiefs and shouts hurrahs on the streets. The fame and the honor of German weapons have been vindicated in the face of world history. Soldiers who were routed at Flanders and in the Forest of Argonne have had their reputation restored through this dazzling victory—over 300 "Spartacists" in the *Vorwärts* building.‡ The days of the first glorious breakthrough of German troops into Belgium, and the days of General von Emmich, who triumphed over Liege, pale in comparison to the deeds of Reinhardt and his generals on Berlin's streets. *Truce negotiators* who wanted to negotiate the handover of the *Vorwärts* building have been hacked down and beaten beyond recognition by government *soldatesca* using rifle butts, making the identification of their corpses impossible. Prisoners were put against the wall and murdered in such a way that their skulls and brains splattered everywhere. Faced with such glorious deeds, who still remembers the shameful defeats at the hands of the French, the English, and the Americans? The enemy is called "Spartacus" and Berlin is the place where our officers understand winning. Noske, the "worker," is the name of the general who knows how to organize victory where [General Erich] Ludendorff failed.

Who would then not be reminded of the victory-high of the "law and order" mob in Paris, and of that *bacchanal* of the bourgeoisie celebrated on the corpses of the Communards, by that same bourgeoisie who had only recently capitulated shamefully to the Prussians, abandoning the country's capital to the invading enemy? Only to then take to their heels themselves, like contemptible cowards! Yet how the manly pride of the bourgeoisie's pampered sons, of those

---

* This article first appeared in *Die Rote Fahne*, No. 14, January 14, 1919. It is translated by Henry Holland from Luxemburg's *Gesammelte Werke*, Vol. 4, pp. 531–6. These are the last words from the pen of Rosa Luxemburg.

† Here, Luxemburg accidentally conflates two historical events—the massacre of some 10,000 Polish insurgents and civilians by tsarist general Aleksandr Suvorov in the Warsaw suburb in Prague in 1794, and the Russian capture of Warsaw during the Polish insurrection of 1830–31.

‡ On January 11, 1919, the workers and soldiers who had occupied the *Vorwärts* building on January 5 were forced to surrender to the numerically and technically superior counterrevolutionary troops. Negotiators whom the occupying forces had sent out to negotiate the handover were assaulted. The 300 revolutionaries who had to lay down arms were whipped and clubbed; several of them were murdered.

"golden youth,"* of those officers, flared up again against the poorly armed and starving Parisian proletariat and their defenseless women and children! How those sons of Mars, who had folded before the foreign enemy, ran riot in their bravery, in monstrous atrocities against the defenseless, against prisoners, even against the dead!

"Order prevails in Warsaw!" "Order prevails in Paris!" "Order prevails in Berlin!" Every half-century this is what the guardians of "order" report from one center of the world historical struggle to the next. And the jubilant "victors" fail to notice that an "order" requiring periodic bloodletting to keep it standing is moving inexorably toward its historical fate, toward its downfall. What was this recent "Spartacus Week" in Berlin, what did it achieve, what did it teach us? Revolutionary proletarians have to give an account of what has happened while still in the midst of the struggle, have to measure, amid the counterrevolution's victory howls, the proceedings and their results against the great yardstick of history. The revolution has no time to lose, and storms forward—over graves that are still open and leaving "victories" and "defeats" standing—toward its great goals. The primary task of fighters for international socialism is to follow its teachings and its paths consciously.

Was the final victory for the revolutionary proletariat to have been expected from this confrontation? Could we have expected to bring down Ebert-Scheidemann and to erect a socialist dictatorship? Certainly not, if one carefully considers all the variables that influence the outcome of these questions. The open wound of the revolutionary cause at this moment in time is the political immaturity of the mass of soldiers, who still allow themselves to be misused by their officers for counterrevolutionary purposes, hostile to the people. This alone is evidence enough that a *lasting* victory for the revolution was not possible in this confrontation. On the other hand, the immaturity of the military is itself a symptom of the general immaturity of the German Revolution.

The countryside, where a large percentage of the mass of soldiers come from, remains largely untouched by the revolution. Until now, Berlin has been virtually isolated from the rest of the empire. Yes, the revolutionary centers in the provinces—in Rhineland, on the Water's Edge,† in Braunschweig, in Saxony, in Württemberg—are body and soul behind the Berlin proletariat. Yet they lack the immediate lockstep of the advance, the direct unity in action, which would make the progress and quick-wittedness of the Berlin working class incomparably more effective. Furthermore—and this merely reflects the

---

* Luxemburg's reference to "*der goldenen Jugend*" (the golden youth) apparently is an established term for pampered officers in Paris at the time of the Commune.

† "*An der Wasserkante*" (On the Water's Edge) is a colloquial name sometimes applied to Hamburg and sometimes to the North German coastal ports collectively—Kiel and Bremen were also early centers of the Revolution.

deeper causes of the revolution's political limitations—the economic struggles, the actual volcanic source that feeds revolutionary class struggle, are still only in their first stages.

From all this it follows that a final, lasting victory could not be counted on in this moment. Does that make last week's battle a "mistake"? Yes—but only if we are talking about an intentional "push," or a so-called "*putsch*"! But what was the starting point for last week's battle? As in all such cases to date, such as December 6 and December 24, it was a brutal provocation by the government! Just like the earlier bloodbath against defenseless demonstrators on the Chausseestraße and like the butchering of the sailors, this time the attack on the Berlin chief of police was the cause of all subsequent events. We see that the revolution does not operate of its own free will, in open country, and in accordance with a plan cleverly concocted by "strategists." Its opponents *also* take the initiative, and indeed they generally make much more use of it than does the revolution itself.

Faced with the brazen provocation from Ebert-Scheidemann, the revolutionary working class was *forced* to take up arms. Yes, it was a *matter of honor* for the revolution to repel the attack immediately with all its energies, otherwise the counterrevolution would have been encouraged to press forward, and the revolutionary ranks of the proletariat and moral standing of the German Revolution in the eyes of the International would have been shaken.

Immediate resistance then spontaneously erupted with such self-evident energy from the Berlin masses that the moral victory was won by the "street" at the first opportunity.

You see, it is a fundamental living law of revolution never to stand still, in inactivity, in passivity, at the step that has been taken. The best defense is a good offence. This elementary rule of every battle applies equally to each step of the revolution. It's self-explanatory and demonstrates the Berlin proletariat's healthy instinct and fresh inner strength that it wasn't content with Eichhorn's reinstatement to his post but it instead moved spontaneously to occupy other command centers of the counterrevolution: the bourgeois press, the semi-official news agencies, and the offices of *Vorwärts*. All these measures resulted from the instinctive recognition that the counterrevolution, for its part, would not accept defeat, but would rather move toward a general show of strength.

And here too we are faced with one of the great historical laws of revolution, against which all the sophistry and arrogance of those petty "revolutionaries" of the USPD sort are smashed to pieces, people who, in every fight, merely look for pretexts for a retreat. As soon as the fundamental problem of the revolution has been clearly defined—and in *this* revolution, that is bringing down the Ebert-Scheidemann government as the first obstacle to socialism's victory—then this fundamental problem rises again and again. With the inevitability of a natural law, each individual chapter of the battle brings the problem's full dimensions again to the fore, however unready the revolution is to solve the problem, however unripe the situation may be. "Down with Ebert-Scheidemann!"—the slogan rises inescapably to the surface in every crisis of the revolution as the single, exhaustive formulation of all partial struggles, and thus, through the revolution's inner objective logic, automatically pushes every conflict to the top, whether one wants it or not.

Because of this contradiction in the early phase of the revolutionary process between the urgency of the task, and the missing preconditions for solving it, individual battles of the revolution end in *defeat*, in formal terms. But revolution is the only form of "war"—this, too, is one of the special laws attached to the revolution's life—where ultimate victory can be prepared for only through a series of "defeats."

What does the entire history of modern revolutions and socialism show us? The first spark of class struggle in Europe, the Lyon silk-weavers revolt in 1831, ended in a heavy defeat; the Chartist movement in England ended in defeat. The rising of the Parisian proletariat in the June Days of 1848 ended in a crushing defeat. The Paris Commune ended in an awful defeat. The entire road toward socialism, as far as revolutionary struggles are concerned, is filled with defeats.

And yet this same history leads systematically and inexorably to ultimate victory! Where would we be today *without* those "defeats" from which we have drawn historical experience, insight, power, and idealism? We stand at the point we have reached today, immediately before the final battle of the proletarian class war, precisely out of those defeats—and we needed *every single* one—defeats that are part of our strength and our clarity of vision.

Revolutionary struggles are the direct counterpart of parliamentary battles. Within the space of four decades, we had any number of parliamentary "victories" in Germany; we were positively striding from victory to victory. And the result, when we came up against the great historical test on August 4, 1914, was a devastating political and moral defeat, a shocking breakdown, an incomparable bankruptcy. Until now, the revolutions have only brought us defeats, but these unavoidable defeats are now piling up guarantee upon guarantee for the final victory in the future.

That being said, the final victory can only come about under *one* condition! The question of why each defeat came about must be asked, whether it resulted from the forward momentum of the battle energy of the masses colliding with the barrier of unripe historical conditions, or whether the revolutionary action itself was hobbled by half measures, indecision, and inner weaknesses.

Classic examples of both cases are, on the one hand, the French February Revolution [of 1848], and, on the other, the German March Revolution [of 1848]. The Parisian proletariat's heroic action in the year 1848 became the vital source of class energy for the entire international proletariat. The deplorable events of the German March Revolution weighed down all of modern German development like a ball and chain. They influenced the exceptional history of official German Social Democracy right up to the most recent events of the German Revolution, right up to the dramatic crisis we have just experienced.

How does defeat in this so-called "Spartacus Week" appear in the light of the aforementioned historical question? Was it a defeat resulting from tumultuous revolutionary energy in an insufficiently ripe situation, or from weakness and indecisive action?

Both! The split character of the crisis, the contradiction between the powerful, decisive, offensive demeanor of the Berlin masses, and the indecisiveness, timidity, and half measures of the Berlin leadership, are the features that have characterized this most recent episode.

The leadership has failed. But the leadership can and must be newly created, from and out of the masses. The masses are what matters; they are the rock on which the final victory of the revolution will be built. The masses were at their peak, they have forged this "defeat" into one link in the chain of those historic defeats that are the pride and the power behind international socialism. And that is why future victory will spring from this "defeat."

"Order prevails in Berlin!" You foolish lackeys! Your "order" is built on sand. Tomorrow the revolution "will rise up again with its weapons rattling,"* and to your horror will proclaim with a fanfare of trumpets:

I was, I am, I shall be!

* "Raise itself up again clashing" is a line from the poem *Abschiedswort* (A Word of Farewell) by Friedrich Freiligrath, a close friend of Marx. Marx published it in the final issue of the *Neue Rheinische Zeitung* after the defeat of the 1848 revolution; the entire issue was printed in red ink. 'I was, I am, I shall be' is a line from Freiligrath's poem *Die Revolution*, written in 1851.

Appendix

ONCE AGAIN, ON ORGANIZATION AND DISORGANIZATION*

In issue 99 of *Czerwony Sztandar*, Comrade R. L. addresses an important issue: "Is the task of the revolutionary workers' movement to organize, that is, to raise revolutionary consciousness among the popular masses and prepare them for battle, or rather to disorganize the government, which, as the PPS believes, is done by expropriating banks and postal trains, or, as was recently the case, by assaulting the police and representatives of the tsarist government in a planned and organized manner?"

Both in this and other articles, our party has always spoken out against the tactic of assault carried out by lone individuals, and invariably juxtaposed it with the tactic of mass struggle and mass demonstrations of all revolutionary people.

To Social Democracy's calm and constructive criticism, the PPS, as usual, has replied with slander. This alone should arouse the suspicion that they are wrong. Let us also, however, take a look at their response to Comrade R. L.'s deliberations. The task of a workers' party, claims the PPS, not only organizes the popular masses; it both organizes the proletariat and disorganizes the government.

The question of tactics—that is, the ways and nature of how workers' parties operate—is an extraordinarily important matter for the proletariat, and we will therefore consider once again how the PPS conceives of its tasks.

The tactic of the proletariat does not only influence the outcome of the revolution and thus the nature of the rights and freedoms we will obtain after the revolution. The tactic also determines whether our proletariat comes out fragmented and disorganized after the revolution or strong, impeccably organized, and ready to take up a fierce struggle in now completely new circumstances.

The latter, as is easy to comprehend, depends precisely on this factor, among others: whether the present tactic of the PPS leads to the organization of the popular masses or whether it introduces disorganization into their ranks.

---

* This article originally appeared in *Czerwony Sztandar* (Red Flag), a newspaper published by the Social Democracy of the Kingdom of Poland and Lithuania (SDKPiL) in May 1906 under the title "Jeszcze raz organizacja I dezorganizacja." It was reprinted in *Gazeta Robotnicza* (Workers' Newspaper), organ of the Warsaw Committee of the SDKPiL, on September 6, 1906. Since no copies of the May 1906 issue of *Czerwony Sztandar* have been found, it has been translated as it appeared in *Gazeta Robotnicza*. The translator is Mathias Foit. Although this article was published anonymously, we have determined that it was written by Luxemburg. It was discovered by Jörn Schütrumpf following the publication of Volume 4 of the *Complete Works*, which is why it appears here as an appendix. For the article "Organization and Disorganization" referred to here, see *The Complete Works of Rosa Luxemburg*, Vol. 4, pp. 179–82.

The PPS believes that it is disorganizing the tsarist government by dint of its fighters killing police officers and carrying out assassinations of generals and other government representatives. Is this really so? Not a bit!

The presumption of the PPS very much resembles the delusions of the tsarist government, which believes that by wrestling single individuals away from the ranks of fighters for our cause, even tens and hundreds of them, it will manage to disorganize and quash the revolutionary movement.

But just as it is implausible to thus disorganize the revolution, so is it fanciful to disorganize the tsarist government via assault, "confiscation," and assassination.

The source and significant causes of the strength and weakness of one and the other—the revolutionary movement and the tsarist government—lie elsewhere, and it is elsewhere that the tsarist government needs to be targeted if one is to disorganize it.

The strength of the tsarist government lies in one thing: in the dim-wittedness of the popular masses. It is from them that the tsarist government wrestles hundreds of thousands of soldiers away each year, still ready to quash the revolution with blood and iron; it is from them that it has syphoned away hundreds of millions of those necessary to maintain the military, police, gendarmerie, officers, prisons, schools of stupidity, etc.

The disorganization of the government began from the moment it failed to meet the needs of any of the social classes, discontentment with the government grew as a result, and its activities started to meet with resistance. The disorganization of the government developed as it began to dawn on the popular masses that they missed something, when they began to issue their demands more and more vocally, and the tsarist government could not and did not want to meet them. Finally, the disorganization of the government passed a milestone when it started a war requiring the expenditure of vast resources of power and energy; when the revolution broke out; when millions of people wrenched themselves toward light, freedom, and bread; and when the tsarist government was unable to satisfy these demands but did not possess enough strength to force millions into silence. The disorganization of the government has, after all, always been the result of a mass movement, of the revolutionizing of the masses, of the government, and the combined needs and demands of millions.

The removal of individuals from its ranks—even the most remarkable ones, even those holding the most senior posts—has had an impact on the disorganization of the government to a very small extent and only temporarily if at all. If the elimination from this world of Plehve—prior to the outbreak of the revolution—caused some havoc within the tsarist government, it is only because it had already been disorganized due to its defeats in the war—and its dependence on society for assistance in that war; not for fear of the bomb did it initiate the so-called "spring" of trust for society (the reign of

Svyatopolk-Mirsky). The assassination of Stolypin, on the other hand, could no longer influence government policies one bit. If concerns over the refusal of a multi-million loan could induce the tsarist government to eventually convene the Duma, then the robbing, that is, "confiscating," of less than a million rubles by the PPS is nothing compared to the tens of millions in monthly deficit caused by stagnation, misery, and the revolutionary attitude of the populace. If the everyday removal from police ranks of individuals most detrimental to the people, as an expression of the revolutionary attitude and climate among the wide masses of society, has a disorganizing effect on the police, then the specially organized assault in which several dozen people dressed in police uniforms are killed merely has the effect of a warning to the tsarist authorities and points to the necessity for better self-organization. Hence the following results: increased repression, "more careful" police selection, the replacement of the police with completely dim-witted, practically Black-Hundredist military troops, etc.* Thus we stand wholly unprepared against the new forces of the tsarist government, and—rather than the other way around—they begin to disorganize us.

That the tsarist forces will not put down the revolution is certain; it does not depend on them, and they are unable to remove whatever caused it and provides it with more and more energy. However, through repression they can make the revolution less organized and more disordered, more anarchic. Instead of mass uprisings with relatively clear and specified aims, we will experience lone assaults by brave militants (or even militant teams!), against the silence of an entire mass, incapable of action, admiring the militants, but not knowing what all of this is really about—whether it is about the Trofim Yemalyanov or giving a "warning" to the tsarist government and reminding it that the PPS has several dozen (or hundreds of) militants and several hundred Brownings;† or whether it is about the Warsaw or Petersburg constitutional assembly; or a republic federated under Russia within the borders of the Kingdom; or, finally, a republic within the Russian state. For our workers follow the lead of socialist parties and sympathize decidedly with their demands, but they have not yet realized how to fight and what to demand at every moment of the struggle.

And under these conditions, the entire "revolutionary" activity of the PPS does not disorganize the tsarist government but introduces that disorganization into the ranks of the proletariat.

---

* This refers to the members, actions, and ideology of the Black Hundreds, a reactionary, monarchist, ultra-nationalist movement in Russia in the early twentieth century. The movement was initiated by aristocrats but mobilized participants from the lower classes in mass violence aimed at Jews and other ethnic minorities as well as labor, socialist, and liberal targets.

† The Browning Arms Company developed many varieties of military and civilian firearms, cartridges, and gun mechanisms. Its rifles and pistols were widely used and commonly referred to as "Brownings."

The entire revolutionary activity of the PPS does not contribute at all to the disorganization of the government, whereas revolutionary Social Democracy may and does contribute greatly– by revolutionizing popular masses, by organizing the revolution. Let each worker be reminded what disorganization of the government was caused by last year's revolutionary uprisings, having drawn entire masses of people into battle; let workers reflect, by comparison, on the meaning of the uprising of the PPS on August 15, which only disorganized the preparatory work for future mass uprisings—and everyone will comprehend instantly not only the futility, but also the harmfulness of the revolutionary belligerence of the PPS.

The tasks of organizing a proletarian movement include not only raising awareness of the aims and means of that movement, but also gaining allies for the revolution who are indispensable to the proletariat in the form of the peasantry, the military, and the petty bourgeoisie. *Czerwony Sztandar* has already discussed the detrimental effect of the tactic of the PPS on this set of tasks to organize popular masses, so we do not pause here but rather briefly recapitulate all of the above.

The task of Social Democracy consists in bringing to the elemental movement of the exploited masses awareness about the aims and means of that movement, and organizing that movement with a view to a new order emerging out of that organization in the future. To rise to that challenge, Social Democracy must focus all its energy on organization and agitation in harmony with its principles, on preparing in this way an uprising of the masses in order to gain their indispensable rights and freedoms. Any departure from this clear and straight road is harmful: firstly, because it diverts our meager forces from essential tasks; secondly, because deluding the masses that their liberation does not rest on them but on a handful of "militants" weakens their self-reliance; thirdly, because, in the minds of the masses, it causes lack of clarity and confusion concerning the ways and means of the struggle for liberation; fourthly, because it creates the conditions not for the organizational, agitational and, as a consequence, simply revolutionary work of Social Democracy, but for the half-anarchistic tactic of "confiscating" funds, supposedly disorganizing the government by killing police officers, destroying bridges and monuments—tactics from which the popular masses derive no benefit.

And the disorganization of the government? It was, it is, and it shall remain the opposite side, the immediate effect of the revolutionary Social Democracy organizing popular masses.

Organizing a revolution—is the only means of disorganizing the government.

A Glossary of Personal Names

Adler, Victor (1852–1918), founder and leader of the Austrian Social Democratic Workers' Party, prominent in the Second (Socialist) International. A political "moderate," he backed the decision of the Imperial government of Austria-Hungary to embark upon World War I.

Albrecht, Adolf (1855–1930), joined tailors' union and predecessor of SPD 1874, leading functionary in the SPD, member of Reichstag 1898–1903 and 1905–18, joined USPD in 1918, chairman of Halle Workers' and Soldiers' Council, elected to Reichstag of Weimar Republic 1920–1924, returned to SPD 1922.

Antrick, Otto (1858–1924), cigar maker and member of the cigar makers' union, active in the socialist movement from 1876, SPD member from 1890, member of Brandenburg Agitation Commission, city councilor in Berlin 1904–06, party secretary in Braunschweig 1906–19; representative in the Reichstag 1893–1903, 1912–18.

Arendsee, Hulda Martha (1885–1953), active in the SPD beginning 1906; worked with Clara Zetkin for women's rights. Identified with the left wing of the SPD, opposed World War I and became part of the USPD. Active in 1920 merger by USPD majority with the KPD. Elected KPD delegate to Reichstag 1924 and 1928. Identified with leadership of Heinrich Brandler, marginalized in KPD circles when that leadership was displaced by Stalin's favorite, Ernst Thälmann. Remained part of KPD, fled to the Soviet Union when the Nazis took power in Germany. Her companion, Paul Schwenk, was arrested during the wave of purges in the 1930s and was saved, in part through her efforts. Returned to Germany after World War II, supporting the Communist regime in East Germany.

Aveling, Eleanor, see Eleanor Marx-Aveling.

Avksentiev, Nikolai Dimitrovich (1878–1943), a leading member of the Party of Socialist Revolutionaries (PSR) in Russia. Member of the moderate wing of the PSR that supported the Russian war effort during World War I. After the overthrow of the tsar, he and his comrades participated in the soviets (democratic councils), while supporting the more moderate Provisional Government. Became minister of the interior of this short-lived Provisional Government headed by Alexander Kerensky, and when it was overthrown by the October Revolution helped initiate armed opposition to the Bolshevik regime. Seeking cooperation with counterrevolutionary forces led by Admiral Kolchak, he found himself under arrest as Kolchak established a military dictatorship. Forced into exile, ended his days in the United States.

Axelrod, Pavel B. (1850–1928), a Narodnik in the 1870s; 1883, cofounder of the Emancipation of Labor Group, an early group of Russian Marxists led by Georgi Plekhanov; 1900, an editor of *Iskra*; after 1903, one of the leading Mensheviks. Opposed the Bolshevik seizure of power; lived remaining years in exile.

Azef, Yevno (1869–1918), active in Russia's revolutionary movement, operating as both an organizer of assassinations for the Socialist Revolutionary Party and as a police spy for the Okhrana, the tsar's secret police. Rose through the ranks to become the leader of the Socialist Revolutionary Party's terrorist branch, the SR Combat Organization, 1904–08. Unmasked as a double agent in 1909 and fled to Germany.

Baden, Max von (1867–1929), German prince, general and politician. Appointed and served as last chancellor of the German Reich and Prussian president in 1918.

Balmashov, Stepan (1882–1902), Russian student who assassinated the Minister of Internal Affairs Dmitry Sipyagin April 1902 in St. Petersburg. Hanged May 1902.

Barrot, Camille Hyacinthe-Odilon (1791–1873), moderately liberal French politician, briefly head of the Council of Ministers under Napoleon III 1848–49, but soon became an opponent. Associated with Adolphe Thiers, who nominated him, after the 1871 collapse of the empire of Napoleon III, as president of the Council of State, but he died having only filled his new office for about a year.

Barth, Emil (1879–1941), prominent SPD activist, joined the antiwar USPD 1917, became a leader of the Revolutionary Shop Stewards January 1918. Considered the most radical of six members of the Council of the People's Deputies ruling the early Weimar Republic, composed of three SPD members (Ebert, Scheidemann and Landsberg) and three USPD members (Haase, Dittmann and Barth). Resigned from the council to protest against Ebert's use of army regulars against revolutionary demonstrations. Rejoined the SPD in 1922. Arrested several times after the Nazis took power in 1933.

Bauer, Gustav (1870–1944), elected to the Reichstag for the SPD in a Breslau constituency. In October 1918, assumed a position in the cabinet of Max von Baden. Remained in this position after Baden resigned November 1918, continued to serve under the Council of the People's Deputies, headed by Friedrich Ebert. Served briefly as chancellor of Germany June 1919–March 1920. After the March 1920 Kapp Putsch, served as vice-chancellor, minister of the treasury, and minister of transportation in other cabinets of the Weimar Republic May 1920–November 1922. His political rise was eclipsed in 1925 when he was tainted by scandal, although he went on to serve as an SPD deputy to the Reichstag from 1926 to 1928 before retiring from public life.

Bauer, Otto (1881–1938), one of the leaders of Austrian Social Democracy and the Second International; founded the theoretical magazine *Der Kampf* in

Vienna 1907; theoretical spokesperson for Austro-Marxism (associated with its "left wing"); wrote important works on the national question. Authored one of the most famous critiques of Luxemburg's *Accumulation of Capital*, to which she responded in her *Anti-Critique*. Adopted a disapproving attitude toward the Bolshevik Revolution in Russia in 1917; was foreign minister of Austria in 1918/19.

Baumeister, Albert (1882–1953), German trade union leader functionary and journalist prominent in the right-wing of the SPD. Active in the International Union of Hotel, Restaurant and Bar Workers; served as secretary to Karl Legien. During World War I editor of *Feldpost* and *Internationale Korrespondenz*, which championed the position of the right wing of the SPD. During the German Revolution of 1918–19 he was an organizer of the Reichstag regiment that fought to quell the Spartacist uprising.

Bebel, Ferdinand August (1840–1913), lathe operator; Social Democrat; member of the Reichstag, 1867–81 and 1883–1913; 1869, cofounder of the SDAP; led the legal and illegal struggle of the party during the period of the antisocialist "exceptional" laws in Germany and contributed in a major way to the founding of the party's central organ, *Der Sozialdemokrat*; 1881–90, member of the regional parliament (Landtag) in the state of Saxony; 1892–1913, one of the two co-chairmen of the SPD; from 1889 on, a leading member of the Second International, and from 1900 on, a member of the ISB.

Beccaria, Cesare (1738–1794), Italian philosopher and politician best known for *On Crimes and Punishments*, a passionate attack on torture and the death penalty that advocated a radical reform of the penal system; his books were an important influence on such U.S. thinkers as Thomas Jefferson.

Bernstein, Eduard (1850–1932), German socialist politician and theoretician, initially a follower of Ferdinand Lassalle, joined the Marxist "Eisenachers" in the 1870s; 1890–1901, lived in exile in London; appointed literary heir of Marx's archives by Engels; regular contributor to *Die Neue Zeit*; from 1896 on, one of the major theoreticians of "revisionism," the view that Marxism should be revised and "modernized"; subject of Luxemburg's polemic in *Reform or Revolution*; member of the German Reichstag 1902–06 and 1912–18; 1906, became a teacher at the SPD's school in Berlin; 1914 resigned from the SPD on pacifist grounds and became a leading member of the USPD; rejoined the SPD 1919.

Berten, Peter (1873–1960), carpenter and active trade unionist who became a shop steward and SPD party chairperson in Düsseldorf, where he also edited the *Volkszeitung* 1909–33 (minus an interval during 1915–18). Drawn to the ideas of Luxemburg while attending the party school in Berlin, part of the SPD left, joined the USPD in 1917, was close to the *Spartakusbund* but in 1922 rejoined the SPD. 1919–28 city councilor in Düsseldorf for the USPD and the SPD, respectively. 1920–21 member of the Prussian constitutional assembly and 1924–33 of the Prussian state parliament. 1921–24 member of the Prussian State Council. Imprisoned several times for short periods after the Nazis took power. Politically active in the SPD after World War II.

Bethmann-Hollweg, Theobald von (1856–1921), German politician. Appointed to various administrative positions in the Prussian government from 1882; president of Brandenburg, 1899; 1905–1907, prime minister of the interior, and 1909–17, chancellor of Germany. A strong proponent of German imperialism and expansionist policies that led to World War I, he favored the ethnic cleansing of Poles and other non-Germans from the empire; forced from power in July 1917.

Biedermann, Alfred (1866–1936), Polish industrial capitalist. Head of a major textile producing firm in Łódź, which he inherited from his father; worked closely with Juliusz Karol Kunitzer in fostering commercial and social interests of the national bourgeoisie in Congress Poland; during World War I moved to Germany and invested in the coal industry.

Bismarck, Otto von (1815–1898), Prussian-German statesman and first chancellor of Germany 1871–1890. A member of the Junker landowning class and extreme nationalist and authoritarian, he was instrumental in Prussia's (and later Germany's) military expansion. He imposed the Antisocialist Laws while trying to buy off sections of the workers' movement by providing some social welfare protections.

Bissing, Mortiz von (1884–1917), German military officer, deputy commander of the VII Army Corps during World War I and appointed governor-general of German-occupied Belgium.

Böhme, Curt (1889–1968), precision mechanic, active in SPD, organized 1916 "Easter Conference of Youth" with Karl Liebknecht; joined USPD 1920, which merged into KPD; returned to SPD 1922; mayor of Allsted 1925–31; driven from public political life 1933; imprisoned in Buchenwald concentration camp 1944–45; rejoined SPD 1945, SED in 1946; held various positions in East German regime.

Bogrov, Dmitry Grigoriyevich (1887–1911), the 1911 assassin of Russian prime minister Pyotr Stolypin. While acting as an anarchist revolutionary, actually an agent of the tsarist secret police, the Okhrana, informing on the activities of anarchists and of the Socialist Revolutionary and Social Democratic parties since 1906. There is controversy over whether Stolypin was killed by revolutionaries to halt a successful and popular set of reforms that Stolypin was promoting (and thereby hasten a violent revolution), or whether the assassination was a plot by ultra-conservative Okhrana elements who detested Stolypin's agrarian reforms and inclinations to foster parliamentary government.

Borgmann, Hermann (1855–1911), hat maker journeyman in Leipzig, joined the union and SPD, moved to Berlin in 1888, where in 1891 he became a partner and manager of the cooperative Deutsche Hutfabrik. Elected to the Berlin council, to which he belonged until his death. One of seven SPD deputies elected to the Prussian House of Representatives in 1908, became chairman of the SPD parliamentary group. At the September 1910 Magdeburg Party Congress of the SPD, he gave the main speech on the voting law debate to which Luxemburg refers in her justification for a motion on the political mass strike in this volume.

Brandler, Heinrich (1881–1967), bricklayer, active trade unionist in 1897, joined SPD in 1901, opponent of World War I; founding member of the *Spartakusbund* and the KPD, for which he became an effective organizer, propagandist, and leader. Replaced Paul Levi as KPD chairman February 1921, garnering criticism for his role in the ill-fated "March Action" and failure to initiate a 1923 revolution in Germany that had been expected by many Communists. In 1928, dislodged by Ernest Thälmann, who was supported by the crystallizing Stalin regime in the USSR, resulting in the formation of a dissident Communist Party Opposition (KPO), which functioned in exile after the Nazis took power in 1933 and continued as the Gruppe Arbeiterpolitik (Labor Politics Group) after World War II.

Brandt, Willy (1913–1992), joined the youth group of the SPD in 1929, drawn to the left-socialist SAP (Sozialistische Arbeiterpartei, Socialist Workers' Party). After 1933, involved in the anti-Nazi underground and an activist in exile. Returned to Germany 1946 and joined the SPD 1948. Mayor of West Berlin 1957–66, leader of the SPD 1964–87, and chancellor of Germany 1969–74.

Braun, Otto (1872–1955), joined the SPD in 1888. A dedicated SPD functionary, rose to the position of chairman of the East Prussian SPD, member of the national executive 1911, and member of the Prussian House of Representatives in 1913. During World War I, upheld the majority SPD policy of supporting the war effort. 1920–1932 served as prime minister of Prussia, going into exile when the Nazis took power in 1933.

Breitscheid, Rudolf (1874–1944), initially a leader of the liberal Democratic Union, joined the SPD in 1912. Opposed World War I, joined the USPD 1917, returning to the SPD in 1922. Served as a senior member of and foreign policy spokesman for the SPD Reichstag group during the Weimar Republic; member of the German delegation to the League of Nations. After the Nazi rise to power, among the members of the Reichstag who voted against the Enabling Act of 1933; soon after fled to France to avoid persecution. After the 1940 German conquest of France, arrested and handed over to the Gestapo in 1941. Died in Buchenwald concentration camp.

Briand, Aristide (1862–1932), studied law at the Faculty of Law of Paris, associated with syndicalist and socialist movements, founded the daily socialist newspaper *L'Humanité* in collaboration with Jean Jaurès. A leader of the

French Socialist Party beginning 1894, elected to the Chamber of Deputies 1902, favored an alliance of the Socialists with the liberal (and pro-capitalist) reformers of the Radical Party. In 1906 accepted a position in the government of Radical leader Georges Clemenceau, which resulted in his expulsion from the Socialist Party. From that time until 1929, served in various governments and assumed the position of prime minister eleven times.

Bromme, Moritz (1873–1926), working-class SPD functionary whose involvement included being elected as Lübeck party secretary in 1909. Known for his autobiography: *The Life of a Modern Factory Worker* (1905).

Buhler, Alfred (1890–1977), joined Association of Lithographers and Stone Printers and SPD 1908; attended courses of Otto Rühle in 1910–1911; member of the Rostock Soldiers' Council during the November Revolution. Member of USPD and then KPD. Active in the KPD through 1920s with lower-level leadership responsibilities; elected to state parliament in Mecklenburg-Schwerin 1924–29; KPD parliamentary group leader briefly. From 1925 involved in internal disputes in KPD, resigned in 1929, for a very brief time rejoined the SPD, remained active as independent activist. Briefly arrested in Nazi period. 1945 rejoined KPD, then became member of SED.

Castan, Ernst Karl (1871–1948), represented SPD in the second chamber of the Saxon state parliament in Dresden 1909 to 1918, assuming a position in the left-wing of the party. For a time after 1919, favored coalition with the KPD, but 1924–1926 agreed with members of his party opposing such coalition. No longer active when the Nazis took power in 1933.

Cavaignac, Louis-Eugène (1802–1857), French militarist and general. 1830, supported the revolution that brought Louis-Phillip to power; stationed in Algeria 1832–1848, instrumental in carrying out the French conquest of the region. Became *de facto* head of state June 1848 and moved to violently crush the revolutionary forces on the streets of Paris; during the week of June 23–26, 1848, responsible for the deaths of thousands. Lost the subsequent presidential election to Louis Napoleon, who had him briefly imprisoned 1851.

Charles I (1600–1649), king of England 1625–49; executed at the end of the English Civil War by the forces allied with Oliver Cromwell.

Chkheidze, Nikolay (1864–1926), Georgian politician prominent in the Menshevik faction of the Russian Social Democratic Labor Party and a key figure in the Russian Revolutions of February and October 1917; from February to September served as president of the Executive Committee of the Petrograd Soviet, until the Bolsheviks won a majority and he was replaced by Leon Trotsky. From February 1918 to March 1921, a leader of a Menshevik regime in Georgia but then forced into exile.

Cohn, Oskar (1869–1934), attorney, Social Democrat; from 1909, a city council member in Berlin; 1912–1918, member of the Reichstag; 1916, belonged to the Social Democratic Working Group (*Arbeitsgemeinschaft*); 1917, became a member of the USPD.

Coligny, Admiral Gaspard de (1519–1572), French nobleman and admiral, close friend and advisor to King Charles IX; disciplined Huguenot leader who was murdered in the Saint Bartholomew's Day Massacre during the French Wars of Religion.

Cunow, Heinrich (1862–1936), SPD politician and theorist. Initially opposed World War I but changed his views, employing Marxist ideas to defend the German war effort. Argued that German imperialism was progressive, sweeping aside antiquated methods of production, fostering modernization and industrial progress. Became editor of the SPD theoretical journal *Die Neue Zeit* when longtime editor Karl Kautsky joined the USPD in 1917.

Dan, Fyodor Ilyich (1871–1947), Russian revolutionary, politician, and one of the Mensheviks' leading theoreticians. Involved in Russia's Social Democratic movement from 1894 on; after the 1917 October Revolution, sharply criticized the Bolsheviks' seizure of power. Left the Soviet Union 1922 and was stripped of his Soviet citizenship 1923. Lived for a time in exile in France, and from 1941 until his death in the United States.

Daszyński, Ignacy (1866–1936), a founder and leader of the Polish Social Democratic Party, which evolved into the Polish Socialist Party; represented a "moderate" trend and served in the parliament of the Austro-Hungarian Empire 1897–1918; supported Austria-Hungary during World War I, served very briefly as prime minster in the new Polish Republic founded in 1918; 1912–26 collaborated with Józef Piłsudski (who evolved from a socialist to a right-wing nationalist and military dictator of Poland).

Däumig, Ernst Friedrich (c. 1866/68–1922), German Social Democrat; 1901–1911, editor of Social Democratic newspapers in Gera, Halle, and Erfurt; 1911 became a regular contributor to *Vorwärts* on questions of culture, education, and military science; 1912–18, chairman of the SPD's Berlin district committee on culture and education; 1917, became a member of the USPD, and secretary in the USPD party leadership May 1918; one of the leaders of the Revolutionary Shop Stewards in Berlin 1918.

David, Eduard (1863–1930), teacher and Social Democrat; 1896, became a leading advocate of revisionism; 1896–97 edited *Plainzer Volkszeitung*; 1898–08 member of the lower house of Hesse; member of the staff and regular contributor to the revisionist organ *Sozialistische Monatshefte*; member of the Reichstag 1903–18; fervent supporter of German expansionism and World War I.

Deutsch, Julius (1884–1968), active in socialist youth movement in Austria-Hungary, close to Austro-Marxist leader Otto Bauer, served on the Italian front during World War I, considered a military specialist and served as war minister in the new Austrian Republic emerging from World War I.

Critical of Bolshevik Revolution, opposed attempted Communist revolution in Hungary, later organized anti-fascist militia of the 1920s and early 1930s, the *Schutzbund*. After World War II, critical of Austrian Social-Democratic leadership for veering away from socialist traditions, withdrew to devote himself to historical and political writing.

Dietz, Johann Heinrich Wilhelm (1843–1922), publisher and politician representing the German Social Democracy in the Reichstag from 1881 to 1918. Supervised publication of correspondence of Marx and Engels; published works by August Bebel, Eduard Bernstein, Ferdinand Lassalle, and Franz Mehring. His publishing house produced the Marxist theoretical journal *Die Neue Zeit*, edited by Karl Kautsky, and the socialist women's magazine edited by Clara Zetkin, *Die Gleicheit* (*Equality*). Aligned with SPD moderates in numerous internal controversies.

Dissmann, Robert (1878–1926), lathe operator, Social Democrat; 1900–1908, head of the German Metalworkers' Union in Barmen-Elberfeld and, 1905–08, in Frankfurt-am-Main; 1908–12, party secretary for the SPD in Hanau; 1912–17, SPD regional secretary for Hesse-Nassau; beginning 1912, city councilor in Hanau; 1917, became a member of the USPD.

Dittmann, Wilhelm Friedrich Carl (1874–1954), carpenter, Social Democrat; from 1899, editor of *Die Norddeutsche Volksstimme* in Bremerhaven and, in 1902–04, of *Die Bergische Arbeitersstimme* in Solingen; 1904–09, party secretary and regional chairman of the SPD for Frankfurt-am-Main and, in 1907–09, city councilor in Frankfurt; 1909–17, again editor of *Die Bergische Arbeitersstimme*; 1912–18, member of the Reichstag; 1916, member of the executive of the Social Democratic "Working Group" (Arbeitsgemeinschaft); 1917, cofounder and one of the chairmen of the USPD; rejoined SPD.

Dobrohlaw, Paul (1870–1946), publican, SPD member, Berlin district councilor (1929–33). One of sixty-two delegates at the 1910 Magdeburg SPD Party Congress to sign Luxemburg's mass strike resolution (*Vorwärts*, September 23, 1910).

Dröner, Ernst (1879–1951), joined SPD 1896; cofounder and chairman of local branch of the Central Association of Clerks in Germany 1897. Cofounder of the Liberation Consumer Cooperative in Elberfeld 1909, member of the board and chairman of the local SPD and managing director of the party newspaper *Freie Presse*. Survived World War I as a private, became chairman of the workers' and soldiers' council in Elberfeld November 1918; took part in the first Council Congress in Berlin. Remained with SPD majority. Played an important role in defending against the 1920 Kapp Putsch, initiating a common front of all workers' parties in an action committee. Remained active in SPD through the 1920s and early 1930s but removed from office and imprisoned several times when the Nazis took power. After 1945 he continued to be active in local politics through the SPD.

Dzerzhinsky, English transliteration of the Russian spelling of the Polish name **Dzierżyński** (see below).

Dzierżyński, Feliks (1877–1926), Polish revolutionary. Prominent figure in the Polish and Russian workers' movements. 1895, member of the Lithuanian Social Democracy; from 1897 on, arrested many times, condemned to internal exile, and escaped; 1900, cofounder of the SDKPiL; beginning 1902, lived as an émigré in Berlin and then in Krakow; member of the SDKPiL's Committee Abroad and, beginning in 1905, of the SDKPiL's Chief Executive Committee; 1906, became the representative of the SDKPiL on the Central Committee of the RSDLP; after 1908, lived as an émigré, mainly in Krakow; in Warsaw in 1912, arrested and again imprisoned; upon his release in 1917, joined the Bolshevik Party; after the Bolshevik Revolution, became head of the Cheka, the secret police.

Ebert, Friedrich (1871–1925), German Social Democrat. 1891–1905, at various times chairman of the Social Democratic party organization in Bremen; 1893–94, local editor and court reporter for the *Bremer Bürger-Zeitung*; 1905, became a member of the SPD executive; 1908, chairman of the Zentralstelle (central office) for the Working Youth of Germany; 1912–18, member of the Reichstag; 1913, together with Hugo Haase, co-chairman of the SPD. A leading representative of reformism and strong supporter of World War I; in 1916, became chairman of the Reichstag group of SPD deputies; on November 9, 1918, named chancellor of the German Empire by Prince Max von Baden; became chairman of the anti-revolutionary Council of People's Representatives; was decisively involved in the crushing of the November Revolution. Remained President of the Weimar Republic until his death.

Eichhorn, Emil (1863–1925), German Social Democrat. Apprenticed as a glass worker, became active in the SPD, working as a full-time official from 1893; headed the SPD press office beginning 1908. Joined with others to form the USPD in 1917, on November 9, 1918, led occupation of police headquarters in Berlin. Took over the office of police chief, set free 600 political prisoners. A January 1919 attempt to dismiss and replace him with an SPD politician provoked mass opposition and a general strike, with Eichhorn declaring at a mass demonstration of 200,000, "I got my job from the revolution, and I shall give it up only to the revolution." This resulted in a chain of events leading to the Spartacist uprising. Became part of KPD when USPD majority merged with it. After expulsion of Paul Levi, in the wake of the disastrous March Action of 1921, affiliated with Levi's Communist Working Group but also retained KPD membership.

Eichhorn, Hermann Emil Gottfried von (1848–1918), Prussian military officer. Served as field marshal general in the forces of Imperial Germany during World War I in the wake of the conquest of the portion of the Russian Empire that is Ukraine, where he assumed the position of military governor.

He was assassinated July 30, 1918, by Boris M. Donskov of the Party of Left Socialist Revolutionaries.

Emmel, Joseph Leopold (1863–1919), German Social Democrat. Became managing director of the *Mülhause Volkszeitung* in Alsace 1902; member of the district council and state assembly; chairman of the precinct organization and the control commission of the SPD in Alsace-Lorraine.

Emmich, Otto von (1848–1915), Prussian general. Led in the bloody 1914 conquest of urban and military targets of Liège (Lüttich) in Belgium.

Engels, Friedrich (1820–1895), German philosopher and socialist. Marx's closest colleague and collaborator; author of such works as *The Condition of the Working Class in England, Herr Eugen Dühring's Revolution in Science (Anti-Dühring)*, and *The Origin of the Family, Private Property and the State;* editor of Volumes II and III of Marx's *Capital.*

Ernst, Eugen (1864–1954), German Social Democrat. Trained as a typesetter, joined Book Printers' Union in 1884 and became a member of the SPD. Held several positions as a party official, chairman of the intraparty oppositional "youth," 1891–93. By the early 1900s active in the top leadership of the SPD, including as business executive of the *Vorwärts* printing house and its custodian 1903–18. In January 1919, the SPD majority leadership chose him to replace USPD radical Emil Eichhorn as police chief of Berlin, which helped set off the ill-fated Spartacist uprising. Worked closely with Gustav Noske, notorious minister of defense in the Ebert administration of the Weimar Republic. With Wolfgang Heine (see below), informed Noske that Luxemburg's body had been found in a sluice in the Landwehr Canal. A town councilor in his native Werder, became inactive during the period of Nazi rule. Rejoined SPD after World War II, participated in the 1946 SPD-KPD merger in East Germany.

Erzberger, Matthias (1875–1921), German publicist and politician. Prominent in the Catholic Center Party. Reich minister of finance, 1919–20. Signed the armistice between Germany and the Allied Powers on behalf of the Reich government. Participated in the Ebert government of the Weimar Republic and was assassinated in 1921 by the right-wing terrorist group Organisation Consul.

Fischer, Richard (1855–1926), German socialist politician and editor. Initially worked as a typesetter in Switzerland, where he joined the socialist movement in the early 1870s; became editor of *Berliner Freien Presse* in 1878; returned to Switzerland during the Antisocialist Laws in Germany, becoming a leading figure of the SPD in exile. In 1902, became a member of German Reichstag; founded and managed the SPD's publishing house, *Vorwärts*, from the late 1890s to 1922. A revisionist who often opposed Luxemburg's positions, avidly supported Germany's entry into World War I.

Fischer, Ruth (actual name: Elfriede Eisler) (1895–1961), Austrian communist.

A founder of the Austrian Communist Party; in the early 1920s became a prominent leader in the German KPD, associated with its ultraleft wing. Took the lead in challenging the ideas and reputation of Luxemburg for being insufficiently Communist. By the late 1920s she and others around her were marginalized and then expelled by followers of Stalin. Late 1940s became a Cold War anti-communist but remained a socialist.

Fleissner, Hermann (1865–1939), Social Democrat. Worked as a carpenter, joined the Woodworkers' Association in 1895, became active in SPD beginning 1884. From 1897 he worked as a reporter for various Social Democratic newspapers and became editor of the *Dresdner Volkszeitung*. 1913–17, member of the central party committee of the SPD and chairman of the Dresden party organization; 1900–03, alderman in Löbtau; 1905–09, city councilor in Dresden; 1909–20, member of the Landtag of the Free State of Saxony. He was in the left wing of the SPD and helped found the USPD in 1917. November 1918, a member of the Council of the People's Deputies of Saxony. Rejected USPD merger with KPD, eventually rejoined SPD.

Frank, Ludwig (1874–1914), German Social Democrat and attorney. Beginning 1904, city councilor in Mannheim; 1905–14, member of the Baden state assembly (Landtag); cofounder of the working-class youth movement in South Germany; 1906–08, editor of the journal *Die Junge Garde*; 1907–14, member of the Reichstag; leading representative of reformism; prominent supporter of World War I, volunteered for military duty and was killed in the war.

Freiligrath, Friedrich (1810–1876), German lyric poet. Joined the revolutionary movement of the "pre–March 1848" period; emigrated to Switzerland in 1845; 1846–48 member of the Communist League; became a close friend of Karl Marx and returned to Germany in 1848; part of the "Young Germany" movement; contributor to the *Neue Rheinische Zeitung*; withdrew from political activity in the mid-1850s.

Friedberg, Robert (1851–1920), German economist and politician. Prominent in the National Liberal Party, in which he headed the parliamentary group. In 1917 became deputy prime minister under Chancellor Georg von Hertling of the Catholic Center Party, tasked (under the watchful eye of Generals von Hindenberg and Ludendorff) with overseeing the last stage of the collapse of Germany's home front. While Hertling's administration made way for that of Prince Maximilian of Baden in the swirl of the November Revolution of 1918, Friedberg shifted from the right wing of the National Liberals to join with more left-wing elements in forming the German Democratic Party (Deutsche Demokratische Partei, DDP).

Frölich, Paul (1884–1953), German Social Democrat and Communist. Born into a working-class family, studied history and social science at the Leipzig Workers' School and joined the SPD in 1902. Active in its left-wing, he became part of the *Spartakusbund* during World War I, then was a founding member of the KPD and of *Die Rote Fahne.* A member of the KPD's central committee, he was forced off that body due to the merger with the USPD. Supporter of the disastrous "March Action" of 1921. Following the departure of the faction around Paul Levi, he rejoined the KPD central committee and was elected as a KPD deputy to the Reichstag for 1921–24, and again in 1928. Expelled from the KPD at the end of 1928 for supporting the so-called "right opposition" associated with Heinrich Brandler, he first joined the Communist Party Opposition (KPO), then in 1932 helped establish the left-socialist SAP (Sozialistische Arbeiterpartei, Socialist Workers' Party). Imprisoned when the Nazis took power but then released at end of 1933. Lived in exile, first in France then the United States, returning to West Germany in 1950. Best known as a biographer of Rosa Luxemburg.

Fuhrmann, Paul (1872–1942), German aristocrat prominent in the National Liberal Party.

Galliffet, Marquis de; Gaston Alexandre Auguste (1830–1909), French general. Coordinated bloody repression of the 1871 Paris Commune. Minister of war in Waldeck-Rousseau's cabinet. This caused a controversy in the socialist movement, since independent socialist Alexandre Millerand was also in the government with the "commune's executioner."

Garibaldi, Giuseppe (1907–1882), Italian general, patriot, revolutionary, and republican. Contributed to the unification of Italy and its establishment as a nation-state. Considered one of the greatest generals of modern times and one of Italy's "fathers of the fatherland." A follower of liberal nationalist Giuseppe Mazzini and of democratic republican government, Garibaldi broke with Mazzini to pragmatically ally himself with conservatives and monarchists in the struggle to create an independent Italy. Involved in revolutionary nationalist struggles in South America while in exile in there. Became international figurehead for national independence and republican ideals, although opportunistic and undemocratic figures more often than not benefitted from the efforts of Garibaldi and his followers.

Garnier-Pagès, Louis-Antoine (1803–1878), French politician. Liberal reformist who fought on the barricades during the 1830 July Revolution that replaced the despotic monarchy of Charles X with the more liberal monarchy of Louis Phillipe. When Louis Phillipe was overthrown in the revolution of 1848, Garnier-Pagès (who was named mayor of Paris) and other less-than-radical figures trumpeted liberal democratic ideals and a romanticized nationalism while distancing themselves from the working class's socialist aspirations. Alienating the working class, the liberal reformers proved incapable of warding off the fake-populist power grab of Napoleon III. Garnier-Pagès was part of the republican opposition to the despotic regime, and he also opposed the disastrous Franco-Prussian War that Napoleon III helped initiate and which caused his regime to collapse. 1870–71, Garnier-Pagès became part of a Government of National Defense that proved as ineffectual as previous such efforts. A crescendo of popular discontent resulted, along with the revolutionary explosion that was the Paris Commune of 1871.

Gewehr, Elfriede (birth and death dates unavailable), German Social Democrat. 1908–09, participant in the third school year of the SPD's Central Party School in Berlin; daughter of Wilhelm Gewehr and cousin of Luxemburg.

Geyer, Friedrich August Carl (1853–1937), German Social Democrat, cigarmaker. 1886–1918, member of the Reichstag; 1895–1918, editor of the *Tabakarbeiter*; 1898–1902, chairman of the Social Democratic Association for the City of Leipzig; beginning 1913, member of the Control Commission of the SPD; during World War I, a centrist; 1916, belonged to the Social Democratic "Working Group" (Arbeitsgemeinschaft); 1917, became a member of the USPD. At the end of 1920 he took part in the unification of the USPD majority with the KPD but left 1921 after the internal party disputes around the "March Action" and by 1922 had returned to the SPD.

Goethe, Johann Wolfgang von (1749–1832), German poet, prose writer, dramatist, and naturalist. Renowned for *Faust*, *Sorrows of Young Werther*, and many other works; foremost representative of nineteenth-century German classicism and romanticism. One of Luxemburg's favorite writers.

Gompers, Samuel (1850–1924), cigarmaker and trade union organizer in the United States. President of the American Federation of Labor from its 1886 founding to his death. In his youth, influenced by the ideas of Karl Marx, but over time became a strong advocate of "pure and simple unionism" kept separate from socialist commitments and radical reforms. By the early 1900s he was an avowed antisocialist and generally favored a bureaucratic-conservative approach to labor questions.

Goremykin, Ivan (1839–1917), Russian conversative politician, prime minister of Russian Empire 1906 and 1914–16. Arrested by the Provisional Government following the February Revolution of 1917. Released by Kerensky but killed soon afterward in a robbery.

Gorter, Herman (1864–1927), Dutch poet and socialist; 1880s, leading member of Tachtigers, group of left-wing Dutch writers; 1897, joined SDAP; 1889, published *Mei*, an epic poem considered an outstanding work of Dutch Impressionism; 1909, broke from SDAP to help form Social-Democratische Partji (SDP) of the Netherlands in opposition to the reformist orientation of the Second International; initially supported Bolshevik Revolution but then became (along with Anton Pannekoek) leading left-wing critic of Leninism; 1921 helped found Communist Workers' Party of Germany, which opposed the Third International.

Gramsci, Antonio (1891–1937), Italian communist. Leader of the Italian

Communist Party, arrested and imprisoned by Mussolini's fascist government in 1926. Over the course of a decade, developed numerous analyses and theorizations in his *Prison Notebooks*, which deal with a remarkable range of historical, cultural, political, philosophical, and socio-economic questions. These have had considerable and influential impact on the thinking of Marxists and non-Marxists alike.

Graupe, Georg (1875–1959), German Social Democrat. Joined SPD in 1900; union secretary of textile workers union in Zwickau, 1906–33; active in various labor and socialist efforts. Took part in World War I, 1914–18. SPD city councilor in Zwickau, sat in Saxon State Parliament, 1919–30, entered Reichstag in 1930. Held in custody by the Nazi regime at various points from 1933 to 1935. After 1946, became mayor of Dommitzsch.

Grenz, Ernst August (1855–1921), German Social Democrat. From 1876, active in labor and socialist movements, involved in metal workers' union; representative in Reichstag, 1903–07 and 1912–18.

Grey, Edward (better known as Sir Edward Grey) (1862–1933), British Liberal statesman and central force behind British foreign policy in the era of World War I.

Grigorjanz, A. (birth and death dates unavailable), Russian Social-Democrat. His reports on the Russian workers' movement circulated in the labor press of various countries. After the Bolsheviks took power, he wrote an article with a critical Menshevik orientation, entitled "Diktator des Proletariats" (Dictatorship of the Proletariat) that appeared in the SPD daily *Vorwärts* on November 9, 1917. Contributed articles to *Vorwärts* 1917–22, notably a 1921 article on the famine in Russia.

Gröber, Adolf (1854–1919), German lawyer and politician associated with the Catholic Center Party, for which he served as parliamentary leader in the Reichstag. Member of the Weimar Republic's National Assembly, involved in helping to draft the country's new constitution.

Groener, Karl Eduard Wilhelm (1867–1939), German general and politician. Enjoyed a successful military career before and during World War I. Worked with the new Social Democratic president Friedrich Ebert to prevent a revolutionary victory during the German Revolution of 1918–19, overseeing the bloody suppression of popular uprisings throughout Germany. Continued to serve the Weimar Republic in various capacities until pushed out of government in the early 1930s, as conservative politicians were preparing an alliance with Hitler's Nazi party.

Grohman, Henryk (1862–1939), German industrialist. Factory owner from Łódź, heir to the business empire established by his father Ludwig Grohman.

Grütz, Willi (birth and death dates unavailable), German Social Democrat. Active and respected working-class SPD militant in city of Remscheid; helped build the USPD, served as a central leader of the Remscheid Workers' and Soldiers' Council during the November Revolution, became a prominent KPD activist in the 1920s. Inner-party disputes led to his expulsion in the late 1920s.

Guchkov, Alexander Ivanovich (1862–1936), Russian conservative politician. October 1906 became leader of the Union of October 17, or Octobrists, which advocated a limited constitutional monarchy while defending the interests of the landed aristocracy. Served as chairman of the Third Duma 1910; voted out of the Duma 1912; raised objections to Tsarina Alexandra's relations with Rasputin, leading to his estrangement from the tsar; served as war minister in the Provisional Government of 1917; supported Lavr Kornilov and other counterrevolutionary forces later in 1917; died in exile.

Guesde, Jules (Mathieu-Basile) (1845–1922), French socialist and journalist. Jailed for opposition to Franco-German War of 1871; originally a follower of Mikhail Bakunin, broke from anarchism and in 1879 became founder of the French Workers' Party; 1890s, represented the "state-collectivist" tendency in the French working-class movement. Later, evolved into a reformist and supported World War I.

Haase, Hugo (1863–1919), German lawyer, Social Democrat. 1894–1910, city councilor in Königsberg; member of the Reichstag 1897–1906 and 1912–18; 1911–16, co-chairman of the SPD (with Friedrich Ebert); 1912–15, chairman of the SPD's Reichstag group; 1914 opposed voting for war credits but did not break party discipline by making his views public; 1916, member of the Executive Committee of the Social Democratic Working Group (Arbeitsgemeinschaft); 1917, one of the chairs of the USPD; 1918, member of the Council of People's Representatives. Assassinated by a monarchist in 1919.

Hackelbusch, Richard (birth and death dates unavailable). German Social Democrat. Member of SPD.

Hänisch, Konrad (1876–1925), German Social Democrat. 1898–99, editor of the *Pfälzische Post* in Ludwigshafen and 1899–1900 of the *Sächsische Arbeiter-Zeitung* in Dresden; 1900–1905, editor in chief of the *Arbeiter-Zeitung* in Dortmund; 1905–06, editor of the *Leipziger Volkszeitung*; 1906–11, once again editor in chief of the *Arbeiter-Zeitung* in Dortmund; until 1914 defended the views of the German left, but during World War I evolved toward a pro-war position; 1915–19, editor of *Die Glocke*.

Haug, Wilhelm (birth and death dates unavailable), locksmith active in SPD, later in the KPD.

Haussmann, Conrad (1857–1922), German lawyer, liberal reformer. Influential in the Demokratischen Volkspartei (DVP, Democratic People's Party) and later founder and leader of the Deutschen Demokratischen Partei (DDP, German Democratic Party), prominent member of the Reichstag 1890–1918. Served in the Weimar Reichstag from 1919 until his death.

Hecker, Friedrich (1811–1881), German lawyer, politician, and revolutionary.

One of the most popular speakers and agitators of the 1848 Revolution. After moving to the United States, served as a brigade commander in the Union Army during the American Civil War.

Heilmann, Ernst (1881–1940), leader of SPD in Prussia, during World War I, a major proponent of *Burgfriedenspolitik* (political truce between political parties during World War I), advocating SPD and trade unions refrain from any actions injurious to the war effort. Elected to Reichstag 1928, arrested by the Nazis in 1933 and sent to Dachau concentration camp, tortured to death in 1940.

Heine, Wolfgang (1861–1944), German Social Democrat. Active in SPD from 1887; member of Reichstag 1898–1918. A leader of the revisionist right-wing of the party, he often clashed with Luxemburg and other leftists; supported Germany's entry into World War I and strongly opposed the workers' and soldiers' councils that emerged during the November 1918 Revolution. Served as Prussian minister of justice late 1918 to March 1919, during which time he helped suppress the Spartakusbund uprising. Fled to Switzerland when the Nazis came to power.

Helphand, Alexander L. (pseudonym: Parvus; also known as Israel Lazarevich Gelfand) (1867–1924), Russian Social Democrat. Became active in German Social Democratic movement 1890s; 1895–96, editor of the *Leipziger Volkszeitung*; 1896–98, chief editor of the *Sächsische Arbeiter-Zeitung* in Dresden; 1902, together with Julian Marchlewski, founded a publishing house in Munich for progressive international literature; 1898–1905, produced a newsletter entitled *Aus der Weltpolitik* (From the World Political Scene); worked closely with Trotsky in formulating theory of permanent revolution, 1904; during the 1905 Revolution in Russia, a member of the St. Petersburg Workers' Council (Soviet); helped produce the newspaper *Nachalo* (The Beginning); 1906–09, on the editorial staff of the *Arbeiter-Zeitung* in Dortmund; supported World War I; in 1915, founded Social Sciences Publishers and edited the weekly *Die Glocke* (The Bell); after the 1917 Bolshevik Revolution in Russia in 1917, offered to assist the Bolsheviks, but Lenin turned him down.

Henke, Alfred (1868–1946), German cigar worker, Social Democrat. Active in Tobacco Workers' Union, joined SPD in mid-1890s; SPD district chairman in Altona, an editor of *Bremer Bürger-Zeitung* 1900–1919, part of SPD's radical left wing, elected SPD deputy to the Reichstag 1912. Opposed World War I, helped found the USPD. Chairman of the Bremen Workers' and Soldiers' Council action committee. Served as a deputy of USPD in Weimar National Assembly. Opposed merger with the KPD. Returned to the SPD 1922. Served in Reichstag as SPD deputy 1932. Mayor of Reinickendorf until 1933. Removed from government service and forced to retire by Nazi regime in 1933.

Hengsbach, Klemens (1857–1940), German carpenter, Social Democrat. A founder of Cologne Carpenters' Association later held a paying office in the German Woodworkers' Association; joined Socialist Workers' Party of Germany 1883, then the SPD. 1893 chairman of SPD in Cologne. Served in Reichstag 1907–12.

Hennig, Auguste (1864–1959), German Social Democrat. Joined SPD 1905, 1908 helped found and lead the Leipzig club for domestic workers. Elected as first female party executive of Leipzig SPD 1908. Attended Second International Socialist Women's Conference in Copenhagen 1910, and together with Clara Zetkin and Käthe Duncker successfully proposed introduction of International Women's Day. Wrote for the periodical *Die Gleicheit* (Equality) and agitated for women's right to vote. Opposed World War I. Joined USPD 1919. After World War II, joined the Socialist Unity Party of Germany (Sozialistische Einheitspartei Deutschlands, SED).

Herschel, William (1738–1822), German astronomer. Discoverer of the planet Uranus.

Hertling, Georg Friedrich Karl Freiherr von (1843–1919), German politician. Long-time leader of the Catholic Center Party and staunch conservative. 1917–18 served as Minister-President of Prussia and Chancellor of the German Empire. Increasingly seen as a puppet of Generals Hindenburg and Ludendorff, who constituted a virtual military dictatorship in the last year of the war, presided over the last stage of the collapse of the German home front—at which point he was forced to resign in favor of Prince Maximilian of Baden.

Heydebrand, Heinrich von (1851–1924), German conservative. From the landowning nobility, became chairman of the German Conservative Party.

Hilferding, Rudolf (1877–1941), Austrian doctor and Social Democrat. Children's doctor in Vienna; 1904–23, co-editor of a journal published in Vienna, *Marx-Studien: Blätter zur Theorie und Politik des wissenschaftlichen Sozialismus*; author of *Finance Capital*; 1907–15, editor of *Vorwärts* in Berlin; 1907, lecturer on political economy and economic history at the SPD's Central Party School in Berlin; opposed SPD support for German war effort in World War I; from end of 1915 to November 1918 an army doctor in the Austro-Hungarian military service; 1917, became a member of the USPD and 1918, chief editor of its central organ, *Freiheit*; 1918, became member of the Socialization Commission. Rejoined SPD and served in several SPD governments 1920s; murdered by the Nazis.

Hindenburg, Paul von (1847–1934), German General and militarist. Led German forces in the Battle of Tannenberg in 1914 and became Germany's Chief of Staff in 1916; President of Germany from 1925 to his death. Appointed Adolf Hitler as Chancellor of Germany in 1933 and signed the Enabling Act, which allowed Hitler to consolidate dictatorial power.

Hitler, Adolf (1889–1945), German fascist. A founder and unquestioned leader of the National Socialist German Workers' Party (NSDAP, Nationalsozialistische Deutsche Arbeiterpartei), popularly known as the Nazis; established a dictatorship, the Third Reich, in Germany 1933; initiated World War II six years later. His ideology combined extreme nationalism and militarism, intertwined with fascist and racist concepts, permeated by aggressive variants of anti-Marxism and anti-Semitism.

Hofmann, Franz Hermann Theodor (1852–1903), German cigarmaker and Social Democrat. Member of the Reichstag, 1892–1903.

Hoffmann, Adolph (1858–1930), German Social Democrat; joined SPD 1876; delegate to founding congress of Second International 1889; elected to Reichstag 1904, and to Prussian parliament 1908; attended Zimmerwald and Kienthal Conferences during war; part of 1917 split that formed USPD; joined KPD as part of 1920 fusion; joined Paul Levi's Communist Working Group in 1921, participating in its fusions with USPD and then SPD.

Hoffmann, Paul (1867–1945), German bricklayer and Social Democrat. SPD activist; elected to Prussian House of Representatives in 1913; during World War I joined USPD; elected to Prussian state assembly, 1919; part of USPD left-wing majority that joined the KPD, 1920; represented KPD in Prussian state parliament, 1921–33; imprisoned by Nazi dictatorship.

Hohenzollern, German royal dynasty. First ancestors mentioned in 1061; over the years, ruled as princes, electors, kings, and emperors within and beyond territories that became modern Germany. Through the efforts of the "Iron Chancellor," Otto von Bismarck, Germany became a unified nation-state dominated by a Hohenzollern monarchy whose leading figures took the title of Kaiser. This "Second Reich" or Empire was forged in 1870 (the first Reich being the Holy Roman Empire, which was said to have existed from 800 AD to 1806). Hohenzollern rule ended with the German Revolution of 1918, replaced by the Weimar Republic.

Holubovych, Vsevolod Oleksandrovych (1885–1939), Ukrainian civil engineer. As a revolutionary nationalist, helped organize the Ukrainian Socialist Revolutionary underground group in 1915 and organized among railway workers. Served as prime minister of the Ukrainian People's Republic January–April 1918, prominent in opposition to the Bolshevik Revolution. He was arrested and his government overthrown in a German-backed coup that installed a dictatorship under conservative aristocrat Pavlo Skoropadsky. After the Skoropadsky regime was dislodged, Ukraine became part of the Russian Soviet Federative Socialist Republic, later Union of Soviet Socialist Republics. In 1931 Holubovych and his wife were arrested by Soviet authorities, and he died in prison in 1939.

Holubovych, Sydir (1873–1938), Ukrainian politician. Studied law at Lviv University; member of Austrian parliament, 1911–1918, and Diet of Galicia,

1913. After World War I became second prime minister of the West Ukrainian National Republic, January 4–June 9, 1919. A founder of the Ukrainian National Democratic Alliance, 1925.

Hörsing, Friedrich Otto (1874–1937), German blacksmith and Social Democrat. Joined SPD in 1894; Executive Secretary of the German Association of Metalworkers in Upper Silesia 1905; SPD District Secretary 1906–14; served in German Army in World War I; chairman of the workers' and soldiers' council of Upper Silesia in 1919; member of Weimar National Assembly, 1919, Reichstag, 1919–22, Prussian Landtag, 1924–33. Cofounder and the first Chairman of the Reichsbanner Schwarz-Rot-Gold (1924–32), paramilitary force defending the Weimar Republic. In 1932, founded the Sozial-Republikanische Partei Deutschlands after he was expelled from the SPD and the Reichsbanner.

Horwitz, Maksymilian Henryk (known by pseudonym Henryk Walecki) (1877–1937), Polish journalist. Political journalist and prominent figure in the Polish and international workers' movement; 1893 went to Belgium as a student from Russian-occupied Poland; 1895, joined the Belgian Workers' Party and the Association of Polish Socialists Abroad and then the PPS; 1899–1901, imprisoned in Russia; 1901–02, in Siberian exile; escaped and went to Switzerland; after 1906 (in Poland), a leading representative of the PPS-L (left wing); 1915, emigrated to Zurich and took part in preparations for the Zimmerwald Conference (1915) and the Kienthal Conference (1916); 1918, returned to Poland and was one of the initiators of the unification of the PPS-L with the SDKPiL to form the Communist Workers' Party of Poland. Perished in the Stalinist purges of the 1930s.

Hutten, Ulrich von (1488–1523), German humanist and poet. Outspoken advocate of the Reformation and ally of Martin Luther; joined anti-papal forces fighting in the Rhine region (the Knights' War of 1522), but after their defeat fled to Switzerland, seeking to join the Reformation movement there. Died in Swiss exile at a lakeside monastery on the island of Ufenau.

Ivan the Terrible (1530–84), Russian ruler. Reigned over Russia as Ivan IV from 1533 until his death. Vastly expanded the territory of Russia by conquering the Khanates of Kazan, Astrakhan and Siberia and was crowned the first tsar of Russia. Under his rule Russia emerged as a powerful and centralized multi-ethnic state. His cruel and relentless repression of the Russian nobility as well as all potential political opponents earned him his sobriquet.

Jagow, Traugott Achatz von (1865–1941), Extremely conservative Berlin police chief 1909–16. 1920 participated in the Kapp Putsch, an attempt to overthrow the new Weimar Republic.

Jogiches, Leo (1867–1919), Polish Social Democrat from Lithuania. Prominent figure in the Russian, Polish, and German workers' movements; Luxemburg's lover from the early 1890s to 1907; initially in Vilnius had connections with the Narodnaya Volya (People's Will) organization, but later as an émigré in Switzerland was closer to the Russian Marxists in the Emancipation of Labor group around Plekhanov; 1893, cofounder of the SDKP (which in 1900 became the SDKPiL) and 1902–14 a member of its main leadership body; 1893, became co-editor of *Sprawa Robotnicza*; 1900, moved to Germany; 1916, a co-organizer of the Spartacus group; 1918, cofounder of the Spartacus League and member of its central leadership body (Zentrale); 1918, member of the Central Committee of the KPD; March 1919, arrested, then murdered in prison.

Kaledin, Aleksei Maximovich (1861–1918), Cavalry General who led the Don Cossack counterrevolutionary ("White") movement in the opening stages of the Russian Civil War. Opposed the February 1917 Revolution that overthrew the Russian monarchy. In the confrontation between General Kornilov and Provisional Government President Alexander Kerensky, he supported Kornilov's intention of establishing a military dictatorship. The erosion of his own military efforts against the Bolsheviks caused him to commit suicide.

Karski, see Marchlewski, Julian.

Kautsky, Karl (1854–1938), German theoretician and SPD leader. Leading figure in German Social Democracy and the Second International from the 1890s to World War I. Married to Luise Kautsky. In 1883 he co-founded the journal *Die Neue Zeit* and was its chief editor until 1917. An ally of Luxemburg in the revisionist debate of 1898; she broke with him in 1910 as he moved closer to reformism with his "strategy of attrition"; 1917 cofounded the USPD; became a strong critic of the Bolshevik Revolution after 1917; returned to the SPD in 1920, when much of the USPD's membership joined the German Communist Party.

Kautsky, Hans (nickname: Igel) (1864–1937), German professor of art. Painter at the Royal Theatre of Prussia, brother of Karl Kautsky.

Kautsky, Luise née Ronsperger (1864–1944), German Social Democratic activist, writer, editor, and translator. Married to Karl Kautsky, associate of Clara Zetkin, close friend of Luxemburg. Served as Berlin city councilor for the USPD, 1920–21. In 1923, published a collection of Luxemburg's letters. 1924, returned with Karl to their native Austria, but in 1938 fled to Czechoslovakia then to the Netherlands to escape Nazi repression due to their socialist affiliations and her Jewish ethnicity. In 1944 she was arrested and deported to Auschwitz concentration camp.

Keil, Wilhelm (1870–1968), German wood turner and Social Democrat. Unionized early, joined SPD 1887; 1896 on the editorial board and 1914 editor in chief of SPD paper *Schwäbische Tagwacht* (Stuttgart); member of the Württemberg State Parliament, 1900–1918; member of the State

Parliament, 1919–20; member of the National Assembly, 1920–1932; Minister of Labor and Food in Württemberg, 1921–23; SPD member of the Parliamentary Council of the American Zone Länderrat, 1947–49.

Kerensky, Alexander Fyodorovich (1881–1970), Russian lawyer and revolutionary. Key political figure in the Russian Revolution of 1917. Prominent in the moderate socialist Trudovik split-off from the Socialist Revolutionary Party. With the February overthrow of the tsar, he was active in two centers of power: the Petrograd Soviet, where he served as vice chairman, and the Provisional Government, where he served first as minister of justice, then minister of war, and finally as head of the government. To maintain stability, Kerensky made an initial alliance with General Lavr Kornilov to crack down on the soviets and on working-class radicals. At the last minute he backed off—fearing that Kornilov would establish a military dictatorship that would also dispense with Kerensky's government. The Bolsheviks, led by Lenin and Trotsky, played a key role in defeating Kornilov and won a majority in the soviets. The overthrow of the Kerensky government followed, and Kerensky himself went into exile in New York City.

Kolb, Wilhelm (1870–1918), German Social Democrat. Leading SPD member in Karlsruhe, where he became one of the first Social Democratic city councilors in the 1890s. SPD parliamentary group leader in the second chamber of the Baden Estates Assembly. On the editorial team of the newspaper *Volksfreund*, supported the paper's embracing the revisionist position of Bernstein. Demanded "superfluous ballast" be removed from the party program, but appeared at the Dresden Party Congress in 1903, incurring sharp reactions from Bebel and Luxemburg. With Ludwig Frank became prominent advocate of SPD creating a broad political bloc with the German People's Party and National Liberal Party. In 1915, he demanded that the SPD "grow beyond the framework of the mere workers' party in order to become a people's party in the best sense of the word."

Kornilov, Lavr Georgiyevich (1870–1918), General in the Imperial Russian Army during World War I, best remembered for the so-called "Kornilov Affair" of August–September 1917. Alexander Kerensky, prime minister of the Provisional Government, appointed Kornilov leader of Russia's military forces, hoping he would be a force for political stability. Kerensky's authority was increasingly undermined by the workers' councils (soviets), with the influential Bolshevik Party under Lenin, calling for an end to the Provisional Government and its replacement by soviet rule. Kornilov sought to lead his military forces into the capital to crush the soviets and execute such leading radicals as Lenin. At the last moment, Kerensky ordered Kornilov to scuttle this plan, which the general refused to do. Kerensky mobilized the soviets to halt Kornilov's efforts and had Kornilov arrested, charged with attempting a coup d'état. After Bolshevik Revolution, escaped from jail and led anti-Bolshevik military forces in the south of Russia. Badly outnumbered, he died in combat.

Krupp, prominent German family and business dynasty. Krupp was organized into the largest company in Europe at the beginning of the twentieth century. The foremost weapons manufacturer for Germany in World War I and World War II, it has produced battleships, submarines, tanks, howitzers, guns, utilities, and hundreds of other commodities.

Kucharzewski, Jan (1876–1952), Polish historian, lawyer, and politician. Member of the Zet political organization, the National Democrats (Narodowa Demokracja) movement, and the National League (Liga Narodowa) until 1911. Resided in Switzerland, writing articles for the Polish cause. Returned to Warsaw in 1917 and, under the auspices of German occupying forces, served as prime minister of Poland from the end of that year to early 1918. After 1920 he dedicated his life to academic work. In 1940 he went into exile in the U.S., where he published many Polish nationalist and anti-communist works.

Kun, Béla (1886–1938), Hungarian Communist. After serving in World War I, during which he became a Communist, he returned to his native Hungary and helped established a Communist Party. In 1919, led a successful coup d'état, formed a Communist-Social Democratic coalition government, and proclaimed the Hungarian Soviet Republic. The new regime collapsed four months later in the face an invasion of hostile Romanian troops but also Communist policies that created great dissatisfaction among the Hungarian populace. Fled to the Soviet Union, working as a functionary in the Communist International and as head of the Crimean Revolutionary Committee from 1920. Assigned to Germany in 1921, helped initiate the "March Action," a poorly conceived Communist uprising. During the Great Purge orchestrated by Stalin in the late 1930s, accused of working with "the class enemy," arrested, interrogated, and quickly executed.

Labriola, Antonio (1843–1904), Italian Marxist philosopher. Originally a liberal, became a Marxist in 1889; one of the first post-Marx Marxists to argue for the critical importance of Hegel to Marxist theory; author of *Essays on the Materialist Theory of History*.

Lafayette, Joseph Marie (1757–1834), French aristocrat and military officer. Fought in the American Revolutionary War, commanding American troops in several battles. After returning to France, a key figure in the French Revolution of 1789–99. Tried to steer a middle course through the years of revolution. In August 1792, radical factions ordered his arrest, and he fled into the Austrian Netherlands. Captured by Austrian troops and spent more than five years in prison. Returned to France after Napoleon Bonaparte secured his release in 1797. After restoration of the monarchy in 1814, became a liberal member of the Chamber of Deputies. During France's July

Revolution of 1830, declined an offer to become the French dictator; supported Louis-Philippe as king but turned against him when the monarch became autocratic.

Lamartine, Alphonse (1790–1869), French author, poet, and statesman, former monarchist, who embraced democratic ideals and opposed militaristic nationalism, shifting in the direction of liberalism in the 1830s, influenced somewhat by the ideas of Saint-Simon. Briefly led the government during the revolutionary turbulence of 1848, as the monarchy was replaced by a republic. Counterposed an idealistic nationalism to working-class socialism.

Landsberg, Otto (1869–1975), German lawyer, Social Democrat; 1903–09, city councilor in Magdeburg; member of the Reichstag in 1912–18; in November 1918, became a member of the Council of People's Representatives.

Lassalle, Ferdinand (1825–64), lawyer, philosopher, initiator of a mass socialist workers movement in Germany fighting for universal suffrage. Close to Karl Marx, but sharply differing in his glorification of the state and secret negotiations with Otto von Bismarck.

Ledebour, Georg Theodor (1850–1947), German journalist, Social Democrat; 1890–1895, contributor to *Vorwärts* and, in 1895–1898, a member of its editorial staff; 1897–1900, editor of the *Sächsische Arbeiter-Zeitung* in Dresden; 1900–1914, contributor to *Vorwärts* and other Social Democratic publications; member of the Reichstag 1900–1918; supported World War I; in 1916, a member of the Executive Committee of the Social Democratic "Working Group" (Arbeitsgemeinschaft); in 1917, a cofounder of the USPD, to whose Central Committee he belonged until March 1919.

Leder, Zdzisław (real name: Władysław Feinstein) (1880–1938), Polish Social Democrat, communist and publicist. Became closer to the SDKPiL during 1901–02, took on leading party functions from 1904. Based in Kraków from February 1904, and from there made regular journeys to the Kingdom of Poland. Worked as an editor for *Czerwony Sztandar* in 1905–06, a period in which his stays in Poland became longer and more regular. Imprisoned from October 1906 to August 1908 in Warsaw Citadel; lived in exile in Berlin, Zurich, and Paris after his release. In 1911, retired from party office and, in 1912, due to the split within the SDKPiL, withdrew from politics. From 1915 to 1918 in Switzerland, he obtained his PhD. In November 1918, he returned to Warsaw, where he was a cofounder of the Communist Party of Poland (initially known as the KPRP, later as the KPP). After being arrested in Poland, he moved to Moscow in 1921, from where he carried out Comintern functions, with periods in Berlin, until 1924. Afterward, did several stints abroad working for the Comintern or as a Soviet diplomat, including periods in Italy, France, and Great Britain. Commissioned by the Comintern in 1929 to write an extensive pamphlet about the life and work of Leo Jogiches. The resulting work was subsequently rejected, and only published in 1976 (by Feliks Tych in Poland). Arrested in Moscow in 1937, he was sentenced to eight years in a prison camp. He died in 1938, en route to the Gulag.

Ledru-Rollin, Alexandre Auguste (1807–1874), French lawyer, politician. For a time seen as a spokesman of the working class; elected to the Chamber of Deputies; used his paper *La Réforme* to popularize political, social, and economic change. His speeches at workers' banquets in various cities, and those of socialist Louis Blanc, heralded the Revolution of 1848. Minister of the interior in the provisional government headed by Alphonse de Lamartine, helped expand the right to vote, but sided with Lamartine and "the party of order" against the radicalizing working-class movement. Lost his influence among workers; led a substantial republican grouping in the 1849 elections but was overwhelmed by the triumphant regime of Louis Bonaparte (Napoleon III), against which he organized unsuccessful protests before going into exile.

Legien, Karl (1861–1920), German trade union leader and Social Democrat. A wood turner, he joined the SPD in 1885. 1887, chairman of the German Association of Turners; 1891, chairman of the General Commission of the German Trade Unions, a position he would hold until its dissolution in 1919. Member of the German Parliament 1893–98, and again 1903–20. He became a leader of the SPD's right wing, fiercely opposing its more leftist factions. Supported the German war effort with "patriotic fervor" during World War I. Committed to the Weimar Republic in the postwar period, in 1920 organized a powerful general strike that defeated the rightist Kapp Putsch.

Lenin, Vladimir Ilyich (real last name: Ulyanov) (1870–1924), Russian revolutionary. From 1903, leader of the Bolsheviks; worked closely with Luxemburg, especially immediately after 1905 Revolution, though differed with her on many issues; after Bolshevik Revolution of 1917, leader of the revolutionary government of Soviet Russia.

Lensch, Paul (1873–1926), German Social Democrat. 1900–02, editor of the *Freie Presse für Elsass-Lothringen* in Strasbourg; 1902–07, contributor to *Leipziger Volkszeitung* and, until 1913, its chief editor; member of the Reichstag, 1912–18; proponent of the views of the German left until 1914. During World War I, evolved into a supporter of militarism, and in the November Revolution of 1918–19, was a delegate from the Council of People's Representatives to the army high command.

Lequis, Arnold (1861–1949), German general who helped lead the genocidal campaign against the Nama and Herrero peoples of Southwest Africa; during German Revolution of 1918–19, active in suppressing left-wing challenges to Ebert's government as Military Governor of Berlin.

Lessing, Gotthold Ephraim (1729–1781), German poet, philosopher, and dramatist. One of the foremost representatives of the European Enlightenment.

Firm advocate of freedom of thought and conscience and defender of the idea of freedom as the most important of human values; critic of established Christianity and other forms of religious dogmatism. Best known for his poem *Nathan the Wise*, also *The Education of the Human Race* and *Laocoön*.

Leutert, Paul (1862–1927), German Social Democrat. SPD member who worked in the painting trade. Councilor in Apolda, 1890–98 and 1908–11. SPD deputy in German Reichstag, 1912–18, representing Grand Duchy of Saxony-Weimar-Eisenach. In 1918 November Revolution, elected by workers' and soldiers' council to Provisional Government of the Free State of Saxony-Weimar-Eisenach. Member of the Parliament of the Free State 1919–1920 and member of the Landtag of Thuringia 1921–24.

Levi, Paul (1883–1930), German lawyer, Social Democrat. Participant in the national conference of leading left-wing Social Democrats in March 1915 in Berlin; an adherent of the International Group (Spartacus Group); Luxemburg's lawyer and colleague during World War I; became a leader of the KPD in 1918, until expelled in 1921. Organized a short-lived Communist Working Group, which soon merged with the USPD and then the SPD. Publisher of Luxemburg's *The Russian Revolution*.

Leviné, Eugen (1883–1919), Russian-born revolutionary and KPD member. Active in the anti-tsarist struggle in Russia as a member of the Socialist Revolutionary Party, arrested but escaped to Germany from Siberia before World War I and was drawn to the Spartakusbund. A prominent activist in the newly formed KPD, became one of the central leaders of the short-lived Bavarian Soviet Republic, after which he was arrested and executed.

Levine, Isaac Don (1892–1981), Russian-born American journalist. Immigrated from the Russian Empire to the United States in 1911; journalist with the *Kansas City Star* and later for the *New York Tribune*, through which he covered the Russian Revolution of 1917. Returned to Russia in early 1920s on behalf of the *Chicago Daily News*. From the late 1920s, increasingly prominent as an anti-communist.

Lex, Anna (born Clocke, married Rudolf Lex) (1870–1950), German Social Democrat. Moved to Dortmund around 1903, active in the Dortmund cooperative movement, helped found an educational association for women and girls of the working classes in October 1904. From 1906, SPD women's representative for the Dortmund-Horde district. 1908, appointed to central Executive Committee of SPD, took part in SPD party congresses and women's conferences up to 1924. 1919–29, member of the Dortmund city council. Served in Prussian state parliament, 1922–24. 1923–33, worked in press commission of *Westfälische Allgemeine Volks-Zeitung*, SPD newspaper for the industrial Ruhr area.

Liebknecht, Karl (1871–1919), German Social Democrat and leading representative of the left. Son of Wilhem Liebknecht. Trained as a lawyer, famous for his defense of socialist leaders; member of the Reichstag 1912–18; refused to accede to the SPD's vote for war credits in August 1914. With Luxemburg, founded Spartacus League and edited its publication, *Die Rote Fahne*. Cofounded the German Communist Party. Arrested with Luxemburg January 15, 1919; summarily tortured and executed by the Freikorps.

Liebknecht, Wilhelm (1826–1900), German Social Democrat, philologist, and publicist. Father of Karl Liebknecht. Participant in the 1848 republican uprising in Baden, after that an émigré, at first in Switzerland and then in England; member of the Communist League and close confidante of Marx; 1862, returned to Germany; 1863, member of the General German Workers' Association (founded by Ferdinand Lassalle) and, in 1864, a contributor to *Social-Demokrat*; correspondent for and authorized representative of the International Workingmen's Association (First International) in Germany; 1869, cofounder, with August Bebel, of the Social Democratic Workers' Party (which became SPD in 1890), and editor of *Der Volksstaat*; 1874–1900 (with an interruption in 1887–88), member of the Reichstag; beginning in 1876, editor and, in 1891 and after, chief editor, of the *Vorwärts*; cofounder of, and leading participant in, the Second International.

Limbertz, Heinrich (1874–1932), German Social Democrat, mine worker, and trade union leader. 1895–1904, "workers' secretary" for the SPD in Iserlohn and, 1904–1907, in Essen; 1907–10, and again, beginning in 1913, editor of the *Arbeiterzeitung* in Essen; 1911–13, head of the SPD Bureau for Rhineland-Westphalia; member of editorial staff of *Volkswacht*; member of the Prussian State Assembly 1919–21; elected to the Prussian State Parliament 1921–24, and to Reichstag from 1924 to his death in 1932.

Liszt, Franz Eduard Ritter von (1851–1919), German jurist and criminologist who favored modern sociological and historical approaches to law. Professor of Criminal Law and International Law at the University of Berlin, served as a member of the Progressive People's Party in the Prussian Chamber of Deputies and the Reichstag.

Lloyd George, David (1863–1945), British politician. Leader of the Liberal Party and prime minister of Britain 1916–22.

Loebell, Friedrich Wilhelm von (1855–1931), Prussian minister of the interior 1914–17. Responsible for organizing the administration during World War I. Issued a decree January 6, 1915, ending the previous practice of viewing Social Democrats as enemies of the state and barring them from public service. As a result of disputes in the government and with the kaiser, resigned from his office in 1917. From 1917 to January 1919, president of the province of Brandenburg; resigned in the wake of revolutionary events.

Lubinsky, Mykola (1891–1938), Ukrainian socialist. Member of the Ukrainian Central Rada, the Lesser Rada and later head of the Ukrainian Socialist Revolutionary Party. Foreign minister under Vsevolod Oleksandrovych

Holubovych and member of the Ukrainian delegation at the Brest-Litovsk Peace Treaty, where he signed the Appeal to Germany to provide military aid to the Ukrainian National Republic. Arrested 1930 and executed 1938, a victim of Stalin's Great Purge. Partially rehabilitated 1989.

Ludendorff, Erich (1865–1937), German general and right-wing politician from the minor nobility. Credited with dramatic German victories on Western and Eastern Fronts during World War I. He and his superior Paul von Hindenburg oversaw German war effort and effectively ran Germany as a dictatorship. After the war, became a prominent right-wing nationalist leader, promoting the "stab-in-the-back" myth that blamed Germany's defeat in World War I on a treasonous conspiracy of Marxists, liberal-minded Freemasons, and Jews. Participated in the failed 1920 Kapp Putsch, followed by the Nazi Beer Hall Putsch of 1923. In 1924 elected to the Reichstag as a representative of the NSFB (a coalition of the German Völkisch Freedom Party and members of the Nazi Party), serving until 1928. Ran unsuccessfully for president in 1925 as the Nazi Party candidate (defeated by his conservative wartime superior Hindenburg). Retired from politics and devoted his final years to the study of military theory, developing the influential concept of "Total War" in a book of that title (*Der totale Krieg*).

Malecki, A. M. (real name: Alexander Rubinstein) (1879–1937), Polish revolutionary. Joined Polish socialist movement in Łódź, moved to Warsaw, became part of SDKPiL leadership in 1906. Resigned from leadership positions in 1909 due to political differences, part of 1912 split of an organized current close to the Bolshevik faction of the RSDLP. After the Russian Revolution, worked for the Communist International 1922–15; taught at various Soviet universities, 1926–35.

Mannerheim, Carl Gustaf Emil (1867–1951), Finnish nobleman, military leader, and statesman. When Finland was part of the Russian Empire, he rose to the rank of lieutenant general in the Russian Imperial Army and was close to Tsar Nicholas II. After the 1917 Revolution in Russia, Finland declared its independence, but there was soon a civil war—with the bulk of the workers' movement pressing for revolutionary change; Mannerheim (with assistance from troops of the German Empire) led successful military onslaught to preserve the established social-economic order. 1939–40, led successful military defense against an invasion orchestrated by the Stalin regime; 1941 joined with Nazi Germany to assist in Operation Barbarossa. When it became clear that Germany was about to lose World War II, Mannerheim was appointed president of Finland (1944–46) to oversee peace negotiations with the Soviet Union and Britain.

Marat, Jean- Paul (1744–93), French revolutionary. A doctor, physicist, and political journalist, he published the outstanding newspaper of the French Revolution of 1789–92, *L'Ami du peuple*; he was a leader of the Jacobin Club and of "the Mountain" in Parliament, and the foremost defender of workers' rights among the Jacobins.

Marchlewski, Julian Balthazar (nicknames: Julek, Juleczek; pseudonyms: J. Karski, Johannes Kämpfer) (1866–1925), Polish Social Democrat. 1889, cofounded Union of Polish Workers (ZRP); emigrated to Switzerland 1893; helped produce the Social Democratic newspaper *Sprawa Robotnicza* with Luxemburg, Jogiches, and Adolf Warski. 1893, a cofounder of the SDKP (which in 1900 became the SDKPiL); 1896, moved to Germany; 1898, became a contributor to *Sächsische Arbeiter-Zeitung* in Dresden and to *Neue Zeit*; undertook the editorship of *Przegląd Robotnyczy* 1900. In 1902, with Alexander Helphand, founded publishing house for progressive international literature in Munich; also in 1902, he became a member of staff of the *Leipziger Volkszeitung*, where he was periodically editor until 1913. 1913–14, with Luxemburg and Franz Mehring, edited *Sozialdemokratische Korrespondenz*; 1915, editor of *Wirtschaftliche Rundschau*. Cofounded the Spartacus group. 1916–18, interned in Havelberg then succeeded in reaching Moscow by way of Petrograd; returned to Berlin in January 1919.

Martignac, Jean-Baptiste Sylvère Gay (1778–1832), moderate royalist French statesman. During 1814–30 Bourbon Restoration under King Charles X, briefly served as minister of the interior. He was part of a current hoping to reconcile the monarchy with ideals of the French Revolution through a liberal-minded constitutional monarchy.

Marx, Karl (1818–1883), German philosopher, revolutionary, critic of capitalism, and founder of historical materialism. Most renowned as author of the *Communist Manifesto*, the *Economic-Philosophic Manuscripts of 1844*, the *Grundrisse*, and *Capital*.

Marx-Aveling, Eleanor (1855–1898), English writer, translator, teacher, and activist in the socialist movement. Youngest daughter of Karl Marx. Helped organize 1890 May Day demonstration for the eight-hour workday; helped found the Independent Labour Party and was elected to its first Executive Committee.

Mehring, Franz (1846–1919), German socialist, historian, literary scholar, and political journalist. 1891–1913, contributor to *Neue Zeit*; 1892–1895, head of the association Freie Volksbühne; 1902–07, chief editor of *Leipziger Volkszeitung*; 1906–11, instructor in history at the SPD's Central Party School in Berlin; 1913–14, with Luxemburg and Julian Marchlewski, edited *Sozialdemokratische Korrespondenz*, and in April 1915, with Luxemburg, the first issue of the journal *Die Internationale*. He belonged to the International Group (Spartacus Group), later renamed the Spartacus League; member of Prussian parliament 1917–18; member of the Prussian House of Deputies, 1917; cofounder of the German Communist Party.

Meyer, Conrad Ferdinand (1825–1898), Swiss poet and author of historical novels, whose epic poem *Hutten's Last Days* (1871–72) had significant impact.

Meyer, Ernst (1887–1930), German journalist and Social Democrat. 1913–15, editor of *Vorwärts*; adherent of the International Group (Spartacus Group); participant in 1915 Zimmerwald Conference and 1916 Kienthal Conference; edited *Spartakusbriefe* 1916; 1918, head of the press department of Soviet embassy in Germany; representative of the Spartacus Group on the Revolutionary Executive Committee, and the Revolutionary Shop Stewards (*Obleute*) in Berlin; in 1918, became a member of the KPD and of its central leadership.

Mignet, François-Auguste-Marie (1796–1884), French historian and politician. Author of influential *History of the French Revolution* and many other works on the Middle Ages and early modern European history. A political liberal, served for many years as a minor official in the government of Louis-Phillipe. Edited a selection of Sismondi's writings entitled *Political Economy and the Philosophy of Government*.

Millerand, Alexandre (1859–1943), French politician. Leading representative of the French Independent Socialists; 1899–1902, minister of trade in the bourgeois cabinet of Waldeck-Rousseau; 1904, expelled from the French Socialist Party for participating in a capitalist government. Subjected to a series of sharp critiques by Luxemburg.

Milow, Marie (birth and death dates unavailable), member of SPD.

Milyukov, Pavel (1859–1943), Russian politician and historian. Cofounder of the Cadets in October 1905. From 1907, member of the Third Duma, leading the Cadet faction. Foreign minister after the February Revolution in 1917. On the side of the Whites after the October Revolution. November 1918 left for Turkey, and from there to exile in Western Europe—first in England, and from 1921 in France. Wrote numerous studies about the Russian Revolutions of 1905 and 1917. A staunch opponent of Hitler during World War II and supported the Soviet Union in that war from 1941.

Mirbach-Harff, Wilhelm (1871–1918), German diplomat. Ambassador in Athens and Bucharest; appointed German ambassador to Russia April 26, 1918; assassinated in Moscow by Left Socialist Revolutionaries, July 6, 1918.

Mirabeau, Octave (1848–1917), French novelist, playwright, art critic, travel writer, journalist, and pamphleteer. Notorious yet highly successful and critically acclaimed, he wrote controversial novels that explore violence, abuse, and psychological detachment.

Molkenbuhr, Hermann (1851–1927), German Social Democrat and longstanding SPD member of the Reichstag. Cigar maker for many years who became involved in the workers' movement. Organized underground after passage of the Antisocialist Laws (1878). Expelled from Germany in 1881, emigrated to the United States, was involved in the Socialist Labor Party, returned to Germany 1884. 1891, member of the program commission that developed the SPD's Erfurt Program; 1911–22, served as one of the chairmen of the SPD parliamentary group alongside August Bebel and Hugo Haase. Advocated the SPD's approval of war credits in 1914 and supported the policy of the party majority during World War I.

Mosse, Rudolf (1843–1920), German publisher. Owner of one of the largest German newspaper groups, including *Berliner Tageblatt*.

Müller, Adolf Gustav (c.1863–1942), German Social Democrat. Joined SPD in 1893, worked for the daily *Münchener Post* and became editor in chief in 1895. Close confidante of reformist-oriented Bavarian SPD chairman Georg von Vollmar, he served in Bavarian state parliament 1899–1919 and was one of the main representatives of southern German reformism. During World War I, on behalf of the SPD and with government support, he worked to influence foreign socialist parties in favor of the German position, building up an international network of agents. Put a representative of the Supreme Army Command in touch with Alexander Parvus and assisted in founding a pro-war Marxist magazine edited by Parvus, *Die Glocke*. Active in the preparation of Lenin's 1917 trip to Russia via Germany, hoping that this would undermine the Russian war effort. From 1919 to 1933, the German Reich's envoy in Bern, first Social Democrat to serve in the Foreign Office.

Müller, Hermann (1876–1931), German Social Democrat. Joined SPD, 1893; 1899–1906, editor of *Gölitzer Volkswacht*; 1906, member of National Committee of SPD; after 1905 Revolution adopted reformist views, sharply opposing Luxemburg's advocacy of the mass strike. Supported Germany's entry into World War I; member of Reichstag, 1916–18; German foreign minister, 1919, during which time he signed the Versailles Treaty with the Allies. Elected chancellor of Germany, 1920. Instrumental in suppressing a workers' revolt in the Ruhr 1920. Leader of SPD parliamentary delegation in 1920s; 1928–30, served as chancellor in a coalition government of the SPD and Centrist parties.

Müller, Richard (1880–1943), German Social Democrat. Transitioned from farm to factory, became a lathe operator, joined the German Metal Workers Union and the SPD in 1906. 1915, became a leader of opposition to World War I among metal workers and a leader of the Revolutionary Shop Stewards, leading strikes in June 1916, April 1917, and January 1918. November 1918, became president of the executive of the Berlin Workers' and Soldiers' Councils. Opposed the call for a revolutionary rising in January 1919. Prominent in the left wing of the Metal Workers' Union and the USPD. Became part of the KPD when it merged with majority USPD. Was aligned with Paul Levi in opposition to the 1921 March Action but remained in the KPD. Expelled from the Metal Workers' Union in 1922 for his communist views and expelled from the KPD in 1924 apparently for factional reasons. Through late 1920s, wrote accounts of his experiences in the German Revolution of 1918–20, maintaining some connection with left-wing currents. Seems to have abandoned politics by 1930.

Necker, Jacques (1732–1804), French statesman and finance minister for Louis XVI. Played a key role during the first period of the French Revolution; tried to introduce modest reforms that went too far for the monarchy but, as it turned out, not nearly far enough for the rising tide of revolutionaries.

Němec, Antonín (1858–1926), Czech Social Democrat, politician, and journalist. Organizer of trade union and socialist movements in the Bohemian region of the Austro-Hungarian Empire, member of parliament from 1897, central leader of Czechoslovakian Social Democratic Party. Active in the creation of the new Czechoslovakian republic after World War I, opposed members of his party attracted to the Bolshevik Revolution.

Nicholas I (1796–1855), emperor of Russia from 1825 until his death. Among Russia's most reactionary rulers, he reigned through brutal autocratic power. Fostered Russian nationalism and repressed the rights of Russia's many national minorities. His crushing of the Hungarian Revolution of 1848 earned him the enmity of democrats and Free Thinkers throughout Europe.

Nicholas II (1868–1918), emperor of Russia from 1894 to 1917. Presided over Russia during its defeat in the Russo-Japanese War of 1904–05 and the revolution that followed; led Russia into World War I, in which 4 million Russians perished. His regime was marked by severe repression and anti-Semitic pogroms as well as political corruption. He was forced to abdicate by the February Revolution and was executed by the Bolsheviks during the Russian Civil War.

Niekisch, Ernst (1889–1967), German writer and politician. A schoolteacher who joined the SPD in 1917, helped found the short-lived Bavarian Soviet Republic in 1919. Briefly joined the USPD, soon returned to the SPD, then broke away as he sought to merge ultra-nationalism and communism, becoming a prominent exponent of what came to be called "National Bolshevism." This was seen by many as aligned with the Nazi movement, although Niekisch was an opponent of Nazism. After World War II, disenchanted with nationalism, embraced Marxist perspectives, becoming a lecturer in sociology at Humboldt University in East Germany until 1953. Disillusioned by the suppression of the workers' uprising, he moved to West Berlin.

Nieuwenhuis, Ferdinand Domela (1846–1919), Dutch socialist, pacifist, and anarchist. Cofounder of the Social Democratic Workers Party of the Netherlands; 1881–91, a deputy in Parliament; corresponded with Marx in 1881; 1890s, a proponent of anarchist views; 1914–18, leader of the pacifist movement in the Netherlands.

Noske, Gustav (1868–1946), German Social Democrat. Trade unionist and SPD member from 1884, chairman of the Brandenburg SPD 1892, elected to the Reichstag 1907–18, developed special expertise on military and colonial issues and supported German colonialism. In the reformist wing of the SPD, he was not much interested in major theoretical debates. Supported German war effort in World War I; 1919–20, served as the first minister of defense in the Ebert administration of Weimar Republic. Used army and paramilitary forces to suppress the socialist/communist insurgencies of 1919, resulting in the murder of Rosa Luxemburg, Karl Liebknecht, and many others. Arrested by the Nazis under suspicion of involvement in assassination attempt against Hitler in 1944 but freed by Allied troops.

Oldenburg-Januschau, Elard Kurt Maria Fürchtegott von (1855–1937), German aristocrat and conservative politician. Member of Reichstag, 1902–12, spokesman for the antidemocratic conservatives. Known for his comment "The king of Prussia and German emperor must always be able say to a lieutenant: take ten men and lock up the Reichstag." In defending the kaiser during a political scandal in 1908, he denounced the vocal SPD critics as a "mob of pigs." Represented the ultra-conservative, ultra-nationalist German National People's Party (Deutschnationale Volkspartei, DNVP) in the Reichstag 1930–1932. 1933, played an important role in persuading his friend President Paul von Hindenburg to appoint Adolf Hitler chancellor of Germany.

Pannekoek, Anton (1873–1960), Dutch astronomer and Social Democrat. Leading Social Democrat from the 1890s; 1898 one of the first to attack Bernstein for revisionism; 1907, one of the founders of *De Tribune*, organ of the left wing of the Dutch Social Democratic Workers' Party; leading figure in Second International; sharp critic of Kautsky's reluctance to oppose imperialism in 1910; from 1910, active with the German left. Wrote one of the first reviews of Luxemburg's *Accumulation of Capital.* During World War I, which he strongly opposed, took part in editing *Vorbote* (Herald), publication of the Zimmerwald Left; from 1920s, important left-wing critic of Bolsheviks, advocated "council communism" based on direct rule by workers' councils.

Parvus, see Helphand, Alexander L.

Payer, Friedrich von (1847–1931), Lawyer, politician, vice-chancellor of Germany during the last year of World War I. First elected to the Reichstag in 1877. Reached height of his political career during World War I when he advocated a negotiated peace with the allied powers and was appointed vice-chancellor. Chairman of the liberal German Democratic Party after the war, remained member of the new Weimar Reichstag until June 6, 1920.

Pieck, Friedrich Wilhelm Reinhold (1876–1960), German Social Democrat. Worked as a carpenter, joined SPD in 1895, became municipal district chairman of SPD in Bremen, secretary of the SPD in Bremen and chairman of its cultural-educational committee. In April 1910, second secretary of the SPD's central educational committee and secretary of its Central Party School in Berlin. A cofounder of the International Group (Spartacus Group). Called up for military service in 1915; went underground in 1917; collaborated on editing *Der Kampf*; October 1918, member of the Revolutionary Executive Committee in Berlin, and November 1918, member of the central leadership body of the Spartacus League. A cofounder of the KPD.

Plehve, Vyacheslav Konstantinovich von (1846–1904), Russian politician and head of police. 1876, prosecutor in Warsaw; 1881, head of the dreaded Okhrana, the secret police; worked to destroy the People's Will organization. Interior minister from April 1902; widely regarded as one of the most reactionary and repressive of the tsar's ministers. In August 1903 met with Theodor Herzl concerning his plans for colonization in Palestine; assassinated by Yegor Sassonov of the Socialist Revolutionary Combat Organization.

Plekhanov, Georgy V. (pseudonyms: N. Beltov, G.V., A. Volgin) (1856–1918), Russian revolutionary and Marxist theoretician. 1880, left Russia to live in exile in Switzerland; 1883, founder of the avowedly Marxist Emancipation of Labor group; author of many books on politics, economics, and philosophy; in 1900, cofounder and co-editor of the newspaper *Iskra* and the journal *Zarya*; generally hostile to Jogiches and Luxemburg from their earliest encounters; after 1903, a Menshevik; sharply opposed Luxemburg at 1907 London Congress of RSDLP; supported World War I; after February Revolution of 1917, returned to Russia; supported the Provisional Government; strongly opposed Bolshevik Revolution of 1917 in Russia; left Russia following the October Revolution.

Poincaré, Raymond (1860–1934), French president, 1913–20. 1902 cofounded a substantial center-right party, the Democratic Republican Alliance. The term "Poincarism" was applied to his politics but had more than one meaning: Georges Clemenceau used it in 1902 to define a young generation of pragmatic conservative politicians; after 1911, it meant "national renewal" in confrontation with Germany; and after World War I it referred to support of business interests.

Poznański, Izrael (1833–1900), Polish Jewish businessman. Established a complex of textile mills in Łódź in the mid and late nineteenth century, making him one of the wealthiest and most powerful capitalists in Congress Poland.

Radek, Karl (full name Karl Bernhardovich Radek; original name Karl Sobelsohn) (1885–1939), Ukrainian born Communist. Activist and writer in the Russian, Polish, and German revolutionary movements. Joined SDKPiL in 1904, participated in the 1905 revolutionary upsurge in Warsaw, responsible for party's newspaper *Czerwony Sztandar*. With other younger SDKPiL members, in 1911 he became aligned with aspects of Lenin's orientation that were at variance with Jogiches and Luxemburg. This resulted in conflict, personal accusations, and his expulsion; remained active in the larger movement. After the Russian Revolution of 1917, played an increasingly significant role in Russia's Soviet Republic, the Communist International, and Germany's early Communist movement. In later years, aligned with Trotsky's opposition to the development of Stalinism, then capitulated to the Stalin regime. Finally, arrested, put on trial, and sent to a labor camp during the Great Purges of the 1930s.

Rauch, Emil (1874–1956), German tobacco worker and Social Democrat. Member of SPD who served in the Reichstag representing Bremen, 1905–11; opposed World War I, active in USPD.

Reinhardt, Walther Gustav (1872–1930), German military colonel. Last Prussian minister of war. First head of the army command in the newly created Ministry of the Reichswehr of the Weimar Republic, under the government headed by Friedrich Ebert. He accepted the position on condition that the Council of the People's Deputies, the revolutionary government as of November 10, 1918, would back the authority of traditional officers against the rival system of soldiers' councils that had emerged in the revolution.

Reitze, Johanne (1878–1949), German Social Democrat. Worked as a maid and in a book printing company before getting married in 1900. Joined SPD 1902. Attended advanced training courses in Berlin and Hamburg, became party speaker and political author from 1907. 1918, played key role in a joint campaign by the civil and Social Democratic women's suffrage movement in Hamburg. Member of Hamburg parliament, 1919–21, and of the Reichstag until 1932. Imprisoned for several weeks in August 1944, as part of the "Thunderstorm" campaign. After World War II, took part in the reconstruction of the SPD and workers' welfare in Hamburg.

Reiwand, Karl (birth and death dates unavailable), German Social Democrat and member of SPD.

Renner, Karl (1870–1950), prominent Austrian Social Democrat. Associated with the theoretical trend of "Austro-Marxism" (associated with its right wing); supported the Imperial government of Austria-Hungary in its decision to embark on World War I; president of the first Austrian Republic 1919–20, and of the second Austrian Republic after World War II.

Reuter, Fritz (1810–1874), German novelist. From Northern Germany; wrote in "Low German," a dialect that is distinct from the official language known as "High German."

Reventlow, Ernst (1869–1943), German naval officer during World War I, extreme and aggressive nationalist writer and journalist. Flirting with the ideas of "National Bolshevism," in 1924 he broke from the German National People's Party (Deutschnationale Volkspartei, DNVP) to form the German Völkisch Freedom Party (Deutschvölkische Freiheitspartei, DVFP) which, in contrast to the conservative DNVP, leaned in a seemingly more left-wing and "*völkisch*" direction (populist, relating to folklore and sense of "peoplehood"). Became an idiosyncratic member of the Nazi party.

Rodichev, Fedor Izmailovich (1854–1933), Russian lawyer and liberal activist. Joined the Constitutional Democratic Party (Cadets) in 1906 and was a member of its Central Committee. He was a deputy of the First, Second, Third and Fourth State Dumas, winning elections to the Third and Fourth Dumas. After the February Revolution, part of the Provisional Government; supported General L. G. Kornilov; after the October Revolution, active in the "White" movement seeking to overturn the Soviet government. From 1922, lived in exile.

Rodzianko, Mikhail Vladimirovich (1859–1924), Russian conservative statesman. Chairman of the State Duma at the time of the February Revolution of 1917. Key figure in events leading to the abdication of Nicholas II of Russia on March 15, 1917.

Rohleder, Fritz (1867–1949), German shoemaker, trade unionist, and Social Democrat; Member of SPD; 1920, joined the USPD; 1922, returned to the SPD.

Roland Holst-van der Schalk, Henriette (1869–1952), Dutch writer and socialist. Active in the proletarian women's movement; radical leftist associated with *De Tribune*; broke from Second International and Dutch Social Democratic Party in 1909 because of its reformism; became leading advocate of revolutionary ideas during World War I; took part in the editing of the theoretical organ of the Zimmerwald Left, *Vorbote*; in 1918, became a member of the Communist Party of Holland. Author of a biography of Rosa Luxemburg.

Rosenfeld, Kurt (1877–1943), German lawyer, Social Democrat. 1906–10, instructor in civil law at the SPD's Central Party School in Berlin; 1910, became city council member in Berlin; 1917, became member of the USPD.

Rutgers, Sebald Justinus (1879–1961), Dutch Marxist theoretician and journalist; civil engineer, employed first by the municipality of Rotterdam, worked on the expansion of the port; 1911–15 director of public works in Medan. Active in the Social Democratic movement of the Netherlands, associated with publication *De Tribune* and member of the revolutionary "Tribunist current," close to the perspectives of Luxemburg. While living in the United States, influential in the left wing of the Socialist Party of America and helped lead the Socialist Propaganda League of America, a forerunner of US Communism. Founding member and early functionary of the Communist International; in the 1920s construction engineer in the Soviet Union. Permanently moved back to the Netherlands in 1938, maintaining membership in the Communist Party of the Netherlands, but no longer prominent as theorist or activist.

Sazonov, Yegor (1879–1910), Russian revolutionary. A member of the Socialist Revolutionary Combat Organization, assassinated Vyacheslav Plehve in 1904.

Scheibler, Karl Wilhelm (1820–81), German industrialist. Originally from Belgium, moved to Russian-occupied Poland in 1848 and helped establish the textile industry in the city of Łódź, building a series of factories and businesses. Became very wealthy during the 1860s, obtaining supplies of cotton for his factories unavailable to other industrialists.

Scheidemann, Philipp (1865–1939), typesetter, Social Democrat. 1900–02, editor at the *Frankische Tagespost* in Nuremberg; editor at the *Offenbacher Abendblatt*, 1902–05; chief editor of the *Casseler Volksblatt*, 1905–11; member of the Reichstag, 1903–18; member of the SPD executive (*Vorstand*) beginning in 1911 and of its central cultural-educational committee beginning in 1913; leading representative of reformism and an arch-militarist during World War I; 1917–18, co-chairman of the SPD, with Friedrich Ebert; beginning of October 1918 entered the government of Prince Max von Baden; November, 1918, became a member of the Council of People's Delegates; contributed substantially to the suppression of the November Revolution in Germany.

Schiller, Christoph Friedrich von (1759–1805), German poet, historian, playwright, and philosopher. One of the most outstanding representatives of the German enlightenment; made important contributions on aesthetics, ethics, and the meaning of human emancipation. His discussion of overcoming the divide between "formal drive" and "sensuous drive" through the realization of the "play drive" anticipates later utopian thinkers and had an especially important impact on the thought of such twentieth-century critical theorists as Herbert Marcuse.

Schlicke, Alexander (1863–1940), German trade unionist, Social Democrat. Joined local union of metalworkers. Joined Social Democratic Association of Frankfurt also in 1890 and became its chair in 1891. Became full-time general secretary of German Metal Workers' Union and was elected its president in 1895. Elected general secretary of International Metalworkers' Federation in 1905. Supported German war effort, forced to step down as Metal Workers' president in 1919 due to dissatisfaction over his role in thwarting workers' actions during World War I. Won election as SPD representative to Weimar National Assembly, elected to the Reichstag 1920 and served until 1930. Minister of Labor in the Württemberg State Government from January to June 1919, and then in the national government from June 1919, until June 1920.

Schmoller, Gustav (1838–1917), leading *Kathedersozialist*, or "socialist of the chair" (academic socialist). Member of the inductive historical school of economics that opposed both classical political economy and marginal utility theory. Advocated social reforms along the lines of a corporatist union of labor and industry. An outspoken supporter of German militarism and imperialism; strong supporter of Bismarck's policies.

Schulz, Heinrich (1872–1932), German Social Democrat. Joined SPD in 1892; appointed chairman of the Social Democratic Party School in Berlin, 1895; worked in SPD press service; in 1906 co-wrote *Leitsätze zum Thema Sozialdemokratie und Volkserziehung* (Guidelines on Popular Education) with Clara Zetkin; 1906–19, worked as managing director of the central education committee of the SPD. Originally in the left wing of the party, went on to support the German war effort and served in the army during World War I. After his discharge, employed by Friedrich Ebert as personal advisor, managing director of the Reich Chancellery, and liaison with the Reich and state authorities. 1919, appointed to the executive of the SPD, and from 1919, chairman of the Central Office for Working Youth. In the Weimar period, chairman of the "Reich Committee for Socialist Education Work," chairman of the "Working Group of Social Democratic Teachers," and head of the "Socialist Cultural Association."

Schumacher, Wilhelm (1880–1938), German SPD militant. Joined USPD in 1917, KPD in 1919. Leader of Garment Workers' Union. Expelled from KPD in 1924.

Sébastiani, Horace François Bastien (1771–1851), French general, diplomat, and politician. Served as Naval Minister, Minister of Foreign Affairs, and Minister of State under the July Monarchy.

Sembat, Marcel (1862–1922), French Socialist politician. Served as member of the Chamber of Deputies of France 1893–1922. Supported Algerians against French colonialists in French Algeria, and spoke out against possibility of world war. With the outbreak of World War I, viewed France as the victim of German aggression and supported the French war effort. Served in the wartime coalition *union sacrée* government as minister of public works. Blamed for coal shortages; unsuccessfully tried to strike a balance between demands of the military, needs of the public, and the interests of the mine owners in France and abroad; he resigned from office. After the war, on the right wing of his party.

Sipyagin, Dmitry (1853–1902), Russian politician. Governor of Courland, 1888–91; governor of Moscow, 1891–93; minister of the interior, 1899–1902. Assassinated by Stephan Balmashov of the Socialist Revolutionary Combat Organization on April 15, 1902.

Skoropadaskyi, Pavlo (1873–1945), a Ukrainian military leader who commanded Cossack forces on behalf of Tsar Nicholas II. The German Army made him hetman of Ukraine in 1918; aspired to reunite Ukraine with Imperial Russia. Overthrown by the Ukrainian Social Democrat Symon Petliura later in 1918.

Skuratov-Belskiy, Grigory Lukyanovich (birth date unknown–1573), also known as Malyuta Skuratov, was one of Ivan the Terrible's most infamous leaders of the secret police (Oprichnina), which murdered thousands of opponents of his rule.

Sonnino, Sidney Costantino (1847–1922), Italian statesman. Moderately liberal; prime minister of Italy (in 1906 and 1909–10); Italian Minister of Foreign Affairs during World War I, he represented Italy at the 1919 Paris Peace Conference.

Soukup, Frantisek (1871–1940), Czech Social Democrat. Became part of the Social Democratic Party in the Austro-Hungarian Empire in 1896; 1904–18, representative of the Czechoslovaks (later the Czechoslovak Social Democratic Party) in the bureau of the Second International. After the creation of Czechoslovakia in the wake of World War I, served as minister of justice (1918–19) and played a major role in the country's parliament in the 1920s and 1930s.

Staab, Wilhelm (1863–1933), German Social Democrat. Joined the SPD around 1885, switched to USPD during World War I. Became a member of the provincial workers' council in 1918, served on the Potsdam city council in 1919, elected to the Reichstag 1920. Returned to SPD, served in Reichstag again from late 1924 to 1930.

Stalin, Joseph (1878–1953), Russian dictator. Born in Georgia, joined the RSDRP while leading strikes there in 1901; active during the 1905 Revolution with the Bolsheviks and assumed important administrative posts following the October Revolution of 1917; in the mid-1920s consolidated total power, and in the 1930s imposed a program of rapid industrialization that cost the lives of tens of millions; his imposition of a totalitarian state resulted in the extermination of most of the leadership of the 1917 Revolution.

Stampfer, Friedrich (1874–1957), German journalist and SPD activist. Editor of the *Leipziger Volkszeitung* 1900–02; from 1902, having moved to Berlin, worked for the SPD's central organ, *Vorwärts*. Adhering to the SPD Majority position of support for the war effort, he became editor in chief of *Vorwärts* after the dismissal of previous editorial team, which was inclined to the left of the party. With a brief interruption in 1919–20, remained in this position until the newspaper was banned by the Nazi regime after the 1933 Reichstag fire.

Stauning, Thorvald August Marinus (1873–1942), Danish Social Democrat; 1896–1908, leader of the Cigar Sorters' Union, 1906 elected member of parliament. 1910, elected chairman of the Social Democratic Party, a position he retained until 1939. A solid reformist, participated as minister without portfolio in the broad multi-party cabinet of Denmark's Social Liberal Carl Theodore Zahle 1916–20. Prime minister 1924–26 and 1929–42.

Stołypin, Pyotr (1862–1911), Russian politician. Became minister of the interior in 1906 and subsequently Russian prime minister, a position he kept until the end of his life. Used brutal methods to crush the Revolution of 1905–06. Subsequently carried out a program of agrarian reform. Died after an assassination carried out with the tsar's knowledge, in Kiev.

Stresemann, Gustav Ernst (1878–1929), German politician. Associated with left-liberal split-off from National Liberal Party, Progressive People's Party (Fortschrittliche Volkspartei, FVP). During World War I, moved to the right, expressing support for monarchy and Germany's expansionist goals. After the war, briefly joined the German Democratic Party (Deutsche Demokratische Partei, DDP), then gathered the main body of the old National Liberal Party (center and right factions) into the German People's Party (Deutsche Volkspartei, DVP), with himself as chairman, based among middle class and upper-class Protestants. The DVP platform promoted Christian family values, secular education, lower tariffs, agrarian subsidies, opposition to welfare spending and to Marxism. Served briefly as chancellor in 1923, and as foreign minister 1923–29, during the Weimar Republic.

Ströbel, Heinrich (1869–1944), German writer, Social Democrat. 1893–1900, editor of the *Schleswig-Holsteinische Volks-Zeitung*, and in 1900–16, of *Vorwärts*; defended the views of the German left for a while but adhered to centrist views during World War I and became member of the USPD in 1917; November 1918–January 1919, chairman of the cabinet of the Prussian Provisional Government.

Südekum, Albert Oskar Wilhelm (1871–1944), German Social Democrat; editor of *Vorwärts* 1895–96, of *Leipziger Volkszeitung*, 1896–98, of *Fränkische Tagespost* in Nuremberg, 1898–1900, and chief editor of *Sächsische Arbeiter-Zeitung* in Dresden, 1900–03; member of the Reichstag, 1900–18; in 1900, became the editor of *Kommunale Praxis*; leading representative of revisionism, supported World War I; 1918, as a member of the German-Ukrainian Company, had a decisive part in the plundering of Ukraine.

Suvorov, Alexander Arkadyevich (1804–1882), Russian general, diplomat, politician. Fought in the Caucasus and in Poland and was repeatedly sent on diplomatic missions to the German courts. 1848 became Governor-General of the Baltic provinces. From 1861 governor general of Saint Petersburg and from 1866, inspector general of the infantry.

Svyatopolk-Mirsky, Prince Pyotr Dmitrievich (1857–1914), Russian general, politician, and police official. Accepted position of governor general of Vilna (modern-day Lithuania and Belarus); credited with successful liberal reforms, defusing national tensions in the province by allowing more rights to the national minorities and stopping pogroms against the Jews. In August 1904, succeeded to the position of minister of the interior after Plehve's assassination. There is controversy over whether he authorized the shooting of demonstrators at a peaceful St. Petersburg protest known as Bloody Sunday (January 1905), but he became the scapegoat for the massacre. Retired from government service February 1905.

Thalheimer, August (1884–1948), German Social Democrat; 1909–12, head of the *Freie Volkszeitung* in Göppingen and, 1914–16, of the *Volksfreund* in Braunschweig; belonged to the International Group (Spartacus Group); 1918, cofounder of the Spartacus League and of the KPD; brother of Berta Thalheimer. Became a leading figure in the KPD and later in the anti-Stalinist KPD-Opposition.

Thälmann, Ernst (1886–1944), leader of Communist Party of Germany (KPD), 1925–33. Under his leadership the KPD was closely aligned with the policies of Joseph Stalin. The KPD under Thälmann regarded the SPD as greater adversary than the Nazis, denouncing non-Communist socialists as "social fascists." Arrested after Nazi regime was established in 1933, beaten, tortured, held in solitary confinement for eleven years. Executed in 1944.

Thiers, Adolphe (1797–1877), French politician and historian. Prime minister of France 1836 and 1840. An opponent of Napoleon III, returned to power in the national elections of February 1871 and sued for peace with the Germans. Fled Paris during the Commune of 1871, directed the government forces that broke through the city defenses, resulting in the slaughter of tens of thousands of communards. Became president following his brutal repression of the Commune, only to be forced from power in 1873 by opposition from the monarchists.

Thomas, Albert Aristide (1878–1932), French politician. Syndicalist, member of the SFIO, supported World War I.

Trotsky, Leon (1879–1940), Russian revolutionary. Joined socialist movement 1897; initially a supporter of the Mensheviks, following 1903 split in the RSDRP; led St. Petersburg Soviet during the 1905 Revolution; published *Nachalo*, a paper that was influential in the 1905 Revolution; moved closer to the Bolsheviks during February 1917 Revolution and joined them later in 1917; people's commissar of foreign affairs, 1917–18, head of the Red Army as people's commissar for naval and military affairs, 1918–25; leader of Left Opposition to Stalin, 1923; expelled from USSR, 1927; founded Fourth International, 1938; murdered by agents of Stalin while he was in exile in Mexico.

Tsereteli, Irakli (1881–1959), Russian Social Democrat. Leading spokesperson of the Social Democratic Party of Georgia and the Russian Social Democratic Labor Party (RSDLP) in 1917, also well known for his oratory in defense of perspectives of the Menshevik faction of the RSDLP in previous years. After the overthrow of the tsar in the February Revolution, took up a leading position in the Petrograd Soviet and accepted a position in the Russian Provisional Government as minister of post and telegraph, and briefly as minister of the interior. After the Bolsheviks seized power during the October Revolution, returned to Georgia, but when that became part of the Soviet Union, went into exile, mainly in France but also in the United States.

Tych, Feliks (1929–2015), Polish Jewish historian and educator. Joined Communist Party in 1948. Carrying out intensive studies in the history of the labor and socialist movements, made important contributions on the life and ideas of Luxemburg. Marginalized by anti-Semitic campaign launched in late 1960s. 1995–2006, Director of the Jewish Historical Institute, member of the Polish Academy of Science and editorial committee member of the Polish Biographical Dictionary.

Tyszka, Jan, see Jogiches, Leo.

Vandervelde, Émile (1866–1938), Belgian socialist. Originally a liberal, joined the Social Democratic movement in 1885; 1886, helped form the Belgian Workers' Party; initially strongly influenced by Jules Guesde; 1894, member of Belgian parliament; 1900–18 president of the Second International; supported the allied war effort in World War I; 1918–21, president of the International Socialist Bureau; 1925–27, minister of foreign affairs.

Wagner, Richard (pseud.: Homo) (1868–1927), German postal worker and Social Democrat. Editor of the *Leipziger Volkszeitung* 1903–05, of the *Norddeutscher Volksblatt* in Bant 1905–08, and of the *Volksfreund* in Braunschweig, beginning in 1908; during World War I, strongly supported the war effort.

Walcher, Jacob (1887–1970), German Social Democrat and Communist. Born into a family of poor religious Protestant farmers, learned the profession of metal working, member of the Metal Workers' Union, joined the SPD in 1906, attended the SPD Party School where he was influenced by Luxemburg. An opponent of World War I, joined the Spartakusbund and was a founding member of the KPD, helping to oversee its trade union work 1919–23. Expelled from the KPD, 1928, became a founder and co-leader of the KPO (Communist Party Opposition), then a leader of the left-socialist SAP (Sozialistische Arbeiterpartei, Socialist Workers' Party) in 1932, with Paul Frölich. He was a mentor of Willy Brandt in this period. After World War II, he returned from US exile to East Germany and joined the communist-led Socialist Unity Party of Germany (Sozialistische Einheitspartei Deutschlands, SED); expelled in 1952 (under the accusation that "Walcher has worked together with the criminal Trotsky and other paid agents"), then reinstated 1957.

Walecki, Henryk, see Horwitz, Maksymilian Henryk.

Warski, Adolf Jerzy (born Jerzy Warszawski) (1868–1937), Polish Social Democrat and Communist. Member of the first proletariat party; cofounder of the Union of Polish Workers and of the SDKPiL; 1892–96, lived as an émigré in France and 1896–1904, in Germany; 1890–1896, worked on *Sprawa Robotnicza*, 1902–13, on *Czerwony Sztandar*, and on *Przegląd Socjaldemokratyyczny* 1901–04 and 1908–10. 1906–12, representative of the SDKPiL in the Central Committee of the RSDLP; took part in the Zimmerwald Conference in 1915 and the Kienthal Conference in 1916; 1918, cofounder of the Communist Workers' Party of Poland. Arrested in Moscow in 1937 and subsequently executed.

Wassermann, Heinrich (1844–?), German Social Democrat. Cigarmaker, moved to Schöningen in 1869, SPD city councilor for many years.

Wellmann, Johann (1874–1932), German Social Democrat. Blacksmith, joined union and SPD in 1893; member of Bremen SPD Executive Committee, 1906–10, Bremen party secretary, 1911–16, SPD central committee member, 1915–16. Remained active in the SPD until his death.

Wels, Otto (1873–1939), German Social Democrat. Paperhanger; 1906, employee of the Paperhangers' Union; 1907–08, secretary of the SPD in the province of Brandenburg; beginning 1908, chairman of the press commission of *Vorwärts*; member of the Reichstag, 1912–18; supported the war effort during World War I; in November 1918, a member of the workers' and soldiers' council of Berlin; helped block radical direction of 1918 Revolution; chairman of the SPD from 1919 until 1939; went into exile after Hitler took power in 1933.

Westarp, Kuno Friedrich, Graf von (1864–1945), German conservative. Director of the police in Schöneberg, 1903; president of the Higher Administrative Court in Berlin, beginning 1908; member of the Reichstag, 1908–18; chairman of the parliamentary group of the Conservative Party, beginning 1912.

Westmeyer, Johann Friedrich (1873–1917), German Social Democrat. 1898–1902, editor of the *Fränkische Tagespost* in Nuremberg, of the *Volkswillens* in Hannover, 1902–04, of the *Schwäbische Tagwacht* in Stuttgart, 1905–11; chairman of the Social Democratic Association of Stuttgart, 1908–17; beginning 1911, member of the press commission of the *Schwäbische Tagwacht*; 1912, became secretary of the First Electoral District of Württemberg; 1912–17, member of the Württemberg state assembly; defended the views of the German left; November 1914, began to edit a newsletter (*Mitteilungsblatt*), which from January 1915, was published under the title *Der Sozialdemokrat*.

Wiese, Minna (birth and death dates unavailable), German Social Democrat, member of SPD.

Wilson, Woodrow (1856–1924), twenty-eighth president of the United States, 1913–1921.

Winnig, August (1878–1956), German politician. Active in trade union movement and SPD, held elected and public offices 1913–21. Became extreme nationalist during World War I, participated in the unsuccessful 1920 Kapp putsch against the Weimar Republic, after which he was removed from his governmental positions by the regime and expelled from the SPD. Gravitated toward Nazism, involved for a time in the "National Bolshevism" tendency along with Ernst Niekisch. Initially welcomed Nazis taking power in 1933, eventually opposed the Third Reich as a Christian conservative.

Wolff, Theodor (1868–1943), German journalist and creative writer; 1909, became chief editor of *Berliner Tageblatt*.

Zetkin, Clara Josephine (1857–1933), German Social Democrat, teacher. Chief editor of the Social Democratic women's publication, *Die Gleichheit* 1892–1917; active in SPD leadership 1895–1917; became secretary of the International Women's Secretariat in 1907; 1910, one of the founders of the annual International Women's Day for equal rights, peace, and socialism; a leading representative of the German left, a contributor to *Die Internationale* and a cofounder of the International Group (Spartacus Group); June 1917 to April 1919, chief editor of the newly founded women's supplement to the newspaper, *Leipziger Volkszeitung*; from 1919 until her death, a leading member of the KPD.

Zietz, Luise (1865–1922), German Social Democrat. Active in the proletarian women's movement; 1908–12, held a seat on the executive (*Vorstand*) of the SPD and until 1916, secretary in the *Vorstand*; beginning 1908, active in the central leadership of the German working-class youth organization; advocated centrist views during World War I; 1917, cofounder of the USPD and a member of its Central Committee.

Zinoviev, Grigori (1883–1936), Russian revolutionary. Joined RSDRP in 1901; member of Bolsheviks from 1903; member of RSDRP Central Committee, 1907; chairman of St. Petersburg Soviet during 1917 Revolution; one of Lenin's closest followers, led Comintern 1919–26; after initially supporting Stalin, broke with him in 1925 and led United Opposition within the Bolshevik Party, with Trotsky and others, from 1926. Broke from Trotsky, capitulating to Stalin, in 1928. Arrested in 1934 and executed in the Great Purges.

Index